JOURNEYS THROUGH CONFLICT

JOURNEYS THROUGH CONFLICT

Narratives and Lessons

Edited by
Hayward R. Alker, Ted Robert Gurr, and Kumar Rupesinghe

A Study of the Conflict Early Warning Systems Research Project
of the International Social Science Council

Rowman & Littlefield Publishers, Inc.
Lanham • Boulder • New York • Oxford

ROWMAN & LITTLEFIELD PUBLISHERS, INC.

Published in the United States of America
by Rowman & Littlefield Publishers, Inc.
4720 Boston Way, Lanham, Maryland 20706
www.rowmanlittlefield.com

12 Hid's Copse Road, Cumnor Hill, Oxford OX2 9JJ, England

Copyright © 2001 by Rowman & Littlefield Publishers, Inc.

All rights reserved. No part of this publication may be reproduced, stored in a retrieval system, or transmitted in any form or by any means, electronic, mechanical, photocopying, recording, or otherwise, without the prior permission of the publisher.

Hayward R. Alker gratefully acknowledges the time and energy that the staff at Morgan Printing has expended on typesetting and indexing *Journeys through Conflict*.

British Library Cataloguing in Publication Information Available

Library of Congress Cataloging-in-Publication Data

Journeys through conflict : narratives and lessons / edited by Hayward R. Alker, Ted Robert Gurr, and Kumar Rupesinghe.
   p. cm
   Includes bibliographical references and index.
   ISBN 0-7425-1027-1 (alk. paper) — ISBN 0-7425-1028-X (pbk. : alk. paper)
   1. Pacific settlement of international disputes. 2. Security, International. 3. Conflict management—Case studies. I. Alker, Hayward R. II. Gurr, Ted Robert, 1936–. III. Rupesinghe, Kumar.

JZ60110 .J68 2001
327.1'7—dc21

2001019737

Printed in the United States of America

∞™ The paper used in this publication meets the minimum requirements of American National Standard for Information Sciences—Permanence of Paper for Printed Library Materials, ANSI/NISO Z39.48-1992.

Contents

Abbreviations	vii
Preface: The Origins of the CEWS Vision	xii
Part I. Building Conflict Early Warning Systems	
1. The Challenge of Developing Conflict Early Warning Systems: A Proposal *Hayward R. Alker, Ted Robert Gurr, and Kumar Rupesinghe*	3
2. The Double Design of the CEWS Project *Hayward R. Alker and Thomas Schmalberger*	32
3. Peacemaking and Conflict Transformation in Guatemala *Luis Alberto Padilla*	56
Part II. Comparative Studies of Prevention Successes and Failures	
4. Could Humanitarian Crises Have Been Anticipated in Burundi, Rwanda, and Zaire? A Comparative Study of Anticipatory Indicators *Barbara Harff*	81
5. Escalatory Dynamics in the Moldova-Dniestr and Chechnya Conflicts *Olga A. Vorkunova*	103

6. Why Are Some Ethnic Disputes Settled Peacefully,
   While Others Become Violent?
   Comparing Slovakia, Macedonia, and Kosovo 128
   Michael S. Lund

7. A Comparative Analysis of Conflict Resolution
   in Angola and South Africa 179
   Vasu Gounden and Hussein Solomon

8. Nonconventional Diplomacy
   Experiences of NGOs and People's Participation
   in Selected Peace Processes 196
   Sanam Naraghi Anderlini, Ed Garcia, and Kumar Rupesinghe

9. Domestic and Transnational Strategies for Managing Separatist Conflicts
   Four Asian Cases 240
   Ted Robert Gurr and Deepa Khosla

Part III: A Prototype Information System for Early Warning Networks

10. A Comparative Look at Early Warning Indicators: PIOOM,
    the State Failures Project, and CEWS Cases 291
    Alex P. Schmid

11. A Synthetic Framework for Extensible Conflict
    Early Warning Information Systems 318
    Thomas Schmalberger and Hayward R. Alker

12. Exploring Alternative Conflict Trajectories with the CEWS Explorer 354
    Thomas Schmalberger and Hayward R. Alker

Part IV: Sharing Informational Resources within Global CEW Networks

13. A Review of Research and Practice in
    Early Warning and Early Response:
    Lessons Learned and Policy Issues 397
    Kumar Rupesinghe and David Nyheim with Maha Khan

References 421

Index 441

About the Contributors 461

Abbreviations

AAAS—American Association for the Advancement of Science
ACCNET—ACCORD Electronic Network
AFRC—Armed Forces Revolutionary Council
AMRSP—Association of Major Religious Superiors in the Philippines
ANC—African National Congress (South Africa)
APFO—African Peace Forum
APHC—All Party Hurriyat Conference
ARMM—Autonomous Region of Muslim Mindano (Philippines)
ASC—Civil Society Assembly (Guatemala)
ASEAN—Association of South-East Asian Nations
BJP—Bharatiya Janata Party
CACIF—Committee of Commercial, Agricultural, Industrial, and Financial Organizations (Guatemala)
CASCON—A Computer-Aided System for the Analysis of Conflicts
CBCP—Catholic Bishops' Conference of the Philippines
CENTO—Central Treaty Organization
CEWS—Conflict Early Warning Systems
CHE—Complex Humanitarian Emergencies
CIA—Central Intelligence Agency (United States)
CIDCM—Center for International Development and Conflict Management
CIPPD—Caucasian Institute for Peace, Democracy, and Development

CNC—Chechen National Congress
CNR—National Commission on Reconciliation (Guatemala)
CNUS—National Committee of Trade Unions (Guatemala)
COCTA—Committee on Conceptual Terminological Analysis, at one time affiliated with the ISSC
CPN—Conflict Prevention Network (European Union)
CPP—Communist Party of the Philippines
CS—Commonwealth Secretariat
CSCE—Conference on Security and Cooperation in Europe
CSEMADOK—Democratic Association of Hungarians in Slovakia
CSFR—Chech and Slovak Federation
CUC—United Peasant Committee (Guatemala)
DDIR III—Data Development for International Research Research Project, Phase III
EAWARN—Network on Ethnological Monitoring and Early Warning of Conflict
EC—European Community
ECOMOG—ECOWAS Cease-fire Monitoring Group
ECOWAS—Economic Community of West African States
EFTA—European Free Trade Area
EGP—Guerrilla Army of the Poor (Guatemala)
EC—European Community
EU—European Union
EWI—East-West Institute
FAO—Food and Agriculture Organization
FAR—Rebel Armed Forces (Guatemala)
FEWER—Forum on Early Warning and Early Response
FLEC—Front for the Liberation of the Cabinda Enclave (Angola)
FMLN—Farabundo Marti National Liberation Front (El Salvador)
FRY—Federal Republic of Yugoslavia
GDP—Gross domestic product
GEDS—Global Event-Data System (Maryland)
GPA—General Peace Agreement (Mozambique)
GRP—Government of the Republic of the Philippines
GVHR—Gross human rights violations
HCNM—High Commissioner on National Minorities
HIC—High intensity conflict
HRNGO—Human rights NGOs
HURIDOCS—Human Rights Information and Documentation System
HZDS—Movement for a Democratic Slovakia
ICON—IPRA Commission on Internal Conflicts and Their Resolution
ICRC—International Committee of the Red Cross
IERRIS—International Emergency Reduction, Readiness, and Response Information System

IFP—Inkatha Freedom Party (South Africa)
IGO—International Governmental Organization
IMADR—International Movement against All Forms of Discrimination and Racism
IMF—International Monetary Fund
IMPD—Institute for Multiparty Democracy (South Africa)
INGO—International Nongovernmental Organization
IO—International Organization
IPRA—International Peace Research Association
IRENE—A UN-related early warning network
IRIN—Integrated Regional Information Network
IRIPAZ—International Relations and Peace Research Institute (Guatemala)
ISA—International Studies Association
ISSC—International Social Science Council
JKLF—Jammu and Kashmir Liberation Front
JPMC—Joint Politico-Military Commission (Angola)
JVC—Joint Verification Committee (Mozambique)
KDH—Christian Democratic Movement
KEDS—Kansas Event-Data System
KLA—Kosovo Liberation Army
KZN—KwaZulu-Natal Province (South Africa)
LDK—Democratic League of Kosova
LIC—Low intensity conflict
LISP—List processing computer programming language
LOC—Line of control
MCC—Mozambique Christian Council
MILF—Moro Islamic Liberation Front (Philippines)
MIM—Muslim Independence Movement (Philippines)
MINUGUA—United Nations mission in Guatemala
MIT—Michigan Institute of Technology
MNF—Mizo National Front (Philippines)
MNLF—Moro National Liberation Front (Philippines)
MNLF-RG—Reformist Group (Philippines)
MNRD—National Movement for Democracy and Development
MPLA—Movement for the Popular Liberation of Angola
MR13—Revolutionary Movement of 13 November
MSPA—Multi-sectoral Peace Advocates (Philippines)
NACC—North Atlantic Cooperation Council
NATO—North Atlantic Treaty Organization
NCC—National Cease-fire Committee
NCCP—National Council of Churches in the Philippines (Protestant)
NDF—National Democratic Front (Philippines)
NGO—Nongovernmental Organization

NIIR—Netherlands Institute of International Relations
NP—National Party (South Africa)
NPA—National Peace Accord (South Africa)
NPA—New People's Army (Philippines)
NPC—National Peace Conference (Philippines)
NPRC—National Provisional Ruling Council (Sierra Leone)
OAS—Organization of American States
OAU—Organization for African Unity
OIC—Organization of the Islamic Conference
ONUCA—UN mission in Central America
ONUSAL—UN mission in El Salvador
ONUVEN—UN mission in Nicaragua
ORCI—Office for Research and Coordination of Information
ORPA—People in Arms Organization (Guatemala)
OSCE—Organization for Security and Cooperation in Europe
PANDA—Protocol for the Assessment of Nonviolent Direct Action. Program on Nonviolent Sanctions and Cultural Survival, Center for International Affairs, Harvard University
PARIS—A Prototype Action Recommender's Information Support System
PARIS-in-LA—A project at USC developing PARIS
PDP—Party for Democratic Prosperity
PGT—Guatemalan Communist Party
PIOOM—Interdisciplinary Research Program on Root Causes of Human Rights Violations (Netherlands)
PKP—The Original Communist Party (Philippines)
PTC—Political Terror Scale
RAND—Research and development think tank (California)
RELATUS—A Computational System for Text Analysis developed by Duffy and Mallery
RENAMO—Mozambique National Resistance
RPF—Rwanda Patriotic Front
RUF/SL—Revolutionary United Front of Sierra Leone
SAARC—South Asian Association for Regional Cooperation
SADF—South African Defense Force
SDUM—Social Democratic Union of Macedonia
SEATO—South-East Asian Treaty Organization
SF—State failure
SHERFACS—Frank Sherman's multiparadigm conflict management data set
SIPRI—Stockholm International Peace Research Institute
SNS—Slovak National Party
SPCPD—Southern Philippine Council for Peace and Development
SRSG—Special Representative of the Secretatry General (United Nations)

TAR—Tibetan Autonomous Region
UFCO—United Fruit Company
UN—United Nations
UNAVEM II—United Nations Angola Verification Mission II
UNDP—United Nations Development Program
UNESCO—United Nations Educational, Social, and Cultural Organization
UNHCR—United Nations' High Commissioner for Refugees
UNICEF—United Nations Children's Fund
UNIPOM—United Nations India-Pakistan Observation Mission
UNITA—Union for Total Independence of Angola
UNMOGIP—United Nations Military Observer Group in India and Pakistan
UNOMOZ—United Nations Operation in Mozambique
UNPREDEP—United Nations Preventive Deployment Force
UNPROFOR—United Nations Protection Force
UNU—United Nations University
URNG—National Guatemalan Revolutionary Unity
USAID—United States Agency for International Development
USC—University of Southern California
VMRO—Internal Macedonian Revolutionary Organization
VMRO-DPMNU—Internal Macedonian Revolutionary Organization—Democratic Party for Macedonian National Unity
VPC—Violent political conflict
VPN—Public Against Violence
YPA—Yugoslav People's Army
ZANU—Zimbabwean African National Union
ZRS—Association of Workers of Slovakia

Preface
The Origins of the CEWS Vision

Peacemakers share a vision of a less violent world and a faith in the existence of real possibilities for achieving it: pathways to peace, journeys through conflict that are, or might be, less violent than those all too visible in the international relations of the twentieth century. If both faith and the intuition of experienced peacemakers tell us that this is possible, the relevant practical–intellectual issue is: how may such a less violent world be concretely achieved? Moreover, can scholars, teachers, and administrators develop better ways to learn from, remember, transmit, convincingly publicize, generalize, and improve upon the practical experiences of those responsible for such successes, as well as of those less successful, as well as the conflict participants themselves?

This book reports on nearly a decade of international social scientific effort to improve the capacities of scholars and practitioners in governmental, intergovernmental and nongovernmental institutions to achieve such goals. The efforts we focus on are those of the Conflict Early Warning Systems (CEWS) research project of the International Social Science Council (ISSC).[1] CEWS fundees were, and are still, grateful for the financial support[2] that has made possible these efforts, as well as the associated scholarly achievements reported on in this book.

Distinctively, CEWS has had a relatively decentralized, multilevel, multinational, multiperspective, peacemaker-friendly, *network approach* to improving intergroup conflict management and violence prevention in the post–Cold War world. This project orientation has been linked to a recognition that contemporary conflicts, associated peacemaking efforts, and related scholarly activities are often complex in many of the same ways. CEWS has focussed on enhancing the production and sharing of information across and among peacemakers and scholars in the multiple nodes of decentralized networks linking researchers to the different societal levels at which today's conflicts, as well as conflict management and violence limitation activities, are organized. Those seen as concerned with the prevention of violent or deadly conflicts through timely action include conflict parties, states, intergovernmental organizations (IGOs), and activist subnational or transnational nongovernmental organizations (NGOs). Within the still powerful limitations of geography, CEWS has sought the multinational enhancement of such capacities as they apply to potentially violent encounters between groups, classes, or "peoples" and states. CEWS's openness to a multiplicity of group, national, and transnational perspectives has been a special feature of its work, carrying over into the way conflict processes have been studied and analyzed. It has worked hard at bridging the many gaps among scholars from different academic disciplines and societal-organizational levels, between quantifiers and qualifiers, and between scholars and peacemakers specializing in conflict mediation, conflict management, and violence prevention. Working in ways intended to be supportive of recent[3] UN-centered efforts to enhance preventive diplomacy and conflict management, CEWS has collaborated with International Alert, the Forum on Early Warning and Early Response (FEWER),[4] and appropriate UN agencies in attempting to learn more about peacemakers' relevant needs, and modestly to help them better achieve their own violence-limiting purposes.

A Brief Prehistory of the CEWS Project

Where did this vision of providing better informational support for decentralized early warning networks come from? Because it serves as a useful background to the work of the CEWS project, and provides information on the development of the CEWS vision during its gestation period, we present here a brief, institutionally linked account of CEWS's prehistory. By its "prehistory" we mean the period of CEWS's original conception and proposal development, before substantial funding, an important narrowing of purposes, and the specific agenda of this book were fully developed.[5] These later specifics will be the subject of chapter 2.

An Antecedent Project of International Peace Research

The CEWS project was stimulated by the convergence of two institutional efforts within a changing world situation. The first was the pioneering work, starting in 1989, of the Commission on Internal Conflicts and Their Resolution (ICON) of the International Peace Research Association (IPRA), a commission headed by Kumar Rupesinghe. With a bibliography of related articles, many from non-North American sources and mostly written in the 1980s, Rupesinghe and M. Kuroda's edited book on *Early Warning and*

Conflict Resolution was becoming recognized as the most authoritative scholarly statement supporting a new, UN-related interest in these topics (Rupesinghe and Kuroda, 1992).[6] As emphasized in Rupesinghe's "Introduction" to that volume, the UN system—broadly defined to include the whole family of UN-affiliated, IGOs and NGOs—was an especially appropriate locus for contemporary conflict prevention, peacekeeping, peacemaking and peace-building efforts. Internal conflicts were, however, a special challenge for the UN—with its charter, inscribed prescription against interfering in the domestic affairs of its member states—which NGOs could help it meet.

New Concerns and Possibilities within the UN System

The cogency of this argument was politically strengthened by a second institutional development. In the winter of 1991–1992, there arose an unusual consensus of all members of the UN Security Council. In their truly remarkable (but rarely cited) January 1992 request[7] to the UN Secretary General for a new agenda for action, the members of the Security Council, speaking through their president, significantly broadened their interpretation of the responsibilities of the Security Council. They included within its purview matters that many would have previously considered domestic or intrastate questions not, according to the charter, within the UN's competence. Thus they welcomed the expansion of UN peacekeeping tasks to include "election monitoring, human rights verification and the repatriation of refugees" as "integral parts of the Security Council's effort to maintain international peace and security." "Some of the most acute problems" were acknowledged to "result from changes to state structures." Sources of instability go beyond "war and military conflicts amongst States"; they include "economic, social, humanitarian and ecological" factors.

This request resulted, five months later, in UN Secretary General's much discussed *An Agenda for Peace* (Boutros-Ghali 1992). There he notes that "the cohesion of States is threatened by brutal ethnic, religious, social, cultural or linguistic strife." He includes within his discussion of how to strengthen preventive diplomacy, "action to prevent disputes from arising between parties, to prevent existing disputes from escalating into conflicts and to limit the spread of the latter when they occur." This broadened, preventively oriented conception apparently grows out of earlier conceptions of preventive diplomacy and conflict management developed by UN Secretary Generals, supportive scholars, and publicists, newly presented as especially appropriate roles for the UN system of organizations in a changed international situation. It responds to the recognition by both seasoned diplomats, secretariat officials, and scholars that international organizations have rarely been conflict preventers; mostly they have been reactive conflict managers, all too often forced to address conflicts only after response-mobilizing violence has occurred. *An Agenda for Peace* further contains a series of recommendations concerning UN peacekeeping, preventive diplomacy, peacemaking (including enforcement actions), and, with much less detail, a recognition of the importance of pre- and postconflict, development-linked peace-building.

Also of special interest for present purposes, the text of *An Agenda for Peace* calls upon NGOs to work with the UN in addressing the changing mix of conflicts in the world today, and includes academic research organizations in this purpose. Directly relevant to present concerns, Boutros-Ghali cites a need to "strengthen arrangements in such a manner that information from . . . a valuable network of early warning systems"[8] can be synthesized with political indicators to assess whether a threat to peace exists and to analyze what action might be taken by the United Nations to alleviate it. In his section on preventive diplomacy, Boutros-Ghali calls for efforts to "rationalize information management systems within the Secretariat . . . [and to] improve information available . . . for the purposes of preventative diplomacy." This call puts the preventive diplomacy theme, echoed from previous UN Secretary Generals, in terms that encourage academic researchers to make specific contributions.

As amplified in the recommendations of a UN roundtable on preventive diplomacy (International Alert et al. 1993), *An Agenda for Peace* includes within its concern the recognition that effective conflict preventing actions require concerted efforts by states, the UN system, and nongovernmental actors, including the global community of scholars. Here, with the idea of relatively decentralized, but information rich, regional and global networks already being emphasized—we have legitimating and motivating bases for the CEWS Research Project. Kumar Rupesinghe, the studies of IPRA's ICON commission, and, subsequently, the activities of International Alert and FEWER gave substance to these motivations.

The Possibility of a Multidisciplinary Research Effort

In 1991 and 1992 Hayward R. Alker served on the executive committee of the International Social Science Council (ISSC) in which IPRA was a full and active member. When asked to review a number of prepublication versions of chapters for the Rupesinghe–Kuroda volume, Alker began to see a number of convergent research possibilities. Just as International Alert's contemporary activities bridged between UN efforts to strengthen its peacebuilding and ICON's research, the CEWS research project of the ISSC was designed to broaden and deepen IPRA's earlier research program on internal conflicts. This meant including contributions from a variety of professional social scientists with other institutional affiliations and skills in a broadened continuation of such activities, as well as enhancing the opportunities of more scholars to learn from the close ties that ICON, Rupesinghe, and International Alert had to in-the-field early warning and peacemaking activities.

In particular, Alker wanted other scholars to benefit from ICON's serious attention to conflict prevention, including especially the refugee problems preoccupying UN officials, and to learn from International Alert's field experience in developing conflict early warning networks. His earlier experience as a consultant for the UN effort to develop in its New York headquarters an Office for Research and Coordination of Information (ORCI) had shown how difficult it was to develop and integrate information generation and analysis activities. The UN needed to get, record, and share accurate field reporting information, put it in the context of its statistical world reports, and coordinate it both with replicably measured news-based event reports of the sort "quantitative" social scientists located some distance from the main conflict interactions tend to favor, and the kind of in-depth, document-based historical analyses practiced by accomplished historians and case analysts. In that effort Alker, Peter Brecke, and the ORCI staff had repeatedly discussed the strengths and limits for UN purposes of quantitatively oriented behavioral research.

Other than mentioning David Singer's pioneering quantitative work on early warning indicators, the ICON volumes paid no attention to other future-oriented North American empirical work on collective security and preventive diplomacy by Ernst Haas,[9] Lincoln Bloomfield (Bloomfield and Leiss 1969; Bloomfield 1988; Bloomfield and Moulton 1997) and other coworkers[10] Alker admired. Nor did it attend to Ted Gurr's impressive, systematic studies of internal conflicts[11] (Gurr 1993a,b), the second and third generation "event data" that Richard Merritt, Dina Zinnes, Ed Azar, John Davies, Gurr, and he had contributed to,[12] or to the series of studies of conflict prevention under way at the U.S. Institute of Peace.[13]

With support from the ISSC Executive Committee, and with the backing of a suggestive research review and proposal prepared by Gurr (1992), Alker proposed to the ISSC's fall 1992 general assembly an ISSC-wide research program, generalizing ICON's work to include more fully other related social science disciplines, keying the research program's development to the convergence of institutional developments mentioned above, opening it up further to a variety of conceptual and methodological contributions of both a quantitative and a qualitative sort. At that meeting, supported by Rupesinghe's oral presentation on the early warning issue and the potential contributions of International Alert, Alker's proposal was approved. At the fall 1994 meeting of the ISSC General Assembly, an appropriately international and interdisciplinary CEWS Steering Group was set up.[14]

The search for financial support continued throughout 1993, 1994, and into 1995. Papers and proposals supporting that effort were developed further. Several conferences, as well as discussions with steering group members, helped in this development. One such influential meeting was a workshop on early warning in the spring of 1993, part of a continuing series sponsored by the Howard Adelman and the Center for Refugee Studies at York University (Adelman 1993). At this meeting Frank Sherman, Gavan Duffy, and others from Syracuse University made special, if often rather technically advanced, contributions.[15] Another influential meeting occurred in the fall of 1993 at the University of Maryland. Building on the Maryland meeting, Gurr and B. Harff edited a special issue of the *Journal of Ethno-Development* on *Early Warning of Communal Conflicts and Humanitarian Crises* (Gurr and Harff 1994) in which Adelman, Alker, Gurr, Harff, and Rupesinghe, among others, articulated some of their views on conceptual, research, and policy needs in the early warning area. This volume represented the first cosponsored publication of the CEWS Research Program, although CEWS-obtained funding for a project-developing steering committee meeting was not obtained until the spring of 1995 from the Carnegie Corporation of New York. The real work of CEWS had begun.

Notes

1. The ISSC is an interdisciplinary confederation of international social scientific professional associations and governmental or nongovernmental social scientific research councils. It is headquartered at the UN Educational, Social and Cultural Organization (UNESCO) in Paris. Else Øyen, its past president, and Lesek Kosinski, its Secretary General, are especially thanked for their inspiration and support.

2. The primary source of funding for the research project has been the Carnegie Corporation of New York. Astrid Tuminez has been an excellent program officer in these relationships. A related project helping to develop an Action-Recommender's Information Support System (PARIS-in-LA) was funded by the Annenberg Center for Communication at the University of Southern California. The assistance of the School of the International Relations and the Center for International Studies at the University of Southern California, which administered the project, are greatly appreciated. So is the encouragement of our work by International Alert and the Forum on Early Warning and Early Response (FEWER), which CEWS joined in the last year and a half of its 1992–1999 existence. Alker has also supported this project personally, aided by the funds of his John A. McCone Professorship at USC. Tom Vest and Anita Schjolset have been able project administrators at USC, where Jafar Adibi, Andrew Blum, Leila Kaghazian, Paul Levin, and especially Thomas Schmalberger have made many different, but special, contributions.

3. Written originally with Boutros-Ghali's writings in mind, these comments apply as well to Kofi Annan's *Facing the Humanitarian Challenge: Towards a Culture of Prevention* (Annan 1999).

4. Both these NGOs have been headquartered in London.

5. This early prehistorical background derives mostly from the first section of the first CEWS ISA paper (Alker, Gurr, and Rupesinghe 1995). It was a substantial appendix to Alker's ambitious multi-project proposal (Alker 1994b) substantially reproduced in chapter 1.

6. Related ICON research publications include Rupesinghe (1992) and Rupesinghe, King and Vorkunova (1992).

7. Quotations here are taken from Security Council Document S/23500, dated January 31, 1992, a five-page "Note by the President of the Security Council" on behalf of the members of a Security Council summit meeting.

8. The Secretary General also refers to early warning systems already existing within the UN on "environmental threats, the risk of nuclear accident, natural disasters, mass movements of populations, the threat of famine and the spread of disease." CEWS uses this language in its self-definition; Alker was hopeful that the social psychologists, sociologists and anthropologists, political scientists, international relations, and international lawyers within the ISSC—in addition to the peace researchers—would be interested in Boutros-Ghali's problematique. Retrospectively, CEWS's somewhat narrow focus on information support systems may have added to the difficulties of interdisciplinary collaboration, just as its UN focus might have limited the interests of those Europeans and North Americans more interested in unilateral or regional responses. As CEWS coordinators, Alker and Rupesinghe were more successful in engaging anthropologists, political scientists, international relations scholars, and political sociologists from among those already

working on early warning questions than they were in enlisting the active participation of the relevant research committees from other international professional organizations.

9. The Haas-Alker-Sherman tradition of extended collective security studies (Haas 1968, 1993; Alker and Greenberg, 1971; Alker and Christensen, 1972; Alker and Sherman 1982; Alker 1993; Sherman 1994) based its early case lists in whole or in part on the quasi-legal agenda decisions of regional and global international conflict management organizations.

10. Such as the relevant, multinationally collaborative work of the empirically oriented global modelers (Deutsch et al. 1997), and the linguistically inspired, "qualitative" work on textual encoding of the artificial intelligence research community (Hudson 1991).

11. Gurr's work on early warning went back at least to the mid-1980s (Gurr and Lichbach 1986). Like that of other specialists in event data and national attributes and interactions, he was experimenting with multivariate statistical approaches to forecasting, and was interested in the possibilities of empirically grounded international relations models capable of supporting counterfactual explorations of alternative futures (Gurr 1993b). Like Alker, Gurr was also grappling with the problem of synthesizing information from qualitative accounts, including case-oriented conflict studies (Gurr and Harff 1994).

12. The two main review volumes of the Data Development in International Relations (DDIR) research effort on events data are Merritt, Muncaster, and Zinnes (1993) and Duffy (1994). Both grew out of a substantial grant from the U.S. National Science Foundation in 1990. Duffy's volume was first suggested to him by Charles Hermann and Hayward Alker after an 1988 International Studies Association panel; it was given more content and development at workshops at Ohio State and MIT, the later organized by Alker and John Mallery, with UN Secretariat participation.

13. Alker was especially impressed by Michael Lund's work there—and had had his earlier views confirmed—by a one day workshop at the U.S. Institute of Peace on August 4, 1994, on conflict prevention. Organized by Michael S. Lund, the meeting consisted mainly of a CASCON demonstration by Lincoln P. Bloomfield and Al Moulton, with additional commentaries by Alker and Brecke based in part on their ORCI experiences. Lund judged Bloomfield's CASCON system (best described in Bloomfield and Moulton 1997) to be the first conflict prevention-oriented computerized information resource (Lund 1994). Brecke included its retrieval and analysis program in his ORCI system design efforts as well.

14. Initial members and their cited affiliations were:

Hayward R. Alker, School of International Relations, University of Southern California, coordinator;
Kumar Rupesinghe, Secretary General, International Alert, co-coordinator;
John Amoda, Director General, International Training Institute for Peace, Lagos;
Hizkias Assefa, Director, Nairobi Peace Initiative, Nairobi;
Ted Robert Gurr, Center for International Development & Conflict, University of Maryland;
Kinhide Mushakoji, Secretary General, IMADR, Tokyo;
Rodolfo Stavenhagen, El Colegio de Mexico, Mexico;
Olga Vorkunova, Institute of World Economy and International Relations, Russian Academy of Sciences.

15. Given the formal, computational, but qualitative orientation of many of the contributions to Duffy (1994), this could be seen as a possibly bridging approach connecting the qualitatively and quantitatively oriented approaches prominently engaged in dialogue within Gurr and Harff (1994).

Part I
Building Conflict Early Warning Systems

1
The Challenge of Developing Conflict Early Warning Information Systems: A Proposal

Hayward R. Alker, Ted Robert Gurr, and Kumar Rupesinghe

This first chapter of our book continues the annotated, historical way we have adopted in our preface of telling the story of the CEWS project. Despite the mixture of vision and hyperbole, grandeur and naivité, the mistakes in judgment and knowledge it reveals, we adopt this presentational strategy to encourage precedential learning from the experiences of our project, its own "data story."[1] It thus builds on the brief "prehistorical" account of the CEWS vision of improved, early warning networks and integrated knowledge bases, as well as the associated proposal development process reviewed in the preface.

After these orientational remarks, we rehearse the broader contextual understanding associated with the post–Cold War beginnings of our project, provide a restatement of our original proposal to fund two separate but linked projects, and list some synergies thought to be associated with the joint funding of both projects.[2] The first proposed project was to create, publish, and make partly available on the Internet and elsewhere, a new set of comparative, interdisciplinary case studies of conflict prevention successes and failures from around the globe. The second project focused on improving the accessibility, analyzability, comparability, and extensibility of preventively oriented, life-cycle structured, conflict knowledge bases, illustratively including the encoded data stories generated by the first project proposal. Its key idea was the development of inexpensive, replicable, multiperspective, open-to-revision, information-handling systems useful to participant-observers preventively trying to find alternative, less violent trajectories for emergent (or ongoing) local or regional conflicts. Such informational support systems could become part of decentralized networks: they could be installed in relatively inexpensive personal computers, workstations and/or computer networks accessible to peacemakers around the world.

Not every idea in this chapter could be accomplished: the CEWS research program became a two-stage research project. Thus chapter 2 continues the discussion of the development of the two-stage research design for the CEWS project, as it was actually funded by the Carnegie Corporation, with lesser levels of support from others. That chapter reports on the important collective discussion of project purposes and related project guidelines at International Alert's London headquarters in 1995 and 1997, and ends with a motivational discussion of the synthetic approach to alternative scenario development undertaken at USC and reported on in chapters 11 and 12 of part III. Because it was available early, compellingly presented, and important in the final stage of the CEWS project, Luis Alberto Padilla's resolution-oriented, transformational account of the tortured journey toward peaceful resolution of the Guatemalan conflict is given a slightly abbreviated account in chapter 3. Although it, and other chronologies and narratives, are available on the CEWS Web site in more complete versions, its inclusion here makes the present volume more internally consistent.

Written and rewritten between 1996 and 2000, part II of this volume contains six comparative case studies of conflict prevention successes and failures composed on the basis of comparative analyses of conflict narratives and chronologies. These essays contain the basic results of the first stage of our latter, more narrowly focussed, two-stage project proposal.

Part III of this volume reflects another two and a half years of work during 1998, 1999, and the first half of 2000. It begins with Alex Schmid's comparative assessment of his own institution's (PIOOM's) approach to human rights early warnings, compared to that of a major U.S. governmental study of Failed States (Esty et al. 1998), using case narratives and chronologies from the CEWS project. Chapter 11, by Schmalberger and Alker, synthesizes analytical approaches, develops and comparatively applies a constitutive modeling approach to coding and graphing multi-episodic, life-cycle–structured conflict trajectories. Describing a prototype information system for early warning network nodes in some detail, chapter 12 presents the core routines of an improved, but partial version of the informational support systems envisioned in chapter 1. Schmalberger's CEWS Explorer makes possible historically grounded explorations of possibly less violent, alternative conflict trajectories.

The concluding chapter comes out of CEWS's initial collaboration with International Alert and its later work with FEWER. Based in part on that experience, Kumar Rupesinghe and David Nyheim review research relevant to the practice of preventively oriented networks of scholars, activists, and government agencies offering conflict early warnings and encouraging effective early responses.

Premises Shaping a Research Program for the Post–Cold War World

CEWS' originating vision of preventable deadly conflicts is at least in part an Enlightenment vision. Two hundred years ago, Immanuel Kant argued that nature's long run secret plan for mankind was "to bring forth a perfectly constituted [republican] state as the only condition in which the capacities of mankind can be fully developed, and . . . that external relation among states which is perfectly adequate to this end." And, Kant argued, "to secure the external security of each state," a "cosmopolitan condition," a "law of equilibrium and unified power" at the international level similar to the domestic arena is required by nature.

> Through war, through the taxing and never-ending accumulation of armament . . . after devastations, revolutions, and even complete exhaustion, she brings them to that which reason could have told them at the beginning, . . . to step from the lawless condition of savages into a league of nations, [a] union of states . . . which is the halfway mark in the development of mankind. (Kant, 1784, reprinted 1963)

Our reactions to these Enlightenment quotations is to put them in more recent historical perspective. It took World War I, and the shattering of European world supremacy, for a League of Nations to become organized and accepted as a legitimate international forum and, under severe restrictions, action agency. When this global union of states failed, another took its place, but only after an even more costly world war. If the mandate of the UN Charter contains a wide ranging, if hard won, recognition of the need for global level cooperation in security matters, the UN's Cold War history does not imply institutionalized acceptance by member states of the appropriate responsibilities for international collective action regarding agreed upon "threats" to "international peace and security." Buoyed by support from nonaligned states, the UN survived and innovated in the peacekeeping domain, but at the price of becoming a secondary arena for Great Power security politics.

If the universalist (and interventionist) language and motivations of the UN Charter still appeals to many in the post–Cold War period, both general and specific sources of opposition and doubt abound. Generally, macro-scripts of world historical development, even those trumpeting the success of liberal markets and politics, are under attack. Globalism and parochialism contend. U.S. congressional responses to such challenges appear to be both isolationist and unilateralist. Canadian reactions are much more positive, but not without their own ambivalences regarding ineffectively supported peacekeeping or peacemaking forces. European social thought is so conflicted that Kant-inspired writers from the Marxist tradition, like Jürgen Habermas, have become the most important defenders of emancipatory Enlightenment goals.[3] In other words:

1. Enlightenment thinking is not dead, but it is under attack.

The Cold War has been ending in fits and starts, with European accommodations somewhat proceeding improvements in U.S.–Soviet relations, and the relaxing of Cold War tensions in Africa and Asia playing itself out with related but different chronologies. Associated with this period has been a spate of "post modern" challenges to Enlightenment projections of improved, more rational modes of human self-governance.

A related trend contradicts Kant's image of a bright beginning for the second half of the history of mankind, one moving toward higher levels of competitive cooperation among integrated republican states. In the later half of the twentieth century, accelerating with the end of the Cold War, we see another tendency:

2. Since the 1970s, there has been an increase in internal conflicts, state or regime shaping controversies, quarrels among noninternationally recognized actors, as compared with conventional, potentially violent, interstate disputes.

Figure 1.1: New Quarrels and Disputes 1945–1993 (Frequency Data from SHERFACS)

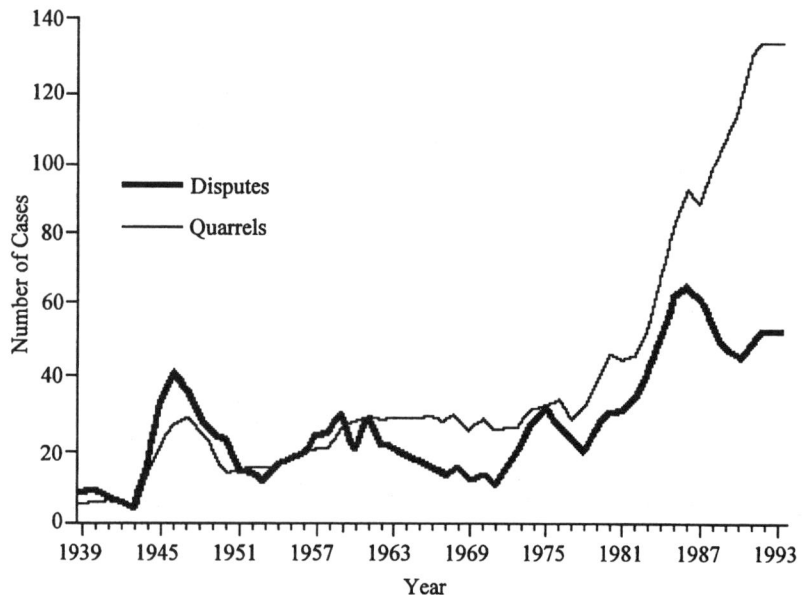

Figure 1.1, taken from Alker and Sherman (1995), spells out one relatively thorough measurement of the relative magnitude and acceleration of such trends. Gurr (1994b) and Wallensteen and Axell (1994) suggest similar, but less conservative pictures of the rapid rise of unconventional forms of organized, inter-group violence. Less than 3, 5, or 10 percent of such violence is described as now being of the "conventional" interstate variety. What then has happened to Kant's world of war-weary republics?

Before becoming too complacent about the ability of "scientific international politics as usual" to map quantitatively such challenges to Enlightenment optimism, we believe our first premise about the post–Cold War world has conceptual, methodological, and paradigmatic implications.

3. Whether they are of the realist or communitarian persuasion, the rapid increase in internal quarrels, conflicts, or wars challenges internationally and comparatively oriented social scientists to develop new and better ways and means for representing and modeling their quantitative and qualitative dynamics.

Consider figure 1.2—a generalization of the Deutschian-Grotian idea that international security relationships need to be arrayed in more than one dimension. For realists, this has been the degree of centralization or concentration of power. Liberals argue with realists about the degree to which national interests are cooperative or conflictful; they want as well to discuss different degrees of "institutionalization." For Grotian or Kantian communitarians, the most important second dimension, perhaps, is a measure of the degree of integration or disintegration of interstate relations. Whole paradigms of international relations are premised on assumptions about its characteristic features, at least in certain situations.[4] Why then should we study the variety of possible security-seeking arrangements mentioned in figure 1.2, in which the UN plays different roles, if the world is "truly anarchic"?[5] Why would one want to study anything other than power balancing and alliance building if pluralistic security communities were not known to have existed?

Just when we are learning to recognize a richer variety of possible international arrangements, the glue constituting the assumed basic units of the state-system, i.e., nation states, appears to be losing its integrative force. Gurr's ISA presidential address (1994b) is titled "Peoples against States: Ethnopolitical Conflict and the Changing World System." It starts with an attack on the assumptions of communications-oriented Deutschean modernization and integration theory that loyalties to larger communities like Canada, the European Community (EC) or an emerging Pan-Africa are the likely future for the world. Even if we grant the success of the EC within its current boundaries, such an integrated future has yet to happen. Reality seems to include a whole series of decaying, overlapping, re-forming collective political identities above and below the level of the states that are the starting points of figure 1.2.[6] The complex, multilayered reality of the present cannot be pictured in the two-dimensional reality of even as complex a diagram as figure 1.2.

This changing reality puts a special premium on relevant and timely, preventively oriented conflict information. Thus it is reassuring that one finds the same sequenced focus in the Fein, Gurr, Harff, Jongman, and Rupesinghe studies highlighted in the *Journal of Ethno-Development* special issue (Gurr and Harf, 1994), the Bloomfield–Leiss and Haas–Sherman analyses emphasized in Bloomfield and Leiss (1969), Bloomfield (1988), and Duffy (1994) and the York conference report (Adelman 1993). Effective early warnings oriented toward preventing conflict escalation or overcoming obstacles to conflict de-escalation must be based on knowledge of more or less changeable actions and situational factors associated with different paths of movement through such sequences or phases of a conflict's history.

Figure 1.2: A Communitarian Sketch of Alternative Security Systems (Alker, 1996a)

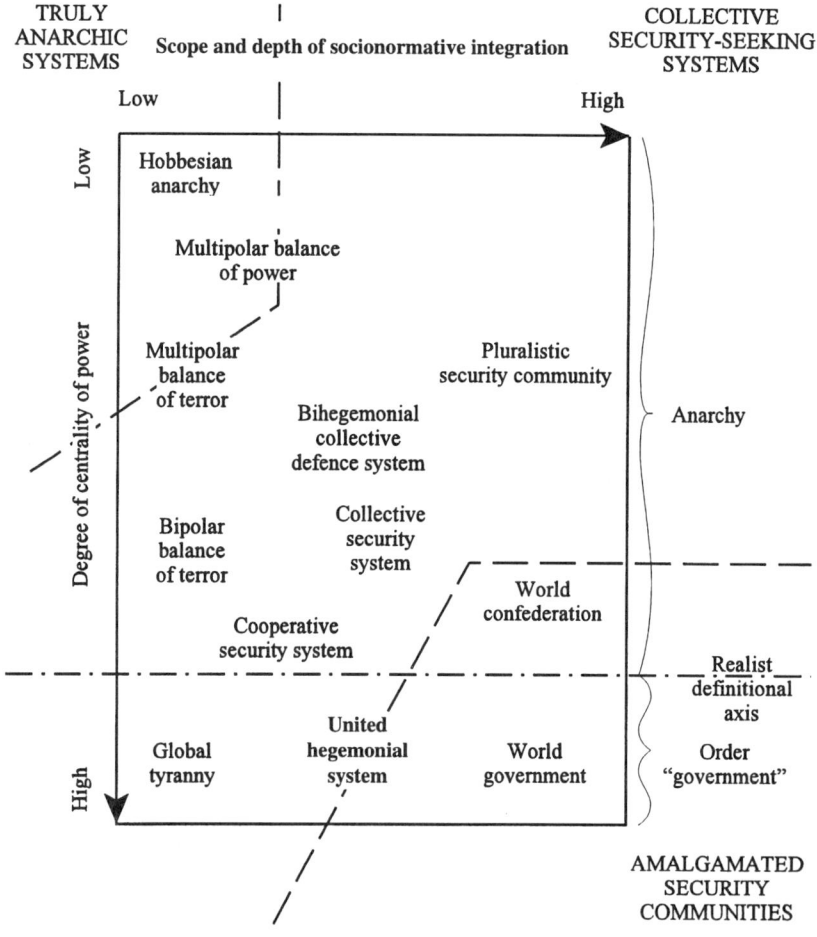

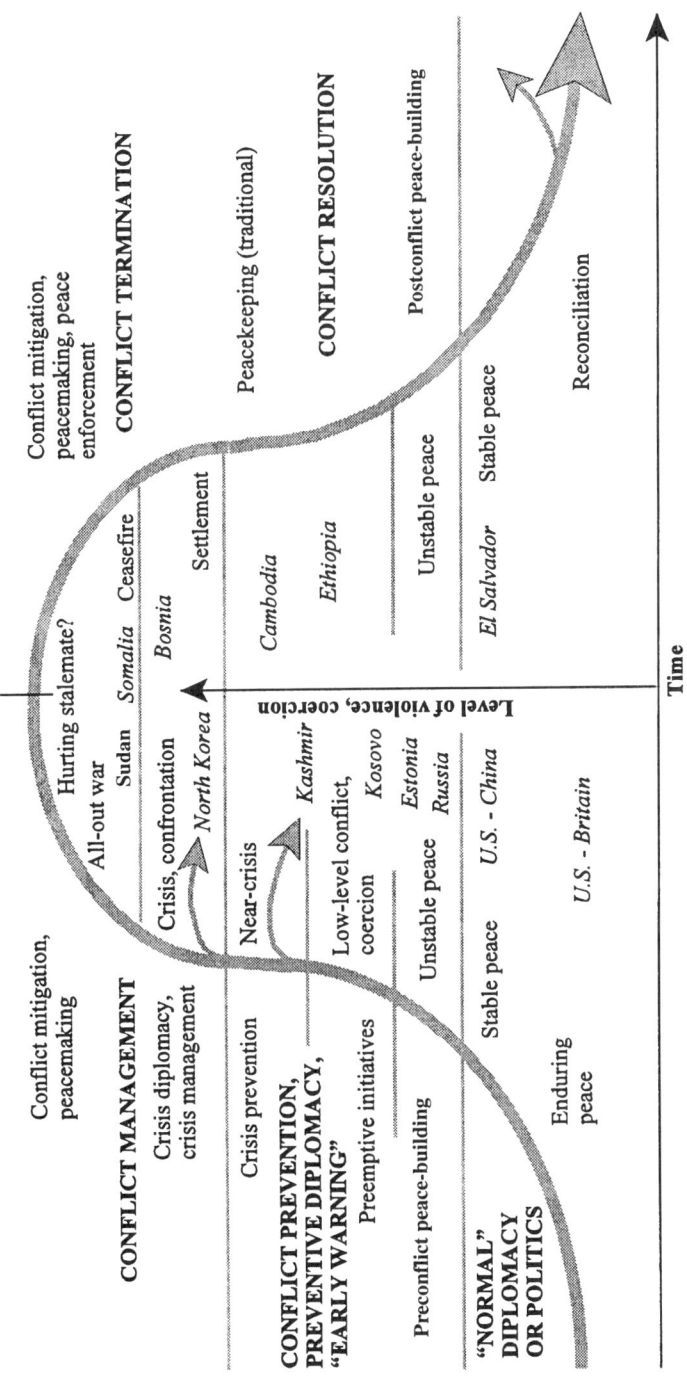

Figure 1.3: The Life Cycle of a Conflict, with Types of Conflict Interventions (from Lund 1994)

4. We define preventively oriented conflict information as information that describes conflicts in terms of conflict-related action sequences and their consequences, by both *conflict parties* and *conflict preventers, managers, or transformers* within or outside of the parties.

5. Describing such conflict histories in terms of previolence early warning indicators, changeable factors leading toward or away from hostility phases, or in terms of multi-option, multiphase life cycles, greatly facilitates informative comparisons among them.

Figure 1.3, taken with permission from a U.S. Institute of Peace handout prepared by Michael Lund (see Lund 1996 for the published version), shows several, especially multiparadigmatic aspects of this complexity. Although the internationally oriented conflict management literature, like the literature on preventive diplomacy, has regularly addressed "stages" of conflict escalation and de-escalation, what is most striking for us about Lund's figure is the way he links (and richly illustrates from recent diplomatic history) these stages of a conflict lifecycle to different paradigms of research. For example, conventional, noncrisis, international diplomacy—often ignored by both journalists and quantitative behavioralists—is linked with early and late stages of such lifecycles.

The crises and conflict management literatures that many researchers link to the writings of Brecher and Wilkenfeld, Claude, George, Haas, Hermann, and others links to a phase placed after an onset phase in which conflict prevention "and early warning"—our addition—is most likely to play a role. Standard peacekeeping, a major literature in the international organization field, is seen as part of a conflict termination stage or process. The conflict resolution paradigms of peace research become part of the settlement or transformation stage of this life-cycle account.[7] To think of such changes as only quantitative is to miss the most important qualitative changes they contain.

Similar points can be made about current attempts to model causally the different kinds of conflicts present in the world system today. Taken from Gurr (1994b, 23) and Fein (1994), figure 1.4 and table 1.1 point toward different modeling approaches to the study of communal conflicts and the humanitarian crises associated with the challenge to the interstate system represented by "internal conflicts." Gurr's approach can be assimilated to the conventional correlational/causal modeling literature, associated with the additional recognition that causal parameters change historically, so they need regular reestimation if they are to be of use for early warning purposes. In many ways compatible with Gurr's rich, disciplined, empirically synthetic efforts, the Fein and Harff models of table 1.1 nonetheless introduce real challenges for quantitative/correlational/causal modelers. How are these "sequential models"—to use Gurr and Harff's nomenclature for modeling efforts especially sensitive to alternative possible trajectories—to be integrated with causal studies? Their proximity to narrative accounts used by traditional sociologists and historians raise many issues we cannot further discuss here (see relevant parts of Alker 1996a).

What we would like to emphasize here, however, is the intriguing way both the "correlational" and the "sequential" modeling/forecasting approaches of figure 1.4 and

Figure 1.4: Processes of Communal Mobilization for Protest and Rebellion (Gurr 1994, 23)

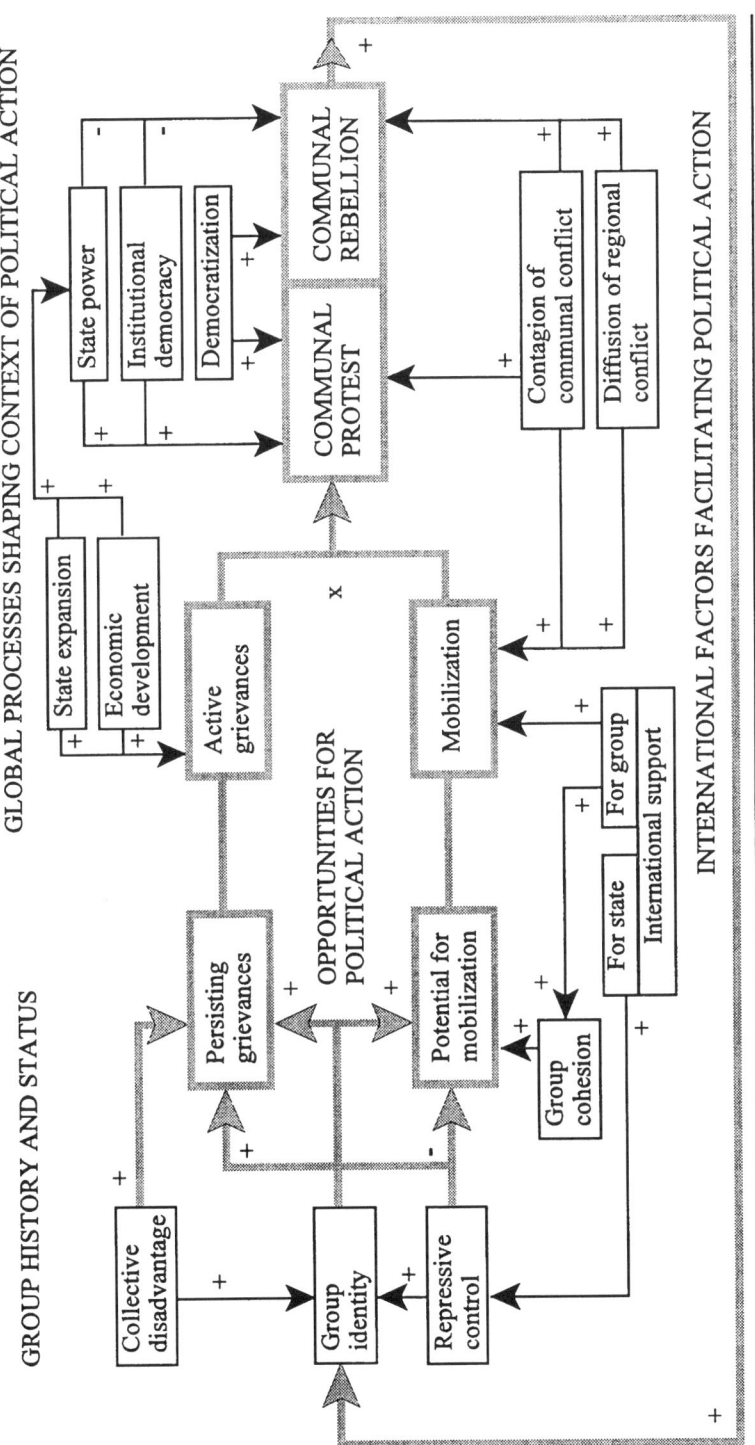

Note: Main processes are in gray; facilitating factors are in black.

Table 1.1: Comparison of Two Sequential Models Forecasting Humanitarian Crises (Fein, 1994, 35; reprinted with permission from the author)

Fein Theory	Harff Model	Agree?
I. Necessary Preconditions		
No check on power	State reliance on coercion vs. democratic experience	Yes
Solidarity/legitimacy, conflict/challenge based on ethnoclass exclusion	Intragroup stratification Salience of group identity (see also Gurr)	Yes
Moral exclusion leading to justification of annihilation of victim	Intervening condition: "commitment to an ideology that excludes categories of people ... from the universe of obligation."	Yes
	Degree of stability in the multipolar system	No*
Past experience Genocide rewarded	Lack of consistent collective ... responses to ethnic strife and/or humanitarian crises	Yes
II. Intervening Conditions		
	Fragmentation of the governing elite	No*
State consolidation Forces of violence	Indicated by lack of restraints on state security agencies	Yes
Ideology	Ideology	Yes
	Charismatic leadership	No*
	Economic hardships that result in increased differential treatment	No*
III. Precipitating or Accelerating Events		
Crisis or opportunity 1. War	Political upheaval (background condition)	Yes
2. Development in regions of indigenous peoples	Victims in the way of development	Yes
Patron's tolerance (no checks by patrons/ allies)	Empty threats of external involvement	Yes
	Increased external support for targeted groups	No
Ethnic/class mobilization and rebellion, or political challenge	Occurrence of clashes between regime supporters and targeted groups	Yes
Political exclusion and discrimination	New discriminatory or restrictive policies	Yes
Escalation of gross violations of human rights	Rapid increase in frequency and severity of life integrity violations	Yes

*In the sense of lack of agreement.

table 1.1 mix together "domestic" and "international" considerations. From a "global to local" top-down perspective, Gurr's figure is atypically sensitive to global processes and international factors affecting "minorities at risk." He wants to use quantitatively estimated versions of this graphical model for early warning purposes. The Fein and Harff sequential models, on the other hand, bring up the "bottom up" irregularities that troubled Alker's tidy communitarian synthesis of systemic possibilities in figure 1.2. Both models are focussed on dependent variables defined in terms of humanitarian/ human rights violations. Not only are indigenous peoples—a subject of some relevant complexity (Stavenhagen 1990)—mentioned as disturbing modern regularities; threatened or actual interventions of international actors into within-state situations also make more complex the "circuits" linking the "domestic" and "international" variables that conventional international theory likes to simplify away.

6. The rapid rise in "internal" conflict challenges the domestic jurisdiction and sovereignty claims of conventional international law so fundamentally that UN practices are changing to accomodate new realities.[8]

Because of their greater legitimacy, NGOs and IGO/NGO coalitions will have a greater role to play when conflict anticipation and prevention come into focus.

7. An appropriate mix of "domestic" and "international" changes in policies and institutions can make a difference.

The implication of an increase in internationally relevant "internal" conflicts for the shaping and reshaping of international society cannot be our focus here. Rather, we want to stress that a constructivist understanding of the development of internal conflicts allows many opportunities for preventively oriented conflict anticipation efforts. Before such conflicts get into the extreme stages at which they are deemed as internationally relevant humanitarian crises involving fundamental and masses violations of human rights, there is much that can be done. Gurr's "Peoples against States" (1994b) gives an empirically supported case for the possibility of successful domestic reforms. Since these conflicts have long fuses, there is time at their earlier stages for appropriate forms of renegotiated regional autonomy arrangements. International and regional interventions in the post–Soviet and Yugoslav cases have contained conflicts they have not yet been able to resolve.

With respect to genocide and politicide, Fein's table 1.2 suggests a constructivist, peace-building sensitivity that is hard to model, but is very worthy of emulation. It lists processes leading away from and toward these kinds of massive human rights violations. Sensitivity to these processes, and the role international actors can play in detecting them, and encouraging the less harmful options, should be a relevant focus for a new research program in this area.

Figure 1.5 (Spencer 1994, 116, revised) provides one model of how coalitions of governmental and nongovernmental actors can collaborate in processing early warning information. Much of this kind of work depends on informal contacts, but coordinated efforts by the major information/data generating agencies, and the field staffs of UN and NGO agencies can become part of a much better handled information flow. How event

**Table 1.2: Processes Leading toward or away from Genocide/Politicide
(Fein, 1994, reprinted with permission from the author)
(potential checks/interventions written in bold and italics)**

g1 (Past Generation)	g2 (Present Generation)	Precipitating Events
Abrupt breakdown Change in regime or Decline in state	State: Nondemocratic weak state Transfer of power/breakdown State consolidation Forces of violence	War with other states or within state
Despotism	Enforcement of civil liberties by GVHR absent or discriminatory ***HRNGO monitoring*** ***Withhold aid*** ***Strengthen civil society***	Escalation GVHR
History of genocide, pogroms, or communal violence	Ethnic hierarchy: political exclusion, discrimination, and severe inequality ***Advise depolarizing structures*** ***International disinvestment*** ***Sanctions***	Ethnic/class mobilization Rebellion or political challenge (fear of elite losing control)
Isolation of indigenous peoples from dominant group related to urban/rural split and undeveloped land	Political economy: Conflict over land use triggered by economic development in regions inhabited by indigenous peoples ***Require human rights and environmental impact reports*** ***Withhold aid*** ***Lobby multinationals*** ***Develop competing uses to protect indigenous peoples***	
Explicit or implicit racism	Victim perceived as or is challenger ***Assist nonviolent challengers through international aid/local NGOs*** Increase visibility	Justification of annihilation of victim
	Ideology: Growth of hate movements Exclusive nationalist, racist, Marxist-Lenninist, or fascist parties rising ***Monitor local press reports of refugees, NGOs, and so on*** ***Denial of recognition*** ***Strengthen domestic opposition*** ***Diplomatic warnings***	Conquest of state
	External control: Protected by international or regional hegemonic state (versus checked by such state) ***Bans on military sales and transfers*** ***International/regional sanctions*** ***Third-party warning to patron states***	Immunity No checks by patrons or allies

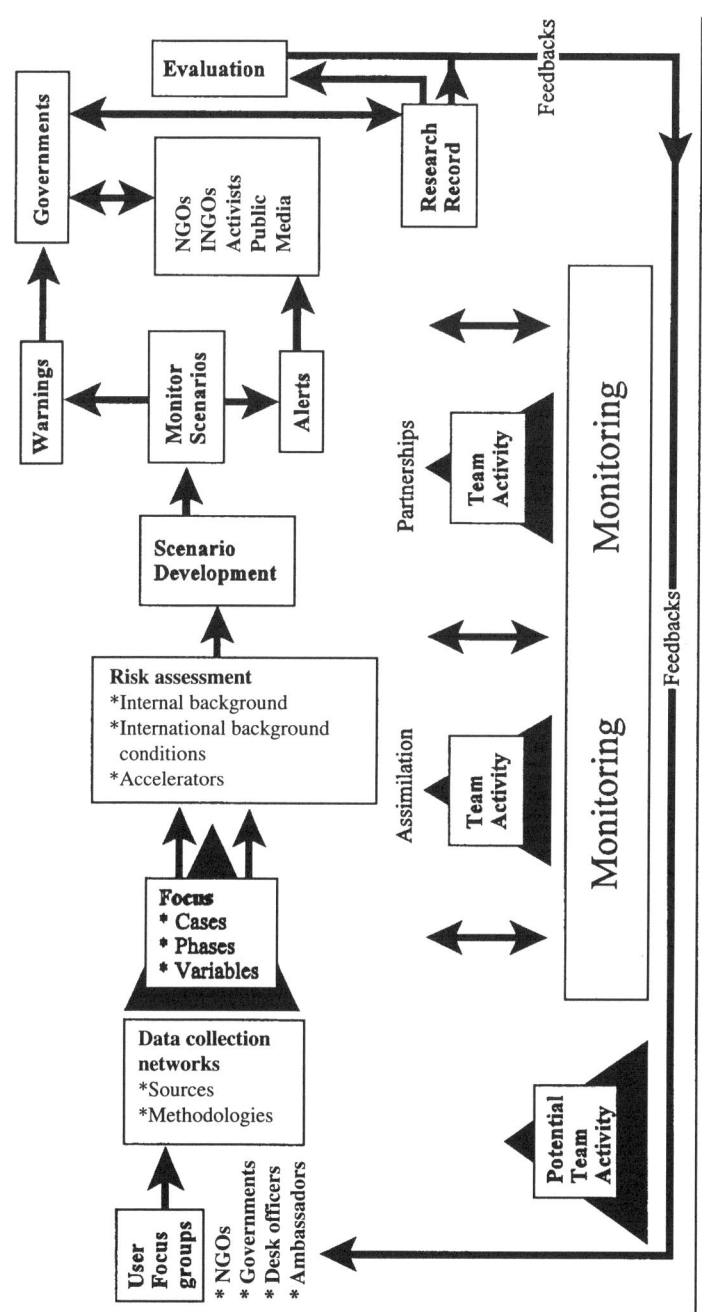

Figure 1.5: Early Warning Flow Chart (revised from Spencer 1994, 116)

data—and Human Rights Watch, Amnesty International or standarized human rights violation reporting (Rupesinghe and Kuroda [1992] describe a variety of such approaches) from the field—can be integrated with research nodes in a global network of regional and international agencies remains to be accomplished. What can be done to improve political will formation concerning the early warning stages of violent conflict prevention activities is only touched upon by the recognition Spencer gives to the role of the public media.

A sobering thought concerns the extent to which past data-making efforts have failed to gather and record information most relevant to conflict prevention success. Can any "quantitative international politics" research list more than ten of Bloomfield's 600-plus conflict exacerbating or abating factors for the seventy disputes he analyzes (Bloomfield 1988)? Can any "data maker" give us a good cite to systematically made collections of qualitative and quantitative material on the fifty-four types of actions that governments can take from the Jentleson–Lund "preventive diplomacy" perspective? (Jentleson and Lund n.d.; Lund 1993).

How much past practice can become the basis for better future performance will depend crucially on the willingness and of conflict management agencies of national governments, transnational agencies, and international organizations concerning to make available of information on their past successes and failures.

In a Deutschean fashion, better institutional memories are a key to the ability to learn from the past how better to cope with the challenges of the future. These are the kinds of data that should be readily available to users of conflict early warning information systems with large, computerized memories.

Project 1: A Global Set of Comparative, Conflict-Prevention Case Studies

Matching Invisible Successes with Painfully Visible Failures

If conflicts that degenerate into large-scale violence are all-too-visible in the world today, successful conflict prevention efforts are often nearly invisible. The lessons of partial prevention successes or painful prevention failures—those where correct anticipations are not forcefully and effectively acted upon—are also hard to find, remember, and learn from when they too are underdocumented. The thrust of this project proposal is to help redress this balance: by matching up from relevant experience a conflict prevention success with a comparable failure, insights concerning paths to prevention can be discovered.[9]

A Volume of Comparative, Conflict Prevention Case Studies

CEWS proposes to commission, oversee, and publish, both conventionally and electronically, a volume of approximately ten comparative case studies of internationally relevant conflict prevention efforts, their successes and failures. At least one failure and one success would be the basis of focused, matched comparisons, although a third possibility could also be incorporated usefully in such a research design. The studies would be chosen by the steering group collectively.

The CEWS coordinators anticipate that both past (since 1918) and future possible violent conflicts will be the focus of attention. If oriented toward the past, the study should contain a brief but analytical history of the chosen conflict or conflicts; for a future possible conflict, alternative scenarios should be developed as to how the conflict in question might be expected to evolve, with or without various kinds of preventive interventions. The most important, case-specific conclusions from the case studies should be about what kinds of long-term and short-term preventive actions by conflict parties or third parties would most likely make (or have made) a difference.

Although most of the cases commissioned by the steering group for special attention will be taken from more recent history, the search for matching cases that reveal alternative pathways to success or failure could go back much further in history. In order to maximize learning relevant to the world of global conflict prevention/management/resolution organizations, we suggest an historical boundary of 1918 for such comparisons.

Here are some possible focuses for such studies. As a conspicuous current example, why did OAU mediations fail before the recent Rwanda crisis, while (so far) international diplomatic mediations have been successful in preventing spillover of Hutu–Tutsi violence into Burundi? Has anything relevant been learned from previous UN or OAU involvements? To take a different set of related cases, what can be learned about conflict prevention from contrasting efforts to end the Sri Lankan conflict with the somewhat more successful efforts over the last several decades to accommodate the Chittagong Hills conflict in Bangladesh? Also reflecting on recent headlines, we can ask why are the Kosovo and Macedonian crises following different paths (so far) than did those in Croatia and Bosnia? There are crucial elements to this case (and others) that are far from the headlines, such as answers to questions like: What domestic or international actions, by which governmental or nongovernmental actors, in the post-1918 and post-1945 nation-building experiences dealt, how successfully, with the ethnic antagonisms we now see, or with others we do not?

In addition to an overview chapter or chapters synthesizing, where possible, the analytic frameworks proposed by the different authors as well as their principal findings, there will be at least two additional overview chapters in which the cases chosen, described, and comparatively analyzed by the case study authors will be compared and contrasted with the more synoptic process-tracing accounts available in existing, globally oriented UN records, news accounts and data sets on conflict management, prevention, and resolution. Alker, Mefford, and Sherman, the scholars primarily responsible for the second project proposed below, will be involved in writing one such historical, systemic comparison. Feedback regarding studies by Gurr, Harff, and Fein will also be solicited, hopefully resulting in a chapter from one or more of their vantage points. And some other group of conference participants may, at London, propose a similar, integrative piece, from a contrasting perspective.

Some of the key decisions about these chapters will be made at a volume review conference, to be held in London in 1996. This conference of chapter authors, steering committee members and some London and Geneva-based early warning practitioners will provide midcourse feedback on draft volume chapters, as well as a chance for chapter authors to influence and even define the ways introductory, comparative, and concluding chapters are written.

It is anticipated that research results will be published in a comparative and synthetic fashion, probably coedited by the CEWS coordinators. Both a regular book (or possibly two, if they break naturally) and a public domain computerized text version are envisioned, comments on which can be circulated and stored by electronic and more conventional means. At least in the computerized version of such studies, commentaries by all participants in the project on each others chapters, as well as by other CEWS Steering Committee members, can and will be encouraged and publicly shared. A two-volume publication format might also allow the wider participation of case-study authors in the comparative, generalizing process.

Globalizing the Research Defining Process

Focused comparisons, based on similarly situated cases with different outcomes regarding conflict prevention will be encouraged, as a way of identifying which types of preventive actions, by which kinds of actors, can and have made a difference in such outcomes. The study itself should contain a relevant literature review, from literatures of the research group's choice, pulling out relevant hypotheses. It is expected that this literature will be of an interdisciplinary and international character; summaries of existing literatures, such as those in Gurr and Harff (1994) will be provided to CEWS-sponsored groups, together with an injunction to propose research frameworks going beyond, or different from those included there.

Looking for focused comparisons of successes and failures allows study authors to choose and develop their own scholarly frameworks as well as encourage their own case-based policy suggestions. In these ways the trans-paradigmatic, as well as the international, character of truthful and useful research results will be encouraged.

Broadening and Empowering the Conflict-prevention Research Community

Uniquely placed to be able to monitor such activities, Kumar Rupesinghe and International Alert will be especially helpful in identifying possible research collaborators. A recent report from International Alert[10] suggests that twenty-eight to thirty have initiatives in the conflict early warning area (eleven in the United States); it gives addresses of sixty individuals and organizations (thirty-one within the United States) so concerned. Supplementing this information is a list of meetings and conferences on such topics: twenty-two of them in 1993 (all but four outside of the United States) and thirty-eight in 1994 (all but three outside of the United States). The wide distribution of these activities suggests a global basis exists for a globally oriented research program on conflict prevention, management, and resolution.

Conflict prevention-oriented research activities outside of North America, the Nordic countries, Japan, and Western Europe are less visible, less well funded, and not as technically advanced as those in the United States, Canada, at the UN and the UN's High Commissioner for Refugees (UNHCR). These deficits appear to occur especially in those regions where there is now the highest level of intergroup armed conflicts and the greatest need for local understanding and preventive responses to them. Thus the capacity to generate new data *and* new frameworks for defining, analyzing, and applying such information must be globalized. The "center-periphery" gap in knowledge production should be narrowed. In this regard, the first project envisions a set of largely qualitative, but comparative case studies of conflict prevention (in Boutros-Ghali's broad sense quoted above), the great part of which would come from outside the United States and Canada. Moreover, scholars will be chosen from different parts of the world, probably in fractions roughly corresponding to the geographic composition of the CEWS Steering Committee, who are interested in, and regionally knowledgeable about, generalizing comparatively from two or more comparable case studies with contrasting outcomes.

Similarly, prospects for successful funding will increase if representatives of local or regional or international organizations interested in conflict monitoring, mediation, management, or prevention are included in the research process. This bridge-building device, besides linking scholars and practitioners, will encourage the development of preventively oriented conflict accounts as well.

Bridging Epistemological, Disciplinary, and Regional Barriers

Conflict preventers deal with maybes, need nots and might have beens. Recognizing the pluralism evident in Gurr and Harff (1994), especially as noted by Howard Adelman in his concluding chapter, the larger design of this proposal is to try to reduce some of the evident differences in national or regional origin, epistemological orientation, discipline-linked descriptive focuses, and analytical methodologies. Put more positively, we want to build a whole that is larger than the sum of the parts of contemporary early warning research.

Specifically, there exist large gaps in style among journalistic observations (whether or not they are checked for accuracy and systematically codified), historical narratives, comparatively structured narrative case studies, statistical models, and computational models of conflict handling practices that need to be overcome if practically relevant knowledge integration and cumulation is to result. We have chosen a methodology of focused historical comparisons as a way of bridging this gap, because it allows cultural, national, and regional differences to be expressed in interdisciplinary framework development, as well as policy-relevant lesson drawing, while at the same time being focused toward scientific generalization making. To further linkages with modeling traditions, the proposed volume (or volumes) and conference are designed to facilitate many-sided contacts among specialists in these approaches.

Less evident in the Gurr–Harff special issue of the *Journal of Ethno-Development* is a tension between locally, culturally, or regionally oriented scholarship and the global orientation of UN, UNHCR, Food and Agriculture Organization (FAO), or Red Cross/Red Crescent early warners, and other globally oriented scholars. In suggesting the participation of representatives of the Gurr–Harff–Fein style of work as well as of the Bloomfield–Haas tradition of computationally grounded studies at the proposed London meeting, we are encouraging a dialogue of such regional and globally oriented perspectives. The International Alert loci for such activities links such scholarly concerns with both regionally and globally oriented early warning practitioners as well.

Project 2: Constructing Inexpensive, Replicable, Networkable Workstations Containing Prevention-Relevant Information

A World Where the CEWS Vision Had Come True

What would the world look like if there were a significantly higher level of popular concern and organizational activity oriented toward effective intergroup conflict prevention? It would be a world where both the possibility and the desirability of avoiding debilitating conflicts would be widely appreciated. Although state sovereignty would still be an important system norm, a common interest in conflict prevention would be more widely recognized by states and citizen groups that had seen both the costliness of a reactive mode of conflict management and some equally salient cases of successful preventive interventions. Systematic comparisons based on integrations of both quantitative and qualitative information largely presuppose a common, global universe of concern that local conflict participants and peacemakers often do not share. In an improved future, it is not clear that globalist orientations would have greatly increased among relevant individuals and groups. But a greater willingness to learn from the appropriately contextualized experience of other regions might be expected to go along with a greater tolerance for other groups' experiences and perspectives.

Additionally, in a preventively oriented world, the overriding importance of international peace and security would mean both greater transnational legitimacy for nongovernmental peacemaking agencies, working together with regional and global international organizations. Increased legitimacy and effectiveness would also be visible in stronger international institutions—like a strengthened OAU, ASEAN, UN, and UNHCR—interested in conflict prevention. Whatever the eventually evolved division of labor, conflict prevention, management, and resolution activities would also be better institutionalized, including alternative mechanisms for redressing intergroup grievances. Popular understanding of the historical development of such institutional capabilities could, and would, be validated by citizens, scholars, and organizational officials with examples where such interventions had been especially valuable, as well as examples where conflict had not been adequately addressed, especially at early stages in their life cycles.

The Construction of Inexpensive, Replicable, Extensible Preventive Information Storing and Handling Systems

This project of the Conflict Early Warning Research Program is designed to foster such a vision.[11] It involves the construction of relatively inexpensive, replicable, networkable personal computers or workstations that could be of great utility for individuals, groups, and organizations interested in enhancing and applying preventively oriented conflict information. An important goal would be to make available for peacemakers in the field, or in relevant bureaucracies, the data bases of several major previous, prevention-oriented studies of intergroup conflict dynamics in the world since 1945, together with retrieval routines for accessing and analyzing such information.

Workstations with CD storage and reading capabilities can be designed and developed that simultaneously store, and make easily accessible, the summary accounts and data codifications of all the research studies mentioned so far in this proposal.[12] Combined with the books elaborating on and analyzing such data sets, these workstations, embodying flexible preventively oriented information handling capabilities, would be valuable resources not only for research scholars, but organizations specialized to conflict prevention, management and resolution activities.

Specifically, data sets associated with the SHERFACS project (Sherman, 1994b; Mallery 1994) describe more than 700 international "disputes" and 1,300 domestic "quarrels" since 1945. Organized in a preventively oriented, actions-within-phases fashion, such a relatively comprehensive data base would be a major component of a CEWS information system, serving as an organizational "spine" of this data base. The relevant data base, extended to June 1994 but not codified, has more than doubled in size. Keyed to UN yearbooks and UN records, as well as Keesing's archives, this data set, more than any other, can provide a framework for organizing and linking the other, preventively oriented data sets mentioned above. If it were continually updated until the present, its outputs could be enormously suggestive, even for regionally oriented scholars and practitioners.

Table 1.3 suggests why this is the case. A search of international disputes within Africa, where the UN was involved as a conflict manager, revealed, for the 1945–1984 period, the cases identified there. Each case in turn is described in detail in terms of the actions taken by primary and secondary parties, as well as management agents, *if* an also described agenda process has brought them into the dispute. The preventive aspect of this data set follows nicely from its expanded use of Bloomfield–Leiss conflict phases. Identified in a summary fashion across the top of the table, these phases allow and suggest what differences early intervention can make. Although it is not suggested

Table 1.3: Early UN Involvement in African Disputes Is Associated with Much Greater Settlement Success
(Data from SHERFACS, 1945–1984; not updated)

	Settled
Dispute (Phase 1)	Somali Independence 1946–1960 Togo Independence 1947–1961 Somali-Ethiopian Border 1950–1961 British Camerouns Independence 1955–1964 Hostages in Chad 1974–1977
Conflict (Violence Threatened) (Phase 2)	South African Race Policies 1946–1960 Repressions in South Africa 1946–1976 Portuguese Territories in Africa 1951–1975 Zaire Independence 1960–1964 Lesotho/Botswana/Swaziland Independence 1960–1969 Southern Rhodesia 1961–1980 Ivory Coast-Guinean Hostages 1965–1967 Djiboutian Independence 1967–1977
Hostilities or Post-Hostilities (Phase 3)	Rwandan-Burundian Independence 1958–1963 Mozambican Border 1963–1975 Ugandan Tyranny 1974–1982
(Phase 4)	Angolan Independence 1974–1976
(Phase 5)	None

	Nonsettled
Dispute (Phase 1)	Namibia 1946–? French Nuclear Tests in Sahara 1959–1963 South African Bantustan Policy 1973–? Uganda–Rwanda Refugees 1981–?
Conflict (Violence Threatened) (Phase 2)	TFDADI 1974–? Cosmoros Independence 1974–? Transkei Independence 1976–? South Africa-Angola Border 1981–?
Hostilities or Post-Hostilities (Phase 3)	Eritrean Civil War 1950–?; Chadian Civil War 1960–? Portuguese-Guinean Border 1961–1975 Angolan Border Security 1961–1975; Tutsi Restoration 1961–1966 Guinean Security (Conakry Raid) 1963–1978 Zaire Civil War 1994–1996; Zambian Borders 1965–1980 Katangan Exiles 1966–68 Equatorial Guinean Post-Independence Tensions 1968–79 Ogaden War 1974–?; Beninese Domestic Security 1975–1978 South African Persecutions 1976–?; Western Sahara 1976–? Botswana-Rhodesia Incursions 1976–1979 Lesotho-South Africa Border Incursions 1982–?
(Phase 4)	Stanleyville Air Rescue 1964–1965
(Phase 5)	Entebbe Air Rescue 1976

that the UN is always the best such intervenor or manager, the percentage of successful conflict outcomes rises from about 18 percent to 64 percent when such involvement occurs in the first or second, prehostility phases of the dispute. The further exploration of the reasons why this is the case is possible within SHERFACS, but clearly the supplementing of even this large data set with case study material is necessary. The updating of the information to current situations is also called for, and being now undertaken.

Bloomfield's CASCON information system now has eighty-five cases in it, plus software for entering new cases and retrieving old ones found to be similar to emerging cases in relevant respects. Software for entering new SHERFACS cases would need to be prepared, making these cases comparable to but less richly specified in terms of conflict-exacerbating and mitigating factors than Bloomfield's cases. Similarly, since Brecher and Wilkenfeld cases (Brecher, Wilkenfeld, and Moser 1988; Brecher and Wilkenfeld 1989, etc.) are publicly available from the Inter-University Consortium at Michigan, and they have a rudimentary phaselike structure as well as supplemental ethnicity information and important codifications of diplomatic responses, at least their coverage since 1945 would be included in the CEWS workstation data base.

The data sets associated with the Gurr, Harff, and Fein papers in Gurr and Harff (1994) would also be included in the data bases of the proposed work station information system. Harff's earlier work on genocides and politicides is also of evident value and relevance. Gurr's updated version of the data set used to estimate predictive regression equations, as in his *Minorities at Risk* data set (Gurr 1993a, b). Both the PIOOM, the Polemos and the Uppsala-SIPRI data sets on the distribution of conflicts over the last decade or so, as published, could be a useful supplement to the above sources. Indications are that they are all available.

Perhaps the most important new source of conflict-related data mentioned in the York Report is the refugee data that Susan Schmeidl has recently exchanged with Frank Sherman for a copy of SHERFACS so that each can integrate the two data sets. Derived from, but going beyond, public UNHCR information, the data need to be broken down from its country-to-country format into conflict specific information sets. It could then be reconnected to a case-based data framework. Since the UNHCR has just put many of its public case studies and other data sets on line, this possibility of access must obviously be explored. If addition, Shin-wha Lee's data on environmental sources of conflict and migration, when available, would be an important supplement to the Gurr data sets.

Although we are interested in collaborating with the event data making projects like GEDS and KEDS described in Gurr and Harff (1994) and Duffy (1994), current plans are to look for other scholars who are interested in linking such data sets to the conflict-specific, case-oriented approach we propose to use in organizing the data bases mentioned above. This is a sizeable undertaking that might be best undertaken by those primarily interested in event data.[13]

Similarly, we are interested in integrating whatever relatively comprehensive case-oriented data sets there are on intergroup or international conflict mediation, such as

Bercovitch's inventory of post-1945 cases, recently reported on in the *Journal of Conflict Resolution*, and several not-yet-comprehensive inventories being collected in Europe. These could be useful in estimating what early preventive conflict interventions might have achieved. But we plan to rely on others for primary data collection efforts.

Making the Data of these Studies More Accessible, Connected, Revisable, and Capable of Supplementation

At the moment, individual data sets for most of the above cited studies are available, or will soon become available. A much more sizeable task than merely merging them onto the same hard disk or CD is the development of ways of cross-linking or co-referencing the corresponding cases in each study. Codebooks also need to be computerized and correspondences established in terms of which comparative and multiple-indicator style studies can be accomplished. The early stage of the project will include the purchase and exploration of a variety of software systems. Standard spreadsheet software, Windows-based data handling systems like Paradox—the current UN standard—will be explored.

Software additions to make it possible to supplement existing data sets, or introduce new ones in such a system include data and codebook entry-facilitating routines, network accessing software and basic data display, and editing and annotating routines. We shall explore and choose from among the publicly available and inexpensive but commercially available routines available for such purposes, initiating a correspondence with current or potential network users outside of North America to see what their special needs are. (The international communication network used by Amnesty International and other such organizations is already a good locus for such inquiries.)

Integrating Qualitative Conflict Assessments with Quantitative Ones

As Helen Fein's work in Rupesinghe and Kuroda (1992) demonstrated early, scholars can code from the annual reports of Amnesty International and the Rights Watch organizations a number of very useful variables. Given the epistemological variability of conflict early warning researchers, however, a fuller compatibility of preventively oriented knowledge bases would derive from the capacity to incorporate on a regular basis textual reports from such organizations, their timely, irregular and annual reports. Because of these organizations' interest in publicizing their findings, we shall explore the extent to which they are willing to make or share them on a computerized basis. Hence a set of text-scanning equipment and associated software will be purchased as well. On such issues the inaugural meeting of the AAAS-Amnesty International-HURIDOCS Canada/U.S. Human Rights Documentation and Information Network, in Washington, D.C., in November 1994, has accelerated the development of networks and sharable human rights information systems.[14]

The integration of qualitative and quantitative information sources is a long-standing issue dividing activists, humanists, and lawyers from many social scientists. Because so much of the refugee case law and the conflict prevention/management/resolution data is organized in a case-by-case fashion, we have adopted that structure as the primary axis for organizing the CEWS knowledge base. But the issue of integration of such different kinds of information will not go away, and we propose to try to take some modest steps to alleviate the problems of varying research style involved.

At the high end of the new information handling technologies, the Feature Vector Editor developed by John Mallery and the RELATUS system developed by Duffy and Mallery (see Hudson, 1990 and several chapters in Duffy, 1994) support simultaneously coreferenced versions of both quantitative and qualitative information, with complex semantic graphs being the common representational device. There are now large grants at the Massachusetts Institute of Technology from the U.S. Department of Defense's Advanced Research Projects Agency for developing such pioneering systems with hermeneutical sensitivities to the perspectives of different groups. More inexpensive versions of such software may soon become available.

At the lower end of computerized integration of diverse information sources, there is the increased use of hypertext modalities for co-referencing different, related information sources. We shall explore whether any such software packages could be used to facilitate the information needs of preventive information systems. One of the most attractive features of Internet networking possibilities is the ease with which hypertext "pages" can be shared from one computer location ("server") to another, thus allowing the interrelation of narratively structured case accounts, like those that many traditional and contemporary scholars prefer to work with and from. The extent to which public domain narrative case studies—such as those being generated by the other major project within this proposal—will be further explored and incorporated as options in the workstation development.

Providing Glossaries of Terms for the UN System and to Conflicts Parties

As the experience of the Librarians at the Center for Refugee Studies attests, once research programs are truly internationalized, there is a rising need for glossaries of technical terms—such as the legal language of refugee-related statutes. An interesting possibility for the proposed work station development is the inclusion of such a glossary.

The Committee on Conceptual and Terminological Analysis (COCTA) research program of the ISSC has developed a hypertext version of a glossary especially relevant to ethnic studies. This seems also to be a promising addition to the proposed workstation. Compatibility and expense questions need to be addressed before such a decision can be made. Surely the addition of multilingual dictionaries would be a related possibility worth investigating.[15]

Adding Country-Specific Data on Human Rights Performance, Human Development and Refugee Flows for Explanatory and Forecasting Purposes

Several sources of data on human rights performance and refugee flows have been mentioned above; Breyer's framework for assessing national human rights performance—which in some cases is an important refugee predictor—is one of the most interesting chapters in the Rupesinghe–Kuroda volume, nicely complementing Fein's work on violations of life integrity. A related set of UN-generated information is the *Human Development Report* (UNDP 1994), a "human security" index that already appears to be suggestive of conflict prone situations, if accompanied by the right (or wrong!) kind of accelerator events. As supplemented by other readily available data sources, with or without adjustments pointing toward conflict-specific data refinements, such information belongs in the information resource base we here propose. It can be highly useful for explanatory and forecasting purposes.

Improving the Persuasive Force of Conflict Prevention Assessments through a Variety of Accessible Analytical Tools

The York Report begins an exploration of unconventional analytical software that can help make conflict prevention analyses more compelling and appropriate. Bloomfield's CASCON system is particularly suggestive regarding "case-based" retrieval possibilities: looking for a case "similar" to a present or emerging conflict, but with associated conflict-mitigating policies, is a good way of suggesting policy ideas for the future. Ironically, Bloomfield's analyses make plain how much future-oriented early warning researchers depend on large amounts of historical information in their minds or bureaucratic memories, from which relevant pieces can be extracted at appropriate times. The idea of "similarity matching" case comparisons has been much developed of late in literatures on precedent logics, "case-based reasoning," "explanation-based learning," etc. See the Schrodt, Alker et al. and Mefford chapters in Hudson (1990), as well as Duffy (1994) for details.[16] We hope to develop from such literatures a second generation version of Bloomfield's basic, heuristic insight.

Beyond the basic statistical routines that often come with current spreadsheet software packages, there are other analytical possibilities that have real potential for history-rich, persuasive impact. A particularly intriguing one is the I2D rule learning software developed by Unseld and Mallery on the basis of earlier work by Quinlan, and all too briefly illustrated in Mallery's chapter in Duffy (1994).[17] This software derives from any irregularly shaped data set, *rules* of engagement or action best fitting the historical record.

Other analytical tools specialized to the comparison, matching, merging, contrasting, and lesson-drawing from new or old data sets will be explored and developed within the limits of resource ability and our human ingenuity.[18]

Some Useful Synergies

If handled productively, the dialectical intersection of these separate project waves, when they criss-cross, should result in a more globalized, scientifically valid, and useful knowledge base available to conflict prevention/management/transformation researchers and practitioners with either a local/regional or global orientation. Some suggested details of this reconciliation have already been given; others will be suggested below.

Obviously, there are more overlaps between these two projects, and between the scholarly work of the ISSC/CEWS Research Program and the work of International Alert. An effort to be complementary to International Alert's own practically oriented efforts has been made.[19]

Facilitating Competitive Integration, Assessment and Reduction of Predictive, Projective, and Preventive Early Warning Indicators

Obviously, much early warning work is done now on the basis of qualitative judgments. With its impressive connections to knowledgeable diplomats, governmental and nongovernmental officials, International Alert provides a unique opportunity for criticism, contacts, information, and advice for the scholars of the CEWS Research Program. Even more interesting, perhaps, is the possibility, at some later date, of joint exercises trying to forecast the emergence of new and dangerous features in a particular conflict situation. A systematic comparison of different qualitative and quantitative approaches to early warning could be undertaken once the relevant information bases were conveniently available to many different users.

Experience with secretariat staff at the UN and elsewhere already suggests a real need for statistical work by scholars to identify which are the most suggestive leading indicators of conflict escalation or de-escalation, as well as refugee flows. Enabling and encouraging scholars to use the gathered data sets, as well as other indicators of their own choice or construction, for the careful uncovering of *equations* or *rules* useful for anticipation purposes, will be a major payoff of the present project. Little systematic work, other than that by Bloomfield and Gurr, has yet been done on this subject.

Linking Case Studies Approaches with more Extensively Defined, Systematically Linked Case History Universes

If our information bases are global in scope, they allow the contextual location of particular conflict developments, vis-à-vis global patterns and trends, as well as locally relevant experiences and precedents. Systemic regularities and possibilities and constraints are also more easily discovered. This style of juxtaposing global and regional trends and possibilities with particular conflicts is another positive research outcome encouraged (but not adequately developed) by the present project. Alker's earlier studies of the operation of the UN Charter system (Alker and Greenberg, 1971, 1977; Alker and Christensen, 1972), like Ernst Haas's work (especially, as in Haas 1983, when it included performance data on regional conflict management IOs), fits within this universal-particular perspective. It uses more detailed versions of data like that presented in table 1.3, which strongly (but only correlationally) supports CEWS's visionary premise that early interventions can be more effective in preventing violent conflicts from developing.

Encouraging the Development of Institutional Memories Within Conflict Management/Prevention Agencies

Visits with the secretariats of the UN and the UNHCR are planned or continuing efforts. Information on the International Emergency Reduction, Readiness, and Response Information System (IERRIS) project within the UN, funded by USAID, is being gathered.[20] Past experience with the ORCI effort in New York suggest that scholarly inputs to such efforts may or may not succeed. At least the coordination of efforts involved may help more people and institutions inside and outside the UN system to understand and comment wisely on each others' efforts. Perhaps the most interesting way in which the SHERFACS data set, augmented as suggested above, may help conflict prevention oriented agencies, is by suggesting a framework in terms of which some of their own institutional memories may be organized. Scholars in the past have sometimes helped organizations see their own histories in a new light; again, for the many different conflict prevention/management/resolution agencies partially tracked by SHERFACS, this possibility intriguingly presents itself.

Toward Global Conflict Prevention Networks: Enabling the Search for Computer Support and Training Programs

There is a mushrooming of interest in computerized information networks in the disaster relief and early warning areas, yet relevant skills are in short supply. Discussions of the use of the Internet, "Relief Net," Togethernet, and PeaceNet abound. Into this discussion, the CEWS research program, working together with International Alert, hopes to insert some relevant experience. The relevant work of the UNU also needs to be better understood. Obviously, International Alert is a leading institutional force working toward the development of conflict prevention networks in different regions of the world. With its talented and experienced membership, the ISSC/CEWS Research Program can support this activity in a variety of ways, many of them indicated above. New case studies, newly financed research groups, new and better integrated information resources, and greater technical networking capabilities, as well as more appropriate analytical software, can result from such collaboration. The net result should be a synergistic relationship of a higher order.

Notes

1. The notion of a "data story," which underlies the project's research design, as well as the summary narratives and their analyses in parts II and III of this volume, will be explicated more thoroughly in chapter 2. The phrase was suggested by James P. Bennett.

2. The main source for the next three main sections of this chapter is the remainder of Alker, Gurr, and Rupesinghe (1995), which parallels Alker (1994b). The following discussion of "synergies" comes, however, from the earlier of these two documents. Some sections have been rearranged, abbreviated, elaborated upon, or modestly updated, as are the citations. But the wording of the main points has generally been kept the same so as to preserve the content of the original unpublished documents that provided the main substantive content for the half-million-dollar proposal that Alker originally made to the Carnegie Corporation of New York. Significant departures from the original document will be indicated in footnotes.

3. Added in 2000, both this explanatory sentence and the first paragraph explicating our first premise point to the arguments among Foucault, Derrida, Fukuyama, Lyotard, Habermas, and others (postmodernists and postcolonialists) about the corruption and failure of Enlightenment ideals. In this literature, related themes have included the end of Western European dominance, the rise of postcolonial ways of thinking about cultural and national identities, the corrupting role of power relations in self-described "scientific" efforts to cumulate knowledge, feminist challenges to male-gendered "sovereign" rationality, the triumph/exhaustion of liberal-capitalist world historical project, the inadequacy of all such macro-historical "meta-scripts," and the obsolescence of the Westphalian international order of sovereign nation states. Two of the best English language collections on these international, epistemological themes are Der Derian and Shapiro (1989) and Appleby et al. (1996).

4. A recent important development of this argument is Wendt (1999).

5. This sentence plays on the double, contradictory meanings of "anarchy" as "chaotic, without rules or order," and as "without superior authorities." Alker's 1986 paper on "The Presumption of Anarchy in World Politics" (reprinted as chapter 11 in Alker 1996a) and Wendt's famous 1992 argument that "Anarchy is what you make of it," re-presented in Wendt (1999), were obvious implicit references supporting this claim when it was originally written in 1995.

6. Beyond the transparent attempt to raise issues associated with "post-positivist" and "postmodern" scholarly orientations, without introducing too much jargon, this elaboration of our third premise suggests how challenging for quantitatively oriented behavioral scientists is the phenomenon that James Rosenau early described as "fragmegration" (Rosenau, 1990). More recently, on the same integration cum fragmentation theme see Clark (1997).

7. Coming at the end of a paragraph that began with a list of seven relatively visible North American students of conflict management, this comment is especially important in that Rupesinghe's ICON project was fully grounded in Johan Galtung's influential thinking about conflict transformation, including his cross-civilizational explorations of conflict life cycles. Full and relevant summaries of this approach, as well as earlier citations to non-North American literatures, are contained in Galtung (1996).

8. In retrospect, it is significant that the press release version of Kofi Annan's September 20, 1999, "Address to the United Nations General Assembly," on the presentation of his annual report on the work of the Organization (Annan, 1999), focuses on this issue.

Just as we have learned that the world cannot stand aside when gross and systematic violations of human rights are taking place, so we have also learned that intervention must be based on legitimate and universal principles if it is to enjoy the sustained support of the world's peoples. This developing international norm in favour of intervention to protect civilians from wholesale slaughter will no doubt continue to pose profound challenges to the international community.

9. This motivational goal has also been partially realized in 1999 by European Center for Conflict Prevention et al. (1999). See also European Platform for Conflict Prevention and Transformation et al. (1999), a study that could be usefully integrated with CEWS work.

10. The specific title of this document, provided by Dr. Rupesinghe probably in 1994 or early 1995, is lost. Similar lists are now available to FEWER members. A recent published "List of Open Access Early Warning Projects" and related data sets is given in Davies and Gurr (1998, 267–280).

11. The detailed outline of the inputs, tasks, and outputs of this project follow closely, in many but not all particulars, upon the recommendations of International Alert et al. (1993) and Adelman (1993). See also Alker (1994a).

12. These issues will be discussed further in chapter 2 and part III.

13. There was no DDIR III project, but Davies, Schrodt, and other event data spcialists are cooperating through FEWER; see chapter 13. A much larger, partly classified event data project is associated with the "Failed States" project of the U.S. government. See chapters 2 and 10, and Esty et al. (1998).

14. AAAS is the American Association for the Advancement Science, which has had an active human rights program focusing on, but not limited to, persecuted scientists. HURIDOCS is a grass roots Human Rights Information and Documentation Systems NGO, headquartered in Switzerland; previously unknown to Alker, Rupesinghe was long associated with it.

15. This proposal made particular sense within the non–English-centered ISSC framework, and corresponded to the interest within the grassroots, bottom-up style of work by librarians and other HURIDOCS, briefly described by Dedring in Rupesinghe and Kuroda (1992). Despite preliminary discussions with COCTA personnel, CEWS never carried through on this proposal. But thanks to Alex Schmid, appointed to the CEWS Steering Committee in its last year and a half, FEWER did develop and distribute such a thesaurus and glossary (Schmid 2000, 1998b).

16. One of the most important points derived from these technical citations in Alker, Gurr, and Rupesinghe (1995) is that both individual human and organizational memories of relevant "precedents" are typically represented not as numerical data matrices, but as qualitative, associative, cross-referenced, semantically labeled networks. These may suggestively be thought of like recursively defined LISP *data structures* capable of becoming revisable, *practical plans or procedures* for action. See the related discussion of historicity in pluralistic security communities in Alker (1996a, 112f, 138–43, 201–206, 386–93). This technically and philosophically important but complicated point was not, of course, elaborated upon in the original Alker proposal.

17. The implied need is for more detailed illustrations and explorations of such inductive, nonadditive algorithms for the constructive derivation of nonuniversalistic but data-matched classificatory concepts. See the discussion in the last section of chapter 2. Based on a reanalysis of grouped CASCON data, Adibi, Alker, Malita, Vest (1998, 97–106) derive practical, contextually nuanced, semantically articulated conclusions about varieties of UN style intervention. To quote their cautionary findings in figure 1 (p. 106): "Neither the actions *nor the absence* of IOs as

mediators/managers in Middle East conflicts had much bearing on the trajectory of these conflicts, except in rare circumstances when at least two moderately helpful economic/resource factors were present (in which case the overall effect was constructive), or when there were more than three profoundly and seven moderately detrimental factors arising from the historical relations of the conflict parties (in which case the overall effect [of intervention] was counterproductive, even if other highly positive factors were present)."

18. Part III delivers on this suggestion, but in ways unforeseen at the time it was first articulated. See the discussion in the later half of chapter 2, as well as Adibi et al. (1998).

19. This brief sentence meant, inter alia, that CEWS's coordinators never intended through CEWS (a scholarly research project appropriate for the ISSC to sponsor) to try to develop early warning networks like those Carnegie and International Alert were developing in Africa, Asia, and the Caucuses. Nor was CEWS itself likely to become an interorganizational collaborative vehicle like the ISSC's large scale projects on environmental assessment and poverty research.

20. Apparently, this was the predecessor to the UN system's IRENE network, which has focussed on humanitarian disasters, not conflict early warning per se. See chapter 13 for related details.

2
The Double Design of the CEWS Project

Hayward R. Alker and Thomas Schmalberger

Following the custom of research programs within the ISSC, by 1994 CEWS coordinators had constituted and gotten approval for a multidisciplinary, globally distributed steering committee.[1] Through the first months of 1995 CEWS Coordinators Alker and Rupesinghe waited for a response to the two-part proposal (mentioned in chapter 1) from the Carnegie Corporation, the foundation they believed was most likely to support their endeavor.[2] As Secretary General of International Alert, Rupesinghe also made contacts with Carnegie and other potential governmental and nongovernmental sponsors seeking support for Alert's field activities, including preventively oriented network development.

This chapter will spell out the design ideas shaping the revised research project that was the result of Carnegie's limited response to this proposal. First it tells of the initial London meeting of the CEWS Steering Committee, at which a more detailed book project was outlined, building on earlier ideas about conflict life cycles. Two years later, when most project participants had completed event chronologies and/or case narratives, a second project meeting was held, resulting in a set of guidelines for a new kind of structured focused case comparisons pointed toward discovering alternative, less violent conflict trajectories. We conclude with a discussion of the two related methodological ideas—computational data stories and multiperspective phase-sequence grammars—shaping the information system design goals of the second, post-case-studies, phase of the CEWS project.

From Research Program to Research Project

Early in the spring of 1995, Alker heard that the Carnegie Corporation was potentially interested in fostering comparative case studies of conflict prevention like those described in Project 1 (chapter 1), but not the systematic merging and integration of different information resources on conflict dynamics in the linked second project in the original CEWS research program proposal. Moreover, because Carnegie was not familiar with CEWS or the ISSC, given the current state of available funds, all that would be formally granted immediately was less than $25,000 for a preliminary project planning meeting at which Carnegie would be personally represented. No funds would be specifically allocated for the setting up and ongoing administration of a CEWS research program.

There was not a whole lot of room for maneuvers directed toward the preservation of a more ambitious ISSC research program, supported and overseen by an international, interdisciplinary steering committee. Not surprisingly, the Carnegie decision fit the known predilection of Jane Holl, the executive director of the Carnegie Commission, and others in the Carnegie network for focused comparison case studies. Thus the possibility existed for doing another volume of focused comparisons like the one that Bruce Jentleson was overseeing for Carnegie (published as Jentleson 2000), but with other participants and a somewhat different focus and approach. And, if most of the CEWS Steering Committee members were to commit themselves to doing such comparative studies, including providing associated event chronologies and/or preventively oriented narratives, an initial meeting of the research program's steering committee could be held, with the larger concerns of that group discussed around the edges of a set of meetings centered on designing a book built up from case study comparisons of some sort.

That indeed was what Alker and Rupesinghe decided to do, proposing a meeting in June 1995 in London at the headquarters of International Alert. Here Rupesinghe could help steering committee members and their Carnegie guest learn about the special needs and accomplishments of conflict prevention NGOs such as International Alert. He and Alker could invite to the meeting at little additional cost a few other European scholars already interested in conflict prevention. Such people might help further specify, strengthen, and carry out the intended book project, whose funding was not yet guaranteed; it might bring a richer mix of conflict prevention specialists into the Carnegie funding picture. Additionally, all workshop attendees could contribute to the discussion of larger possibilities for the research program. But without additional funding—and no likely other sources were in view—a research program in name was well on the way to becoming a funded research project in fact.

With the administrative help of Thomas Vest Jr. and the London staff of International Alert, the London meeting was exciting and successful in its immediate, if reduced goals.³ In conjunction with what must have been a favorable report on the meeting by Carnegie's designated representative, the key document supporting Alker's revised proposal was his December 1995 report on that meeting (Alker 1994b). Because it also helped sustain interest in the CEWS project at the ISSC, whose executive committee had commented on the slowness with which CEWS was proceeding, we include the substance of its content below, in a somewhat reorganized form. While burdensome, writing and distributing such reports is an important part of the direction, administration, and history of such research activities.

A Report on the First Meeting of the CEWS Steering Committee

Written primarily for those not familiar with International Alert, with IPRA's work on internal conflicts, or with the evolutions in conflict understanding associated with international peace research more generally, the first part of the 1995 report reviews some of their main concerns under the disarmingly simple theme of getting acquainted. In reality, most of the people Rupesinghe brought into the project were peace researchers he already new through IPRA, so the main extension of understanding was probably on the part of those at the meeting (or in the intended audience of the report) not so familiar with either the ICON project or with International Alert.⁴

Getting Better Acquainted

In London, Ed Garcia personally introduced the concepts and practice of participatory peacemaking that many peace researchers and International Alert favored with only passing reference to his impressive work (Garcia, 1993). After the meeting, trying to go beyond the deceptively simple terminology of the rest of the peace researchers' self-introductory discussions, Alker found the chapters by Gurr, Galtung, Rupesinghe, Nordstrom, Lawson, the Spencers, Lederach, and Ryan in Rupesinghe (1995) most helpful. Those not familiar with IPRA thinking could probably not find a better introduction to the distinctive developments in the discipline of peace research during the previous several decades than Galtung (1996).⁵

From the perspective of a relative newcomer to the International Alert world, the opportunity to observe some of the early warning, conflict prevention, and conflict resolution activities of its practitioners put flesh on sometimes abstract-sounding concepts, such as conflict transformation.⁶ Garcia's illustrative discussion of International Alert's West African activities, especially concerning a kidnapping crisis in Sierra Leone, heightened shared understandings of participatory, or "grassroot" style conflict transformation.⁷ International Alert's interest in peace maintenance through the careful and sustained development of social infrastructures relevant to conflict prevention in both Africa and the former Soviet Union was also expressed.⁸ Not surprisingly, a common theme was the existence of a space between officially sanctioned international peacemaking efforts and the interactions of conflict participants, a space in which such organizations as International Alert can play a constructive role.

Later in the meeting, evidence was presented of International Alert's role as a user of, and contributor to, publicly available information resources relevant to its peacemaking purposes. This included a demonstration of its HURIDOCS-based bibliographic database,[9] containing many "gray area" literatures not available in conventional social science libraries (Dueck et al. 1993). The list of Alert's regularly contacted Internet bookmarks was one particularly impressive product of that presentation, greatly multiplying the sources known to several Internet-literate workshop participants. Alert's extensive use of conference groups and other information sources available through the Green Net and the global Association for Progressive Computing probably resonates with the experience of many human rights or environmental activists. But it contrasts with the relative preoccupation of most quantitatively oriented North American social scientists: for them the Bitnet, the World Wide Web, international wire services, consortium data archives, and news-based event files are, or were, likely to be more familiar information sources. Beyond and behind the obvious state and interstate organizational contacts, one saw in Alert's London computers specific links in what could be described as a multicentered, multilevel, self-organizing, transnational, complex system. Optimistically, this reflected a "post-modern" civil society of "cooperative mechanisms grouping parties to conflict, local and international nongovernmental organizations and individual experts . . . [needed to] maximize the global community's peace building capacities" (Rupesinghe 1995, 65).[10]

A Revised Research Proposal

Building on this continuing, mutual education process, the meeting's main business was the revision and elaboration of the research proposal for a series of comparative case studies of conflict prevention success and failures in Alker, Gurr, and Rupesinghe (1995), represented in chapter 1. Most workshop attendees, and some who could not attend, sent brief outlines of the cases they would like to study within that framework. A preliminary book outline based on the further discussion of these memos, and related analyses, is given in table 2.1.

Several supporting arguments for the elaboration of a balanced, comparative study of conflict prevention successes and failures stand out. Rupesinghe's original suggestion was that at least equal attention be given to relatively successful cases.[11] First, conflict prevention successes are usually much less visible than their failures, so an instructive, balanced approach, giving ample attention to how the successes were achieved, was clearly desirable and needed. Public fatalism is often linked to a lack of knowledge of these less visible successes.

Second, there is the need for improved, prevention-relevant institutional memories. In the international sphere, damage repair efforts have too often overridden damage prevention efforts. The desire to shift toward more proactive intervention strategies calls up the need to have better, accessible institutional memories of how successes have been, or might be, achieved. When they get to a certain stage in their institutional development, key personnel in practically oriented conflict handling agencies usually recognize this need.[12]

Academic discussions of relevant precedents for inclusion in historically oriented early warning information systems, libraries, or data banks suggest that comparable, instructive, accessible accounts of relatively successful interventions are not readily available. The wisdom of experienced preventively oriented practitioners has rarely been systematically recorded in sufficient detail,[13] critically checked and then rigorously analyzed for lessons generalizable beyond their contexts of origin.[14] If preventively oriented organizations are to reuse and rewrite such conflict prevention histories for their own early-phase warning or intervention purposes, it is important that these multi-institutional memories be created and progressively improved upon. Those somewhat familiar with different IGO and NGO archives felt such richly usable institutional memories had not yet been achieved.

Third, a real, synthetic convergence appeared possible between conventional social scientific approaches to conflict management, conflict resolution, and conflict transformation, and those favored by peace researchers. This emergent consensus was built around the idea of a possibly repeating, multistage conflict cycle, as preliminarily sketched in the earlier version of chapter 1 (Alker, Gurr, and Rupesinghe 1995). For Alker, an important stimulant toward this recognition was Michael Lund's independent praise for Lincoln Bloomfield's soon-to-be-published CASCON conflict information system (Bloomfield and Moulton, 1997) at an earlier meeting at the U.S. Institute of Peace. The information in CASCON is based on case studies of management interventions going all the way back to Bloomfield and Leiss's 1969 book *Managing Small Wars*. Alker and Sherman's studies of the collective security-seeking practices of the UN system, Brecher and Wilkenfeld's similar studies of the League of Nations, and the UN's crisis management practices fit closely with the Bloomfield–Leiss life-cycle categories.

In his own study of preventive diplomacy (Lund, 1994, 1996; see figure 1.3), Lund generalizes the Bloomfield–Leiss conflict stages. His highly suggestive life-cycle conception integrates the normally separate phenomena and literature of:

1. "normal" diplomacy
2. conflict prevention and preventive diplomacy
3. conflict management, including crisis diplomacy, peacemaking, and peace enforcement
4. conflict termination, including traditional peacekeeping
5. conflict resolution, including post-conflict peace building
6. a return to normal diplomacy, or international politics, with its presumption of stable peace between at least some of the states in question

Grounded in an equally rich, overlapping literature on conflict mediation and transformation, as previously noted in this chapter, Rupesinghe (1995, 76–78) refers to "the life of a conflict" with stages comparable to those of human life: formation, escalation, endurance and stagnation, termination, and renewal. He is sympathetic with Johan Galtung's relevant interest (at the level of civilizational contrasts and overlaps) in non-Western ideas of nonlinear, organic, cyclic processes. Inspired by Daoist and Buddhist thought, Galtung suggests that we think less linearly and more cyclically about conflict processes and transformations; waxing and waning stages are followed by self-transformations to higher or lower levels. Conflicts rarely completely disappear.[15] Civilizational sensibilities, then, lie behind certain differences in understanding integrative conflict resolutions, or transformations, but working middle grounds can be found by those of different backgrounds who look hard enough for such meeting places.

Methodological Revisions of the Structured, Focused Comparisons Approach

Upon reflection, as the above discussion of different approaches to conflict resolution or transformation should have made clear, the London meeting was a productive site for discussing serious conceptual and methodological issues in research on conflict prevention. This was a fourth, especially important, area of convergent concerns among London workshop participants.

Without full specification, but citing Gurr and Harff's comparatively oriented work (1994b), the original CEWS proposal (Alker 1994b; Alker, Gurr, and Rupesinghe 1995) had mentioned Alexander George's methodology of structured, focused comparisons (George 1979; George and McKeown 1985). It did so because of the evident productiveness of the series of foreign policy and diplomatic case studies undertaken by George, his associates, and students. The London meeting, during which Alker had promised to Carnegie's representative to make the case for using George's approach,[16] turned out to be an excellent occasion for talking about its strengths and weaknesses in an audience not dominated by policy-oriented U.S. social scientists. For our purposes, an alternative was to emerge.

At first, discussion focused on the ambiguities inherent in the "success" and "failure" codings of the dependent variable around which case selection is organized in the structured, focused comparisons approach. The convergent interest in conflict life cycles meant that alternative trajectories, rather than simpler dependent variables, would be the focus of our attention.[17]

Reflecting the conflict transformation perspective described above, several important, case-based arguments motivated the emergent group consensus that the matched, focused comparison approach was not the most appropriate one for CEWS's purposes. Although there was general agreement that one could usefully isolate a certain "successful" aspect of a conflict transformation process for comparative purposes, the costs of such abstraction could be considerable:

1. More culturally or contextually oriented approaches are predisposed to look for partly unique, situation-specific factors as determinants of prevention,

management or resolution outcomes; these are especially difficult to match across cases.
2. This situation-specific orientation has a practical side, the concern with building on, and empowering, local, specific, conflict-transforming actors and enhancing their locally available resources and resolution-sustaining capabilities. These are not "success" variables as normally conceived in short-term, externally oriented, diplomatic studies.[18]
3. Conflict transformation processes often produce mixed, precarious, and reversible outcomes not adequately codified by "success," "partial success," or "failure" dependent variable measurements. Here the "intervening from afar" quality of much Great Power-inspired policy research pushes the scientist toward clear "success" (or "failure") judgments when a sensitive observer more accurately should see a lot more complexity and instability, including the sources of enduring difficulty that transformation-oriented research is particularly concerned with.
4. This time-sensitive criterion instability is multiplied by the variety of relevant participant perspectives and conflict features at local, communal, state, regional, and transnational or international (NGO and IGO) levels.

All these problems are enhanced with the complex, multiphase, processual aspect of conflicts is cut short or analytically ignored by methodologies not focusing on more complex life cycle histories. The big story about complex, protracted communal conflicts is often one of several years, or decades, in length. Repeated failures in one or two phases can sometimes be followed by surprising, often sudden successes, the results of complex interactions of processes at different levels, with overlapping by different participants, stakes, and time spans. One can fruitfully describe the South African struggle and the secret Israeli–Palestinian negotiations in terms of such complexities.

Trajectories also often have surprising transformations in them, successes leading to new problems, or even new failures. Thus certain successes in the last minute efforts of Perez de Cuellar to produce an agreement in the El Salvador civil war became problems, or stumbling blocks, at later stages of the process. Certain redistribution-related aspects of the land reform agreements were not implemented.

Thus the steering committee and its guests converged on generating and using *comparable histories* of conflict processes, where the preventively oriented efforts by indigenous parties and external parties (as managers, mediators, facilitators, third parties, infrastructure developers, etc.) were carefully observed and potential or actual differences in trajectories noted.[19] Situated chronologies of conflict-related events, attempted interventions, plus judgments as to missed opportunities, would be parts and products of such studies. A record of both realized and unrealized possibilities for early warnings and preventive actions more generally should be part of each case account. Although some cases might not be covered all the way until some "final" resolution was observed, reasonably large segments of the conflict life cycle, including *complex trajectories* (such as those with reversed paths back into violence) should be sketched. The studies would be pointed toward the drawing of multiple lessons about the role of situational features, and alternative strategies and tactics for reducing violence, conceived in a multilevel, phase-sensitive fashion. Paralleling Alexander George's terminology, the approach could be described as seeking to make *preventively-focused, life-cycle structured, trajectory comparisons.*

A Preliminary Volume Outline

Given the emergent consensus on our methodological orientation, it was clear that comparisons among at most three cases could be sustained in a chapter of moderate length. Two cases might indeed be better than three because of the level of detail envisioned. Making publicly available narratives or chronologies would mean that chapter summaries thereof could be shorter. Comparisons with, and information for, more data-oriented frameworks of analysis would be facilitated. A triad of derivative conclusions from case analyses and interpretations was sought. Academic reports and, it was hoped, policy briefings would follow. Conclusions to our study should obviously include comparative reflections written from such practical, as well as more formally academic, perspectives.

To this preliminary sense of our volume's orientation, two additional chapter ideas were added through group discussions. First, Kinhide Mushakoji suggested that we should not become too fact bound, that we consider nonempirical cases of conflict prevention efforts. This imaginative invocation of a tradition of simulation or gaming studies finds resonance in both the preventive diplomacy and peace research literatures.[20] This interest converged with Alker's concern with developing or routinizing scenario-writing skills for preventive diplomacy type simulations, information systems, and training exercises. The use of comparable case histories as partial precedents for new, preventively oriented interventions requires at least a tacit grammar of such historical reuse possibilities.

Finally, Alex Schmid felt there was a need for the systematic, comparative assessment of the individual early warning and preventive action efforts revealed by our case studies. Since his organization, PIOOM, has made a major effort at developing institutionalized, routinized, and quantitative ways of anticipating gross human rights violations, the matching up of our more historically oriented, comparative approach with his efforts, and those Gurr has been associated with,[21] seemed a good topic for an additional "meta chapter" in our volume.[22]

Project Contributor Guidelines and the 1997 London Workshop

After further explorations and negotiations about administrative arrangements, on behalf of CEWS, through the School of International Relations at the University of

Table 2.1: The December 1995 Table of Contents for Alarms and Responses

Part I: Introduction
Chapter 1: The Challenge (Alker, Gurr, Rupesinghe)
Chapter 2: Relevant Past Research (Rupesinghe +)
Chapter 3: A synthetic framework for developing and analyzing preventive case histories (Alker +)

Part 2: Case Studies (order not determined)
- Islamist Movements: A comparative study of conflict transformations (J. Amoda)
- Prevention Successes and Failures: El Salvador compared with Guatemala, or perhaps Chiapas (R. Stavenhagen, L. A. Padilla and/or Clingendael project participants)
- Nonconventional Diplomacy: Evolving NGO strategies illustrated by Central American and African examples (E. Garcia and K. Rupesinghe)
- Multilevel Strategies for Conflict Reduction: A comparison of Southern African experiences (V. Gounden, E. Cairns, or their recommendees)
- Prospects for Transforming Regional Conflicts in Asia: Chitttagong Hills, Tibet, and Kashmir (T. R. Gurr)
- Strategies for Avoiding Humanitarian Crises and State Failure in Zaire, Burundi, Rwanda (B. Harff)
- Kin Conflicts in Central Europe: Preventive experience in the Yugoslav wars, Hungary-Slovakia relations, and around Macedonia (M. Lund)
- International Prevention Strategies and Their Consequences for Human Security: The Gulf War and Cambodia cases (K. Mushakoji)
- The Evolution of Conflict Prevention Strategies in Russia and the Successor States: Moldova and Chechnya (O. Vorkunova)

Part 3: Analyses and Conclusions
Chapter 13: Early Warnings and Preventive Actions: A summary assessment. (A. Schmid of PIOOM, perhaps plus Gurr and Harff)
Chapter 14: Preventively Oriented Trajectories and Scenarios (Alker and Mushakoji)
Chapter 15: Some Policy Implications (K. Rupesinghe)

Southern California, in March 1996 Alker submitted to the Carnegie Corporation a request for nearly $250,000 to conduct "A Comparative Study of Conflict Prevention Successes and Failures." The new project proposal built on the report recapitulated in the last section. The bulk of the grant was for honoraria for chapter contributors, but it also included money for another London meeting, a contributors' workshop in June 1997, halfway through the grant period.[23] Administrative assistance was modest, but mailing, telephone, copying, conference, and travel expenses were included.[24]

Shortly after being notified of the project proposal's acceptance, at Gurr's suggestion, Alker drafted and distributed in late July 1996 a six-page set of draft guidelines for contributors to the CEWS comparative study (Alker 1996b). This document was designed to help clarify features of the draft narratives and/or chronologies that was the first part of the authors' work, as well as an appropriate rationale for case selection, the substantive focus of the intended comparative and analytical chapters, and financial arrangements.[25] It was distributed ten months before the planned midproject workshop.

The introductory section envisioned comparative and analytical chapters of approximately thirty to forty-five double spaced pages, based on descriptive narratives or chronologies of at least ten pages per case and, possibly, preliminary "chronological outlines." The need for public descriptions of violence preventive "successes" or "partial successes" was repeated, with an emphasis on "covering the main phases and tracks (to date) of the conflicts and preventive efforts by local, national, international, and transnational (NGO) level interveners." The proposal-related materials re-presented in the present volume were referenced, as well as the text of the successful proposal to Carnegie.[26] We reproduce here, without significant change, that memo's two main substantive sections, omitting its concluding section on financial arrangements. They represent significant improvements on earlier statements on case selection, phase descriptions, and chapter focus.

On the Selection and Phased Description of Our Cases

The first section of these guidelines suggests considerations relevant to the selection, justification, and phased description of cases included in the present study. It derives from the previously mentioned documents, but has been updated to reflect correspondence with several planned contributors. Sending it out in a preliminary fashion may yet help a few final case choice decisions, but its primary utility should be to help concretize what we need in our respective chapter drafts, and the associated conflict/prevention chronologies/narratives.

With respect to the case choices and the justification of these choices, the mentioned project documents contain several relevant considerations. Clearly, our interests have several dimensions:

1. We want most of our cases to be ones in which violence prevention or termination was attempted, and may or may not have succeeded. Some successes should be included: they are often relatively invisible and understudied; on the other hand, a conflict prevention failure with no or tardy and inadequate preventive interventions might be the perfect second or third case for contrasting/highlighting/assessing the effectiveness of preventive/management actions.

2. We want most of the conflict cases we study to be those with international (intergovernmental and/or nongovernmental), as well as national and/or local preventive involvements—a multilevel, perhaps even a multitrack set of

prevention/management involvements—the richness of which should be extended as well to the parties and factors shaping the conflict.

3. The conflicts must have a sufficient history (of several "phases," probably including a situation where intergroup violence was threatened), so that we can seek to account for why the conflict increased or decreased in its intensity, violence levels, or length over these phases; conflicts only in the earliest phase cannot be usefully compared in these regards.

4. Conflict processes and preventive efforts should be described in appropriate phased ways. The revised project proposal and inaugural meeting report emphasize two conflict phrase frameworks. The first is the extensive one Lund discusses and graphs in his work (1996), just published by the U.S. Institute of Peace; an earlier version of the relevant figure was used in Alker, Gurr, and Rupesinghe (1995) and included as figure 1.3 in this volume. The second set of life-cycle or phase distinctions, also previously discussed, comes from Rupesinghe's chapter in his edited collection on conflict transformation (1995). But we have left the preliminary choice of phase categories up to our case authors, and have suggested a number of other relevant possibilities. Like the Rupesinghe collection, the Alker, Gurr, and Rupesinghe paper (1995) is also broader on this point: Alker and Sherman (in SHERFACS and its predecessor database) have used Bloomfield and Leiss's phase categories, which are similar to Lund's, but not quite as elaborate as Lund's or Spencer's Early Warning Flow Chart, presented in modified form as table 2.1. Fein, Gurr, and Harff, on the other hand, have simpler, but still important phase-like distinctions, also discussed in chapter 1. Preliminary chronologies and draft chapters should follow one or more such life cycle/phase descriptions, justified and carefully applied to the cases in question.

5. Such a conception also allows for ambiguities associated with different perspectives, time frames, and standards of assessment. We want conflicts whose partly ambiguous histories can still be usefully compared as to the situational/infrastructural sources of their violence trajectories and the differences made by various interventions, at different levels or on different tracks, with respect to violence levels/expectations and overall settlement outcomes or transformations.

The Focus of the Case Comparison and Analytical Chapters

Given the broad geographical distribution of cases in the original volume outline (table 2.1), and the anticipated further discussion of life cycle possibilities and explanation/understanding frameworks in our own volume, on what should the individual case study chapters focus? How can they be written so that the subsequent, purely analytical chapters can maximally benefit from our book's earlier chapters? First, each of the comparative case chapters should include a brief discussion of the choice of cases, and how and why their comparative analysis is expected to prove illuminating.

Second, there should be a brief recapitulation of major case events and trajectories, making explicit reference to the chronologies/narratives that will separately be made available to volume readers (perhaps via a diskette, or a publicly accessible computer location). A tabular overview would be a good way to make this brief but succinct. The emphasis should be on the primary topic the chronologies/narratives are designed to address: the major activities and situational characteristics significantly constituting or affecting the conflict's development as well as those constituting or affecting conflict prevention/management process(es), especially their "successes and failures," variously conceived. Each of the two or three cases being studied should be so summarized.

Third, there should be an analytical treatment of the phasing and life cycle notion used to give descriptive shape to the preventively oriented account in the chronology/narrative outline of each case. The nonlinear, synthetic sequencing idea suggested, but not adequately elaborated upon, in the proposal was that of conflict process life cycles, with waxing and waning stages, and with self-transformations to higher or lower levels being more likely than final "resolutions." Although periods of instability and vacillation do happen, recognition of shifts to new phases or cycles can usually be made, however; the chapters should be explicit in describing and justifying how this was done. And a preliminary assessment of the utility of these case framing ideas should be offered. Discussions at the anticipated London workshop may lead us further toward a more integrated approach, life cycle/phase structures but that should be a collective decision based on working drafts, not an editorial dictate.

Fourth, there should be a case-specific, context-sensitive discussion of how and why different turning points in the case trajectories should be considered as "contributing, or failing to contribute, to intergroup violence preventive success." The broad conception of preventive diplomacy offered by Boutros-Ghali, and extended to the multiphase, multiparty, multilevel conception outlined herein should be helpful in this regard. As quoted above, such successes include "action to prevent disputes from arising between parties, to prevent existing disputes from escalating into [violent] conflicts and to limit the spread of the latter when they occur." For many life cycle notions, such meanings are more or less explicit in the phase descriptions, but the complexities and uncertainties of such descriptions need explicit attention.

Moreover, as the successful proposal and the inaugural report emphasize, accounts of these upturns, downturns, and periods of vacillation or stagnation need to be supplemented with available, if incomplete, evidence concerning slower "infrastructural" changes in deeper ecological-economic, cultural, and other sociopolitical practices, including "the rooting of peace constituencies, effective civil institutions, and the development of cultures of tolerance and negotiation." This last quotation repeats Rupesinghe's language from the 1995 Inaugural Meeting Report. Such analyses may well have to go beyond the "events" focus of chronologies/narratives. They need to address what Braudel or Gurr would call "conjunctural" or "structural" features, usually slowly changing, of these situations.

Finally, there should be an effort to interpret, explain, account for, and suggest lessons from the observed and discussed features of "success and failure" in the cases in question. Here both the theoretical frameworks already suggested in Alker, Gurr, and Rupesinghe (1995), additional relevant literatures, and the insights from comparisons across the cases analyzed in the chapter, are especially relevant. Another task of the 1997 London workshop should be the development of more widely shared understandings of the relative interpretive and explanatory efficacy of the explanatory and preventive frameworks reviewed there.

The 1997 London Workshop and the Double Design of the CEWS Project

The 1997 workshop proved to be a businesslike meeting, with most present already having met at the earlier London meeting. A few new faces were added.[27] We will first discuss challenges faced by authors of the comparative chapters, followed by a discussion of the analytical chapters.

The draft guidelines proved to be a challenging assignment for the writers of CEWS's comparative chapters. For the 1997 London workshop, most authors distributed preliminary versions of their descriptive narratives or chronologies, but gave out or orally presented only very preliminary comparative discussions of them. Although all authors were considered experts in their subject matter, their coverage of the perspectives of the different parties to a conflict varied, depending a good deal on the level of their detailed knowledge of their cases.[28] Those like Padilla, Anderlini, and Garcia, who were primarily oriented toward conflict management and violence prevention, gave more details about third-party actions, if not always their perspectives. Some, like Barbara Harff, preferred event chronologies that told the reader little of the intentional calculus within which particular actions were taken; others, like Vorkunova, provided narratives of a similar, quasi-objective sort. Joined to a deep interest in predicting likely violence, perhaps realistically in such cases where the violence has not yet happened, such accounts revealed very little of the choices made by those one would want to hold responsible for their actions. Most authors suggested at least one or two points in their accounts where alternative pathways to peace might have been found—alternative journeys through conflict, or conflict trajectories—but some did not, preferring to wait for a later stage in their analysis. Attention to the contributions of geopolitical, social or ecological infrastructures varied, although writers identified with "Third World" African or Latin American contexts of Cold War-era conflicts were more likely to link resolutional difficulties with Super Power machinations by one or both of them than was usually the case in "First" or "Second" World literatures on these conflicts. The extent of track-specific policy relevant lessons varied too, with most scientifically trained authors being more reluctant to generalize in this way from either a track-focused, an institution-specific, or a more synoptic perspective.

One could read these ambiguities into the project specific designs and texts given above. Indeed, according to Astrid Tuminez, support for different approaches and international perspectives not strongly represented in the Carnegie Commission had been an important reason for the Carnegie Corporation's support. Knowing of the national, disciplinary, and epistemological diversity of project participants, one could expect that some of the ambiguity and some of the "either/or" language in such specifications was intentional, trying to keep a diverse group all under the same tent, so to speak. Indeed it was, but for additional reasons.

Both old and new readers of the material in chapter 1 would have good reasons to suspect that a special concern of Alker, and perhaps to a lesser extent his coauthors, was with the reconciliation of diverse methodological approaches to conflict prevention studies. Too simply, such differences have been described as those between "quantitative" and "qualitative," "humanistic" and "scientific," "policy-oriented" and "objectively oriented" research approaches. Moreover, Alker believed, and had argued repeatedly, that institutional memories in conflict management and prevention organizations, whether NGOs or IGOs, could not avoid such differences once they found it desirable to encode in their institutional memories informative records about their past successes and failures. Surely deadly intergroup conflicts are articulated through many voices, just as an elephant has many parts that the proverbial blind men had a hard time picturing together. But he still believed that at least one and preferably several interdisciplinary syntheses of information codification processes would greatly improve the capacities of such organizations to recognize their differences and coordinate their activities, to share in the learning from their and others' mistakes, and to contribute to the violence-transforming capacities within emerging civil societies at the regional, transnational, international, and global levels.

For such purposes, *a diversity of approaches to answering the same set of questions was required*, although some of their silences on key guideline themes was frustrating. Indeed, initially presenting several different life-cycle approaches to conflict was part of a designed effort to evoke new alternatives or syntheses, and to make better methodological choices from among these or older, existing approaches. These goals could be achieved only partially of course, and through time-consuming discussions, editorial commentaries, and rewritings. Project authors and volume readers are the most relevant judges of the extent to which the editors of this volume have succeeded in such purposes.

The two-stage design of the CEWS project, then, was to generate comparative studies of typical questions asked by preventively oriented conflict researchers, and then to have concretely illustrated second-order discussions of the discipline-linked conceptual/analytical frameworks from which the concrete comparative studies were undertaken. A synthesis of project frameworks inclusive enough to support a wide range of scenario possibilities could only be taken in a later effort, after they had been proposed, developed and illustratively applied.

Paralleling the two project proposal of chapter 1, but on a much less ambitious scale, the actual CEWS project reported on in this book was thus designed to have multiple studies within two stages.[29] Part III of this volume contains two such comparative and synthetic studies of analytical frameworks, although not necessarily those originally envisioned. The first one—described above as an effort that Mushakoji and Alker would undertake to go beyond the data in the interests of constructing alternative scenarios—requires a more detailed discussion, to be given in the final section of this chapter. Suffice it to say that on Schmalberger's lead it develops a way of incorporating both the quantitative and qualitative frameworks of analysis used by other CEWS authors into a robust conflict life-cycle framework that is then empirically amplified to support counterfactual scenario explorations.

The second comparative effort is more competitive than synthetic. Illuminated by a large selection of the CEWS project's specific case accounts, it is Alex Schmid's comparison of early warning adequacy of indicators suggested by the PIOOM project and those used in the much discussed State Failures project. Since the frameworks used by Schmid and the State Failure project were known to Alker and Schmalberger when they developed their own synthesis of CEWS project frameworks, it is appropriate to begin part III with Schmid's chapter, presenting their own efforts at approach comparison and scenario development based on actually observed phase sequences. In a similar spirit, the final chapter, in part IV, gives a state of the art review of FEWER's early warning and early response practices, allowing reflective comparisons with the approaches of each individual chapter in parts II and III.

Generating Scenarios from Data Stories and/or Phase Sequence Grammars

If CEWS began as a vision of informationally empowered networks of practically oriented early warners or violence preventers, a crucial historical presupposition was that alternative, less destructive trajectories were possible for at least some serious intergroup conflicts.[30] Derived from such a belief is the imperative of finding such pathways. In this respect, the emancipatory vision of Alker's writings on emancipatory peace research (inspired by Galtung–Habermas–Ollman critical theory, mostly collected in Alker 1996a) was that at least the beginnings of these alternative journeys could be found *inside* the conflicts themselves, as real, *immanent, violence-reducing possibilities* within humanly motivated intergroup relationships.

But such a possibilist ontology is hard to represent in conventional statistical fashion, even if we think of codified, measurable, causally related, event sequences. For this vision to be realized, event sequences have to be seen as elements that are combined into stories. Depending on how sequences of events are combined, different stories result. For either participants and/or observers, each story reflects different motivations or cultural backgrounds, and entails different choices that produce different consequences from which different morals are inferred. Different stories need to be told regarding the different kinds of early warnings (Davis and Gurr 1998, 3). Observable conflicts going through, and possibly repeating, less or more violent phases can be said to *contain* their pasts or more desirable possible futures only if they are thought of more deeply *as event-generating or event-constituting processes or relationships* with multiple, situation-linked potentials. If scholars are ever to get to a place where they can scientifically describe conflict processes the way Helen Fein has done in figure 1.2—with practical suggestions for avoiding various disasters as parts of their narrative reconstructions– Alker's proposal is to have real cases be represented as revisable and reapplicable computational procedures, as LISP-computer-programlike *data stories*.[31]

Such representations would be very different tools for early warning research than David Singer's preference for time series correlation-regression equations (Singer and Wallace, eds. 1979) or the regression equation and neural net prediction procedures used in the Failed States study (Esty et al. 1998). Cases represented as data stories could have choices, plots, and morals within them; similarly conflict sequences could be reinterpreted as fitting into conflict narratives of the sort that nonquantitative traditionalists have always preferred. Like the findings of the more quantitative approaches, their contents could be publicly and scientifically debated. Accessible data would not be vectors of attributes or numbers; it would look more like the partly reusable, episodic memories of innovative peacemakers and revered institutional leaders. At a more complex level, conflict narratives could analogously have lessons associated with them.

The PARIS-in-LA Project

Without support for the second project in the original CEWS proposal, none of the above had much choice of being realized. Shortly after *New Directions in Events Data Analysis* (Duffy 1994) was published, Frank Sherman died. However his friends tried, no one was found who was willing and able to continue coding collective security conflict management practices in the SHERFACS tradition. So that second project would have been very hard to realize in its fullest version.

As a gifted cross-culturally sensitive peace researcher, political scientist, and peacemaker, Kinhide Mushakoji had helped preserve the idea of developing alternative scenarios at the inaugural CEWS meeting, but he was unable to contribute any more to the revised, funded CEWS project than an extraordinarily stimulating set of reflections on culturally different ways of narratively encoding, more or less ambiguously, the morals of potentially violent interpersonal or intercivilizational encounters.[32]

But the sun of possibility rose again, when Alker was able in late 1995 to get a modest sum from the Annenberg Center for Communication at the University of Southern California for a jointly undertaken, CEWS-inspired study of news-based and case-based ways of synthesizing preventively oriented conflict descriptions from a subset of Bloomfield and Moulton's CASCON data base, a corresponding set of Haas's collective security case codings, and a set of about twenty corresponding SHERFACS cases. With the resources and talents available over the next two years, Alker, Shankar Rajamoney, and Dwain Mefford were unable to write text parsers or story grammars powerful enough computationally to represent lesson-embedded conflict prevention narratives, despite Roger Schank and Robert Abelson's prior existing illustrations of such an approach (Alker 1996a, 200–206). But together with the PARIS-in-LA Web site (accessible from the CEWS Web site), the published report on the project (Adibi, Alker, Malita, and Vest 1998) did evidence some important learning.

First of all, even with the cooperation of Haas, Bloomfield, and Moulton, and a complete set of Sherman's information files, it was hard work to establish case boundary correspondences, a preliminary effort before an Alker–Mefford–Sherman style inductive grammar of phase sequences could be constructed from a merged data set. Designed to be more inclusive than Haas's and Butterworth's earlier studies, Sherman's universe of interstate disputes and intrastate quarrels still didn't agree exactly with their or Bloomfield–Moulton's case delimitations. More careful coordination of episodes, cases, and intercase affiliations was needed.

Moreover, the CASCON codings of measures or factors tending to exacerbate or cool down a particular conflict were as difficult to unpack and coordinate with others' views as Haas's equally seasoned judgments of the multiple contributions of management agent actions to their success or failure of their efforts. Without the living copresence of the original coders, fully articulated coding practices/manuals, and the extensive materials they used for their codings, and the ability to argue and clarify the multiple international perspectives involved, both the replication and unpacking of judgments were too difficult.

Hence, without ever intending to substitute automated procedures for responsible human judgments, PARIS-in-LA authors learned how appropriately modest that project's contributions must be. A survey of possible ways of using context specific information in making policy response recommendations was published (Adibi, Alker, Malita, and Vest 1998). While including a concrete, highly suggestive illustration of Quinlin's C4.5 algorithm for inducing situation-specific *rules* for successful UN intervention practices from the a subset of 30 CASCON Middle Eastern case phases, it only sketched ways in which a new computer science research paradigm—called "Data Mining" and "Knowledge Discovery from [Large] Data Bases"—could explicate the locally relevant circumstances of successful preventive actions *inside of* the beginning story/narrative of an emerging conflict. Programs needed to be developed that simulated the opening-seeking sharable memories of generations of peacemakers. Possibilities for more peaceful trajectories "seen inside" an emerging conflict needed to be constructed/computed on the basis of extensive "knowledge/data/memory" networks of related cases somehow constitutively connected to that specific conflict. Adibi's doctoral dissertation was to continue that quest. Clearly, the careful study of a single data set, and the development of hypothesis-shaped inductive procedures for mining such information from coordinated partial mergers of several overlapping data sets could take years. So our own efforts in a single project, or even two related ones, should be thought of as "prototype" studies making specific contributions to a larger, long term goal.

Carnegie's Concluding Grant and Schmalberger's "Dangerous Liaisons"

Late in 1997 or early in 1998 the relevant Carnegie Corporation staff person suggested to Alker that he could make one more proposal to them to help support the conclusion of his ISSC/USC/CEWS project. Doing this meant that CEWS could make several presentations at international academic meetings, work with FEWER on a more policy-oriented meeting, and continue to exist as a funded ISSC research program, even though the steering committee was not funded to meet. But how was the book to be finished?

During the 1996–1997 academic year, through a visit to Los Angeles funded by the Swiss National Science Foundation, Alker had become deeply familiar with Thomas Schmalberger's dissertation research on the Cuban Missile Crisis (Schmalberger 1998). Within the logical consistency required by computational simulation, this dissertation systematically explored alternative interaction sequences that shed light on how the Cuban Missile Crisis could have been prevented, or brought to an earlier conclusion, or led to war. Working from a case for which transcripts of crucial U.S. deliberations, Soviet documents, Cuban interpretations, as well as extensive public and diplomatic records that were newly available, Schmalberger reconstructed both the typifications and the inferencing rules by which U.S. decision-makers recognized threats, strove to protect vital U.S. interests, and tried to shape the outcome of an extraordinarily dangerous and important international crisis. One could say that he reconstructed the lifeworld of these policy makers.

Schmalberger was influenced by Husserl's phenomenological approach to the constitution of experience, and its sociological application by Schütz and Garfinkel. He followed David Sylvan's computational formalization of Kripke's innovative semantic modal logic approach to counterfactual inferences about possible worlds (Sylvan and Majeski 1998). In this way of thinking—which goes all the way back to Aristotle, and resembles Bertell Ollman's and G. E. Moore's discussion of external (contingent) and internal (necessary) relations—constitutive relations (more crudely, variables) are those which name, identify or mould something's identity or essence. Schmalberger's constructive approach to the reconstruction of conflict trajectories, the choices parties might make, and possible transformations in their meaningful development, builds crucially on participants' sense of *possible next steps* by each party. Following this lead, one could try to develop empirically grounded, grammarlike rules for what different parties saw as *possible subsequent conflict phases* without directly attempting to compose the data story or stories for each case in the data set.

Even though Schmalberger's case study was much more detailed in its informational bases and its modeling approach than anything that could shortly be done with the twenty or so CEWS case descriptions and analyses then becoming available, Alker proposed to Carnegie that Schmalberger and a Web site developer be funded for the final year of the CEWS project. Given the delays becoming apparent in getting revised final chapter drafts from CEWS case study contributors, that delay in scheduling seemed doubly fortunate. A preliminary paper (Alker, Schmalberger, Blum, and Schjølset 1999) became available in time for public presentation and discussion at the International Studies Association and at a FEWER-cosponsored workshop.

The approach that Schmalberger proposed, once he became more familiar with the CEWS project, focuses on the relationships by which different conflict phases are constituted from their essential and contingent features by both parties and observers. It suggests relatively simple graphical ways for representing life-cycle structured conflict trajectories with multiple episodes, which may differ according to the perspectives of different parties. Although Schmalberger's approach initially tends to sidestep some of the most complicated causal determination issues that Alker had long been interested in, it produces operational ways of representing and exploring the "contested historicities," the time-ordered collective self-understandings of continuing human communities (Alker 1996a, 386–391; Alker, Schmalberger, Blum, and Schjølset 1999) that are immanent within pluralistic security communities (see figure 1.2). A simpler version of Schmalberger's thesis approach seemed likely to mesh with the rich but uneven set of alternative possible journeys through conflict suggested by CEWS comparative case study authors. With further revisions and extensions, building on the work of all other CEWS contributors, the results of this collaboration are available for the readers' consideration in chapters 11 and 12, and on the CEWS Web site.

With reluctance, Rupesinghe supported Alker's proposal at the December 1998 meeting of the general assembly of the ISSC, that CEWS end as an ISSC research activity on May 31, 1999, the last date of its Carnegie funding. Energy clearly did not exist in the steering committee for continuing to try to fund CEWS's activities in the absence of substantial Carnegie support. In calling for a positive final assessment of the CEWS project, Alker promised that a book reporting on CEWS activities and accomplishments would soon appear. He argued that FEWER's accomplishments, led by Rupesinghe and Nyheim, and modestly encouraged by CEWS's support, were an important positive spin off of CEWS activities. By the summer of 1999, good drafts existed of most book chapters, and a preliminary, prototype version of a CEWS Web site, including the CEWS Explorer, had been created. Further improvements and a final manuscript have taken an additional year.

We see the termination of the CEWS project as a new beginning, the chance for its developments to be applied and developed by users in the early warning and early warning research communities. Further developing the CEWS Web Site as a way of providing tools to different conflict prevention specialists at different points in regional or global networks is an exciting possibility that we hope to help realize.

Notes

1. The original members of the steering committee are listed in the last endnote of the Preface. ISSC guidelines suggested not more than two members from any one country and active participation from at least three of ISSC's disciplinary organizations, and the discussion of the

CEWS project at the ISSC General Assembly had encouraged Alker and Rupesinghe to get more involvement in CEWS from the conflict-related subunits of the psychological and anthropological global organizations. Each of the coordinators drew on their previous associations in meeting these guidelines.

2. Under David Hamburg's leadership, a principal project area of the Carnegie Corporation of New York was conflict prevention research. In 1994 and 1995, they were developing a whole series of studies through the Carnegie Commission on Preventing Deadly Conflict, established in May 1994, headed by Hamburg and Cyrus Vance. The major report of this effort is found in Carnegie Commission on Deadly Conflict (1997). A recent Web site containing summaries of many of their studies is www.ccpdc.org.

3. Among the guests, Alex Schmid was particularly active. Among members or anticipated members, Ernst Gellner (who died shortly afterward, but had expressed an interest in CEWS Steering Committee membership) and Ed Cairns were not able to attend. Because Alex had good professional credentials as a Dutch historian and sociologist, it was possible to incorporate him into CEWS activities under ISSC guidelines. Schmid eventually became a member of the CEWS Steering Committee.

4. From the vantage point of the year 2000, it appears that here was also some important two-way communication between conventional academic social science as practiced, inter alia, in the United States, and the varieties of Latin American, African, and Asian peace research represented at the meeting. See below.

5. An equally systematic and more recent review especially focused on destructive and constructive conflict processes is Kriesberg (1998), while Jentleson (2000) and Leatherman, DeMars, Gaffney, and Väyrynen (1999) are perhaps the two most closely parallel volumes of case studies with which the present volume's findings might profitably be compared and integrated.

6. In Rupesinghe (1995, 201), Lederach suggests the gradual shift toward "conflict transformation" conceptualizations and away from the term "conflict resolution" to be an attempt to avoid "the connotation of a bias toward 'ending' a given crisis or at least its outward expression, without being sufficiently concerned with the deeper structural, cultural, and long-term relational aspects of conflict." Rupesinghe (1995, 73–77) contrasts an "integrative or transformational approach" to protracted internal conflicts with rationalistic, problem-solving discourse aimed at finding win-win solutions in the mutural interests of the parties. The former approach emphasizes the reality that protracted conflicts are more often transformed to new stages in a possibly cyclic process, than they are finally resolved. Therefore an appropriate, long-term perspective sees multiethnic conflict transformation as a slow process of "the rooting of peace constituencies, effective civil institutions, and the development of cultures of tolerance and negotiation to resolve potentially violent disputes." For the well-read expert, this language obviously contrasts with much of the U.S. policy-oriented writing on conflict management and resolution.

7. In addition to Rupesinghe's evocative discussion of the empowerment of local actors as "architects, owners and long-term stakeholders" in a sustainable peace process (Rupesinghe 1995, 80f), John Paul Lederach (Rupesinghe 1995, 207ff.) and Carolyn Nordstrom (Rupesinghe 1995, 93ff.) are particularly suggestive about reliance on local cultural resources and a multi-level approach to peacemaking, including grassroots, regional/sectoral and top leaders at the national and international levels.

8. Again we find a theme emphasized throughout Rupesinghe (1995). Gurr (in Rupesinghe 1995, 1–30) is particularly suggestive on the ways restructurings in autonomy, containment, assimilation, cultural pluralism, and power-sharing have sometimes enabled

conflict prevention infrastructures. See also Gurr and Harff (1994), discussed in chapter 1, for similar claims.

9. The work of the Human Rights Information and Documentation System (HURIDOCS) is briefly described in Hans Thoolen's contribution to Rupesinghe and Kuroda (1992, 178). The patient development by librarians and others of internationally stable coding/cataloging/retrieving conventions on such subjects gives dignity to the oppressed through the careful, reliable, comparable reporting of the indignities they have suffered. This seemingly modest contribution to collaboration among different elements of the human rights community has nonetheless paid big dividends, as when Sharon Rusu easily transferred computerized versions of many expensive Canadian research results to the Center for Documentation on Refugees at the Geneva headquarters of the UN High Commissioner for Refugees. Staff of the U.S. Immigration and Naturalization Service, when interviewed at the time by Alker, indicated their own reliance on this documentation work.

10. A more open, constructive linking to the guarded "post-modern" thematics of the original CEWS proporal (see chapter 1) was intended in the report's use of this language.

11. A more inspirational version of this idea is realized in European Centre for Conflict Prevention et al. (1999). Significantly stimulated by Kumar Rupesinghe in his capacity as director of the Coexistence Initiative of the State of the World Forum (which discussed the project at its November 1998 meeting in San Francisco), this volume should be read in conjunction with a series of similarly sponsored, somewhat more analytical regional volumes on conflict management and prevention activities. The first regional volume is European Platform for Conflict Prevention and Transformation et al. (1999). Related reports are publicly available at www.euconflict.org.

12. Alker's emphasis here came from his long association with systematic empirical studies of collective security and preventive diplomacy practices—e.g., the Bloomfield, Brecher-Wilkenfeld, Haas-to-Sherman traditions standing behind the second project proposal in chapter 1. A fair number of the peace researchers present were not familiar with these studies; some probably felt that their analytical frameworks were too simplistic and/or inappropriately mathematical. Recall that the second project proposal in chapter 1 mentioned without justification a 1918 beginning date for matching case selection. That date makes most sense to those like Alker, Bloomfield, Brecher, Haas, Lund, and Wilkenfeld, trying to learn from, and improve upon, the partly institutionalized collective security practices of the League of Nations, the United Nations, and associated regional security organizations.

13. Based on a recognition of such a need, the Yale United Nations project, funded by the Ford Foundation, has been putting oral histories with UN crisis managers in a publicly accessible, on-line format. When available, they can be used by CEWS scholars or their successors.

14. To clarify this thought in the 1995 memo, we note the following. The summary quality of most statistically oriented academic studies is just too highly abstract for most practitioners for most practical purposes. Academic differences in scope, detail, and methodology can also be bewildering. By 1995, Bloomfield (1988) had built his richly detailed database from an original sixteen cases up to something like sixty-six cases; Brecher, Haas, and Gurr had differently delineated data bases with total numbers of cases in the hundreds. Sherman had coded approximately 700 international disputes and 1,000 domestic intergroup quarrels for the 1945–1985 period, amplified by computational "text models" of summary narrative accounts. For details, see Hudson (1990) and Duffy (1994).

15. By way of subsequent clarification, see Galtung (1995, 51–64); and the systematic development of conflict theory in Part II and civilizational theory in Part IV of Galtung (1996). Citations to many of his relevant earlier writings are given in the latter source.

16. Although never asked to bring up or argue for this approach, Alker thought it appropriate to do so. Alker and Gurr were both very familiar with the relevant literature. In particular, Alker had regularly taught it as insightful, probing, theoretically grounded, skeptical U.S. policy-oriented research; on the other hand the need for better representations of constitutive and causal relationships in humanistically motivated social scientific research on practical reasoning is a principal conclusion of his 1996 book.

Besides Hamburg (a psychiatrist) and John Steinbrunner (a political scientist), George was the only other primarily academic American social scientist on the Carnegie Commission on Preventing Deadly Conflict. The executive director of that commission, Jane Holl, studied with George and served under General Schwartzkopf.

The willingness of the Carnegie Corporation to support an approach significantly different in its methodological orientation than the variant of George's approach that Jentleson was to use in his work for the Carnegie Commission must be publicly and gratefully acknowledged. Working in a European venue under ISSC guidelines for steering committee membership provided the constructive context for such a development. Surely, scientific research on peace and conflict should not be limited to methodological approaches favored by the scholars of one or a few countries or disciplines.

17. Using variants of the Bloomfield–Leiss approach, Frank Sherman and his collaborators had been able empirically to distinquish more than seventy types of trajectories (Sherman 1994b, 88).

18. Note here Alker, Gurr, and Rupesinghe's (1995) emphasis on developing fuller, life-cycle structured conflict histories for enhancing practically useful shared institutional memories is in tension with a more surgically focused study of the relative impact of particular management "tools." The latter are often thought of as externally applied, in a particular phase of a complex and protracted social conflict. The tension is not an absolute one, but it does materially affect preferences concerning research designs.

19. Hopefully more clearly stated, this paragraph is a substantially rewritten version of two paragraphs in Alker (1994b).

20. Lincoln Bloomfield, Thomas Schelling, and the RAND Corporation all have claims on the reemergence of anticipative "political military exercises" in the early Cold War years. "War gaming," of course, has a longer history. Within the peace research community, Harold Guetzkow, Paul Smoker, and Hiroharu Seki have made special contributions to this mode of inquiry.

21. The implicit reference here, made explicit in the next textual page of Alker (1994b), is to the "State Failure" project commissioned by the U.S. Central Intelligence Agency's Directorate of Intelligence. In London, Gurr briefed steering committee members about the project, from which a variety of scholarly publications are now becoming available. An early version of a project report (Esty, Goldstone, Gurr, Harff, Surko, Unger, and Chen 1998) was presented at the February 1995 meeting of the International Studies Association.

22. Having reproduced exactly the tentative title and table of contents from Alker (1994b), except for a volume subtitle ("A comparative study of contemporary international efforts to anticipate and prevent violent conflicts"), we omit here the last section, a page and a half titled "Other Activities of CEWS." These reflected the high interest at the London meeting of engaging seriously and comparatively with the soon-to-be-published reports of the U.S. government's "State Failure" project, in which Gurr and Harff, among CEWS participants, were participating. The similar, but much less elaborate, computational data analyses of the Humanitarian Early Warning Systems effort in the UN Secretariat in New York, and the effort at the UNHCR to reduce to a useful size

their preliminary set of early warning indicators, were also of related interest. Given our continued interest in such tasks, "the decision was, for now, to concentrate our limited resources on doing the comparative study of early warning and prevention successes and failures detailed above" (Alker 1994b,11).

Since the revision of the original research proposal was our principal task, those ideas in it that stimulated interest on the part of steering committee members were of first importance. Although there was, as reported, genuine interest in the analytical use of the idea of a conflict life cycle, clearly there was much less interest in globally or systemically scoped, historically oriented "quantitative" or "computational" studies by Bloomfield, Brecher, and Wilkenfeld, or the Haas–Alker–Sherman tradition. The preliminary title and contents in table 2.1 reflect these priorities, but keep partly alive, through the suggested contributions of Schmid, Alker, and Mushakoji, these earlier, larger interests.

23. At the 1995 London meeting, many present had argued that new funding was needed for them to complete the anticipated chapters and the publicly accessible narratives or detailed, but summary chronologies, hence the proposal emphasized honoraria—a form of authorial payment not requiring overhead payments to the University of Southern California. Travel costs to come to the second London meeting were provided for at least one author of each comparative chapter; to the extent that such funds were available and requested, similar or lesser levels of support were available for authors of the analytical chapters.

24. When necessary and possible, Alker supplemented his CEWS budgets by the use of research assistance provided through his John A. McCone Professorship and by his own personal funds. Reporting to USC administrative authorities, the ISSC, and the Carnegie Corporation about both substantive activities and budget related expenditures was a time-consuming task. Thomas Vest Jr, and Anita Schjølset provided exemplary assistance in this regard.

25. In the middle of the funded project period, partial honoraria beyond an initial infusion of funds were geared to the achievement of the chronology/narrative stage of the work, and evidence of the beginning of a comparative assessment.

26. With the guidelines, Alker included copies of his peace-research-oriented "Emancipatory Empiricism" chapter (Alker 1996a), and encouraged others to share copies at their cost of their most project relevant writings. Since it had not gone through the consensus building discussions associated with key project documents, it was obviously more personal and less authoritative a statement. But this chapter was cited in the draft guidelines, and subsequently played an important role in the shaping of the second stage of the CEWS project, as will be described in more detail below. No negative reactions to the guidelines or to this chapter were received during the two years of the related Carnegie Grant.

27. Despite valiant efforts, because of traveling difficulties in Africa, John Amoda was unable to attend, and Vasu Gounden could participate only in the last day of our discussions. Ed Cairns, Rodolfo Stavenhagen, and Hizkias Assefa did not participate, nor did invited author Barbara Harff. Ted Gurr made a presentation on her behalf. But Michael Lund and a new member of the steering committee, Marianne Heiberg, did come and participate actively. Hugh Miall was a particularly helpful guest participant, suggesting several new areas in which CEWS might expand its work, but funds and personnel for such activities were not found. Had he not been from the discipline of peace research, given ISSC guidelines about multiple disciplines in ISSC Steering Committees and/or projects, he might well have been asked to get more actively involved.

28. Project contributors differed in the extent to which they had participated in "large N" or "small N" case studies, and intensive single case studies. Policy-oriented discussions of single

case failures were also on the minds of participants. Some CEWS members had access to the intensive, multiaspect studies of the Rwandan genocide written in 1995–1996, and summarized and discussed further in Adelman and Suhrke (1999).

29. Recalling the language of the revised proposal in table 2.1, one will see that there has been an editorial shift toward a greater focus on analytical frameworks, the anticipation of pathway alternatives, and early warning practices. In a field with a variety of scholars publishing different books on conflict prevention, in which Carment and James (1998), Davis and Gurr (1998), Haass (1998), Jentleson (2000) and Wallensteen (1998) are important recent contributions, this focus seemed to be CEWS's comparative advantage as well as closest to its original ISSC mandate.

Individual CEWS authors were encouraged to make their own policy recommendations. On the more applied side, in May 1999 CEWS and FEWER jointly sponsored an early warning workshop at the Dutch Foreign Ministry focused on FEWER's concrete issue concerns and CEWS project accomplishments, to the extent that they were relevant to them.

30. This final section is jointly authored by Alker and Thomas Schmalberger.

31. Omitting italics, Lesson 10 of his "Emancipatory Empiricism" reads: "Think of conflict and cooperation case descriptions as LISP encodable data stories. These descriptions are then executable programs, situation specific practical accomplishments, procedural enactments that constitute the cases, analogous to, but possibly different from the practical actions constituting the observed actions they refer to" (Alker 1996a, 350). Schmalberger rightly adds that complex issues concerning functional and object-oriented programming are riding just below the surface of this notion, as James Bennett, its originator, was doubtless aware.

32. See Alker and Mushakoji (2000), which appeared in a relevant ISSC publication and is available on the CEWS Web site. Had the editors had more time and space prepare the present volume, a revised version of this conversation would have been included in part III as another example of engaging different prevention-oriented research approaches.

3
Peacemaking and Conflict Transformation in Guatemala

Luis Alberto Padilla

One of the main goals of the Conflict Early Warning Systems (CEWS) research project is to provide knowledge about the causes and determinants of success and failure in conflict prevention, management, and resolution. In this chapter we will use the theoretical framework of such authors as Johan Galtung, Ted Robert Gurr, Kumar Rupesinghe, Ronald Fisher, and John Paul Lederach in order to analyze the nature of the peace process in Guatemala with special attention to the peacemaking and conflict transformation phenomenon, and also to the prevention of potential conflicts in the near future.

The Guatemalan peace process can be characterized as being essentially a peacemaking process[1] with the mediation of both (in different stages) an internal mediator or "conciliator" (the Catholic Church) and an external mediator, or "moderator" (the United Nations). The aim was to put an end to violence and solve/transform an internal armed conflict. Concerning the conflict itself, we assert that the Guatemalan conflict is intrinsically of an ideological and political nature, with roots in the violent U.S. intervention in Guatemala (1954) to overthrow the democratic and legally elected government of President Jacobo Arbenz Guzmán. The government was perceived by Washington at that time as a "communist" government mainly because of the agrarian reform, (which affected U.S.-owned plantations and corporations), and because of its nationalist and modernizing policies. (For more on the U.S. intervention in Guatemala, see Gleijeses 1991; Schlesinger and Kinzer 1983; Schlesinger 1978; and Jonas 1991.)

Thus, according to this view the Guatemalan armed conflict was essentially a political and military conflict between the state and an insurgent movement (the Guatemalan National Revolutionary Unity or URNG) and therefore it fits Kumar Rupesinghe's definition of intrastate conflict between government and other parties "who are either victims or unequal parties to the conflict" (Rupesinghe 1992, 23). Therefore, we can assert that the Guatemalan conflict was simultaneously external and internal. In other words, the insurgent movement represented an ideological and nationalist response to the violation of national sovereignty and to the national trauma generated by the U.S. intervention in 1954, and at the same time the conflict was over governance and authority, because it also expressed popular demands for democracy and political participation.

Consequently, the Guatemalan conflict can be considered not only as an ideological conflict in the sense that it was a result, or negative side effect, of the cold war extrapolated to Guatemala—mainly by the U.S. administration decision in the context of the witch-hunt of the times of McCarthyism—but also as a conflict over democracy and governance. In other words, it was a revolutionary war between the insurgents and the government aimed at displacing the authoritarian regime imposed by the U.S. intervention of 1954 through guerrilla warfare.[2]

Thus the absence of democracy and of the rule of law, illegal repression through "disappearances," extra-judicial killings, torture, human rights violations, and the ban of all leftist parties, popular organizations and trade unions are also fundamental causes of the conflict, and therefore, clear issues for its resolution. The fact that the issues of democracy and governance were included in the agenda for negotiations between the URNG and the government (as it was stated in the Framework Agreement of April 1991 signed in Mexico City) is a clear demonstration of this proposition.

It took more than forty years to end a conflict that had basically been created as a result of political ignorance, misperceptions, and misunderstandings, as well as spurious economic and shortsighted social (Guatemalan) and corporate (foreign) interests. Thirty years of guerrilla warfare and hundreds of thousand deaths, with the resulting destruction, refugee problems, backwardness, and obstacles for economic and social development, were not a small affair, for the Guatemalan people, or just another instance of low intensity warfare as the U.S. military and strategy experts used to call the conflict in the 1980s. It was a real national and social tragedy, a catastrophe that provoked a wave of violence of such a magnitude that it devoured an entire generation of Guatemalans.

Could the conflict have been prevented? How was it that, in spite of the general situation of crisis and near "state failure" that the country endured at the beginning of the past decade,[3] it was impossible to realize or to prevent what was going to occur, especially regarding the mass killings of Indian peasants and the large scale mobilization of the indigenous population both as guerrilla combatants and as "civil patrols" or soldiers in the army troops.[4]

Another concern is related to the peace process, both in its recent past and regarding the future: What lessons can we derive from the development of the peace process inaugurated by the Central American Peace Agreements of Esquipulas in 1987 and the subsequent (1991) negotiation process in Guatemala?

The Guatemalan peace process finally reached an end with the signature of the Agreement for a Firm and Lasting Peace in Guatemala City on December 29, 1996. In this paper we will describe the peace process as an example of successful conflict resolution with the mediation of the United Nations.[5] What are, therefore, the main features of the peace process?

First, as we have already stressed, the conflict was ideological and political but it also had a Mayan indigenous or ethnic component. That means that even if it is true that the Guatemalan armed conflict can not be qualified as an ethnic war, or ethnopolitical conflict,[6] the indigenous population was not solely involved in the conflict but suffered the most terrible wave of violence since the times of the Spanish invasion, the so-called *conquista* (conquest) in the sixteenth century. The majority of casualties and civilian victims were among them.[7] That is why the item of indigenous rights was included in the negotiations agenda.

Consequently, the explanation for one of the main agreements of the peace process, the Agreement of Identity and Rights of the Indigenous Peoples, is associated with the fact that both parties were aware that the situation of the indigenous peoples was not only a fundamental issue of the peace process, but also a mechanism for prevention of conflict, and somehow also an instrument of early warning for potential ethnic conflict in the near Guatemalan future. Furthermore, the issue was one of the most crucial points of the negotiations (it took more than one year to reach an agreement), even though the parties were not supposed to be legitimated to speak on behalf of the Guatemalan ethnic groups.[8]

Another important feature of the Guatemalan peace process is that it is closely related to the Central American peace process, for without the Esquipulas agreement of 1987 there could have not been a peace process in Guatemala. The general situation in Central America at the beginning of the 1980s was one of conflict and crisis: both the FMLN and the URNG were in war against their governments in El Salvador and Guatemala, while the "contras" (armed and financed by Washington) were fighting against the Sandinista government in Nicaragua with the support of Honduras. Mexico, assisted by the "Grupo de Contadora" (Colombia, Venezuela, and Panama), tried hard to find a negotiated solution through the Contadora mediation effort, which failed at the last minute when Honduras—under White House pressure—refused to sign the *Acta para la Paz y la Cooperación en Centro América*.

The Esquipulas accord was the result of a summit meeting of the five Central American presidents convoked by Guatemalan President Vinicio Cerezo, who was democratically elected in Guatemala in 1985 and took office in January 1986. The first meeting was held in Guatemala the same year, the second took place in Guatemala City in August 1987, and the result was the signature of the Esquipulas II Peace Accord. The accord established a procedure for negotiations in order to achieve peace through political means. The overriding characteristic of the peace agreement was that the Central American presidents agreed not only to address the causes of conflict as an essential element of the negotiations, but also to promote both democratization and sustainable development as a fundamental means for both conflict resolution and *peace building*, using the term in Galtung's sense of "overcoming the contradictions at the root of conflict formation" (1996, 103).

Furthermore, the Central American presidents agreed to request the presence of the United Nations as facilitator, mediator, conciliator, and, in sum, key actor in the regional peace processes.[9] This was an outstanding resolution if one recalls that this sovereign decision was made in the context of the confrontation between the United States and the Soviet Union, as well as under circumstances in which Washington was trying to overthrown the Sandinista government in Nicaragua and did not at all like the idea of a peaceful conflict resolution that could have consolidated a revolutionary government perceived in the White House as a client of Moscow and Havana. Another interesting trait of the agreement is that the direct appeal to the United Nations is far from the regional schema of the Organization of American States (OAS), privileged by U.S. foreign policy, and it signified a call for UN intervention in conflicts of an essentially internal nature, which is against the prescriptions of paragraph 7, article 2 of the UN Charter.

Finally, it is also important to mention that in Central America the peace process is the result of the democratization process. In other words, the settlement of armed conflict was possible because democratic regimes were established. Even if the nature of the democratic regimes was incomplete, "in transition," or under army vigilance (or of the Sandinista Front in the Nicaraguan case), democracy lays the basis for peace and not the other way around.

In the following pages we will describe the most important events of the Guatemalan peace process, including the historical roots of the conflict. We will analyze the nature of third-party intervention, the nature of the agreements, and their importance for the future in terms of the peace-building process and the prevention (early warning) of potential future violent conflicts.

Historical Roots of the Armed Conflict in Guatemala

The Central American republics are old independent states. In 1821 the independence from Spain allowed the establishment of the Central American Federal Republic until 1838, when the federation was dissolved and the five unitarian states of the republics of Guatemala, El Salvador, Honduras, Nicaragua, and Costa Rica came to life. The federation could not continue because of the rivalry among national oligarchies (the struggle among *liberales* and *conservadores*), divorced economic and commercial interests within the regional elites, and the constant intervention of foreign powers such as the United States and Great Britain using the well-known practices of *divide ut impera*.

The primary interest of both powers in the region, at that time, was the construction of an interoceanic canal using the San Juan River and the Great Lake of Nicaragua as an interoceanic water way.[10] William Walker, an American "soldier of fortune," led a military expedition to Nicaragua and took possession of the country, where he stayed several years until his defeat (and subsequent death by shooting) by a Central American army under the command of the Guatemalan Marshall Zavala. In the meantime the British continued to consolidate their possessions in the Caribbean coast of Guatemala, Honduras, and Nicaragua. They forced the Guatemalan government to give up Belize by way of signing a "treaty of boundaries" (1859) in order to legitimize the occupation of the Guatemalan territory known afterward as British Honduras.

The war of Augusto Cesar Sandino against the U.S. intervention and occupation of Nicaragua in the 1920s and the U.S. intervention in Guatemala in the '50s are two historical examples of the "big stick" policy that Washington applied to Central America in those years, partly because of the economic interest of U.S. corporations with investments in agriculture (banana plantations), communications (railroads, telegraphs), and electricity, and partly for geopolitical reasons.

In the case of Guatemala the restoration of democracy in 1944 allowed the access to power of a nationalist young generation with the will to modernize and develop the country. Presidents Juan José Arévalo (1945–1951) and Jacobo Arbenz (1951–1954) did a lot of work in that direction, especially in the fields of education, health, welfare (social security was established at that time, and the first code of labor was enacted), and public works. Arbenz wanted to compete with the U.S.-owned monopolies in railroads and electricity, so he decided to build a road to the Caribbean Sea ("carretera al Atlántico"), a national maritime port (Santo Tomás de Castilla), and a hydroelectric power plant known as Jurún Marinalá. He also enacted an agrarian reform law that affected the interest not only of Guatemalan landlords but also of the United Fruit Company (UFCO), a U.S. agricultural corporation that had—unfortunately for the Guatemalan government—among its legal advisors both U.S. Secretary of State John Foster Dulles and the CIA director, his brother, Allen Dulles, and had among its share holders both John Moors Cabot (assistant secretary of State) and Henry Cabot Lodge (U.S. Ambassador to the United Nations).[11] If we add the strong nationalistic and ideological rhetoric of the leftist politicians, the influence of the small Guatemalan communist party within the government, and the international context of cold war and U.S.—USSR confrontation, we have all the ingredients for the explosive cocktail that broke out in the so-called "Guatemalan revolution" in the period of 1944–1954.[12]

Therefore, the invasion of the country by a small military corps under the command of Colonel Carlos Castillo Armas in June 1954 was just a smoke screen in order to prepare the conditions for the coup d'etat organized by U.S. Ambassador John D. Peurifoy. Only two military gestures marked the nationalist reaction of the army: the battle of Gualán in June 1954, and the attack and defeat of Castillo Armas's so-called liberation army by cadets of the military academy ("Escuela Politécnica") on August 2, 1954. Afterward, an authoritarian government was established, the leftist parties were outlawed, hundreds of people went into exile while others, less fortunate, were killed or imprisoned, and, of course, the agrarian reform law was repealed. The communist party became clandestine and started to organize a resistance movement. In November 1960 a group of young army officers decided to rebel against the government of General Miguel Ydígoras Fuentes. The rebellion failed, but as a result of the events, links of collaboration were established between certain officers and the leftist clandestine movement, and the first guerrilla organizations initiated their actions.[13]

The first stage of the Guatemalan revolutionary war, during the '60s, is clearly influenced by the Cubans, particularly by the ideas of Ernesto "Ché" Guevara, as they were divulged by the book *Revolution in the Revolution* by the French intellectual Regis Debray, about the guerrillas as a sort of "core" (*foco*) for the revolution. The FAR and the MR13 operated with this strategy in the oriental region of Guatemala, in Sierra de las Minas, and in Izabal, but they were defeated by the army in a ruthless and bloody military campaign during the years 1967–1970. This campaign was accompanied in the cities by a wave of terror against real or suspected communist leaders or leftist intellectuals and by the operation of death squads in charge of political assassinations and "disappearances" of people.

The survivors of the military and terrorist campaign of the '60s reorganized the guerrillas for a second stage of the revolutionary war in the mid-1970s as political and military organizations that appeared in the western highlands, in the northern Petén province, and in the central volcanic range of the southern coastal lowlands with two new organizations: the Guerrilla Army of the Poor (EGP, *Ejército Guerrillero de los Pobres*) and the People in Arms Organization (ORPA, *Organización del Pueblo en Armas*), and one surviving entity of the first stage: the FAR or Rebel Armed Forces (*Fuerzas Armadas Rebeldes*). In this new stage of the war the insurgents decided to establish their strongholds in the indigenous region of the country (the eastern region and mountain range Sierra de las Minas used by the FAR at the first stage is, by the contrary, a *ladino* region). They established a geographical distribution for military operations: EGP in the northwestern highlands and lowlands (*ixcan*), ORPA in the central volcanic range, and FAR in the northern lowlands. This employed a more complex military strategy based in the ideas of the Vietnamese General Nguyen Vo Giap about the extended popular revolutionary war or *guerra popular revolucionaria* that must be deeply rooted in the people as the main actor of the revolution and as the *conditio sine qua non* for the triumph and access to power. These three organizations, along with the communist party (PGT, *Partido Guatemalteco del Trabajo*), coagulated in 1982 in order to form the *Unidad Revolucionaria Nacional Guatemalteca* (URNG, National Guatemalan Revolutionary Unity).

The URNG's strategy for this second stage of the war was successful in the sense that the guerrillas looked for and obtained massive support for their military effort and that they also succeeded in organizing thousands of people through popular organizations such as the *Comité de Unidad Campesina* (CUC, Peasant United Committee) or the *Comité Nacional de Unidad Sindical* (CNUS, National United Committee of Trade Unions), and even the student movement both at the national University of San Carlos and at the level of secondary public schools. The URNG also obtained support of many priests and religious people mainly linked to the Catholic Church and of all sorts of NGOs and organizations in the United States, Canada, and Western Europe.

However, in the military field, the URNG was not capable of resisting the monstrous and ruthless military campaigns of 1981, 1982, and 1983 that we have already mentioned when citing Le Bot, and that had as principal trait the cruel attack against the civilian population in order to "remove the fish from the water," as the Guatemalan military used to say at that time, in a cynical parody of Mao's well-known expression "the guerrilla moves within the people as the fish in the water."

The Peace Process and the Nature of Third Party Intervention

As a result of the military stalemate provoked by the army's counter insurgency campaign, the URNG decided to change its strategy and emphasize political action, especially abroad. It is not clear if at that time the insurgents were genuinely committed to a negotiated settlement of the armed conflict; their political discourse and actions were in any case addressed in that direction. With the help of activist of the so-called Solidarity Committees with Guatemala that were established in North American and Western European countries since the beginning of the '80s, they started a well-organized campaign searching for political support and financial assistance.

NGOs, cooperation agencies and even governments expressed their sympathy for the rebels. Rigoberta Menchú, daughter of a well-known peasant and indigenous Guatemalan leader who died during the assault by police forces at the Spanish Embassy in Guatemala City (1980), won the Nobel Peace Prize, and this rallied a wave of support and solidarity from indigenous peoples all over the world. With the support of Amnesty International and other international human rights organizations Guatemala was included in the agenda of all the international organizations dealing with human rights.

The Stage of Prenegotiations and the Role of the Internal Mediator: 1990–1994

At the national level the democratization process started in 1986, and the peace processes opened by Esquipulas in both Nicaragua and El Salvador continued to exert pressure on the Guatemalan government to open bilateral talks with the rebels as had been done with the Sandinistas in Nicaragua and the FMLN in El Salvador. But the army refused, arguing that the Esquipulas accord stipulated negotiations with the "legal" opposition and not with armed rebels. Nevertheless, as a result of the Esquipulas agreement a *Comisión Nacional de Reconciliación* (CNR, National Commission on

Reconciliation) was established. Appointed as chairman of the CNR was Monsignor Rodolfo Quezada Toruño, a Roman Catholic priest and bishop of Zacapa who received the official title of *conciliador* (conciliator).

After a meeting with the insurgents in San José de Costa Rica in 1988 and with the support of the process of consultation that he went through with different sectors of the civil society in the years 1988 and 1989 (the national dialogue), Monsignor Quezada decided to initiate a round of "preliminary negotiation" talks with the URNG. Thanks to the good offices of the government of Norway, a second meeting with the rebels took place in Oslo in March 1990. As the government still refused to have any direct contact with the rebels, Monsignor Quezada proposed a mechanism that was a real innovation for third-party intervention in peace processes: The preliminary negotiation talks were held with representatives of different sectors of the civil society, including leaders of the legal political parties, entrepreneurs and businessmen, priests and church members, trade union and popular organization leaders, and scholars and professors from the academic community. The URNG accepted the mechanism and on March 30, 1990, the Basic Accord for the Search of Peace by Political Means (*Acuerdo Básico para la Búsqueda de la Paz por Medios Políticos*) was signed.

As a consequence, five meetings were held in this manner. The first meeting, between the URNG and the legal political parties, took place in Spain in June 1990, and it was followed by a meeting with representatives of the private sector—business and corporations—in Ottawa, Canada, on September 1, 1990. A third meeting, this time with representatives of the religious sector, took place at the end of the same month in Quito, Ecuador. Finally, guerrillas and representatives of popular organizations, trade unions, and the academic community gathered in Mexico at the end of October 1990. As a result of these conversations, important issues were discussed and some relevant understandings reached. For instance, in the Escorial Agreement—signed by representatives of the URNG and of the political parties—both sides recognize the need to initiate a process of constitutional reforms and to promote popular participation in order to make institutional changes aimed at social justice, the respect for human rights as an "independent development," social welfare, and so on. Also, the URNG stated that it would not oppose the presidential elections (held in November 1990 and January 1991) and stated its willingness to refrain from acts of sabotage during the electoral process.

There was no joint communiqué from the Ottawa meeting with the private sector (CACIF, the leading entity of agricultural, commercial, industrial, and financial organizations) in September 1990, but both sides recognized the need for a peaceful solution of the armed conflict, and the URNG—in accordance with the CACIF declaration—expressed a willingness to respect "human liberties." The meetings with the religious, labor, popular, and academic sectors held in Ecuador and Mexico produced interesting joint communiqués that emphasize the need for a negotiated political solution to the armed conflict, respect for human rights, democratization, and economic and constitutional reforms. Representatives of these sectors also called for a "direct dialogue between the URNG, the army and the government." Jorge Serrano Elías, a former member of the National Commission of Reconciliation who signed the Oslo Agreement, was elected president of the republic in January 1991. He was the only candidate who stated his willingness to initiate a direct dialogue between the URNG and the government without conditions.

What was the role played by Monsignor Quezada? Was he a conciliator or a mediator? How can we assess his performance? All the meetings were convoked and chaired by the Bishop of Zacapa, who acted officially as a conciliator with the following duties on the basis of the Oslo Agreement:

> . . . to propose initiatives to the parties to arrange for and maintain dialogue and negotiation actions, making this a dynamic process, and to summarize converging and diverging positions which may arise between the parties. He will have the authority to propose initiatives and solutions for them with the purpose to be discussed and agreed upon, and to perform all of those duties which ensure the correct fulfillment of his commission. (IRIPAZ 1992)

It is interesting to note that afterward, when direct bilateral negotiations between the URNG and the government were initiated and the Mexico Agreement was signed (in April 1991), the duties of the conciliator according to the Oslo Agreement were ratified, and it was added that:

> As part of this context, it is also the duty of the conciliator, in addition to those contained in other paragraphs of this document to: a) call the meetings which have been agreed on; b) to be the keeper of documents produced as a result of the meetings and to issue certified copies of them to the parties; c) appoint his advisors; and d) provide for breaks during the meetings. (IRIPAZ 1992)

From the perspective of theory, it is clear that the intervention of Monsignor Quezada was not reduced to the role of a simple conciliator. He acted as a real mediator.[14] In this sense, it is interesting to note also that his intervention can be qualified as one of an insider partial mediator.[15] As we know, both impartiality and neutrality have been recognized as essential to every successful mediation effort. Yet, recent research work underlines the fact that the emphasis on impartiality comes from the inability to realize that mediation is a really structural extension of bilateral negotiations (Bercovitch, Agnoson, and Willie 1991). In this sense, it is perfectly possible to see the mediator as a sort of "assistant" or facilitator of negotiations, so to see him as an "impartial outsider" does not reflect what actually occurs. That means that in certain special cases the influence-persuasion role of the mediator is better attained not when he is "impartial" and lacking ideological biases but rather when the mediator has resources—leverage—that one or both contenders value as positive. Evidently, in the case of

Monsignor Quezada both contenders at that time valued as positive his position as a bishop of the respected and influential Catholic Church, even if the Guatemalan church historically has not been impartial and has had bias for the oppressed and the poor or for the powerful and dominant, depending on the historic period and the political balance of power.[16]

UN Intervention: The Role of the Outsider Neutral 1994–1996

In the Oslo Agreement, the parties also decided to ask for the presence of the United Nations as an observer and "guarantor" of the fulfillment of the agreements. The UN Secretary General appointed Francesc Vendrell as observer to follow up the process. What kind of assessment can be made concerning the results of this first stage of negotiations? Undoubtedly they were very important and useful, even if we take into account the two years of stagnation. At the beginning of the '80s the armed conflict in Guatemala was in the stage of "search for mutual destruction"[17] and by April 1991, thanks to the process opened by Monsignor Quezada and the National Commission on Reconciliation, the government and the URNG decided to initiate a process of direct bilateral negotiations of peace. The signature of the Mexico Agreement fixed the procedures of the negotiations, the role of the mediator and of the UN observer, and opened the way for the signature of the Queretaro Agreement on the issue of democracy and democratization. Unfortunately, as we will explain later on, the negotiations were blocked during the discussion of the human rights issue and it was impossible for the mediator to make the parties transcend the incompatibilities. From July 1991 until January 1994 no further agreement was reached.

What kind of factors were determinant for this situation? In part it was the nature of the issue. As we have pointed out elsewhere (Padilla, 1994), the success of a mediation process is linked to the type of issues that seem feasible in a given conflict. In the case of Guatemala, it is important to take into consideration the fact that the nature of the conflict was transformed in the middle of the '80s from an ideological conflict to one over governance and democracy.[18]

This conflict transformation phenomenon was the consequence of an evolving international and internal context. In the international field the collapse of communism and the fall of the Soviet Union was a determinant factor. In the internal arena it was the struggle for human rights, as well as the support and solidarity from democratic countries of North America and Europe, that were decisive in the change of mentality and attitude of the guerrilla commanders, who changed their Marxist-Leninist ideology for a democratic and pragmatic approach. Thus the importance assigned to human rights and the rule of law as a fundamental issue for conflict resolution and the displacement from ideology to the issue of security.[19] Therefore, it seems quite clear why for both the government and the guerrillas a different kind of mediator was needed: a mediator with muscle[20]—with more leverage—that could be in capacity to offer guarantees for security and respect for human rights.

The so-called Framework Agreement of January 1994 provided for this change in the third-party model of intervention, and from the insider partial the schema moved toward the *outsider neutral*—the United Nations—and, by request of both parties Boutros Boutros-Ghali appointed Jean Arnault, who played a decisive role in the peace process for three years and now is the chief of the UN Mission in Guatemala (MINUGUA).

Other Types of Third-Party Intervention: The "Group of Friendly Nations" and the Civil Society Assembly (ASC)

The Guatemalan peace process was innovative also in the new types of third-party intervention that it produced. The idea of the Group of Friendly Nations was probably the result of the different kind of participation than its members had had in the recent past concerning the peace process. The United States, for instance, changed its role after the fall of the Berlin Wall and the end of the Cold War. From a Cold War warrior the White House became an advocate of peace,[21] thus facilitating its participation in the group. Traditionally, Mexico has been interested in a peaceful settlement of the Guatemalan armed conflict for a number of reasons: by virtue of its position as a neighboring country with more than 1,000 kilometers of borders, because of the presence of more than 50,000 refugees in Chiapas, Tabasco, and Quintana Roo and the presence of the Guatemalan guerrilla at the frontier zone, and because the guerillas had their headquarters in Mexico City. Venezuela and Colombia were in the group due to their participation in the Contadora Group.[22] Spain and Norway were the European members of the group: Spain was interested in the peace process not just for cultural reasons but also because of tragic events such as the assault and burning of the Spanish Embassy in Guatemala City in 1980, and because of the Spanish support for the first attempt of direct bilateral peace talks between the URNG and the government in a meeting held in Madrid in 1988 and the ulterior meeting of El Escorial in the prenegotiations framework. Finally, Norway is a country with a very important policy of support for peacemaking all over the world, and also expressed the well-known permanent policy of the Nordic countries in favor of human rights and peaceful conflict resolution.

The *Asamblea de la Sociedad Civil* (ASC) is another example of an interesting third party intervention because the actor (the "assembly") was a direct result of the "framework agreement to continue the peace talks" signed by the URNG and the government in January 1994 after more than two years of deadlock. At that occasion both parties agreed to call upon the United Nations to transform its own role as an observer into the role of a moderator—in fact a mediator with muscle as we have seen before—but also they decided to keep Monsignor Quezada Toruño in the peace process as chairman of a consultative body where all the civil society sectors that participated in the prenegotiation talks organized by the CNR in 1990 had representatives.[23]

The scope of this chapter does not allow us to make a fuller assessment of the participation of these two important third-party actors in the peace process, but in general terms we do think that their intervention was positive and valuable.

The Nature of the Peace Agreements

Another interesting feature of the Guatemalan peace process is that the parties agreed to negotiate a very complex list of agenda items, and that most of them were "substantive matters." That is, both parties agreed to negotiate those issues that concerned the causes of the conflict: the absence of democracy and the rule of law; the human rights violations; the kind of role that the army must play in a democratic society; the strengthening of democratic institutions and civil democratic authorities; the economic, social and agrarian inequalities and problems; the recognition of the indigenous peoples' cultural identity and rights; and the need for constitutional and legal reforms. These items received priority, which meant that the so-called operative items chronologically were situated at the end: the cease-fire and demobilization of the guerrillas. That is why the negotiations took such a long time—from April 1991 until December 1996, more than five years. Table 3.1, starting with the result of the first direct meeting between the URNG and the Government,[24] summarizes the contents of each agreement.

Conclusion

Thinking back to the main focus of this chapter, prevention successes and failures regarding peacemaking and conflict transformation in Guatemala, as well as to the questions regarding the need to acquire knowledge about the causes and determinant factors of successes and failures in conflict prevention and conflict management and

Table 3.1: Guatemalan Peace Accords, 1991–1996

Date/Place:	April 26, 1991 Mexico City
Event & Actors:	Accord on the procedure for the Search for Peace through Political Means (Mexico Accord); URNG and the Guatemalan government with the mediation of the CNR chaired by Monsignor Quezada Toruño.
Content:	The government and the URNG agreed to start a negotiation. They fixed an agenda of substantive and procedural items and also decided that the agreements and their implementation and execution would be verified by the CNR, the UN and any other international organizations both parties agree to designate.
Date/Place:	July 25, 1991 Queretaro, Mexico
Event & Actors:	Quezada Toruño Queretaro Accord

Table 3.1 (Continued)

Content:	Agreements on the process of democratization including: 1. The meaning of democracy. 2. The need for the rule of law, respect for human rights, subordination of the armed forces to civilian authorities, respect for indigenous rights, respect for social and economic rights.
Date/Place:	January 10, 1994 Mexico City
Event:	Framework agreement to resume the negotiations between the URNG and the government.
Actors:	URNG commanders, government officials, and the UN representative Jean Arnault.
Content:	Both parties agreed to: 1. Ask the UN Secretary General to designate a moderator. 2. Ask the Catholic Church to designate Monsignor Quezada to chair a "civil sector assembly." 3. Ask the governments of Colombia, Mexico, Norway, Spain, United States, and Venezuela to integrate a group of Países Amigos ("friendly nations"). 4. To meet again to consider a human rights agreement and a calendar of discussions in order to finish the peace process in December 1994.
Date/Place:	March 29, 1994 Mexico City
Event:	Comprehensive Human Rights Agreement.
Actors:	URNG, UN moderator, and the government.
Content:	Among other important issues, the government and the URNG agreed to ask the United Nations to send a special mission to monitor the fulfillment and implementation of the accord.
Date/Place:	March 29, 1994 Mexico City
Event:	Calendar Accord
Actors:	URNG, government, UN moderator
Content:	It established the calendar for negotiations as well as the precise agenda items: refugees; truth commission; indigenous rights;

Table 3.1 (Continued)

	social, economic, and agrarian issues; the role of the army; URNG's legal reincorporation; cease-fire; constitutional reforms; chronogram for the implementation of agreements.
Date/Place:	June 17, 1994 Oslo, Norway
Event:	Accord for the resettlement of the population uprooted by the armed conflict.
Actors:	URNG, government, UN moderator
Content:	Important provisions concerning the guarantees for a safe resettlement of both internal and external refugees as well as for economic and social welfare of the returned people.
Date/Place:	June 23, 1994 Oslo, Norway
Event:	Accord for the establishment of a commission in charge of the historical clearing up of the human rights violations and the crimes that provoked the suffering of the Guatemalan people.
Actors:	URNG, government, UN moderator
Content:	Said commission should elaborate a report containing the results of done investigations and offer objective elements to realize and understand what took place during this period of time, and finish the impunity.
Date/Place:	March 31, 1995 Mexico City
Event:	Accord on the Identity and Rights of the Indigenous People.
Actors:	URNG, government, UN moderator
Content:	Recognition of the Mayan cultural identity, it has provisions against discrimination; for the protection of culture and languages, sacred places and spirituality; recognition of customary law and traditional authorities, for the implementation of 169 ILO convention, etc.
Date/Place:	May 6, 1996 Mexico City
Event:	Accord on Social and Economic Aspects and Agrarian Situation.
Actors:	URNG, government, UN moderator

Table 3.1 (Continued)

Content:	Democratization and participative development; empowerment of citizens and their participation at local, communal, municipal, and regional levels; education, health, social and human development; economic measures, etc.
Date/Place:	August 22, 1995 Panama
Event:	Contadora Declaration.
Actors:	Guatemala political parties
Content:	In meeting the Central American political parties, the Guatemalan political leaders agreed to considerate the Peace Accord as state compromises and therefore to promote the necessary new laws or legal reforms.
Date/Place:	September 19, 1996 Mexico City
Event:	Accord on the Strengthening of Civilian Authorities and on the Army's Role in a Democratic Society.
Actors:	URNG, government, UN moderator
Content:	Reform of the Armed Force and reduction of military expenditures; reform of the intelligent services; cleansing of security forces; strengthening of civilian authorities through development councils, among other mechanisms.
Date/Place:	December 4, 1996 Oslo, Norway
Event:	Final Cease-Fire Agreement.
Content:	Complete cease-fire.
Date/Place:	December 7, 1996 Stockholm, Sweden
Event:	Accord on Constitutional Reforms and Electoral Laws.
Content:	It summarizes the constitutional and legal reforms originated in the accords.
Date/Place:	December 12, 1996 Madrid, Spain
Event:	Accord establishing the bases for the URNG's incorporation to legal political activities.

Table 3.1 (Concluded)

Content:	Law on National Reconciliation (Amnesty Law).
Date/Place:	December 29, 1996 Guatemala City
Event:	Accord of Chronogram for the Implementation, Verification, and Achievement of the Peace Accords.
Content:	It establishes a calendar and also the schedule and other operative matters of the peace accords.
Date/Place:	December 29, 1996 Guatemala City
Event:	Accord for a Firm and Lasting Peace.
Actors:	URNG, the Guatemalan government, and the UN moderator. As witnesses of honor several chiefs of state signed the accord together with UN Secretary General Boutros Boutros-Ghali.
Content:	Final declaration with a list of principles and fundamental concepts as well as the acknowledgment and gratitude for the third parties, among them the Países Amigos (Mexico, Norway, Spain, United States, Venezuela, and Colombia), the Asamblea de la Sociedad Civil, and the United Nations.

resolution, it seems evident, in historical retrospective, that the case of Guatemala is a clear example not only of failure to prevent a major internal conflict but also of the incapacity of a great power to understand and to deal with a small independent country in its immediate periphery. The Guatemalan case thus reflects the inability of the United States to manage concrete conflicts with the kind of approach and methodology that should have been appropriate, such as the UN peacemaking approach.

In other words, the armed conflict unchained by the U.S. intervention in 1954 against the democratic and legally elected regime of Jacobo Arbenz demonstrated that the use of the world level (geopolitical) bipolarity approach to analyze and elaborate policy actions addressed to concrete situations in countries other than the strategic contender was dangerous and erroneous. In order to contain an absolutely unreal takeover of communism (and of the Soviet Union) in Guatemala, Washington played the sorcerer's apprentice, liberating forces impossible to control afterward—evil forces that sowed the seeds of discord, violence, and civil war in the country.

Equally pernicious for Guatemala was the U.S. interpretation of complex national political facts and processes with the Manichean lens of ideology: communism vs. anticommunism. This was especially destructive as this lens was applied to a non-industrialized, agrarian country, with almost no working class at all, struggling to modernize both its economic and political systems, "guilty" of suffering from the influence of a small group of communist intellectuals as the major source (and explanation) of the political conflict with a U.S. government then ruled by officials with personal interests in the U.S. corporations established in Guatemala, and that later—that same decade—left the country.

All the minor problems provoked by the agrarian reform could have been resolved through negotiations, and the relatively "major" problem of the influence of the communists in President Arbenz's Cabinet could have been easily solved, if not with negotiations, at least with financial assistance for the legal moderate opposition parties in order to give them the means to win the 1956 scheduled elections. That, of course, would have required that a foreign policy based on the principles of the U.S. Constitution, international law, and democracy could have prevailed in the perceptions (and decisions) of U.S. policy makers. And that, in turn, seems rather difficult in the light of an examination of their biographies, because it illustrates a curious entanglement of ideology with personal interests in personages as John Foster Dulles (U.S. Secretary of State), Allen Dulles (CIA director), John Moors Cabot (Assistant Secretary of State for Inter-American Affairs), and Henry Cabot Lodge (U.S. Ambassador to the United Nations, and former senator of Massachusetts, the state where UFCO's headquarters were located).

Therefore, the use of violence to "solve" the "Guatemalan problem" was not just a wrong U.S. foreign policy decision—and a major failure of bilateral U.S. foreign policy,[25] which engendered the monstrous cycle of three decades of insurgency and counter-insurgency in a context of violence, terror and military dictatorship. It was also, intrinsically, an unintelligent decision that showed the incapacity of the CIA to understand the real Guatemalan situation and the complex social and political processes underlying the Arbenz measures of economic modernization and social welfare, as well as its inability to manage the conflict adequately. All these facts have been demonstrated with scientific evidence in the historical works of Stephen Kinzer, Stephen Schlesinger, Susan Jonas, Richard Adams, and Piero Gleijeses (among others) who we quoted earlier in this chapter.

We would have imagined that after the 1954 events in Guatemala, the Cuban experience, as well as the Vietnamese, Iranian, Dominican, and other similar experiences, the U.S. government would have not incurred in the same kind of mistakes and erroneous policies. Unfortunately, the same error was made again in the beginning of the '80s in Central America, with the insistence on policies of military solutions for Nicaragua, El Salvador, and Guatemala without considering the fact that those conflicts were essentially of a social and political nature.[26] This is why, at the same time that we can argue that the overall U.S. foreign policy toward the region in the '80s was a clear example of failure, we can also conclude that the sovereign decision of the five Central American countries to start a serious peacemaking effort with the support of United Nations—due to the Esquipulas Peace Accord signed in Guatemala in 1987—is an interesting case of successful conflict resolution. It is interesting mainly because the peace accords are the result of a very innovative and unique negotiation process, especially in El

Salvador and Guatemala, as we have underlined in this chapter.

Concerning the situation of the Central American region during the times of bipolarity and East-West conflict there are some major conclusions that we can reach. First of all, the U.S. policy toward Central America during the Cold War is a case of major failure of the realist power politics paradigm of international relations, based on considerations of the balance of power, as it was recommended by the outstanding theorists of the epoch, such as Hans Morgenthau or George Kennan. It seems as if the realist paradigm's macro-approach did not fit the small scale conflicts of the region, which required the kind of micro-approach finally—and fortunately—used by the Central Americans themselves: peace talks with an agenda that addressed the real issues—poverty, human rights violations, absence of democracy, backwardness and absence of a modem economic system, insecurity and absence of the rule of law.

Consequently, Esquipulas II and the peace agreements signed by the Central American presidents in 1987 are good examples of the success and efficacy—in a concrete historic situation—of the peaceful conflict resolution approach embedded in chapter 6 of the UN Charter, or, in other words, of the idealist, Wilsonian paradigm, opposed to the balance of power realist paradigm. As we have pointed out elsewhere, that means that "the United Nation's peacemaking and peace building efforts, particularly in Central America, are among its outstanding accomplishments . . . [The lesson is] that this type of UN work must be emphasized and, simultaneously, that the corresponding techniques and procedures must be improved and developed through education and training."[27]

Another important conclusion concerns the relatively new phenomenon of UN intervention in internal armed conflict. From our point of view, the Central American case clearly demonstrates that UN intervention in internal armed conflicts, both as mediator and as monitor of peace accords in order to verify the fulfillment of the agreements, is a fundamental role of the UN that, as we have already mentioned, must be enhanced and promoted in the future. In other words, peacemaking (peace through negotiation and mediation) and peacebuilding (peace through development and democratization) must be emphasized in internal armed conflict resolution.

The Central American example demonstrates that the techniques suggested by the idealist paradigm can be as effective (and certainly less expensive) than those inherent to the mechanisms of peace enforcement or peacekeeping.[28] Particularly for weak and small countries the use of the principle established by article 2 paragraph 3 of the UN Charter ("all member states shall settle their international disputes by peaceful means in such a manner that international peace and security and justice are not endangered") can be used in both internal and international conflicts, and furthermore it is a very useful tool not only to recover peace but also as a means to strengthen national sovereignty in relation to world powers.

Concerning the Guatemalan internal armed conflict, the longest and more difficult to resolve of the region, the peace process can be seen as an interesting theoretical case of analysis in peace research precisely because it is a success story of peacemaking and conflict transformation. The explanation for this success is linked to three major points:

1. The political opening and the democratization process initiated in 1986.

2. The pragmatic (unintended) "contingency approach" used by both parties in the negotiation process[29] that allowed the intervention of all sort of parties: both *insider partial* and *outsider neutral* mediators called *conciliator* and *moderator* in two different and clearly defined stages of the peace process), as well as the third-party *consultations*, with actors like "the group of friends" and the "civil society assembly," without forgetting the prenegotiation talks with different social sectors from June to October 1990.

3. The decision to include substantial issues (causes of war, structural violence) in the negotiations agenda instead of just dealing with the so-called procedural issues of cease fire, legal reincorporation to political life (the "amnesty" issue), and the demobilization of the insurgents.

Finally, it should be stressed again that the Guatemalan internal armed conflict was essentially of an ideological and political nature. In the 1980s massive involvement of the indigenous population added the social ingredient but it never became an ethnic conflict. Thus, the Accord of Identity and Rights of the Indigenous Peoples can be seen as an instrument of early warning and conflict prevention: the recognition of the indigenous rights to their language, identity, and culture is a mean to prevent ethnic struggle for cultural rights in the near future. Consequently, the assessment about the efficacy of that accord cannot be done in present times, but what will be said of it in the future depends on its implementation.

Notes

1. We use the *peacemaking* concept in the same sense as Boutros Boutros-Ghali ("between the tasks of seeking to prevent conflict and keeping the peace lies the responsibility to bring hostile parties to agreement by peaceful means. Chapter VI of the Charter sets forth a comprehensive list of such means for the resolution of conflict," 1992, 20). Therefore, it is essentially a negotiation process with third-party intervention (good offices, conciliation, mediation).

2. The guerrilla warfare became of "small scale type" after the army's military offensives during the years 1982 and 1993, if we use the terms of Esty et al. (1995 and 1998).

3. The conflict was exacerbated by the armed guerrilla struggle, which—between 1979 and 1983—took the form of a large scale and intense civil war with thousands of deaths mainly among the civilian indigenous population in the central and western highlands, all in the middle of a regime crisis with massive human rights violations.

4. Barbara Harff and Ted Robert Gurr include Guatemala in table 1—"Victims of Genocides and Politicides since World War II"—in Gurr and Harff (1992). The authors point out that "the essential quality of all these episodes is that the state or dominant social groups make a concerted, persistent attempt to destroy a communal or political group, in whole or in part. We distinguish between two types of episodes. In genocides the victimized groups are defined primarily in terms

of their communal characteristics. In politicides, by contrast, groups are defined primarily in terms of their hierarchical position or political opposition to the regime and dominant groups." Indeed, both kinds of group repression were used in Guatemala, especially during the period 1979–1994: genocide against indigenous communities suspected of supporting the guerrillas in the countryside by the mere fact of being Indians (". . . 'guilt' is established not by action or association, but is assigned to all those who share the defining ascriptive characteristics"), and politicides against the leftist-Marxist opposition (especially against intellectuals, students, professors, trade union or popular leaders in the urban areas). However, the figures of victims presented in the Harff and Gurr table (30,000 to 63,000 victims for the period 1963–1994) are underestimated. For instance, we can quote very different figures for the period 1981–1983: "The statistics are staggering. Over 440 villages were entirely destroyed; well over 100,000 civilians were killed or disappeared (some estimates including those of top church officials, range up to 150,000); there were over one million displaced persons (1 million internal refugees, up to 200,000 refugees in Mexico—Inforpress 1988c, 107–110; Americas Watch and BPHRG 1997, 73ff; church and UN sources)" (Jonas 1991, 149).

5. It is interesting to recall that President Jacobo Arbez tried to obtain the intervention of the United Nations in 1954 in order to find a solution for the interstate conflict with the United States. Washington did not accept the Guatemalan request on the grounds that it was a matter for the regional organization, the OAS. The United States exerted political pressure on England and France in order to obtain the abstention of both countries. Only four delegates voted for Guatemala in the Security Council on June 25, 1934: the USSR, Lebanon, Denmark, and New Zealand (Gleijeses 1991, 329–332).

6. Ethnic wars or ethnopolitical conflicts are related to *identity conflicts* (Rupesinghe 1992). The concept of "ethnopolitical conflict" is used by Gurr (1993).

7. To give an idea of the kind of repression and violence that occurred in indigenous areas, we will quote a French scholar. ". . . De 1981 a 1983, des dizaines des hameux et villages, la trés grande majorité dans les communautés indiennes, ont été détruits et leur population massucrée partiellement ou entiérement. Plusiers dizaines de milliers de personnes ont péri et des centaines de milliers ont été déplacées . . . L'armée, qui donne la chiffre de 440 hameux et villages détruits, en rend responsable la guérrilla. En réalité la quasi totalité des massacres ont été perpétrés par des militaires ou des para-militaires. De son côté, l'un des principaux dirigeants de la guérilla, estime (à plus de 35,000 morts) le nombre des victimes du conflit dans les années 1981–1983. . . ." (Le Bot 1992, 202–207). Figures and information about this terrible period in the history of Guatemala can also be found in several reports of the epoch (1980–1985), among them the reports of Amnesty International, the Inter American Commission for Human Rights, the special rapporteur of the UN Human Rights Commission, the Vicount Colville of Culross, and also in Falla (1992 and 1995).

8. At the negotiation table there was no representation whatsoever of the indigenous people. Only after the Asamblea de la Sociedad Civil (ASC, "civil society assembly") was created in January 1994, a "Mayan sector" was able to present its views, which were then channeled through the ASC to the negotiation parties.

9. The Esquipulas Peace Accord is at the one of four UN missions in Central America: ONUCA and ONUVEN (Nicaragua), ONUSAL (El Salvador), and MINUGUA (Guatemala).

10. In 1850 a maritime transportation agency organized trips to the North American far west, loading passengers in New Orleans and sailing via Nicaragua, on the San Juan River and the "Gran Lago," reaching the Pacific Ocean and eventually California after a short distance by road

in Nicaragua. The trip was safer and less weary by comparison with the traverse of the deserts of the Midwest and the dangerous Indian territories.

11. Susan Jonas gives the following explanation: The United States could not tolerate the Guatemalan Revolution for several reasons. First, the Arbenz government regulated existing U.S. interests there and threatened prospects for future investments. In the postwar era of capitalist expansion, U.S. investors (and the U.S. government, which was heavily influenced by these interests) were unwilling to accept any regulations or to work with revolutionary nationalists governments. The Eisenhower administration (1953–1960) was heavily influenced by UFCO with the Dulles brothers both members of UFCO's law firm, and UFCO itself played a significant role in orchestrating support for the intervention. The overthrowing of Arbenz is one of the clearest examples in modem history of U.S. policy being affected by the direct ties of public officials to private interests (Jonas 1991, 31–32).

12. Notwithstanding, our point of view is that the main historic responsibility for the events of 1954 lie on the U.S. government not just in respect to fundamental principles (the violation of the UN Charter, the ideals of the U.S. Constitution and the American people's democratic ideology) but also for pragmatic reasons: there was no real need to "solve" the conflict by military means. If both the Guatemalan ruling economic class and the Eisenhower administration could have waited for the elections planned for 1956, they could have had a democratic solution with the election of a "conservative" Guatemalan administration, as was the case in the Nicaraguan elections of 1990, when Daniel Ortega was defeated by Violeta Chamorro. Therefore, it is clear that the U.S. government overreacted for ideological reasons and as a result of the pressure of corporations like UFCO and the personal interests of the Dulles brothers and State Department officials like John Moors Cabot and Henry Cabot Lodge.

13. The army rebellion was addressed against the corruption of the Ydígoras administration but it also expressed the malaise within the army for events seen as new violations of national sovereignty. At that time a military expedition was being organized and troops were trained on Guatemalan territory (on a private estate: la finca "Helvetia") by the CIA in preparation for the invasion of *Bahia de Cochinos* against the Cuban revolutionary regime. It is easy to understand that Fidel Castro's ulterior support for the Guatemalan rebels is linked to these events. The guerrilla movement was organized with the name Rebel Armed Forces (Fuerzas Armadas Rebeldes, FAR), still one of the military organizations belonging to the URNG, whose commander in chief, Pablo Monsanto, signed the Peace Accord of December 29, 1996, in Guatemala City. The first commander in chief of the FAR was former army officer Luis Turcios Lima, killed in 1967. Another guerilla group was organized in the 1960s with the name Movimiento Revolucionari 13 de Noviembre (MR13) by another former army officer, Marco Antonio Yon Sosa, who died in combat in 1970.

14. Ronald Fisher and Loraleigh Keashly proposed a typology of third party intervention in conflicts consisting of conciliation, mediation, mediation with muscle, consultation, arbitration, and peacekeeping. Conciliation "involves a trusted third party providing an informal communication link between the antagonists for the purposes of identifying the major issues, lowering tension and encouraging them to move toward direct interaction such as negotiation to deal with their differences. The important distinction is that the third party does not propose alternatives for sealing the dispute. . . . Mediation involves the intervention of a skilled and experienced intermediary who attempts to facilitate a negotiated settlement to the dispute on a set of specific substantive issues. The mediator usually combines individual meetings involving each party's representatives

with joint negotiating sessions, and uses reasoning, persuasion, the control of information and the suggestion of alternatives to assist the antagonists in finding an acceptable agreement" (Fisher and Keashly 1991, 33).

15. The concept of "insider partial" is used by Wehr and Lederach (1992).

16. In colonial times, Fray Bartolomé de las Casas, a Dominican priest, was the first defender of the indigenous peoples, and he succeeded in establishing autonomous indigenous communities under the benign control of the church and not under the ruthless and despotic power of the so-called *conquistadores* (conquerors). During the epoch of the U.S. intervention in 1954 Archbishop Rossely Arellano acted as an ally of Washington and of the soldier of fortune Castillo Armas. On the contrary, in the times of the revolutionary uprising in the 1980s, the Catholic Church was more or less aligned with the insurgents, even if the Guatemalan clergy did not share the approach to social problems of the "theology of liberation" that prevailed in other Latin American countries, including Brazil, Colombia, and Peru.

17. Fisher and Keashly describe the stages of conflict escalation as discussion, polarity, segregation, and search for mutual destruction (1991, 35–36).

18. Regarding the concept of "conflict transformation" it is interesting to quote Raimo Värynen (1991, 6–7), "The transformation of conflict may be either intended or unintended. In the former case actors, rules and substance of the conflict are deliberately redefined in order to create better preconditions for instrumental political action to solve the disagreement.... The unintended transformation process is usually a by-product of broader social and economic changes that the actors have not planned and cannot avoid, but to which they have to adjust. The transformation perspective suggest that conflict resolution is not only a form to stepwise rational action in which the actors involved try to adjust their competing interests to each other. It is also associated with everyday and broader historical changes transforming the scope, nature, and functions of collective violence." Obviously, the Guatemalan situation that we are describing (the URNG's change of objectives at the beginning of the '90s) is a good example of "unintended" conflict transformation.

19. Human rights and the rule of law are closely linked to security, and in the perspective of a peaceful resolution of the Guatemalan conflict—and the transformation of the URNG from a military actor into a political actor—it is evident that "guarantees for security" (for the former combatants) became a crucial point to discuss and to resolve.

20. Mediation with muscle (or power mediation) is defined by Fisher and Keashly as a mediation in which a third party uses leverage or coercion "in the form of promised rewards or threatened punishments. In a very real sense, the third party becomes a member of the negotiating trade and bargains with each party using carrots and sticks, to move them to a negotiated settlement. This form of mediation often kids to settlements which have future implications for the third party as a provider of continuing benefits and or the guarantor of the agreement" (1991, 33). It is easy to see the MINUGUA in Guatemala as both the provider of continuing benefits—in terms of international financial cooperation—and the guarantor of the agreements of peace.

21. The Reagan administration was never convinced of the value of the Esquipulas peace process. They even tried to avoid signing the accord and for that purpose Secretary of State George Schultz was sent to Guatemala at the last minute. However, the Bush administration changed the U.S. position and after the meeting of El Escorial between the political parties and the URNG (convened by National Commission of Reconciliation) that took place in Spain in May 1990, Bernard Aronson, Assistant Secretary of State for Latin American Affairs, sent a message of congratulations and support to Monsignor Quezada (IRIPAZ 1992, 60–61).

22. The Contadora Group was the result of a meeting held in the island of the same name in Panama's territorial waters. Mexico, Venezuela, Colombia, and Panama worked as mediators between 1993 and 1985 in order to stop a direct U.S. military intervention against Nicaragua, which was feared in those years. Another interesting development of the group was that it got the support of Brazil, Argentina, Uruguay, and Peru. These countries later became the Grupo de Rio, actually the most important permanent summit consultative mechanism for policy coordination and agreement of all the Latin American countries.

23. Except for the powerful CACIF—the leading organization representing business and the private sector.

24. Except for a meeting that took place in Madrid in October 1997 with no results at all, because the government wanted the unconditional surrender of the guerrillas. A few months after the meeting, the Guatemalan ambassador in Spain who organized the encounter, Danilo Barillas, and who was also a prominent leader of the then ruling Christian Democratic Party, was killed by a death squad in Guatemala City.

25. Nevertheless, ironically, the CIA's covert operation for Guatemala received the code name of "Operation PB SUCCESS" and during the epoch was presented by the U.S. mass media as a success story and generally applauded by American public opinion and the U.S. political establishment of those years. It is only recently that this "official story" started to be reviewed at the academic community in the light of well-documented and rigorous historic studies. It could also be interesting to start working within the U.S. bureaucracy in order to change the official U.S. assessment of the Guatemalan PB SUCCESS operation, which in fact was a real tragedy for Guatemala.

26. This policy was implemented by the Reagan administration under the name of "roll back in low-intensity conflicts." It is interesting to recall also that the "military solution" strategy is mainly based—as we have already mentioned—on the well-known realist paradigm of international relations, which has been predominant in U.S. foreign policy since the beginning of the Cold War and it is quite different from the idealist and Wilsonian paradigm that informs the UN Charter (except for chapter 7 and the measures of peace enforcement) (Padilla 1995).

27. Padilla, 1995, 93.

28. In similar terms an American scholar wrote about the Salvadoran peace process that it "created a precedent for mediation of civil conflict by the office of United Nations Secretary General. It was successful in that the proactive role developed by the mediator served to advance the process to a final accord ending twelve years of armed confrontation. However, the leverage wielded by the Secretary-General's office throughout the negotiations rested on two pivots: the moral authority of the United Nations as a peacemaker, and the unusual degree of international interest, especially on the part of permanent members of the Security Council, in ending the Salvadoran conflict" (Burgerman 1995, 119).

29. "A contingency approach to third-party intervention is based on the assessment that social conflict involves a dynamic process in which objective and subjective elements interact overtime as the conflict escalates and de-escalates. Depending on the objective—subjective mix, different interventions will be appropriate at different stages of the conflict. Rather than being limited to particular strategies by the assumptions that are made, the contingency approach challenges all parties to entertain a complex view of the conflict, and to develop and adapt strategies from a range of options" (Fisher and Keashly 1991, 34).

Part II
Comparative Studies of Prevention Successes and Failures

4

Could Humanitarian Crises Have Been Anticipated in Burundi, Rwanda, and Zaire?
A Comparative Study of Anticipatory Indicators

Barbara Harff

Burundi, Rwanda, and Zaire have been hotbeds of communal violence that have claimed hundreds of thousands of lives since their independence. In Burundi, beginning in 1965 and ending in 1973, some 100,000 to 200,000 Hutus died as a result of widespread systematic killings, tolerated or initiated by the Tutsi-dominated government. In Rwanda in 1963–1964, between 5,000 and 14,000 (primarily) Tutsis died in a series of massacres initiated or tolerated by the Hutu-controlled government. In what was to become Zaire, beginning in February 1964 and ending in January 1965 anticolonial rebels killed up to 10,000 educated Congolese, missionaries, and other Europeans. In Zaire, some 3,000 to 4,000 tribal and political opponents of President Mobutu were executed, massacred, or tortured in the years 1977–1983. In 1988 between 80,000 and 100,000 people, primarily Hutus, died in Burundi, and again in 1994 between 25,000 and 50,000 Tutsis and their Hutu allies died. In 1994 alone, between 500,000 and 1 million Tutsis and moderate Hutus died in Rwanda (Harff 1992b, 32–36).

Chances are that we will see new cycles of violence, a mixture of massacres, genocides, and politicides in these countries. These events are not inevitable and should not be blamed on traditional communal animosities. Rivalries between Hutus and Tutsis in Rwanda and Burundi have existed for a long time, but were exacerbated by the colonial experience, ruthless leadership, corruption on the local level, foreign meddling, and external support for local rebels. Heterogeneity alone does not produce conflict, but lingering antagonism can be ignited given the right mix of incentives and provocations. This chapter describes and analyzes the events that led to the genocide that began in April 1994 in Rwanda, traces the evolution of the series of massacres that began on October 21, 1993, in Burundi, and describes events in Zaire from April 1990 to May 1992—a period of high instability that contributed to the eventual disintegration of the state itself (in 1997). With Mobutu's reassertion of power in 1992, which can partially be blamed on a series of international diplomatic errors, the country was heading toward disaster (Emizet 1997, 53).

Our goal is to identify conflictual events that were instrumental in leading to the three crises of the 1990s described above. We further identify all cooperative events that may have contributed to a decrease in violence in all countries. The rationale of the approach is described in greater detail below. It is designed to test my argument that the close monitoring of prespecified events believed to be contributing factors to genocidal violence gives us a tool to predict the onset and magnitude of genocide (Harff 1996, 1998; Harff and Gurr 1998).

Systematic Monitoring, Risk Assessment, and Early Warning

A curious aspect of "early warning" and "risk assessment" research is that the terms are often interchangeably used but rarely defined. Equally puzzling are claims that early warning signs are abundant, that is that policy makers receive "enough" information, but typically fail to heed warnings. Such lofty generalizations are often accompanied by suggestions that researchers really ought to concentrate on developing strategies that would mobilize reluctant policy makers into action (Adelman 1996).

Having been to many conferences on early warning, I am only too well aware that at present no system exists that enables policy makers to reliably anticipate escalation from crises to conflicts. By and large the policy community relies on area or country specialists to assess conflict potential. There are a few efforts under way to systematize information, and evaluate or develop monitoring capabilities that may allow for better cross national risk assessment (for example, Ahmed and Kassinis 1998; Brecke 1998; Jenkins and Bond 1998). The State Failure project in its latest phase project is a striking exception: it is a data-driven study on the correlates of state failure from 1955 to 1995, and includes four categories of conflict: regime crisis, revolutionary and ethnic wars, genocides, and politicides. Results are encouraging: a few simple models help to explain complex phenomena (Esty et al. 1999). The latest effort uses the accelerator methodology applied here to link the background conditions to the onset or avoidance of state failure. The results potentially bridge the gap between developing watch lists and recognizing the signals that suggest that a state failure is imminent. The methodology used here and its connection to conflict resolution are described in greater detail below.

Risk assessments are typically "good enough" explanations of why particular conflicts occur. They are based on general models that identify "preexisting patterns with historical roots" (Lent 1996, 77). The data for projects such as Gurr's Minorities at Risk survey are periodically updated, which allow for continual reassessment of which ethnic minorities are more likely to contribute to internal instability (Gurr 1993a, 1998, 2000). This effort, although a tremendous improvement in developing better risk assessments of ethnic conflict, is only the first step in the direction of developing early warning capabilities. What we need, depends, of course, on what we think early warning capabilities should enable us to do. At minimum, I think that early warning capabilities should enable us:

1. to provide reliable estimates of conflict potential
2. generate "warnings" months in advance of serious escalation
3. enable analysts to differentiate among different types of conflict

If in place, such a system would allow diplomats and activists to "buy" time for developing appropriate responses to each particular stage of conflict development and ideally, in the long run, to prevent escalation.

This is the approach I think is best suited for early warning purposes. High risk situations should be identified using risk assessments such as those provided by the Minorities and State Failure projects and then monitored on a daily basis. Systematic monitoring is the essential tool that would allow us to identify the prespecified, critical factors that are responsible for the escalation or diffusion of a conflict. All prespecified factors are operationalized as events. Typically the factors mentioned are those that are likely responsible for conflict diffusion or escalation. Of course we need to prespecify different sets of factors for different kinds of conflicts. At the present state of research we need not to be concerned about parsimony, rather we should indulge and add other factors that are more specific and/or are more regionally and culturally sensitive. Such models, once refined, should enable us to forecast both the likely magnitude and the precise onset of a conflict.

Initial work in the State Failure project concentrated on developing early warning models for ethnic conflict, abrupt regime transitions, genocides, and politicides. The first two models were tested using twelve African cases, including four retrospective cases of each type and four control cases. In this chapter I report the initial test of an accelerator model of genocide on three African cases. The cases are Rwanda in 1994, a case of genocide; Burundi in 1993, which was often cited as a "lesser" case of genocide; and Zaire in 1990–1992, a case with the potential of developing into a genocide. The State

Failure project is currently (mid-2000) testing this model on a larger sample of cases from a number of world regions.

Structural Conditions of Genocide and Politicide

Considerable time and effort has been given to defining and redefining the term genocide. My definition of genocide and politicide parallels those of other genocide scholars (Fein 1993b, chapter 2) and includes those characteristics that describe the general phenomena. Genocide is defined here as the promotion, execution, and/or implied consent of sustained policies by governing elites or their agents—or in the case of civil war, either of the contending authorities—that result in the deaths of a substantial portion of a communal and/or politicized communal group. In politicides groups are victimized primarily because of their political opposition to the regime (Harff 1992b, 27–41).

Background and intervening preconditions of genocide and politicide have been identified by Harff (1996, 47–49) and Fein (1994, 31–35) and examined in comparative studies (for example Fein, 1993a, b). In late 1998 the State Failure Task Force was asked to develop and test systematically a structural model of genocide and politicide derived from previous work. The universe of analysis included 127 instances of state failure between 1956 and 1998 as identified in the State Failure study. This set includes thirty-one conflicts that led to geno/politicide (previously identified by Harff in a long-term study that began in 1984) and ninety-six failures that did not. Logistic regression was used to identify the variables that distinguished between the occurrence and nonoccurrence of geno/politicide, lagging the variables two years prior to the onset of genocide (for the problem set) and four years after the onset of state failure (for the control set). The most recent analysis correctly classifies 79 percent of all cases.[1]

The theoretical argument (Harff 1996) identifies a number of international preconditions of geno/politicide including shifting global alliances, political upheaval (warfare) in the region, and the degree of threat of collective regional and unilateral responses. The post–Cold War international system brokered new alliances and did away with others. There are no new long-term alliances in sight and old alliances (NATO) have appeared more fragile. In this fractured world the policing of rogue states has become less certain and potential perpetrators are less likely to be deterred by the threat of collective action. An offsetting factor is a country's economic status. Resource-rich countries are more likely to be scrutinized by the international community; conversely countries of low international economic status can literally get away with murder. Several of these international variables were included in the structural analysis and proved to be significant, as shown in table 4.1.

A larger number of internal preconditions of genocide were specified and tested. Democratic experience reduces the risks of geno/politicide because democratic elites seldom use repressive measures to deter opposition groups. Conversely a history of elite reliance on coercion to maintain power, usually associated with autocratic regimes, increases the risks. Moreover geno/politicides often occur during or in the aftermath of internal political upheavals such as ethnic war, regime crisis, and revolutionary war, therefore countries with a recent history of internal war and state failure are at greater risk. Other internal factors that are postulated to increase the risks of geno/politicide are strong

Table 4.1: Structural Preconditions of Geno/Politicide in Three African Cases[a]

Theoretical Variables	Indicators	Observed Effects	Burundi 1992	Rwanda 1993	Zaire 1990
International Factors					
Status of regime	Trade openness[b]	Lower risk	Low	Low	Low
Regional	Magnitude of upheaval conflict in bordering states	Higher risk	High	High	High
Internal Factors					
Type of regime	Autocratic regime	Higher risk	Autocratic	Autocratic	Autocratic
Cleavages	Religious homogeneity	Higher risk	Homogeneous	Homogeneous	Homogeneous
Internal upheaval (1)	State failures in last decade	Higher risk	Yes	Yes	Yes
Internal upheaval (2)	Magnitude of civil conflict in last decade	Higher risk	High	High	High
Discrimination	Ruling elite represents only some ethnics	Higher risk	Yes	Yes	Yes
Exclusionary ideology	Elite committed to an exclusionary ideology	Higher risk	No	Yes	No

[a]Theoretical variables are discussed briefly in the text. The indicators shown here are those tested in the State Failure project's logistic regression analyses of the preconditions of genocides and politicides from 1956 to 1998 (Harff, Surko, and Unger, forthcoming). The risk profiles for Burundi, Rwanda, and Zaire show their ratings on these variables for the first year in which accelerators are coded.

[b]Trade openness is the total of a country's imports plus exports as a percentage of gross domestic product. Burundi, Rwanda, and Zaire all had low trade openness, hence greater susceptibility to geno/politicide, prior to the period coded.

group identities in heterogenous societies, a high degree of factionalization within communal groups, and elite contention along ethnic lines. Ideology and charismatic leadership are strong intervening factors. In particular, risks of geno/politicide are greater in countries where elites are committed to an ideology that excludes categories of people defined in terms of class, belief, or ethnicity from the universe of obligation.

Indicators were available only for some of these internal and intervening variables. Those that were statistically significant in logistic regression analysis are listed in table 4.1. In summary, the results show that since the mid-1950s geno/politicides have been most likely to occur in countries that have had low trade openness, internal upheavals, autocratic regimes, elite contention along ethnic lines, and exclusionary elite ideologies. Religious homogeneity is the only empirically identified risk factor not anticipated in the general theoretical arguments. Zaire, Burundi, and Rwanda were high on most of these risk factors in the early 1990s, as shown in the three right-hand columns of table 4.1.

Accelerators, Triggers, and De-accelerators

The concepts of accelerators, triggers, and de-accelerators are the basic elements of processual models, which are based on the assumption that all conflicts proceed through stages of development similar to life cycles. Such phases may include early dispute phases, actual conflict phases, and posthostility phases. Given the logic of my effort to advance early warning capacities, the following analysis emphasizes prehostility and hostility phases and the early stages of the posthostility phases. A promising effort to link the accelerator and de-accelerator variables to conflict phases, with special application to the Burundi data described in this chapter, is reported in chapter 10.

Typically, background and intervening factors described in general models are to some degree present or co-occur at the time when accelerating factors first appear. Accelerating variables operationalized as events are events that move conflict along a predictable path. They are linked to general factors, can be feedback events, but also have an independent impact; that is, they may be aspects of general conditions identified in the static model (described above) but they also carry their own momentum. In contrast, triggers are onetime significant events that are likely to trigger escalation, that is, to push a conflict to the next phase, for example, the hostility phase. De-accelerators are significant events that diffuse or halt conflict escalation. In future work accelerators will be weighted as having low, medium, or high impact. Here we did not weigh accelerators because no formal analysis such as time-series or probability assessments has been attempted, because of the small number of cases and lack of control cases. The State Failure project has experimented with weighted categories of accelerators, but formal analysis has not been completed. Our goal here is to introduce the basic method, develop detailed chronologies, and compare and contrast cooperative and conflictual events.

As mentioned above accelerators are operationalized as events. A example of an accelerator variable in our model of genocide and politicide is external support. This variable is operationalized as statements of support, promises and delivery of material support, and promise and delivery of military support—events that are regularly reported by journalists and other informed observers, and are subject of monitoring over time. An example of a de-accelerator is a regional meeting at which adversaries negotiate their differences (a cooperative event). A typical example of a triggering event is the execution or assassination of a top political leader. At present we use the Global Events Data System (GEDS, directed by John L. Davies) at the University of Maryland's Center for International Development and Conflict Management (CIDCM) to identify and code events reported by Reuters World Service for prespecified periods in the cases chosen. The full text of articles is retrieved, reviewed, and coded; on-screen help notes guide coders through discussion of what and how relevant information should be coded. Listings of categories of accelerators appear in Harff (1996, 50–52) and in Harff and Gurr (1998, 576–579); types of de-accelerators are listed, with dates of specific events, in Appendix 1 of this chapter.

Conflict Phases and Interventions

The editors of this volume propose to use phase categories to structure our narratives and analyses. Broadly understood that idea is compelling since it builds on a trajectory notion, to use Alker's terminology. But in accelerator analysis it is problematic. Original phase research as developed by Bloomfield and Leiss (1969) and advanced by Azar (1980), Sherman (1994a), and Alker (1974) emphasizes an action-reaction process, resembling a dialectic mode of thinking. The assumption is that certain drivers carry the seeds that lead to the next phase. But accelerators are not necessarily actions that prompt reactions. Accelerators may trigger some further activity, de-accelerators may stop action altogether, but neither are necessarily related to each other nor are they always reactions to some previous event. The reasons may be found in our theoretical understanding of the nature of genocide and the kinds of actions that escalate to genocide. Typically such actions are one-sided and initiated by the perpetrator state or governing authority. In pure genocides victims often do little or nothing (they do not react) and in the classic cases of genocides (for example the Holocaust), they are killed because of who they are, not because of what they do. Action-reaction sequences are more typical in politicides, where opponents often do react to government repression. Thus, the following analysis makes selective use of the phase categories.

An original intent of the CEWS project was to identify international efforts that help (or have helped) to settle ongoing conflicts or to prevent their escalation. Laudable as this effort may be, it is also somewhat limited. For example, despite the enormous literature on how and who should settle conflicts, the problem of *when* best to use *what* type of mechanism and by *whom* has neither been solved nor can it be easily solved, especially in the absence of an early warning system. More specifically, retroactive analysis enables us to identify efforts that we think led to a peaceful settlement of disputes, but can we be sure? We need to be able to calculate at which time parties are ready to sit down and talk, and what means are readily available to further peace or at least stop escalation. In many cases the available means work best in the early stages of conflict development, whereas stopping a serious situation that has already escalated to armed violence is a different matter. In the latter situations costly international efforts are needed (typically of a military nature) to prevent more bloodshed. Such efforts, even if they are attempted, can come at inappropriate times and sometimes may contribute to renewed or prolonged fighting. And, if such an intervention did take place at a time international action was thought to be warranted, do we know for sure whether other means could have sufficed to halt escalation, or conversely that a potentially serious situation may have fizzled out due to some other circumstances?

The effort here is to trace conflict development and simultaneously to identify cooperative behaviors, that is to identify those events that were crucial in conflict diffusion and escalation. Clearly, if we see patterns of cooperative behavior that coincided with or were followed by conflict escalation, this suggests that conflict resolution efforts were either inadequate or wrong-headed. This modest study follows conflict development in three countries and identifies those cooperative and conflictual events that either diffused or escalated conflict development. To draw causal inferences about accelerating and de-accelerating events in three cases is somewhat tendentious, but more formal analysis is bringing us closer to the envisioned goal of developing good warning capabilities (Harff, Surko, and Unger, forthcoming).

Burundi: Massacres and Repression

Instability has been a given in postcolonial Burundi. After a series of coups, massacres, and a genocide, we see a continuation of these patterns in an ethnically divided nation-state. The latest round of violence began in 1992 only to end in yet another coup in October 1993, followed by massacres.

We coded daily events twelve months prior to the outbreak of the massacres mentioned above (the hostilities phase) and twelve months past their onset. The pattern is depicted in figure 4.1. These are the key events. First, Burundi is the mirror image of Rwanda, whatever happens in Rwanda affects Burundians and vice versa. In November 1992 Burundi expels Rwandans, claiming that Rwandan groups inside Burundi plan to launch attacks inside Burundi. In February 1993 Rwandan militants loyal to the Hutu president protest oppositional activities seen as attempts to hijack the government. Opposition youths respond by going on a rampage. Young Hutu militants begin to kill Tutsi opponents, violence escalates in the countryside. On March 21 the leaders of Burundi, Tanzania, Uganda, and Rwanda meet to discuss common projects and problems. The Burundian government promises presidential election in June—this is the first time that Burundians have an electoral opportunity to challenge dominance by the Tutsi minority. In April the prime minister accuses Hutu political leaders of taking ethnically divisive stands contrary to prior agreements that do not allow parties to run on ethnic platforms. In May a leading Hutu opposition politician is assassinated.

Multiparty elections take place in June and President Buyoya, a Tutsi in power since a coup in 1987, surprisingly is beaten by Ndadaye, a Hutu. The Belgian government

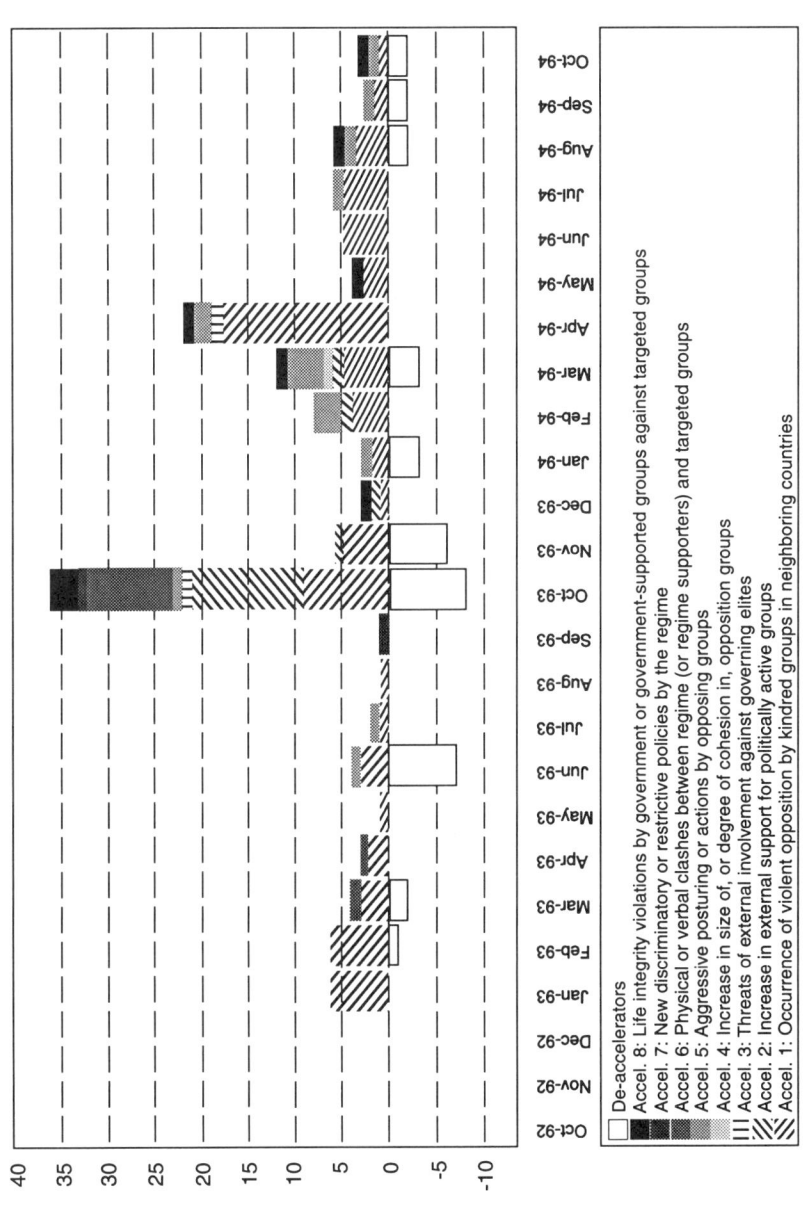

Figure 4.1: Burundi Accelerators by Month

praises Burundi for smooth and honest elections. International observers endorse the elections. Rwandan President Habayarimana (a Hutu) congratulates Ndadaye. For the first time since independence in 1962 both countries are run by Hutus who are representative of the overwhelming majority of both Rwandans and Burundians. In June, 2,000 minority Tutsi university students protest the elections. In neighboring Zaire ethnic Rwandans battle Zaireans, and about 1,000 people are killed. At the end of June, Burundi holds its first parliamentary elections since the new president took power, and Hutus win an overwhelming majority. In July the army foils a coup attempt against the president, and five senior military officers are detained. As a gesture of goodwill 500 political prisoners are released (July).

In September 1993 outside observers warn of an impending coup if the new government does not stop its purges of Tutsi political leaders. Of the twenty-three members of the Cabinet, nine are Tutsis, but prominent Tutsi governors, mayors, head of schools, and others are purged. In October the army (led by Tutsi officers) stages a coup; Ndadaye is killed and mass violence ensues. The international community condemns the coup (Germany, Belgium, and the United States among them), some suspend aid (the United States and Germany), and tens of thousands flee to neighboring Rwanda. Ethnic fighting ensues in the countryside, with Hutus killing Tutsis and vice versa; in six days the death toll is estimated in the thousands. The UN Security Council condemns the coup. Regional leaders meet to discuss the coup. Surviving government leaders have taken refuge in the French Embassy; Uganda offers to send troops, and France offers military advisers. In November the Burundi premier and army leaders talk, and the Organization of African Unity sends an envoy. The UN says no to peacekeepers. A French protection force arrives in Burundi. In December the United States resumes its aid program, refugees return, and the European Community grants more than $2 million to aid refugees. An interim Hutu president is selected in January 1994. Violence continues as the Tutsi-dominated army does little to prevent bloodshed. In February the OAU plans to send African peacekeepers. A new prime minister is appointed (a Tutsi). The fighting continues between Hutus and Tutsi army forces, despite the government's appeals for peace. In April the presidents of Rwanda and Burundi are killed in a rocket attack on their aircraft and turmoil engulfs Rwanda, resulting in genocide—most victims are Tutsi. Refugees from Rwanda flee to Burundi. In September Burundi selects its new president to replace the interim government—Ntibantuganya, a Hutu, is elected and a Tutsi prime minister is reappointed. In October a new power-sharing agreement is reached between the political factions.

The above description also identifies some of the precursors of genocide in Rwanda. Many observers expected that the massacres in Burundi would lead to a full-fledged genocide, but fortunately genocide was avoided. It is likely that events in Rwanda affected both sides in Burundi. Hutus and Tutsi political leaders took steps to avoid the cataclysm that ensued in Rwanda. Figure 4.1 does not show the more typical slow buildup of accelerators escalating to genocide. Instead we see recurring violence offset by many instances of international and domestic cooperative behavior that seemed to avert the worst-case scenario. There are two significant events that may have triggered communal violence, one the election of the first Hutu president, and second the death of the second president in the downing of his airplane, an event prompting genocide in Rwanda but not in Burundi. What stopped escalation in Burundi was the continuation of talks among political and army leaders and efforts on all sides to continue to build a different polity in Burundi, one aimed at stable power-sharing by the two major communal groups. Uganda's President Museveni may have been correct when he told foreign correspondents in October 1993 that he did not believe that Burundi was ready to adopt a Western style democracy. In a country torn apart by communal bloodshed stability may come at a price, namely that of minority rule or at best a carefully engineered power-sharing agreement prior to any more conventionally democratic political formula. Economic hardship (abundant in Burundi) has contributed throughout to a lack of trust in the capabilities of elected officials.

No pronounced increases or decreases in accelerators are shown in figure 4.1. The only accelerator of any significance is accelerator 1, which refers to violent opposition by kindred groups in neighboring countries (Rwanda). There are isolated clashes and instances of aggressive posturing by opposition groups, but overall oppositional activities is low. International engagement is low throughout. There is international praise for fair elections (June 1993), the UN sends an envoy one week after the coup, and in January 1994 it approves a small mediation team. There is no evidence of international interest in Burundi. Prior to the coup we have a low-level conflict phase. In the aftermath of the coup oppositional activity includes killings and massacres, with the Tutsi dominated army reacting by massacring Hutu radicals. Conflictual activities peak five months post-coup. From November 1994 onward we see a pattern more closely resembling an action-reaction process, i.e., violence begets violence. The peak periods, not surprisingly, coincide with the onset of genocide in Rwanda. Cooperative efforts in Burundi are discussed in greater detail in the final section.

Rwanda: Genocide

Tutsi exiles of the Rwanda Patriotic Front launch a major invasion from bases in Uganda, prompting sporadic ethnic violence between the Hutu army and Tutsi civilians. Intermittent negotiations lead to the Arusha accords (August 1993) but the mobilization of Hutu militias continue. The death of the Hutu president in an air crash (April 1994) triggers genocide against Tutsi and Hutu moderates; the RPF is in effective control of the country by July 1994. Following is the narrative of key events leading to and following the Rwanda genocide of April–June 1994, shown graphically in figure 4.2.

In April 1993 a UN team comes to Rwanda to work out details of a plan to replace French troops with a UN peacekeeping force. Rwanda's rebel movement (Tutsis) accuse the government of violating a March cease-fire. In May the Rwandan government and rebel forces agree to cut their forces by about 19,000 men, representing about half of

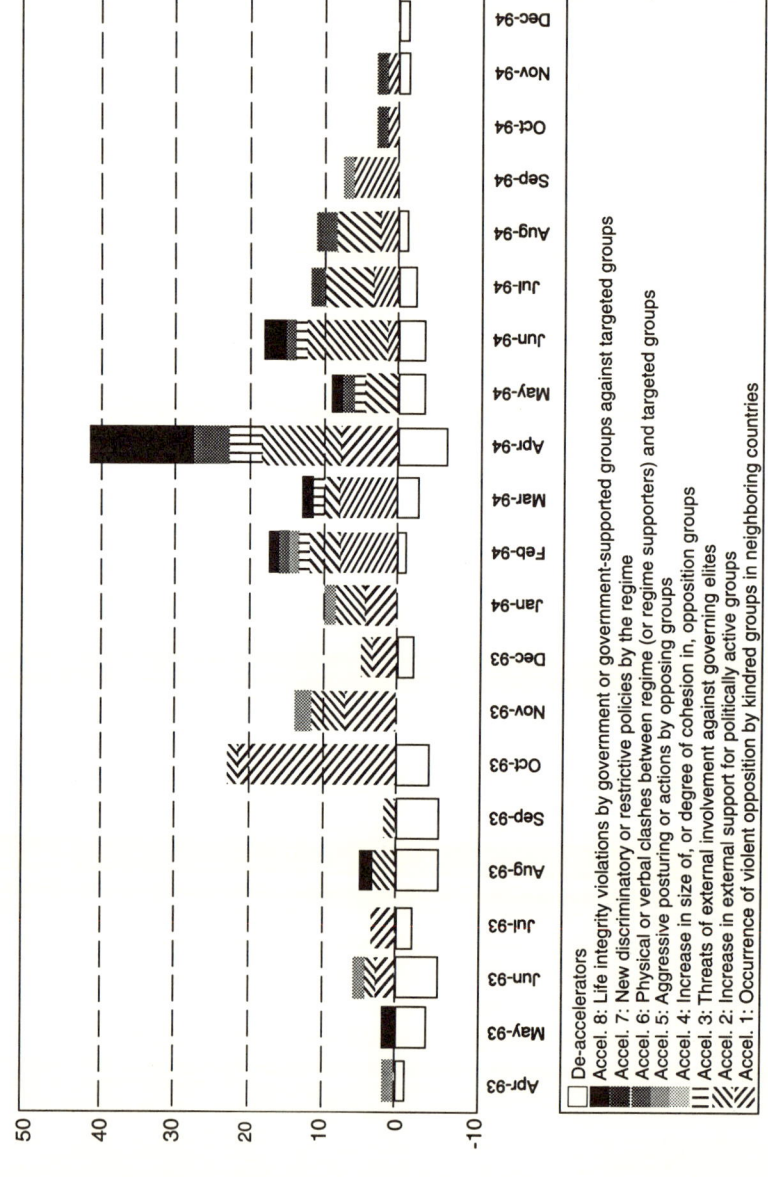

Figure 4.2: Rwandan Accelerators by Month

the combined forces. Gunmen shot dead a leading Hutu politician. Both sides agree (in Arusha, Tanzania) to bring home 650,000 peasants, who had fled the civil war during the previous months. The agreement is signed on May 30, 1993. One day later sixteen people are killed when two grenades explode in a small town in western Rwanda. The United Nations is expected to agree to deploy an observer force along Uganda's border. The first refugee relief convey reaches Rwanda from Uganda on June 9.

The rebels (the Rwanda Patriotic Front) and the government under President Habyarimana announce that they will sign a power-sharing agreement in Tanzania. The UN Security Council decides to send 100 military observers to the Uganda side of the border with Rwanda (June 22). Ethnic Rwandans and Zaireans clash in Zaire, and about 1,000 people are killed. The signing of the Arusha peace pact that caps more than one year of on-and-off negotiations is delayed (June 23). Tanzanian mediators say that talks are under way (July 14). The fighting in Zaire continues, and the number of Rwandans killed nears 3,000. In early August the RPF forces and the Rwandan government sign a peace agreement in the presence of foreign representatives. The United States hails the peace agreement and praises the parties; France especially praises Tanzania for its mediating efforts. The UN promises to station a peacekeeping force numbering at least 600. A prominent Hutu politician is killed; sacked from a government job the previous year, he was accused of involvement in massacres against Tutsis. The Ugandan and Rwandan presidents meet to heal relations (September); Uganda was thought to have aided the rebels. Rebel leaders and the president meet in mid-September. The president of Rwanda asks for aid and rapid deployment of the peacekeepers (October). France promises aid.

The coup in Burundi takes place, and more than 70,000 refugees enter Rwanda. Hutu politicians from Burundi also seek refuge in Rwanda. Massacres continue in Burundi. At the end of October 1993 the Rwandan president declares seven days of mourning for the assassinated president of Burundi, Ndadaye (both are Hutus). The UN High Commissioner of Refugees says that 342,000 Burundians fled to Rwanda.

In November 1993 the UN peace monitors take up positions in northern Rwanda, and sixty-five Belgian troops arrive. In mid-November rebels kill forty people in the northern region, the first clash since the June peace agreement. The Belgian foreign minister condemns the killings. An additional twenty people are killed at the end of November, when rebels break the cease-fire. Crowds cheer rebels troops when they enter the capital of Kigali (end of December). The rebels name five ministers to serve in the interim government, but political wrangling delays its formation. The UN approves the additional deployment of peacekeepers (January 1994). At the end of January, human rights groups called for a ban on arms sales to Rwanda. Residents of Kigali flee due to ethnic tensions. Christian churches team up with trade unions and aid agencies to break an impasse and form a new government (February). The Belgian foreign minister visits Rwanda and urges those involved to work toward a broad-based transitional government.

Two prominent politicians are killed at the end of February, and Belgium voices concern about the renewal of violence. The UN Secretary General condemns the killings.

Uganda's President Museveni visits Rwanda in early March. The UN and Belgium warn that Rwanda risks the withdrawal of peacekeepers unless the new government is in place within the next few weeks (mid-March). Gunmen kill the director of a tea plantation, his wife, and three children in a UN-supervised peace zone (mid-March). The UN renews its commitment for four months in April; Tanzania's president warns Burundian and Rwandan leaders that without peace their countries are doomed for annihilation. The presidents of Rwanda and Burundi are killed in the downing of their plane in Rwanda. Violence ensues: on April 7 the prime minister is killed, and gangs of youth kill people settling tribal scores. Eleven Belgian peacekeepers are killed; government forces participate in the killings. France and Belgium put their African troops on alert. Thousands of Rwandan refugees pour into Tanzania. A cease-fire among various factions is declared (April 8) and a new president takes power. France lands 280 soldiers in Kigali to help evacuate its citizens, and vows not to intervene in the fighting. In mid-April battles rage in Kigali, massacres take place in the countryside, and the bloodshed continues throughout the country. Hutu radio stations spread hate messages against Tutsis. Hutus kill 1,180 Tutsis in a church in one among many massacres. The UN pulls out most peacekeepers, but a force of 270 remains (mid-April). The OAU accuses the UN of abandoning Rwandans. At the end of April the rebels declare a cease-fire, but refuse to meet government officials; France criticizes rebels for shunning talks. By mid-May 500,000 Rwandans are believed to be dead. By the end of May the rebel forces control more than half of the country. The UN authorizes 5,500 peacekeepers. Ugandan President Museveni criticizes Rwandan government officials. The United States, after first avoiding the term, now says a genocide occurred in Rwanda (June). Hutu militias butcher 170 Tutsis sheltered by missionaries (mid-June). The rebels participate in an OAU summit conference and agree to a cease-fire. Ten thousand Tutsis march in the capital Bujumbura to protest a French-sponsored peace plan (a proposal for active intervention). Britain backs the French plan, NGOs oppose it, and the UN Security Council approves Operation Turquoise. French paratroopers crack down on Hutu militias (end of June), and protect Tutsi villagers. Rebels attack French safe zones.

In July 1994 the rebels declare victory and name a Hutu president. At the end of July Tanzania recognizes the rebel-held government. The UN, U.S. and E.C. promise massive aid for Rwanda. The new government plans a war tribunal to try those responsible for the genocide. U.S. troops arrive to help rebuild crucial infrastructure. At the end of August, UN officials denounce a reign of terror in the Hutu-dominated refugee camps in Zaire. The World Bank promises help. In October violence and killings continue in camps and in the south. At the end of November a new interim government is installed. In December it opens a transitional parliament and promise elections within five years.

There is little doubt that communal and political violence in Burundi had an impact on Rwanda, amplified by the large influx of refugees. But, despite the Arusha Accords and attempts to reconcile warring factions, differences were too deep. Both sides were intransigent and would or could not agree on a power-sharing formula. The downing of the plane killing the presidents of Burundi and Rwanda was the final trigger that led to the ensuing bloodshed. Efforts by the international community were inept, too little, and too late.

Figure 4.2 show three distinct phases: a preconflict phase with low-level conflictual activities and high-level cooperative activities (April 1993 to October 1993), is followed by a conflict phase with high-level conflictual activities and low-level cooperative activities (October 1993 to April 1994). This leads to a conflict phase with high-level conflictual activities accompanied by a slight increase in cooperative activities ending in September 1993. Again we see reactions to violence in Burundi, especially after the coup in Burundi (October 1993). International involvement almost ceases after the Arusha Accords are signed (August 1993), with the notable exception of a small UN peacekeeping force arriving in November 1993 to monitor the implementation of the accords. It is clear that the inability of leaders to form a transitional government added fuel to the fire. International threats to withdraw support seem foolish in light of increasing tensions and bloodshed. In March, the Belgian defense minister said he would urge the UN to draw up a more flexible mandate, which ideally would increase its enforcement powers. The mandate for the peacekeepers was too limited and inflexible to allow for direct intervention, i.e., peace-enforcement to stop the slaughters that ensued in the aftermath of the Burundian ethnic slaughters.

Zaire: Autocratic Leadership and Democratization

The period from April 1990 to May 1992 was crucial for Zaire. The context is Mobutu's feeble attempt to democratize the country, which Emizet observes could have led to "new international arrangements or total chaos" (1997, 45). Chaos could have lead to genocide, politicide, or ethnic war. Groups openly opposed to Mobutu—the Luba-Kasai and Lunda or Banyarwandans—potentially were ideal scapegoats. In fact the Banyarwandans were targets of communal violence during the period in question. The key events in this period are sketched below and summarized graphically in figure 4.3.

At the beginning of April 1990 Mobutu announces a radical shake-up in the Zairean political landscape. He orders huge pay raises for civil servants and promises to double student grants. Despite his announcements, opposition forces plan to hold antigovernment rallies to demand Mobutu's resignation and an end to corruption. Government forces prevent the rallies. In a gesture of goodwill Mobutu releases political prisoners (April 24) and names a new prime minister—a first step in multiple changes that may lead to a multiparty system. At the end of April influential rightists form a new party. When government opponents demonstrate to show their support for newly released opposition leader Etienne Tshisekedi, Zairean paramilitary forces open fire, killing five and injuring several. One student thought to be an informer for the government is killed by fellow student in a series of protests in early May. On May 21 sympathetic Zambian students march to protest the killings. In Belgium protesters ransack the Brussels office of the Zairean news agency. News of the killings of up to 100 students at a university in the southern city of Lubumbashi prompts the government to announce the establishment of a commission to investigate the murders, allegedly by Mobutus presidential guards.

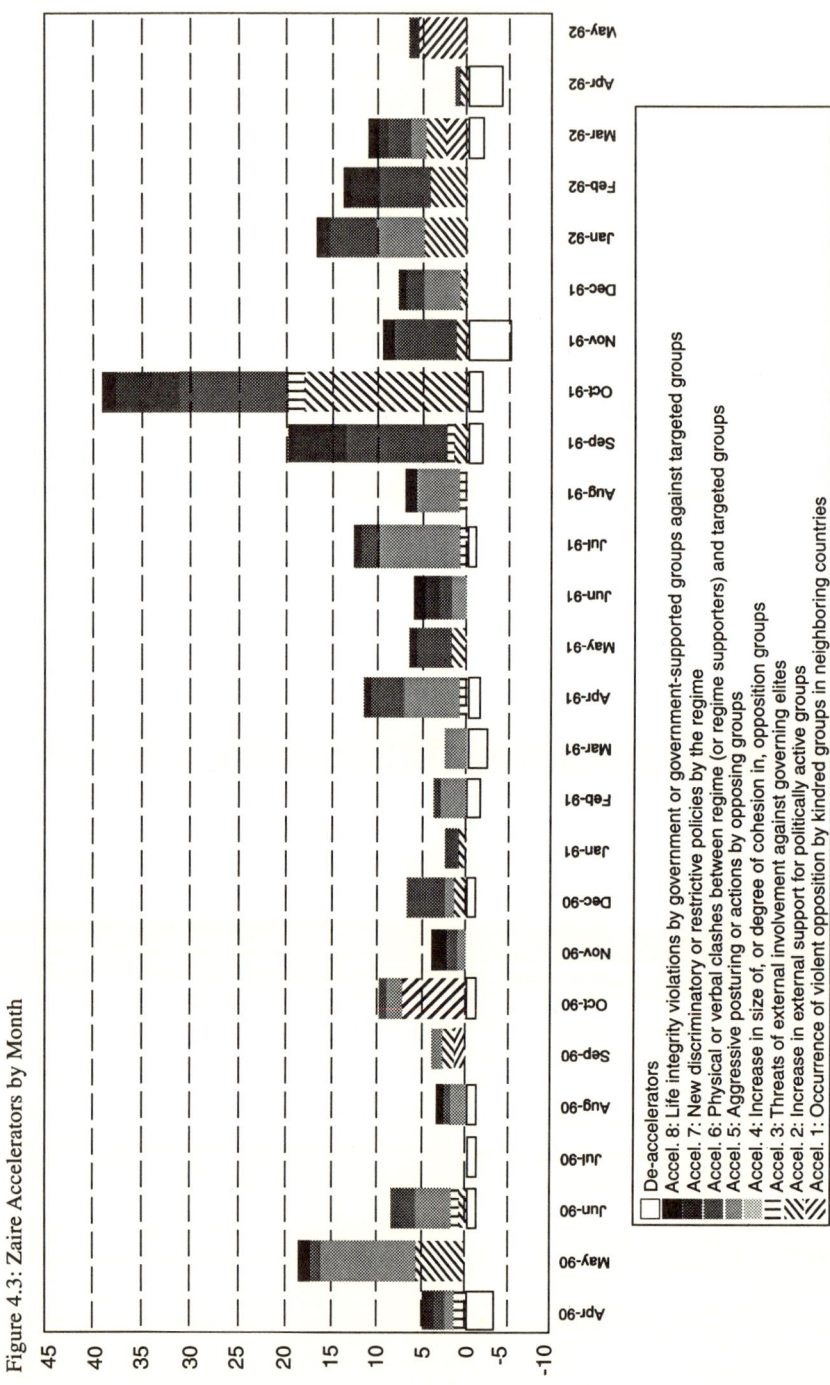

Figure 4.3: Zaire Accelerators by Month

Belgium suspends a loan to Zaire and the EC urges a probe of the massacre. Zairean doctors and teachers strike, demanding higher wages, and defy government orders to return to work. The Zairean commission publishes details of additional student unrest, leading to arrests of some government officials. Religious leaders in Zaire and Belgium press for greater openness and democratization. At the end of June the government suspends striking professors and lecturers.

On the bright side, a large majority in the parliament supports a new constitution that cuts Mobutu's power and permits trade unions (June 30, 1990). The parliament passes a law establishing a multiparty system (July 17); the law was proposed by Mobutu and allows three legally recognized parties. The Zairean opposition wants a transitional government with at least half of the Cabinet posts given to opposition leaders. In September, on a tour of Europe and North America, former prime minister Karl-I-Bond, now an opposition leader, condemns the democracy move as a sham. Nelson Mandela of South Africa pleads for solidarity between the peoples of Zaire and South Africa (September 9). Zairean, Rwandan, and Ugandan leaders meet on security and trade in Uganda (September 11). Mobutu denies reports that he wants to leave Zaire. Taxi and bus drivers go on strike at the end of September. Amnesty criticizes Zaire for continued human rights abuses, and Mobutu angrily denounces the report. When fighting breaks out in Rwanda, France, Belgium, and Zaire send troops. In October Mobutu lifts restriction on parties. In mid-October Zaire claims to have stopped its support for the Rwandan rebels. The Rwandan president arrives in Zaire for talks.

In November 1990 the Zairean army arrests and wounds hundreds of people prior to a political meeting of opposition groups that was authorized by authorities. In December food riots lead to the death of some protesters when troops fire into the crowds. Mobutu opponents ask for his resignation, and a U.S. congressman calls for free elections. In January 1991 Zairean radio and TV workers strike for higher wages, followed by government workers in February. Some agreements are reached to end strikes by teachers and government workers. In March a new prime minister is named to oversee the change to a transitional government before multiparty elections. On March 31 Zaire names a fifty-two-member transitional government. Students ransack the home of some newly appointed members of the transitional government. Again the Zairean army fires on opposition protesters in Lubumbashi, killing one and wounding dozens. Mobutu goes on a holiday in France (May 7) with the promise to return. At the end of May people are killed by troops in a central town during antigovernment rallies. In June the two main opposition leaders, Karl-I-Bond and Etienne Tshisekedi, are detained by police. In July the opposition calls on the army to abandon Mobutu, for the first time directly challenging Mobutu. Mobutu in a surprise move names his chief opponent, Tshisekedi, prime minister (July 22), and he promptly turns him down. On the eve of Zaire's democracy conference 80,000 rally in Kinshasa to declare their opposition to Mobutu (July 30), and the conference is boycotted by hard-line opposition leaders. Dozens of protesters are killed in September. The United States suspends aid in response to the country's continued human rights abuses and lack of economic reforms. Throughout

September riots continue and foreigners flee the country, assisted by their governments. Riots wreck the capital of Kinshasa; soldiers loots stores and homes. At the end of September under Western pressure, Mobutu declares his willingness to share power with his opponent; Tshisekedi becomes prime minister. The U.S. government supports the new transition government, but the French government is divided over withdrawing all support from Mobutu.

In mid-October 1991 the first opposition-led government takes power, but Mobutu keeps critical portfolios. Mobutu claims that the new government was not legally sworn in, consequently it is locked out of its offices by troops loyal to Mobutu. Tshisekedi is sacked by Mobutu, and riots erupt. Opposition leaders call for peacekeeping forces. The EC calls for Mobutu to reform or face consequences (October 26), Canada suspends aid, South Africa closes its trade mission. Tshisekedi declares his government the only legitimate government (November 1). Nigeria launches a mediation effort, holding talks with Mobutu and Tshisekedi. The OAU urges Mobutu to find solution to conflict. On November 22 Mobutu signs an agreement with opposition leaders to end the conflict; Karl-I-Bond becomes prime minister, though some opposition leaders are unhappy with the choice. In December the national conference on democratic reform resumes. After heated debates the presidential parties boycott the conference and it breaks down.

In January 1992 the EC suspends all aid. Protesters clash in Kinshasa with government forces. An aborted coup leaves two dead and strengthens Mobutu's rule (January 23). The opposition calls for a general strike. In February troops kill thirteen in a church protest led by radical Catholic priests. Belgium, France, and the United States condemn the shootings. The opposition calls for a global boycott, Japan suspends aid in March, and the pope urges backs the democracy movement. At the end of March thousands of Zaireans flee to Uganda. On April 4 the national conference on democracy restarts and opposition leaders quickly proclaim themselves to be the supreme decision-making body of the country. Mobutu visits Egypt in search for Arab support. At the end of April Kinshasa university reopens after a one-year break. In May Belgian companies return to Zaire. Mobutu appears willing to cede power, but in fact remains in power until overthrown in May 1997 by rebels based in Eastern Zaire and backed by the Rwandan Tutsi government.

The Zairean events, in figure 4.3, show a predictably different pattern from that of Rwanda: no geno-politicide took place. We see a medium-level of conflictual activities accompanied by low-level cooperative activities from April 1990 to April 1991. Increasing violence eventually forces Mobutu to share power, which leads to violent responses instigated by Mobutu loyalists. International responses vary from none to the EC and Belgium urging probes of an alleged massacre that took place killing 100 university students, and intermittent announcements that occasionally lead to brief suspensions of aid (e.g., by the United States). We see a classical pattern of action and reaction. Opposition leaders and followers, strengthened by what they perceive as international support (mostly verbal), engage in protests, strikes, and other oppositional activities, countered by more restrictive or sometimes conciliatory measures by the Mobutu government. Mobutu uses carrot-and-stick methods by appointing or sacking political opponents to prominent positions until he is forced to concede some powers. International involvement is largely reactive, that is, whatever happens between Mobutu and his followers and opposition forces elicits some limited response among Western governments.

Conclusion

It is apparent that conflictual events (accelerators) far outweigh cooperative events (de-accelerators) in the periods coded. This is to be expected, given the volatile histories of all three countries. However, significant differences emerge. Zaire at times shows high levels of conflictual activities, but cooperative activities rarely ever cease. For a complete list of de-accelerating events, by type and date, see the Appendix. Burundi's relatively low levels of conflictual events are accompanied by relatively high levels of cooperative events. By contrast, in Rwanda, cooperative activity is highest six months prior to the conflict and ceases almost entirely four months prior to the outbreak of genocide. Much has been written about the failure of the international community to get involved in a more timely and effective fashion, but rarely do we know six months prior to the event what to expect. This effort may bring us a bit closer. The model is prespecified to identify factors leading to genocide. Thus, in Rwanda, the display of conflictual and cooperative events in figure 4.2 shows clearly a much sharper increase of accelerators accompanied by a steady decrease in de-accelerators in late 1993. This kind of assessment, if available, could have been used in November of 1993 to alert international policy makers that the situation was rapidly deteriorating. The following is a brief attempt to analyze the cooperative events that appear to have been significant in averting genocide in Burundi and Zaire.

The Burundi conflict was intensified by what happened in Rwanda. A comparable "spillover" effect can also be observed in Rwanda. In Burundi isolated clashes and aggressive posturing took place seven months prior to the October 1993 coup and ensuing massacres. Regional and international cooperative activities during the same time-period was always low. The elections in June 1993, which brought a Hutu president to power, were praised by outside observers as fair. In July 500 political prisoners were released by the new regime. The coup and killing of the president in October led to widespread killing; note that four months prior to the coup the international community disengaged. Immediately after the coup, political leaders urged reconciliation and some negotiations occurred. UN peacekeepers were requested by the government and a small contingent was approved (in November) by the UN Security Council. In January 1994 a new Hutu president was elected. International neglect possibly contributed to internal instability during the crucial period of transition to democracy. The coup and massacres were condemned but few efforts were made to support the democratically elected president.

Twelve months prior to the genocide in Rwanda some cooperative events occurred, but ceased about five months prior to the onset. A flurry of international activities accompanied the last phase of the killings but slowly lost momentum three months after the killings began. Of all cooperative events the Arusha Accords of August 1993 stand out as an attempt to establish a permanent peace in Rwanda. With Tanzania acting as the host, and with international observers, facilitators, and representatives of the OAU and UN present, international engagement was at an all-time high. But, given its strong military showing the Tutsi rebels of the RPF were able to secure significant advantages in the future power-sharing agreement, whose implementation in turn was delayed by the Habyarimana regime. The death of Habyarimana unleashed extremist forces loyal to him. The Arusha Accords, hailed at first as a success by outsiders, probably contributed to the further deepening of cleavages between moderate Hutu factions and extremists. The extreme factions were either under-, or not-at-all, represented. In short, Western ideals of conciliation, power sharing, elections, and other problem solving devices may have not been appropriate to a sharply divided nation already at war and unaccustomed to democratic norms.[2]

Partisan support by France (for the Habyarimana regime) and Uganda (for the RPF rebels) added further fuel to the fire. The French attempt to establish safe havens for refugees during the last stage of killings aroused further suspicions by the victorious RPF leaders that the French actively supported the perpetrators of the genocide. Humanitarian relief did come from NGOs (postgenocide), but, unfortunately, were probably also construed as self-serving or partisan efforts. Cautious international support for the new regime, combined with long-term aid, may do more to secure peace than genocide tribunals or attempts to democratize states that are not ready for it.

The inefficient nature of international involvement in the three cases presented is all too apparent. Conflicting Western interests in Zaire may have allowed the oppressive regime of Mobutu to continue until internal forces gathered enough power to overthrow him five years later. Burundi and Rwanda suffered and continue to suffer from malign neglect by the international community. The French for better or worse were the arbiters of international engagement. It was only after massacres and genocide had killed more than 1 million people that the international community asked for action and showed its willingness to get involved, albeit mostly symbolically. The Rwandan government is largely on its own when it comes to punishing the perpetrators of genocide. In contrast to the silence of the international community at the early stages of the genocide, voices are now heard that criticize the handling of the accused murderers. I rest my case.

Notes

1. The definitions and descriptions of the four types of state failure, and coded data on all current cases, are posted on a University of Maryland Web site, address www.bsos.umd.edu/cidcm/statefail.

2. For other researchers' analyses of the Arusha Accords see Clapham (1998) and Prunier (1995, chapter 5). Two general works on the management of civil war in Africa are Rothchild (1997) and Zartman (1994).

Appendix 1: The Data on De-accelerating Events

International De-Accelerators

Visits by High-level Foreign Delegations	Zaire 2/97 Rwanda 2/94, 5/94, 6/94 Burundi (none)
Foreign Statements of Support for Reconciliation Measures	Zaire (none) Rwanda 8/94 Burundi 6/93, 10/93
UN Negotiations/Good Offices	Zaire (none) Rwanda 4/94, 5/94 Burundi 9/94
Promise of Foreign Economic Aid	Zaire (none) Rwanda 10/93 Burundi (none)
Regional Summit Meetings	Zaire 1/92 Rwanda 9/93, 9/93, 3/94 Burundi 3/93
Trade and Economic Agreements	Zaire (none) Rwanda (none) Burundi 2/93
Delivery of International Relief Aid	Zaire (none) Rwanda 6/93, 10/93 Burundi (none)
Withdrawal of Foreign Troops Favoring One Warring Faction	Zaire (none) Rwanda 10/93 Burundi (none)
UN Peacekeeping Deployments	Zaire (none) Rwanda 4/93, 6/93 Burundi 11/93

Appendix 1 (continued)

Domestic De-Accelerators

Statements by Leaders Urging Reconciliation	Zaire 3/92, 4/92, 4/92, 4/92 Rwanda 8/94, 7/96 Burundi 10/93, 11/93, 1/94, 3/94, 8/94
Negotiations between Factions	Zaire (none) Rwanda 5/93, 9/93, 3/94, 4/94, 5/94, 6/94 Burundi 10/93, 11/93, 9/94
Announcements of Multiparty Election Dates	Zaire 7/90, 1/92 Rwanda (none) Burundi 3/93
Requests for UN Peacekeeping	Zaire (none) Rwanda 9/93, 10/93 Burundi 11/93
Refugee Settlement Agreements	Zaire (none) Rwanda 5/93 Burundi (none)
Mutual and Unilateral Cease-fires	Zaire (none) Rwanda 4/94, 5/94, 6/94 Burundi (none)
Rebels Join Multiparty Political System	Zaire 10/90 Rwanda (none) Burundi (none)
Disarmament Agreements between Warring Factions	Zaire (none) Rwanda 5/93 Burundi (none)
Democratic Elections Held	Zaire (none) Rwanda (none) Burundi 6/93
Lifting of Security Measures	Zaire (none) Rwanda 8/93 Burundi 10/93, 11/93
Peace Agreements between Warring Factions	Zaire (none) Rwanda 6/93 Burundi (none)
Release of Political Prisoners	Zaire (none) Rwanda (none) Burundi 7/93, 8/94
Formation/Reform of Governments	Zaire 9/91, 11/91 Rwanda 8/93, 12/93, 3/94, 11/94, 12/94 Burundi 7/93, 10/93, 1/94, 10/94

5
Escalatory Dynamics in the Moldova-Dniestr and Chechnya Conflicts

Olga A. Vorkunova

In his *Agenda for Peace*, former UN General Secretary Boutros Boutros-Ghali defines preventive diplomacy as "action to prevent disputes between parties, to prevent existing disputes from escalating into conflicts and to limit the spread of the latter when they occur" (Boutros-Ghali 1992, 11). This definition focuses on the objectives of preventive action and neglects its instrumental aspects. A broader definition has been adopted by Lund (1996, 37): "action taken in vulnerable places and times to avoid the threat or use of armed force and related forms of coercion by states or groups to settle the political disputes that can arise from destabilizing effects of economic, social, political, and international change."

A comprehensive concept of conflict prevention and preventive diplomacy was defined in the final report of the workshop on "An Agenda for Preventive Diplomacy: Theory and Practice" (1996) in terms of:

> special actions, policies, procedures or institutions that are called for in situations where existing means seem unlikely to peacefully manage the

destabilizing effects of economic, social, political, and international change and thus they are applied by governmental or nongovernmental bodies or the protagonists themselves in order to keep states or groups within them from threatening or using violence, armed force or related forms of coercion as the way to settle interstate or national political disputes.

In this chapter we, like Väyrynen (1995), prefer a more comprehensive and functional definition of preventive diplomacy, including the following key elements:

1. conflict prevention, i.e., preventing disputes from arising between parties
2. escalation prevention, i.e., preventing both vertical and horizontal escalation of hostilities
3. postconflict prevention, i.e., preventing the reemergence of disputes

In this context the two chosen case studies refer mainly to escalation prevention after the outbreak of violence and post-conflict prevention.

The Moldova-Dniestr Conflict

Origins and Background Conditions

There is a risk of misperceiving the nature of this conflict as essentially ethnic. But ethnicity was not the cause of the conflict, rather its effect. It is multidimensional and includes territorial issues, questions of national identities, ethnicity, security, democracy, ideology, religion, power, and other factors.

The deep-rooted historical, social, economic, and political factors increase the potential for violent conflict in the Dniestr region. The historical controversy over possession of Moldova still persists today.

In the Middle Ages, the territories of Moldova and Romania were divided into several princedoms dependent on the large neighboring states. During the last half of the fifteenth century Moldavia was governed by Prince Stephen the Great, the ultimate symbol of freedom in present-day Moldova. During the eighteenth century, Moldavia and Walachia were brought under the supervision of Turkey, but came under Russian dominance in 1812. This territory between the Dniestr and Prut rivers—Moldova—was called Bessarabia. After the Crimean War (1853–1856) the areas were again overtaken by Turkey, but were allowed to pursue more autonomous policy. In 1859 they elected a common prince and adopted the name of Romania in 1862. After the Russo-Turkish war (1877–1878), Romania was compelled to cede Bessarabia to Russia, but regained the territory at the outbreak of the Russian Revolution (Graeger 1995, 41). A greatly expaned Romanian state existed during a short period between the two world wars and did not include the territory of the present Transdniestria, which was incorporated in the Soviet Union as an autonomous Moldovan republic within Soviet

Ukraine. On March 27, 1918, the Bessarabian Parliament "Sfatul Tserij" voted for unification of territories between the Prut and Dniester rivers. In Northern Bukovina the population, following the disintegration of the Austro-Hungarian Empire, expressed itself on November 3, 1918, in the Bukovina Popular Assembly as being in favor of reunification with Soviet Ukraine.

During the Russian Civil War (1919–1922), the territory that is currently Moldova (Bessarabia) was seized and annexed by Romania. During this period (until 1940) the Romanian state supported a policy of forced "romanization" of Moldovan territory. The Soviet Union regained control of the Bessarabia and the west bank of Dniestr River under the Ribbentrop-Molotov Pact in 1940, when the enlarged Moldova received status of a union republic within the USSR. The territory west of Bessarabia remained within the borders of Romania. Ethnogenesis of Moldavians and Romanians goes back to the Roman Frakijskij population of the Balkans, which included Iranians, Slavic, and other elements.

The Moldovian Romanians—at 2.8 million—constitute 64 percent of the population; Ukrainians, 600,000 (14 percent); Russians, 562,000 (13 percent); Gagauzi (Turkish-speaking Orthodox), 153,000 (6 percent); Bulgarians, 2 percent; Jews, 1.5 percent; and 1.8 percent of the population represents other nationalities. As Graeger (1995) points out, the majority of the Russian population (approximately 70 percent of the Russians) is concentrated west of the Dniester and particularly in Chisinau (Kishinev). Seventy percent of Ukrainians and almost all Bulgarians also live west of the Dniester. Together, these three groups make up a substantial fraction of the total population west of the Dniester River. The remaining 30 percent of the Russians live to the east of the Dniester River. This area covers approximately 15 percent of the Moldovan territory, and was settled in the early 1940s. The population of the area consists of 40 percent Moldavian Romanians, 30 percent Ukrainians, and 30 percent Russians.

As part of the former Soviet Union, Moldova was a moderately developed republic within its agrarian-industrial structure. The most developed region in Moldova has been Transdniestria (*Nezavisimaya gazeta*, March 2, 1994, 3). It covers approximately 12 percent of the Moldovan territory, was home to 17 percent of the total population in Moldova, produced 34 percent of agricultural production (vegetables and fruits), 33 percent of industrial, and 56 percent of consumer production in Moldova. The largest electric power station in Moldova is Dniestrovskaja in Transdniestria, and produces 90 percent of the total electric power. The main transport and gas lines are located on the west side of the Dniestr River. The composition of rural and urban population in 1989 has been 52.5 percent and 47.5 percent in comparison with Kazakhstan (42.4 percent and 57.6 percent), Azerbaijan (46.5 percent and 53.5 percent), Russia (26.1 percent and 73.9 percent) and Lithuania (31.2 percent and 68.8 percent). The proportion of the rural population is higher among Moldovans and Gagauzs than among any other ethnic groups in Moldova. This archaic structure of the Moldovan economy was compensated by its openness, with a highly trade-oriented industrial agricultural sector. Moldova was specialized in internal labor division on crops production. It was the highest specialized republic of the former Soviet Union, and was totally dependent on exchange of industrial production and energy. In 1988 it had its crops production estimated in rubles: 112,800 rubles in comparison with the total Soviet Union, 17,000; the Russain Federation, 18,000; Kazakhstan, 3,200; Lithuania, 46,000; Azerbajian, 59,400 (*Agropromyshlenij kompleks of the Soviet Union* [statistical book], 1990, 46).

The socioeconomic development of Moldova and its level of sociopsychological modernization have contributed to the susceptibility of local intellectuals to nationalist propaganda. Similar socioeconomic development is seen in the South Caucasus and Kazakhstan, and the further violent development in Alma-Ata (Kazakhstan) in 1986 and the violent conflicts in Georgia and Azerbaijan thus support this thesis. The possibility of the emergence of violent conflict in Moldova was higher than in other parts of the former Soviet Union.

The scenario of violent conflict development was characteristic for the majority of regions in the European part of the former Soviet Union. It consisted of several phases: national-political revival and development of self-consciousness, consolidation of national political leaders and emergence of independent political structures, participation of "patriotic" forces (nationalistic) in the parliament fighting, attainment of political power, and declaration of independence.

The first signs of a nationalist revival became manifest in 1987–1988. Moldovian intellectuals were concentrated around the literature journal *Kodry*. These groups constituted the nucleus of the Moldovan Popular Front (Narodnyi Front). It announced as its main objectives: the dominant position of the titular Moldovan language and culture, the attainment of political power and political independence, and unification with Romania. The Popular Front slogans soon became popular, explained perhaps by the fact that in the late 1980s Moldovian culture experienced a deep crisis as the result of forced russification processes, especially in urban areas. The percentage of mixed marriages was especially high during this period. The problem of the suppression of the Moldovan language was real for the majority of the Moldovan population. The first mass actions since 1989 were against Russians and Jews.

The roots of the Dniestr conflict run deep. The immediate cause, however, can be traced to the Moldovanization of national life, i.e., the replacement of Russian as the dominant language, and de-Sovietization aroused fear among the Slavic (Russian/Ukrainian) minority within Moldova. This population, which formed a majority within the Transdniester region, was also fearful of the ethnic ties of the majority of the Moldovan population to Romania and of agitation by some nationalists in Romania and Moldova for eventual union of the two states. All the developments described above raised fears of the loss of national identity, social status, and economic security. In response to these fears, Slavic nationalists called for creation of the Dniester Republic and proclaimed their independence from Moldova.

As the summary of findings in the Appendix makes clear, there were abundant signals in all symptomatic violence categories to indicate the upcoming crisis in Moldova. These might have given time to Russia, Moldova, and Ukraine to react in an adequate manner in order to de-escalate the situation had they been available. It is obvious from the violent clashes in Bendery and Tyraspol that this has not been indicated, and that Moldovan leaders behaved in a counterproductive manner. They chose the use of force coupled with the demand to unite with Romania, which led to escalation rather than de-escalation (see Appendix, table 5.1).

The decline of the central authority and the strengthening of regional forces, based upon nationalist sentiments as well as erosion of the basis for dialogue, the escalation of hostile rhetorics and the escalation from rhetorics into the use of force constitute the general elements of the internal conflict in Moldova.

National Liberation and Formation of the New Independent State

The Language Act of 1989 was the trigger in the conflict between the Russian minority in the Dniestr region and the Moldovan authorities, and it affected radical rhetorics of the Popular Front and the sense of vulnerability and fear among Russian minority concerning the demand for reunion with Romania. The presence of threat and discrimination (fears of being relegated to occupying a lower economic and social status in Moldova) heightened the importance of protecting the Russian community's social identity. At this time, the conflict can therefore be described as an intrastate conflict around Dniestria within the Soviet Union.

Moldavia adopted the name Moldova on June 5, 1990, and declared itself an autonomous Soviet Republic on June 23 in the same year. The nationalistic pro-Romanian Popular Front received 40 percent of the seats of the Moldovan Supreme Soviet in March 1990. The Communist Party was the only registered party for these elections, but opposition candidates were allowed to run as individuals. The origins of the Popular Front's dominance in parliament lie with the creation of a coalition between independent supporters and the nationalist wing of the Communist Party. The Popular Front's line was dominating in Moldovan policy until 1992. Members of the Popular Front, who were in power, made no attempt to integrate members of all minority communities in the process of governance, or to solicit their support for the new state.

The escalation was fueled by the provocative policies of the central Soviet authorities, who supported the establishment of different international fronts and international movements in the republics of the former Soviet Union, including Moldova. The central government presented the idea of the Union Treaty. In doing so, it decided that the treaty should have its basis in autonomous regions of the republics and suggested that autonomous formations had equal rights with the republics to sign the Union Treaty. There were no autonomous provinces in Moldova, but after the declaration of equal rights for the regions that had acquired the status of republic and the autonomous provinces based on the Union Treaty, several national-political elites started fighting to get autonomous status in Moldova. They included elites from Gagauz and Transdniestria. A referendum on independence for Dniester was held on January 28, 1990, and the region declared itself as the Transdniester Moldavian Soviet Socialist Republic within the Soviet Union on September 2 the same year. Leaders of Gaguzia have proclaimed independence within the framework of Moldova's borders in the summer of 1990. Economic reasons affected the Gagauz decision, as Gagauzia was comparatively more dependent on Moldova than Transdniestria.

In 1993 the Gagauz deputies returned to the Supreme Soviet of Moldova. Political elites as well as economic elites were ready for compromises with the Moldovan leadership. One reason has to be seen in the economic dependence of the Gagauz economy, which was connected to the Moldovan economy. Basically, the economy of the southern regions—traditionally occupied by wine production and light industry—was strongly integrated into the Soviet and Moldovan economies. Despite the economic crisis, the agrarian economy of Gagauzia was easily adapted to new conditions thanks to the naturalization of the economy (*Novoe vremya* 1993, 10–13).

The announcement of Moldovan as an official language in the republic, the closing of Russian schools, the adoption of a Law on Citizenship (June 5, 1991), which gave privileges to Moldovans, the "Moldavization" of the state apparatus, the "cleansing" of research organizations, the discrimination of local governance in regions with a compact minority population (under the rule on local governance), and the negotiations with Romanian leaders on the issue of further unification—these were manifestations of Moldovan nationalism as being offensive. Slavic minorities have experienced a sense of insecurity, threat, and injustice. As a reaction, the most politically organized minorities, including Slavic and Gagauz, opposed the growing assertiveness of Moldovan nationalism.

In June 1990 Russia declared independence from the USSR, which affected the Moldovan Supreme Soviet decision to declare the republic to be sovereign. Mircea Snegur was chosen as president of the Moldovan Republic. The first clashes broke out in the town of Dubosari between Moldovan government troops and militant civilian groups from Transdniestria in November 1990.

In March 1991 presidential elections were held in Transdniestria, together with a referendum on future membership in a successor state of the Soviet Union. With the exception of the Moldovan Romanians in the villages, an overwhelming majority favored a union governed from Moscow.

During the first half of 1991 the situation in Transdniestria was rather stable. Opinion polls showed that the population in the region favoured the Declaration of Independence of Moldova (53 percent), supported the territorial-administrative reforms (41 percent), were for radical economic reform (62 percent), for participation of Transdniestrian deputies in the Moldovan parliament (45 percent), and for the establishment of a department on Transdniestr issues (41 percent), and that 19 percent considered the main cause of tension in Moldova to be nationalism and discrimination. However, during the second half of 1991 and in 1992 the Popular Front engaged in repression toward minorities and strengthened its line for unification with Romania.

Transdniestria supported the organizers of the Soviet coup in August 1991. The Moldovan government, however, denounced the attempted coup and arrested several prominent persons, which triggered a new wave of ethnic uprisings, a monthlong blockade of railways, attacks on police stations, and the occupation of public buildings. As Graeger (1995) pointed out, the first armed combat between Moldovan government troops and the Dniestrian Republic National Quard—supported by the former Soviet 14th Army stationed in the region and Cossacks from Russia—took place in December 1991. The issue of the unification with Romania was discussed during the meetings of Druk-Iliesku (January 1992) and Snegur-Iliesku (February 1992). The unification was planned for the end of 1992. The Popular Front Congress, which was held on February 15-16, 1992, adopted the program of unification between Moldova and Romania. These plans of unification with Romania underpinned a potential outbreak of violence.

In the further development, Moldovan nationalism increasingly turned "offensive," claiming the right to reestablish Moldovan leadership over Transdniestria. For this purpose military forces were used to suppress the autonomous province. This, in turn, fueled nationalist tendencies in Transdniestria, and contributed both to the establishment and activation of paramilitary units in the province and to new signs of Transdniestrian independence, including military forces, a national currency, etc. This was challenged by the extremism of the majority population, leading in turn to secessionist claims among the ethnic minorities of Moldova.

As Camplisson and Hall (1996) argued, the unionists, dominance at the political level in Moldova ended in July 1992 when a government of national consensus was established and some portfolios were reserved for representatives from Transdniestria and Gagauz.

During this period an early third-party intervention was vital for peaceful conflict transformation. There was an opportunity to encourage and facilitate negotiation between then contending parties: Moldovan central authorities and the autonomous province—the Transdniester Moldavian Soviet Socialist Republic. But no action was taken at the time. Lost opportunities in the first half of 1991, when the conflict was internal to the Soviet Union, negatively affected further dynamics toward violence.

The escalating confrontation between the parties to the Moldova-Dniestr conflict progressed in phases. An escalatory process may be defined as the maturation of the crisis and violence phases.

Emergence of the Intra-State Conflict (March-August 1992)

Events in the first half of 1992, in particular armed clashes between Moldovan police and "Dniester insurgents," and the seizures of arms from military arsenals, raised the prospect that intrastate communal violence may turn into civil war. Attacks on the police headquarters and road blocks led to fighting on March 1 and 2, 1992. As Graeger pointed out, in March alone fifty people were killed and at least 5, 000 fled to Ukraine. The increased use of violence by the parties to the conflict shifted the balance from political to military action.

Fighting escalated in mid-March 1992 when Dniester Republic Guards and Don Cossacks attacked Moldovan police units in three villages in the Dubosari region in an attempt to eliminate the last remaining Moldovan police presence on the left bank of the Dniester. Russian forces also blew up two highway bridges over the river.

Paramilitary forces in the region grew with the arrival of Slavic volunteers and Cossacks from the Don region. Reaction to the fighting came rapidly. On March 15 the Ukrainian Foreign Ministry issued a statement expressing concern about the involvement of the Cossack volunteers from the Don region in the armed conflict in Moldova. The statement described Cossacks fighting on the side of the Dniester Republic as mercenaries, whose involvement violated international legal norms. The following day, the Ministry for Foreign Affairs of Ukraine called for a cease-fire in the Moldovan conflict over the Dniester Republic and offered to mediate, adding that refugees were crossing into Ukraine. Within a week the number of refugees who had fled to Ukraine numbered 3,000.

On March 16 representatives from the large indigenous Ukrainian population living in the Transdniestria appealed to the Supreme Soviet of Ukraine and to Ukrainian President Leonid Kravchuk to help prevent conflict in their region from spreading. Heavy fighting continued with the initiative in the hands of the Dniester volunteers. At the same time, mass demonstrations in Chisinau (Kishinev) demanded arms and criticized Moldovan President Mircea Snegur and his government for not declaring a general mobilization. The same day, Snegur announced a unilateral cease-fire to go into force on March 18 and asked Dniester forces to honor it. Kravchuk responded to the crisis by imposing a special regime in a fifty-kilometer zone along the Moldovan-Ukrainian border to prevent infiltration of arms and armed troops.

This temporary cease-fire did not put an end to the conflict. Rumors and protests multiplied, especially as it became more evident that Russia was supporting the Dniester Republic. On March 18 the Moldovan government protested the Russian State Bank's decision to open accounts in the self-proclaimed "State Bank of the Dniester Republic." On March 24 the Moldovan parliament described the March 20 appeal from the Russian Parliament on the conflict in the Dniester region as an "unfriendly act" and blamed it for interfering in the "internal affairs of another state."

At the Helsinki foreign ministers' conference, Moldova protested the activities of insurgent forces operating on the left bank of the Dniester River. They were supported by the Romanian government, which issued a statement condemning these activities. On March 24, following the Helsinki meeting of the Conference on Conflict and Cooperation in Europe (CSCE), the foreign ministers of Romania, Moldova, Russia, and Ukraine issued a joint statement saying they would continue their efforts to resolve the conflict in Moldova and announced that they planned to meet again in April.

None of these diplomatic moves put an end to the fighting, which in the last week of March escalated from sporadic raids into planned acts of sabotage and large-scale fighting. On March 26 Igor Smirnov, president of the Dniester Republic, signed a decree ordering partial mobilization of men up to the age of forty-five. Smirnov justified the action on the grounds that the Moldovan government was actively preparing for combat operations.

The fighting that emerged in Moldova on April 2, 1992, grew out of weeks of escalating violence. On March 29 President Snegur declared a state of emergency throughout Moldova, calling on separatists of the Dniester Republic to surrender their arms and acknowledge the authority of the Moldovan government. He ordered Moldova's security forces to disarm illegal armed formations that were backing the Dniester "pseudo-state." Snegur appealed to Parliament on March 31 with the statement that time for negotiations between the two sides had run out, and that it had become apparent that leaders of the Dniester Republic were not interested in resolving the conflict in a peaceful manner.

Each side called upon the other to back down but prepared for the worst. On March 30, Snegur warned that his government would take "all the necessary measures" to restore its authority in the breakaway Dniester Republic and threatened to take back an offer to guarantee the region the status of a "free economic zone." The leader of the Dniester Republic, Igor Smirnov, stated on the same day that his supporters would do everything possible to protect their region, including turning part of the area's industry over to military production. There were also reports of more sporadic violence and a number of new casualties.

The Transdniestria leadership responded with a call to arms and appealed to Russia for protection. The Russian Foreign Ministry issued a statement calling on Moldovan authorities and all parties concerned to act strictly in accordance with the norms of international law, legality, and respect for the rights of individuals and ethnic minorities.

When the escalating of violence forced the Russian government to play a more active role in the Moldova-Dniestr conflict, it sought to resolve the problem by "peace enforcement." To promote political compromise, horizontal escalation in Moldova was stemmed by preventive action of the Russian troops. The deployment of the Russian 14th Army in Moldova was a unilateral action within the framework of Russian military operations in the post-Soviet territories. It was not set up by the UN Security Council and had no mandate given to peacekeeping and peace enforcement.

Between December 1991 and April 1992 it was difficult to determine the loyalties of the Russian 14th Army deployed in the Dniestr region. The 14th Army commander has announced his intention to become Commander of the Armed Forces of the Dniester Republic and to transform 14th Army into the nucleus of that state's armed forces. However, the existence of the Russian military force had its impact on the policies of parties to the conflict in a positive way and helped control the spread of violence.

Boris Yeltsin signed a decree on April 1 that placed the 14th Army and several other units deployed in Moldova under Russian jurisdiction. The report said all troops in Moldova had been subordinated to the Confederation of Independent States (CIS) commander-in-chief and that Colonel General Vladimir Semenov, then commander of CIS ground forces, had been named Russia's representative for all Russian troops in the area. A Moldovan deputy defense minister immediately labeled the decree illegal, stressing that all forces in Moldova, except those on the left bank of the Dniester, have been placed under the legal jurisdiction of Moldova.

Subordinating these troops to Yeltsin's control permitted him to use that part of the armed force that is Russian and perhaps even obtain military cooperation from several other states. Statements by leading officials implied that Yeltsin was considering use of force. Russian Foreign Minister Andrei Kozyrev, for example, was quoted by ITAR-TASS on April 1 as saying that Russia "will be protecting the rights of Russians in other states of the CIS. This is top priority. We shall be protecting their rights firmly and will be using powerful methods if needed" (*Nezavisimaya gazeta* 1992).

Experts from the Ministries of Foreign Affairs of Moldova, Romania, Russia, and Ukraine gathered in Chisinau on March 31 to discuss a solution to the Dniester conflict. The participants were quoted before the meeting opened as saying that they would be guided by the Helsinki agreements on stability of borders and would seek a peaceful resolution while preserving Moldova's integrity. However, these talks were unsuccessful.

Special Moldovan Inner Forces attacked Bendery on the same day, leaving at least ten people dead. The attack was described as one of the heaviest actions in the breakaway Transdniestria region during that month, and the possibility of another meeting being scheduled later that month (April) between the four countries was proposed.

Russian military presence in the region played the decisive role in conflict termination and containment. Moldovan authorities insisted on redeployment of the 14th Army first in 1991, but grassroots movements, especially womens' groups (The Women's Union for Support of Transdniestria) organized a blockade of the railway route. In fact, the 14th Army supported the secession aspirations of Transdniestria in conflict with Moldova.

The situation had not improved by May and as the crisis deepened, on May 9, the forces that previously belonged to the CIS reverted to the control of the newly formed Russian National Army, which created a direct confrontation between Russian and Moldovan interests.

Additionally, more violations of the cease-fire were reported on May 9, 10 and 11. President Snegur appealed through the UN Security Council to the world community, asking it to intervene and stop Russian aggression in his country, which he claimed was causing Moldova's search for a political solution to the country's problems to fail. In June, Yeltsin offered to withdraw the 14th Army from Moldova, but his plan encountered heavy opposition from Russian military officials. They claimed that more than half of the army's personnel were local inhabitants who wanted to defend their "homeland" and that even if this were not the case, there were no apartments in Russia for servicemen, should they be returned.

On June 23 Radio Ukraine reported a change in its position toward the Moldovan conflict. President Kravchuk called for the left bank of the Dniester to be given the status of an autonomous republic within Moldova. This was the first time Kiev had recognized or supported Transdniestria's calls for the federalization of Moldova.

On July 3 President Yeltsin held talks with Moldovan President Snegur and they agreed in principle on a sequence of steps designed to settle the conflict. The agreement included: implementing a cease-fire, creating a demarcation corridor between the forces, introducing "neutral" peacekeeping forces, granting "political status" to the left bank of the Dniester by the Moldovan Parliament, and ultimately scheduling bilateral negotiations on withdrawing Russia's 14th Army. Yeltsin also agreed to resume deliveries of Russian goods to Moldova, which had been previously agreed to, but had since been halted. Although these agreements were a step in the right direction, they have been disappointing.

Similar attempts by CIS institutions have been equally unsuccessful, though in a July 6–7 Moscow meeting, the heads of states from the CIS agreed to create and deploy what they called a joint "peacemaking" force of between 2,000 and 10,000 soldiers to eastern Moldova within the next few weeks. This force, consisting of soldiers from Russia, Ukraine, Belarus, Romania, and Bulgaria, would have the mission to enforce and monitor a cease-fire and keep the forces of both sides in the Dniester region separated.

Despite continuing controversies, on July 21 a peace agreement was signed in Moscow by Presidents Yeltsin and Snegur. Just after this agreement was signed, in a July 31, 1992, interview printed in *Literaturnaya Rossiya*, then General Alexander Lebed fueled the controversy by criticizing the Moldovan government as being "criminal" and "fascist" and calling for a "Nuremberg trial." He said that his army was a "local" army and the "Dniester people have a right to this army" (*Literaturnaya Rossia* 1992).

In early June, the Dniester separatists proposed to transform Moldova into a federation of three republics: Moldova, Dniester, and Gagauz. Moldovan President Snegur immediately rejected the proposal. He reiterated that Chisinau (Kishinev) had offered to negotiate some form of territorial autonomy, but something short of federalization. This proposal, in turn, was dismissed as unacceptable by the Dniester government. On August 13 and 14, the president of Transdniestria announced that the republic intended to form its own army and at the same time General Lebed said his (14th Russian) army would help create this new army. In late August, Russia again seemed to hasten progress toward resolving the crisis. On August 26, General Pavel Grachev, at the time Russian defense minister, signed an agreement with Major General Pavel Creanga, the Moldovan defense minister, on withdrawal of Russia's 300th Paratroop Regiment from central Chisinau.

The Situation in September–December 1992

By early September it seemed as if the Moldovan government was seeking to "soften the crisis" through compromise. On September 16 and 17 the second round of bilateral talks to decide the terms of the withdrawal of the Russian 14th Army from Moldova were held in Chisinau but were unsuccessful. The association between a political solution to the Transdniestrian conflict and withdrawal of the former Soviet 14th Army has further complicated the negotiations. Due to the active and central role of the army in Dniester, the withdrawal of the Russians is a necessary condition for a solution.

In an October 15 interview in *Izvestiya*, former Russian defense minister, General Pavel Grachev, added to the uncertainty over the 14th Army's intentions, when he stated that "the withdrawal of the 14th Army from the Dniester area will only be possible when the conflict in the region is settled." He also noted that "14th Army units were manned by personnel from the region and that they would refuse to accept withdrawal unless the conflict was over" (*Izvestiya* 1992).

Moldovan President Snegur told a group of Russian journalists visiting Chisinau on October 16 that Moldova will continue to resist its transformation into a "federation of republics" and the creation of a Dniester republic with an army, security services, border guards, and other attributes of statehood. He reiterated, however, Moldova's willingness to grant the left bank of the Dniester self-government, with political, economic, and cultural autonomy, within an "integral and indivisible" Moldova. This was yet another example of Moldova's unwillingness to recognize any insurgent attempt to formally divide its republic.

The third round of negotiations for withdrawal of the Russian 14th Army from Moldova achieved no concrete results. The proposals of both sides were rejected: the Russian side offered to "disband" some of their units and transfer their equipment to "local authorities" rather than withdraw units; the Moldovan authorities insisted that units be withdrawn and "left bank" residents not be drafted into the Russian army for compulsory military service. Consequently, the stalemate continued.

The main argument behind normalization of relations between Transdniestria and Moldova was economic. Until 1993, the economic situation in Transdniestria was better than in other regions of the former Soviet Union. Prices were rather low. But this temporary "economic surprise" has come to an end: inflation and unemployment rose while production decreased. Then integration with a stronger state became a necessity. Political independence and one's own currency could not solve economic problems. The economic situation had its impact on the approach for compromises with Moldova. At the same time, the political leadership in Moldova changed in favor of more liberal and moderate leaders. The Agrarian-Democratic Party won parliamentary elections in 1994. The second largest faction in the Parliament became the Socialist Party and "Yedinstvo" became the third. The Popular Front divided into the bloc of peasants and intellectuals and allies of the Christian-Democratic Popular Front.

Stalemate and Shift to Political Balance

At the end of January, representatives from Moldova and Transdniestria held another round of negotiations in Bendery, where they approved the basic principles for settling conflict in the region. These included principles for recognition of characteristic features of the formation of regions and principles dictating what kind of status the Transdniester region receives in the Republic of Moldova. According to the agreement the Transdniester region is a part of the Republic of Moldova, but it has its distinct features in comparison with other regions of the republic. Therefore, it should be given special status, but not at the expense of the republic's territorial integrity and sovereignty.

Details of the agreement were later released in a statement from Chisinau on February 11. Anatol Tsaran, the leader of the Chisinau delegation from the mixed parliamentary commission established to oversee a peaceful settlement of this conflict, further clarified the Dniester region's status. He stated that the region would be granted "administrative self-government on condition that the unity and integrity of Moldova is maintained."

In a surprising turn of events, Petru Lucinschi, first secretary of the Moldovan Communist Party from 1989 to 1991, was elected chairman of the Moldovan Parliament. Lucinschi was reputed to be liberal and proreform and was closely tied politically with Mikhail Gorbachev when he was General Secretary of the Communist Party of the Soviet Union. In his inaugural address to the parliament Lucinschi pledged "to focus on settling the Dniester conflict politically and on pursuing balanced relations with Romania and Russia." At the same time, the presidiums of both the Dniester and Gagauz Supreme Soviets demanded that the Moldovan Soviet Socialist Republic be changed "into a federation of three equal republics—Moldova, Dniester, and Gagauz—and its accession to the Commonwealth of Independent States (CIS)."

The prospects for resolving Moldova-Dniestr conflict peacefully were better in the spring of 1993 than before. In May 1993, the Moldovan and Russian presidents agreed in principle on arrangements for procedures and deadlines for a withdrawal of the Russian 14th Army.

In 1993 direct negotiations were opened with the Transdniestrian leadership. At a meeting with the Moldovan Parliament Chairman Lucinschi, Prime Minister Sangheli, and Dniester Republic President Smirnov, the sides agreed to pursue a political dialogue and to focus at this stage on restoring economic links.

During this current stage the situation in Moldova was filled with periods of tension separated by short periods of relative calm as the two (or more) sides attempted to sort out their interests and make attempts, however feeble, to resolve the conflict. The attitude of the parties themselves in conflict, such as Moldova-Dniestr, contributed to its continuance, but the stalemate in 1993 helped buy time and develop new, constructive conflict solutions.

The permanent mission of CSCE in Moldova was officially opened on April 25, 1993. The work of the mission helped to reduce the level of mistrust among the conflicting parties and to promote the start of a permanent process of negotiations. It maintained an active dialogue for creation of the necessary conditions for mediation. OSCE[1] could not recognize Transdniestria as an independent state and consider it as a component part of the Republic of Moldova. As Ataman argued, report No. 13 prepared by CSCE mission in November 1993 was one of the important inputs of the mission for encouraging dialogue, restraint, and compromise between the parties.

A real dialogue was started after the spring of 1994 when the president of Moldova and the leader of Transdniestria signed a framework document concerning the format of negotiations. Each side created independent expert groups that submit directly to the presidents. These groups were supposed to negotiate a political agreement with the assistance of the mediators from OSCE and Russia. Initial mediated negotiations were quite difficult because, while each side verbalized and argued in support of their positions, the subject in discussion and the role of the mediators was not quite clear.

In January 1994 the Moldovan government accepted in principle the peace plan proposed by the CSCE.

The Moldovan constitution of July 28, 1994, establishes the "permanent neutrality" of Moldova, and prohibits the stationing of foreign troops on Moldovan territory. On October 21, 1994, the Russian Federation and the Republic of Moldova signed an agreement on complete withdrawal of the 14th Army and all associated equipment from Moldova within three years (*Diplomaticheskij vestnik* 1994). However, the Russian 14th Army was transformed into Operational Group of Russian Forces. During 1996–1997 twenty-six units of Operational Group of Russian Forces were transformed and reduced. Russia initiated a new formula for the peacekeeping forces in Transdniestria that includes units of the Russian, Moldovan, and Dniestrian forces under the Joint Military Command that patrolled the security zone along both banks of the Dniestr River (*Nezavisimaya gazeta* 1999).

With enormous stockpiles of weapons and ammunition deployed in the Dniestr region the crisis in Transdniestr could easily develop into a civil war with connections to a series of active or latent armed conflicts in the region.

In 1996 a stabilization of the situation was connected with the fact that both sides were ready to make concessions. Conflict prevention activities including external Russian intervention for preventive purposes had kept the situation from escalating to the large-scale use of violence. Peace enforcement actions of the Russian 14th Army had the purpose to restrict the conflict to the noncoercive phase and further containment. The presence of the 14th Army in the Dniestr region had a calming effect in terms of easing any interethnic tensions arising from perceptions that Moldovans abused Russians.

As Camplisson and Hall (1996) pointed out, on June 17, 1996, Presidents Snegur and Smirnov agreed on the outlines of new constitutional arrangements to end the conflict.

The breakthrough in conflict prevention became visible in 1997 when a "top down" strategy of conflict prevention was carried out by the leadership of the Russian Federation. It was fueled by perspectives of NATO enlargement. The demand to preserve Moldova in the Russian sphere of interest contributed to efforts to prevent escalation.

During this period (1997–1998) the aim of Russia and Ukraine was to avoid new violent escalation by mediation efforts and confidence-building measures aimed at preserving the territorial integrity of Moldova. A plan proposed by Dniestria involved a free confederal association, while Moldova proposed a special status for Dniestria with a concentrated Russian population.

On May 8, 1997, a Memorandum on Basic Principles in Relations between Moldova and Transdniestria was signed in Moscow. However, the proposed draft Declaration on Transdniestria State (February 1998) does not coincide with the memorandum. The Transdniester leaders want a confederative solution, where the Dniestrian Republic has the status as a sovereign state, as does Moldova. The Moldovian government wants a solution that would give the Dniestrian Republic considerable local autonomy and the legal right to self-determination if Moldova should relinquish its status as an independent state, i.e., reunite with Romania (*Nezavisimaya gazeta* 1998). The disputing parties are still not willing to resolve their differences.

As the economic situation in Moldova deteriorated by the end of 1997, Moldova administration had to cope with permanent economic difficulties and a growing "black economy" sector (48 percent of the Moldovan economy). As a result, communists won the national elections in March 1998. It was a devastating defeat for the Agrarian-Democratic Party, which lost mandates in the parliament.

Preliminary Conclusion

The Moldova-Dniestr conflict is an evident example of inadequate alertness to growing hostile rhetorics and human rights abuses. The reasons could have been psycho-cultural factors, which played a dominant role in the Moldovan nationalist revival. With regard to the dynamics of the Moldova-Dniester conflict, it appears that the decline of the central authority and the strengthening of local forces in Moldova, based upon nationalist sentiments, challenged counter-measures from the Slavic regional forces in Dniestria and narrowed the basis for dialogue. The reactions by the federal government, which neglected indicators for the coming crisis, may be understood in light of the fact that the Moldova-Dniestr contradiction was used in the central political struggle between Communists and radical-Democrats.

In the posttotalitarian countries coming out of the former Soviet Union, election outcomes have often been less than expected in democratic terms, because of the underdeveloped nature of their civil societies. As in Moldova, the government and the parliamentary structures tended to loose legitimacy, but this was not seen as constituting an immanent threat of militarization or the use of violence. Many of the subsequent events were seen as internal affairs, and it was difficult to find a traditional trigger to act on.

Therefore, future parties to the conflict or potential mediators did not take the opportunities for preemptive prevention that were given. When escalation from hostile rhetorics had transformed into the use of force and a violent conflict phase was on its way, Russia practiced its coercive diplomacy to prevent large-scale civil war in the region. Preventive action was launched when fighting already happened. This was too late to stop the conflict dynamics, but not too late for maintaining stability in the region. The preventive action served to contain violence or threats of violence in a region of high importance for the Balkan theater of military actions. It was preventive action after the arming of militias.

Although late, actions were taken at a moment when matters still could be channeled in a stabilizing direction. Preventive action aims at preventing situations from entering a limited violence phase. This, then, was not achieved, and it is likely that the legacy of some of the violence in Dubosari region and Tiraspol (1992) will have an impact for a long period to come in Moldova. The central government in Moldova still does not have control over Transdniestria.

Because the main strategic powers of the region were only vaguely interested in Transdniestria, Russia took the role as a mediator and would also have been the only possible regional candidate to coordinate a preventive effort. There was, however, a rivalry between Russia and Ukraine, which affected the handling of the issue.

The role of the Russian 14th Army deployed in the Dniestr region should not be overestimated, but at the same time it succeeded in containing the conflict. The risk of escalation would be higher without the preventive deployment of the Russian military forces.

The outside world did not act early to find a peaceful solution to this conflict before the outbreak of violence through, for instance, regional peace conferences. Instead, it let the conflict have its course; perhaps this lack of action was a preferable course, in a sense serving as structural conflict prevention or limitation. OSCE entered into the conflict in Moldova in early 1993, in the aftermath of violence. However, the OSCE mission later provided a more active mediation role, which kept the conflicting parties in constant communication and contributed to preventing the conflict from turning violent by encouraging the parties to continue dialogue.

The Chechnya Case

Chechnya was the first of the autonomous North Caucasian republics to declare independence. In 1990 a Chechen National Congress (CNC) was convened, proclaimed a sovereign Chechen republic, and drew up guidelines for a new constitution and separate armed forces. The leadership in Moscow, however, feared that the Chechens would provoke further secessions throughout the Russian Federation. The situation in Chechnya was marked by a complex network of external and internal factors that contributed to economic and political uncertainty and rising social tension.

Background Conditions of the Chechen Conflict

Russian military involvement in the Caucasus started early in the eighteenth century, and in 1785–1791 the first major rebellion in Chechnya against imperial rule took place. In the early nineteenth century several Georgian princedoms and Abkhazia appealed to join the Russian Empire; several successful military campaigns against the Ottoman Empire and Persia made it possible to consolidate control over Transcaucasus. However, resistance in the North Caucasus continued, and it was only in 1864 that the Caucasian war was over.

The status of the North Caucasian republics was determined in 1936, but some changes took place in 1944. The Chechen-Ingush Republic was disbanded (both peoples were blamed for collaboration with Nazi Germany in 1942 and deported to Kazakhstan) and Chechens and Ingush were rehabilitated and allowed to return in 1957. At the same time, their republic was reestablished, with somewhat changed borders.

In 1989, Russians made up 23 percent of the population of Chechen-Ingush Republic, but intensive migration has since sharply reduced this figure.

On November 27, 1990, the Supreme Soviet of the Chechen-Ingush ASSR adopted a Declaration on the State Sovereignty of the Chechen-Ingush Republic. This declaration did not cause particular concern, despite the implicit upgrade in status from that of autonomous republic within the Russian Federation.

The CNC was held in the spring of 1991 and called for early parliamentary and presidential elections, for adoption of a new consitution and a law on citizenship, and for a referendum on the republic's status. The CNC set as prerequisites for signing a treaty with the USSR or Russia the unconditional recognition of the Chechen nation's right to independence, compensation for crimes committed against the Chechen nation, trials of the guilty, and establishment of a government based on democratic principles.

The "National Revolution" in Chechnya (August–December 1991)

The political situation in Moscow has its impact on events in Chechnya. Zavgaev was then in Moscow to sign the proposed Union Treaty. Almost all officials in Grozny either favored the attempted coup or avoided taking sides by calling in sick.

In contrast, on August 19, Dudaev and the CNC executive committee issued a decree denouncing the organizers as "a group of government criminals," appealed to "the population of the Chechen Republic to show perseverance, determination, and courage in defending democracy and human dignity," and called for "a campaign of civil disobedience." Large demonstrations in Grozny's main square supported Dudaev and the CNC. Zavgaev, who returned from Moscow on August 21, could not regain control of the situation in Chechnya; on August 22 Dudaev's armed supporters seized the Grozny television station; on August 24 they pulled down Lenin's statue in the town center; by the end of August a national guard was formed; on September 1–2 the third session of the CNC passed a resolution transferring power in Chechnya to its executive committee; and on September 6 the National Guard stormed a meeting of the Chechen-Ingush Supreme Soviet, forcing Zavgaev to sign an "act of abdication."

On September 11, Gennady Burbulis and Mikhail Poltoranin were dispatched from Moscow by the federal leadership to try restore order. On September 14, Ruslan Khasbulatov, a Chechen elected in 1990 to the RF Supreme Soviet from Grozny and its acting chairman after June 1991, arrived in Grozny. On September 15, at a special session of the Chechen-Ingush Supreme Soviet, he persuaded the deputies to remove Zavgaev and to disband, in anticipation of new parliamentary elections, which were set for November 17. The political struggle between the radical nationalist forces, grouped around Dudaev and pushing for independence, and the conservative nomenklatura, trying to preserve the status quo, continued.

Instability in North Caucasus increased after October 1991, when the Chechen Republic declared its independence. On October 8, the presidium of the RF Supreme Soviet adopted a Resolution on the Political Situation in the Chechen-Ingush Republic, which expressed "serious concern regarding the situation in the Chechen-Ingush Republic" where "the escalation of violent actions by illegal formations is continuing" and "the life, rights, and property of citizens of the Chechen-Ingush Republic are subject to growing danger." The presidium then declared that the provisional council was the only legitimate state power in the republic, that this provisional council should take all necessary measures to stabilize the situation, that "illegal armed formations" should hand in their weapons by midnight October 10, and that the forthcoming elections should be held on the basis of the Russian Federation's existing legislation.

On November 7, President Yeltsin declared a state of emergency in the Chechen-Ingush Republic. The newly elected Chechen Parliament responded by voting emergency powers to Dudaev, who ordered martial law in Chechnya and mobilized the National Guard. When planes carrying Russian troops landed at the airport near Grozny, their deployment was blocked by Chechen forces.

On November 10, the RF Supreme Soviet voted to withhold the confirmation of Yeltsin's state of emergency decree.

Stalemate in 1992–1993

After Russia's failure to reassert sovereignty over Chechnya in November 1991, an extended stalemate developed. Chechnya attempted to assert the prerogatives of an independent sovereign state, while Russia continued to regard the Chechen Republic as part of the Russian Federation and subject to its laws. Chechnya for three years managed to function effectively outside Russia's control, refusing to participate in any federal initiatives including the elections/referendum in December 1993. That did not provide for internal stability, and the contradictions between the Chechen parliament and President Dudaev, elected in October 1991 by a very questionable ballot, escalated to confrontation. In March 1992 an attempted coup was crushed by force, and in June 1993 President Dudaev, in a last resort to avoid a referendum on a vote of no-confidence authorised by the parliament, used his troops to dissolve it and to dislodge the opposition from Grozny to the Nadterechny district bordering with Stavropol krai. Limited clashes and terrorist activities continued after this.

Increasing instability in the Chechen Republic in 1992–1993 was related primarily to the competition between several major teips (clans), which started to struggle for control over oil, drug trafficking, and arms smuggling. In 1993, several presidential decrees and government orders were issued in Moscow for tightening control on the Chechnya borders—but with little practical effect, since Daghestan was not particularly interested in implementing those while the border between Chechnya and Ingushetia was not even demarcated after the split. The first half of 1994 saw increasing demands in Russia to seal off Chechnya, due to several incidents with hostage-taking and highjacking in Stavropol and Krasnodar krai, all of which involved Chechens. An official propaganda campaign was intensified in Moscow depicting Dudaev's regime as criminal, illegitimate, and losing popular support.

Moscow authorities pursued a policy of peaceful coexistence with the Grozny authorities until the spring of 1994. However, nationalists in Moscow wanted to reassert Russian rule by force. Liberals wanted to bring Chechnya within the framework of the Russian Constitution and the rule of law by means of a process of peaceful negotiation. The average Russian was angered by stories of Chechen abuse of local Russians and saw Chechnya as a dangerous center of mafia activities. Local opposition in Chechnya to Dudaev had grown because of the republic's failure to win international recognition. Some districts of Chechnya had come under the control of the opposition, notably Nadterechny raion, dominated by Umar Avturkhanov, who in December 1993 organized a provisional council as a potential alternative government for Chechnya and appealed to Moscow for assistance.

In the spring of 1994 Yeltsin and his advisers decided to provide financial and military assistance to the opposition in Chechnya in hopes that Dudaev could be overthrown and that a reconstituted Chechen government would accept the Russian Constitution and the status it granted to the Chechen Republic.

By the summer of 1994, the internal clashes in Chechnya had escalated to full-scale civil war. Several groups of opposition consolidated their control on Nadterechny district and established bases in other areas, threatening to reduce Dudaev's control to the capital Grozny. For Moscow it became increasingly tempting to extend its support for the opposition in order to bring into power a more controllable regime. This support initially included financial aid and some military equipment; but Dudaev played rather skillfully on discord among the opposition leaders and defeated their uncoordinated attacks. In early November, central authorities in Moscow decided to secure for the opposition a clear military superiority; But the decisive assault on Grozny on November 26 was repelled, with heavy casualties. Moscow tried to deny any involvement, but several dozen Russian officers captured by Chechen government forces confirmed that they had been hired by the Federal Counterintelligence Service with consent of the military authorities.

Since then the nature of conflict has changed. The opposition forces were demoralized, not so much because of the military failure as because of the connections with Moscow. Dudaev was able to turn his case from fighting with opposition into standing firm against external intervention.

Russian Intervention in Chechnya (December 1994–September 1996)

Russia's full-scale military intervention was launched on December 11, 1994, as an "order-restoring" operation aimed at "disarming illegal groupings." Up to 40,000 troops with some 500 armored vehicles marched toward Grozny from three directions: northern (from Mozdok), western (through Ingushetia), and eastern (through Dagestan). But the western and eastern groupings immediately faced massive resistance that seriously hampered the offensive and led to unexpected casualties. Only by the end of December were the Russian troops able to tighten their blockade of Grozny, but the armoured assault of December 31 was defeated with heavy casualties. That left the commanders of the operation with only one military option: indiscriminate bombardment of residential areas accompanied by slow advance of crack forces into the city. Despite forecasts of a quick victory, Russian troops made slow progress in advancing on Grozny, held up by unarmed civilians as well as by Chechen troops and a lack of supplies and seasoned soldiers.

The Chechen forces are made up of the National Guard and other regular army units, including many soldiers with Afghan war experience, and the volunteer militia, subject also to central command and discipline, in which a great proportion of able-bodied Chechen males participate, some on a part-time basis. By mid-January 1995, Chechen fighters abandoned the presidential palace in Grozny and retreated to their bases in countryside, intensifying the guerilla warfare across the whole territory of the republic. The Russian forces were unable to contain the guerilla movement by the Chechen insurgents.

President Yeltsin declared the military phase of the operation "effectively over" but it was clear that only the army could hold back Dudaev's forces. Moscow continued its efforts to set some puppet government, but there was little doubt that the captured territories would remain politically uncontrollable. The price of this "victory" appeared enormous, both in terms of the army's own losses and in terms of casualties among the civilian population and the destruction of the economic infrastructure.

Conflict Resolution and Postconflict Prevention (1996–1997)

After 1996 the Russian Federation turned to a new strategy—more consequent—where the main emphasis seemed to be on the need to abandon the attempts to solv the conflict by force. Missions by then-secretary of the National Security Council, Alexander Lebed, on August 14–15 and on August 21–22, became an important input in preventing the further escalation of violence as a result of General Pulikovskij's ultimatum.

On August 27, 1996, the commander of the Russian forces in Chechnya, General Vyacheslav Tikhomirov, and then top separatist commander Aslan Maskhadov signed an accord to reinforce a six-day cease-fire. The agreement called for planned joint Russian-Chechen patrols to start operating in Grozny. Secretary Lebed presented his peace initiative.

On August 31, 1996, Alexander Lebed and Aslan Maskhadov signed a Statement on Basic Principles of Relationship between the Russian Federation and the Chechen Republic (Khasavurt Agreements). Both sides agreed to abandon the use of force while the question on Chechenya's status was postponed until December 31, 2001.

The outbreak of violence in the North Caucasus during the spring of 1997 has threatened to freeze the negotiation process between Russia and Chechnya. However, further projects on economic rewards to Chechnya seemed to be more effective as tools in the prevention of the reemergence of hostilities.

During the meeting between Russia's President Boris Yeltsin and Chechnya's President Aslan Maskhadov on May 12, 1997, a political agreement normalizing relations between Russia and Chechnya and a banking agreement were signed and agreement on the oil industry seemed on its way. The oil issue is the main positive factor in the stabilization of future relations between the Kremlin and Chechnya and in postconflict reconstruction. Russia is interested in controlling the route chosen for the transport of so-called early oil from the first phase of exploitation of the Caspian oil through the Chechen segment pipeline to the Black Sea port of Novorossyisk. Chechnya is also interested in oil transit through its territory as one of the main sources of money for economic reconstruction.

Conclusion

The first common feature of the situations in Moldova and Chechnya is that Russia is not the third party to address problems in both regions. However, in Chechnya Russia has transformed its strategy from reactive measures through military intervention and coercive means in preventive diplomacy to diplomatic and positive economic instrument (more precisely economic assistance). In the case of the Chechen war measures were taken by Russia to stop the increase in the intensity and magnitude of violence in 1996 when there was a decision to execute a full-scale bombing of Grozny and Lebed's fast involvement and diplomacy stopped the further escalation.

The Chechen war was "a strange war" from the pure military strategy point of view. Military means served political objectives—more precisely, sides in the struggle between different top official groups in Kremlin. Thus the shift from military coercive measures to diplomatic and economic tools is explained by interests reflecting a political struggle in the presidential elections. In this context the Chechen war became a decisive issue in the Russian presidential campaign.

Russia's failure in the Chechen war was a result of its lack of a clearly formulated and consistent policy toward the Caucasus in general and the North Caucasus as a very special part of the Russian Federation in particular. While one of the declared goals of the intervention was to restore the integrity of the federation, this could prove highly counterproductive by reinforcing the centrifugal trends.

Preventive diplomacy is not effective where there are no legitimate central governmental institutions and state power is weak. Preventive diplomatic efforts are more effective when major powers, regional powers, and neighboring states consider uncontrolled conflict escalation as a major threat not only to national and regional security, but to global security as well. If a major power or regional powers use the conflict in their national interests or as a tool to weaken its international opponents, then such policies enhances the likelihood of preventive failure. The level of tension and the disposition to use violence in Chechnya greatly increased when political controversies were intensified by mass media reports.

In comparison with the Moldova-Dniestr conflict, the use of force in the Chechen conflict could hardly be treated as preventive deployment. The Russian intervention rather contributed to the territorial escalation than horizontal conflict containment. Developments since 1998 are not included in this analysis.

1. During the course of the conflict, The CSCE changed its name to the Organization for Security and Cooperation in Europe (OSCE).

Appendix: Symptoms of Violence in These Two Cases

We have constructed our mode of indicators for the measurement of the comparative magnitude of internal tension and destabilization. We shall partly describe them in terms of the sequential phase concepts introduced in chapter 11, starting with dispute and crisis phase conflict trajectories.

Our approach is to identify signals as symptoms of eight types of violence, derived from the typology of direct, structural and cultural violence developed by Galtung (1996) and the inner tension and inner conflict of opposing parts. From the standpoint of the amount of violence the signals are divided into four types:

Type 1: Faint signals (weaker than weak)
Type 2: Weak signals
Type 3: Strong signals
Type 4: Hyper signals

Faint and weak signals refer to dispute and crisis phases, while strong and hyper signals are properties of crisis and limited violence phases.

Faint signals. Faint signals differ from weak and strong signals by the absence of direct violence expectations. They include:

- stagnation in economy and political development
- economic crisis
- decay of central political power
- articulation of contradiction without violence
- conscientization and polarization of contradiction
- mobilization of conflict facilitators
- articulation of contradiction with slight verbal violence

Weak signals. These include:

- articulation of contradiction with slight verbal violence
- articulation of contradiction with slight physical violent acts

Strong signals. These include:

- articulation of contradiction with higher levels of verbal violence, hostile rethorics
- articulation of contradiction with direct incidental violent acts accompanied by killing (destruction of life and property), murders, fights, blockades of railways, etc.

Hyper signals. These include:

- articulation of contradiction involving violence on a still larger scale, followed by deep and lasting sociopolitical consequences

For the Moldova-Dniestra conflict, these indicators are given in table 5.1.

Table 5.1 Signals as Symptoms of Violence: Moldava–Dniestr

Faint Signals	
General Development	Economic crisis and decay. The general decay of central political power. Shifting of the centers of power from the federal level to republics. Emerging of nationalisms.
Moldovan Actions	Nationalistic reactions to forced "Russification" policies. Increasing dissatisfaction because of a stagnating economic and political development. The Language Act of 1989.
Dniestr Actions	Increasing dissatisfaction "because of a Popular Front Slogans." Fear that increased "romanianization" would demote them to second-rate citizens.

Weak Signals	
Moldovan Actions	Shifting from a defensive toward an offensive orientation within Moldovan nationalism. Agitation for eventual union of Romania and Moldova. The Popular Front Congress, which has adopted the program of unification between Moldova and Romania.
Dniestr Actions	Demands for the creation of a free economic zone. Demands for increased political autonomy. Reemerging of anti-Moldovan nationalist tendencies. The creation of the Dniestr Republic independence.

Strong Signals	
General Development	Increasingly violent rhetorics.
Moldovan Actions	Growing popularity of the "Greater Romania idea." Rejection of the plans for an autonomous status of Transdniestria. First use of armed force in November 1990 to crush protests of Dniestr potential. Discrimination of Russian and Jews minorities within the new Moldovan Constitution.
Dniestr Actions	Manifest anti-Moldovan statements in the Dniestr election campaign. Blockade of railway.

Hyper Signals	
General Development	Increasing violence in Dubosari region, Tiraspol 1992.
Moldovan Actions	March 29, 1992 declaration of a state of emergency throughout the Moldovan Republic.
Dniestr Actions	Organization of paramilitary forces by Dniestr Russians. The announcements of secession in Transdniestria March 26, 1992. A decree ordering partial mobilization of men up to the age of forty-five.

For the Chechen case, these indicators for the second of two episodes are given in table 5.2. The first episode of the case was an intra-republican conflict between governing elites and national-radicals in Chechnya. The second episode concerned the transformation of the intra-republican conflict into conflict between the republic (Chechnya) and the Federal Center (Moscow).

Table 5.2 Signals as Symptoms of Violence: Chechnya

Faint Signals

General Development	The general decay of central political power. Emerging of nationalism.
Opposition Actions	Mobilization of opposition. Establishment of the Chechen National Congress in November 1990.

Weak Signals

General Development	Conflict between the Russian and central Soviet Union governing elites. Competition for power among republican elites.
Republican Power Actions	Decay of political power. Republican governing elites ignore opposition actions.
Opposition Actions	Executive committee of the Chechen National Congress declares the sovereignty of the Chechen-Ingush Republic on May 25, 1991. The Supreme Soviet of the Checheno-Ingushetia is declared illegal. All-national Congress of the Chechen People (former Chechen National Congress until June 1991) decides to abolish the Supreme Soviet in June 1991. Changes in the composition of the All-national Congress of the Chechen People toward national-radical forces.

Strong Signals

General Development	The attempt of coup d'état in August 1991 in Moscow.
Republican Power Actions	Zavgaev signs the act of renunciation of power. The extreme session of the Supreme Soviet of Checheno-Ingushetia. The Supreme Soviet of Checheno-Ingushetia declares its self-dissolution on December 15, 1991. Meetings in Grozny and seizure of TV center in August 1991.
Opposition Actions	Seizure of the House of Political Education by National Guard and radical forces on September 6, 1991.

Table 5.2 (continued)

Hyper Signals

General Development	Decay of central political power.
Chechen Actions	Accession to power by Dudaev in October–November 1991. Meeting in Grozny in November 1991 against the Russian actions.
Russian Actions	Diplomatic intervention of the delegation from the Russian Supreme Soviet in August 1991. Decree of President Yeltsyn on the State of Emergency in Checheno-Ingushetia on November 8, 1991. First attempt to use the Russian Army against Chechnya in November 1991.

6
Why Are Some Ethnic Disputes Settled Peacefully, While Others Become Violent?
Comparing Slovakia, Macedonia, and Kosovo

Michael S. Lund

Bosnia, Somalia, Congo, and many other recent civil wars all reveal that, once political conflicts become militarized, third parties find it extremely difficult and financially and politically costly to terminate them and heal the societies that have been torn apart. Due to these frustrations as well as humanitarian concern, increasing numbers of world leaders and other observers have been calling for "preventive diplomacy" or "conflict prevention," i.e., early action to keep tensions and disputes from escalating into destructive violence in the first place. But while preventive initiatives are increasingly launched, what is required for effective prevention is only beginning to be understood.

To identify policy responses that have the best chances of fostering peaceful resolution of a possible violent intrastate conflict requires analysis of an emerging conflict's various ingredients and their relative weight and interactions in the particular case. Empirical analyses of emerging conflicts that identify which factors are the most significant in a given situation can provide clues as to what mix of responses, among an array of possible options, is likely to achieve the most leverage.

Yet how to undertake such a diagnosis of a deteriorating political situation is not clear. A limitation of many extant conflict analyses is the failure to structure their explanations economically in a way that can be replicated and tested in further studies and that show some connection to possible policy options. The main existing approaches to analyzing unstable situations that may become violent conflicts each have serious shortcomings. The usual information that busy policy makers draw on to interpret a country's status, for example, is a hodge-podge of intelligence cables, news sources, country profiles, advocacy pieces, and perhaps some personal experience or an analogy from a similar context. These sources look at the conflict from very different angles, thus leading to widely differing policy conclusions. Though such varied analyses each embody implicit theories about the causes of a conflict, their assumptions are rarely made explicit and thus are not tested. Even if a more in-depth description of a given conflict is provided, these tend to catalog a large number of factors that have contributed somehow or other. Or, they emphasize one factor to the exclusion of other important ones, based on the intuitions or most familiar policy domain of the author. Thus, the policy maker has no reliable way to know which factors are the most important. Although each conflict is unique in its particular situational details, the most likely factors that should be examined in a given case cannot and need not be infinite in number.

Studies of large numbers of conflicts that seek statistical correlations between their outcomes and various hypothesized causal factors may be more rigorous, and they help to focus on the small number of factors that prove to be the most powerful overall. But this does not help the policy maker decide whether and how much the most significant factors identified in general are operative in the particular case he or she is trying to address. Early warning studies and syntheses of conflict case-studies can reliably suggest a richer yet still relatively small set of sources of conflicts that can be translated into checklists to consider in each particular situation. A common limitation of this genre, however, is that they usually search only for "negative" factors that may lead to the outbreak of violence; they tend to ignore factors that may be having a braking or violence-inhibiting effect as a political situation unfolds. While they provide clues as to known harmful elements that the policy maker might seek to reduce, they do not indicate where opportunities may exist where proactive engagement might buttress local conflict capacities. Most research has focused on active wars by looking retrospectively at their many causes, but very few studies have examined cases of potential war, to identify the elements that preserved their peace.

In sum, few existing approaches to diagnosis are both empirically reliable and inclusive of both possible causes of conflicts and conflict-managing capacities so that policy makers are offered a number of promising entry points. An empirical method is needed for particular cases that combines economy, depth, and attention to existing peace capacities.

One way to reduce some of the complexity and achieve an ordered policy-relevant account of the main factors affecting the course of an emerging conflict is to compare pairs or sets of countries in which the same overall global-systemic and national-level challenges generated new political tensions and disputes, but the countries differed in terms of whether they handled the disputes peacefully or through violence. If the broad historical and regional forces that challenge many countries are held more or less constant, but their differing conflict trajectories are compared, certain features may be found to be associated with these differing outcomes. This "similar system" comparative method can reduce the great number and variety of sources of conflicts that are likely to result from studying either single cases in great depth or large numbers of very differently-situated cases. It also allows the analyst to identify "positive" as well as "negative" factors that mediate between the broad global-systemic forces and the outbreak of violence that have enabled vulnerable situations to maintain peace rather than led them to violence. Such key factors may tend to be more policy-manipulable.

The purpose of this chapter is to illustrate how such a comparative approach can target critical entry points for effective preventive interventions. An empirically-informed, structured comparison of various possible sources of conflicts in three similar cases is used to identify why political tensions and disputes led to peaceful political negotiations in some situations, but led to convulsing national conflicts in others. These key "swing" factors thus suggest promising entry points for preventive actions.

Similar Challenges, Differing Outcomes

The fundamental geo-political and ideological changes during the past ten years that arose from the collapse of communism and the faster spread of globalization represent the kind of pervasive global-systemic forces that provide a common basis for comparing different countries' responses. Many nations in the former Communist bloc as well as in the Third World have been challenged to make major changes in their economic and political practices and institutions, such as privatizing their state industries and holding multiparty elections. These new policies have variously caused widespread economic hardship and political uncertainty, and they have heightened intercommunal tensions.

These changes loomed especially dramatically among the postcommunist polities of the former Soviet bloc. The discrediting of communist ideology and the economic and political reforms initiated by Mikail Gorbachev led in 1989 to the removal of Soviet political controls and reduced centralized economic management in Eastern Europe and the republics of the Soviet Union. In 1991, they led to the breakup of the latter into fifteen newly independent states. The republics of communist Yugoslavia were also affected. The deconstruction of communist controls sparked intense national debates and negotiations among elites, political parties, and newly mobilized social groups on fundamental issues such as constitutions; the territorial boundaries of their states vis-á-vis their ethnic communities; the relationship of local government authorities to central governments, especially in federal states; the structures of their economies, and their new foreign policies, security alliances, and trade relations. Because of the potential for violence arising from these multiple sources of different interests, almost all the countries of Eastern Europe and the Balkans were described in the early 1990s as possible "powder kegs."

As it happened, the result in some of these potential hotspots, such as Yugoslavia, were in fact secessionist conflicts resulting in violent civil wars. But a greater number of the new nations did not in fact explode, such as Czechoslovakia and Russia (at least in general so far). Instead, they handled their multiple tension without violence or armed force. In these instances, issues that could have led to violence were instead avoided or negotiated largely through nonviolent political processes such as bloodless revolutions or negotiated social pacts.

Cross-Border Ethnic Affinities

In particular, one source of disputes that faced many of the newly independent states in the whole region of the former Soviet Union and Central and Eastern Europe was the existence of "kin-group" ties across new borders. As countries replaced or dissolved their Communist Parties, the euphoria of having political freedom from previous central controls led many newly dominant ethnic groups that lived within a newly empowered national or subnational jurisdiction to want to eradicate the signs of their past domination by a former central governments, such as the USSR and the Socialist Federal Republic of Yugoslavia. These ascendant ethnic groups within the new polities often sought to codify in legislation and public policies their own supreme position as a distinct people with their own state or republic. Whether the local nationalist sentiment was pressing for full independence or simply greater devolution of power, the dominant local group's ascendancy tended to result in discrimination against, and fear of, other ethnic groups that were living within the same jurisdiction and that formerly had been protected by a more inclusive governmental entity.

Such treatment was widely experienced among the many dispersed communities of ethnic Russians who were left stranded as newly independent states emerged out of the former Soviet Union. Discrimination was felt or feared by those, such as Russian-speakers in Estonia and Crimea, who had migrated or been sent to the area in sizeable numbers from the old "center." Though they may have lived there for years or decades since the days of the former regime, they now found themselves in a new political community. Examples of the same phenomenon in Yugoslavia as it dissolved were the Serbs in Croatia and the Albanians in Macedonia. On their part, the dominant ethnic groups in these jurisdictions often became suspicious that the minorities, especially those who had ethnic kin in a nearby former "mother" state, were planning secession or irredentist movements that would disrupt the newer polity and seek to redraw its borders, so that the minority could be embraced once again by a state in which they had been a majority.

In sum, a particularly widespread problem in the new politics of the former Soviet Union, in Russia, and in eastern and central Europe involved the rights and the loyalties of ethnic groups that had become minorities under a new governmental authority but that formerly had been majorities or at least enjoyed more political power, under a previous communist regime and the Soviet bloc system. According to the previous official communist doctrine and policies these groups had been brethren living in solidarity within states or across states, but the emergence of new political boundaries quickly shifted the ethnic balance of power within many states and subnational political jurisdictions. Yet no clearly established constitutional and political order existed to spell out and enforce the respective rights of the new majorities and minorities.

Although the residual cross-border ethnic "kin group" affinities throughout the former communist states of Eurasia provided many opportunities for ethnic disputes and conflicts to arise, however, they manifested themselves in quite varied degrees and ways. The bloody Yugoslavian wars among Croatia, Serbia, and Bosnia are a well-known outcome, and other situations with similar elements led to violence in Nagorno-Karabakh, Moldova, and Chechnya. But less recognized is the fact that, though arising during roughly the same period and often in nearby areas, many if not most of the tensions arising from such cross-border "kin-groups" did not lead to violent conflicts at all. Examples where relations remained peaceful include those between Macedonia and Serbia, Bulgaria, Albania, and Greece; Hungary and four of its neighbors; and between Russia and the Baltic states, Ukraine (over the Crimea), and Tatarstan.

Why, when facing similar systemic challenges and though showing common signs of serious strains, instability, or even sometimes low-level violence, did societies like Estonia and Macedonia avoid destructive violent conflicts over these affinities across borders, while nearby societies like Moldova and Bosnia did not? Surprisingly little research has focused explicitly on this compellingly interesting theoretical as well as practical question. This chapter seeks to identify the crucial factors that appear to have made the difference between peace and war in countries that faced the same basic challenge of having ethnic kin-groups living on both sides of new borders.

Disputes in Three Post-Communist States: Differing Courses and Outcomes

The three ethnic conflicts examined here involved the following kin-groups and states: Ethnic Hungarians in Slovakia, 1989–1998; Ethnic Serbs in Macedonia, 1991–1999; and Ethnic Serbs in Kosovo, 1989–1999. All these newly ascendant "host" polities faced serious challenges in defining their new political identity. On the one hand, they had majorities who expressed aspirations for some degree of greater self-determination, but on the other, they had minorities whose ethnic brethren lived in sometimes powerful supportive states or entities right next door.

The chronological narratives accompanying this chapter that trace the differing courses that each country's disputes took show that the three conflicts reached differing degrees of accommodation or hostility. To highlight the differences in the conflicts' course and latest status, the narratives put the background and events in a common comparative framework relating to the stages and levels through which conflicts can evolve. The narratives also indicate when and how various intraregional parties in or near to the conflict arena, as well as international actors from outside the region, took preventive actions to inhibit an escalation of the dispute or conflict. More specifically, the conflicts followed these individual trajectories:

- The Hungarian-Slovakian dispute emerged out of the preexisting communist order of ostensible harmony into an unstable peace resulting from the reawakening of Slovakian nationalism and its drive for independence. The Hungarian minority's kinship with Hungarians across the border in Hungary influenced the relations between Hungary and the new state of Slovakia. But while periodic ethnic tensions arose within Slovakia and between it and Hungary, no incidents of violence occurred, and Slovakia never reached a point close to internal rebellion or interstate war. Over the course of the 1990s, ethnic issues moved toward conflict abatement and partial settlement, although they continue to be irritants.
- The relations between Serbs and ethnic Macedonians in Macedonia and their respective governments also went through uncertainty following Macedonia's independence declaration in 1991. An unstable peace was characterized by occasional shows of force by Serb troops on the northern border, but no killings or prolonged use of armed force. By 1995 it had moved toward conflict abatement efforts and partial settlement, until it was suddenly put at considerable risk once again due to the outbreak of the Kosovo civil war. But to the surprise of many analysts, Macedonia continued to be resilient in the face of several external and internal strains on its cohesion.
- The worst scenario by far occurred in Serb-Albanian relations in Kosovo. During the communist era, these relations were maintained in a uneasy equilibrium punctuated by periodic violent demonstrations and episodes of state crackdowns on dissenters. In the early post-communist period in 1989, the relationship changed abruptly to a situation of near-crisis that subsequently fluctuated between tense polarization and imminent violence. In 1998, it abruptly shifted to a full crisis, mass violence, and civil war, followed by a NATO-led international peace enforcement action against Yugoslavia.

Why did Slovakia's and Macedonia's ethnic relations reach moments of higher tension, but not escalate into violent hostilities, while Kosovo's kin-group conflict ultimately became a deadly civil war resulting in international military intervention? If we can identify elements that varied consistently in the differing cases being compared, they may explain why these conflicts took one route or another. This analysis can then reveal entry points evolving potential conflict situations for appropriate policy interventions in other evolving potential conflicts.

Differing Societies, Institutions, Leaders, or International Involvement?

To find explanations for the three conflicts' differing levels and outcomes, this chapter will "test" several leading distinguishable hypotheses. The hypotheses are not picked from the air but are grounded in recent research. The current interest in conflict prevention may tend to assume that a situation with serious tensions and the potential for violence conflicts that does not in fact escalate has been prevented from doing so by some third party preventive intervention, i.e., an exogenous factor. However, another explanation may very well lie with endogenous factors in the conflict arena itself: the issues or forces that could lead to violence simply were not sufficiently powerful in the case to produce escalation, or, these forces were powerful enough but were counteracted by other forces. In considering the reasons why the three conflicts compared here escalated or not, therefore, it is appropriate to refer to the literature that concerns the causes of violent conflicts, such as empirical individual conflict case-studies and syntheses of case-studies of conflicts (e.g., Carment and James 1998; Ayres 1998, Levy 1996), and also to the (much smaller) literature about situations where tensions and issues arose but preventive actions appear to have avoided violence (e.g., Jentleson 2000; Wallensteen 1998). These "causes of conflict" and "prevention" literatures have focussed on four rather different sets of explanatory variables. These sets deal with favorable or unfavorable societal conditions; actions or events brought about by leaders and elites; political processes and institutions; and international influences.

Societal theories of conflict point to broad, underlying characteristics of a society's history, culture, economy, demography, and social structure, such as its past ethnic relations, gross disparities in the life opportunities enjoyed by a society's various identity groups, or economic decline. Societal conditions are past or continuing forces that characterize the broad environment of the major protagonists in a conflict and present them with various constraints or opportunities. These abiding "givens" either cannot be changed at all by particular actors, or they are amenable to policy decisions but slow to change.[1] *Action* explanations focus on the behavior, overt or covert, of the major influential political leaders and elites in a society and of their governments, such as manifested in the public rhetoric of "ethnic entrepreneurs" and the policy decisions which often shape the direction of public events in a conflict arena.[2]

A third set of causes of violent conflicts has been introduced into recent literature and policy discussions more recently. These concern favorable or unfavorable *political institutions and processes* that may structure the expression of interests in the potential conflict situation. If differing interests are accommodated through the access and opportunity for bargaining and negotiation that are afforded by participatory mechanisms such as elections, rather than blocked by exclusive ones, or the expression of interests is separated by decentralized governmental institutions, rather than centralized ones, coercion and violence can more easily be avoided. Lacking such channels of political and policy representation, violence becomes more likely.[3]

These three ways to explain conflicts focus on factors arising within the conflict arena itself or its immediate regional context. But whether a political conflict breaks out in violence may indeed be determined also by *major international actors* outside the immediate region. As already suggested, the impetus behind the recent interest in conflict prevention arises from the view that timely, effective intervention by major third parties such as multilateral organizations and major states can often spell the difference between peaceful resolution and human tragedies. Thus, a fourth explanation of the course of the three conflicts may concern whether the overall international response to the situation was effective as prevention. Did Slovakia and Macedonia differ from Kosovo because of differing degrees and forms of engagement by major actors in the international community?

The point of laying out these four types of explanation is not that one or another approach will necessarily be the single correct one. It is rather that in approaching a given potential conflict, analysts and the policy makers they may advise may need to consider several kinds of variables. For one thing, which factors are most influential in a particular setting, and to what degrees, may determine the extent to which such growing conflicts may be preventable at all. It is possible that the more that societal factors are unfavorable, for example, the more difficult it is for institutions and leaders to prevent violence from occurring, and thus also for third parties to prevent it.

Second, each of these types of explanation points to quite different "entry points" in a conflict situation, some long-term and some short-term, that domestic or international policy makers may find it the most cost-effective to address. The differing entry points suggest very different types of intervention instruments among the wide range that have come to be considered as potentially conflict-preventive. For example, societal explanations tend to look to programs of overall economic development, economic structural reform, psycho-social transformation and healing, or perhaps complete partition (Kaufman 1996). These policies (sometimes called "structural" or "deep" prevention) address the fundamental conditions that affect whole populations and thus tend to be achievable only over the long-term. Institutional explanations see democratization and civil society building policies (also often classified as "structural" or "deep" prevention) as needed. Action theories, however, tend to suggest remedies using various interactive techniques such as third-party mediation or diplomatic and military pressures, which operate in the short-term to diffuse disputes and resolve substantive issues (sometimes called "direct" or "light" prevention). Whatever international engagement may have occurred in a studied case can also be categorized in terms of these two varieties.

Assessing Alternative Explanations

We turn now to examine the various domestic and international factors that each of the types of argument have claimed as the most powerful explanatory variables. This section assesses three societal factors, two institutional factors, one action or behavioral factor, and the international influences. With regard to each explanation, it examines and compares evidence from the three cases to judge the extent and ways those factors were significant influences on the course of the conflict.[4]

Past Group Relations: Violent Conflict or Accommodation?

One factor that has been identified as critical in explaining the likelihood for contemporary hostilities between ethnic, religious, linguistic, or other identity groups is the extent there has been violent conflict, coexistence, or active cooperation between them in the past (see Miall 1992). At one extreme, bitter, deadly, and protracted conflicts may have recently occurred. To the extent there are fresh memories of bloodshed perpetrated by another group against one's kin, political activists can more easily conjure up those atrocities to instill further distrust and incite a following to take up arms once again. Subjugation or repression that falls short of taking lives is a milder form of hostility along this spectrum. Killing or domination both tend to create and perpetuate a culture of coercion, in which all sides assume that gaining their interests requires eliminating or subduing others. Alternatively, past relations may reflect no violent conflict or relatively tolerant relations. An authoritarian system that included groups in more or less equal clientele relationships can maintain peace, even though the mutual interactions between groups might not have been extensive. The most favorable history would have seen groups participating jointly in governmental decisionmaking, such as through wide access to competitive multiparty elections.

Accordingly, we compare the nature of the past relations of the three pairs of groups prior to the post–Cold War decade. Did Kosovo escalate into violence while the other two cases remained at the level of political tensions because the former groups had more violent relationships in the past?

Ethnic Hungarians and Slovakians

Beginning in the ninth century as the Magyars settled into the Danube plain, Slovakians came under the domination of Hungarian kings, who sometimes ruled harshly. Although Czech Hussites spread Protestantism to Slovakia during the Reformation, the Habsburgs who succeeded to the Hungarian throne in 1526 restored Catholicism and ruled Slovakia until 1918. Under the dual monarchy of the Austro-Hungarian Empire, Hungarian rulers assumed direct control in 1866 over an area that included present-day Hungary and parts of present day Slovakia, Croatia, Vojvodina, Transylvania, and Ukraine. In 1867, they began a policy of forced magyarization, which led many Slovaks to emigrate.

The collapse of the Austro-Hungarian Empire in World War I led to the establishment of the first Republic of Czechoslovakia. Many Hungarian civil servants, teachers and other professionals had their jobs taken away and were forced to leave the country. Their numbers dropped from an estimated 880,000 in 1910 to 650,000 in 1921. The Hungarian population living in Slovakia thus became a minority in the newly formed Czechoslovakian state. The Treaty of Trianon of 1920 reduced Hungary to one-third of its historic territory, two-fifths of its prewar population, and two-thirds of its Hungarian population. It also removed 83 percent of its iron and 58 percent of its railways, and put severe limits on the size and armaments of its armed forces and police, especially in comparison to the post–World War I forces of its neighbors.

This treatment following the war led many Hungarians to feel they were victims of the settlement and they passionately supported revisionism. This stance took the form of aggression when Hungary sided with the rising Axis powers, and with German help, regained some of its former territory from Czechoslovakia in 1938 and 1939, from Romania in 1940, and from Yugoslavia in 1941. But from 1944 to 1948, these annexations were again voided, and many Hungarians were blamed for bringing war to the Czech republic and for collaboration with the Nazis. The liberated Czech government deprived ethnic Hungarians of their citizenship, many civil rights, and their property. Hungarian schools and cultural institutions were closed, and many Hungarians were sentenced to forced labor. Thousands were expelled or exchanged with Hungary. Under the Communist regime starting in 1948, official doctrine espoused the equality of all ethnic groups within Czechoslovakia, and domestic policies sought to balance the interests of the various ethnic groups. But during this period, minority interests tended to be submerged under the renewed sentiments of Slovak nationalism.

In sum, during most of their mutual history, Hungarians and Slovakians alternately dominated the other, and each group often imposed severely repressive policies. But although the armed actions during the world wars caused a number of deaths, no major violent conflicts occurred in recent memory explicitly between ethnic Slovaks and ethnic Hungarians. "There is little tradition of any sort of violence in this region" (Zielonka 1972, 12).

Ethnic Serbs and Macedonians

In a whole chapter devoted to Macedonia, Robert Kaplan's *Balkan Ghosts* reflects the "weight of history" thesis by describing Macedonia as the real source of World War I and other barbarisms—"a historical and geographical reactor furnace . . . (where) the ethnic hatreds released by the decline of the Ottoman Empire had first exploded, forming the radials of twentieth-century European and Middle Eastern conflict. Macedonia was like the chaos at the beginning of time . . . the original seedground not only of modern warfare and political conflict, but of modern terrorism and clerical fanaticism as well" (Kaplan 1994, 51–56). But this blanket characterization fails to capture the mixture of affinities and antagonisms in the relations between ethnic Serbs and ethnic Macedonians.

During the nineteenth century, the current area known as Macedonia was subjugated under the Ottoman Empire. As the Ottoman Empire waned in the 1880s and ethnic Macedonian nationalist consciousness first began to rise, Serbia sought to exert cultural influence over Macedonia, which it called South Serbia. But Serbia was only one of several states that competed for influence there. In the Balkan Wars of 1912 and 1913, Serbia fought over the area against Bulgaria and Greece, and Macedonians on the Bulgarian side were killed by Serbs and vice versa. Following Bulgaria's defeat in the second Balkan War, Serbia achieved control. Following Bulgaria's occupation of the area during World War I, Macedonia was again brought under a Serbian king in the first Yugoslavia, known as the Kingdom of the Serbs, Croats, and Slovenes. During World War II, Macedonians and Serbs both fought for Tito's partisan forces against Fascism, as represented in the occupying forces of Bulgaria, Nazi Germany's ally until late in the war. Under federal communist Yugoslavia, Macedonia became a republic legally equal to Serbia. Through recognizing Macedonia's own language, church and history, Tito sought to give it a distinctive political and cultural identity as a counterbalance to the Serbs within the Yugoslav federation.

In sum, Serbs and ethnic Macedonians, at least as politically self-conscious groups, have not fought violent battles against each other in recent times. The Serb-Macedonian relationship has been considerably less hostile recently than, for example, the animosity that arose between Serbs and Croatians from the horrible atrocities perpetrated during World War II by the Ustashe and Chetniks respectively.

Ethnic Serbs and Kosovar Albanians

Serbs first settled in present-day Kosovo in the sixth and seventh centuries and established a state, but they still harbor deep resentment at their defeat by the Muslim Turks in a battle in 1389 in Kosovo's Polje Field and the subsequent Turk invasion. Beginning in the late nineteenth century, ethnic Albanians began to move into Kosovo and become numerically dominant. Serbs were expelled from the area several times when under Muslim rule, during the Balkan wars, and during World War I, but their occupations of the area also saw them ruthlessly seek to serbianize it and expel Albanians. During World War II, German and Italian authorities allowed Kosovo to be linked for a while with Albania. Mutual atrocities and expulsions were common between local Albanian groups who collaborated with the Axis forces of occupation from Germany and Italy, and the Serb Chetniks or Partisan Communists comprising many Serbs, who sought to liberate the area. In the post–World War II period, in response to Albanian pressures, Tito provided some recognition to Albanian interests to the extent that was politically useful, such as the granting of Kosovo's status as an autonomous republic in 1974. But the periodic Albanian nationalist clashes with the federal government in violent demonstrations, punctuated by occasional harassment of individual Serbs, were also suppressed. These clashes reached their height in 1989, when the existing Albanians protested the removal of the elected local authorities in favor of officials more loyal to President Slobodan Milosevic. Mass riots were answered by police crackdowns that killed a number of Albanians, arrests of political leaders, and wholesale expropriations of jobs and institutions.

Comparing the relationships in these three pairs of groups prior to the end of the Cold War, none could be said to be amicable, but the amount of past hostility varied greatly. The least hostile relations existed between Serbs and Macedonians, for they had not either fought or subjugated each other recently. The Hungarians and Slovaks had a more estranged relationship because of past periods of direct domination and harsh treatment. In Kosovo, because ethnic Albanians and Serbs have engaged in recurring violent hostilities against each other for several recent decades in which many members of each group were killed, theirs was clearly the most hostile relationship.

Current Relations: Segregation or Association?

This factor refers to the social distance or contact that normally exists between members of identity groups in a society. The assumption is that the less that identity groups interact with each other in ordinary life, the more they will be predisposed to engage in violent conflict when tensions and disputes arise. Social distance allows unwarranted suspicions and distrust to arise in groups' mutual perceptions, and increases the difficulty of their understanding each others' perspectives and needs.

This dimension may be reflected at the level of local communities in terms of whether the ordinary members of each group live and work in the same places, and thus are in contact or physically separated by virtue of their residence and daily routines. One group may be primarily farmers and others urban workers, for example, or their rural communities may be concentrated geographically within different areas. Alternatively, groups may have considerable mutual interaction within urban areas.[5]

The degree of heterogeneity in the wider society, that is, the number and similarity in size of identity groups, may also tend to increase mixing (Stroschein 1996). Groups that are very small may be inclined simply to assimilate as individuals into the dominant society, whereas groups that constitute a larger proportion of the total population have a greater incentive to organize themselves to pursue common interests because they stand to gain from establishing a social presence and political voice. Some studies suggest that societies with either one homogenous identity group or many small identity groups will be less subject to violent conflicts than societies with just two groups of moderate and more equal size.[6]

Another factor shaping this dimension is the number of socioeconomic and cultural characteristics that differentiate groups from each other. They may differ on or possess in common their physical features, language, religion, social class, and social and cultural institutions. Hostile conflict is more likely to the extent that groups differ in many such respects, because this generates more diverging interests, which can become politicized and pursued through coercion, and fewer shared interests exist to counteract or offset these competing interests.[7] Conversely, however, where identity groups share some features, even though they may still differ on others, the potential for violent conflict is thought to be reduced because shared "cross-cutting" identities offset the other differences and limit the range of interests over which groups might be motivated to fight with each other.

Ethnic Hungarians and Slovakians

Because Communist policy had suppressed nationalist sentiments and denied that differences among minority groups' interests existed, the incorporation of Slovakia into a federal Czechoslovakia had not led to policies promoting greater integration between Slovakians or other ethnic groups, and the ethnically defined borders between the Czech and Slovak republics were not questioned. In the early 1990s, only 300,000 Slovaks live in Bohemia and 53,000 Czechs lived in Slovakia. A similar attitude was evident within Slovakia. But with the arrival of electoral democracy, the proportions of minorities in the population and their presence in certain areas became more salient in political life. According to some political party analysts, Slovakia's politicians waged especially turbulent and fractious party politics and had more difficulty building government coalitions than did politicians within the Czech Republic, largely because of the existence of its two major ethnic identity groups (Evans and Whitefield 1998, 135).

While ethnic Hungarians constituted about 3 percent of the federation's population, according to the 1992 census, they comprised about 11 percent of the 3 million population in Slovakia (Stroschein 1996; Evans and Whitefield 1998, 118). The Hungarians are by far Slovakia's largest minority group, with about 600,000 people. Slovakia is home to six other ethnic groups, but each only comprises approximately 1.5 percent of the population or less. In terms of location, more than 92 percent of Hungarians live in a continuous strip of land along the southern border of Slovakia, in which they comprise about 62 percent of the population. That Hungary is immediately adjacent intensifies the ties the Hungarian minority feel with their ethnic brethren across the border. Many ethnic Hungarians in Slovakia have relatives in Hungary, some of whose families may have fled from those areas into present-day Hungary after Trianon. An obvious cultural difference between the groups is language, for Slovakian is a Slavic tongue and Hungarian is Finno-Ugric. Economically, Hungarians in Slovakia are generally considered to be somewhat better-off than the average Slovak (Zielonka 1972, 17f).

At the same time, however, many administrative districts in that region have highly mixed ethnic Slovak and Hungarian populations (Strochein 1996). About sixty percent live in small villages, but the larger towns provide points of contact, since Slovakia has become highly industrialized, and agriculture accounts for only 6 percent of GDP. Also, due to centuries of coexistence, there are few significant distinguishing physical marks of identity between Hungarians and Slovakians. The dominant religion in Czechoslovakia, among those who were religious, was Catholicism, and about 60 percent of the general population in Slovakia are now Roman Catholic. Eight percent are Protestant, and Protestant evangelism is active. But apparently neither of these faiths is concentrated more among Slovaks than Hungarians. About 65 percent of ethnic Hungarians are Catholic and many attend mass in Slovak. Thus, both groups share a strong Catholic affiliation (Stroschein 1996).

Overall, the geographic and linguistic differences of these groups are offset somewhat by their physical similarities, shared religions, and considerable everyday contact, especially in the mixed areas.[8] Although an opinion poll early in the post–Cold War era (1991) found that a significant proportion of Slovakians wanted Hungarians to move to Hungary, analysts do not think the groups consider each other as alien and they interact frequently. Nor do the Hungarians share all the same interests with their kinfolk in the mother country.

Ethnic Serbs and Macedonians

A similar combination of geographic separation with cultural affinities characterizes Serb-Macedonian relations in Macedonia. Serbs tend to be concentrated in strips of the country adjacent to the northern border with Serbia, such as in and around the town of Kumanova. The Serbs in Serbia share with ethnic Macedonians a Slavic language, although Macedonian differs somewhat and is close to Bulgarian. The groups also share the Orthodox religion, although in 1967 the Macedonian church was allowed to establish its own organizational hierarchy, rather than be governed by the ecclesiastical authorities in Belgrade. More immediately, they share the feeling of a threat from the Albanians, with whom they both differ in both language and religion. Their contact is probably increased also because ethnic Macedonians constitute the largest population group in the country (65 percent), while Serbs are a very small portion (2 percent).

Ethnic Serbs and Kosovo Albanians

This pair shows much more pronounced cultural and geographic differences. Albanians are Muslims and Serbs Orthodox, although the Albanians' Islam is neither vigorous nor political. They also differ in language. Kosovo is dominated demographically by Albanians. Before the 1998 war, there were 2 million Albanians and about 150,000 to 200,000 Serbs living there. Pockets of Serbs lived throughout the capital city Prishtina, and they are concentrated in certain other towns around Kosovo. Although some Serbs and Albanians in Kosovo live near to each other in the same towns, while others occupy their own communities, the groups nevertheless have pursued their daily work and lives in entirely separate channels. Since 1990, Kosovar Albanians have set up their own governmental, political, educational, and social services, separate from those of the federal government but tolerated by it, and this clearly reduced whatever social contact existed previously to a minimum. Because this segregation is due to recent Serb repression as well as Kosovar aspirations, it reflects the respective groups' political mobilization, considered below, rather than geographic and cultural factors alone, however.

All in all, the three pairs all speak differing languages, but they experience differing degrees of physical separation and cultural difference. The Serbs and Albanians in Kosovo clearly have the most geographic, cultural, and institutional differences and least association.

Economic Decline or Growth?

Another factor creating potential for intergroup conflict is the extent that groups are in competition for the natural and other material resources that they depend on for their livelihoods, such as land, water, education, and jobs. A declining economy increases the possibility for conflict because all groups want to maintain or improve their position, but there is less and less to go around of the means to do so. In primarily rural societies, this competition may be reflected by increasing population to land ratios, inequitable land ownership, and scarce grazing areas and water supply. In more industrialized societies, competition may arise over social assets such as education, jobs, housing, and health services, as reflected in comparative rates of children in school, unemployment rates, and infant mortality rates. Pressure for key resources may be especially affected by a society's birthrate and whether it has a "youth bulge"—the proportion of population between the ages of 15 and 30, for this could mean a large proportion of the population is seeking to enter a constricted labor market. Conflict may arise also out of from simple "greed," if there is competition over the ownership of natural resources that can be exported for profit, such as minerals and oil, and the proceeds from these assets are not distributed widely, or these riches enable a leader to recruit and arm a following through which he can wrest control of the society by force.

Whether economic decline actually generates intergroup competition and thus ethnic political tensions is a function not simply of the status of economic indicators, however. It is also influenced by the extent of the governmental control of the economy, and thus whether the allocation of vital economic and social goods such as jobs and education opportunities is determined by governmental decisions and political leaders. A related indicator is the size and budget of the military, since these employees of the state can also be used for political purposes. Because a growing market economy holds at least the prospect of expanding opportunities for all, as long as the fruits of growth are broadly distributed, it can reduce the sense of economic competition and thus the potential for conflict. The growth of such an economy is reflected in aggregate figures such as economic growth rate; gross domestic product (GDP) per capita; income per capita; and primary product exports as a percentage of GDP. However, in states with large public sectors relative to private sector opportunities, economic competition gets played out over access to government jobs and benefits. Especially when transitioning political systems are becoming more open to political competition through democratic elections, competition for vital resources can become more salient because central political decision makers decide their allocation in a more public and visible way than many dispersed private employers would. Politicians can use state goods as favors in return for political support, whereas more market-oriented and privatized economies provide fewer assets for use as political patronage.[9] Intra- or interstate conflicts can also arise from economic decline, because incumbent statist regimes may try to scapegoat certain groups or other nations as the source of the scarcity problem, thus encouraging hostility toward them.

In sum, violent conflict does not arise from poverty or even economic disparities per se, but its potential is increased to the extent groups have to compete, especially in the political arena, over the allocation of existing or prospective levels of vital or highly valued socioeconomic resources.

Ethnic Hungarians and Slovakians

Although it had one-third of the population, Slovakia had been subsidized by the Czech and Slovak Federation to the extent of half the federal budget. The economy in Slovakia underwent a steady decline in the last decade of communism, which developed into a severe economic crisis in the early 1990s. Much of this decline resulted from the emphasis during the Cold War on heavy industry and military production, which required importing raw materials from Soviet Union. When these industries became less competitive in a more open international economy and raw material supplies declined, recession hit Slovakia's arms industry from 1988 to 1992. Overall, from 1990 to 1995, Slovakia experienced drastic drops in output and rises in prices. Real GDP declined every year from 1990 to 1993, including a 15 percent drop in 1992, and though it began to rise in 1994, 1995 output was only 84 percent of that in 1990. Inflation during that period fluctuated between 7 percent and 58 percent; the unemployment rate was between 10 percent and close to 15 percent from 1991 through 1995.

Interestingly, Hungary showed roughly similar sharply declining figures to those of Slovakia. By 1995, output had dropped to 86 percent of its 1991 level. Inflation increased by 33 percent in 1991 over the previous year and was still increasing by 28 percent in 1995. Unemployment started at 2.5 percent in 1991, but rose to a high of 12.7 percent in 1992, remaining at 10.4 percent in 1995.

But the Slovakian government was notably slower in the early 1990s than either the Czech government or Hungary to institute economic reforms. Indeed, one reason for the breakup of Czechoslovakia was the unwillingness of Slovakian leaders to move as fast as the Czech leaders to enact economic reforms. In the June parliamentary elections of 1992, one of the worst years of economic decline in both Czechoslovakia and Hungary, conservative liberals (free marketers) came to power in Bohemia as Vaclav Klaus's Civic Democratic Party campaigned successfully on the perception that Czech voters favored the continuing of economic reforms. He received 33 percent of the vote, while the Left bloc got only 14 percent. In Slovakia, however, Vladimir Meciar increased his popularity with the opposite theme of slowing reforms, as 60 percent of the electorate voted for his or other nationalist parties or socialist parties. In these years, Slovakia's parties did electoral battle more over issues of Slovakia's political status and differing ethnic rights than over economic issues and ideologies (Evans and Whitefield 1998, 119, 130).

Some attribute this difference to political culture: "Eastern influence in Slovakia produced more collectivist social attitudes than was the case in Bohemia..." (Zielonka 1972, 10f). But Slovakia also had much old heavy industry and munitions plants from the Cold War era and could adjust less easily to the need for new technology. The Czech republic was already the more advanced economy and so stood more of a chance of increasing its ties with the West through trade and investment. Some analysts argue that the extent of economic decline was actually similar in the Czech and Slovak regions, but that in the latter, nationalistic politicians were able to resist reforms because they associated marketization and its social costs with the reform policies of the federal government that had victimized the Slovaks, a theme that appealed to the many Slovaks who were eager to be politically independent. Subsequently, Slovakia's greater resistance to the market was due in part to the political power of its industrial managers. They found they could lobby more successfully than their Czech counterparts to keep their state jobs and increase state spending by taking advantage of the antimarket nationalist line taken by the major parties (Appel and Gould 2000).

On their part, Hungary's economy had already experienced considerable liberalization during the Cold War, and in the post–Cold War era, was attracting possibly about half the foreign capital going to the former Soviet Union and Eastern Europe. The Hungarians were aware that their economy was one of the strongest in the former Soviet bloc and that ethnic turmoil risked losing the benefits of investment from the West (Schopflin 1994, 16).

Ethnic Serbs and Macedonia

Due to Tito's increasing indebtedness and the decline in the Yugoslavian average income during the 1980s, the Republic of Macedonia shared with all the Yugoslav republics severe economic decline. Macedonia was one of the poorest Yugoslav republics and thus, like Slovakia, was heavily dependent on federal redistributive policies. After the 1991 independence declaration, the country's general standard of living fell drastically. From 1990 to 1994, real GDP fell nearly 35 percent. Gross social product per capita fell from U.S. $1,419 in 1987 to U.S. $720 in 1993, and per capita income in 1994 was U.S. $790. Trade flows fell by about 10 percent, and total investment by two-thirds, while known unemployment rose from 17 to 20 percent, possibly even to 30 percent, with many of working-age dropping out of the labor force.

This decline was considerably worsened by austerity policies imposed from outside Macedonia by governments or international bodies. The UN sanctions against Yugoslavia of November 1991 and May 1992 are estimated to have cost the country U.S. $3 billion by 1995 in lost trade, in relation to an annual government budget of $1.2 billion. The Greek government's trade embargo was estimated to have cost $330 million in lost exports in its first year alone. The International Monetary Fund (IMF) began implementing economic reforms when Macedonia became a member in December 1992 and the World Bank opened an office in Skopje in February 1993. More than 1,000 industries were closed or privatized. These policies reduced consumption, limited wages, laid off workers, and increased the burden on welfare and pension costs, just when government revenues were also declining. A further fiscal burden was added with UN membership in 1993, when Macedonia had to repay a certain portion of the former Yugoslavia's loans. Though Serbs were possibly somewhat poorer on average than ethnic Macedonians, privatization actually may have hit ethnic Macedonians relatively harder because they held more jobs in state-owned industry.

Ethnic Serbs and Albanians in Kosovo

Kosovo also has been one of the poorest and neglected areas of Yugoslavia. It is very densely populated, for ethnic Albanians have one of the highest birthrates in Europe, and something like 50 percent of its population is under 25 years old. These demographics have created considerable pressure on existing land, housing, and jobs. Even apart from the Yugoslav government policies that removed Albanian control over critical needs by fiat, in the 1980s Kosovo's unemployment rate was considerably higher than Macedonia's or the other countries, a statistic that Serbs experienced as much as Albanians. Then, with martial law imposed in the 1990s, federal policy pushed Albanians out of their jobs in the civil service, police, social services, and schools. Many were evicted to make room for Serbs who were enticed to move into Kosovo during this period by jobs in newly built factories and housing. Recent unemployment is estimated to reach 70 percent. The UN economic sanctions also affected Kosovo. In addition, though strangely little mention is made in most recent commentary on Kosovo of the rich reserves under the earth of lead, zinc, nickel, and other valuable metals that have been tapped by the mines around Trepca, these natural resources have undoubtedly been in the calculations of the Serbs and Kosovars who have been fighting to keep control of this territory, in addition to the more frequently mentioned matters of the Serbian monasteries and holy places.

Certain factors have helped, however, to offset this economic competition. In response to their expulsion from jobs and other needs, the Albanian political movement, the LDK, set up an alternative government, school system, social institutions, health services, and media, staffed by unemployed workers and professionals who often volunteered their labor, and financed by taxes on Albanian workers in Europe. Kosovo Albanians have been allowed to travel and emigrate to work in western Europe via Skopje and Ohrid, and the remittances of workers' earnings have helped to maintain the area's standard of living. Thus, this parallel economies may have kept glaring objective economic gaps from opening up that would compound the linguistic, religious, and political differences between Serbs and Albanians. Still, on both sides economic goods were obviously allocated along ethnic lines in local economies for political reasons.

In sum, all three of the host post-communist societies had poor economies during the Cold War era and thus were seriously challenged by exposure to global competition of their deteriorating statist economic-support systems and the decline of regional trade networks. The chief difference among them relevant to their conflict potential may be that Macedonia adopted market reforms fairly actively, while Slovakia and Yugoslavia resisted economic reform. While this difference in state policies and economic structures put Macedonia under a tremendous economic strain, it may also have lowered the political stakes of economic competition compared to what they were in the less reformed economies. With interest groups and ethnic groups in the latter focusing on the available supply of state-owned goods and other economic resources, political leaders were under more pressure to appeal to nationalist themes and thus to use public assets, declining though they were, to gain support from and reward their followers.

Ethno-Political Mobilization or Quiescence?

Whatever sources of potential conflict may derive from past conflicts, social fragmentation or economic competition and structure, they will not lead to violence unless the population groups affected subjectively feel that they belong to the same "identity group" and become organized into self-conscious political movements that pursue their interests and grievances in collective ways. Thus, the degree of political mobilization and organization is critical if latent conflicts of interest are ever to become manifest as the bases on which groups actually take concrete actions, such as using armed force to obtain their goals.

Ethnic nationalism is an ideology that seeks a distinct, ethnically defined subnational political jurisdiction or independent state. A sign of its activation is seen when nationalist sentiments become the basis for organizing political movements, political parties, or other organizations that can take political or military action. Often, nationalist groups formulate national myths and political ideologies to strengthen their internal cohesion and to recruit members to help advance their political agenda. Their making common cause is often fostered, moreover, by their ill treatment by more dominant groups. Where two or more communities are highly mobilized behind differing nationalist visions with regard to the same territory, their perceptions of each other can become highly antagonistic and lead to violent conflicts. An identity group's size in relation to the other groups within a given political jurisdiction may enhance the likelihood it will mobilize and aspire to nationalism.

A group's ethnic mobilization can increase as well to the extent that it receives external support from neighboring countries with whom it shares ethnic affinities. Thus, it is important to consider the extent of which the minority receives various degree of support in the neighboring state with which it has those ties.

Ethnic Hungarians and Slovakians

Ethnic Slovakians have developed a fairly sharp sense of common identity by looking back to a long history of frustrated aspirations for self-rule. This included several short-lived opportunities for self-government that were overtaken by more powerful empires, states, and peoples, particularly Hungarians and Czechs.

Following a period of habitation by Germanic tribes, Slovaks settled in the area in the sixth or seventh centuries, but were taken over by Avars and incorporated into Greater Moravia in the ninth century, until the Hungarian monarchy took control in the eleventh century. Slovak nationalist and cultural consciousness emerged in the late eighteenth century and were encouraged after the Hungarian revolution of 1848 by the policies of the Habsburg central administration that favored non-Magyars. But the Austro-Hungarian accommodation of 1867 returned control of Slovakia to Hungary, which then imposed programs of forced magyarization.

Slovak nationalists saw the formation of Czechoslovakia in 1918 as a way to escape Hungarian domination, but they were still under Czech tutelage. In response to the centralist regime in Prague, however, the Slovaks declared autonomy as Germany threatened Czechoslovakia, and they became nominally independent under German protection. Germany's harsh policies sparked an uprising in August 1944, however, and when the Soviet and Czech armies occupied Slovakia, it agreed to join the Czechs of Bohemia, Moravia, and Silesia to form Czechoslovakia in a state that promised equal status. Although Slovakia was given some autonomy, this was soon eroded, especially when the communists took control in 1948. Some Slovak activists were imprisoned in the early 1950s.

Political autonomy did not return until shifts toward federalism were made in 1960 and 1968. In 1968, a constitutional amendment made the state into a federation with separate governments and parliaments in the two capitals. Slovakia then became the Slovak Socialist Republic with its own National Council and equal representation in the Federal Assembly of the Czechoslovak Socialist Republic. But the "normalization" occurring after the subsequent Warsaw Pact invasion deprived the federation of meaning, as the Communist Party bureaucracy in Prague continued to manage centrally.

With the end of the Cold War and the Velvet Revolution in 1989, Slovak leaders renewed their aspirations for power-sharing and sought to renegotiate a new federal constitution. Within a year after the communists gave up power in 1989, the views of all the larger parties in Slovakia began to change from civic values to specific Slovak issues, the harm that government reforms were bringing to Slovakia, and the desire for independence. The Slovak leaders' interest lay not so much in democracy as in Slovak autonomy (Stroschein 1996). Extreme Slovak politicians spoke of possible secession and the creation of an independent home guard. Slovakian nationalist feelings grew to such a degree that one commentator warned in the year just preceding the breakup that "The Czech and Slovak Federation (CSFR) currently faces the most severe ethnic problems in the entire region of Central Europe" (Zielonka 1992, 10). The first to benefit from this feeling was the nationalist Slovak National Party, which was formed in March 1990 and gained parliamentary seats in June in both the Federal and Slovak assemblies. Other such parties were formed, although their radicalism lost them support by the 1992 elections, and the movement for independence was taken up by the Movement for a Democratic Slovakia (HZDS). Although Slovakia had the same formal political arrangements as the Czech Republic, democratization in Slovakia was producing a nationalist and statist political culture, led by Prime Minister Vladimir Meciar.

The apotheosis of a Slovakian nationalism was attained in January 1993 with the establishment of an independent Slovakian state, whose constitution starts with the words, "We, the Slovak nation . . ." In 1990, Slovak nationalists expressed anti-Hungarian views when they pressed for a new law making Slovak the only official language. The achievement of Slovakia's independence then magnified the question of the political status of its minority groups. From 1993 to 1998, except for a brief interim from March to December in 1994, Slovakia's parliament and government have been dominated by strongly nationalist Slovakian parties (Kelley 2000, 5).

Ethnic Hungarians in Slovakia also have developed a strong sense of ethnic identity and have organized themselves into several political parties, but more recently. In the interwar years, several Hungarian parties formed in Slovakia and contributed several members of parliament, and other parties had Hungarian wings. Immediately after the fall of communism in Czechoslovakia in 1989, the Hungarian minority in Slovakia formed four new major Hungarian parties. These parties supported the federal state and differed mainly with regard to the approach to economic reforms. Two formed a coalition that won seats in the parliament in 1990, and a third party joined the Public against Violence (VPN) in the coalition that won control of the government. But that liberal government suffered the political fallout from the economic deterioration in the first two years of economic reform, and lost power in Slovakia in 1992 to the more nationalist new HZDS, the neo-communist party of the Democratic Left, and the extreme nationalist SNS. Nevertheless, three Hungarian parties won seats in parliament, and all won seats in elections in local districts and autonomous districts. Currently, the coalition of the main Hungarian political parties is the third largest political entity in Slovakia.

Of course, the Hungarians in Slovakia identify themselves as a part of a larger ethnic community who live mainly in a neighboring country. This larger community is imbued with a sense that several times in the past, it ruled a large area outside the present state's boundaries but had this taken away. Hungary was occupied by the Romans and eastern tribes until Charlemagne took it over about 800 A.D. In the fifth century, a nomadic people speaking a Finno-Ugric tongue known as the Magyars had begun moving into the area and, in 892, joined the Holy Roman Emperor Arnulf in subduing the Moravians. Settling into the Hungarian plan, they controlled a large area of central Europe until defeated by Otto I, which led to the conversion of the Magyar leader to Christianity, the crowning of a famous Magyar king named Stephen, and the acceptance of a Western feudal system involving peasants' rights.

But the Mongol invasion of 1241 wiped out the local dynasty by 1301, thereby ending Magyar independent rule until 1918. Ottoman Turk incursions in the fourteenth century led to its division into a western part under the Habsburgs, and two eastern parts under indirect and direct Turkish rule, until the Habsburgs assumed absolutist control, ruthlessly crushing revolts against their tyrannical rule. A revolution in 1848 led to a declaration of independence that was short-lived but was followed by concessions to the Magyars in 1867 under the dual Austro-Hungarian monarchy. World War I led to the division under the Trianon Treaty of 1920 of the empire's population between Russia, Yugoslavia, Czechoslovakia, Romania, Austria, Poland, and Italy. Hungary was reduced to one-third of its historic territory, two-fifths of its prewar population, and two-thirds of the Hungarian people. Its autocratic governments in the interwar era variously promoted better treatment of the Hungarians in neighboring states, revision of borders to restore ethnic Hungarian areas to the state, or complete recovery of its former borders. This irredentist sentiment then took the form of aggression when Hungary, with German help, regained some of its territory from Czechoslovakia in 1938 and 1939, from Romania in 1940, and from Yugoslavia in 1941. But Germany's defeat led in 1945 to a pro-Soviet government in Hungary and the communist Hungarian People's Republic in 1949. In 1956, the Hungarian uprising against Soviet control was crushed.

Just as it had spurred Slovakian nationalism, the post-Cold War period released suppressed revisionist sentiments that Hungary had harbored ever since the Trianon Treaty. The 3 million Magyars living outside Hungary are the largest expatriate minority in Europe. The Hungarians in Slovakia thus tend to look toward Hungary for political support. When the Hungarian parties opposed the post–Cold War separation of Czechoslovakia, they threatened to ask for help from Hungary if abandoned by Prague. But although their area was once under Hungarian governments, Hungarians in Slovakia have not generally expressed the wish to revise the current borders. The Hungarian minority has not sought statehood, but rather pressed for enhanced minority rights within the established state of Slovakia.

In Hungary itself and in its government, views on this score in the post–Cold War era have been generally moderated, and at times expressed moral repulsion at the previous stances and the suffering that past Hungarian regimes caused. Now democratic, the government, as well as all the other states in the region, are reluctant to support any revisionist claims (Zielonka 1972, 16). The high ethnic homogeneity of Hungary also has made it politically stable, so the government is better able to exercise discretion in deciding its ethnic policies. At the polls, its governments have even felt pressure against too much emphasis on ethnic incitement (Schopflin 1994, 17).

Ethnic Serbs and Macedonians

At the time that Macedonian cultural consciousness first arose in the late nineteenth century, there were competing notions even locally about whether the emerging Macedonian identity was intertwined with Bulgaria or distinctive to the Vardar (roughly present-day) area. A local nationalist movement mounted a rebellion to wrest the area's independence from the Ottomans, but it was brutally crushed, thus only creating some heroes who would inspire later activists. Macedonia's decision to achieve independence was much less predictable than Slovakia's two years later, in view of the former's relatively less fervent brand of nationalism. Ethnic nationalist Macedonians were assertive in the local debate over independence, but they were a relatively recent phenomenon compared to the other nationalist causes in Yugoslavia. Most ethnic Macedonians were profederation and shared with Serbia a wariness toward the ethnic nationalist Albanians who straddled their two republics. That Macedonia's independence did not emerge from a vigorous grassroots ethno-nationalism was seen when the Internal Macedonian Revolutionary Organization–Democratic Party for Macedonian National Unity (VMRO–DPMNU) had to be revived to form a political party that could represent ethnic Macedonians in the 1990 election. And though it gained 37 of 120 parliamentary seats, more than any other party, it could not form a government. Macedonia's first government was made up of nonparty experts.

Macedonian nationalism was hampered by the fact that the republic has had two sizeable identity groups. The 1994 census figure for ethnic Macedonians is 66.5 percent. Albanian leaders have claimed Albanians constitute 40 percent of the population. The 1991 census estimated a little more than half that number, but Albanians boycotted it because it did not count as citizens many Albanians who had fled to Macedonia from Serbian repression in Kosovo. The 1992 citizenship law required fifteen years' residence for other groups, whereas all ethnic Macedonians from the former Yugoslav republics were granted citizenship automatically, regardless of how many years they lived in the country. Nevertheless, the 1994 census, sponsored by the Council of Europe in part because of this controversy, put their number still at 22.9 percent, but it also did not count the emigres.

The country also comprises an estimated 4 percent ethnic Turks, 3 percent Roma, 2 percent Serbs, 2 percent Macedonian Muslims, and .04 percent Vlachs. Because Serbs thus constitute a very small base from which to recruit a political movement, they have a strong incentive to work within the dominant Macedonian parties and structures. But their small numbers might have been compensated by active support for their interests from Yugoslavia. The ultranationalists to the right of Serbia's President Milosevic espoused a vision of a Greater Serbia that included Macedonia. In 1991, the ultranationalist leader of the Serb Radical Party, Vojislav Seselj, said, "Three states will come out of Yugoslavia—Greater Serbia, Small Croatia, and even smaller Slovenia. . . . And Macedonia has always been the Serb territory . . . Macedonians, Moslems, and Montenegrins are fictitious nations." A large number of the Yugoslav electorate felt that the independence of Macedonia had not been illegitimate, believed that its language was not distinctive, and viewed the renegade republic as a straying part of what used to be Serbia. But although provocateurs attempted to organize the Serbs in Macedonia in 1991, little direct political or financial support has been given directly to the Serb cause in Macedonia. Apparently, the small Serbian community in Macedonia was not feeling so oppressed that they have wanted to publicly agitate against the government or vocally appeal to Serbia for support.

Ethnic Serbs in Kosovo

Serbs regard Kosovo as the cradle of their culture and share a national myth in which a huge loss was experienced when the Turks destroyed their ancestral medieval kingdom and expelled the Serbs in the humiliating Battle of the Polje Fields in 1389. Because the Turks subsequently favored Albanians, Serbs now identify Albanian political activists with the Turk intruders. Probably the most crucial turning point in the breakup of the Yugoslav federation occurred in Kosovo in April 1987, when Slobodan Milosevic embraced the Serb discontent being expressed by a crowd at a rally in Kosovo. In later speeches at huge Serb nationalist rallies that were televised to the nation, he gave voice to an underlying Serb resentment by inveighing against the privileges being gained by the Kosovo Albanians and the other rising ethnic groups.

Many Albanians inside and outside of Yugoslavia also trace their ancient national roots to Kosovo. Since the late nineteenth century, Kosovo had become the center of a growing Albanian population and nationalist movement. The League of Prizren, their modern nationalist movement, was organized in that town in 1878. The population increases have become more dramatic since the early 1960s. In 1961, they were 68 percent of the population, and by 1981, 78 percent. As tensions rose and Kosovo's economy fell further behind other regions of the country, more and more non-Albanians, including Serbs and Macedonians, emigrated. As a primarily rural people, the Albanians have had one of the highest birth rate in Europe and due also to economic outmigration by Serbs (only in part spurred by their ill treatment by Albanians), Albanians comprised 90 percent of the 1 million population by 1993.[10]

The contemporary Kosovar political movement was spawned in the immediate post–Cold War years. In July 1990 Albanian MPs in the provincial parliament declared Kosovo an independent unit within Yugoslavia. When the federal authorities then closed the parliament and university, completely took over the government, and shut down the Albanian media, ninety members of the suspended parliament declared in September the creation of the republic of Kosova. As several opposition parties emerged, the literary scholar Ibrahim Rugova galvanized much of the Albanian leadership behind the Democratic League of Kosova (LDK). In May 1992 the LDK elected its own parliament and established the Republic with Rugova as president. The Kosovo Albanian movement has said it received only moral and political support from individual Albanians in Macedonia and Albania. The government of Albania has given vocal moral support and supplied many educational materials to Kosovo schools. Kosovo Albanians are also tied through family, economics, and frequent travel to the Albanians living in western Macedonia. Many Albanian leaders studied or taught at Kosovo's Prishtina University, and after its forced closing in 1989, migrated to Macedonia.

All the paired ethnic communities drew on their respective national myths and formed ethnically based political parties and other social and political organizations in order to achieve ethnically oriented policies or political authorities. But there were obvious differences in the extent they each aspired to and attained exclusive ethnic political control. The Slovakian desire for a national state was longstanding and not matched by any equally aggressive local Hungarian ethnic nationalist movement. Macedonian nationalism is not as virulent, and its minority Serbs launched no challenge to the sovereign government. In Kosovo, however, a deep-rooted Serbian nationalism was matched by an equally deep-rooted Albanian nationalism that it has sought to thwart, only stimulating greater determination and political organization, until in 1998 it took an open militarized form.

Accommodating or Unresponsive Government?

Although contending groups may each have a sense of common identity and be mobilized politically, violent conflict may not arise because satisfactory channels exist for them to pursue their perceived needs through nonviolent means. These channels may include sharing decision-making authority, having access and participation rights in lawmaking and executive administration, having recourse to procedures for settling disputes through negotiation, and enjoying the fruits of policies that allocate government and public policy benefits and services broadly, even if not competely equitably. The most accommodating form of government might be highly egalitarian constitutional democracies with multiparty competition and minority rights. It is widely argued that democratic systems are likely to be more stable because they assure some degree of representation by all major identity groups, and a group's treatment is not dependent simply on the shifting fortunes of constantly contending for spoils or the upper hand. But the required degree of accommodation can be achieved short of a fully developed social democracy, such as some power-sharing in executive and representative institutions Where at the other extreme, states are dominated by certain majority or minority identity groups that restrict the ability of other groups to have their needs and interests addressed, violent conflict may result if the excluded group gains the means to wage armed struggle.

Civil conflict may also arise when the problem is not so much repressive or exclusive government as it is ineffective government. A government that is ineffective in providing essential public services, such as sanitation and security, breeds cynicism and apathy among the citizenry. These conditions can then lead to anarchy and become violent through a takeover of government by the military or alternative elite factions, in the name of restoring order, or by a popular insurrection, both with possible violent counterreactions from the usurped authorities and their followers.

Ethnic Hungarians and Slovakians

In precommunist Czechoslovakia, ethnic Hungarians in Slovakia were able to organize political parties and participate in political life. Although they had equal rights in theory with other groups under communism, any form of nationalist activity was strictly suppressed. With the push for democratization from the Velvet Revolution in 1989, Czechoslovakia held free presidential, parliamentary, and local government elections that allowed for multiparty participation, the government allowed NGOs and free speech, and an independent judiciary operated, although these institutions were still weak (Zielonka 1972). Along with other groups, Hungarians were allowed to set up their own cultural and political associations, such as the Democratic Association of Hungarians in Slovakia (CSEMADOK).

While Slovakia was still part of the Federal Republic, the Hungarians could get some support for their cause from other minorities in Parliament. But as the cause of Slovakian nationalism achieved its goal of an independent state, Hungarian political and cultural freedom and rights were curtailed. There were even fears that the anti-Hungarian demonstrations organized by Slovak nationalists in 1990–1991 might reflect sentiments that would lead to the expulsion of Hungarians from Slovakia, as happened to 100,000 Hungarians in 1945–1948. Even before the breakup into two states in January 1993, Hungarians complained that Slovak authorities were hostile to their demands for full nationality rights, and their numbers in the Slovak National Council and the government, as well as in the Federal Assembly and government, did not increase. New Slovak language and land laws were burdensome and resented. Efforts were made by Meciar's government in 1993–1994 to limit the ethnic Hungarians' electoral power and political cohesion through reorganizing administrative districts throughout Slovakia. A shortage of Hungarian teachers and schools was not addressed.

But political channels for representation and advocacy did exist in the form of a multiparty system and were used. The interests of ethnic Hungarians were either worsened or slightly improved, depending largely on the shifting policies of whatever coalitions of parties gained power, and whether the Hungarian parties were invited into those coalitions. In the 1994 elections, the coalition of Hungarian political parties received 10 percent of the vote. By the late 1990s, Hungarians were enjoying increasing access to government decision making. As a result of the most recent elections in September 1998, a Hungarian party was included in a four-party governing coalition.

In Hungary, electoral politics influenced the degree of support successive governments gave to their ethnic brethren in Slovakia. The Josef Antall government's rhetorical support to Hungarians living in the neighboring states stemmed in part from his party's need to maintain a fragile coalition with the nationalist Hungarian party. However, in the parliamentary election of 1994, the government actually suffered at the polls from the extent its rhetoric avowed concern for the external Hungarians. Many in the electorate began to tire of the theme and thought the government should be more concerned over its own voters. The subsequent coalition formed by the Hungarian Socialist Party Alliance of Free Democrats under Prime Minister Gyula Horn was thus able to carry out a more conciliatory foreign policy.

In both countries, the parties' continuing temptation to cater to Slovak or Hungarian nationalism stemmed in part from the need of leaders to establish a base of political support amid a general atmosphere of basic apathy and cynicism that has characterized both political systems since the postcommunist revolution. As a result of the economic decline and political wrangling that has been typical within governments and parliaments, all party governments were often ineffective in providing basic services and this has disillusioned many voters. Crime, for example, rose 40 percent in Czechoslovakia and 35.4 percent in Hungary in the first nine months of 1991, compared with the same period in 1990. Turnout for the second round of 1991 local elections in Hungary was only 28.9 percent.

Ethnic Serbs and Macedonians

Issues of representation and the legitimacy of the governmental process have not been salient in Serb-Macedonian relations within Macedonia. This is due not only to the Serb community being only 1.2 percent of the population, but also because much greater tensions existed between ethnic Macedonians and the country's second-largest ethnic group, Albanians. Indeed, ethnic Macedonians have felt some common affinity with Serbs in that both have felt threatened by the Albanians living within the respective boundaries of Yugoslavia and Macedonia. Were the Serbs to make up a larger proportion of the population, they likely would have increased government responsiveness to their interests, since Macedonia has been governed by two multiparty coalitions that have included some members of the smallest communities such as Turks.

Executive and legislative power-sharing was required as early as the 1990 elections, because nationalist parties competed not only against each other but with nonethnic parties, and no party gained a majority, so the first government was made up of nonparty experts. After it fell in a no-confidence vote in July 1992, the government consisted of a coalition that parcelled out portfolios among three parties. Although the strongly anticommunist, anti-Serbian Macedonian nationalist party, VMRO–DPMNU, gained 37 seats of the 120 in the next elections, which was more than any other, it failed to assemble a new government. The Alliance of Macedonia thus formed a coalition among the Social Democratic Union of Macedonia (SDUM, the successor to the communists), the Liberal Party, and one of the ethnic Albanian parties, the Party for Democratic Prosperity (PDP). The lack of a two-thirds majority hampered this government from enacting reforms, however, and boycotting Albanian and VMRO deputies often left it without a quorum. The alliance strengthened its power in the second parliamentary elections in October 1994, gaining a clear two-thirds majority with ninety-seven seats. The PDP also has a number of vice ministerial jobs. The political weight of ethnic Macedonians is not only partly counterbalanced by Albanians; both groups face some pressure from Turks, Serbs, and other ethnic minorities as well.

Because the government has been multiethnic, it has been inclined toward relatively even-handed policies. Although data specifically on government treatment of Serbs goes beyond the capacities of this study, we can gain some sense of how government policy would treat the Serbs were they to constitute a larger minority from policies toward the Albanians. Regarding Albanian education and employment grievances, for example, government officials agree there is serious imbalance. The country's main university, in Skopje, had only 1.7 percent Albanian students in 1994, although it sought a quota of 10 percent. But they point to modest changes that are in fact showing up, such as in teacher training, police training and the composition of the army. These issues remain unresolved and continue to cause interparty and intragovernment public accusations and rancor. But though ethnic controversies continue to provoke tense demonstrations, they are still generally pursued through the cabinet, parliament, the Constitutional Court, the bureaucracy, and electoral process, or they are handled through special negotiations on particular issues.

Overall, although the internal conflict in Macedonia has avoided violent politics and totally polarized political camps, it is hard to judge whether the increasing recent ethnic ferment since 1997 means Macedonia's relatively accommodating institutions and political processes are weakening or becoming gradually stronger. Rather than boycotts, the 1997 elections saw several political parties aligning, campaigning vigorously, and incorporating their more radical youth wings. A tax scandal was followed by Cabinet reshuffling and the prime minister initiated direct talks with opposition parties. By further institutionalizing its political and public policy disputes, Macedonia's domestic politics possibly was slowly maturing.

Ethnic Serbs and Albanians

In the case of Kosovo, government fiat and police coercion deprived Kosovo's Albanians of any representation in Yugoslav government and even pushed Albanians out of their jobs in the civil service, police, social services, and schools. Many were evicted to make room for Serbs who were enticed to move into Kosovo during this period by jobs in newly built factories and new housing. Even a modest agreement in 1997 to allow Albanian students to reenter the state university was not implemented.

But although the Yugoslav government sought to curtail the power of opposition parties and limit the independent media, its policies toward Kosovo were not symptoms of an utter lack of democratic processes within the rump Yugoslavia. The government of the former Yugoslavia in Belgrade has been dominated by the Serbian Renewal Party under Slobodan Milosevic, who has felt pressure to maintain his power from even more ethnic nationalistic parties, whose members he occasionally asked to join his government. But anti-Albanian views are held widely throughout the Serbian population, and none of the opposition parties has been willing to grant the LDK's demands for self-government. Thus, even if the Together alliance that demonstrated against Milosevic in 1996 and early 1997 had not fragmented and more democratic forces had come to power, Serb Kosovo policy would not necessarily have become more progressive, since none of the opposition movement showed support for more Kosovo autonomy and would have actively engaged the Kosovo issue.

In sum, the Slovakia case involved the continuous opportunity for some power-sharing, so electoral politics were usually the source of ethnic discrimination but were sometimes also a channel for alleviating it. Macedonia's government was open to Serb participation in politics and allowed for some degree of minority representation for Serbian parties, and may have been even more so if their numbers had been substantial enough to elect more representatives. Regarding Kosovo, Yugoslav institutions for representation existed but they were increasingly usurped by one party and its leader, who used martial law to lock Kosovars out of the official legal government. Subsequently, any possible entrees such as elections were shunned by the Albanians. The impact of this government repression was undoubtedly blunted by the Kosovars' creation of an alternative government, which the Yugoslav government tolerated. At a deeper level, in all three countries unmobilized public distrust and cynicism of government has meant that politics were continuously vulnerable to populist demagoguery, political paralysis, and discriminatory government policies.

Moderate or Divisive Leaders?

Changes toward democracy that provide new opportunities for masses to participate in politics may actually create new opportunities for demagoguery, for election campaigns can become platforms for ethnic mobilization. Latent conflicts of interests and open tensions can be turned into violence when key political leaders who represent the antagonistic communities worsen relations by acting in provocative, threatening, and uncompromising ways or incite their constituencies to take hostile actions against opponents. Such "ethnic political entrepreneurs" can use public speeches, for example, to instill fear in a group by raising the specter that other groups intend to do them harm. This can prompt them to take preemptive actions, or at least support them, which in turn elicits fear and violent reactions from the other side in a self-fulfilling prophecy (the "ethnic security" dilemma). Alternatively, however, leaders can significantly affect their public's political temperature by making conciliatory gestures and discouraging xenophobic attitudes.

In all three cases in the late 1980s, individual leaders who had been communist officials mow sought to achieve greater political control for their respective ethnic groups and thus had great opportunities to influence the course of each of the three conflicts. Table 6.1 gives the names of the incumbents of two kinds of positions in the three cases

Table 6.1 Two Types of Polity Leaders

Case	Focus polity leaders	Neighboring polity's leaders
Hungarians in Slovakia	Prime Ministers Vladimir Meciar, Josef Moravcik	Prime Ministers Josef Antall, Gyula Horn
Serbs in Macedonia	President Yiro Gligorov	President Slobodan Milosevic
Serbs in Kosovo	Kosova President Ibrahim Rugova	President Slobodan Milosevic

for the period under study. The "focus polity leaders" led a majority ethnic community in a political jurisdiction in which an ethnic minority resided whose fellow ethnics were the majority in a neighboring and more powerful state. The "neighboring polity leaders" headed the government where the minority in the focus polity was in the majority. As we shall see, the style with which these individuals played their respective roles differed greatly, especially with respect to whether they related to their counterpart and situation in a unilateral, belligerent way or a cooperative reciprocal way.

Ethnic Hungarians in Slovakia

In Slovakia, the primary contributor to ethnic tensions was the focus polity's leader for most of the period, Vladimir Meciar. Meciar was prime minister in pre- and postindependence Slovakia until 1998, except for when his party lost the reins of power briefly in 1991 and 1994. Under Czechoslovakia's first postcommunist government, Meciar held the post of minister of the Interior and Environment. In the first postcommunist parliamentary election of June 1990, he was elected as a VPN deputy to the Federal Assembly and became the Slovak prime minister in the federation, from which position he negotiated Slovakia's independence with Vaclav Klaus. The functioning of the Slovak government until 1998 was largely dominated by the agenda of Vladimir Meciar and the nationalist coalitions he headed under the Movement for a Democratic Slovakia (HZDS).

Meciar's rise to power and maintenance of it can be explained in part by his ability to play on Slovakia's latent nationalism and insecurity about its status during a period when voters were having increasing influence. He became prime minister of Slovakia by pressing for more autonomy under a federation. When chairman of the HZDS, he made speeches around the country suggesting Slovaks were poor because of exploitation by the Czechs for seventy years and by the Hungarians for centuries earlier. Though Meciar distinguished himself from the first ostensibly independent Slovak state, which was a puppet of Nazi Germany, he was a nationalist-populist who purported to defend Slovakia's interests against real or imagined enemies, and he fed in a simplistic way the resentments and sense of injustice felt by the Slovak people about their exploitation by Hungarians and Czechs.

Meciar's success was due not simply to a popular message, however, but also his political tactics. Meciar has been described by former political allies as "using authoritarian or dictatorial methods of blackmailing, and browbeating even his allies, seeking head-on challenges with anyone who crosses his path, and being unable to compromise or work together with those whose opinions differ even slightly from his own." While in power, he often hit back at anyone who disagreed with him, claiming they harmed Slovakia's interests. Throughout his career, he displayed a continuing tendency to push for his own way by legitimate or illegitimate means, compromising only when he had to. Since he had once been a boxer, his belligerent style caused Meciar to be caricatured as the former pugilist who bullied his opponents.

While minister of the Interior, Meciar was believed to have used his access to secret files to blackmail people. Meciar frequently used key positions in government institutions such as the police and major industries as patronage, and tried to reduce the powers of President Michael Kovac. While keeping a tight rein on the state media, he attacked the independent media by accusing them of being financed from abroad, and constantly sought to apply economic pressures on them, including having his supporters or allies buy them up. A charismatic, intuitive manipulator and maneuverer who sidelined potential rivals in his own party, no one could stand up to him until President Kovac's feud with him in 1993–1994.

Meciar's divisive style was often destructive even for the parties and governments which he led. Yet he was able to return to power in subsequent elections and recapture control of key positions. The VPN became divided due to demands from the nationalist wing around Meciar for more autonomy from Prague. After his government fell in April 1991, the prime minister post went to Jan Carnogursky, leader of the Christian Democratic Movement (KDH), so Meciar and his allies formed a new opposition party, the Movement for a Democratic Slovakia (HZDS), which called for a new, confederal relation with the Czech government. He became prime minister again when they won the June 1992 elections for parliament, the Slovak National Council, over the post-communist party of the left, the KDH, the SNS, and the Hungarian Coalition. But the HZDS then began splitting up due to feuds between Meciar and the foreign minister, and a HZDS-led coalition fell apart apparently because of Meciar's efforts to control the ministries held by the other parties. The HZDS ruled as a minority party until entering another coalition in October 1993.

President Kovac's stand-off with Meciar peaked in early 1994 when his state of the nation address was boycotted by Meciar's party. Kovacs questioned Meciar's competence in appointing the secret service head and obtained from Parliament a no-confidence vote that removed his party from office in March, replacing it with a government headed by the foreign minister Josef Moravchik until the elections of September and October. These elections garnered Meciar's party more votes than any other party, however, and another HZDS-led coalition was formed in December. Meciar then sought to consolidate the power of the prime ministership. In June 1996, he demonstrated his style of divide and rule again when the junior coalition parties Slovak National Party (SNS) and the Association of Workers of Slovakia (ZRS) tried to pressure him to give them more spoils of privatization, but they were shown they could be replaced. The HZDS was allowed its full term to run out until the September 1998 elections, but in the meantime, the other parties faced efforts by the HZDS to change the electoral law to help its own chances.

Because individual leaders can have unusual influence in transitional settings, some analysts seek the roots of extreme ethnic nationalism through psychological analyses of the leaders' personalities and their upbringing. Here, we can only point out Meciar's rather troubled quest to achieve respect. In his youth, he reportedly had taken up boxing to avoid his father's threats to beat him when he got into street fights, and he fought in six amateur bouts. Joining the Communist Party at twenty, Meciar was an apparatchik in its youth movement and rose to other political offices. But "normalization" in 1969 removed him from office and from the Communist Party because of his progressive views. He left politics to obtain a law degree and worked as a lawyer for sixteen years until he returned to politics in 1989 as a leader in VPN, which forced out the Communist Party. At that point, he discovered the advantages of promoting Slovak nationalism as the route to power.

In office, although not an all-powerful autocrat, Meciar was able to use his political cunning and intimidating tactics to take advantage of the frequent state of disarray. He could use the office to shape the direction of government policy because of the discretion available to him and the fact that the political opposition was often divided. The only brakes on his executive power were President Kovacs and his government's inability to obtain a parliamentary majority large enough to change the constitution. But when seen to have made a major mistake and losing power, he was repeatedly able to regain power because of his popularity. His "little boy lost" appearance was said to appeal to peasant women who massively voted for him. Ultimately, Meciar's rule was possible because of the immaturity of the electorate and its general lack of faith of Slovaks in political institutions. He was simply Slovakia's least unpopular politician, with whom more of the distrustful electorate could identify than with others.

On their part, Hungaria's leaders were generally less inflammatory, but provided some basis for anxiety in Slovakia. In the early 1990s, Hungarians insisted Hungary had no territorial claims or intention to use force to assist their fellow nationals abroad, even in extreme situations. Although a government policy statement in 1990 did refer to their right to self-determination, the government expressed its concern about the human rights of the Hungarian minorities through established international channels such as the CSCE. At this time, Hungary-Czechoslovakia relations were more constructive than before World War II, and better than between Hungary and Romania. Vaclav Havel and a former president of Hungary, Matyas Szuros, issued a statement in March 1990 that condemned the expulsion of Hungarians from Slovakia in 1945–1948. Yet Budapest reminded Prague of the rights of its Magyar minority, and pushed for legal and administrative changes to meet the minority's demands.

Nevertheless, Hungary's neighbors had some reason to remain suspicious that there was a hidden agenda of revisionism, based not simply on memories of the policies of Hungary's interwar governments but Budapest's reaction to the Yugoslav crisis. After the new Serbian constitution of 1990 drastically reduced self-government in Vojvodina, Hungary had expressed strong support for the rights of the province's 400,000 Hungarians. One Hungarian party there called not only for cultural autonomy for Hungarians, but also for Vojvodina to be part of a united Hungary. At a time when Croatia was openly anti-Serbian, Budapest arranged a secret arms deal whereby 10,000 Kalashnikov rifles were delivered to Croatia. After the Serbia-Croatia war had erupted and a border change was possible between them, the Hungarian government raised its own claim to the areas in Serbia where Hungarians lived. Prime Minister Josef Antall claimed that the Trianon and Paris Peace Treaty had stated that Vojvodina should become part of Yugoslavia, not Serbia, which was seen as clearly revisionist by politicians in Serbia, Vojvodina, and Romania.

However, as Slovakian nationalism became more virulent and led to independence, Hungary's policy at first was quite aggressive but later moderated due to pressure from its own electorate as well as international actors. Antall made statements that were interpreted as threatening to Slovakia when he suggested he was premier of all the Hungarians, including those across the borders in Romania and Slovakia. A general view in 1991 was that if Czech broke up, Hungary's influence in Slovakia could become greater, with the potential for leading to a revision of it borders. Hostility had been growing also between Hungary and Bratislava over the Gabcikovo power plan project on the Danube. After committing itself to the project, Hungary pulled out in 1989 under pressure from its environmentalists, while Slovakia was determined to go ahead on its own.

Subsequently, Hungary played a role in Slovakia's ethnic controversies through support of the Hungarian minority by giving financial aid to Hungarian political and cultural organizations in Slovakia and urging Hungarian political parties to form a coalition. Overall, however, the Hungarian government attempted to diffuse tensions by reassuring Slovakia of the security of the border. While strains have remained because Slovakia has continued some of its discriminatory policies, subsequent Hungarian governments have placed more emphasis on good relations with its neighbors, so the chances of rising tensions have lessened.

By and large then, there were constraints on the lengths to which the inflammatory rhetoric by both Slovakian and Hungarian leaders during the years 1990 to 1994 would be allowed to go. Observers have ventured that the outbreak of the wars in Croatia and Bosnia in 1991 and 1992 may have led all these leaders to the tacit conclusion that it was not worth risking bloodshed over these issues and that political solutions needed to be found.

Ethnic Serbs and Macedonians

The markedly less aggressive style of President Kiro Gligorov of Macedonia was reflected in both his relations with his counterpart Milosevic in the former Yugoslavia and his policies toward minorities in Macedonia. Macedonia was poor and heavily dependent on Yugoslav federal redistributive policies, and thus was not inclined to secede. Most ethnic Macedonians were profederation and shared with Serbia a wariness toward the ethnic nationalist Albanians who straddled their two republics. But in the spring and summer of 1991, Yugoslavia's dissolution was occurring de facto through armed hostilities between Slovenia and Croatia, on the one hand, and the Belgrade government, on the other. Gligorov concluded that unless Macedonia seceded, too, its people and the Bosnians would be left as minorities in a Serb-dominated rump Yugoslavia.

But Macedonia's declaration of independence in September 1991 required Gligorov to labor to avoid provoking Serbian nationalists into preventing the secession. A former communist technocrat, he lived up to his nickname, "the fox," by adeptly maneuvering to independence, but then pursuing a policy he called "active neutrality." The Macedonian government pledged friendly relations with all neighbors. After parliament voted that the Serbian-dominated Yugoslav People's Army should leave, Gligorov negotiated an agreement whereby it completely pulled out by April 1992.

But the only peaceful secession that has occurred in Yugoslavia was not achieved simply by Gligorov's tactful diplomatic style and acumen. His counterpart, Serbia's President Milosevic, was not known for equivalent reciprocity, but was probably restrained from his characteristic aggressive style largely by a set of fortuitous circumstances. Whether or not Milosevic was inclined to block Macedonia's exit, fortunate timing avoided the need to test Milosevic's ultimate intentions. The Yugoslav Army's (YPA) withdrawal from Macedonia began a few weeks before Bosnia's independence declaration of sovereignty in March 1992, which was followed by heavy fighting there. Milosevic had decided he actually could not afford both to keep troops in Macedonia and to fight the Bosnian war. He apparently concluded that he could let Macedonia go for the time being, without necessarily giving up on its later becoming part of a Greater Serbia. Because the YPA took every weapon and piece of equipment it could carry and destroyed the rest, the new Macedonian state was defenseless. Milosevic believed that Macedonia, left economically dependent and exposed to the depredations of what were known as the "three wolves" (Albania, Bulgaria, and Greece), would crawl back to Serbian protection. This view was reinforced by the collateral impacts on Macedonia of the UN economic sanctions against the FRY. Another factor possibly mitigating a hostile Serbian response was the advantage of Macedonia's allowing oil to "leak" through the UN embargo to Serbia, which gave it fuel for its trucks and tanks and gave Macedonia a useful black market. Gligorov also profited from the demographic circumstance that Belgrade lacked a fifth column of discontented Serbs in Macedonia.

Yet Yugoslavian-Macedonia relations were not based on equality but continued to be governed by a possible threat. The specter of Yugoslavian irredentism was maintained up until perhaps the Kosovo crisis of 1999. The Serbian radical Seselj, for example, sought to exploit the discontent of Macedonia's Serbs, by assisting Serbian nationalist cells in northern Macedonia during the early independence years. In later years, the pro-regime Belgrade press and Serbian ultranationalists continued to see "South Serbia" as going through a trying transition on the way to eventual reunion. In a press conference with the Greek foreign minister in November 1993, Milosevic referred to Macedonia in doubting terms and spoke of a Serbian confederation with Greece. After the 1994 census, the Serbian press rejected the results by claiming Macedonia actually had ten times the number of Serbs recorded.

Also, Yugoslav Army forces would periodically make incursions into Macedonian territory across its northern border. It is unclear whether their tendency to eventually back off was due to the fact that they ultimately did not want or were unable to go beyond minor troublemaking to invade or intimidate Macedonia, or whether the UN preventive deployment force that Gligorov had asked to be stationed at the border dissuaded them of the high political costs that further infractions would incur.[11] But Serb armed forces were at least testing the Macedonian government and the peacekeeping force.

The moderation of Gligorov and other FYROM leaders made more of a difference with regard to its policies toward its minorities, since here, they were in a stronger position to affect the situation. Although reflecting the power sharing and logrolling that were required under Macedonia's coalition governments, Gligorov and other Macedonia government and party leaders showed a begrudging but generally cooperative attitude to the demands made by Macedonia's minority groups, among whom the Albanians represented the most significant politically. Gligorov also established generally good relations with Albanian President Saul Berisha, which helped to avoid escalation of domestic tensions. The two exchanged several mutual assurances when ethnic group demonstrations arose, arms smuggling incidents were discovered, and other incidents threatened the fragile ethnic balance in the country, and they met several times to pledge mutual respect for the two countries' borders.

Ethnic Serbs and Kosovo Albanians

From 1989 to 1998, the relationship between the leaders of Kosovo and Yugoslavia under Slobodan Milosevic's influence clearly exhibited the most hostile open behavior of the three under review. On the one hand, an ambitious but insecure autocrat brutally oppressed the Kosovar people, and on the other hand, the Kosovars were led by a nonviolent but determined and often uncompromising political leadership under the LDK of Ibrahim Rugova, which eventually gave way to armed militants. This put Kosovo ethnic relations in a continuously high state of mutual hostility and distrust until it broke out in armed rebellion in 1998.

In 1987 and 1989, the federal government fell under Milosevic's growing influence. Although he was a committed socialist party official at the time, he decided to assuage the rising Serbian resentment of the gains made by the Albanians under Tito, by revoking Kosovo's 1974 autonomous status, removing duly elected local leaders, and imposing a crackdown on the marches and miners' strikes in that year and early 1990. These actions confirmed for many Albanians that they could not survive under the existing political relationship with Yugoslavia. But Rugova explicitly adopted a strategy of nonviolence inspired by the Eastern European civic movements, Mahatma Gandhi, and Martin Luther King Jr. He and the other Kosovo elite intellectuals and community leaders have clearly shaped the political outlook of several generations of Albanians through educational and cultural institutions. The Albanians boycotted what few opportunities there were for political engagement with Serbs, on grounds that only international mediation would suffice. The LDK's program sought to reclaim Kosovo's autonomy, which they expressed as the right to their own republic or independence. Rugova variously called for an international administration and UN protectorate. In short, for a whole decade, two parallel separated communities operated in uneasy relations. Two polarized groups viewed the same events with diametrically opposite renditions. What Albanians described as wholesale ethnic cleansing of Albanians out of government, industrial, and other jobs, Serb officials say was necessary because Albanians left their jobs, and the mines and other facilities had to be kept operating.

Until 1998, the Serb-Kosovo conflict involved mainly recurrent street demonstrations and police crackdowns. The Albanians' leverage was weak because FRY police power was dominant. Mass violence was kept at a low level simply because the Kosovars were overpowered by Serbian security forces and the JNA. FRY MIG jets frequently flew over the capital, Prishtina, to remind the population who was in charge. Although the LDK's nonviolent doctrine made a virtue out of necessity and sought to attract international support, it also helped keep a volatile situation from escalating into all-out revolt.

These political dynamics began to change in November 1995, however, raising the chances of an outbreak of violence. The Dayton Accords accepted Croatian and Bosnian ethnically defined borders achieved in battle but did not require Milosevic to address Kosovo human rights violations. With the Kosovars exhausted by years of martial law, high unemployment, deteriorating health and other basic community needs, Albanian activists began to question out loud whether the LDK's patient nonviolent strategy had failed by not reaping its due international reward. The established LDK leadership came under pressure to show the benefits of peaceful parallelism. In late 1997, the Serb-Albanian stand-off began to escalate rapidly to an unprecedented level of confrontation, violence, and military action. The threshold that had been maintained of nonviolent action was crossed when a small Albanian guerrilla movement, soon to be known as the Kosovo Liberation Army (KLA), began to attack Serb police stations and other officials and Albanian collaborators. A year had elapsed since a Rugova-Milosevic education agreement had been signed, and members of the largest Kosovo Albanian student organization, seeing no way to get an education to qualify for jobs, carried out nonviolent demonstrations in Prishtina that pressed for the agreement's implementation. Though announced and highly disciplined, several demonstrations met with bloody Serb police crackdowns. In late February 1998 government paramilitary police began indiscriminate and destructive attacks using mortars and then tanks, artillery, and infantry on houses and villages suspected of harboring leaders of the KLA. By June, these had killed more than 200 Albanians, including many women and children, and several thousand refugees were moving about the countryside and into Albania seeking shelter and safety. The escalation was shifting the Kosovo crisis from a nonviolent and repressive modus vivendi to an entirely different level at which thousands of radicalized and emboldened Albanian youth were now willing to die in an all-out civil war.

Although it had provoked a militarization of the conflict, the KLA was too weak to wrest control of Kosovo from the Yugoslav army. Thus, its effect was to provide Milosevic with an excuse to try to finally break the back of the vexsome Kosovar cause. Evidently, having lost influence over Montenegro and facing a worsening Yugoslav economy, he was trying to shore up his political support by either vanquishing the budding Albanian guerrilla movement, and/or provoking a higher stakes international crisis from which he might exact needed economic and diplomatic concessions. The LDK held a new round of elections March 1998 in which Rugova's leadership and popularity was barely confirmed. Although international ultimatums elicited a first-ever direct Milosevic-Rugova meeting and interparty negotiations, even as the shelling of villages intensified, the question by now was whether, even assuming the doubtful proposition that the negotiating parties were inclined to mutually acknowledge the futility of continuing the armed combat now unleashed and could reach some agreement, any compromise would be accepted by their respective riled-up constituencies.

Overall, the leaders in three host polities of Slovakia, Macedonia, and Kosovo showed very clear differences in the style with which they handled policy differences between their respective ethnic constituencies and the hostile actions through which they pursued their political agendas. Similarly, in the respective neighboring countries, the top leaders in Hungary and Serbia who also had opportunities for ethnic appeals handled them in rather different ways overall, although not always consistently. They also differed in the extent to which inclinations to act unilaterally and arbitrarily were successful.

In Slovakia, an ambitious leader used ethnic themes to aggrandize power wherever possible, but he was checked periodically by other parties and politicians, and most policies were carried out largely through normal legislative means. Although he exhibited the same kind of demagogic behavior as Milosevic, Meciar was restrained to some extent by opponents within his own party and by opposition parties, and he lost power twice due to his unilateral political style. Meciar was able to return to power through his charismatic appeal to the nationalist elements in the Slovak electorate. His counterparts in Hungary were more restrained by both temperament and circumstances. In Macedonia, despite the small number of Serbs in the society, moderate leaders diligently avoided any confrontations with Serbia over Serb ethnic issues or border disputes, and Milosevic saw little immediate advantage in pressing their cause. In Kosovo, however, belligerence characterized one side and meekness the other, until access to arms allowed the latter to use force to try to rectify the imbalance. Marked since the early 1960s by periodic demonstrations and police repression, the relationship between these two polarized communities had maintained an unstable status quo until the outcome of Dayton invited extremists to try armed force. Even a momentary engagement on the education agreement was overtaken by escalating political violence and military mobilization. Subsequent events unleashed almost all of the fears in the widely anticipated Kosovo scenario.

In all the cases, however, the extent of low or high levels of violence depended as much on what individual politicians could get away with in view of the prevailing distributions of military and political power and popular sentiments, as with the leaders' individual temperaments and political styles. Defenseless Macedonia in 1991–1992 had no choice but deference toward the FRY and neutrality in the Yugoslav wars. Although less enduring, a similar calculus of power realities explains Rugova's practice of nonviolent politics. When deciding whether or not to "play the ethnic card," several of these group leaders obviously took into account whether doing so would best serve their own constituencies and thus increase their chances of continued tenure.

International Engagement or Neglect?

A final possible explanation of the differing courses and levels of the three conflicts concerns the extent that the affected societies and governments were influenced in a peaceful direction by major international forces and actors. Two sorts of international influences on intrastate conflicts can be distinguished: the degree of economic and diplomatic integration of the country into the international system, sometimes called "structural" or "deep" conflict prevention; and more ad hoc "hands-on" actions taken in response to specific issues arising in group relations, sometimes called "direct"or "light" prevention.

Peace is believed to be more likely to the extent that countries are linked economically and politically to other states within their own region and the wider international system. Studies suggest that the extent to which there are trade links between a country and other trading partners, for example, violent conflict is less likely (Esty et al. 1998, 1999). Trade apparently offers actual or potential economic benefits in which key actors in the society develop a strong stake. In addition to economic integration, institutionalist theory suggests that multilateral organizations, both global and regional, can play a role in addressing tensions through maintaining diplomatic communications, setting standards, and brokering agreements over particular disputes. Whether through such international organizations or done outside their channels, international influence can also be exercised through various diplomatic, military or other short-term responses that are made to specific events and actions within societies as a conflict situation unfolds.

Slovakia and Hungary

As Czechoslovakia, Hungary, and Poland shed their communist doctrines and institutions, they became interested very early in reaping the benefits of joining the West's international organizations, chiefly the European Community (now Union) and NATO. Consequently, they sought to participate in the intermediate opportunities on the way to these memberships provided by the EU Association Agreements and NATO's Partnership for Peace. These goals were not always pursued steadily or consistently, however, due to the countries' differing bilateral and multilateral approaches to integration with the West, their preoccupations with domestic power struggles, the orientations of changing leaders, and mutual disputes (Zielonka 1972, 37).

Initially, each sought integration on its own, rather than multilaterally. Their harboring of mutual suspicions and old national stereotypes of each other, vying for preferential treatment from the West, and diplomatic wars, however, blocked efforts to increase cooperation, such as agreeing to liberalize trade (Zielonka 1972, 41). But when these states failed to gain early admission into the desired Western institutions, some of their leaders sought to promote pan-European schemes for security cooperation. In 1990, Czech Foreign Minister Jiri Dienstbier proposed a new European security treaty among all the CSCE members that would commit them to peaceful settlement of disputes, mutual security assistance, and an executive security commission. After the failed Soviet coup of 1991 and the dissolution of the Soviet Union, cooperative relations at the regional level got a boost because the Central Europeans realized they no longer had special bargaining power with the West but were in competition for Western support with the Baltics, Ukraine, and Russia. Regional cooperation began to be seen not as an end in itself, but as an interim step needed for all of them to join Western institutions.

Meeting in the city of Visegrad, Poland, the leaders of Czechoslovakia, Hungary, and Poland discussed the potential for cooperation in security, economics, environment, and minority issues. The goal was to restore their countries' independence and democracy, as well as develop a plan for integration with the West. They agreed to seek to develop common economic policies, to coordinate their efforts to join the EC and EFTA, to begin trilateral military inspections, and to discuss border regulations. They also signed several bilateral treaties. A Central European Cooperation Committee was set up in April 1992 as a forum for trade consultations with the possibility of a free trade zone. These actions reflected a sense that they shared a common destiny in relation to the West that distinguished them from other Eastern and Southern European states. Although not a formal structure and largely a consultative body, the Visegrad Three, or Triangle (later the Visegrad Four with the separation of the Czech Republic and Slovakia), provided a framework for regional dialogue and cooperation on many controversial issues, including ethnic questions, and it signalled their recognition that mutual cooperation was important for eventual integration into the West.

During the same period, although the Western powers were not willing to grant immediate entry to the EC and NATO, they did use the offer of eventual benefits from membership as their chief means to influence the foreign and domestic policies of these states. They hoped this leverage would entice the states to establish regional economic cooperation, reach stable security relations and boundary agreements with one another, and adhere to the standards of the CSCE/OSCE (of which all the states involved were already members) regarding minority rights, democratization and rule of law, as well as the inviolability of borders. Hungary and Czechoslovakia were admitted to the Council of Europe in late 1990. The EC reached an association agreement with these states and Poland in November 1991, under which trade barriers would be gradually dismantled over ten years, and regular political dialogue would be undertaken.[12] Whether the actual policies of the states made progress in fulfilling these standards, or violations of standards occurred, was more or less continuously monitored by the OSCE, World Bank, and other bodies, and informally through the extensive media coverage of politics and policies in Eastern Europe. Where a state's performance was judged lacking, the partial benefits were withheld.

The attitude of Slovakia's leaders towards European integration was always more ambivalent than the others, however, both before and after its independence. When Czechoslovakia signed the EC Association Agreement in 1991, it was expected that if the two republics were to split, the agreement would have to be renegotiated and that the poorer Slovakia might not obtain the same agreement. After Slovakia did split from the Czech Republic, while Czechoslovakia adopted market reforms earlier than many other communist states, Slovakia balked at the stepped-up pace of economic reform. Though Slovakia's foreign policy officially included the goal of joining Western institutions, the government's actual behavior repeatedly spoke otherwise.

It joined the Council of Europe in 1993, but failed to fulfill its commitments (Duleba 1997). It signed an Accession Agreement with the EU in 1993, but when the EU issued a series of demarches in 1994 and 1995 in response to the Slovak Parliament's purges of civil service personnel, restrictions on media organizations, and actions against the political opposition and the presidency, the government did not respond with any explanations of its behavior. Slovakia was the object of more such demarches than any other Visegrad government (Duleba 1997). Thus, Slovakia's application for an association agreement was not taken up on the grounds that its human rights record fell short. Visiting Western leaders such as Madeleine Albright, then-U.S. Ambassador to the United Nations, and Hillary Clinton expressed concern over Meciar's policies, and he was not invited to major capitols to meet with major European leaders.

Similarly, NATO decided in 1991 to develop institutional relations with all the Eastern European countries except Yugoslavia and Albania through the establishment of the North Atlantic Cooperation Council (NACC), which holds annual ministerial meetings. The Western European Union also made them observers in the WEU Assembly and initiated contacts with officials and academics. But in 1997, Slovakia was dropped by both NATO and the EU from their lists of the first governments that might be invited to join the organizations. While the three other Visegrad states were allowed to join NATO in 1999, Slovakia was left out.

Slovakia's relations with Germany were also telling. Though Germany was Slovakia's second-biggest trading partner after the split, German relations deteriorated especially after Meciar's reelection in 1994, and Meciar was not invited to meet with Chancellor Helmut Kohl. Slovakia blocked progress on agreements with Germany regarding illegal aliens, technical assistance, and cooperation in other areas because it refused to accept Germany's post–Cold War name. Investment from Germany and other countries slowed dramatically, largely due to skepticism about Slovakia's commitment to democratic and market reforms.

In short, though Meciar made efforts to establish relations with key governments such as Germany and the United States, apparently believing the West could not ignore Slovakia, analysts doubt that he actually wanted to join the EU. He also spent much time developing close ties with Russia and Belarus, both of which he saw as following a different model of development. Thus, the energy with which Slovakia pursued links and agreements with the West and its neighbors was weak and fluctuated considerably, depending on who its leader was.

The broad "carrot" strategy of the EC and NATO was supplemented by more direct initiatives whereby U.S. and European organizations attempted to diffuse ethnic conflict in Slovakia by engaging officials and community leaders in official or nonofficial dialogues on specific issues. Western organizations and NGOs were the major third parties to get engaged in the problem of minorities in Eastern and Central Europe, including the tensions between the Hungarians and Slovakians in Slovakia. The CSCE office of the High Commissioner of National Minorities (HCNM) was designed to get directly involved in ethnic policy issues throughout the CSCE member countries before they escalate. Accordingly, the energetic and widely respected first incumbent of the office of the HCNM, former Dutch Foreign Minister Max van der Stoel, visited these two countries frequently, although his visits apparently were not welcomed by Meciar. Western NGOs, sometimes working through local NGOs, conducted a variety of workshops among community leaders, such as from churches and synagogues, and local government officials.

In 1993, the European Union launched a diplomatic initiative known as the Stability Pact, which was intended as a mechanism to encourage dialogue between and within potential members regarding border and minority disputes. The EU held a series of bilateral meetings and roundtable discussions with these countries. Under the auspices of the Pact, Hungary and Slovakia finally signed an agreement in 1995 calling for the inviolability of borders and guarantees of minority rights. The agreement merely created a framework for relations between the two countries, however, without resolving specific disputes. Implementation of this agreement was delayed by disagreements over the composition of a joint committee on minorities. Hungary insisted that ethnic Hungarians be included on the committee, while Slovakia maintained that minority representation was not necessary. Thus, international incentives fostered engagement on the Hungarian minority's grievances, but were not able to maintain momentum in resolving them. Nevertheless, the settlement of the Gabcikovo dam dispute and various efforts to moderate ethnic relations within Slovakia reflected the influence of international third parties as well as positive actions by the two countries.

In sum, although the Slovakian government expressed a strong desire for diplomatic and security ties to West European and other international organizations, its policies and political process—in addition perhaps to its smaller economic significance—undermined its ability to achieve its goals with the West, at least until the 1998 change of government. In sharp contrast, Hungary remained considerably more open to Western influence than Slovakia, although the pace of Hungary's pursuit of multilateralism as well as bilateralism varied some, depending on its differing leaders.

Macedonia and Yugoslavia

At first, the republic of Macedonia's potential internal conflict did not receive the attention of high-level U.S. or European officials. But in late 1991 and early 1992, though occupied with the Croatia and the possible Bosnia war, governments had to decide whether to recognize Macedonia's independence declaration. Despite the fact that the European Community's own Badinter Commission advised against recognition for Croatia and Bosnia-Herczegovina but recommended it for Macedonia, in January 1992, the EC flip-flopped these recommendations for the sake of members' solidarity. Relenting to intense German pressure from Foreign Minister Hans Dietrich Genscher, it recognized Slovenia and Croatia and supported their admission into the UN, but it turned down Macedonia. Whether "preventive recognition" would have eased the situation or would have done harm, as it had when used to avoid war in Croatia, is uncertain, but the option was not tried.

Nevertheless, each republic whose independence was generally recognized became a member of the CSCE and the Council of Europe. In addition, Macedonia sought earnestly to join NATO and the EU. The next year, Macedonia was admitted to the Partnership for Peace and began receiving IMF and World Bank loans, and joined the latter in 1993. It has also sought to maintain and increase trade with its neighbors, including its former occupier, Bulgaria. However, much of the trade it cultivated was reduced by UN sanctions of November 1991 and May 1992 and the Greek embargo.

In contrast, as the federal government of Yugoslavia witnessed various republics secede, there was no impetus for it to join new international organizations beyond the UN and CSCE. Then, once it was implicated in the wars in Croatia and Bosnia, the rump Yugoslavia lost existing memberships other than the UN, so it no longer shared any international organization with its former republics. Its extensive trade with Macedonia was maintained. Following its suspension from the CSCE in 1993, Yugoslavia under Milosevic denied the renewal of the Observer Mission that had been established in Kosovo, Sandjak, and Vojvodina the previous year. Only after the Dayton Accords of 1995 were diplomatic relations restored for the FRY, and then eligibility for membership in international financial institutions became a possibility.

Regarding international engagement with specific disputes, Macedonia was notable for taking the initiative. In late summer of 1992 President Gligorov requested international observers to monitor the border with Serbia. In early fall, U.S. President George Bush urged the CSCE to place observer missions in the still peaceful areas of rump Yugoslavia to discourage the emergence of ethnic tensions and alert the international community to their earliest signs. The CSCE Council of Ministers (CoM) authorized the CSCE Spillover Monitoring Mission for Macedonia on September 18 and gave it the job of monitoring the northern border. With a staff of six to eight, the mission continuously tracked economic, social, and political events in the country, and observed its demonstrations and political rallies. It established contact with the major political parties, held roundtables to encourage dialogue among government officials and party leaders, and helped conciliate policy disputes regarding minority interests.

In November, in a visit to UN headquarters, President Gligorov requested a UN peacekeeping force to help buttress the weak Macedonian army. The world's first multilateral preventive deployment set up observation posts by January 1993, composed of

500 Canadians, who were soon replaced by 700 Swedish, Norwegian, and Finnish troops; 300 Americans supplemented this force in July 1993. The deployment's mandate was to patrol the Macedonian side of the 240 kilometer-long Serbian and 180 kilometer-long Albanian border, to monitor and report developments that could threaten Macedonia, and "by its presence, deter such threats from any source, as well as help prevent clashes which could otherwise occur between external elements and Macedonian forces, thus helping to strengthen security and confidence in Macedonia." The mission's civilian police worked with the government's police and civil authorities in border areas with large proportions of ethnic minorities. Military and civilian commands also did extensive visitation in local communities and started several humanitarian and other demonstration projects to create goodwill. The aim was to help villages with vulnerable populations from falling through the government's safety net.

The six-month reports of the UNSG in 1992 and 1993 saw the mission as still needed for external threats, but called attention to the effect of a military presence in calming the country itself. Subsequent reports emphasized the possible threat from internal political tensions. Thus, the resident Special Representative of the Secretary General (SRSG) was encouraged to use his offices in cooperation with the country authorities to foster political dialogue among the major ethnic communities. As the head of UNPREDEP, SRSG Henryk Sokalski engaged in active dialogue with political leaders of ethnic groups in the country, as well as maintained contacts with high officials in Albania and the FRY. He used quiet diplomacy to offer suggestions relating to the rights of ethnic communities. Civilian staff continuously monitored and analyzed internal political developments such as elections.

Paying short visits lacks the advantages of an ongoing presence in the country, but the HCNM, Max van der Stoel, used the discretion and relative visibility of his roving portfolio to visit Macedonia frequently. Addressing the differences among government, party and community leaders, including Albanians and Serbs, the HCNM pressed for better employment and educational policies, and promoted a continuing roundtable between the government and minority groups. Particularly when local controversies flared up that could exacerbate the poor relations of the two communities or risk spreading civil unrest, the HCNM sought to wield his prestige and skills to allay tensions, such as when he proposed the Tetovo University controversy be handled through a new law on education. Also, below the level of the national political leadership at which UNPREDEP and the OSCE operate in Macedonia, as in Slovakia, a number of U.S. and other NGOs launched conflict resolution training and civil society promotion projects at the national and grass-roots levels.

Kosovo and Yugoslavia

Yugoslavia's loss of international memberships affected these relations even more than those with Macedonia. Kosovo under the LDK had long sought to join the community of nations, but because of the fear of worsening the conflict by causing a breach of Yugoslav sovereignty, the would-be state of Kosova was recognized by few governments. Thus, international engagement in Serb-Albanian relations in Kosovo had to take the form of diplomatic demarches and other issue-specific actions.

To buttress the CSCE mission placed in Kosovo in September 1992, President Bush issued a "Christmas warning" in December to then-Serbian President Milosevic against increased Serbian internal pressures. This stated that in the event of conflict caused by any Serbian action, the United States was prepared to use military force in Kosovo or Serbia proper. The message clearly meant air strikes or some other military response. These warnings were repeated by President Clinton in March 1993 and by the State Department that October. In addition, adding the 300 U.S. troops to UNPROFOR on the Serbian border was meant to be a further message to Serbia to stay out of Macedonia.

The Bush and Clinton warnings to Milosevic sought to deter increased repression, and UNPREDEP provided an uncertain bulwark against massive refugee flows into Macedonia. But the FRY authorities held the upper hand in Kosovo and, unlike the Macedonian government, did not initiate any further international governmental missions, having ejected the initial OSCE mission in July 1993. Because the FRY's legal sovereignty limited how much the international community could become involved politically, on-the-ground engagement was confined mainly to humanitarian relief from Mercy Corps International, Oxfam, and the Catholic Relief Service for the badly deteriorating health and social conditions.

The lack of a high-level international diplomatic engagement in Kosovo did lead other NGOs subsequently to try to fill the gap by engaging Albanians and Serbs in dialogue. Following the Dayton Accords, for example, several track-two initiatives approached the Kosovar leadership and President Milosevic to urge dialogue. After a failed EU initiative in early 1996, discussions by the Italian NGO Communita'di Sant Igidio, with EU and U.S. government encouragement and U.S. funds, achieved a breakthrough education agreement between the LDK's Rugova and Milosevic on September 3. This called for reopening all levels of the Kosovo government schools to Albanian students and teachers, including the teacher training colleges and faculties of the University of Prishtina. The plan was to start within a month under the supervision of three representatives from both sides. Both parties were under increasing pressure to produce results for their respective constituencies. Milosevic's party was coming up for reelection in November, and at this point, he was earnestly seeking access to World Bank and IMF funds for Yugoslavia (removal of the "outer wall of sanctions"). The talks also allowed Rugova to produce concrete benefits for a Kosovo Albanian electorate that was hearing criticisms of his leadership by other leaders of the community. But Albanian students began to return in some numbers only after the conflict escalated over a year later. The United States and Europeans also negotiated to place cultural offices in Prishtina in 1997, which U.S. officials saw as a way to establish an official U.S. presence in Kosovo.

Because eventually, no less than thirteen governmental initiatives were tried and sixteen NGO efforts made, it cannot be argued that Kosovo escalated because of utter international neglect. But no robust and sustained multilateral effort was made to address the political sources of the continuing threat posaed by the two community's almost total polarization. It was not until the violent escalation of the conflict that high-level and sustained diplomatic action was undertaken by the United States; a UN contact group comprised of the United States, Britain, France, Germany, Italy, and Russia; and various governments. Aimed as they were at stopping the continuing spiral of violence, however, these sanctions, conditional diplomatic carrots, and mediation efforts, though necessary, were less preventive than reactive, and were not effective. Though the new Serb armed activity clearly fit the criteria of the Christmas warnings, no U.S. military actions were taken until March 1999.

From early 1998 to early 1999, the familiar features of an escalating international crisis came into play: attacks and counterattacks by "thugs" and "terrorists" causing further spiraling violence; an equivocal, disjointed international response in the form of the Contact Group holding high-level meetings and sponsoring mediation attempts; UN Security Council resolutions and sanctions; expatriates financing increased arms shipments and joining the two armies; and sympathizing powers lining up on both sides. An agreement was reached that led to a large, hastily-deployed OSCE observer mission, the Kosovo Verification Mission, but violence and cease-fire violations led to its breakdown and another failed settlement at Rambouillet in February 1999. This was followed by NATO bombing of Serbia and massive ethnic cleansing of Kosovo, and finally, capitulation by Milosevic.

All in all, international engagement did not ignore any of the three countries facing tensions, but the extent of early international integration of the three polities differed significantly as did the extent to which international diplomacy, official or nonofficial, got involved with significant inducements in emerging interethnic tensions and issues. Interest was shown very early by the West in the three Visegrad countries, and specific incentives were offered due to ensure their peaceful transition, due to their greater economic importance and potential. But though Slovakia as an independent country was open in theory to integration, and its price tag, reform, it was largely indifferent to its practice, and thus was denied the promise of such benefits early on and instead viewed with skepticism. Demarches and a few mediation efforts tried to improve its policy behavior, but without a carrot so visibly in view. Although Macedonia was eager from the start, it was also ignored for a while, and at some risk, was at first jilted in its efforts until its strategic importance was soon recognized. It then received a great deal of attention in a variety of ways that operated close to the ground, including a symbolic form of military protection as well as internal political dialogue and increasing amounts of aid. The rump Yugoslavia did not and could not pursue integration actively after a certain point and became increasingly hostile. With regard to Serb-Kosovo relations, a hypothetical kind of deterrence was introduced at a fairly high level of crisis to avoid the militarization of the conflict. But the deep divisions and grievances between these highly mobilized groups were not significantly addressed through either diplomatic efforts or economic incentives until the conflict escalated into sustained violence in 1998.

Conclusion

We have compared seven possible leading determinants of the course of ethnic disputes within countries where at least one group has ties with kin across the border. Table 6.2 summarizes the differences among the cases that were associated with the rising and falling but moderated tensions existing in Slovakia and Macedonia, on the one hand, and the high tensions and periodic confrontations in Kosovo resulting in civil war, on the other. Certain patterns are clear.

Table 6.2: Groups in Conflict

Key Variables	Hungarians in Slovakia	Serbs in Macedonia	Serbs in Kosovo
Recent Hostilities	Low	Low	High
Social Segregration	Low to moderate	Low	High
Economic Competition	High	High	High
Ethno-Political Mobilization	Moderate	Low	High
International Isolation	Moderate	Low	High
Unresponsive Government	Low	Low	High
Leaders' Behavior	Moderate to high	Low	High
International Neglect	Low	Low	Moderate

Slovakia, Macedonia, and Kosovo did not differ discernibly from each other on any one or two factors, but rather, several. Indeed, they differed to some degree on all but one factor, economic decline. Apparently, the likelihood of violent conflict arising between major ethnic groups is governed by a combination of factors, including the extent that: there was violence or coercion in the past between them; they differ in multiple societal and cultural respects and have little interaction; they are highly conscious of their respective identities and are organized into separate political movements, parties, or governmental machinery; the government structure permits little participation by both groups simultaneously or is in effect divided between them; at least one of the leaders on one side accentuates these divisions through statements and policies; and the countries affected have limited diplomatic ties and direct engagement in domestic issues by major international bodies.

This multifaceted explanation suggesting that violent conflicts are contingent on several ingredients debunks some fashionable analyses of conflicts in academic as well as policy circles that tend to rely on a single societal, institutional, behavioral, or international factor. The primordialist argument gets some support from the fact that the two most hostile relationships had contended with one another over at least several decades before the Cold War ended. However, the existence of "ancient hatreds" was not determinative of violence; past bloodshed or a history of antagonism apparently were not sufficient. Although not equalling the bloodshed between Serbs and Albanians and the recent Yugoslav repression, the lengthy history in which Hungarians and Slovakians alternately dominated each other arguably may have held just as much potential for violence. Yet that conflict did not in fact escalate. These two most contentious relationships also corresponded to two more sociologically distinct communities, in which fears and distrust instilled in the past could be nurtured rather than challenged.

Another popular societal or structural argument, that violent ethnic conflicts result from so-called root causes such as a poor economy and economic decline, has even less support. The extent of economic decline and competition did not appear to differ across these cases, nor were economic inequalities worse in one than in another. A related economic argument, that rapid market reform and resulting austerity can precipitate violent conflict, is actually contradicted here. Despite the initial strains that they caused, the system that adopted considerable structural adjustment and endured it, Macedonia, remained the most peaceful. Slovakia and Yugoslavia may have risked higher levels of hostilities by shielding themselves from economic change. This maintained the link between achieving political power and possessing state assets and thus perpetuated the notion that a group's economic position could be maintained or improved only through zero-sum competitive politics.

But institutional differences may have been important, too. The extent that organized ethnic nationalist political parties who prevailed could virtually monopolize their states, as in Yugoslavia, or their control was attenuated, as in Slovakia and Macedonia, albeit in differing degrees, appeared to depend on the electoral strength of the other political parties, and thus the degree of access that alternative leaders had to parliamentary and executive offices. Even limited access to power-sharing put some check on nationalist extremes in Slovakia, and probably less so in Yugoslavia, through the support and protection provided to the autonomous or semiautonomous operations of local governments, the judicial system, and other agencies of the state. Thus, the extent of constitutional checks and balances also helped to temper the level of conflict.

Especially interesting is the considerably qualified evidence for the behavioral or "agency" arguments, either that individual top leaders, especially possibily pathological ones, who become ethnic entrepreneurs can gather elite cliques to foment ethnic violence more or less on their own, or conversely, that moderate individual leaders can make a difference. The two most nationalist and belligerent leaders, Meciar and Milosevic, also had the ugliest histories to work with. In addition, however, Meciar was arguably as manipulative and unbending a leader as Milosevic, yet Slovakia did not escalate into violence. He seems to have had more constraints on his behavior, whereas Milosevic used his somewhat freer hand to crack down viciously. On the other hand, those leaders with less divisive and more accommodating styles did help to keep their conflicts under control. Gligorov, Rogova, and, perhaps, Antall, were they to have chosen to do so, could have increased the temperature of their respective conflicts by inciting their ethnic brethren more than they did. Instead, they presented their counterparts with mild opponents who appealed to international principles. Yet in the first two instances, because they lacked political or military power, the political costs were perhaps too high to proceed otherwise. In Antall's case, the ethnic card was probably not worth playing for the leader of a relatively secure state. To have a real fight may require dyads composed of two determined and opposed nationalist forces. In short, the simple idea that ethnic conflicts arise from the machinations and depredations of individual demagogic leaders, or that moderates can make a difference all by themselves, must take into account the specific situational and shifting opportunities and restraints, including differing balances of military and political power, that shape individual leaders' differing choices.

Overall then, relatively hard-to-change societal conditions such as past violence and highly estranged societal relations of groups may increase the possibility of violent escalation, but they do not make it inevitable. Several other more contingent political factors are needed before a community's past treatment, social distance from other groups, or poor economic straits lead to violent conflict. These contingencies include a highly politicized sense of group identity, the mobilization and aggregation of group interests through political organizations, governing structures that create exclusive dependency on the state, leaders' interpretations of the reasons for one's plight and a course of action, a present threat to one's position, and finally, permissive institutions that put few obstacles in the way.

The view also gets some support that ethnic conflicts with these features can still be prevented from actually escalating and the level of hostility can be moderated through timely and robust interventions of international actors. The hostilities do seem to be influenced by the extent and further prospects of economic and political integration of the polities and the degree to which that integration was supplemented by more "hands-on" attention to specific domestic ethnic issues. But the status of intergroup relations and polarization in Slovakia and Macedonia was much lower in the first place than in Kosovo, and the leaders and elites in Hungary, Macedonia, and Kosovo could restrain the level of aggression, repression, or reaction.

These covarying elements are undoubtedly mutually reinforcing, although we do not know which are most powerful and may drive the others. Past hurts inflicted on one's group are harbored in separated communities and help to engender early ethnic nationalist aspirations, which require political organization. Left unchallenged and undiluted in stagnant managed economies, these feelings and institutions can be revitalized by ambitious leaders, when the next period of global change and domestic political uncertainty opens up opportunities to advance a group's position or presents new threats to it. If two such mobilized communities live in the same polity, their exclusive mentalities will clash over matters of ultimate control. When the nationalist leaders are the incumbents in government, they tend to use the state for that cause, avoid economic and political reform, worsen their already poor economies, and abridge minority rights. All but the most powerful international pressures and incentives are ignored except where they may assist that program. Because such policies are incompatible with emerging international standards, they tend to be shunned internationally. Although they thus have more rein to continue their policies, this stimulates reaction from their nationalist opposites and conflict escalates.

That kind of vicious cycle, or conflict syndrome, seems especially apt to the Kosovo-Yugoslavia relationship. Compared to its tamer counterparts, the Serb-Albanian conflict distinguishes itself from the other two by lying on the extreme end of all the factors. Kosovo was apparently the most hostile conflict, to the point of civil war, because there had been significantly more violence in the recent past; Serbia was less integrated internationally; its government was not only less unaccommodating but repressive and largely unchecked by effective opposition; and international positive incentives, pressures, and mediation to prevent escalation were neither sustained nor robust. But although this led to war and the other cases have found peace so far, the differences among the three cases on all the dimensions are gradual and not sharp. This suggests there can be a middle ground between vicious and virtuous circles, such as Macedonia may be in. In other words, although the mutual reinforcement of several factors led to a isolation and violence that made international preventive intervention more and more difficult, even in the negatively spiralling cases, there may be several points before a definitive turning point is reached and when vigorous attention to several of the factors can begin to break the cycle of deterioration.

More specifically, in view of the similarities between Slovakia and the rump Yugoslavia, and yet the eventual peaceful transition of the former, it is possible to argue that, rather than almost totally isolating Yugoslavia by casting it so readily as a pariah state, a more consistently vigorous strategy that maintained the prospect of positive incentives for Milosevic upon good behavior, while also supporting the strengthening of his political opposition to compete electorally, and vigorously promoting direct dialogues with rewards for progress on specific Kosovo issues such as the 1997 education agreement, may have created some brakes on the escalation of that conflict. A degree of accommodation over Kosovo may have avoided the KLA violent actions in 1997–1998 that subsequently led to all out rebellion, repression, escalation, and international military action.

These conclusions provide preliminary findings or grounded hypotheses for further research on the central question of why some ethnic disputes become violent while others remain peaceful. In the meantime, their multifacted explanation holds implications for prevention policy making. Some social scientists may persist in pursuing the holy grail of the few most statistically powerful causal variables that they can find numbers to measure in a large universe of cases. But because violent conflict escalation in particular places is dependent on the strength of several apparently interacting factors, policy analysts and policy makers trying to formulate appropriate prevention responses should avoid one-dimensional "magic bullet" remedies that any such single factor or causal explanation may imply. To be more relevant and effective, responsible decision makers should examine, in each individual situation they face, the weight of several major generic factors that are likely to be at work, such as the factors described above, and thus arrive at the particular configuration of factors that are most important in that case. This method reveals several areas of leverage or entry points that could and should be attended to, ideally simultaneously or in some prioritized sequence. Effective prevention calls for moving some sufficient number of those targetted factors in the right direction to inspire a virtuous circle. But consequently, these policy makers will find they will need to join with other international and domestic actors in order to aggregate enough resources to influence those several entry points.

Notes

I am indebted to the research assistance of Wendy Betts, especially regarding the preliminary research and writing of the chronology of the Slovakia case. The chapter draws on research done for " 'Preventive Diplomacy' for Macedonia, 1990–1998: Containment Becomes Nation-Building," in *Opportunities Missed, Opportunities Seized: Preventive Diplomacy in the Post-Cold War Era* ed. Bruce Jentleson, (Lanham, Md: Rowman & Littlefield 1998), 173–208.

1. Two recent influential analysts epitomize structural theories. Robert Kaplan sees "Balkan Ghosts" of past ethnic hatreds still haunting that region. Samuel Huntington pinpoints Yugoslavia as lying on top of a deep fault line that divides two clashing regional cultural civilizations. Both analysts judge that country to be especially prone to recurring turmoil because of the powerful undercurrents of past group animosities or persisting cultural divisions that will tend to override any short-term influences on their politics. Societal factors also have been cited in retrospective explanations of particular conflicts that have escalated, such as when a supposed pervasive political culture of "the Balkans" as a region is invoked to explain its recent conflicts (e.g., Gallagher 1998; Bookman 1994). The problem, however, is that not all potential Balkan conflicts actually erupted. Either societal explanations are not helpful, or these factors varied significantly in particular Balkan conflict arenas. We cannot dismiss the relevance of such factors, but need to look closely to see if the historical, cultural, and other backgrounds of the conflicts showed significant differences, for those might still help to explain their differing levels of hostility.

2. These two sets of factors parallel recent academic and policy debates. The two main positions in a debate about the sources of "ethnic conflict"—primordial versus instrumental theories—represent societal and action theories, respectively. Societal and action theories also correspond to the debate in international relations between realists and constructivists, as well as the wider debate in social science between "structure" and "agency" in explaining collective behavior. They also show up in policy makers' and journalists' accounts. Though practitioners often pride themselves in eschewing "academic theories" in favor of practical pursuits, one view journalists often repeat about ethnic conflicts is that "the X-ians and the Y-ians have been fighting each other for centuries." Whether always accurate or not, attributing recent violence to deep and abiding animosities in X-Y relations follows the logic of societal explanation. Recent policy discussions of the causes of the violent conflict in Kosovo, for example, have reflected this theory. Alternatively, journalists and policy makers have also widely seen this conflict as resulting from the manipulations and actions of Yugoslav President Milosevic. Invoking some reviled individual

leader is an example of action theory. These offered interpretations simply illustrate how the discourse of "op-eds" and policy decision making cannot escape theory.

3. In some research, such institutions and processes are also called "structural," or systemic, but this collapses the difference between factors, on the one hand, over which decision makers have considerable control, such as the redistributive effects of social policies and constitutional arrangements, and, on the other hand, conditions that are less easily changed except over time, such as a society's age distribution.

4. The following analysis is not intended as a complete and thorough assessment of all data pertinent to the variables introduced. It simply does an initial review of pertinent sources in order to present some preliminary findings that can be used as hypotheses in further research.

5. Underlying conditions that may shape the degree of separation or integration in a society include the extent the society has become industrialized and urbanized, the national economy is based on market competition, and the amount of resulting commerce and travel within and outside the country. These conditions all tend to increase the socioeconomic and physical mobility of minority groups, and thus their contact with other groups. Some believe such contact can result in more cosmopolitan attitudes and thus higher tolerance of others.

6. Homogenous groups will tend to share more interests, contact, and methods for resolving disputes. At the other extreme, highly pluralistic or atomized societies make it difficult for the sponsors of political movements or armed actions to unify forces to launch threats to stability. For such movements to make gains requires bargaining, logrolling, and compromise to satisfy many competing interests. The fragmented distribution of power among them also engenders confidence in any one group that its interests can be accommodated to some extent.

7. When Samuel Huntington describes Macedonia and Serbia as "cleft countries" that exist on the main fault lines between two regional civilizations, he employs a version of the social distance explanation in which the emphasis is on the multiple cultural differences of religion, language, and historical experience. It is assumed that such a cultural gulf will continue to be powerful forces that fuel current tensions, no matter what other more situational factors may come into play.

8. Some analysts believe that greater alienation exists within ethnic Slovakia's population between its urban and rural members than between them and the ethnic Hungarians.

9. We could regard such differences in state economic policy making as an institutional factor and thus place them under section 6, since it is shaped by the policies of governments. But it is reviewed here, rather than be confused with official institutions affecting representation of political and policy demands.

10. The Albanian attacks on Serbs have been grossly exaggerated in Serb tracts. On the several sources of the Albanian population concentration since 1981, including a high Serb abortion rate, and the distorted Serb reaction to Albanians (Malcolm 1998, 329–333, 336–339).

11. A UN official in Macedonia expressed the view that Serbia was unlikely to invade, and the UN liaison in Belgrade believed Yugoslav officials were largely indifferent to Macedonia. In September 1994, the UN Secretary General stated that Serbian troops did not seem to want to provoke confrontation.

12. Actually, its provisions fell considerably short of many of the membership, trade, and labor desires of the Eastern signatories. From the point of view of the expectations and hopes of most officials in these countries, the Western responses to their desires for integration in economics and security fell far short of what they desired. But basically, they were in a weak position to get their demands met.

7
A Comparative Analysis of Confict Resolution in Angola and South Africa

Vasu Gounden and Hussein Solomon

In an address, UN Secretary-General Kofi Annan noted that

... since 1970 Africa has had more than 30 wars fought on its territory, the vast majority of which have been intra-state in origin. Fourteen of Africa's 53 countries were afflicted by armed conflicts in 1996 alone. These accounted for more than half of all war-related deaths worldwide, resulting in more than 8 million refugees, returnees and displaced persons. The consequences of these conflicts have seriously undermined Africa's efforts to ensure long-term stability, prosperity and peace for its people. (1998, 7)

Since these words were uttered a few months ago,[1] little has occurred that detracts from the image of the African continent as being crisis-prone. Consider here the border war between Ethiopia and Eritrea and the recent rebellion in the Democratic Republic of the Congo. These suggest an urgent need for peace researchers to understand the root causes and trajectories of conflict in order to understand when and how to intervene in a conflict to achieve a successful resolution. This is precisely what this chapter seeks to accomplish by means of employing a comparative perspective of two case studies: one, South Africa, a success, and the other, Angola, a failure.

Several factors make these two case studies appropriate in contributing to the comparative perspective. First, both conflicts have a life history of about twenty years. Consequently, the conflict trajectory can be assessed in phases. Second, both countries are developing countries in the Southern African region, and both countries have historically contributed to each other's security dilemma. Consider in this regard, apartheid South Africa's repeated military invasions of Angola in support of Jonas Savimbi's Union for the Total Independence of Angola (UNITA) and against the Movement for the Popular Liberation of Angola (MPLA), which, in turn, supported the African National Congress' (ANC) *Umkhonto weSizwe* (Spear of the Nation).

Third, in both countries there were ideological and ethnic overtones to the conflict. In the case of Angola, this was played out in the fact that UNITA portrayed itself as capitalist and pro-West and the MPLA was portrayed as Soviet Marxist. In the South African case, the Inkatha Freedom Party (IFP) projected itself as a staunch supporter of the free enterprise system, while the ANC was viewed as socialist in orientation. With the demise of the Cold War and the ideological precepts it engendered, conflicts in both countries increasingly took on ethnic dimensions. In Angola, the MPLA was seen to represent the interests of the Mbundu and the mesticos, while UNITA was seen as the guardian of the Ovimbundu ethnic group. In South Africa, some sectors of the South African population viewed the conflict between the ANC and Inkatha as tensions between the Xhosa and Zulu population groups respectively.

Fourth, to a certain extent, in both countries the conflict also revolved around the personalities of leaders to the extent that Dr. Mangosuthu Buthelezi was synonymous with Inkatha and Dr. Jonas Savimbi was synonymous with UNITA.

Moreover, in both cases violence prevention was attempted. In the case of Angola, the effort failed and led to greater levels of violence. In the South African case, the efforts were successful and led to a peaceful election. In addition, in the Angolan case study there were two parties involved in the mediation and the effort was conducted essentially by international mediators. In the South African case, there were many parties to the mediation and intervention efforts were undertaken by international, national, and local actors. Furthermore, both government and nongovernmental actors were involved.

An additional important difference in the contexts of the conflict situations was the fact that in the South African scenario the environment was characterized by a grassroots peace culture that grew organically from the need to deal with an unprecedented wave of violence that had developed soon after the negotiations had begun.

As a consequence of this violence the leaders of the several political parties engaged in the negotiation process and signed a National Peace Accord (NPA) that was brokered by the business and religious sectors in South Africa. The NPA made provision of the establishment of regional and local peace committees in every locality in South Africa.

The result was the spontaneous development of a national "peace culture" from grassroots level to the national political leadership. This "culture" did not end the violence, but arguably, it did mitigate the violence. It was the buffer that insulated the peace process and ensured that despite the high levels of violence in the country, the negotiation process could continue.

This "national peace culture" from the grassroots level to the national leadership was conspicuously absent during and after the Angolan peace process that led to the Bicesse Accords. Consequently, the peace process was not protected from the ongoing violence that resulted from sporadic clashes between troops of both sides, and more importantly it had the effect of not bringing the general populace into the negotiation arena, as was the case in South Africa. This latter effect, of bringing the general population into the negotiation process, is the guarantor of any negotiated peace. Without "buy in" from the general population, implementation of a peace agreement is extremely difficult.

A Brief Narrative on the Nature of the Conflict in Angola and South Africa

The Angolan conflict began as a struggle for independence and national liberation from Portuguese colonial rule during the first months of 1961. By the time of independence on November 11, 1975, political rivalries between the two major nationalist groups—the MPLA and UNITA—who were fighting for independence, degenerated into a vicious civil war that seemed to have no end. With the assistance of the Cubans, the MPLA emerged the victor of the national liberation struggle and formed the government of independent Angola. This victory, however, was violently contested by Jonas Savimbi's UNITA. In the context of the Cold War, this conflict acquired ideological undertones with UNITA being seen as pro-West and the MPLA as pro-Soviet. The demise of global bipolarity shifted the emphasis from an ideological paradigm to an ethnic one. Various attempts were made to resolve this conflict, with the Bicesse Accords of May 31, 1991, being the most significant and resulting in an election a year later. However, these Accords failed to bring peace to the sixteen-year-old conflict as UNITA challenged the results of the 1992 elections, a product of the Bicesse Accords. The inevitable result was renewed fighting that resulted in more than 120,000 people being killed in eighteen months of fighting. This is almost half the number of people killed in sixteen years of civil war preceding the Bicesse Accords.

In the case of South Africa, its first democratic elections in April 1994, marking the demise of apartheid, were threatened days before the elections were to happen by the refusal of the Inkatha Freedom Party (IFP) to participate in the elections. The implications of the IFP's nonparticipation was almost certain to be increased levels of violence in KwaZulu-Natal. This would have had the potential of awakening other disparate groups in the country to violent opposition to the peace process, thereby plunging the entire country into a dangerous cycle of violence bordering on full-scale civil war.

In a series of international and national governmental interventions complemented by nongovernmental efforts the IFP agreed, in the eleventh hour, to participate in the elections. Although this development led to a peaceful transition from apartheid to democratic governance, the agreement itself became a source of continuing conflict between the government, led by the majority African National Congress (ANC) party of Nelson Mandela, and the IFP of Gatsha Buthelezi. The significance of this latter issue has diminished over the last four years and is testimony to the fact that the guarantor of a sustainable peace process is the development of a broader peace culture that can assist in building trust and sustaining peace.

The important issues for peace researchers are: Why did the conflict persist in Angola while it was resolved in the case of South Africa? Why did interventions prove successful in the one case and unsuccessful in the other?

Theoretical Framework

It has often been said that theory is a construct that assists us in selecting and interpreting facts. In this sense, theory is intensely practical. Consequently, a comparative study of conflict resolution efforts in South African and Angola will be of little practical utility unless this was contextualised within a broader theoretical framework which would assist us in determining the strengths and weaknesses of specific intervention efforts and allow us to draw conclusions that would have a wider applicability.

For the purposes of this chapter, the conflict transformation model of Kumar Rupesinghe (1995) will be employed. Several reasons may be advanced to justify the utility of such a model in the comparative study of conflict and conflict-resolution attempts in Angola and South Africa. In the first place, unlike conflict-resolution models, which cannot escape the label "Made in the West" and a product of the Cold War's emphasis on interstate rivalry, Rupesinghe's model lays its stress on internal conflicts and, as such, is more appropriate in a post-Cold War Third World environment where such intrastate conflict is the norm.

Second, because of the multidimensional nature of the protracted social conflicts plaguing much of Africa, Rupesinghe emphasizes the need for an "understanding of nonlinear peace-building processes. Because of the complexity of many existing and emerging conflicts, a multisectoral approach to conflict transformation is needed" (1995, 65). This multisectoral approach is a far more holistic approach to conflict transformation and, as such, allows it to be far more flexible in application than most conventional models that tend to be rigid, resulting in a gap between theory and reality. This gap between words and actions adversely affects the quality of research findings. This is an issue that Rupesinghe emphasizes when he notes that "[w]e can speak of conflict processes—conflict transformation, conflict endurance and stagnation, and conflict transformation and renewal. . . .

However, as with human existence, conflict development is also solely linear and does not lend itself to neat compartmentalisation; it is rather a multidimensional, multifaceted process" (1995, 77–78).

Third, Rupesinghe's multisectoral approach requires that the number of actors involved in the peaceful transformation of a conflict needs to be increased to reflect all constituencies of broader society. This fact was crucial to the success of the South African case. Several factors account for this. First, all constituencies of society have a stake in peace and the peace process needs to be "owned" by them if it is to succeed.

Second, it is these constituencies that would be playing a key role in postconflict reconstruction. This is an important point if one considers Rupesinghe's contention that the peaceful transfer of power is not meaningful transformation. Meaningful transformation also includes sustainable structural and attitudinal changes within broader society and the emergence of new institutions to address outstanding issues (Rupesinghe 1995, 77).

Third, the involvement of nonstate actors is also vital in situations of intrastate conflict where the state cannot play the role of nonpartisan broker because the state may often be a party to the conflict.

Finally, the inclusion of nonstate actors also reflect a broader theoretical point that the dominant realist state-centric paradigm, which so dominated international relations during the Cold War era, is under threat, that, ultimately issues of peace and security revolve around people as opposed to states.

Therefore, in summary, the conflict transformation model of Rupesinghe argues that "coming to an agreement on outstanding issues is of secondary importance to addressing the overall conflict process and coming to terms with the temporal aspects of conflict" (1995, 76). The conflict transformation model of Rupesinghe has several component parts:

a. Prenegotiation stage
b. Understanding root causes
c. Ownership of the peace process
d. Identifying all the actors
e. Identifying facilitators
f. Setting a realistic timetable
g. Sustaining the effort
h. Evaluating success and failure
i. Strategic constituencies
j. The role of outside peacemakers
k. The role of local peacemakers

The next section is an analysis of the Angolan and South African conflict resolution processes in relation to each of the components of the model as elucidated above.

A Comparative Look at Conflict Resolution Efforts in the Angolan and South African Cases

Prenegotiation Stage

According to Rupesinghe, the aim of this stage is to bring conflicting parties into the negotiation process with the purpose of

> the outlining of a logistical framework and timeframe for negotiations, and the setting of ambitious, yet realistic, goals for each stage of initial negotiations. The "strategic intent" of the pre-negotiation phase is to reduce intractability, to formulate and design a process which can bring parties to the negotiating table and to begin the trust and confidence-building necessary for a successful negotiating exercise. (Rupesinghe 1995, 80)

An important point to assess the success of the prenegotiation stage (and, indeed, the entire negotiation process) is why conflicting parties come to the negotiation table. Do they really want to peacefully resolve their conflict (reduce intractability) or is it just a tactical maneuver to buy time to pursue the military option allowing one's forces to be regrouped and resupplied?

In the case of Angola, the changed international and regional environment resulted in a mutually hurting military stalemate. From the perspective of the MPLA, the disintegration of the Soviet Union removed one of its main sponsors for weapons. The withdrawal of Cuban troops, which formed part of the deal to secure UN Resolution 435 and the independence of Namibia, also weakened Luanda's capacity to sustain its war effort. This changed strategic environment, however, also adversely affected UNITA's military option. The end of global bipolarity resulted in the United States being less willing to militarily aid its former surrogates fighting to defend capitalism. In addition, the withdrawal of South African forces from Namibia meant that UNITA could no longer count on the South African Defense Force (SADF) to come to its aid in its fight against the MPLA.

This military stalemate was clearly evident in the battle for Mavinga in December 1989. The MPLA armed forces launched a massive assault on this town and managed to drive UNITA out but not far enough to claim a decisive victory. There were losses numbering thousands on each side. The result of the battle was the government coming to the realization that a military solution was beyond its capacity. On the part of UNITA, it could not face another offensive like this without major losses on its side.

Clearly, then, the warring parties came to the negotiating table not as a result of any change of heart, but simply because the military option at that stage was no longer viable and because of the pressure to negotiate by international sponsors such as the United States, Russia, and Portugal. But it is also clear that both sides viewed the military option as a viable alternative should they not have their desires satisfied through negotiations. Thus, in violation of the Bicesse Accords, the MPLA shifted approximately

20,000 of its elite troops into a paramilitary police force, while UNITA kept its heaviest weapons and more than 25,000 battled-hardened fighters hidden in the bush.

Thus, in the Angolan scenario the prenegotiation stage was already doomed and with it the Bicesse Accords. The conflicting parties came to the negotiating table for the wrong reasons hoping to continue to play the zero-sum games they played out on the battlefield so destructively. In this way, compromise was anathema and trust was nonexistent. It was a negotiation to be dictated by Washington, Moscow, and Lisbon but had no relevance to the situation on the ground in Angola. The international environment had changed but this had not yet had a significant impact at the local level in Angola.

In the South African case, while political parties came to the negotiating table with fixed position, they maintained a flexible posture to ensure that negotiations did not stalemate, although all parties played brinkmanship to the extreme. Besides the willingness to compromise, the other distinctive character about the South African case is that the willingness to talk peace came from local actors themselves and was not engineered by international brokers. However, it must be noted that this willingness to compromise also related in large measure to the various parties having a true appreciation of their relative strengths and weaknesses. The IFP and white right-wing parties knew that their bargaining power derived from the threat of violence by their followers. Equally, the ANC and the National Party (NP) government, recognized the potential of these groups to destabilize any agreement. This threat provided the countervailing balance that provided one of the necessary incentives for compromise.

In addition the presence of a national peace culture, as alluded to earlier, assisted the peace process. An important distinction between the Angolan and South African cases was the fact that in Angola you had two conventional armed forces matched against each other with each controlling formidable armed forces that were well equipped with heavy weapons and that controlled significant sectors of the country. This was not the case in South Africa, where the only party that controlled significant military capability was the South African government. However, most, if not all, of the protagonists to the conflict had the potential to unleash violence that ranged from mass demonstrations to armed massacres with guerillalike hit-and-run tactics that were extremely difficult to control.

The countervailing balance of power was understood well by the ANC and the NP and resulted in their utilizing the "carrot and stick" approach to deal with the IFP. Thus on February 28, 1994, Nelson Mandela made a passionate plea to the nation for peace and this was seen by the IFP as a sign that the ANC was willing to make further concessions. On the same day, President De Klerk declared that he will deploy troops in KwaZulu-Natal to counter any move by King Goodwill Zwelithini and the IFP to secede from the republic. Thus while compromise and concessions were used to lure recalcitrant parties to the negotiating table and also as a face-saving device; the alternative was also revealed in stark terms. In this way, minimax as opposed to zero-sum games prevailed.

South Africa was also blessed with leaders who understood the imperatives of the national interest and the need for ethnic, regional, and other sectarian interests to be subsumed under its rubric. This was made abundantly clear in Mandela's address in 1990 to a huge public rally in Durban, soon after his release from twenty-seven years of imprisonment, where he appealed to ANC supporters to end political violence and embrace reconciliation in the national interest.

This overarching concern with the national interest as well as a true appreciation of their relative strengths and weaknesses (thereby understanding how far they can push for their demands) on the part of political parties formed the basis of a common middle ground. The identification of this common middle ground and its expansion formed the basis of third-party intervention to reduce intractability in this prenegotiation stage. In this way trust and confidence between parties could be established.

Understanding Root Causes

Rupesinghe (1995, 81) notes that it is abundantly clear from recent experiences in Somalia and the former Yugoslavia that there is the need for a thorough understanding of the root causes of a given conflict. It stands to reason that any successful intervention is premised on knowledge of how and why the conflict started in the first place. Addressing the sources that generated the conflict would then form the basis of the resolution to the conflict.

In the case of Angola, it is difficult not to escape the stark fact that the root causes of the conflict had less to do with ideological (capitalism versus communism) and ethnic (Ovimbundu versus Mbundus) considerations and more to do with the unsatiated desire for complete control on the part of leaders who utilized such considerations as vehicles for their own naked political ambitions. Consider in this regard that in the 1992 elections large sections of the Ovimbundu voted for Mbundu candidates and vice versa. As for ideological considerations these were largely put to rest with the disintegration of the Soviet Union and the almost unseemly haste with which Marxists in the MPLA rushed to embrace the free enterprise system. As for UNITA's concerns regarding the presence of Cuban troops in Angola; these were also met when the last 119 Cuban troops from Angola arrived in Havana on May 27, 1991.

Apart from personal ambitions, another underlying cause of the conflict was (and continues to be) the fear of domination. The levels of trust are so low in the Angolan case and the history is so checkered by indications of complete control of the levers of power that the politics of fear is as dominant a theme as is the politics of power. One of the main failures of the Bicesse Accords was its inability to recognize this fact and prepare the ground for a politically inclusive settlement as opposed to a "winner takes all" outcome.

In the case of South Africa, the desires of political leaders for irrational and uncontrolled political aggrandizement was less of a problem. Specific problems, rather, were identified by political parties as accounting for their antagonism and, on the part of the IFP, their threat of nonparticipation in the first democratic general elections to be held in the country.

Thus, in the case of the IFP their points of contention were the issue of a double ballot, the entrenchment of the Zulu monarchy in the new constitutional dispensation, and the nature and extent of the devolution of political power from central to regional governments. While these were, indeed, thorny issues it did open up the process and set the agenda for third-party intervention. The lesson to be learned from this is that it is always easier to resolve a conflict where issues of divergence are clearly put on the agenda and where such issues go beyond the mere hunger for power among political elites.

Ownership of the Peace Process

According to Rupesinghe (1995, 81), the sustainability of the peace process is also dependent upon the "empowerment of local actors so that they become the primary architects, owners and long-term stakeholders in the peace process." International pressure, Rupesinghe notes, is not applicable in many intrastate conflicts plaguing the world today. Even when "successful," such imposed settlements do merely serve to postpone the conflict as there is little internal support and root causes of the conflict are not addressed.

The truism of this statement is clearly borne out in the Angolan situation where the Bicesse Accords was, in large measure, imposed on the parties. In this sense, too, the real architects of the accords were U.S. Secretary of State for African Affairs Herman J. Cohen; Soviet Deputy Foreign Minister Vladimir Kasimirov; U.S. Secretary of State James Baker; Soviet Foreign Minister Aleksandr Bessemertnylch; and UN Secretary-General Javier Perez de Cuellar, as opposed to Eduardo dos Santos and Jonas Savimbi. Small wonder then, that throughout the talks leading to the Bicesse Accords fighting has continued. This is indicative of the fact that the Angolans themselves did not own the peace process and therefore did not feel obliged to obey its terms.

In the South African case, the situation was reversed. The role of outside mediators such as Dr. Henry Kissinger, Lord Peter Carrington, and British Defence Secretary of State Douglas Hurd were minimal. Even the important and vital role of Professor Washington Okumu, the Kenyan mediator who played a major role in brokering the IFP's entry into the elections, was largely complemented by the efforts of several other South African peace brokers who worked in trying to influence different constituencies. Archbishop Desmond Tutu and the Reverend Frank Chikane are the most notable local actors who were involved in brokering the IFP's entry into the elections. In this way, the peace process was truly owned by all parties and, more importantly, by South Africans in general, and as such they had a vested interest in its maintenance.

Identifying All the Actors

Rupesinghe stresses the importance of identifying all actors (big and small) and bringing them to the negotiating table. Failure to do this could result in the alienation of key stakeholders and role-players from the peace process.

In the case of the Bicesse Accords in Angola little effort was expended on bringing the factions comprising the Front for the Liberation of the Cabinda Enclave (FLEC) to the negotiating table. Little wonder that they issued a statement on July 31, 1992, saying they would boycott the elections and carry on an armed struggle until independence for Cabinda was won. This was to prove disastrous for the Angolan state and for postconflict reconstruction since FLEC was operating in oil-rich Cabinda, on whose revenues Luanda was almost completely dependent.

In the case of South Africa, the emphasis was on an all-inclusive process of twenty-six parties including large and powerful ones such as the ANC, NP, and IFP, as well as comparatively smaller and weaker ones such as the homeland governments of QwaQwa and Gazankulu. From the start the main political actors realized that an inclusive process meant that the outcome of the negotiations would be more credible among South Africans generally and that such an inclusive process also increases the number of stakeholders who would then serve to sustain that agreement.

Identifying Facilitators

Rupesinghe notes that it is crucial to identify in the design of a peace process appropriate facilitators "who have the background knowledge, analytic and mediation skills to make a positive contribution to the design process" (1995, 81).

In the case of Angola, because the peace was imposed and the architects were outside sponsors, facilitators came from these sponsoring countries and these, too, were imposed upon the belligerents. There were no internal facilitators on whom the parties could agree. This once again underlined the fact that the Bicesse Accords was not owned by Angolans themselves.

In the case of South Africa, the situation was reversed. South Africa has a large and experienced pool of facilitators such as Archbishop Desmond Tutu who greatly contributed to the peace process. Moreover inside the political parties there were a large and vocal propeace lobby whose proponents were well schooled in the art of facilitation and negotiation.

These skilled negotiators and facilitators were present at both the regional and national levels. An example is the region of KwaZulu-Natal, which was the scene of the highest levels of violence immediately preceding and during the negotiations. In this case the IFP's Frank Mdlalose and the ANC's Jacob Zuma, both skilled mediators, played an important role in brokering local peace efforts.

At the national level the main protagonists to the conflict, the NP and the ANC, both had skilled negotiators who had formal training and vast experiences in the art of negotiations. The ANC team was led by Cyril Ramaphosa, a trade union leader who honed his negotiation skills over years of negotiations in the labor-management arena. The NP negotiation team was led by Roelf Meyer, a seasoned negotiator who had received formal negotiation training and who honed his skills in government over several years. This meant that there was the necessary resources, skills, and goodwill in South Africa to facilitate the resolution of the conflict and to sustain such a peace effort even after agreement was reached.

Setting a Realistic Timetable

Rupesinghe emphasizes the importance of setting a realistic timetable, from the identification of root causes and significant actors, through such phases as cease-fires, to the elaboration of mechanisms of political and social accommodation, for the success of the peace process. A timetable that attempts to do too much over a short period of time may result in most tasks not being done or being done very badly (such as demobilization of former combatants). This could then serve to undermine the credibility of the entire peace process. On the other hand, a timetable that results in protracted peace negotiations over a considerable period of time may result in the momentum for peace being lost. Both options are equally dangerous.

In the Angolan case, the Bicesse Accords called for the formation of a national army, the establishment of government administrations all over Angola, and the institution of a multiparty system. Elections were to be held between September and November 1992 and these were to be prepared for. A Joint Political-Military Commission (JPMC) was to be established and charged with overall responsibility for the peace process, including the cease-fire. The UN Angola Verification Mission II (UNAVEM II), under the direction of the JPMC, was responsible for policing the transition. In addition, the accords committed UNITA and the MPLA to demobilization; and UNITA was to convert to a political party, presenting its candidates in national presidential and legislative elections. Clearly, it was impossible to accomplish all these tasks within fifteen months, but this was precisely what the accords bound them to do.

In the South African scenario, flexibility in one's negotiating posture and flexibility around time-scales were the watchwords to ensure an all-inclusive process. Consider the following. On January 8, 1994, the IFP threatened to boycott the elections. At this stage, the IFP had until January 24, 1994 (until the special parliamentary session), to find a compromise and become involved in the elections. On March 5, 1994, way after this deadline, the IFP announced it would consider registering, pending international mediation. On March 7, 1994, the South African government announced it was prepared to extend the election registration date and on April 25 (two days before the election), the South African Parliament sat to effect amendments to the constitution to enable the IFP to participate in the elections.

The important lesson to be learned from the South African scenario is that the government displayed no flexibility regarding the election date of April 27, 1994, thereby preventing protracted negotiations resulting in the loss of a peace momentum. At the same time, the government displayed considerable flexibility to ensure that the all-inclusive character of the negotiations was maintained and that root causes were being addressed in the process (the role of the Zulu king, the power of provinces). In this way a realistic timetable was maintained.

Sustaining the Effort

According to Rupesinghe (1995, 82), a "comprehensive approach to peace requires an adequate investment of financial resources, patience and a sustained commitment from sponsors."

In the Angolan case, clearly this commitment on the part of the sponsors was lacking. For example, the international community erred by underresourcing the peacekeeping operation with a mere 400 observers. This translated into one observer for every 333 soldiers, whereas in Namibia there was one observer for every six soldiers. Part of the reason for this could be that the international community's attention was deflected elsewhere to Iraq and the Middle East.

More specifically damaging was the ambivalent response on the part of international sponsors, especially the United States, to Savimbi's rejection of the results of the 1992 election, which was hailed as relatively free and fair by the United Nations, and which UNITA lost. An unambiguous condemnation of UNITA's actions may have resulted in their coming back into the process and the civil war that followed in the immediate post-1992 period may have been avoided. Instead, UNITA may have been encouraged by the ambivalence of the United States.

In the South African case, as was mentioned above, international sponsors played a minimal role and most of the effort to sustain the process (even after Inkatha participated in the 1994 elections) was left in the hands of the parties themselves. This they successfully accomplished since inclusion was stressed even after the 1994 period. Consider in this regard the May 27, 1996 high-level meeting between the ANC and the IFP that resulted in a closer working relationship and recognition of the IFP as a liberation movement. In addition, at this meeting it was acknowledged that there were no major ideological differences between the ANC and IFP.

One of the reasons to bring the IFP and ANC closer together was the nature of the South African constitutional engineering process and the final constitution itself. The process itself sought consensus as opposed to majority domination. This influenced the manner in which both the ANC and the IFP have been conducting their politics. There was a major shift away from confrontation to cooperation, thus reducing tensions. Both parties made concessions regarding policy issues and, as such, the IFP dropped the demand regarding international mediation.

This thawing of relations can be seen in several ways. When the National Party chose to leave the post-election Government of National Unity, the IFP chose to stay in it with IFP leader, Chief Mangosuthu Buthelezi, continuing to be minister of Home Affairs and, on various occasions, in the absence of President Mandela, he wore the mantle of acting-president of South Africa. At the time of writing there is much speculation regarding the integration of the IFP into the ANC with Buthelezi being offered the deputy presidency of the country under President Thabo Mbeki since Nelson Mandela has decided to step down.

Evaluating Success and Failure

Rupesinghe (1995, 82) notes that a crucial element "of any peacekeeping design should be a process of evaluation which indicates whether the main interests of the parties are being addressed, the precedents and principles used in searching for a solution (and whether they were useful), the obstacles encountered and factor which led to progress, alternatives and missed opportunities, co-ordination with other peacemaking activities, and what could be learned from the process."

In the Angolan case, such a built-in system evaluating success and failure was not designed into the process. If it was, perhaps the parties and international sponsors would have asked why, throughout the negotiations leading up to the Bicesse Accords, fighting on the ground continued. Part of the problem could also have been an unrealistic timetable (as explained above) that made no provision to evaluate whether each of the requirements of each phase were being met. Another problem that may have hindered an evaluation of success and failure is that the root causes were not properly spelled out. As such, it would be difficult to assess whether issues of divergence were being addressed or not.

In the South African case, this clearly was not the case as problem issues were clearly put on the agenda, thus progress toward a resolution of the conflict could be assessed in terms of whether these root causes were being addressed. In the case of the IFP the demands included the future role of the Zulu king in any constitutional dispensation as well as the devolution of power between the central and provincial governments. Having put this on the agenda, the parties could now look at ways to resolve these problems and it was on this basis that success or failure could be evaluated.

On January 18, 1994, following talks between the government and King Goodwill Zwelithini, President De Klerk informed the king that adequate provision was to be made for the entrenchment of the Zulu monarchy in the envisaged KwaZulu-Natal constitution. Moreover, on the following day a meeting was convened among the government, the ANC, and the Freedom Alliance, of which the IFP was a part. The focus of this meeting was on the powers and functions of provinces; provincial constitutions; safeguards for provincial status; self-determination, and the two-ballot issue. On February 6, 1994, the ANC threw its weight behind a demand to have the Zulu King enshrined as a constitutional monarch over the entire province of KwaZulu-Natal.

To once more underline the central thrust of this argument: knowing what the points of divergence are forms the basis for the successful resolution of the conflict and, hence, this is the first step in the evaluation of success or failure of the peace process.

Strategic Constituencies

Rupesinghe also identifies the need for strategic constituencies to sustain peace processes. According to Rupesinghe (1995, 82), these include "relevant nongovernmental organizations, the media, human rights and humanitarian institutions, peace institutions, religious institutions, independent scholars, fomer members of the military, members of the business community, intergovernmental and government officials and donors. To maximize their impact, various constituencies would form strategic alliances focused on particular conflicts, aspects of violent conflict or the overall goal of prevention."

In the Angolan case no such peace constituency existed, with civil society being relatively underdeveloped. Consequently, there was not a sufficient domestic propeace lobby to sustain the process before and after the signing of the Bicesse Accords.

In the South African situation, things were dramatically different. South Africa has a strong and vibrant civil society nurtured by their opposition to apartheid. This proved in many instances a deciding force during negotiations when faced with recalcitrant parties playing the role of spoiler.

Throughout the period of the negotiations leading to the April 27 elections, public opinion in favour of the elections was voiced through the media, mass marches throughout the country, and mass religious and political rallies. The South African Chamber of Business also strongly came out in support of the elections. NGOs such as the Institute for Multiparty Democracy (IMPD) also played a role in getting the IFP to participate in the elections. On March 31, 1994, at a time when the IFP leadership was still ambivalent regarding their position, the IMPD released the results of its survey that indicated most people, including the majority of IFP supporters, would vote in the election. From the perspective of the IFP, what gave this survey greater credibility was the fact that the director of the IMPD was a former secretary-general of the IFP.

Public opinion was, perhaps, most dramatically displayed in the case of the Boputhatswana homeland government, which on March 7, 1994, announced that it would not to participate in the April elections. Mass popular uprisings occurred, which resulted in the toppling of the Mangope regime on March 11, 1994. Public opinion so overwhelmingly in favour of the elections was possibly one of the factors that pushed the IFP to participate in the elections for fear of following the route of the Mangope regime.

The Role of Outside Peacemakers

Rupesinghe (1995, 84) notes that traditional "diplomacy and outside nongovernmental peacemakers have important roles to play in mediating the mitigation or resolution of violent internal conflict." This was clearly borne out in the recent Norwegian intervention on the Israeli-Palestinian question, which resulted in the Oslo Peace Accords.

On the other hand, the role of outside peacekeepers can adversely affect negotiations as was the Angolan experience. As was illustrated above, outside sponsors did not commit sufficient resources to sustain the peace effort. In addition, they misunderstood conditions on the ground and drew up an unrealistic timetable.

Moreover, the Angolan peace process raises interesting questions regarding the motivations and interests of third parties who seek to mediate. Consider in this regard the short-lived Gbadolite Peace Accords. Seizing the opportunity presented by the 1988 New York Accords, President Mobutu Sese Seko convened this initiative six months later. But this initiative was as much about Angolan peace as it was about bolstering Mobutu's international image. President Mobutu's manipulation of the parties, by feeding them with false information as to what each had agreed to with him in private, led to no agreement being secured. To the contrary, it led to the hardening of attitudes.

In the South African case, as was mentioned above, the role of outside peacekeepers was minimal. A strong case could be made to argue that even the role of Professor Washington Okumu was one of facilitation, selling the basis of compromise already largely reached between the parties. The South African experience, once more, underlines the need for ownership of the peace process to reside with local actors.

It is important to note, however, that Professor Washington Okumu's success in facilitating dialogue derived from his twenty-odd year relationship with Chief Buthelezi and the enormous trust that existed between them. It could be argued that this factor was a crucial link in the chain of peace that was used to secure the peace process.

The Role of Local Peacekeepers

Rupesinghe (1995, 85) emphasizes the role of local peacemakers who are influential "members of local communities with a first hand knowledge of conflict, actors, the political and economic situation and the cultural background will have a distinct 'comparative advantage' over other potential peacemakers wishing to act as third-party mediators." The role of these local peacekeepers take on added importance if one considers the erratic and ambivalent role played by outside peacekeepers, as was displayed in the Angolan case. More disconcerting though is the fact that in the Angolan case there were no local peacekeepers, which meant that parties were increasingly dependent on the attention of outside sponsors. In 1991 the Angolan crisis was dominated by the Persian Gulf crisis. It can be argued that had local actors been given the resources to mediate in the Angolan conflict their closeness to the conflict and deeper understanding of the nuances may have brought a sharper appreciation of what was possible within a realistic framework and a more sustained presence that may have yielded a different result.

As was previously mentioned, South Africa had such local expertise and these were utilized. Thus, Archbishop Desmond Tutu chaired the meeting between Nelson Mandela and Mangosuthu Buthelezi. The archbishop understood each individual very intimately since he had a personal relationship with each of them, he was familiar with the cultural nuances of African culture and tradition, and was acutely aware of the political and economic dimensions of the South African milieu.

Conclusion

Utilizing the theoretical framework as espoused by Dr. Kumar Rupesinghe, it is abundantly clear why the Bicesse Accords failed whereas intervention to avert the crisis was much more successful in South Africa. One crucial aspect, lacking in the above analysis however, was the role played by culture.

Angola's political history, unlike South Africa's, is mainly militant. The militant political culture developed through history as a response to Portuguese colonialism, which was extremely brutal and left behind a strong legacy of underdevelopment and poverty. Since the thirteenth century, indigenous Angolans have resisted colonialism for decades before finally succumbing to the Portuguese onslaught with the support of Boer settlers. The post–World War II period witnessed a significant rise in Portuguese brutality as well as the rise of nationalism. Angolan nationalism was met with hostility, suppression and brutality. The frustration and lack of legitimate ways of channeling grievances led to the formation of armed liberation movements. Independence from colonial rule, as was mentioned above, did not bring about peace; rather conflict escalated between UNITA and the MPLA. For the next two decades, Angolan society became highly militarized, battle-hardened and violently socialized. Under these conditions, civilian culture and civil society could not develop independently from the state. The war peaked in 1988 with far-reaching effects that paralyzed the infrastructure, caused hundreds of thousands of casualties, and displaced many more Angolans.

Unlike South Africa, warring factions in Angola sought control of the state. The state machinery is a symbol of power and wealth. Angola is well endowed with natural resources that could turn around the economy within a short period of time. The presence of oil in Angola further complicated the dimensions of the war. Oil, alone, can pay for Angola's development in the same way gold paid for industrialization in South Africa. In this way, the Angolan conflict could not be viewed against the same background as South Africa.

Furthermore, South Africa's conflict was low intensity and interest-based as opposed to Angola's one that is resource-based. The political differences between the IFP and the ANC were over strategies to bring down apartheid while in Angola it was for the control of the state and its resources. It was therefore much easier to contain the IFP as it had very little stake nationally that could have otherwise complicated the transition process. The IFP never sought national leadership, but rather intended to retain its traditional support at KZN province. An understanding of these dynamics formed the basis of compromises and concessions reached.

Unlike South Africa, the Angolan conflict involved powerful actors who had independent power bases, and each faction was backed by a superpower. The MPLA had access to oil and other resources while UNITA controlled large areas suitable for agriculture and rich in gold and diamonds. Some analysts estimate that UNITA accrues more than U.S. $500,000 from the illegal diamond trade. This is a budget that sustains smaller economies like Zambia. This also meant that both UNITA and the Angolan government had sufficient resources at their disposal to purchase sophisticated weapons. Under these same circumstances, it is highly unlikely that either side could have conceded defeat. These conditions also militate against minimax strategies and encourage parties to play zero-sum games.

What the above demonstrates is that over and above a thorough understanding of the technical aspects of the peace process, third parties seeking to resolve a conflict also need to understand the broader context in which such intervention takes place. This context or background includes both an understanding of political culture as well as an assessment of the nature of vested interests and how that impacts on the broader conflict.

This chapter began with an overview of conflict in Africa. Perhaps it would be ideal to conclude on a more optimistic note. In recent months, South African Deputy

President Thabo Mbeki has popularized the term of an "African Renaissance" to describe the resurgence of the continent. One aspect of this Renaissance is Africans accepting more responsibility for their own actions. This has been eloquently expressed by OAU Secretary-General Dr. Salim Ahmed Salim:

> OAU Member States can no longer afford to stand aloof and expect the International Community to care more for our problems than we do, or indeed to find solutions to those problems which in many instances, have been of our own making. The simple truth that we must confront today, is that the world does not owe us a living and we must remain in the forefront of efforts to act and act speedily to prevent conflict from getting out of control. (1997:4)

Note

1. This chapter was written in 1999.

8
Nonconventional Diplomacy
Experiences of NGOs and People's Participation in Selected Peace Processes

Sanam Naraghi Anderlini, Ed Garcia, and Kumar Rupesinghe

In recent years nongovernmental organizations and institutions, civic movements, and individuals have increasingly engaged in peacemaking and conflict transformation efforts in situations of violent intrastate conflict. Drawing on concrete particular experiences in Mozambique, Sierra Leone, and the Philippines during specific phases of each conflict, this chapter will explore the conditions that offer nongovernmental and citizen groups the opportunity to participate in peacemaking, and compare the strengths and limitations that such groups may have relative to their official counterparts. By breaking the peace process into three critical phases, it will examine the conditions necessary to enable NGO involvement, and the key areas and activities in which such groups can participate effectively. In doing so, it highlights the benefits of cooperation and complementarity when nonstate groups, governments and intergovernmental organizations come together to make and build sustainable peace.

Introductory Reflections

Intrastate conflicts arise out of a complex range of issues. Typically sociopolitical factors are tied together with economic issues and questions of identity. The actual triggers of violence and hostility may be difficult to determine, but there is little doubt that once violence does erupt, intrastate conflicts and civil wars can strike at the very core of society, rapidly reducing opportunities for moderation. As fear, mistrust, and violence spread, even the most close-knit communities can become polarized. Under such conditions normal political discourse becomes virtually impossible. Often the initial political dispute, fueled by the politics of intimidation and fear, degenerates into extreme positions with little room for compromise and hardly any space for the middle ground.

This intense polarization and, in effect, dehumanization of the "other" reduces opportunities for even basic dialogue between opposing sides. Those political leaders willing to engage in talks or compromise inevitably face recriminations from their own followers. Those who do step forward face increased risks of isolation within their own side, as there are always certain elements who continue to wage war and derail any progress that is made. Consequently, at the official level too, the spaces for dialogue and negotiation virtually disappear.

Political dialogue and negotiations alone are by no means the final solution to such conflicts. Rather they are the first step and a critical element that pave the way toward seeking a solution. In other words, sustainable peace comes when the core social, political, and economic factors that initially culminated in violence are reassessed and changes implemented. But without that initial communication between the conflicting parties, without a degree of trust and willingness to explore areas of common concern, or without an understanding of each other's priorities and fears, it is unlikely that any tangible change could be wrought. So creating that first opportunity for communication and sustaining the space for dialogues is a small but critical element of peacemaking.

Rigorous analyses of conflict situations demonstrate that even in the most difficult situations there are opportunities to initiate breakthroughs and communication that allow parties to begin considering negotiated solutions. Some of these opportunities may be advanced through nonconventional diplomacy by nongovernmental and citizen groups. These groups are generally recognized by all sides as having some moral influence. They also have the possibility of working in discreet and nonthreatening ways.

Such efforts may be undertaken, for example, by religious leaders or communities, who often have the capacity to network across regions, and the moral authority to convene significant sectors of society. Organizations emerging from the humanitarian aid, development, and human rights community can also become involved. They often have programs and partners in conflict areas, and the networks and resources needed to address the international arena as well. They can encourage and accompany the work of grassroots groups and organizations from within the regions of conflict. Finally, local groups can become involved. They have in-depth knowledge about the issues and conditions surrounding the conflict. Often they have direct access to the perpetrators of violence and the political leadership. Finally, they have a direct stake in the outcome of such conflicts, as their quest for peace is closely linked to their people's struggle for survival.

The Rationale for Choosing Our Case Studies

This study on nonconventional diplomacy explores selected experiences of the participation of NGOs and people in working to bring about peace in different political contexts and under diverse conditions. We first examine the mediating work of the Rome-based Catholic lay organization Sant Egidio in Mozambique, which resulted in the signing and implementation of a general peace agreement. The second case study is that of the contributions of an NGO (International Alert) in the peace efforts in Sierra Leone, West Africa, which resulted in a short-lived peace accord that was rolled back by a series of military actions. The third case study is the mobilization for peace by citizens' groups in the Philippines that has, so far, resulted in the articulation of a peace agenda and initiatives taken by people. To date, although only a part of a peace agreement has been formally ratified by the parties to the conflict, nevertheless peace efforts have resulted in significant advances in building consensus and strong foundations for the future.

The armed conflict in Mozambique between the forces of Frelimo (the government) and Renamo (the rebels) raged for more than a decade before the conditions made it possible for Sant Egidio to attempt to build on previously failed peacemaking initiatives. Sant Egidio itself had done extensive preparatory work, but it was not working alone. During a significant period of time in Mozambique it relied on partners in the country and in Europe. As a lay Catholic institution, the group already had extensive contacts across the country through the Catholic Church, and was itself a direct provider of humanitarian aid to all sides. The move toward initiating dialogue and communications between the two sides came in 1989, at a time when the international geopolitical climate and the thawing of the Cold War favored an end to the conflict. Within Mozambique, the two sides had reached a "hurting" stalemate (Zartman, 1995, 3–17). There was widespread war fatigue among the population, and elements on each side of the political divide, calling for an end to the devastating war. Nationally and internationally, the conditions were favorable for a negotiated settlement. Moreover, Sant Egidio received substantial moral and financial support from the Vatican and the Italian government as well as appropriate assistance from other governments and institutions. They had legitimacy in the eyes of both parties in Mozambique, and they were fully respected by the international community, including the United Nations.

Sierra Leone presented a different political climate altogether. The five-year war caused immense destruction resulting in the displacement of nearly half the population. The violations of rights and atrocious behavior on the part of the combatants on both sides had resulted in the general condemnation of the war. Moreover, war fatigue had set in. Internationally, the Sierra Leone military government, represented by the National Provisional Ruling Council (NPRC), and the Revolutionary United Front of Sierra Leone (RUF/SL) were put under severe pressure to end hostilities in a country that had become among the poorest in the world. But there was no space for negotiations. To draw attention to their cause, the RUF/SL had taken foreigners and nationals hostage in 1994, and because of this the NPRC and the international community had refused to even consider negotiations. After discussions with the NPRC and the intergovernmental organizations, International Alert (IA) initiated radio contact with the RUF/SL. With assistance from the International Committee of the Red Cross (ICRC), the hostages were finally released, and the path was opened for "talks about talks" in 1995. By early 1996, the Ivory Coast government was hosting formal talks between the two sides. The principal mediator was the foreign minister of the Ivory Coast, but the facilitators included the United Nations, the Commonwealth Secretariat (CS), the Organization for Africa Unity (OAU), and IA. The talks progressed and stalled momentarily, until a first short-lived peace accord was signed in November 1996 in Abidjan. As the only NGO involved, IA experienced certain difficulties that could have been overcome by more effective burden sharing (as in the case of Mozambique). So this case study reveals not only the particular opportunities that NGOs may have, and the critical roles they could play, but also the limitations and obstacles they may encounter.

The peace process in the Philippines involving the government and the National Democratic Front offers a valuable case study on the role of people's participation in advancing efforts for peace in situations where the parties to the conflict hesitate to be directly involved in formal political negotiations. In the Philippines, formal talks had broken down after the promise of the people's power revolution in 1986 had been held in check by successive military coup attempts. Thus, it took nearly a decade of work before the on-and-off talks resulted in some preliminary agreements. During the negotiations, there were no external mediators or facilitators, and there were no significant advances on the formal diplomatic front. But nonconventional diplomacy and parallel efforts by citizens' groups and NGOs did create opportunities for peace. Religious groups and academia joined with NGOs and people's organizations (e.g., labour unions and community groups) to launch the National Peace Conference, to which other sectors of society were invited to articulate a peace agenda. Efforts to encourage dialogue were initiated by a gathering of multisectoral peace advocates and supportive institutions. Conditions were such that the main thrust of the peace process could be characterized as consensus-building supported by consultation processes undertaken by the citizen groups with diverse sectors of society on key issues such as human rights and humanitarian law, economic and political reforms, issues that subsequently fed into the official negotiations process. Unlike Mozambique and Sierra Leone, for most of the time between 1986 and 1996, the substantial efforts for peace took place not around the formal negotiating table but around the informal spaces for peace created by a spectrum of citizen-based groups.

Through examining these different case studies, this chapter hopes to give a better understanding of the contributions and limitations of nonconventional diplomacy in the making and building of peace. We will examine the importance of cooperation with other significant players, the conditions that provide a more favourable environment for the participation of NGOs and citizen groups, and the phases or stages in which their contributions can be most or least effective.

Understanding Peace Processes

It is helpful to recognize that peace processes, like conflicts, go through different stages or phases. Existing research in this field provides insights into the life cycles of conflicts. In one study on violent conflicts, for example (Lund 1996), the life history of a conflict is analyzed as: war (varying from low-intensity to all-out war), crisis (involving levels of actual or potential political violence), unstable peace (including tensions but where violence is either absent or sporadic), and stable peace (where disputes are generally settled in nonviolent ways), as well as durable peace (where "positive peace" prevails). Another study (Rupesinghe 1994) identifies five broad phases in the lifecycles of protracted conflict situations: conflict formation, conflict escalation, conflict endurance, conflict reduction, and transformation—categories employed to define the various stages when disputes between conflict parties arise, develop, and either stagnate or are transformed into situations where nonviolent ways of settling differences become possible.

These phases are not necessarily linear at all times nor are they irreversible. Protracted conflicts can last for decades. There can be stagnation, periods of intensity and calm, or reversals at each phase. But the life-cycle model does provide a framework for greater conceptual clarity.

Peace processes similarly cover a wide spectrum. Peace negotiations, the best-known stage in a process of peace, represent but one moment. Though essential, they nevertheless do not exhaust all the possibilities of actions or initiatives that such a process may require. For negotiations to take place, prenegotiations are necessary, be they formal or informal. For a political settlement to succeed, implementation of the provisions of an accord in the postnegotiation period is vital. In other words, it could be said that peace processes have three broad phases; preparation, transformation, and consolidation (see figure 8.1).

Within each phase there may be a number of shorter stages and steps. In the process of peacemaking, just as in conflicts, there can be reversals and stagnation. Finally, it is important to recognize that by definition peace processes are ongoing and multifaceted efforts, not one-off initiatives.

Figure 8.1: Phases of a Peace Process

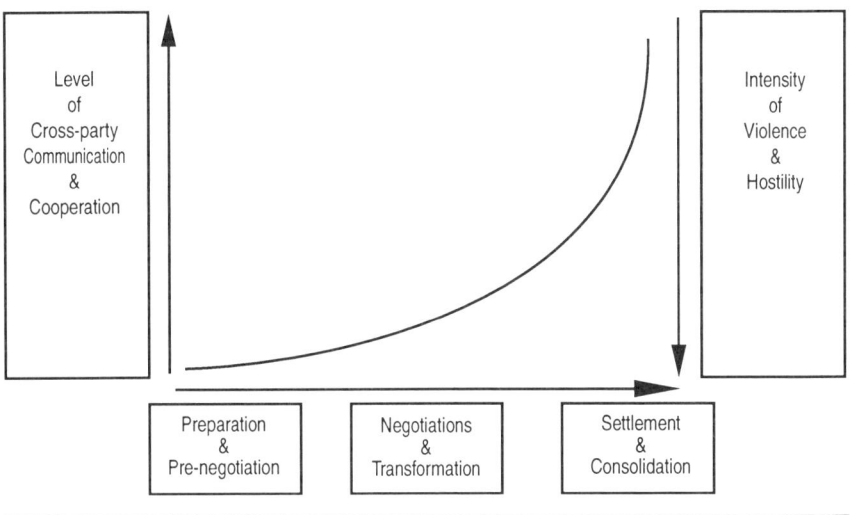

NGO Contributions to Peace Processes

Preparations and Prenegotiations

Generally, the "preparation" or prenegotiations phase takes place while the violent conflict is either ongoing or a stalemate has been reached. It is normally a time when parties are extremely polarized and the space for official dialogue is either limited or nonexistent. However, the absence of talks does not imply the lack of a willingness to talk. It is here that NGOs can generally play a role and contribute to the initiation of peace processes. As independent and impartial entities they are able to maintain a low profile and work discreetly and patiently to encourage a space for dialogue between low profile representatives from each side. They can sound out the concerns and grievances of either side, and can seek out common issues as well as clarify their real differences.

Through these efforts they can gradually help to build a degree of trust and personal relations with and between adversarial groups. By initiating the "talks before talks" process, they can help generate a mutually acceptable agenda of issues to be dealt with at the official level. In this way, when official talks begin, the ground may be set for a degree of consensus and understanding on all sides. Moreover they can help avoid surprises or hidden concerns that could otherwise derail official talks. In effect, through time and patient facilitation, nonstate groups can help to set the stage for, and generate mutual willingness to enter into, official negotiations.

Negotiations and Transformation

If and when official talks begin, NGOs can play an immensely useful role as facilitators supporting the mediation processes and contributing toward demystifying the conflict by breaking it down into separate stages or components. They can provide technical and material support through the provision of information and examples relating to other peace processes and the resolution of similar situations. They can help identify and explore new approaches to conflict and peace issues. In addition, NGOs can assist and offer training in conflict resolution, negotiations, and problem-solving skills. Through seminars and role-playing sessions they can help adversaries to appreciate each others' perspectives, so that there is better understanding, trust, and capacity to address the conflict nonviolently. Through advocacy and lobbying of international organizations and outside governments, they can help raise the profile of a given conflict and draw attention to the critical issues. Moreover, by expanding the process of consultations to community groups and civil society, NGOs can also ensure that the official peace process takes into account the needs and concerns of the grassroots communities. As official talks get under way, international and national NGOs can play a critical supplementary role in generating and sustaining peace processes.

Settlement and Consolidation

In many ways, getting the signatures on a peace agreement is just the beginning. A new set of problems may arise once the signatures are in place, as oftentimes in the course of negotiations difficult compromises have been made that are not acceptable to all sides. As the middle ground unites, the suspicions and fears at the extremes create fragmentation. Break-away factions emerge willing to unleash violence to derail the peace process once more. This is a fragile point in the peace process; on the one hand, the hardships wrought by war are still a fact of daily life, while, on the other hand, people are being asked to lend a helping hand to advance the process. The leadership on all sides is also put to the test. On the one hand they have to rely on the goodwill and trust of the people, but on the other hand, they still have to strengthen that trust and ensure that they keep the promises that were made during the negotiations period.

For combatants, it is an equally difficult time. The prevalence of arms in the conflict zone and the presence of landmines in some areas may present problems. If resettlement is not properly planned, demobilized fighters face hardships in cities and the countryside, often desperate for food and shelter. In cases such as Mozambique, the fighters had few other skills to rely on. The end of war was equated with a hard struggle for survival. The temptation to return to fighting, to join up with other factions, or to use their weapons (against civilians) to get food and shelter can be great.

Under such arduous circumstances, NGOs have found a role to play. They are often well-placed to identify and recognize potential indicators for the emergence or resurgence of actual violence. They can be effective in helping to monitor cease-fires, human rights violations, political repression, social and economic trends, and have greater flexibility and fewer constraints than state-based organizations to raise warnings and alerts regarding the resurgence of violence. Moreover, they can make substantial contributions toward the reconstruction and reconciliation of society helping to address concrete issues relating to social, economic, and political change (see also Carnegie Commission on Preventing Deadly Conflict 1997).

Sharing the Burden

However, although nonstate groups can contribute enormously toward generating peace and complementing peace processes, they rarely have the political or financial clout required to ensure compliance with agreements, to hold parties accountable for their actions, or to provide incentives or enforce leverage when necessary. Nonconventional diplomacy, therefore, is best exercised within the context of a multitrack process where there is burden-sharing and a division of labor. In other words, the official efforts of state-based actors and intergovernmental diplomacy need to be supplemented with the contributions of nonstate actors or organizations to ensure a comprehensive approach.

This sharing of responsibilities can be simultaneous—so that there is parallel activity at different levels, or on different issues, or it can be consecutive—so that different actors take on specific tasks at various times during the peacemaking process. In this way, the strengths and expertise that each players brings to peacemaking or peacebuilding can support the actual or potential efforts of all the others.[1]

Peace Process Experiences: Sant Egidio in Mozambique, 1977–1992

The three cases studies in the central parts of this chapter help to illustrate the points raised previously. The time frames covered vary in each case, but the focus is on the phases during which peacemaking attempts were initiated. Our first focuses on the chance for peace associated with Sant Egidio's role in Mozambique, 1977–1992.[2]

As the Mozambican civil war entered its thirteenth year in 1990, the Rome-based Catholic lay institute of Sant Egidio hosted a series of low-profile talks between members of the opposing sides. These talks lasted two years and helped lay the foundations the General Peace Agreement (GPA) that was finally signed between the government of President Joaquim Chissano and the rebel movement, Renamo, in Rome on October 4, 1992.

From the outset, Sant Egidio's efforts were supported by the Vatican, the Italian government, and later by the United Nations, the U.S. government, a number of European and Southern African governments, and the British businessman Tiny Rowland.[3] Furthermore, the final peace agreement was the cumulative result of the Sant Egidio talks and a series of regional African initiatives that were taking place concurrently. However, by virtue of its work and connections within Mozambique, Sant Egidio seized on an opportunity to initiate dialogue between the two sides at a time when other efforts seemed to have failed. The case study below provides a background to the Mozambique civil war, and a chronological analysis of Sant Egidio's involvement and the key events that led to the peace agreement of 1992.

Background

European colonialism in Mozambique dates back to the fifteenth century. The Portuguese arrived there in 1498 and for the next 400 years settlers and traders flocked to the coastal regions. Gold and ivory were the early attractions but as the slave trade flourished in the ninteenth century, Mozambique became a main exporter of humanity. Until the 1880s the settlers had little to do with the indigenous populations living in the north, central, and southern regions. But the 1885 Berlin Conference established the rules for a final European scramble for land in Africa. Portugal was given the rights to the inland areas of Mozambique and Angola. Lacking the necessary resources to make its claim, however, Portugal turned to Britain for support. The British, wary of German expansion in the region and concerned about the status of their own colony Southern Rhodesia, willingly aided the Portuguese.

The British-Portuguese cooperation lasted into the twentieth century, with the British establishing themselves as the regional economic power, developing ports and transport links to the coastline of Mozambique, and the Portuguese sending a steady supply of unskilled Mozambicans to work in the mines of South Africa.

The situation altered after 1932 when the fascist Salazar regime took power in Portugal. The new government was keen to assert its own control in the colony. Lisbon-based companies were encouraged to develop trade in the colony and thousands of semiskilled workers began to emigrate. Over the next forty years, in an effort to avoid land reforms in Portugal itself, the fascist government virtually "dumped" thousands of landless peasants in Mozambique. The number of emigres rose to 250,000, but the nature of Portuguese rule did not change. In the hinterland the authorities cooperated with the traditional tribal leaders, while on the coast the emigres dominated every aspect of society. The indigenous population was kept illiterate and unskilled and nothing was done to prepare Mozambique for eventual independence.

In 1960 the UN General Assembly recognized the need to dismantle the colonial yoke in resolution 1514 (XV), but Portugal refused to adopt the resolution. By 1962, however, the Frente da Libertacao de Mocambique (Frelimo) had been launched. It was the first independence movement in more than 400 years. Yet Frelimo found the Portuguese unwilling to negotiate, and thus by 1964 the call for independence turned into a military struggle. The fight for independence lasted eleven years, until 1975, when the fascist government was toppled in Portugal and Mozambique was granted independence by the incoming government.

But all was not well. The affluent educated and skilled Portuguese fled the country, destroying their property in their wake and leaving behind an unskilled and illiterate population. Mozambicans lacked even the most basic skills needed to run the economy.

In an effort to ensure production, Frelimo opted to nationalize the social services, land, and rented properties. Where businesses had been abandoned, Frelimo established a state-run intervention system appointing administrators to each business. But where owners had stayed, they were left in peace to run their businesses. Despite the difficulties, there was a sense of optimism in the country and Frelimo had widespread support.

Throughout the late 1970s, Mozambique embarked on a program of modernization coupled with socialism, and by 1977 Frelimo had declared itself a Marxist-Leninist party and Mozambique a one-party state. People who were not members of Frelimo did not suffer direct prejudice, but certainly had limited opportunities to advance toward local or national significance. Yet as 1980 approached, the majority consensus was favorable to the government, and with the economy improving, Mozambique was optimistic about the advent of a new decade.

The Sequence of Conflict Phases

The Dispute Phase (1977–1980)

However, despite its domestic popularity Frelimo's ascent to power in 1975 was not entirely unopposed. There were a number of smaller movements vying for power in the country, but none had Frelimo's widespread and organized urban and rural support. On a regional level, there was a strong degree of opposition from the white minority government of Southern Rhodesia, and the apartheid regime in South Africa. As an ardent supporter of Robert Mugabe's Zimbabwean African National Union (ZANU) and the African National Congress (ANC) of South Africa, Frelimo placed itself in the front line of attack from its two neighbors. One of its first acts in power was to close the borders to Southern Rhodesia, preventing them access to transport and trade routes.

Seen as an symbol of direct hostility, the Rhodesians took to sponsoring a small group of antigovernment protesters, initially dominated by disgruntled Portuguese who had fled Mozambique. By 1977 there was a steady flow of Mozambicans joining the rebel group, mainly coming from the Mozambican Diaspora and mining communities of South Africa. Andre Matsangaissa, an ex-Frelimo army commander sent to correction camp on account of thieving, was among the early recruits. He escaped the camp to join the rebel movement and was soon nominated as leader. By mid-1977 the movement that had operated under a series of different acronyms chose Resistencia Nacional Mocambicana, or Renamo for short.

Until 1980 Renamo was in effect a subdivision of the Rhodesian security forces, but fighting Frelimo. Matsangaissa's death during a raid led to internal conflict and ruptures among Renamo's leadership. Afonso Dhlakama eventually took the lead, but with the 1980 the Lancaster House Agreement that led to the emergence of the new Zimbabwean state, Renamo was thrown into further turmoil. The movement was "on the road to destruction."[4]

But during that period South Africa was beginning to take notice of Renamo's presence. So instead of closing down Renamo's activities, the Rhodesians passed the reins on to their South African military counterparts. New training camps were set up in South Africa, and young Mozambican peasants, some through coercion and threats, others voluntarily, joined the movement. Once they had joined, they had little choice but to remain, for those caught trying to escape were executed immediately.

Frelimo's foreign relations were important. Concurrent with the regional developments, international events were also beginning to affect Mozambique. First, its vehement antiapartheid stance, and second, nonalignment. Aware of the pitfalls that foreign aid could bring to underdeveloped countries, at independence Mozambique chose not to join the IMF, the World Bank, and the Lomé Convention. But in a world carved up by Cold War rivalry, nonalignment and neutrality were not easily tolerated. This independent stance threatened the apartheid regime in South Africa, and proved unacceptable to the incoming Republican administration of U.S. President Ronald Reagan in 1980. The United States was not only vociferously hostile to the Marxist states of Angola and Mozambique, but also advocated "constructive engagement" with South Africa.

The South Africans, meanwhile, viewed the United States' willingness to engage in "constructive engagement," while maintaining an openly hostile line toward its neighboring states, as a signal for the intensification of attacks on Mozambique. South Africa's main objective was to maximize destabilization and inhibit development in the region. From 1981 they stepped up their commando attacks and raids into Mozambique, attacking both ANC members and Mozambicans. The U.S. government did nothing to discourage these actions. With increased resources and training, Renamo's presence throughout Mozambique increased. By 1981 up to 7,000 rebels were active, up from less than 1,000 during the Rhodesian-command days. Although Renamo's primary source of support was South Africa, the group maintained its independence and leadership.

Phase Two: Crisis and Limited Violence (1981–1984)

The conflict gathered momentum between 1981 and 1984, as the apartheid regime in South Africa mounted its destabilization policy in the continent's southern cone. Renamo's operations spread from the central provinces down into the southern regions of the country. Major transport and communications arteries were targeted and destroyed. Agricultural production was disrupted as fields were mined, properties destroyed, and peasants and rural populations driven into Maputo and other cities. Amid this violence, the entire southern African region was also hit by the worst drought of the century. Combined with a rise in oil prices, a world economic recession, and a sudden hike in interest rates, Mozambique's exports and the country's ability to cope with the consequences of the drought were effected severely.

Preliminary attempts at negotiations occurred. The sustained violence and devastating famine impelled the Mozambique government (still a one-party state under the control of Frelimo) to engage in negotiations. The first attempt to end hostilities came on March 16, 1984, when President Machel met Prime Minister "Pik" Botha of South Africa at the border town of N'Komati to sign the Agreement on Nonaggression and Good-Neighborliness. Mozambique was to close down the ANC military bases in its territory; in return, the South Africans were to halt their support of Renamo. South Africa reneged. With airlifts and transport routes through Malawi, it continued to supply Renamo with food, medication, and weapons, including large numbers of landmines.

The Mozambican government took a different approach by deciding to negotiate directly with Renamo. However, aware of the critical role that South Africa played in its support for Renamo, the Mozambique government insisted that the talks be facilitated and mediated by the South African government. South Africa eventually complied and the regime offered its "good offices" to bring about a negotiated solution to the conflict. Machel accepted, stating that his government would give amnesty and assist in the full reintegration of all Renamo members who surrendered voluntarily.

Three rounds of negotiations took place from May to October 1984. But the mediators were neither impartial, nor did they engage in thorough consultations with either side. An atmosphere of mistrust permeated the talks as statements were misinterpreted. Eventually failure was declared and both sides took on more extremist positions. Machel publicly stated that "Mozambique will not negotiate with kidnappers, bandits and criminals. Instead Mozambique will wipe them out, and that day is not far off" (Vines 1991, 4) On the other side, Renamo demanded the country's presidency for itself.

Phase Three: Intensification (1984–1988)

The failure of the talks led to further intensification of the conflict between 1985 and 1986. Neither President Machel's accidental death in 1986 nor the ascension of the more moderate Joaquim Chissano into the presidency had much effect. By 1987 Renamo had gained substantial ground across the country and was receiving indirect encouragement and backing from a number of conservative and right-wing governments in the West. The war was taking a heavy toll on the government, forcing President Chissano to modify many of Frelimo's original policies and positions vis-à-vis the international community.[5]

Meanwhile, Renamo's reputation as the "Khmer Rouge" of Africa had also spread. In 1988, following the publication of a U.S. State Department report, attitudes toward the movement shifted radically. The Gersony Report (named after its author, Robert Gersony) stated that Renamo used excessive violence against the civilian population, including "burying alive, beating to death, forced asphyxiation and drowning, and random shootings" (Hume 1994, 15). Despite backing from a number of right-wing organizations in the United States, Renamo's hopes of U.S. aid and assistance were eliminated. Moreover, its own ideological underpinnings and organizational structure were shown to be ambiguous and malformed. Domestic and regional pressure was also mounting on Renamo to enter into negotiations.

Prenegotiations (1988–1990)

Although the conflict escalated throughout the mid-1980s, there were already sectors of society, notably religious leaders, and other regional actors attempting to initiate a peace process. As early as 1984, the Mozambican Christian Council (MCC), which united seventeen of the country's Protestant churches, set up the Peace and Reconciliation Commission. They argued that "dialogue is the way forward in any dispute"—an approach that received official rebuff. During the same period, the country's Catholic Church, which already had an ambivalent relationship with the government (due to its historic ties with the Portuguese), publicly called for dialogue between the government and Renamo. But at the time President Machel refused.

By 1987, under the presidency of Chissano, the Catholic Church was finally permitted to openly recognize the parties to the conflict as well as the possibility of dialogue. Chissano also gave the MCC the go-ahead to conduct a dialogue with Renamo, along very carefully defined guidelines. Between 1987 and 1988, the MCC, joining forces with the Catholic Church, held a number of meetings with Renamo representatives in the United States and in Kenya. President Moi also took an interest in the negotiations. By November 1988, the church activities had become public. The Peace and Reconciliation Commission continued with their efforts, meeting Renamo officials and outlining their objectives. Though aware of Renamo's hostility toward the government, the commission became convinced of the group's fatigue and willingness to end the conflict.

In effect, some of the internal conditions necessary for initiating dialogue (war fatigue, stalemate) existed. Externally too, the regional and international political arena was changing. In South Africa, the domestic political situation was witnessing changes and a gradual shift away from the principles of apartheid. With antiapartheid sentiments rising, international tolerance (especially in the United States and United Kingdom) of apartheid had diminished substantially, and South Africa was under both external and internal pressure to change. Internationally, the fall of the Berlin Wall and collapse of Communism toward the end of 1989 and 1990 brought the advent of a new era of optimism and willingness to engage in ending the proxy wars of the Cold War years.

Negotiations started in August 1989 but quickly faltered as it became evident that the groundwork was still lacking. The government rejected Renamo's demands for recognition as an active political force in Mozambique, and Renamo back-tracked on its original acceptance of the existing political order in the country. These talks reached an impasse. However, the process made the Renamo leader, Afonso Dhlakhama, acutely aware that for Renamo to gain legitimacy in the eyes of the world, continued negotiations and the participation of the international community were essential.

In the same year, the British businessman Tiny Rowland and the U.S. government also became involved, pushing for direct government-Renamo talks, within a wider regional context. Rowland's multinational corporation, Lonrho, had major business interests in Mozambique and throughout the region. As the war continued and the destruction escalated, Lonrho's interests were badly affected. The company's expenditure on security forces was very high, and no amount of protection money to Renamo's leadership (an estimated $500,000 per month at one stage), was enough to guarantee the safety of its land or transported goods. In 1989, based on Rowland's advice and knowledge of the region, Lonrho's strategy changed. Tiny Rowland became personally involved in the quest for peace. Through high-level contacts with regional governments and Renamo, he arranged for direct meetings between Frelimo and Renamo representatives. Although both sides agreed to participate initially, Renamo's representatives never arrived at the designated meeting point in Malawi.

It was important that Sant Egidio had developed links with Mozambique. The Catholic lay community of Sant Egidio[6] traces its ties to Mozambique during the mid-1970s when a Mozambican priest, Don Jaime Goncalves (later to become the archbishop of Beira Province, Mozambique) forged close personal ties with many of the community's members while studying in Rome in 1976. After Goncalves returned home, Sant Egidio initiated the Committee of Friends of Mozambique in Italy and continued its links with the Catholic Church in Mozambique. The Vatican, with its strong ties to the Portuguese government of the colonial era, had strained relations with the government of the independent state, but through the continued mediation of Sant Egidio, representatives of the Mozambican government began informal meetings with Vatican officials by 1982.

As the armed conflict worsened during the 1980s, Sant Egidio began sending aid to the Beira diocese. As early as 1982, Sant Egidio made its first contact with Renamo, when negotiating the release of a number of hostage missionaries. Over the next few years, a relationship of mutual trust and understanding began to develop.[7] In parallel to their humanitarian assistance, the community also facilitated meetings between the pope and Presidents Machel and Chissano, with the real breakthrough coming when the pope agreed to visit Mozambique in September 1988.

Advancing the opportunities for peace was possible. By 1990 Sant Egidio had developed strong ties within the Mozambican government and the church groups around the country, as well as with Renamo. It was regarded as a trusted and impartial intermediary in the conflict. Moreover, given its role as a principal provider of humanitarian aid to all regions, the group had legitimacy and leverage in the eyes of both sides. In Italy, the government and the Vatican agreed to support Sant Egidio's peacemaking efforts. Thus, its offer to facilitate high level talks between representatives of the Mozambican government and those of Renamo at the community's discreet compound in Rome was eventually accepted. Dhlakama arrived in Rome in February 1990.

Negotiations

The first direct meetings between Renamo and Mozambican government officials finally took place at Sant Egidio's headquarters in July 1990.[8] But it was an inauspicious beginning as the two sides disagreed on the extent of third-party participation and mediation, and the order of the agenda and events. It took a further round of talks before both sides agreed to recognize the team of observers (two Sant Egidio members, an Italian parliamentarian, and Bishop Goncalves) as the official mediation team.

A third round of talks was first canceled, and later reinstated following U.S. support for the Rome process and a series of meetings between the mediation team and regional heads of state. Finally in December 1990, an agreement was reached on maintaining a partial cease-fire along major transport routes, and on providing humanitarian agencies access to the conflict zones. A Joint Verification Mission (JVC) was also appointed, with Renamo nominating Kenya, Portugal, the United States, and Zambia, and the government asking Congo, France, the USSR, and the United Kingdom to be members.

The next four rounds of talks, held over a one year period, tackled issues of political and electoral reform. As the talks stalled and faltered, accusations of a breach of cease-fire were made by both sides, and inevitably little humanitarian aid reached those in need. But the presence of the JVC and the signed agreement offered some reassurance to both parties.

Renamo sought support from the Portuguese government and the United Nations, but both refused to interfere in the Rome process. The indications were that all parties (regional and international) were supportive of, and recognized the Sant Egidio talks as the official negotiations. Any assistance given was aimed to supplement and enhance that process.

Transformation

In an effort to surmount a number of major obstacles, the mediators drew up a series of protocols, each tackling specific issues and each demanding concessions from both parties. Once again with support from external observers, the two sides agreed to sign Protocol One. It indicated that the government was to tolerate and not impede Renamo's international contacts, while Renamo acknowledged its compliance with Mozambique government laws after the cease-fire. The two sides also agreed that a joint commission with UN participation would supervise the implementation of the General Peace Accord. In essence it was a substantial breakthrough, establishing mutual political recognition.

Shortly afterward, Protocol Two on Criteria and Modalities for Forming and Recognizing Political Parties was signed. The critical issues incorporated were that the government had authority to register political parties, and that Renamo would be given provisions to begin activities as a political party once the peace agreement was signed. Protocol Three on electoral reform took more months of negotiation. But finally with U.S. advice and encouragement, Renamo agreed to postpone discussions on constitutional reform and to sign the agreement.

By June 1992, all sides agreed to include the U.S. and Portuguese governments formally into the peace process. But there was little progress being made on the question of military reform. As the negotiations process in Rome ambled on, a humanitarian crisis was mounting in Mozambique itself. Aid agencies and major donors applied pressure on both sides, but still no significant progress was made. Frustrated by the delays in Rome, in July a summit meeting between President Mugabe, President Masire of Botswana, Dhlakama, and the U.S. ambassador to

Botswana was arranged by Tiny Rowland. The meeting gave a positive boost to the proceedings, and Dhlakama agreed to face-to-face talks with Chissano.

In early August, at an African summit in Rome, Chissano and Dhlakama met in the presence of Mugabe and Rowland and agreed to a further meeting in October. But behind the scenes there were still numerous obstacles. Renamo feared for their security after the peace agreement was signed, and there were signs of dissent amongst the ranks of both sides. In a series of smaller meetings with the mediators who were engaged in shuttle diplomacy, issues such as the size of army, reform of the police, and the future of secret service were discussed. However, the mediation team lacked the authority and means to enforce any agreements, so the UN was invited in.

Consolidation

By October 1992, a number of the issues were finally resolved. Regional governments including South Africa were supportive, the UN was to send monitors and troops to uphold the agreement, and the Italian government agreed to donate U.S. $10 million toward Renamo's transformation into a political party. After two years, and with the involvement of regional and European governments, the United States, the UN, a major international corporation, not to mention Sant Egidio itself, the Rome General Peace Accord was signed.

Reflections

There is little doubt that the resolution of the Mozambican conflict came as a result of the conjuncture of several different factors domestically and internationally. In broad terms, four categories can be identified.

First, within the context of international politics, the demise of the bipolar Cold War era and the ending of apartheid ensured that external support for Renamo was diminishing. These factors are further coupled by the impact of the Gersony report, which dramatically changed U.S. attitudes to Renamo, and President Chissano and Frelimo's shift toward more centrist politics and inclusion into international institutions. Second, at a domestic level the country was reaching a point of collapse. Socioeconomic infrastructures were all but destroyed. Another humanitarian crisis and widespread famine were threatening the nation, and the vast refugee and internally displaced populations were growing restless. Neither the government nor Renamo could maintain effective control over these factors. Third, Sant Egidio's role as third-party facilitator was critical. Sant Egidio had a long-standing and trusting relationship with key figures on both sides. Its network of churches ensured its access to all parts of the country, and its vast humanitarian aid contributions made it a credible entity in the eyes of all sides. As a facilitator Sant Egidio had no independent gains to make or agendas to press during the process. Given it had the full backing (morally and financially) of the Italian government and the Vatican, its role was accepted by other international actors (e.g., the UN, and the U.S. and European governments). Fourth, it is critical to appreciate that throughout the two years that led to the eventual peace agreement there was consistent support for the process and path towards peace from a variety of stakeholders. Tiny Rowland played a critical role, as did the church groups in Mozambique and across the region. Regional and international governments supported the process despite the obstacles and reversals. Ultimately the success of the peace process and agreement lay in the fact that there was a shared willingness in both parties to agree on the necessary steps toward peace, and a willingness among the international community to provide all necessary assistance to implement these steps. These steps included compromise on political and military issues, including demobilization and disarmament, elections, socioeconomic reform, and substantial financial support to transform Renamo into a national political power.

Peace Process Experiences: Confronting Obstacles in Sierra Leone, 1994–1996

Our second peace process review will be focused on the 1994–1996 period of the peace efforts in Sierra Leone, one characterized by the confronting of obstacles. On November 30, 1996, Sierra Leone's President Alhaji Ahmad Tejan Kabbah and Corporal Foday Sankoh, leader of the Revolutionary United Front of Sierra Leone (RUF/SL), signed a Peace Agreement in Abidjan, the Ivory Coast. It was, however, short-lived.

Communications between the conflict parties and the guarantors of the peace accord soon broke down as effective compliance with the comprehensive provisions of the agreement was not forthcoming. For example, the Neutral Monitoring Group that was to verify the end of hostilities and the disposition of armed forces could not be set up. Internal dissension within the respective camps eventually led to a break-up of the Committee for the Consolidation of Peace, whose task was to oversee the accord's implementation. More seriously, this rupture led to the resumption of hostilities thereafter followed by the military coup of May 1997 that was supported by some factions within the RUF/SL. Subsequent efforts by relevant regional organizations and, in particular, the ECOMOG forces led by Nigeria helped restore the civilian government in February 1998.

This brief section limits itself to the period of the peace process in Sierra Leone prior to and leading to the Peace Agreement from 1994 to 1996. During this initial phase, International Alert (IA),[9] an NGO working for the peaceful resolution of conflicts, was involved in supporting official efforts to reach a negotiated political settlement. The principal mediator and host to the talks was the foreign minister of the Ivory Coast government. The talks were facilitated by the UN, the OAU, the Commonwealth Secretariat, and IA.

Background

West Africa represents a turbulent region in the continent, with its share of civil wars and coup d'etats that have caused the loss of lives, the devastation of national economies, and the destruction of homes resulting in refugee flows and the internal displacement of people. At the heart of this subregion lies Sierra Leone.

British colonial rule ended there in 1961. Independence initially brought the Sierra Leone People's Party to power. The All People's Party of Siaka Stevens assumed office in 1967, but not before a military coup and counter-coup ushered in their wake violence and factionalism, political patronage and repression, economic mismanagement and chronic corruption. After nearly a quarter of century of one party-rule, the politics of exclusion was entrenched. Aptly described as a period of political failure and corruption, this period once again triggered a coup d'etat in April 1992, led by Captain Valentine Strasser and the National Provisional Ruling Council (NPRC). The NPRC was composed of young military officers who initially adopted certain objectives: end the war, end administrative corruption, reform the economy and restore multiparty democracy. However, their initial objectives were soon overshadowed by their ineptitude in government and their own propensity for corruption.

First Conflict Phase: Crisis and Violence (1991)

It was in this context that in March 1991 an armed rebellion broke out, and the RUF/SL, led by Foday Sankoh, a former army corporal, launched attacks from the eastern and southern parts of the country. The group recruited disaffected rural people and former dissident students, and its objective was to secure a democratic civilian government in the country. But in the military struggle between government and rebel forces terror tactics were employed and civilians attacked. Violence spread throughout the country (Richards 1997).

The Sierra Leone military forces sought support from the Nigerians, Guineans, and the United Liberation Movement for Democracy in Liberia, and countered the RUF/SL's advances successfully. Government troops had recaptured much of the rebel-held territory by 1993.

Second Conflict Phase: Escalation (1993–1995)

In 1994, however, the RUF/SL resumed its attacks. The conflict escalated further, spreading more widely into northern parts of the country. UN estimates indicated that approximately 47 percent of the country's total population was either internally displaced or refugees in neighboring countries. Figures also indicated that 70 percent of educational facilities were destroyed and only 16 percent of the country's health centers functioned (UNDP 1995). Countless children were trained as soldiers. As a result of the war, the country's armed forces increased from 3,000 members to an estimated

16,000 soldiers. However, resources were limited. Thus, many of the soldiers were ill-trained, ill-equipped, ill-disciplined, badly clad, and hardly paid. Many were forced to eke out an existence by raiding villages, plundering and pilfering. Civilian populations throughout the country grew terrified of these "sobels"—soldier-rebels. The RUF/SL gained ground and continued to bolster its numbers. Both sides in the conflict were accused of gross human rights abuses (Amnesty International 1995). The government sought further military assistance by hiring Executive Outcomes, a private security firm mainly composed of former South African soldiers, in exchange for mineral concessions (Rupesinghe with Anderlini 1998, 55f).

Preparation and Prenegotiation, Creating a Framework for Peace

IA had embarked on a discreet program aimed at responding to the subregional challenges for peace in West Africa as early as December 1993. Although it believed that the internal armed conflicts in Liberia and Sierra Leone had their unique causes, it recognized the importance of taking the subregional context into account when attempting to address each conflict. At the time, a former west African journalist was among IA's staff and was able to make contact with the parties. Following discreet consultation with international and regional parties, IA held a series of meetings with OAU and UN officials. A visit was also arranged to meet with one of the subregion's most seasoned diplomats, Amara Essy, foreign minister of the Ivory Coast, and then president of the UN General Assembly, to explore possible efforts to help mediate talks between the parties to the conflict in Sierra Leone. In Freetown, IA held discussions with NPRC representatives and made radio contact with the RUF/SL, which led to preliminary talks. Together with the Nairobi Peace Initiative, IA organized a conflict resolution workshop in Dakar, Senegal, at which RUF/SL representatives met with other Sierra Leoneans in an informal problem-solving setting.

During this period, despite mounting international pressure for an end to the violence, the conflict continued to intensify. However in April 1995 the RUF/SL took a number of Sierra Leoneans and foreign workers hostage. The international community refused to enter into talks with them so long as the hostages were still captive. Under such circumstances, there seemed little chance of peace talks getting under way.[10]

Overcoming Obstacles to a Process

IA fully supported the international diplomatic community's position that no dialogue was possible unless the hostages were released, however it sought to explore a means of releasing them. In consultations with the International Commitee of the Red Cross (ICRC) a decision was reached to attempt to secure their release. The Sierra Leonian government was consulted and its approval sought. A plan was made, and following three weeks of trekking into the bush and face-to-face negotiations with the

RUF/SL leadership, the hostages were released into IA's care and escorted to the Guinean border into the care of the ICRC. This event proved to be a significant step toward creating a more conducive climate for talks.

There were, however, other significant obstacles. To sustain a process of peace in Sierra Leone meant dealing with both political and logistical problems. Establishing reliable and secure communication links with the parties to the conflict under the most difficult circumstances was an initial hurdle. Nigerian, Ghanaian, and Guinean troops were involved in the war efforts through the invitation of the NPRC government. Helping to bring out a delegation from the bush to engage in talks posed many difficulties in this preparatory phase of the process at a time when the other state-related facilitators were not yet fully engaged.

Furthermore, the RUF/SL hardly had any experience in formal diplomacy and little in their representatives' backgrounds prepared them for formal negotiations. They had expressed their desire to receive technical assistance since they felt afraid of becoming "casualties of peace." At the same time, the NPRC was a military regime that generally acted in cautious fashion, discussing possibilities of talks while continuing to pursue the military option.

In the ensuing months, IA's role in the Sierra Leone peace process was one of catalyst and subsequently cofacilitator. During the prenegotiations phase, IA helped prepare the ground by putting together relevant peace-related material, sharing copies of peace accords formulated in other conflict areas for comparative purposes, making available compilation of resource material on rebuilding war-torn societies, documents of human rights and humanitarian law, as well as reports by Amnesty International on Sierra Leone.[11]

The Third Phase:
Negotiations and Transformation (Abatement)

The situation took a distinctive turn as a change of guards—a palace coup—took place at the beginning of 1996 when Brigadier General Julius Maada Bio displaced Captain Strasser. In his first public broadcast, General Bio stated his support for a return to civilian rule and a commitment to ending the war, and participating in the talks process. In the space of a few months, with support from the international community (the UN, Commonwealth Secretariat, and the OAU), the country entered into national elections. Simultaneously a round of formal peace talks got under way in the Ivory Coast between the RUF/SL, the NPRC government (under General Bio's leadership), and representatives of the incoming civilian government of President-elect Ahmad Tejan Kabbah.

In this phase of the peace process, assurances were sought from all quarters that the talks would be sustained even as the delicate period of transition to civilian rule was then taking place simultaneously. As talks were about to take place in Yamoussoukro in March 1997, IA led a peace mission to Sierra Leone to consult with and brief leaders of the incoming civilian government, including the president-in-waiting's special representative who was set to join the talks. He participated in the discussions that produced a joint communiqué which adopted three critical measures: the maintenance of the cease-fire, the adoption of humanitarian measures to ensure that relief aid reach people on both sides of the conflict-affected areas, and general provisions for the future of peace talks (International Alert 1997, Appendix 2).

These steps in turn enabled a consensus to emerge on the establishment of three joint working parties (on the peace accord, encampment and disarmament, demobilization and resettlement of combatants), which formed the core of the joint communiqué signed in Yamoussoukro on April 23, 1996, by both President Kabbah and Corporal Sankoh, leader of the RUF/SL, in the presence of the president of the Ivory Coast (International Alert 1997, Appendix 2).

Comprehensive discussions in working group and plenary sessions from May 6 to 28, 1996, resulted in a common single text, a draft peace agreement with twenty-eight articles, and an annex, which reflected significant consensus. The parties failed to reach agreement on two critical issues—principally, the timing or the synchronization of the withdrawal of the private military outfit Executive Outcomes and the disarmament of the RUF/SL. It was therefore agreed to suspend the sessions to give time to the parties to consult with their respective constituencies and explore ways to move forward. Nevertheless, the cease-fire remained in force for as long the parties remained committed to negotiations.[12]

Consolidation and Reversal, a Rare but Missed Window of Opportunity

Sustaining momentum and rebuilding confidence in the precarious in-between period of the talks from June to November 1996 was a critical task that determined whether the talks advanced or were scuttled. The draft text existed on paper, but already it was evident that the tenuous cease-fire was difficult to sustain on the ground for lack of both vigorous political will and a way to properly monitor how forces behaved on the ground. Without proper verification, the situation could easily deteriorate.

To overcome deep suspicions that had resurfaced, intense shuttle diplomacy of diverse kinds and exchange of communications thus continued. It was not until after the consultations with combatants and the RUF war council in November 1996 that the process resumed in earnest. The ICRC and a representative of the Ivorian government accompanied the RUF leader to the Kailahun District and the Kangari Hills to discuss the content of the peace agreement and the alternatives provided by the possible transformation of guerrilla to political force.

In the last days of November 1996, the remaining issues seemed finally resolved with the adoption of a compromise formulation on the contentious issues, including the repatriation of all foreign troops still in Sierra Leone. Monitoring groups were likewise identified (an internationally constituted group and joint group composed of both government and guerrillas). Dubbed as the Abidjan Accord (International Alert 1997, Appendix 1), the peace agreement was signed on November 30, 1996, at official ceremonies held at the presidential palace. The UN, the OAU and the Commonwealth were named as moral guarantors and the Commission on the Consolidation of Peace designated to ensure compliance.

But it proved to be a rare window of opportunity for a peace that existed for an all-too brief period. In early 1997, as the parties to the conflict faltered in fully implementing the terms of the Agreement, serious disputes arose. This resulted in the breakdown of communications and the inability to set up joint verification for the cease-fire and demobilization process. In May 1997, a military coup launched by breakaway factions of the army—the Armed Forces Revolutionary Council—and the RUF toppled the civilian government. Sierra Leone was once again cast into conflict with foreign troops entering the arena again. Finally, in early 1998 a counteroffensive by a subregional force of the ECOMOG led by Nigeria resulted in the ouster of the combined AFRC-RUF forces and the restoration of the civilian government.

Peace Process Experiences: The Philippines, 1986–1998

In February 1986, the massive popular uprising later coined as "people's power" ousted a dictatorial government in the Philippines. This collective effort of people from diverse walks of life, brought together by common aspirations, conspired to bring about the downfall of a regime that enjoyed super-power support for nearly two decades of the Cold War. It opened spaces for greater people's participation hitherto absent in Philippine society, a process we shall review for the period 1986-1998.

This period was not without its challenges. The new government that had assumed power on the shoulders of people's power was confronted by forms of violent resistance on three fronts: rebellion from within the ranks of the armed forces, manifested in six attempts at coup d'etats; the Moro National Liberation Front, largely representing the Moro peoples in Mindanao and others in the southern Philippines; and the National Democratic Front representing the Communist Party of the Philippines (CPP) and the New People's Army (NPA), which was engaged in armed struggle for nearly two decades. This brief section will discuss the efforts of people and their organizations to contribute to the peace process relating to the particular armed struggle waged by the Communist Party.

Background

The period of Spanish colonial rule dating from the 1500s to the 1890s was characterized by periods of repression and insurrection, struggles around land and the imposition of taxes. In 1898 the Philippines witnessed the first revolution and a successful struggle for independence in Asia. But this victory was short-lived as the Philippines was ceded to the United States under the infamous Treaty of Paris in 1902.

The period 1902 to 1946 was the time of U.S. colonial rule, characterized by the first armed struggle against the United States in Asia. U.S. Congress passed the Tydings-McDuffie Act providing for Philippine independence after a ten-year commonwealth period, interrupted by the Japanese occupation from 1941 to 1945. U.S. rule eventually ended in 1946, although major U.S. military bases remained in the country.

Between 1946 and the 1950s agrarian unrest in Central Luzon and in the sugar haciendas of the Visayas led to the armed struggle of the Partido Komunista ng Pilipinas (PKP), the original Communist Party. Throughout the 1950s and early 1960s successive governments attempted and, to a large extent, failed to address deep-seated causes of social unrest in a profound and durable manner. In 1965 Ferdinand Marcos assumed the presidency and won an unprecedented second term, which he extended by the declaration of martial law, using the armed rebellion as a pretext for staying in power.

Phase One: Crisis (1969–1972)

In 1969, the New People's Army, the armed wing of the new Communist Party, was formed. Initially a small armed band in the plains of Luzon, it grew dramatically, particularly after martial law was declared in 1972. Repressive rule spread considerably as government attempted to quell dissent over food and transport prices, poverty and inequality, and restrictions on the rights to freely organize and assemble.

Phase Two: Escalation (1972–1986)

During the next fourteen years, massive human rights violations, torture, extrajudicial killings, disappearances, and internal displacement of people escalated dramatically. Corruption among the top ranking officials was endemic, while the majority of the population suffered marginalization. On the eve of the declaration of the martial law, less than half of the country's families were poor. By the time Marcos was ousted from power, nearly two-thirds of the population lived below the poverty line.

In 1983, Senator Benigno Aquino, returning from exile, was assassinated on the Manila International Airport tarmac. His death resulted in mass popular protest in Manila. The "parliaments of the streets" erupted into the scene. By February 1986, people's power had deposed a tyrant. Marcos and his inner circle were transported by U.S. helicopters into exile. But by the time Marcos was toppled, the NPA had grown to more than 25,000 regular fighters, deployed in sixty-six guerrilla fronts.[13]

Phase Three: Abatement, Exploring Negotiated Paths

Upon taking office, President Corazon Aquino demonstrated her willingness to take a path of compromise and negotiations by releasing 500 political prisoners. Among them were top leaders of the CPP, the NPA, and the National Democratic Front (NDF). Preliminary talks with the NDF began in May 1986 as the government of the Republic of the Philippines designated representatives to the negotiations. The NDF likewise appointed representatives to a full-time panel to engage in talks. Meanwhile, a Constitutional

Commission was established to draft a new fundamental law to supersede the old Charter that had been designed during the period of martial rule.[14]

The government's willingness to engage in dialogue with the revolutionary movement, however, seemed to have been undermined by preemptive actions taken by the still powerful armed forces. Nevertheless, despite numerous hurdles and initial setbacks, preliminary agreements to lay the ground for talks were reached on a sixty-day cease-fire, and a guarantee of safety and immunity for rebel leaders, to be monitored by a National Cease-fire Committee (NCC) and seven subregional divisions.

To address popular expectations to end the violence—both structural and repressive—resulting from long-term disputes over land and governance, formal negotiations were agreed upon. In January 1987 talks dealing with substantive issues commenced. Dispute over the framework for the talks was among the initial hurdles, and it appeared that the process would stall. However, the negotiators overcame the hurdle by focusing on issues where they could find a minimum of consensus. The compromise framework for the negotiations, titled "Food and Freedom, Justice and Jobs," expressed the principles that seemed to move the parties toward some common ground. The government's chief negotiator, the respected former Senator Jose W. Diokno, argued that despite ideological differences that separated the two sides, nevertheless, they were concerned with similar challenges and recognized that the solutions to major socioeconomic problems were complex and interrelated. Moreover it was explicitly stated that since these problems were internal to the Philippines, solutions sought should serve Filipino, not foreign, interests.

A Phase Transition:
Formal Talks Break Down and Cease-Fire Collapses

Yet despite the goodwill and intentions of both sides, the talks failed to address the substantive issues. With the military undertaking actions that seemed to undermine the civilian government and the communists pursuing a strategy of their own, the talks soon collapsed.

Events took a turn for the worse just weeks later. A peasant demonstration ended in the massacre of eighteen people—mainly farmers. Reports and rumors of an impending military coup and threats to the security of the peace panel members undermined the confidence and trust in the talks process. The coup was unsuccessful, but the reservoir of goodwill that had been generated soon dissipated. The cease-fire agreement was broken and the formal talks collapsed.[15]

The attacks and counterattacks by government and revolutionary forces intensified. The government was faulted for its military operations and human rights abuses. The CPP/NPA intensified their struggle after several top leaders were once again arrested. Military personnel and local politicians, and U.S. servicemen in the military bases were targeted in urban areas. Within the CPP itself, internal mistrust was rife resulting in purges against so-called deep penetration agents. In effect, the cycle of violence had turned vicious, and the levels of mistrust between the two sides as well as within their ranks dramatically reduced the space for dialogue and peacemaking.

Renewed Preparation and Prenegotiation, Seeking People's Participation[16]

As the violence escalated, major church groups renewed their call for a return to concerted peace efforts. Among them the Catholic Bishops' Conference of the Philippines (CBCP), the Association of Major Religious Superiors in the Philippines (AMRSP), and Protestant church groups such as the National Council Churches in the Philippines (NCCP) issued pastoral letters and national appeals for peace. From 1986 to 1987 they contributed to the talks by advocating land reform proposals and solidarity for the poor.

The Coalition for Peace, a citizens' group drawing together NGOs, community groups, academicians, and eminent people, also continued their campaign, calling for humanitarian cease-fires, the observance of international humanitarian law, and supporting the formation of peace zones in selected rural areas of conflict. Local networks continued their collaboration with international NGOs and UN agencies such as UNICEF. Numerous conferences and conventions were organized to focus on the resumption of peace talks, with specific emphasis on political reform, economic dilemmas, the role of the military in a democratic society and people's participation in peacemaking.

In this period, for example, International Alert was also involved in helping to organize the first international conference on conflict resolution in the Philippines, held in a university campus. It cooperated in setting up the workshops on electoral and political reforms, and on the role of the military in the period of transition to democracy.[17]

In brief, even during the period when formal peace talks were recessed, thanks to a network of citizens and institutions, the peace process continued advancing. Their efforts were harnessed to ensure that communication continued on various levels including advocacy for a peace agenda, the support for peace issues, the efforts to catalyze new channels of communication to discuss issues such as human rights and humanitarian law. In other words, citizens and their organizations committed to maintaining and developing the spaces for dialogue sustained public pressure and placed peace issues high on the country's agenda (National Peace Conference 1993).

Building Networks of Peace in a Spiral of Violence

The president declared the 1990s as a "Decade of Peace." But the government's words were not sufficiently backed by adequate and sustainable programs. Amnesty International's report (1990) indicated that more than 200 real or suspected critics or opponents of government policies, including human rights activists, church workers, trade unionists, and peasants were killed in apparent extra-judicial executions by government or government-backed forces and dozens reportedly "disappeared." The following year, Amnesty International reported: "The NPA was likewise held responsible for the killing of at least 80 people in 1990, reportedly committed by the urban-based assassination squads known as 'sparrow units' " (Amnesty International 1991).

Yet communication between the two sides did not break down completely. Discreet, unofficial, and informal exploratory meetings between representatives of the government and the NDF took place in Italy and the Netherlands in the presence of intermediaries as well as within the sanctuary of religious houses, facilitated by peace advocates. A number of more public gatherings also took place, giving rise to new peace efforts and greater public participation in addressing critical issues. These efforts contributed to the agenda of the negotiations.

In October 1990, the three-day National Peace Conference (NPC) brought together participants from fourteen major sectors (such as farmers, workers, urban poor, indigenous people, women, among others) and three major religious faiths. Nearly a year of pre-conference consultations reaching a broad cross-section of society resulted in a number of consensus documents that later formed the basis for "Basic Peace: Peace Agenda of Four Sectors" (Coalition for Peace 1993).

The Multi-Sectoral Peace Advocates (MSPA) brought together representatives from sectors of society and independent organizations focusing principally on putting the official peace negotiations back on track. With the presence of the International Committee of the Red Cross, the MSPA participated in a joint technical committee with Cabinet representatives, and presented all parties to the conflict with a draft memorandum on upholding human rights and humanitarian laws. Parallel efforts were made through the organization of a People's Caucus composed of progressive people's organizations and NGOs that, together with the NPC, generated national-level recommendations during the consultations held by the National Unification Commission in late 1992 to mid-1993.

The NDF and the government launched tentative initiatives, but never simultaneously. In June 1991, for example, the National Democratic Front (NDF) announced the suspension of offensive military operations in the areas affected by the Mount Pinatubo volcanic eruptions. This humanitarian cessation of hostilities was seen as a confidence-building measure, but the Government's response came belatedly a month later.

Another substantive breakthrough seemed possible in September 1991. The Philippine Senate voted to reject the extension of the Military Bases Agreement between the U.S. and the Philippine governments. This issue had been identified as a principal obstacle to any future peace agreement and the NDF had offered a unilateral truce if the bases agreement was terminated. The Senate's rejection of the military bases was welcomed by a unilateral cease-fire declaration from the ranks of the CPP/NPA. It was short-lived. The NDF claimed that the government supported efforts to undermine the Senate veto by recourse to a possible referendum on the issue.

As the 1992 national elections drew closer, a Peace Vote campaign was launched to raise public awareness on social justice and peace issues. Public forums involving the presidential candidates were organized, and peace organizations made efforts to evaluate the performance and platform of candidates according to certain criteria. The impact of the campaign was made manifest when newly elected President Fidel Ramos focused on the need for a comprehensive peace in his first State of the Nation address in July 1992. Congress later took the initiative to repeal the Anti-Subversion Law, which previously made the Communist Party of the Philippines illegal and penalized membership in the party and similar organizations.

Negotiations and Transformation

Direct talks between the government and NDF leaders in the Netherlands appeared to make gains toward substantive negotiations in September 1992. The Hague Declaration of September 1992 provided workable guidelines for the holding of formal negotiations without preconditions. It was however not vigorously followed up. Differences over interpretation and other procedural matters, such as safety guarantees for NDF members and safe conduct passes for certain areas, posed new obstacles.

It must be noted that no mediators or facilitators were involved in these negotiations. Only observers were allowed at times. Although the government of the Republic of the Philippines (GRP) and NDF negotiations were held largely in private venues in the Netherlands, no international mediation was requested. In contrast, the Government Moro National Liberation Front (MNLF) negotiations received international support provided by the Organization of Islamic Conference; talks were hosted by the Foreign Minister of Indonesia.

Official talks, which had been suspended several times due to procedural and political disagreements, recommenced in June 1996. Nearly two years later on March 16, 1998, a Comprehensive Agreement on Human Rights and Humanitarian Law was signed and jointly issues by the government of the Republic of the Philippines and the NDF. This agreement paves the way for other similar accords on socioeconomic reforms, political, electoral, and constitutional reforms, and disposition of armed forces. It also manifests the role that nonstate actors can play addressing human rights and humanitarian laws, having been involved in earlier stages of tackling the difficult question of the monitoring of human rights abuses and the parties' compliance with international laws.

As a new government was elected to take office in July 1998, the talks were recessed. Nongovernmental and people's organizations, meanwhile, continued their unceasing efforts to advance the peace process that has become "theirs" as much as the direct parties to the conflict. Following years of broad consultation since the 1990 National Peace Conference they have reformulated their peace agenda for the post-Ramos period, essentially proposing that social reform, poverty alleviation, a more equitable distribution of wealth and income, and broader political participation "form the core of governance" (National Peace Conference 1998). They have identified concrete legislative initiatives, executive policy directions and other "doables" within the context of a broad peace process to lay the solid foundations of peace that can be sustained.

Unlike the Sierra Leone or Mozambique cases discussed above, the Philippines conflict and peace process at the time of this chapter's composition had not reached a point of significant resolution. The aim of this discussion has been to demonstrate the role of "peoples participation" in sustaining the "process" toward peace, even as the official negotiations between warring parties has reached an impasse.

NGOs and Peace Processes:
Necessary Conditions and Possible Contributions

No two conflicts are ever the same. But there are always common themes and characteristics that can be identified, and thus lessons to be learned. Similarly, although every peace process takes a different path, there are always common elements that can be understood and considered.

As discussed and illustrated above, peace processes pass through different stages. Our aim in this section of the paper is to identify the critical and sensitive factors that arise at each phase, and to assess the specific contributions that NGOs and civic groups can make toward conflict prevention and resolution throughout the process. As mentioned in the introduction, it must be recognized that the causes of conflict are often deep-seated and structural in character, leading to deeply felt injustices. Therefore it is important to remember that to bring about sustainable peace, peacemaking efforts should aim not only to raise the key issues, but also address them comprehensively and concretely. Otherwise there is a danger that all that is achieved is a pause in the conflict.

The Preparatory Phase:
Creating Spaces for Dialogue and Building Trust

Among the first casualties of war are truth and trust. Communication often breaks down, perceptions predominate, opposing groups are demonized, and trust undermined. These essentially intangible issues are among the first obstacles that need to be overcome early on in most peace processes.

Moreover, the rhetoric of extremism on both sides often prevails, offering supposedly clear-cut, no-compromise positions and pandering to an unrealistic ideal. Reason and moderation are to a large extent marginalized. Moderates who attempt to carve out a middle ground so as to face their adversaries, to understand their grievances, and explore mutually acceptable resolutions, often face grave danger. Typically this "middle ground" is unstable and fragile. The simple act of dialogue with "the enemy" is regarded by many as collusion and subversion. When that middle ground caves in, there is rarely physical or conceptual space for communication. Arguably, therefore, the initial steps toward peace require the creation of spaces for dialogue and communication.

These efforts demand discreet and patient work often best undertaken by individuals or groups from within civil society or by impartial and neutral third parties. In Mozambique, the local church groups played a significant roles, to some extent, preparing the ground for Sant Egidio's eventual intermediation. In Sierra Leone, International Alert's involvement and particularly their contribution to the release of the hostages provided opportunities for further talks. In the Philippines, it was largely the force of popular support and civic action that led, in the first instance, to the change in government—from dictatorial to democratic—and, subsequently, to negotiations between the government and the guerrilla forces. These preliminary efforts can help to discover common spaces and to direct the course of the conflict into new territory. Undoubtedly, the full resolution of a conflict requires more time and effort. But these early actions during which the two sides can discuss mutual concerns, and begin to understand each other's priorities, can help lay the foundations for an eventual peace process.

Without dialogue, there is no chance to build trust between the parties; without mutual trust these negotiations are virtually impossible and the implementation of agreements vitiated. Trust is a critical element, but it must be built slowly and earned over time. The dilemma, of course, is where and how one starts: without communication there is no chance of building trust; without a modicum of trust, however, there are often slim chances of meaningful communication.

Sharing the Burden

In each of the brief case studies reviewed above, establishing communication and trust not only took time, but also occurred at different levels of the social and political strata relevant to the peacemaking process. In the case of Mozambique, the international political conjuncture arising at the end of the Cold War, the weakening of apartheid, and the favourable policies of the Italian government, provided a unique opportunity for developing contact between the two sides. In other words, much of the external support, given to Renamo and Frelimo to sustain the war, was diverted toward negotiations that led to ending that war.

Within this new climate, Sant Egidio was able to play its role effectively, by providing a low-profile setting for the talks. The Italian government and the Vatican ensured that at the international level, Sant Egidio's efforts were legitimized and supported by influential bodies such as the European Union, the United Nations, regional African governments, and other governments such as the United States.

At the grassroots level, Sant Egidio's efforts would not have been so successful, had it not been for the ongoing activities of local Mozambican church groups, both Protestant and Catholic. Despite their own historic animosities, the two groups came together in their call for a cessation of hostilities. With their wide network of organizations down to the grassroots level, the religious institutions not only understood the situation but also knew the significant players. Moreover, as providers of humanitarian aid, they had access even to the most remote areas throughout the country, including Renamo-held territory. This gave them the legitimacy to exert pressure for talks to take place. Finally, because Sant Egidio operated its own humanitarian aid program through the church network, it was able to establish links with the Renamo leadership. Over a number of years, Sant Egidio's members were able to build a sufficiently trusting relationship with Renamo, which gave them the leverage to encourage Renamo to the negotiations table in 1990.[18]

In Sierra Leone, the conditions were very different. A window of opportunity began to open in 1995, and the chances for dialogue increased after the hostages were released by the RUF. However, the NPRC military regime balked and failed to take full advantage of the opportunity created to accelerate the cessation of the war. The international community, including the OAU, the Commonwealth Secretariat, and the UN, attempted to exert pressure, but with little success. In part, this was somehow due to some unwillingness to recognise the RUF/SL as a viable political force or a legitimate dialogue partner, as had taken place in Mozambique with Renamo.

It was not until January 1996, when a new leader from the NPRC ranks announced readiness to engage in direct talks, that formal negotiations were put back on track. The political environment was unstable, uncertain and in flux. Nevertheless, the talks did continue through three changes of government. Moreover, despite the poor lines of communication between the negotiations team in the Côte D'Ivoire and the RUF/SL leadership in the rain forests, agreements were reached resulting in joint communiqués leading to cease-fires and corridors for humanitarian assistance.[19] But the level of trust between the two parties remained weak.

Furthermore, the inability of the representatives of the facilitating organizations and the Côte d'Ivoire mediator to work with single-minded focus created unnecessary difficulties made manifest when serious problems arose in the implementation phase of the accord. This inability to decisively overcome the lack of trust between the two parties and the absence of more vigorous support from the regional governments and the international community were critical factors that jeopardized what was a unique opportunity for peace in the war-torn West African subregion.

The Philippines presented yet another situation. The desire for negotiations and dialogue emerged from citizen groups through the grass roots. After the breakdown of the first formal talks in 1987, localized efforts such as the creation of peace zones, and regional and national conferences, and widespread consultations provided the impetus for dialogue at a higher political level. However, efforts were hampered by actions taken by recalcitrant elements within the military who did not look favorably at the negotiations. Nevertheless, despite these obstacles, citizens' movements and NGOs unceasingly advanced the peace process (Garcia 1993).

In all three cases but in different degrees, it was somehow the work of NGOs and groups that led to the initial breaking down of barriers and the opening of the lines of communications. Sant Egidio and the religious community in Mozambique, citizens groups in the Philippines, International Alert and the International Committee of the Red Cross in Sierra Leone, were helping to pursue efforts even while the conflicts still raged, and before any states or international state-based institutions were fully engaged. The NGOs had the advantage of working discreetly over a period of time, preparing the space and breaking new ground.[20]

Preparing the Ground with Talks before "Talks"

Having created that initial "space for dialogue," other issues remain: what steps need to be taken, by whom, to build the necessary level of trust among the parties to the conflict? What specific issues need to be raised at this early stage, to ensure that later, more public talks are sustained?

This prenegotiations period provides the best opportunity for NGOs and members of civil society to contribute to the building up of peace processes. First, familiarity with local cultures that involves navigating through traditional customs and ways of doing things is indispensable. Second, preparing the grounds for talks requires patience and a nuanced understanding of personal relations and detail. It is a task best done away from the glare of public attention and formal diplomacy. Generally, talking before "talks" is a sine qua non if official talks are to take place and become meaningful.

The aim is to create a secure and informal environment in which differences can be aired and common concerns and anxieties shared. In other words, to the extent possible, the intractability and complexity of a conflict may be divided into interrelated components, which can be tackled separately. Adversaries can be given a chance to view the conflict from each others' perspectives, so that their understanding of the grievances of their adversaries increase. This process is also an essential factor in agenda setting. If the conflict is not "unpacked," so to speak, into more manageable components there is constantly the danger of "overloads" that can lead to dead ends.

An essential first step is the creation, or strengthening, of a mutual desire for peace. In certain experiences, this has been done by conveying, the economic, social, and psychological costs of war to both sides, and comparing the mutual benefits of peace. It has also been done through exerting sufficient pressure by offering incentives to both sides. In cases of intrastate conflict where the two sides have reached a mutually hurting stalemate, or reached a point of war fatigue, there is a greater willingness to consider compromise and negotiations.

In Mozambique, for example, the 1984 N'Komati talks failed primarily because the South African apartheid regime was still fully supportive of Renamo. Renamo had no real incentives to cease fighting. The Sant Egidio talks, on the other hand, came at a time when South Africa's support for the guerrillas was waning, and when the government's ability to fight the rebels was also severely limited. Moreover, fighters on both sides were suffering from war fatigue. Fear of punishment and the need for survival had replaced the rhetoric of the unreal as the driving forces for waging war. Realizing its internal weaknesses and decreased external support, Renamo signaled its willingness to enter into talks with the government. The signal was conveyed through the network of church groups working in Renamo-held territories. There was need to explore concrete ways to take advantage of opportunities that arose.

In Sierra Leone, the political and military conjuncture in mid-1995 provided a rare opportunity for meaningful peace efforts. Moreover, the levels of brutality had become unacceptable, causing the displacement of nearly half the population; the parties to the conflict had committed unspeakable violations of basic rights as attested to by Amnesty International reports (Amnesty International 1995). Additionally, the kidnapping of foreigners and Sierra Leoneans drew attention to their cause and plight causing the international community to condemn their actions. However, no peace process was possible while the hostages were still captive.

As an independent and impartial NGO, with a recent history of project work in the subregion, IA was then well-placed to initiate communications with the group. To avoid misunderstandings and suspicions, IA consulted with the NPRC government and the international community before embarking on the hostage negotiations. It took these opportunities to explore potential peace talks, once the hostage crisis was resolved. In other words, the NGO not only identified a potential opportunity for initiating talks, but was committed toward consolidating that opportunity and making it viable.

As the ICRC's experiences in conflict regions elsewhere in the world attest, these were substantial risks being taken by an NGO. However, it was believed that creating a chance for the RUF/SL to meet with official international representatives, once the hostages were free, was a good opportunity to build trust and encourage small steps toward a negotiated political path (International Alert 1997, 14–18).

Another way of identifying opportunities for peace can be to seize upon political conjunctures such as a change in the political leadership of either side, shifts in the policies of external supporters, or a season of economic hardships, and transform them into peace conjunctures. In the Philippines, it was people's power that toppled the Marcos regime and installed the Aquino government. Once the new government was in place, the civic groups took the opportunity to press guerrillas and the government into talking about peace. Similarly, in Sierra Leone the stage was set for talks between the RUF/SL and the NPRC, but Captain Strasser's unwillingness to negotiate with them led to discontent within his own ranks. The change in leadership, with Brigadier General Bio taking charge, created the necessary momentum to start the official talks.

In the Philippines, civic groups similarly played an active and critical role not only in identifying deeply entrenched societal inequalities that contributed to the conflict, but also in helping to provide ideas in the drafting of new legislation and measures to overcome these obstacles. Throughout the peace process, when high level talks broke down and the conflict reignited, these groups maintained their grassroots support and continued their work. Each time the talks recommenced, the efforts of the civic groups made a significant and positive contribution.[21]

Enlisting Support by Identifying Facilitators and Mediators

Given that peacemaking is not unilinear but to a great extent a protracted process with recurring problems of deadlocks and stalemates, enlisting the support of individuals from relevant parties to the conflict and from the world at large is an indispensable component for sustaining the effort. Although this appears to be a straight-forward process, nevertheless it often is difficult and potentially divisive.

If they are trusted sufficiently by all sides, mediators and facilitators can help maintain the momentum of the negotiations even when faced with serious obstacles. If talks break down, they can provide channels of communication between disputants. They can offer safety nets, so to speak, to ensure the process does not unravel entirely. They can help to nurture the adversaries and encourage trust among them. However if there is any ambiguity in their actions, or any perceptions of partiality, they themselves can be among the causes of failure (Annan 1998, paragraphs 22–23).

Furthermore, given the range of tasks that must be undertaken during a peace process, and the varying priorities of each side, it is important to ensure that different mediators and facilitators are involved, and that they collaborate together on specific tasks, and coordinate their efforts at different stages; excellent relevant insights for academics and practitioners may be found in Wallensteen (1995). South Africa's mediation attempts in 1984 between Frelimo and Renamo was a classic case in point. The regime took an arrogant and overbearing approach trying to push solutions on to both sides, particularly the Mozambican government. Ultimately its actions triggered more extremist reactions from both parties.

Six years later in Rome, among the first issues discussed was the composition and role of the mediation team. Frelimo rejected Kenyan presence while Renamo questioned the participation of Zimbabweans in the mediation efforts. Renamo pressed for Portuguese, United States, and UN involvement, while Frelimo rejected such high-profile presence for fear of compromising its sovereignty. Sant Egidio itself was overtly questioned by the Kenyan government, forcing the mediation team to visit Kenya and dispel any suspicions and mistrust.

The issue was ultimately settled with great clarity. Both sides agreed to a mediation team composed of two Sant Egidio members, an Italian government representative, and a representative of the Mozambican Catholic Church. A team of observers composed of U.S. and European government representatives and the UN was also present. It was agreed that they would help establish monitoring mechanisms and provide technical and financial support once agreements were reached in Rome. But Sant Egidio's major role as mediator and facilitator was officially recognized by both parties and all governments concerned. There were no ambiguities, or distrust about them, giving them the freedom to focus on the resolution of the conflict rather than their own role (Sengulane and Goncalves 1998; Vines 1998).

In Sierra Leone, although the Ivory Coast government's role as mediator was fully supported by both sides, there was a degree of misunderstanding between the facilitating intergovernmental organizations and the NGO during certain period of the talks. IA's role was at times never fully acknowledged or employed to maximum advantage by the other third parties. Moreover, the RUF/SL at times perceived itself as negotiating from a disadvantaged position. They did not have a level of technical assistance and advice given to Mozambique's Renamo, for example, when engaging in official diplomatic discourse and in attempting to convey their demands and concerns. Furthermore, because the negotiations team of the RUF was to a great extent isolated from its council of leaders in the bush, it was unable to reflect and consolidate its position vis-à-vis the government. By contrast, Renamo's negotiators took weeks off from the negotiations to regroup and assess their position. Although the international community grew disgruntled at times, they still supported the process and gave the rebels a degree of freedom.

The ambiguities surrounding IA's role were never fully resolved either. The organization was quickly deemed to be partial to the RUF/SL. Its provision of documentation materials including copies of other peace agreements and declarations that were made available to all the parties and the assistance given to representatives of the RUF/SL in interpreting international human rights standards and other instruments as well as helping to more clearly articulate their positions for purposes of the negotiations were, at times, perceived negatively.[22] To some extent, the RUF/SL's reliance on nonstate parties was a consequence of their mistrust of the state-related organizations involved. In the perception of the Sierra Leone government and the intergovernmental organizations, however, IA may have overstepped the boundary between neutral assistance and partial advice.

This lack of clarity and trust amongst the third-party participants meant that, at times, there was no concrete consensus or uniform message being transmitted among them during the talks and in their aftermath. Consequently, when hostilities resumed it was difficult, if not impossible, to harness all efforts to bring together the parties and ensure their full compliance with provisions of the agreement. The RUF/SL retreated into the bush, expelling (and arresting) their own moderate negotiators, and spurning the efforts of the UN military mission to set up the monitoring mechanism.

In essence, the critical issues arising from the involvement of mediators and facilitators remain, first, the need for multitrack efforts to tackle different aspects of the process, and, second, the need for coherence and synergy within these efforts. In other words, all third parties involved must ensure that their efforts do not result in a proliferation of efforts that can weaken the peace process.

Transformation:
Substantive Issues Raised, Complementary Actions Taken

Working without Illusions and Overcoming Obstacles

Peace processes are long-term efforts that require the capacity to work without illusions. Undoubtedly, negotiations are merely the first steps in the task of transforming situations of conflict. Obstacles abound and can be overcome, but these efforts take time and change cannot come overnight.

Peace talks are often stalled due to a lack of common understanding on a mutually acceptable agenda, structured as such. Negotiators may arrive at talks without a thorough knowledge of their adversaries' key demands, their priorities and the issues where some room for compromise may exist. They thus find themselves deadlocked, with limited room for maneuvre (Moreno 1998).

Adversaries normally have different priorities, and may propose different timetables and agendas for discussion. For example, governments make demands for a complete cease-fire and disarmament before entering into political negotiations. On the other hand, the opposition may demand political reforms before agreeing to any cease-fire or disarmament. This difference can become sufficiently serious so as to scuttle the entire process of talks and negotiations. Finding solutions to these deadlocks, by identifying specific demands, exploring areas of potential compromise and creating flexibility and space for maneuvre can become major challenges for mediators and facilitators, as well as the parties to the conflict themselves.[23]

To work without illusions may mean recognizing the long and arduous character of a process that can involve a variety of activities from scenario-setting exercises to attending workshops on negotiation and problem-solving in which the two sides are exposed to alternative solutions and comparative experiences. Before high-level political meetings take place, research-assisted, problem-solving workshops arranged in series can help develop relations as well as provide options and alternatives for the parties. They can be expanded to include wider citizen-based participation, as demonstrated by the Philippines, so that the different and complex causes and effects of the conflict are identified and tackled. It is in this area where NGOs and civic groups can complement the efforts of their official diplomatic counterparts. They have fewer restrictions and may find better opportunities to explore new and more creative methods of engaging adversaries in communication and relationship building.

Building Blocks for Peace, Stages, and Issues

In peace processes, the aphorism holds true that "the perfect is often the enemy of the good." The demands of either side in a conflict are often difficult to implement in full, and their general programs normally articulate long-term aspirations that often require years to realize. Thus, the ability to compromise based on mutually acceptable principles is generally the norm for viable outcomes. To do so, the capacity to focus on certain options, though imperfect, may be seen as building blocks that can either form part of the total package, or that can be improved as long-term processes are broken down into viable stages. Similarly differences on substantive questions can be tackled separately, issue-by-issue, and with a sense of realism.

In the case of Mozambique, the agreement on a partial cease-fire, which was more symbolic than actual, was still sufficient for both sides to continue with the negotiations. Similarly, in the midst of a long deadlock, it was the mediators who suggested the drafting of Protocols I and II. In these documents, the government acknowledged Renamo's international political legitimacy and promised political reform. The actual reforms did not take place immediately, but the protocols were clear statements of intent on the government's part and were enough to boost Renamo's sense of security and freedom, and restart the talks process.

It is not sufficient to merely draft agreements without giving attention or resources to the mechanisms needed for their eventual implementation, and monitoring. In the short term, Protocols I and II were a means to certain objectives—to kick-start a flagging process. But the issues raised in those documents were substantive, and had to be tackled concretely in the medium to long term. This aspect of peace talks requires patient and detailed work. Disputants often contest each point, and will use every opportunity to backtrack or reinterpret the initial agreements, to further their own objectives.

In this regard, NGOs and civic groups can play an important role by bringing the agreements and issues to the public, and holding all sides accountable to their word. The greater the levels of people's participation in the peace process, the greater the chances that disputants will uphold their promises and observe the agreements. With the eyes of the world on them, it is more difficult to break a cease-fire agreement or backtrack without losing credibility and support.[24]

Furthermore, states and international diplomacy may seem to overwhelm and subsume substate groups in direct talks. These entities may normally not have sufficient experience of international diplomatic procedures and language. Neither are they normally adept at articulating their demands and concerns, nor proficient at drafting documents and agreements stating their demands. Given the already tense atmosphere of such talks, it is not unlikely that such seemingly minor issues become major obstacles. The groups may feel certain pressures. They may be distrusting of their official international mediators, and they may ultimately refuse to negotiate. In the Mozambique situation, Renamo's leadership was extremely wary at every stage. In Sierra Leone, the RUF/SL negotiators were also suspicious. In both circumstances, it was the NGOs, Sant Egidio, and IA that seemed to provide some measure of confidence that allowed them to trust the process more. They provided comparative peace agreements, and thus helped to show ways in which they could articulate their concerns in the language and style of international diplomacy and peace accords. These efforts, although not always welcomed by the intergovernmental organizations, may have been indispensable to some of the progress achieved in the talks.

Protecting Civilians and Combatants, Addressing Humanitarian and Legal Concerns

Violence inflicted on noncombatants and hardships suffered by civilian communities are among the most immediate concerns of all sides in a war. War and conflict research reveals that increasingly, much of the violence committed by combatants is not against each other, but against unprotected civilian populations. This fact compounds the conditions of abject poverty and ill-health wrought by war. It is for this reason that initiatives taken by local, regional, or international organizations to protect the lives and rights of the civilian population, particularly children, women, the elderly, and the disabled, including those of combatants de hors de combat, are placed high on the agenda of peace efforts. Once again, the difficulty is not the drafting of legislation or agreements, it is the creation of monitoring mechanisms and effective institutions to address complex issues such as impunity, war crimes, and the treatment and remuneration of victims.[25]

Among the key objectives of any peace agreement must be provisions for the promotion and protection of human rights and humanitarian principles. NGOs, particularly those working in the domain of human rights issues, have a substantial contribution to make toward identifying the difficulties, helping to monitor adversaries and ensuring that all sides comply with any agreements that are reached.

In Mozambique, the Sant Egidio talks created a pattern of normative behavior for Renamo and the government. The success of the multitrack efforts was in ensuring that monitoring mechanisms were in place soon after the peace agreement was signed, and the both sides were held accountable for their actions.

Another aspect of this problem is impunity. The "truth commissions" in Latin America and South Africa have progressively tackled this problem. Victims of human rights violations are given an opportunity to tell their truth, and perpetrators of crimes are either identified or become subjects of appropriate judicial processes. It is not a perfect solution, especially since high-ranking military personnel directly responsible for the crimes are seldom brought to justice. But for the families of victims, knowing the truth about their long-disappeared relatives can be an important first step toward the healing of psychological and emotional wounds.[26] Once again, although truth commissions are now a recognized form of process in the regions mentioned, they originate from concerns of sectors of civil society and the pursuit of justice by human rights victims.

Tackling Questions of Governance, Including Political Reforms and Alternatives

In every peace process there comes a time when armed opposition forces have to be transformed into legitimate political actors, and combatants integrated into civil society. In tackling issues of governance where the gun, so to speak, is removed from politics, a number of related issues are discussed and agreed upon. This undertaking can become a difficult and a treacherous time for the prospects of a durable peace. It is normally during this period that the issue on the disposition of armed forces can be agreed upon, which involves the demobilization of combatants and their resettlement. If this transition process is managed fairly and transparently so that neither the parties to the conflict nor the public feels betrayed, then the process can generally be sustained.

To better understand this process it is best to put this in the context of the question of governance that involves putting in place significant electoral and political reforms, including police and military reforms, and, to some extent, constitutional reforms. To ensure a stable transition, it is important to give all sides ample time to prepare so that more inclusive systems are established while transparent and regular mechanisms of popular consultation are put in place. Governance is a broad issue, and one of its pillars is the electoral process. Governments, for example, may prefer earlier elections, giving their opponents less time to establish national networks and institutions. It is thus important to ensure sufficient funds, and technical assistance for both sides. In Mozambique, Renamo was finally given a trust fund of an estimated $10 million by the Italian government, to help transform the group into a viable political force.

The UN maintained a strong presence in the country for four years in preparation for the elections. The elections were in fact postponed when it was felt that the country was not ready for conducting truly representative electoral exercises. The church groups played a critical role in encouraging the population, particularly in the rural areas, to register for voting. Moreover, in certain areas, particularly Renamo-held areas, people were encouraged to vote for the rebels. In part, this was done to bring Renamo into the political fold, to ensure them a place in the public political arena and to establish that it was no longer compulsory to vote for Frelimo representatives. It was believed that Renamo would return to armed combat if they fared badly in the elections. In Sierra Leone, however, not only was a trust fund to convert the RUF into a mainstream political movement not readily available (although a provision existed in the accord) but also national elections in fact took place even before formal negotiations were concluded.[27]

Consolidation: Agreements Implemented and War-Torn Societies Rebuilt

Disarmament, Demobilization, and Monitoring Mechanisms

Even after the agreements are signed and the protocols are drawn up, the actual process of disarmament and demobilization can be fraught with difficulties. Combatants and their leaders are reluctant to surrender weapons, which not only offer security, but are often their sole means of survival. In many cases, the country may be awash with small arms, landmines, and other light weapons, which are easily concealed or acquired. Drawing up an inventory or calculating the number of weapons in existence is virtually impossible. Furthermore, it is also necessary to provide real incentives to combatants to give up their weapons.

For example, in Central America weapons buy-back programs were created, allowing combatants to sell their weapons at a standard, but above-market, rate. Although initially controversial, the program proved highly effective and has been replicated in other parts of the world. Diverse skills training programs exist for reintegrating combatants into civil society. These issues can be addressed and included in agreements, but without designated resources it is difficult for these programs to be implemented.

At times, the recognition that members of the combating forces may be integrated into a joint military force or incorporated into the armed forces can also provide some measure of security. Moreover, it is important to establish monitoring mechanisms to ensure that all sides comply. In the case of Mozambique, the international Joint Verification Committee (JVC) was dispatched early in the talks. It did not succeed in monitoring the partial cease-fire effectively, but it did introduce an element of accountability into the actions of both sides. It also signified the international community's commitment and willingness to assist in the peacemaking process.

Similarly, UNOMOZ was created immediately following the signing of the General Peace Agreement (GPA). UNOMOZ remained in Mozambique for more than two years, assisting in the demobilization process, monitoring the disarmament, and the preparation of the elections. It offered security and stability to both sides, while simultaneously holding all parties accountable. Furthermore, the international community and the guarantors of the GPA provided aid and technical support to Mozambique for the rebuilding of its infrastructures and national economy.

In Sierra Leone, however, the initial cease-fire agreement that helped improve the climate for the talks may have raised unfounded expectations. No nationwide monitoring mechanisms were established in the country although Articles 11 and 12 of the 1996 Agreement called for the formation of a Joint Monitoring Group (primarily composed of representatives of the parties to the conflict) and a Neutral Monitoring Group (from the international community), to monitor cease-fire violations and other breaches of the accord. A Demobilization and Resettlement Committee constituted by that agreement was to have addressed issues of disarmament, demobilization, and resettlement. Funding was promised, and provisional timetables proposed. However, events overtook their implementation. Moreover, the parallel measures on the socioeconomic, political, judicial, and human rights spheres, all included in the 1996 Abidjan Accord, did not receive the attention necessary to create a more positive momentum in the process.

Economic Reforms and the Peace Dividend

In the context of most conflict situations, the restructuring of the national economy leading to improved sources of livelihood and resulting in an economic recovery that effectively benefits people in urban and rural areas is a priority concern for all sides. But combatants are often reluctant to surrender their weapons, which often offer both security and a means of survival. So it is essential to devise programs that offer realistic economic alternatives. The problems and difficulties are of course countless; combatants may lack the necessary skills for civilian jobs, agricultural land and transport routes may be heavily mined, and the economic structures that do exist cannot provide the necessary numbers of paid jobs for all. But if the aim is to ensure that communities and combatants do not resort to the use of arms again, then it is essential that concrete programs of social and economic reform are developed.

These issues can be raised, during the course of a peace processes and negotiations. They may not be fully resolved, but measures and guidelines on how they are addressed can perhaps be designed and agreed upon. The peace dividend has to be converted into something tangible, concretely benefiting different constituencies and improving the lives of people who otherwise would have been drawn into the spiral of violence. In the short term, this approach helps to minimize the recurrence of violence. In the longer term, it can diffuse the causes of future conflicts at the grassroots, especially if these causes are deep-seated and structural in character. However, to do this effectively there is a need for sufficient consensus and will, resources and technical advice. Experiences in other conflict situations provide numerous lessons.

Peace accords in Central America, South Africa, and other conflict regions indicate that provisions dealing with the socioeconomic concerns of disadvantaged people such as land or ancestral domain, the use of mineral and natural resources, and the protection of the environment, including seas and water resources, are essential. It is also important to search for and create effective mechanisms and forums through which socioeconomic issues can be discussed by all sectors of society and where mutually acceptable priorities can be set. In certain situations, providing appropriate venues where citizens can articulate their own social, and political concerns and demands are critical ingredients of the peace process. These issues should not be underestimated. They can make a substantial difference to the medium to long-term success of the peace.

The experience of the National Peace Conference and related networks in the Philippines that brought together peasants, fisherfolk, women, urban poor and indigenous peoples, and others, for example, demonstrates the importance of broad-based social participation in the formulation of a peace agenda. Such work goes beyond the period of negotiations and ensures that agreements become the foundations for sustainable peace that can be "owned" and nurtured by the people. It is essential that such efforts are supported and that resources are made available.

Sustaining the Process by Mobilizing People and Building a Culture of Peace

A peace agreement normally is a key ingredient or element of a peace process. A sound process, however, not only aims to end the war, but also looks toward the reconstruction of society while contributing toward a culture of peace. It can draw on people's participation and involvement so that the longer-term process of peacebuilding directly impacts on the improvement of people's lives. In other words, the final peace agreement is not only a legal document, but can somehow provide a practical guide defining issues within a certain timeframe. This undertaking may require a comprehensive program based on a broad framework embracing the social, political, economic, and military spheres.

Moreover, if the grass roots are not consulted and included during the peace process, or if they experience few of the benefits of the new situation, their grievances may remain unresolved. They can grow indignant about the broken promises of the peace process, and more distrusting of their own leadership and the adversaries. Splinter groups can form unleashing more and different forms of violence. Peacemaking and peacebuilding are not tasks of politicians, diplomats, or military personnel alone. Communities in the regions of conflict can be involved. If the will to make peace is strong enough at the roots it will ensure that the leadership of conflict parties will focus constructively to the challenges of the peace process.

In Mozambique, peacebuilding was a multilateral and international process. It benefited from a timely umbrella of concern. It succeeded because the national political hierarchy cooperated with their international counterparts, and coordinated their activities with NGOs and church groups. Through UNOMOZ and other sources, technical and financial resources were made available to both sides, but they were also held accountable for their actions. Undoubtedly, there were clashes and tensions between Renamo and Frelimo, and among the international facilitators, but the common desire and will to sustain the peace overcame these differences.

Conclusion

It is not possible to cover all the issues related to the role and possible contributions of NGOs and civic movements to peace processes.[28] However, it is clear that nonconventional diplomacy has a significant place in complementing, not supplanting, other efforts that are crucial to peacemaking. Undoubtedly the need for cooperation and coordination with state-based organizations and international diplomatic structures cannot be underestimated. Parties involved in the process, be they mediators, facilitators, or external advisers, should work in conjunction with the official negotiations' track to advance the process. The moral and financial guarantors of the agreement must have the ability and willingness to hold parties accountable, and to use the necessary leverages, political and financial. Finally, people and their organizations could participate and should take responsibility to ensure that critical issues relating to socioeconomic and political reforms are tackled in an effective and timely manner.

Within this vast spectrum, NGOs and civic groups have their own unique role to play. On one level, as the Philippines and Mozambique cases show, civic and religious groups can often articulate the concerns of the people. By themselves, they do not have the sufficient human, political, technical, or financial resources to achieve durable outcomes to complex situations. But as part of a wider network, they can perform precise tasks very effectively at each stage of the peace process. Moreover, NGOs and civic groups do not have the capacity to address the critical economic and political causes of conflict, but they can prepare the grounds so that such issues are tackled more effectively. It is in this context therefore, that nonconventional diplomacy should be set.

First, in the prenegotiations phase, NGOs and civic groups are often best placed to generate spaces for dialogue even while a conflict is ongoing. Sant Egidio, International Alert, and the people's groups in the Philippines, among others, demonstrate how they can become effective at that stage. They can work discreetly, over long periods of time, on a highly personal level to build trust and encourage constructive steps for peace. Because of their unofficial status and the informal approaches they can initiate, they can create an environment in which opponents meet, talk informally, air their views and share their concerns, without fear of reproof or shame. They can also work toward building grassroots awareness and support for the resolution of conflict. From localized forums to organized workshops and seminars, they can identify and draw on different strata of society so as to expand spaces for dialogue. By drawing on the experiences of other conflicts and peace processes, they can help expose the adversaries and members of the communities to the issues that need to be addressed and solutions that may be available, thus providing complementarity to the efforts of others. Moreover, by undertaking these tasks, NGOs and civic groups can help to create more favorable conditions for the next phase of official negotiations.

Second, once the negotiations phase commences, NGOs can continue to play a subsidiary role by helping to ensure that relevant factors and issues are considered to help conduct sound negotiations. When required, NGOs can be called upon to provide technical assistance and nurture the process. Particularly, if official talks are stalled, NGOs can help maintain less official channels of communication to sustain the dialogue. They can help encourage opponents to consider each obstacle independently and to formulate mutually acceptable agreements at every stage. In other words, when confronted by the possibility of stalemates or seeming dead ends they may provide alternative approaches or even discreet face-saving devices that may help advance the process. Once again, by helping to consolidate the foundations of the negotiations process, and ensuring that issues critical to all sides are adequately addressed, NGOs contribute toward strengthening the agreements and improving the climate in which the implementation phase is undertaken.

Finally, NGOs and civic groups can play a significant part in the consolidation phase, when a peace agreement is put into operation. Significant tasks such as demobilization of combatants and disarmament can be the responsibility of a joint international/national force. Maintaining adherence to the peace agreement and timetables, and keeping all sides accountable is primarily the task of the agreement's official guarantors who can exercise political, financial, and military leverage. The responsibility for the reconstruction of the nation's major infrastructure often falls into the hands of the government. Given the wide spectrum of international and national NGOs existing in the world today, cooperative work undertaken within a coherent framework could be highly effective in rebuilding trust and strong working relationships. They can help generate small scale economic programs for ex-combatants and civilians; create local and national forums for political debate and consultation; contribute educational materials, health care, and social services such as caring for orphaned children, women, the war's disabled populations, and refugee repatriation. They can draw attention to the issue of de-mining fields, social justice, establishing truth commissions, and securing legal assistance for war crimes tribunals.

Long after the international community and media have lost interest in the region of conflict, NGOs continue to work within the communities. Organizations rooted in the regions of conflict have a direct interest in pursuing their work. They are, after all, members of societies where the issues of war and peace are literally matters of life and death. Because the choices are stark, and the impact on their lives and their futures are direct, their commitment to making and building peace should be neither underestimated nor ignored.

Notes

1. See the relevant sections on "Burden Sharing" and "MultiTrack Diplomacy" under the chapter on "The Diplomacy Continuum," in Rupesinghe and Anderlini (1998, 112–115).

2. The historic information noted below was gathered from various sources, especially Vines (no date) and Hume (1994).

3. As director of Lonrho, a multinational British-based corporation with diverse interests in the Southern African region, Tiny Rowland had the necessary financial means and the political connections to wield a degree of influence with Renamo and regional governments.

4. Dhlakama's own writings are quoted in Vines (1991, 17).

5. Initially, Frelimo had taken a nonaligned stance in the international community but given President Reagan's deep-rooted intolerance of left-wing and Marxist governments, Mozambique was forced to modify its position.

6. Sant Egidio was founded in 1968, when a group of religious students decided to establish a charitable organization as a means of expressing their commitment to society. By 1994, the community had more than 100,000 members worldwide, working with 300 local groups across Italy and throughout Europe, Latin America, and Africa.

7. By 1984 Sant Egidio's involvement in the provision of humanitarian aid had also increased. In 1985 the "ship of solidarity" transported 3,500 tons of aid. In 1988, a further 7,000 tons were sent. Throughout that time, at home and across Europe, Sant Egidio developed a network of regional groups and committees to help collect funds and materials, while also spreading information about Mozambique's crisis. Inside Mozambique itself, a new network of mainly local parishes gradually emerged, helping those suffering from the war. Strong ties were also forged with local missionaries working in mine-ridden areas and Renamo-controlled territory. Communication with Renamo also continued to develop, so much so that by 1989, plans were being drawn for Dhlakama to visit Rome.

8. The detail of events listed in this section are quoted from Hume (1994) and Vines (no date).

9. International Alert (IA) is an NGO founded in 1985 with the specific mandate to work toward the prevention and resolution of intrastate violent conflicts. By 1995 IA had approximately fifty permanent staff at its London headquarters and had established close working relations with a wide network of national, regional, and international organizations involved in conflict resolution practice, skills training, and mediation.

10. For a comprehensive account of the Sierra Leone peace process, see International Alert (1997).

11. For a selection of relevant documents, see International Alert (1997, 87–97), as well as Amnesty International (1995) and various urgent action appeals made by Amnesty International.

12. See "A Report on the Peace Talks from February to May 1996: Searching for Common Ground," in International Alert (1997).

13. Military estimates also placed the figure at 23,200 regulars operating in sixty-five of the country's seventy-four provinces in the mid-1980s (Ferrer and Raquiza 1993).

14. The Philippine Constitution was drafted from June to mid-October 1986, and ratified in a plebiscite on February 2, 1987, by more than two-thirds of the electorate.

15. An analysis of the 1986–1987 talks has been written by Maris Diokno, herself a participant in the talks, and now director of the Third World Studies Center at the University of the Philippines.

16. Our terminology here follows Garcia (1993).

17. The book *Waging Peace in the Philippines* records the proceedings of the international conference; other IA-related publications were Garcia (1993) and National Institute for Policy Studies (1992).

18. Conversations with Dom Matteo Zuppi of the Comunita Sant' Egidio.

19. Joint Communiqués, Abidjan and Yamoussoukro, March 26, and April 23, 1996, in International Alert (1997, Appendix 2).

20. In the Joint Communiqué issued at Yamoussoukro, March 26, 1996, during the early phases of the talks the following acknowledgment was made by both the Sierra Leone government and the RUF: "The two Heads of Delegation expressed their sincere appreciation to the ICRC for providing valuable support for the peace process and in particular for facilitating the presence of the leader of the RUF/SL and his delegation at the summit by providing them transport facilities. Special recognition was also given to the role of International Alert who have played a great part in bringing about this historic meeting."

21. See Ferrer and Raquiza (1993) and Coalition for Peace (1993), and subsequent documents on social reform produced by the people's organizations that had been convened in this consortium built around the goal of a just peace.

22. See Appendix 3, "A Compilation of Peace Accords, Material on Cease-Fires and Confidence-Building Measures, Material on Human Rights and Truth Commissions, and Articles on Related Issues," and Appendix 4, "International Resource Material on Rebuilding War-Torn Societies," in International Alert (1997).

23. The example of recent efforts in Northern Ireland provides key lessons. See Rupesinghe (1998).

24. Especially relevant is Appendix 8, "Some Proposed Steps to Strengthen the Involvement of Civil Society in Pursuing Peace," of International Alert (1997).

25. A number of relevant articles are Hayner (1994); Zalaquett (1993); and Zalaquett's contribution to the 1994 IDASA volume, *Dealing with the Past: Truth and Reconciliation in South Africa*. The discussion on the International Criminal Court and the Amnesty International papers as well as those of other organizations participating in the 1998 Rome meetings are equally illustrative of the approaches to these important issues.

26. See the sources in the previous endnote.

27. See Article 17 of the 1996 Peace Agreement, "The Parties shall approach the international community with a view to mobilizing resources which will be used to establish a trust fund to enable the RUF/SL to transform itself into a political party." A brief discussion on the issue of elections and negotiations is found in the section on "Reconciling Different Positions" in International Alert (1997, 44).

28. Issues such as healthy economic development and sound electoral processes clearly contribute toward achieving sustainable peace.

9
Domestic and Transnational Strategies for Managing Separatist Conflicts
Four Asian Cases

Ted Robert Gurr and Deepa Khosla

Pessimists have characterized the first post–Cold War decade as the age of ethnic warfare and state collapse, of "conflicts unending" (Haass 1990) and "pandemonium" (Moynihan 1993). The generalization is overdrawn. It is true enough that many new communal wars broke out in the immediate aftermath of the Cold War, especially in the post-Communist states and in Africa. Global monitoring and analysis by the Minorities at Risk project, however, show that the surge peaked in the early 1990s. Whereas thirty-six new ethnopolitical rebellions began between 1988 and 1992—an average of seven per year—only twelve began between 1994 and 1998 (see Gurr 2000, chapter 2). Others also have documented and commented on a general decline in serious armed conflicts since the early 1990s (Wallensteen and Sollenberg 1998).

The decrease in communal warfare is due in part to the growing capacity of states and international organizations to contain and accommodate the demands of communal groups for greater rights and autonomy. The 1990s saw a pronounced global increase in negotiated settlements of separatist wars. The minorities project has identified seventeen such settlements between 1991 and 1998. Another ten separatist wars were contained during the same period, most of them by cease-fires and peacekeeping operations that open up longer-run opportunities for negotiated settlement. The net effect of the post–Cold War shift toward constructive management of armed conflicts within states is this: the number of ongoing separatist wars declined from twenty-nine at the end of 1990 to fourteen at the end of 1998 (Gurr 2000, chapter 6).

Several separatist ethnic conflicts have been transformed by negotiated settlements in Asia, including insurgencies fought by the Moros of the southern Philippines (armed conflict 1972–1996, autonomy agreements implemented in 1990, 1997–2000) and the Mizos of Northeastern India (armed conflict 1962–1986, statehood in the Indian Union in 1986). In other Asian countries—in Burma, Indonesia, Sri Lanka, and elsewhere in India—protracted communal conflicts have thus far been resistant to settlement.

This chapter compares the relatively successful settlements in the Philippines and India with failed efforts at accommodation in Kashmir and Tibet.[1] Our objective is to understand the character, consequences, and outcomes of domestic and international initiatives that were intended to manage and transform these four conflicts. The cases include two serious separatist conflicts that have been settled and two ongoing conflicts that have serious implications for regional security in the near and more distant future. The two groups that have achieved substate autonomy after a period of armed conflict and negotiation are the Moros of the Philippines and the Mizos in India. The ongoing conflicts center on the autonomy demands of Muslim Kashmiris in India (armed conflict 1989 to present) and Tibetans in China (episodic armed conflict 1959–1989, ongoing low-level resistance).

The cases chosen have these similarities:

- All involved protracted rebellions.
- The challenging groups had some degree of international support for rebellion.
- All posed some degree of regional security threat.

The cases are dissimilar in these key respects:

- As of mid-2000 there is little evidence of movement on the Tibetan dispute whereas conflict in Jammu and Kashmir escalated in the spring of last year following a major Pakistani-supported rebel incursion across the Indian side of the Line of Control.
- Despite regional autonomy agreements, some important underlying issues of conflict for the Moros and Mizos remain unresolved, including continued immigration of outsiders and low levels of economic development relative to other regions.
- In the Moro case, but not the others, an international organization (the Islamic Conference) was actively involved in promoting a negotiated settlement.

The following questions will be addressed in the case studies. At what phases in each conflict were initiatives taken and which actors, whether principals or third parties, initiated them? What immediate circumstances and motives led to the initiatives? How did the initiatives relate to developments (a) in the challenging group, (b) in the regime, and (c) in the international environment? And what short-term and long-term effects did they have on conflict transformation and settlement? Many other issues that are potentially relevant to the origins and resolution of protracted communal conflict fall outside the scope of our detailed analysis. They include the "root causes" of communal challenges to the state, the differing concepts of communal and national identity held by the principals, the impact of uneven development, and the potential supporting role of grassroots organizations and second-track diplomacy. Our approach is essentially a pragmatic or policy-making one: Taking the larger context as given, what initiatives have had what effects on the amelioration of armed secessionist conflict?

Other Studies

Good comparative studies of separatist conflicts in Asia have been published in the 1990s. Ahmed (1996) focuses on South Asia, showing how state-led modernization has helped politicize communal and regional identities and, as a consequence, has inspired separatist and communal challenges. Ganguly (1997b) tests alternative theories of ethnic political mobilization using information on ten secessionist movements in the Indian subcontinent. Gopinath (1991) examines how international forces have shaped the separatist campaigns of Muslims in Thailand and the Philippines, while Linter (1994) explores the links between separatist insurgencies, the opium trade, and state policies in Burma.

But we know of no comparative studies of strategies for managing or transforming communal conflicts in the region. On that topic it is necessary to refer first to case studies. Examples include chapters by Singer (Sri Lanka) and Anderson (Assam) in Montville (1990), and by Shastri (Sri Lanka), Liddle (Indonesia), May (Philippines), and Dreyer (China) in Brown and Ganguly (1997). Also relevant are general comparative studies of international conflict management strategies. Three are of particular interest to this study. One is Dixon's empirical study of the relative efficacy of six types of third-party conflict management techniques in settling 640 interstate disputes during the Cold War. He found that mediation and communication had consistently positive effects in preventing escalation to more intense phases of conflict and in promoting peaceful settlement. These two techniques even had positive effects on that subset of disputes that involved ethnic and irredentist issues (Dixon 1996).

The second is Regan's study of third-party military and economic interventions in eighty-five intrastate ethnic and ideological wars between 1944 and 1994. He reports that mixed military and economic strategies are much more likely to lead to a cessation of hostilities than either one alone, and that ethnic conflicts are more susceptible to successful intervention than ideological ones. The probability of success ranges from 0.07 (military or economic intervention in ideological wars) to 0.49 (mixed strategies in ethnic wars) (Regan 1996).

Finally, Walter compares negotiated settlements of interstate and civil wars between 1940 and 1990, asking why only 20 percent of civil wars were ended by peace agreements compared with 55 percent of interstate wars. She concludes, based on an analysis of outcomes of forty-one civil wars during this half-century, that the key problem is lack of guarantees on the terms of settlement. The presence of external (third-party) security guarantees for political and military power-sharing is the only factor that has a strong positive effect on negotiated settlements (Walter 1997). Her analysis does not distinguish between ideological and ethnic wars.

However, these studies fail to analyze conflict-management initiatives by the principals themselves. Most of the fourteen major initiatives identified in the four studies below originated with the principals; in the Mizo case a settlement was reached with minimal engagement by third parties outside India. This study begins with the assumption that it is essential to study the joint effects of domestic and third-party management strategies on the outcomes of internal ethnic wars. Hence our focus on the interactions between domestic and third-party initiatives in de-escalating separatist conflicts.[2] We begin with a series of analytic distinctions.

Phases of Conflict

We define the success or failure of conflict management initiatives according to whether they lead to a phase shift away from high-level hostilities. The most widely used scheme for characterizing the phases of international conflict was devised by Bloomfield and Leiss (1969) and subsequently modified by Sherman (1994a) and others. Their six phases are listed elsewhere in this volume. In Dixon's 1996 study, cited above, two levels of success of conflict management techniques are defined in phase terms: preventing escalation (e.g., a shift from the dispute phase to the hostilities phase) and promoting settlement (e.g., a shift from the hostilities phase toward posthostilities phases).

It is necessary to modify the Bloomfield–Sherman–Dixon phases to represent better the distinctive characteristics of internal wars. Unlike international disputes these are conflicts in which actors within states mobilize to challenge state authority. Case and comparative studies suggest that more fine-grained distinctions are needed to represent their dynamics. Therefore we distinguish the following phases, using categories that parallel those used by Sherman (1994a):

Phase I. Conventional mobilization. A political/communal group organizes in pursuit of collective objectives, relying on conventional and nonviolent strategies of political action.

Phase II. Militant mobilization. A political/communal group organizes in pursuit of collective objectives, developing capacities for disruptive and violent strategies of political action.

Phase IIIa. Low-level hostilities. A political/communal group makes limited, localized, selective use of disruptive and violent strategies; the regime makes limited and selective use of reactive force.

Phase IIIb. High-level hostilities. A political/communal group, or the regime, or both use intense, widespread, and organized armed violence against their opponent.

Phase IVa. Talk-fight. Discussions and negotiations are pursued, or cease-fires are declared, while substantial armed violence continues. Fighting may be done by the principals themselves (for example as a bargaining tactic) or by factions that reject dispute settlement.

Phase IVb. Cessation of open hostilities. Fighting largely ceases but one or both principals remain prepared to resume armed violence if settlement efforts fail.

Phase V. Posthostilities phase. Interim or partial settlements are in place and accepted by most parties and factions; demobilization, disarmament, and stand-downs are under way.

Phase VI. Settlement phase. A final settlement or agreement is accepted by most parties and is being implemented.

Criteria for Successful Conflict Management

Two criteria are used to evaluate the positive outcomes of conflict management initiatives. First, the initiatives lead to some degree of accommodation between the interests of the principals. That is, each party must attain some of the objectives for which it fought. In the case of communal challengers this usually means some mix of recognition, participation in governance, and material benefits; in the case of states it usually means an end to armed resistance by communal rebels and acceptance of the state's authority. Note that this criterion rules out situations in which communal conflicts end because of one party's military victory or mutual exhaustion. The second criterion is a substantial and sustained phase shift away from armed conflict. Conflicts do not necessarily progress regularly through the six phases identified above but may oscillate episodically among them. The success of conflict management initiatives can be judged by operational rules similar to those used by Dixon: modest success can be claimed if a conflict in Phase II or IIIa does not escalate to a higher level; if a conflict in Phase IV does not revert back to Phase III; and if a Phase V conflict does not revert to Phase IV. We also consider the durability of phase shifts. In our assessments we distinguish between short-term shifts (those lasting less than a year) and long-term shifts (more than a year).

Management Techniques: Who Uses What?

A broad distinction is made in this chapter between two kinds of actors who can initiate management techniques: principals and third parties.

The principals are the entities that represent the regime and ethnic challenger, any or all of whom may have reasons to seek a settlement. Regimes may propose cease-fires or amnesties, may initiate public or secret discussions with rebel representatives, or promise reforms contingent on a settlement. Challengers also frequently initiate peace moves. They may do so directly, as when a liberation army declares and observes a unilateral cease-fire, or through a political organization that issues a list of principles for settlement. In the case of Tibet the principal initiatives have come from the Tibetan exile organization based in India. The challengers are often represented by multiple and competing entities. In the later stage of the Mizo insurgency the elected Union Government of Mizoram was a party to the conflict, along with the military and political wings of the Mizo rebels. Similarly in Kashmir the National Conference coexists with armed rebels and, after the 1996 elections, controlled the state government. We treat all such entities as principals, though with the observation—developed in the conclusion—that elected regional governments may function in ways analogous to third parties.

Third parties include other governments in the region, major powers elsewhere, regional and international organizations, and nongovernmental organizations (NGOs). The diverse roles of these parties are illustrated in the four cases, except that initiatives by NGOs have played at best a supportive role in the Asian separatist conflicts under study (Behera, Evans, and Rizvi 1997). Moreover our chronologies do not identify any Asian examples of sustained second-track diplomacy initiatives.

The following types of conflict management techniques are used with some frequency (see Dixon 1996, 658; Harff 1992a; Lund 1996, 203–205; Regan 1996, 342). This list is intended to be comprehensive but not exhaustive. All these techniques, except peacekeeping, have been attempted at least once in the four Asian cases, appeals and concessions being by far the most commonly used.

Norm-based appeals, resolutions, condemnations. From third parties, also from principals within the country in conflict.

Communications. Informal diplomatic consultations and offers of good offices by third parties; exchanges of information and views, "talks about talks" among principals.

Proposals. Stipulation of principles, issues, possible reforms (by third parties or principals) that could lead to negotiations and settlement.

Concessions. Unilateral or tit-for-tat changes in action such as cease-fires, withdrawal of forces, lifting of restrictions, release of captives, etc.

Incentives. Provision of economic and political incentives to principals, including elections, appointment of group members to government bodies, humanitarian and developmental assistance, security guarantees, diplomatic representation, etc.

Observation. Fact-finding missions, commissions of inquiry, on-site monitoring by third parties.

Mediation. Negotiations convened by third parties, including conciliation and adjudication.

Coercive diplomacy. Threats and implementation of diplomatic and economic sanctions.

Peacekeeping. Internationally sanctioned peacekeeping operations.

Military intervention. Supply or transfer of troops, equipment, or intelligence and logistical support to parties in conflict, or cutoff of aid previously provided.

How the Case Studies Are Organized

The case studies consist of three elements. First there is a summary account of each conflict that identifies key issues and traces political developments. Embedded within these accounts are analyses of conflict management initiatives. Second, rather than providing a comprehensive catalog of conflict management efforts we identified major initiatives in each conflict, three each in the Moro and Mizo conflicts and four each in the Kashmir and Tibet disputes. Each initiative involved the investment of substantial political capital by one or several parties and was regarded by observers as a potential turning point in the conflict. Actors, motives, techniques, and consequences of each of these initiatives are summarized schematically in tables that accompany the text. The third element is a detailed chronology of each case that contains most of the information used for the summary account and analyses of initiatives. These chronologies, updated to mid-July 1999, are available on the Conflict Early Warning Systems Web site.

The Moros

The Moros are a conglomeration of tribal groups (including the Tausug, Maquindanao, Maranao, and Sulu) associated through a common religion: Islam. They primarily reside in the southern portion of the Philippines on the islands of the Sulu Archipelago, and on Mindanao and Palawan. Islam in the Philippines dates back to around 1280 A.D. Over the centuries, Muslim Sultanates and other political organizations emerged in conjunction with the development of a local folk-Islamic tradition.

The Philippines were colonized by the Spanish in 1565. However, the Spanish, like future outsiders, were never able to fully control the Muslims. It was the Spanish though who labeled the Philippine Muslims as "Moros," a term they first used in a derogatory sense toward their historic enemies, the Muslims of North Africa and southern Spain.

Three centuries later, the Treaty of Paris of 1898 ceded the Philippines to the United States. For nearly two decades, the southern Moros resisted U.S. control. In 1935, the Commonwealth of the Philippines was created. Fearing that they would be dominated by the majority Christian population, some Muslim leaders unsuccessfully attempted to keep the south under U.S. administration. Muslims were partially integrated at the national level through appointments to the Commonwealth's Senate.

World War II temporarily defused Muslim concerns as a coalition was formed among Moros, Christians, and the United States to combat a Japanese occupation that reportedly engaged in "unparalleled atrocities." The Philippines gained its independence in 1946. The subsequent opening of Moro lands, especially in Mindanao, resulted in extensive migrations of mostly Christian settlers. The indigenous Muslim groups on Mindanao feared that their status was quickly eroding due to what they perceived as central government bias toward the Christian settlers. Disputes over land and resource allocations ignited sporadic conflicts between the settlers and the Moros throughout the 1950s and 1960s.

In 1961, a federal representative of the Muslim Sulu region called for self-government for the region, and by the end of the decade Moro organizations and leaders were actively pressing claims for autonomy and/or secession. The immediate trigger for the emergence of a militant Moro movement was the 1968 incident referred to as Operation Merdeka by the Philippines government and the Jabidah Massacre by Muslims. The government asserted that some twenty-eight Muslim army recruits were killed after they mutinied against not being paid for several months. The Moros argued that the soldiers mutinied because they were being trained for clandestine pro-Philippines operations among the predominantly Muslim peoples of Sabah and North Borneo (Malaysia). No charges were made in the incident.

The lack of government response to the soldiers' deaths added fuel to existing Moro grievances. Primary among these was the increased migration of Christians to the southern region, which deepened Muslim fears that they would be overwhelmed. The Christians were also viewed as the primary beneficiaries of the government's economic and political programs in the economically disadvantaged region.

In 1969, traditional Moro leaders established the Muslim Independence Movement (MIM). It demanded an independent government, claiming that integration with the Philippines was impossible. Some ninety Moros, who later formed the MIM's military arm, the Blackshirts, were sent to Malaysia to begin guerrilla training (Mercado 1984, 157). Among this group was Nur Misuari, who rose from modest origins to become a political science instructor at the University of the Philippines. He was representative of a new class of Moro activists that did not belong to the traditional aristocratic and religious elite and favored, among other things, a modern guerrilla approach. In 1971, under Misuari's leadership, they formed the Moro National Liberation Front (MNLF) and its military arm, the Bangsa Moro army.

Conflict Management Efforts

The first effort to peacefully settle Moro claims for autonomy occurred in 1975. From 1969 until martial law was imposed in 1972, there was widespread violence in the south as the MIM's military arm, the Blackshirts, violently clashed with the Illaga, a Christian militia movement formed in 1970. During this time, the Moros consolidated their movement under the umbrella of the MNLF, resulting in a force that ranged from 5,000 to 30,000 fighters. The ability of their leader, Nur Misuari, to obtain support from Islamic states enabled the organization to launch armed attacks against the Marcos government and Christian groups.

From 1972 to 1975, Libya was reported to be the Moros main patron, supplying some $3.5 million in financial and military assistance. Neighboring countries such as Malaysia and Indonesia, along with Saudi Arabia and Iran, also reportedly supported the Moros in the early years, including a short-lived 1973 oil boycott against the Philippines. The Malaysian state of Sabah was actively involved in backing the Moros until the mid-1980s, providing transit routes and hosting some 100,000 refugees.

Finally, the Organization of the Islamic Conference (OIC) gave political and logistical support, including recognition of the MNLF as the legitimate representative of the Moro people. It also initiated fact-finding missions and created a Quadripartite Commission that helped establish a framework for talks between the two sides. At no time did the Association of Southeast Asian Nations (ASEAN) or the United Nations engage in the dispute.

The imposition of martial law in the Philippines in 1972, mainly in response to escalating violence in the south, is believed to have closed off any nonviolent options for the Moros (May 1988, 53). Fidel Marcos generally adopted a two-pronged strategy to the insurgency: on the one hand, he promoted economic development along with conceding some religious demands, while on the other, he tried to militarily defeat the rebels. By the mid-1970s, the insurgency was responsible for some 35,000 to 60,000 deaths, 31,000 to 54,000 injuries, and 260,000 to 350,000 displaced persons (Rodil 1993, 17).

The first formal talks between the MNLF and the Philippines were held in 1975 in Jeddah, Saudi Arabia, under the auspices of the OIC. No progress was reported as Misuari reportedly wanted the Marcos regime to make an a priori declaration that an autonomous region would be established with a separate government and army. The OIC's efforts to develop an acceptable negotiating framework led to negotiations in Tripoli from November to December 1976. (See table 9.1: Management Initiative I, July 1975–December 1976, for details.)

On December 21, 1976, the Tripoli agreement was signed between the MNLF and the Philippines government under the sponsorship of the OIC. The accord granted autonomy in thirteen geographic areas of the south and committed the government to undertake all the necessary constitutional provisions.

However, by April of the next year, disagreements emerged over the implementation of the Tripoli Agreement. MNLF chief Nur Misuari objected to government plans for a referendum to ratify the autonomous region, likely because by now Muslims were a minority in the south. The referendum was held nonetheless and three provinces chose to opt out of the proposed autonomous region while a majority of voters rejected proposals such as allowing the region to maintain its own security forces. The MNLF now began to press for full independence.

At the eighth Islamic Conference in Libya in May 1977, the MNLF was granted observer status. However, the OIC refused a Moro demand to enact economic sanctions against the Philippines; instead the Quadripartite Commission extended its mediation efforts.

Table 9.1: Management Initiative Moros I, July 1975–December 1976

Conflict Phase at Onset of Initiative: Phase IIIb. High-Level Hostilities

Motives

Philippines Government

- Reduce international pressure due to reported human rights abuses under martial law.
- Help curtail growing support for the Moros from the OIC and other Muslim states.
- Marcos is concerned about the Moros's military capabilities, who while unable to overthrow the government, remain a significant armed threat. The growth of the Christian right and its violent activities also poses a challenge to the regime.

Moros

- Rebel force is exhausted following the large numbers of militant and civilians deaths since the early 1970s.
- Fear of withdrawal of external support from the OIC and Muslim states if they do not open talks.
- Growth of a militant Christian right threatens the capabilities of the Moros to challenge state authorities.

OIC

- Help ensure that the MNLF's demands do not escalate to independence as this could set a precedent in member countries.
- Concern that the conflict might spread to embroil neighboring states such as Malaysia.
- Protect Muslim kin from state repression and promote their well-being.

Interacting Motives

- All the parties seek to de-escalate the conflict, although for different reasons.
- The government and the OIC are likely worried about the spread of Islamic extremism.

Table 9.1 (continued)

Management Techniques

Principals:

- Philippines government
- Moros: Norm-based appeals; concessions

Third Parties:

- The Organization of the Islamic Conference: norm-based appeals; communications; proposals; observation; mediation
- Libya: Military intervention; Norm-based appeals
- Malaysia: Military intervention; Norm-based appeals

Short-Term Consequences:

- Phase shift to IVb. Cessation of open hostilities
- The accord is a diplomatic coup for the Organization of the Islamic Conference, which has actively attempted to resolve the dispute since the early 1970s.

Long-Term Consequences:

- Shift to phase IIIa. Low-Level Hostilities
- Divisions emerge within the MNLF.
- International support for the Moros declines likely due to Misuari's demand for independence.
- The Tripoli Agreement does, however, provide a framework for subsequent negotiations between the two sides.

The year 1977 has been described as a watershed for the Moro National Liberation Front (May 1988, 57). The rebels were militarily weak as many had been killed while others had sought refuge in Sabah or the Middle East. Divisions had arisen over the Islamic nature of the movement, whether to pursue autonomy or independence, and whether to continue using the Tripoli Agreement as the basis for negotiations. The MNLF split into three major factions: the original MNLF, the Moro Islamic Liberation Front (MILF), and later the MNLF-RG (Reformist Group).

The Philippines government founded Autonomous Regions 9 and 12 in March 1979, following its interpretation of the Tripoli Agreement. Regional assembly elections were boycotted by the MNLF. Throughout the next five to six years, Nur Misuari (in self-exile in Jeddah) focused on gaining international recognition and support for the Moro cause. In 1984 the OIC reconfirmed the MNLF as the sole legitimate representative of the

Bangsa Moro people, but by this point the MNLF reportedly had only 14,000 members. Widespread disenchantment with the Fidel Marcos regime culminated in the People's Power Revolution in 1986. The subsequent election of Corazon Aquino as president and the end of military rule led to Nur Misuari's return from exile and the initiation of talks with the new regime. (See table 9.2: Management Initiative II, September 1986–May 1987, for details.) A cease-fire and amnesty program were announced in September 1986. However, efforts to unite the disparate Moro groups failed and armed attacks against government targets by the MILF and the MNLF-RG continued.

On January 4, 1987, the Jeddah Accord was signed between the government and the MNLF. In this case, no outside parties were directly involved in the negotiations. The agreement proposed autonomy for the entire island of Mindanao. Talks in April to work out the details deadlocked over the extent of the proposed Muslim area as the government offered Autonomous Regions 9 and 12 while the MNLF argued that all of Mindanao and the three nearby islands be included. The next month, following MNLF accusations that the government had violated the cease-fire, Misuari returned to the Middle East.

Corazon Aquino proceeded with the implementation of the Jeddah Accord by creating the Autonomous Region of Muslim Mindanao (ARMM) in August 1989. A subsequent referendum to ratify the new region was boycotted by both the MNLF and Christian groups. Only four noncontiguous provinces voted for its creation and they formed the ARMM. Regional elections held the following year resulted in a former MNLF member being elected as governor.

National elections in the Philippines in May 1992 were won by the party of Marcos' former defense minister, Fidel Ramos. Upon taking office as president, Ramos committed himself to reaching political settlements with all of the country's armed groups including the Moros and the communist New People's Army (NPA). A National Unification Commission was created to undertake the negotiations.

Following the urging of Libya and the facilitation of the OIC, formal talks between the government and the MNLF opened in Jakarta, Indonesia, in April 1993. (See table 9.3: Management Initiative III, April 1993–September 1996, for details.) By November, a cease-fire agreement was reached and a committee established to help resolve the problems confronting Muslims in Mindanao. The cease-fires were continually extended over the next three years.

As talks continued, some Moro groups refused to participate and sought to derail negotiations by attacking government and civilian facilities. Along with the MILF, another group, the Abu Sayyaf, was alleged to be responsible for a May 1995 attack that resulted in more than fifty civilian casualties. This was reported to be the single worst attack since the Moro insurgency began. Meanwhile, the Ramos government sought to redress economic difficulties in the south through improvements in infrastructure and development of the agricultural sector. An $80 million agreement was signed with foreign investors to develop Mindanao.

By December, a tentative settlement between the MNLF and the government was reached, covering some 70 to 80 percent of the issues on the table. The integration of

Table 9.2: Management Initiative Moros II, September 1986–May 1987

Conflict Phase at Onset of Initiative: Phase IIIa. Low-Level Hostilities

Motives

Philippines Government

- Eliminate the costs of the insurgency that are draining the government's resources and diverting policy attention from the country's dismal economic conditions.
- Negotiating with the MNLF could reduce the growth of extremist Moro groups.
- Corazon Aquino is eager to gain international support for her new democratic government and talks with the Moros would send an important signal.

Moros

- MNLF leader Misuari is under pressure from his membership to settle for autonomy instead of pursuing independence.
- Misuari is concerned that he is losing control of the movement as splinter groups such as the MILF are able to launch sustained violent attacks against the regime.
- International support for the MNLF has sharply declined.

Interacting Motives

- Both principals are feeling the costs of the insurgency and are worried about extremists.

Management Techniques

Principals:

- Philippines government: Norm-based appeals; concessions
- Moros: Norm-based appeals; concessions

Short-Term Consequences:

- Although the MNLF refuses to participate, the institutional framework for an autonomous Muslim region is established.

Long-Term Consequences:

- The creation of an autonomous region provides for limited Moro self-governance and implementation of some economic development policies.
- Other Moro groups that favor setting up an Islamic state begin to pose a more disruptive challenge to the government than the MNLF.
- Christian resentment against a Muslim autonomous region is tempered as it only encompasses four provinces.

Table 9.3: Management Initiative Moros III, April 1993–September 1996

Conflict Phase at Onset of Initiative: Phase IIIb. High-Level Hostilities

Motives

Philippines Government
- President Ramos wants to eliminate the costs of the twenty-year insurgency.
- The regime wants to negotiate an agreement with the MNLF while it still retains broad support. It is worried that extremist groups might soon become the major players.

Moros
- The MNLF is losing its support base due to war weariness and the expansion of extremist groups and Misuari is also under pressure from the OIC.
- The Christian population in the south continues to grow. Already, the Muslims are a minority and could become less influential over time.

OIC
- Attempt to stop extremism and its potential diffusion in the region.

Indonesia
- Indonesia offers to take the lead role as it is likely concerned about the development of similar movements in its own country. Further, since Indonesia has not actively supported the militants it may be more acceptable to the Philippines government.

Interacting Motives
- All parties are seeking to counter the influence of extremist Islamic groups.

Management Techniques

Principals:

Philippines government: Norm-based appeals; concessions; incentives

Moros: Norm-based appeals; concessions; incentives

Third Parties:

Organization of the Islamic Conference: Norm-based appeals; communications; proposals; incentives; mediation

Indonesia: Norm-based appeals; communications

Table 9.3 *(continued)*

Short-Term Consequences:

- High-level hostilities continue.
- The implementation of the autonomy accord allows for economic development policies to be instituted in the south while also drawing some initial foreign investment.
- Some 100,000 refugees in Sabah, Malaysia return home.
- The OIC's successful mediation increases its regional and international stature.

Long-Term Consequences:

- Shift to Phase V. Post-Hostilities.
- As institutional structures are in place for the Muslim autonomous region, organizations such as the World Bank are willing to provide loans.
- While many MNLF members have demobilized, concerns remain that some will return to violence due to the limited benefits accrued so far.

---

the rebels into the army, the geographic area of the autonomous region, and the holding of a referendum remained the main sticking points. By this time, Muslims were estimated to constitute only 40 percent of Mindanao's population, about 4.9 million of the country's population of some 69 million.

In early 1996, the MNLF and the Christian group, the Illaga, agreed to cease hostilities. However, violent attacks by the MILF and Abu Sayyaf persisted against both civilian and government targets. A potential deadlock in March over interpretations of the 1976 Tripoli Agreement led both the OIC and MNLF leader Misuari to fear that the hands of radical Moro groups could be strengthened.

Following meetings brokered by the OIC, a peace agreement was realized on June 23, 1996. Under the accord, a Southern Philippine Council for Peace and Development (SPCPD), run by the MNLF, was founded. It is guided by a consultative assembly of local officials and NGO representatives to pave the way for autonomy. The new region includes fourteen provinces; this was basically the area agreed upon in the Tripoli Agreement. A referendum, expected to be held later this year, will determine whether the residents support the council's rule. By 1996, the Moro campaign had cost some 100,000 lives—half of these rebels, 30 percent soldiers, and the remaining civilians. The government had spent an estimated $3 billion, an average of 40 percent of its military budget, over the course of the insurgency.

While the accord led to widespread protests by Christian leaders and residents, who now constituted a majority in the south, President Ramos vowed that its provisions would be implemented. The Moro Islamic Liberation Front and Abu Sayyaf also rejected the settlement, pledging to continue their violent campaigns for genuine autonomy and/or independence.

On September 2, the peace agreement was formally signed in Manila between the government and the MNLF in the presence of Indonesia's Foreign Minister Ali Alatas and OIC Secretary-General Hamid Algabid. Since 1993, Indonesia had hosted a number of rounds of formal talks while the OIC actively mediated these sessions. MNLF leader Nur Misuari was elected governor of the Autonomous Region of Muslim Mindanao (ARMM), receiving 90 percent of the votes. Some 80 percent of the residents participated. In October 1996, he was appointed as head of the regional Development Council, which received a $1.2 billion aid package from the federal government.

While the Moro Islamic Liberation Front (MILF), the next largest group, continued its violent attacks against state authorities it also opened negotiations with the Ramos regime. Despite numerous violations, a cease-fire agreement reached in July 1997 was continually extended to allow for preparatory talks. Formal peace talks between the 10,000 strong MILF and the government opened in October 1999 and were still underway in early 2000. The military has continued its operations against Abu Sayyaf, asserting that it is only a terrorist organization. The death of the founder and leader of Abu Sayyaf in 1998 allegedly dealt a severe blow to the organization, which is reported to have about 200 members. Both of these groups favor some form of Islamic rule in the south.

Implementation of the provisions of the autonomy accord is still proceeding as of mid-2000. However, grievances over limited economic benefits coupled with delays with the rehabilitation and integration of former MNLF rebels have led a minority of MNLF members to join the MILF or Abu Sayyaf or resort to extortion. Continuing violence in the south has limited foreign investment and although the government and agencies such as the World Bank are providing various forms of assistance, it is unlikely that tangible benefits will be visible to the average person in the near future. Economic conditions and other indicators such as literacy rates indicate that the south already lags far behind the rest of the country. The long-term success of the autonomy agreement likely hinges on the government's ability both to provide greater material benefits and also to subdue the remaining militant groups, either through negotiations or military victory.

The Mizos

The approximately 650,000 Mizos—also referred to as Lushais after their primary area of residence, the Lushai Hills—are of Tibeto-Burmese origins. They live throughout the northeastern border areas of India and maintain close links with tribal groups in both neighboring Bangladesh and Burma. As with the Chittagong Hill Tribals in modern Bangladesh, the British occupation of the Indian subcontinent in the late 1800s markedly changed traditional Mizo social structures. Missionaries were able to convert the vast majority of the population to Christianity. The British abolished the traditional elective Lushai chieftaincy system, instead granting certain influential families the hereditary privilege to rule.

The Mizo Union was established in 1946 to oppose the British-imposed political system. It formed close ties with the Indian Congress Party and subsequently supported the incorporation of the Lushai Hills into the Indian state of Assam in 1947. However, the delayed and limited responses of the Mizo Union and the Assam government to a massive famine in 1959 led discontented Mizos to form a new organization, the Mizo National Famine Front. Led by Laldenga (Mizos traditionally use one name), a former army officer who had also worked in the administration of the local district council, the organization was renamed the Mizo National Front (MNF) in 1962 to reflect members' desires for autonomy or secession.

In local elections later that year, the MNF won a significant number of seats. To press its claim for independence, it sought and received military aid from the government of East Pakistan. Reports suggest that China also provided similar assistance. In 1966, barely six months after the second India-Pakistan war, the armed wing of the MNF launched Operation Jericho, a major military strike against key civilian and military centers in the Lushai Hills. The 1,000-odd rebels captured the capital, Aizawal, and raided government treasuries and arms depots in other towns. By March of that year, the central government wrested control from the MNF. Many MNF members including its leader, Laldenga, fled to East Pakistan to escape arrest.

In the late 1960s, to prevent a resurgence of Mizo militancy, Indian Prime Minister Indira Gandhi embarked upon a large-scale reorganization of villages in the Lushai Hills. Following the British Malay model, thousands of villagers were relocated in hamlet areas, their houses and crops burnt (Bhaumik 1996, 159). With their traditional source of livelihood gone, the villagers became reliant on government handouts. The program was finally halted in 1970 after complaints from local opposition parties. Throughout the late 1960s, the MNF continued sporadic armed attacks against government targets. While it unsuccessfully attempted to gain international recognition for its independence campaign, the MNF did form links with rebel groups in Nagaland and the Arakan in Burma, and with Mizo kin in India's Manipur and Tripura regions.

Caught in the crossfire in the aftermath of the 1971 India-Pakistan war that led to the secession of Bangladesh, the MNF suffered a major political and military defeat. Indian forces swept the Chittagong Hill Tracts in Bangladesh and destroyed MNF bases. Further, the organization split as its intellectual cadres surrendered and Laldenga fled again, this time to Burma.

Within India, efforts to satisfy autonomy demands resulted in the 1972 North-Eastern Areas (Reorganization) Act, under which Mizoram was given the status of a Union Territory and three other states were created. While this met some Mizo grievances, it still did not address issues such as MNF desires for the protection of the Mizo culture and lifeways and a halt to continual migrations of Bangladeshis in the northeast. Fearing that they would be overwhelmed by the Bengalis from Bangladesh, indigenous peoples throughout the region have launched violent campaigns to check these migrations.

Conflict Management Efforts

The first formal talks between the MNF and the government of India were held in early 1976 although the process leading toward negotiations began some three years earlier. Following its expulsion from the Chittagong Hills in Bangladesh, the MNF moved its operations to Burma's Arakan province. Indications are that China increased its military support to the Mizos to offset the loss of their East Pakistani patrons (Ali 1993, 39–40). In 1973, MNF leader Laldenga offered to open talks with the government. His suggestion was supported by the local Congress Party, which had recently merged with the Mizo Union and won the Union Territory elections the previous year. However, Prime Minister Indira Gandhi asserted that violence in Mizoram first had to end.

In August 1975, Laldenga made his second overture to begin negotiations. The Indian government's recent negotiation of the Shilling Accord—a peace settlement with the Nagas—was a blow to the Mizos who had formed links with Naga rebel organizations. Laldenga returned from exile the following January and held secret negotiations with New Delhi. (See table 9.4: Management Initiative I, August 1975–March 1978, for details.) The next month a tentative agreement was signed between the two parties in which the MNF acknowledged that Mizoram was an integral part of India and that any settlement would be in line with the constitution. Further, Laldenga agreed that the MNF would cease its violent campaign and that the rebels would surrender.

During the two years after the February 1976 agreement, MNF leader Laldenga attempted to consolidate his control over the rebels and obtain widespread support for the interim accord. Meanwhile, with the end of the National Emergency (1975–1977) and subsequent elections, a new Janata Dal government led by Moraji Desai took over in New Delhi. In March 1978 the federal government broke off talks. The breakdown reportedly was due to the government's rejection of Laldenga's demand that he be granted an interim government position prior to the holding of elections in Mizoram (Bhaumik 1996, 180–181).

Talks between the two sides resumed in April 1980, shortly after Indira Gandhi was reelected as prime minister. (See table 9.5: Management Initiative II, April 1980–January 1982, for details.) A cease-fire agreement was implemented in August. Divisions within the MNF arose again, particularly between the military and civilian wings. As Laldenga was unable to persuade all the rebels to cease their operations, attacks against government targets and Bangladeshi migrants—likely by members of the military wing—continued despite the cease-fire.

Early in 1982, Indira Gandhi launched another crackdown against the MNF, banning the organization and arresting hundreds of members. New Delhi asserted that Laldenga was using the talks to strengthen his movement and escalate its violent activities. It also contended that Laldenga wanted the elected Mizoram government dismissed and the MNF to be allowed to form an interim administration. The MNF leader claimed that India intended to end the dispute by military force.

The activities of the MNF were severely curtailed for the next few years as its leader was again in exile and some 800 MNF members had been arrested, killed, or

Table 9.4: Management Initiative Mizos I, August 1975–March 1978

Conflict Phase at Onset of Initiative: Phase IIIa. Low-Level Hostilities

Motives

Indian Government
- Reduce international pressure due to reported human rights abuses during the imposition of a National Emergency (1975–1977).

Union of Mizoram Government
- The ruling Congress Party has established its presence in the area through its relations with the top twenty Mizo families that dominate the region's economic structure.
- It seeks to expand its political base by helping to promote a negotiated settlement.

Mizos
- Rebel force is exhausted and is able to launch only limited attacks from the Chittagong Hill Tracts in Bangladesh and Arakan Province in Burma.
- China withdraws its military/financial support to the group, asserting that it will now only aid ideological movements.
- The MNF's leader, Laldenga, has been in exile in Pakistan and Bangladesh for the last five years. Along with fears that he is losing touch with the Mizos in India, there are concerns about the growth of new Mizo organizations such as the Peoples' Conference.

Interacting Motives
- Both Prime Minister Indira Gandhi and MNF leader Laldenga are worried about the extent of their control over their constituents and need to undertake some action to assert their dominant roles.

Management Techniques

Principals:
- Indian government
- Mizos: Norm-based appeals; concessions
- Union of Mizoram government: Norm-based appeals

Third Parties:
- Bangladesh: Military intervention
- Burma: Military intervention

Short-Term Consequences:
- The MNF returns to the use of violent tactics, primarily from its bases in Bangladesh and Burma, although divisions between its civil and military factions deepen.
- A newly formed Mizo group, the Peoples' Conference, vies for the allegiance of the Mizo population. The conference wins local elections in 1978 and again in 1979 after a brief period of federal rule.

Long-Term Consequences:
- While the accord does not address underlying issues like Bangladeshi migration or the protection of Mizo culture and lifeways, it does provide the framework for the second initiative to resolve the dispute (1980–1982).
- The electoral victories of the Peoples' Conference raise doubts about the popularity of the Mizo National Front and its leader, Laldenga, who has spent most of the past five years in exile.

Table 9.5: Management Initiative Mizos II, April 1980–January 1982

Conflict Phase at Onset of Initiative: Phase IIIa. Low-Level Hostilities

Motives

Indian Government
- Following her large countrywide electoral victory, Prime Minister Indira Gandhi seeks to remove a thorn from her side as the Mizos are no longer a significant challenge.

Mizos
- The MNF is worried about the rise of the Peoples' Conference, fearing it has lost its support base.

Interacting Motives
- The talks provide both Gandhi and Laldenga with an opportunity to expand their control over their constituencies. Prime Minister Gandhi is attempting to centralize control at the federal level while Laldenga is seeking to ensure his support among his group members and the Mizo population at-large.

Management Techniques

Principals:
- Indian government: Concessions
- Mizos: Concessions; Norm-based appeals

Short-Term Consequences:
- Laldenga is ordered to leave India. He goes into exile in London.
- The fragmented Mizo movement is further weakened due to a security crackdown.

Long-Term Consequences:
- Many of the issues in dispute are settled during this round of talks, setting the stage for the final negotiations in 1984.
- The MNF is no longer able to pose an effective challenge to state authorities due to internal divisions, a lack of external support, and the state's military campaigns.
- Low-level hostilities continue.

---

surrendered to authorities. After the local Congress Party won a majority in Mizoram's election in 1984, Indira Gandhi announced that she was ready to resume talks with the MNF. (See table 9.6: Management Initiative III, October 1984–June 1986, for details.)

Mizoram's new Congress government provided a major impetus for the resumption of talks. There was a mood of war-weariness among the population and growing resentment against the continual violence. The union territory's Chief Minister Lalthanhawla was eager to promote stability and as a major concession, he offered to resign his position in the hopes of promoting a settlement.

To fulfill the government's preconditions for negotiations, the MNF agreed to cease its military activities and again pledged that the area was an integral part of the Indian union. At this point, there were reported to be fewer than 1,000 armed fighters. The movement was again divided between those who favored continued warfare and those who wanted to rejoin the political process.

Negotiations between the government and the MNF were set to open in October 1984. But the assassination of Prime Minister Indira Gandhi late that month postponed the talks for another month. She was succeeded by her son, Rajiv, who subsequently won an overwhelming majority in December's federal elections.

Regular meetings between the two sides resulted in the elimination of most points of contention by April 1985. The provision of full statehood for Mizoram was agreed upon. Issues that remained included the provision of an amnesty for the rebels and the MNF desire to participate in an interim administration. In October the two sides reached a deal on the surrender of arms by Mizo rebels. In June of the following year, India's Cabinet gave its approval to the peace accord. A Memorandum of Settlement was signed on June 30, 1986, between the Union Home Secretary, MNF leader Laldenga, and Mizoram Chief Minister Lalthanhawla. This was the third accord negotiated by the Rajiv Gandhi government to end an insurgency—the others were in Assam and the Punjab.

In August, Mizoram was formally declared the twenty-third state of the Indian Union. The remaining aspects of the settlement were implemented over the next year, including the surrender of the MNF rebels. The MNF won state elections in March 1987, becoming the first insurgency movement to be elected to rule an Indian state. Laldenga assumed the chief ministership.

In contrast to many other regional accords in India, the 1986 Mizoram settlement has thus far succeeded in ending open conflict. However, a number of key issues still remain to be settled. Primary among these is the large-scale presence of Bangladeshis (Bengalis) in Mizoram. Mizos fear that they will become a majority in their region, contending that the Bangladeshis already benefit disproportionately from limited economic and educational opportunities. Although Mizoram has a very high literacy rate (over 80 percent), it remains economically behind much of India. Pressures for economic development are thus likely to increase.

Finally, desires for the formation of a Greater Mizoram that would encompass Mizo areas in India and Burma are still alive among a limited segment of the population. Were this movement to gain broad support, it could lead to the emergence of a new conflict that could engulf much of the northeast region.

Table 9.6: Management Initiative Mizos III October 1984–June 1986

Conflict Phase at Onset of Initiative: Phase IIIa. Low-Level Hostilities

Motives

Indian Government
- The Congress Party has established its presence as a legitimate force in Mizoram and hopes to end the minor insurgency as New Delhi is confronting more serious rebellions in the Punjab and Assam.

Mizos
- The MNF is a depleted force of 250–400 fighters and is able to launch only sporadic armed attacks. Its leader is in exile in London.
- Public support for the violent campaign has declined. Protests held in Mizo areas reflect the population's war weariness.

Union of Mizoram Government
- Desires a return to normalcy after two decades of warfare while still preserving the culture and lifeways of the Mizos.

Interacting Motives
- All three parties are weary due to the protracted dispute. It is clear that the MNF is no longer a military threat but it is still able to conduct limited attacks against both state authorities and Bengali migrants.

Management Techniques

Principals:
- Indian government: Concessions; norm-based appeals; incentives
- Mizos: Concessions; norm-based appeals
- Union Government of Mizoram: Norm-based appeals; concessions; incentives

Short-Term Consequences:
- There is a shift to Phase V. Post-Hostilities.
- Mizoram achieves full statehood, ending the twenty-year Mizo insurgency.
- The Mizos are empowered to protect their culture and lifeways and make some progress on limiting outsiders entering the region.
- The MNF agrees not to support insurgencies in Tripura and Manipur.
- Relations between India and Bangladesh improve due to the end of Bangladeshi support for the Mizos coupled with joint efforts to stem the cross-border migration of Bengalis.
- The rehabilitation of the rebels proceeds on schedule and the other aspects of the agreement are implemented.
- The MNF wins the state's first elections. Laldenga becomes chief minister.

Long-Term Consequences:
- There is a shift to Phase VI. Settlement.
- The MNF becomes a regular political party and engages in the electoral process.
- Mizoram and Arunchal Pradesh are the only two regions among the seven northeastern states that do not face violent insurgencies in the late 1990s.
- Some problems remain unsettled, including migrations by Bangladeshis, economic development concerns, and the desire of a limited group to unite Mizos in neighboring areas.

The Kashmiris

It has been more than fifty years since India and Pakistan waged their first war over the territory known as Jammu and Kashmir. The roots of the dispute date to the decolonization and subsequent partition of the subcontinent into the states of India and Pakistan. Princely regions such as Jammu and Kashmir were allowed to join either of the new countries based upon geographic and demographic realities. Independence was not an option although this was favored by Sheikh Abdullah, the region's most popular leader, and his National Conference Party. The Hindu maharajah of the Muslim-majority region of Kashmir negotiated standstill agreements with the two countries that became independent in August 1947.

However, in October of that year a tribal rebellion broke out in Western Kashmir and large numbers of Pakistani troops joined in. The Maharajah appealed to New Delhi for aid. But this aid was conditioned on Kashmir's accession to India. The Maharajah complied on October 26, 1947. The rebellion was crushed shortly after Indian forces entered Jammu and Kashmir.

The dispute was then referred to the United Nations, where agreement was reached to hold an international plebiscite to determine Kashmir's status. A UN commission visited the area to investigate and make arrangements for the plebiscite. Following another Pakistani incursion, the UN Military Observer Group in India and Pakistan (UNMOGIP) was created to monitor a cease-fire implemented in 1949. By this time, the ceasefire line left one-third of the territory under Pakistani control (this area is referred to as Azad or Free Kashmir) and the remainder under India.

Throughout the 1950s, various UN representatives attempted to mediate the dispute between India and Pakistan. However, all the draft proposals on demilitarization of the cease-fire line and the holding of a plebiscite were rejected. At least twelve bilateral meetings were also held from 1953 to 1972 but no settlement was reached. During this period, Pakistan became a member of SEATO and CENTO, U.S.-developed alliances to combat the Soviet threat. In response, the Soviet Union utilized its veto in the UN Security Council to stop any resolutions against India.

In 1956 Jammu and Kashmir, the only Muslim-majority region in India, was proclaimed a state of the union. Prime Minister Jawaharlal Nehru declared that a plebiscite was no longer necessary as the region's Constituent Assembly approved the merger. By the late 1950s, it became clear that the United Nations was either unable or unwilling to implement any of its proposals to resolve the conflict. Moreover, neither country was prepared to make any tangible concessions (Lindgren et al. 1991, 47).

The attention of the international community turned toward Vietnam and the Arab-Israeli conflict in the 1960s. No international mediation efforts were undertaken regarding Kashmir. Talks held between India and Pakistan during 1962–1963 failed as India had just suffered a humiliating defeat in its 1962 war with China, which captured the Askai Chin, in the eastern part of Jammu and Kashmir (Ganguly 1996a, 150).

Protests by the majority Muslim population in Kashmir in 1963 reportedly signaled to Pakistan that the time was ripe to capture the remaining territory. This was reinforced by both limited Indian responses to Pakistani incursions in the Rann of Kutch in January 1965 and active campaigning by the residents of Azad Kashmir (the one-third of territory controlled by Pakistan) who have supported reunification with their kin through either incorporation in Pakistan or the establishment of an independent state. In September, the second Indo-Pak war broke out when the Pakistani army crossed into Jammu. The war was short-lived (less than three weeks) as the United States and Britain imposed arms embargoes against both combatants. U.N. Security Council resolutions called for a cease-fire that was monitored by a temporary U.N. India-Pakistan Observation Mission (UNIPOM). The status quo in Kashmir was reaffirmed in the Soviet city of Tashkent as the USSR mediated a peace settlement.

The bifurcated nature of the Pakistani state, with its east and west wings divided by the expanse of India, rendered a natural barrier to efforts to unite the Muslims of Pakistan. In the 1950s, Bengalis in the east, although numerically superior in Pakistan, agitated against what they perceived as unequal treatment as, among other things, Urdu was declared the national language. In 1970, the electoral victory of the Bengali Awami League under Mujibur Rahman threatened the power base of western-based military and political leaders. The Pakistani army launched a massive campaign in East Pakistan to eliminate the Awami League and its military arm, the Mukti Bahini, which now believed that a separate state of Bangladesh was the only answer.

Throughout 1971, Bengali refugees fled to India to escape reported human rights abuses by the West Pakistani military. India allegedly supplied various forms of aid to the Bengalis to deepen dissension in Pakistan. In December, following the influx of some 10 million refugees, New Delhi militarily intervened in support of the East Pakistanis. The resulting war lasted less than a month. The second successful secession movement in the post-World War II era resulted in the creation of the state of Bangladesh (the first instance was Singapore's peaceful separation from Malaysia).

Conflict Management Efforts

The successful secession of Bangladesh occurred as a result of the third war between India and Pakistan within barely four decades. The negotiations of this peace settlement continue to have a bearing on the two countries' efforts to resolve the long-standing dispute in Jammu and Kashmir.

In July 1972, Indian Prime Minister Indira Gandhi and her new Pakistani counterpart, Zulfikar Ali Bhutto, met in the Indian resort town of Simla to work out issues such as prisoner transfers, the division of assets, and the establishment of a new line of control (LOC) in Kashmir. (See table 9.7: Management Initiative I, July 1972–October 1993, for details.) Pakistan had just suffered a major military defeat at the hands of its main rival.

This was a jubilant period for India. The dismemberment of Pakistan was regarded as a clear rejection of the two-nation theory that Mohammed Ali Jinnah had espoused

Table 9.7: Management Initiative Kashmiris I July 1972–October 1993

Conflict Phase at Onset of Initiative: Phase I. Conventional Mobilization

Motives

Indian Government

- Seeking Pakistani and international acceptance of its dominant position in South Asia.
- Attempt to set the agenda for future talks, especially regarding Jammu and Kashmir.

Pakistani Government

- No real choice as the initiative follows its military defeat.

United Nations

- Trying to stabilize the situation, especially regarding the cease-fire line in Kashmir.

Management Techniques (1972)

Principals:

- Indian government: Proposals
- Pakistani government

Third Parties:

- United Nations: Norm-based appeals; communications; observation (UNMOGIP)

Short-Term Consequences:

- The dismemberment of Pakistan means that it can no longer challenge India's control over Kashmir through the use of conventional weapons.
- The agreement solidifies India's dominant role within the region.
- The limited nature of support Pakistan receives from external allies is likely indicative of the trend that international actors are not predisposed to intervene in these regional disputes.

Long-Term Consequences:

- Differing interpretations over the Simla accord continue to hinder negotiating efforts.
- A nuclear weapons race begins on the subcontinent. Pakistan focuses on building both its conventional and nuclear capabilities, especially through aid from China.
- Jammu and Kashmir Chief Minister Sheikh Abdullah signs an agreement with New Delhi that relinquishes some of the autonomy that the state had under a 1952 accord.

to create a Muslim state of Pakistan. Further, India believed that the obstacles toward its historical destiny as the dominant regional power had been removed. There was a much smaller Pakistan, a grateful new state of Bangladesh, and while the United States engaged in sabre-rattling during the Bangladesh war, it ultimately allowed Indian military intervention to ensure the secession. The Soviet Union had earlier signed a Friendship Treaty with India, affording New Delhi with a counterpart to the growing rapprochement between the United States and China.

As part of the Simla Agreement, the two countries, along with the United Nations, agreed that the 1971 ceasefire line in Kashmir would be the new LOC. This was where any agreement ended. Until present, India asserts that the Simla Agreement mandates that all disputes between the two countries be settled within the framework of bilateral talks. Pakistan, on the other hand, argues that the LOC is not a permanent border and that external actors such as the UN should manage any conflict resolution efforts. To this day, the UNMOGIP maintains a small presence at the cease-fire line.

During the 1970s, India exerted its new-found regional muscle. In 1974, it conducted a peaceful nuclear explosion, leading Prime Minister Bhutto to retort that Pakistanis would rather eat grass than not follow in kind. The following year, New Delhi annexed the tiny Buddhist kingdom of Sikkim, consolidating its control in the northeast.

Any efforts to internationalize the Kashmir dispute by Pakistan or other interested observers in the 1980s were overshadowed by the 1979 Soviet invasion of Afghanistan. Pakistan's frontline position made it the main conduit for military and financial aid to the mujahadeen, which proved advantageous for President Zia ul-Haq as he was able to extract large military and financial concessions from the United States. The spiraling arms race between India and Pakistan reached a new level in 1986 when Pakistan became a de facto nuclear power.

While there had been no direct negotiations between India and Pakistan since the 1972 Simla Agreement, developments within Jammu and Kashmir set the stage for the insurgency that began in 1989. New Delhi's efforts to centralize control through policies such as the dismissal of Farooq Abdullah's democratically elected National Conference government in 1984 were widely viewed as the beginning of Kashmiri alienation (Varshney 1991, 1015). Farooq, the son of the father of Kashmir, Sheikh Abdullah, succeeded his father who died in 1983. For the first time, Islamic parties coalesced to form the Muslim United Front to contest the 1987 state elections. Charges of harassment and vote-rigging overshadowed the victory of a coalition of the local Congress Party and the National Conference. Widespread anti-India demonstrations followed.

The reported fixing of elections and dismissals of state governments—referred to as part of the deinstitutionalization of Indian politics—limited the development of a genuine opposition and foreclosed political participation by a new generation of middle-class Kashmiris (Ganguly 1996a). In comparison to previous instances, the Pakistani government and activists in its Azad Kashmir region were reportedly able to exploit widespread discontent. They began providing safe sanctuaries and military and economic aid to Kashmiri rebel groups such as the secular Jammu and Kashmir Liberation Front, which has sought independence since its founding in 1976, and the Hizb-ul Mujahadeen, which emerged in early 1990 and has favored union with Pakistan.

By 1990, Jammu and Kashmir was in the throes of a major insurgency as President's Rule was imposed, rebel groups and security forces engaged in regular armed attacks, and strikes and protests were commonplace. Some 300,000 Hindus in Muslim-majority areas fled to Hindu-dominant Jammu or other parts of India. A flare-up between India and Pakistan that raised the prospect of a war between the de facto nuclear powers was averted in early 1990, allegedly after U.S. National Security Adviser Robert Gates met with both sides and helped initiate limited confidence-building measures. Analysts strongly disagree, however, over both a reported Pakistani threat to use nuclear weapons and the importance of U.S. efforts to defuse the crisis (Cranna 1994, 69; Hagerty 1995–1996).

While Pakistan continued its campaign to internationalize the Kashmir dispute, India remained steadfast that it would only participate in bilateral talks. Various human rights groups, the Organization of the Islamic Conference, and Western nations criticized both India and the rebels for widespread human rights abuses. The United States partially cut India's foreign aid budget. Pakistan's reported support of the rebels also drew international censure.

In October 1993, shortly after Benazir Bhutto became Pakistan's prime minister, India's leader Narasimha Rao offered to open talks toward a comprehensive solution to the Kashmir dispute. Meetings between their foreign ministers were held in early January 1994. No progress was reported and no further talks were scheduled. (See table 9.8: Management Initiative II, October 1993–January 1994, for details.) The attempt to begin negotiations influenced one of the largest rebel groups, the Jammu and Kashmir Liberation Front (JKLF), to announce a unilateral cease-fire and offer to suspend violence if India opened negotiations. New Delhi did not publicly accept the offer. About thirty Kashmiri groups had united under the banner of the All Party Hurriyat (Freedom) Conference to press collectively for the holding of a plebiscite. However, divisions over leadership, ideology, strategy, and objectives periodically erupted in violence among the contending groups. The kidnapping and occasional killing of foreigners, wich began in 1991, has also continued.

In October 1994, Indian Prime Minister Rao proposed that local elections be held in Jammu and Kashmir. (See table 9.9: Management Initiative III, May 1994–October 1996, for details.) Almost unanimous rejection followed from Kashmiri separatist groups who asserted that they would only settle for a plebiscite. New Delhi tried to appease the militants by allowing Hurriyat representatives to attend an Organization of Islamic Conference meeting in Casablanca and by offering businesses tax breaks to promote development.

Violence in the Kashmir Valley increased in the first half of 1995 following the military siege and destruction of the Charar-e-Sharief shrine near Srinagar. Hindu temples and government structures were destroyed in retaliation. During this period, Prime Minister Rao renewed his calls for elections, announcing that they would be held in

Table 9.8: Management Initiative Kashmiris II October 1993–January 1994

Conflict Phase at Onset of Initiative: Phase IIIb. High-Level Hostilities

Motives

Indian Government
- Attempt to deflect international criticism regarding human rights abuses.
- Counter the growth of the Hindu-nationalist Bharatiya Janata Party that favors a hard-line military stance.
- Help to ease concerns among Muslims in India following the destruction of the Ayodhya mosque and the security forces' attack on the Hazrat Bal shrine in Kashmir.
- Reduce the costs of the insurgency as India faces similar campaigns in its Punjab and northeastern states.

Pakistani Government
- Provides an opportunity for Prime Minister Bhutto to build both domestic and international support for her new regime.
- Help ensure continued international support from Muslim states and the Organization of the Islamic Conference.
- Likely concerned about the costs of supporting Kashmiri insurgent groups given the limited gains that have been realized.

Third Parties
- Primarily concerned with reducing/eliminating human rights abuses in Jammu and Kashmir. In the case of the UN, its mission is to monitor the line of control that divides Pakistani-controlled Azad Kashmir from Indian-held Jammu and Kashmir.

Interacting Motives
- Both countries are concerned about the costs incurred due to the insurgency and are also hoping to garner international support for their respective positions.

Management Techniques

Principals:
- Indian government: Norm-based appeals
- Pakistani government: Military intervention; norm-based condemnations

Third Parties:
- Nongovernmental Human Rights Organizations: Norm-based appeals, condemnations
- The Organization of the Islamic Conference: Norm-based appeals, condemnations; concessions
- United States: Coercive diplomacy
- United Nations: Observation (UNMOGIP)

Short-Term Consequences:
- Opens the avenue for talks between the two countries, some twenty-one years after their last meeting, which led to the Simla Agreement.
- Helps both countries to ease domestic and international criticism.

Long-Term Consequences:
- High levels of violence continue.
- Paves the way for future talks between the two states.

Table 9.9: Management Initiative Kashmiris III May 1994–October 1996

Conflict Phase at Onset of Initiative: Phase IIIb. High-Level Hostilities

Motives

Indian Government
- Reduce international censure due to human rights abuses.
- Contain the growing strength of the Hindu-nationalist Bharatiya Janata Party.
- Help break the military stalemate and open the avenue for moderates to emerge.

Pakistani Government
- Offers to open talks to help ensure international support for its position.
- Islamabad is likely concerned that elections could lead to decreased support for unification with Pakistan.

Kashmiris
- Population is war weary, especially as the conflict has reached a military stalemate.
- The secular and pro-independence JKLF is concerned about losing support to either its main pro-Pakistan rival, emerging splinter groups, or those who take part in the September 1996 state elections.

National Conference
- Attempt to gain popular support as it participates in the state elections.

Third Parties
- The various international governmental and nongovernmental organizations are primarily concerned with the degree of violence and human rights abuses. The UN mission is to monitor the line of control that divides the two countries.

Interacting Motives
- All the parties are concerned about how state elections will influence their positions.

Management Techniques

Principals:
- Indian government: Norm-based appeals; incentives; concessions
- Pakistani government: Norm-based appeals, condemnations; military intervention; concessions
- Kashmiri militant groups: Norm-based appeals, condemnations; proposals
- National Conference: Norm-based appeals

Third Parties:
- International organizations (including NGOs): Norm-based appeals, condemnations
- The Organization of the Islamic Conference: Norm-based appeals
- United Nations: Observation (UNMOGIP)
- European Union: Observation

Short-Term Consequences:
- Restoration of the political process. Following elections, the Jammu and Kashmir legislature convenes for the first time since 1990.
- The National Conference attempts to restore normality through offers to open talks with militant groups and the establishment of a human rights commission.
- Although the major rebel groups in the Hurriyat Conference refuse to participate in the elections, the first talks since 1989 are held between the government and four former rebel leaders. The JKLF offers some concessions to supportopening negotiations.

Long-Term Consequences:
- The emergence of moderates through the electoral process provides the population with an alternative to the militant groups.
- The high degree of violence continues; divisions among Kashmiri insurgents deepen.

December 1995. Postponements due to the unstable situation ensured that Kashmiris did not go to the polls until September 1996.

Meanwhile, Farooq Abdullah, whose National Conference government was dismissed when the insurgency began in 1990, reemerged on the political scene demanding that Jammu and Kashmir be given its 1952 status, which allowed central control over only defense, foreign affairs, and communications. New Delhi offered the 1975 agreement as the basis for negotiations. That accord permitted the state to repeal any federal laws that impinged on its autonomy. The right-wing Hindu nationalist Bharatiya Janata Party (BJP) walked out of Parliament to protest Rao's autonomy plan.

Uncertainty over the final outcome of federal elections in India marked the first half of 1996. A coalition government was finally formed in June under H. D. Deve Gowda, who led the fourteen-party United Front. In the nine months that Gowda held office, he initiated what has been described as a major restructuring of India's foreign policy. Gowda settled long-standing water disputes with neighboring Bangladesh and Nepal and offered to open talks with Pakistan. His "good neighbor" approach emphasized Indian support of and cooperation with its smaller neighbors and sought to expand regional economic ties. He also became the first Indian leader since the insurgency began to visit Muslim areas in Jammu and Kashmir.

Following three years of efforts, state elections were held in Jammu and Kashmir in September. Abdullah's National Conference won an absolute majority, capturing fifty-seven out of eighty-seven assembly seats. The BJP and the Congress Party followed with eight and seven seats respectively. Despite a boycott called by the APHC, about 50 to 53 percent of the electorate cast ballots for a record 142 candidates. The exception was Srinagar, the heart of the insurgency, where about 30 percent of voters participated. Only sporadic violence marred the monthlong polls that were generally viewed as free and fair. Gowda's ability to ensure that local leaders contested the elections coupled with his offer of maximum autonomy were believed to be critical in allowing for the first state elections in seven years. Some analysts concluded that the vote was in favor of autonomy and reflected the war weariness of the population.

The All Party Hurriyat Conference (APHC) rejected a call to hold talks with the new chief minister, who promised that autonomy would be implemented within a year. Abdullah formed a committee to recommend avenues to safeguard and restore autonomy and promote cordial relations with the central government. His efforts to restore normalcy did not, however, result in a reduction of violence. The number of bomb explosions and grenade attacks increased by year's end. More than 25,000 people have reportedly died since the insurgency began in 1989.

In February 1997, Indian Prime Minister Gowda paved the way for talks with Pakistan over Kashmir, while reiterating that India would not give up the area it controls. (See table 9.10: Management Initiative IV, February 1997–May 1999, for details.) The offer followed Nawaz Sharif's overwhelming victory in Pakistan's general elections that occurred due to the dismissal of the Bhutto government. Gowda also announced $2.1 billion in aid while he visited the state.

Table 9.10: Management Initiative Kashmiris IV, February 1997–May 1999

Conflict Phase at Onset of Initiative: Phase IIIb. High-Level Hostilities

Motives

Indian Government
- Reduce the costs of the insurgency and further the return to normalcy in Jammu and Kashmir following the successful holding of state elections.
- Limit Pakistani and growing Afghani support for the insurgents.
- Deflect international censure that follows its May 1998 nuclear tests.

Pakistani Government
- Islamabad is concerned about its ability to influence militant groups coupled with the potential impact of the 1996 elections in Jammu and Kashmir.
- It is seeking to promote development through the expansion of regional economic ties.
- Deflect international censure that follows its May 1998 nuclear tests.

National Conference
- Supporting talks between India and Pakistan is viewed as vital to restoring normalcy to the state and would help consolidate the party's hold on power.

United States and United Nations
- Primarily concerned with limiting Pakistan's and India's nuclear and ballistic weapons programs and helping to ensure that a crisis does not escalate to interstate hostilities.

Other Third Parties
- NGOs are concerned about human rights abuses. Afghanistan seeks to help promote the cause of its Muslim brethren.

Interacting Motives
- All the parties, with the likely exception of Afghanistan, are concerned with reducing the current and potential future costs of the insurgency.

Management Techniques

Principals:
- Indian government: Concessions; incentives; proposals; norm-based appeals, condemnations
- Pakistani government: Military intervention; proposals; concessions; norm-based appeals, condemnations
- Kashmiri militant groups: Norm-based appeals, condemnations; proposals
- National Conference: Norm-based appeals, condemnations; proposals; concessions; incentives

Third Parties:
- United States: Norm-based appeals, condemnations; communications; proposals
- United Nations: Observation (UNMOGIP); norm-based appeals
- Afghanistan: Military intervention
- NGOs: Norm-based appeals, condemnations

Short-Term Consequences:
- Implementation of limited agreements including the establishment a hotline telephone link between the leaders of the two countries.
- India's and Pakistan's open declaration of their nuclear weapons status in May 1998 and the 1999 Kargil crisis increase interstate tensions and raise the potential of a full-scale interstate war that could have escalated to the nuclear level. The crisis is defused when Pakistan agrees to facilitate the withdrawal of the rebels.
- Violence in the state increases after Kargil. The exclusion of Kashmiri militant groups from the negotiating process severely limits the possibilities of a permanent settlement.

Talks between the secretaries of the foreign ministries of India and Pakistan were held in March in New Delhi. The APHC and other Kashmiri leaders criticized both India and Pakistan for not including Kashmiri representatives in the negotiations. APHC Chairman Mirwaiz Umar Farooq contended that his organization could play a meaningful role by urging militants to suspend their violent operations in conjunction with an Indian scale-down of security operations.

The United States supported the resumption of the India-Pakistan dialogue and reiterated that along with cuts in the two states' military arsenals, the Siachen Glacier area should be demilitarized and noninterference in each other's insurgencies accepted. China, Pakistan's regional ally, and the OIC also expressed their support for the talks. Beijing has not supported either Pakistan's claim to Kashmir or insurgent groups in Azad Kashmir or India's Jammu and Kashmir state.

In mid-May 1997, Indian Prime Minister I. K. Gujral (who replaced Gowda) met with Pakistani Prime Minister Sharif at the summit of the South Asian Association for Regional Cooperation (SAARC) in the Maldives. This was the first bilateral meeting between the leaders of the two countries in four years. India and Pakistan each agreed to release more than 200 civilian detainees, to establish a direct telephone hot line between the prime ministers' offices and to consider easing travel restrictions between the two countries. The seven South Asian leaders also agreed to form a free trade zone by 2001. Greater economic ties between India and Pakistan were expected to help normalize relations as reports indicated that business people in Pakistan favored opening trade, whereas previously they feared that they would be economically swamped.

Meetings between the foreign secretaries of India and Pakistan in June 1997 resulted in an eight-point agenda for bilateral talks, in which working groups would be created to address various issues, including Kashmir. Analysts asserted that India-Pakistan relations had never previously been at such a favorable phase. While Sharif and Gujral held face-to-face meetings two times over the next six months, negotiations bogged down over the establishment of a working group to address Jammu and Kashmir. Pakistan contended that Delhi was backtracking on setting up the group while India asserted that it was waiting for a response to proposals it had submitted to Islamabad.

Meanwhile, in Jammu and Kashmir, violent conflict continued as sporadic clashes between Indian and Pakistani troops occurred across the Line of Control and militant groups continued their separatist campaign. Following the massacre of some two dozen Hindu villagers, Hindu groups demanded the creation of a separate Hindu homeland within Jammu and Kashmir. The Indian and Kashmiri governments claimed that the level and scope of violence had declined since the 1996 state elections while other observers indicated that there had been no discernable change.

The collapse of Gujral's United Front Coalition in November 1997 set the stage for federal elections held in February 1998. The Hindu nationalist Bharatiya Janata Party won the largest number of seats and formed a new government with the support of small regional parties.

Barely two months after Atal Bihari Vajpayee had assumed the prime ministership, India shocked the international community by openly declaring its nuclear weapons capability. On May 11, 1998, Delhi conducted three nuclear tests and, despite widespread international condemnations, it followed up two days later with another couple of test explosions. The election mandate of the BJP had always stressed that India should develop nuclear weapons; however, these assertions were generally dismissed as electoral rhetoric.

Less than three weeks later, on May 28 and May 30, Pakistan responded in kind with seven nuclear test explosions. Islamabad contended that Pakistan's declaration of its nuclear weapons status was required to ensure its national security and that it followed the limited sanctions enacted by the international community in response to India's tests. U.S. and Japanese sanctions were also imposed against Pakistan.[3] Kashmiris responded to the two countries' nuclear tests by stepping up their military campaign for a UN-sponsored referendum to decide the region's future status.

While international efforts focused on convincing India and Pakistan to join global treaties banning nuclear testing and proliferation, a September meeting between the two prime ministers prompted a resumption of bilateral talks. Prime Ministers Sharif and Vajpayee also agreed to reopen a hot line telephone link and to establish the first direct bus service between the two countries. Meetings between the foreign secretaries of India and Pakistan in October focused primarily on the issue of Jammu and Kashmir. No progress was reported. The next month the two sides met again to consider issues such as reducing cross-border tensions in the Siachen glacier, cross-border terrorism, and economic cooperation. Again, no real progress was made. Kashmiri Muslim groups continued their militant and civil disobedience campaigns to protest their exclusion from the negotiations and to press for autonomy/independence and an end to human rights abuses in the region.

In February 1999, Indian Prime Minister Atal Bihari Vajpayee visited Pakistan as part of the ceremonies to inaugurate the first direct bus service between New Delhi and Lahore. He was the first Indian leader to visit Pakistan in a decade. Demonstrations against a potential thaw in bilateral relations occurred in both countries. A joint statement issued by the two prime ministers, referred to as the Lahore Declaration, committed both states to undertake immediate steps to reduce the risk of an accidental or unauthorized use of nuclear weapons and to work together to combat terrorism and promote human rights. Along with agreeing to continue talks on a broad array of issues, including Jammu and Kashmir, India and Pakistan agreed not to interfere in each other's internal affairs. Some analysts viewed the declaration as a strong political commitment to normalize relations.

However, tensions between the two neighbors increased sharply just two months later when India and Pakistan successfully tested their most advanced ballistic missiles. The coalition government led by the Bharatiya Janata Party also collapsed in April, requiring the third national election in India in just over three years. In the September-October polls, the BJP-led coalition won a majority of seats.

In Jammu and Kashmir, the insurgency reached a new level in May when Indian troops discovered about 500 to 1,000 militants occupying a series of border outposts in the Kargil region on the Indian side of the LOC. The occupied area overlooks the only major highway between Srinagar and Leh and it is extensively used during the summer to restock military provisions for Indian soldiers in the Siachen Glacier area. India alleged that the majority of the militants were Pakistani army regulars, along with Pakistani and Afghan mercenaries, who had invaded the territory from Azad Kashmir. Pakistan denied the claim. Concerns over a potential escalation to a full-scale interstate war that might involve the use of nuclear weapons led the United Nations, various Western countries, Russia, and China to offer to mediate the Kashmir dispute. India again rejected any third-party involvement.

After ten weeks of often heavy fighting, which claimed more than 1,000 casualties and included the first use of Indian air power at the border since the 1971 India-Pakistan war, U.S. President Clinton secured an agreement with Pakistani Prime Minister Sharif to withdraw the militants from Kargil. By late July only sporadic fighting was reported as most of the rebels had withdrawn to Pakistan. Opposition parties in Pakistan contended that the rebel withdrawal was a major blow to the Kashmiri self-determination campaign. Dissatisfaction with Sharif over Kargil, among other reasons, led to a military coup in Pakistan in October.

It is unlikely that any substantial progress will be made on the Jammu and Kashmir issue in the near future. Since the Kargil incursion, India has hardened its stance, stepping up its military crackdown in the region while asserting that talks cannot be held until Pakistan stops promoting cross-border terrorism. Pakistan's military rulers were supportive of the Kargil incursion and are only likely to engage in talks in an attempt to deflect international pressure.

It is also unlikely that the Kashmir issue can be delinked from India and Pakistan's nuclear and ballistic weapons programs. This has added another complication to an already extremely complex situation. While the National Conference government in Jammu and Kashmir continues its efforts to ensure a return to normalcy, violence has actually increased in the past year. Further, neither the central nor state governments have drawn Muslim militant groups into negotiations, nor have they adequately addressed some important concerns of most residents, primarily widespread human rights abuses by security forces or pro-India militias. In the final analysis, any negotiations toward a lasting settlement must include Kashmiris (not only the militant Muslim groups but also Hindus and Buddhists) as participants, a move that both India and Pakistan have so far rejected.

The Tibetans

An estimated 5.4 million Tibetans inhabit one of the world's most geographically remote and isolated regions. Nestled among some of the earth's highest mountain ranges, the Himalayas to the south and the Kunluns to the north, the vast plateau of Tibet lies at an altitude of about 14,000 feet. This isolation allowed the Tibetans to develop a unique culture and social structure with a feudal theocracy of Buddhist Lamas led by their spiritual and political leader, the Dalai Lama. Although periodically forced to pay homage to powerful Mongol, Manchu, or Chinese suzerains, Tibet maintained de facto independence until the People's Republic of China invaded its territory in 1950.

The Tibetan government reluctantly signed a seventeen-point agreement with Peking that guaranteed the Dalai Lama's traditional political rule and the protection of local religious and cultural customs. However, centralized Chinese control of the area, often through the suppression of dissent, coupled with numerous violations of the 1951 accord, resulted in a massive Tibetan uprising in 1959. In March of that year, the current Dalai Lama and more than 50,000 supporters fled to India and set up a government-in-exile in Dharamsala. Thousands of Tibetans died in the military revolt against Chinese rule.

In response to China's actions, the United Nations passed two resolutions that called for respect for the fundamental rights and freedoms of the Tibetan people, including the right to self-determination. However, neither the UN nor any individual countries actively intervened in the conflict.

In the first thirty years of direct Chinese rule, Tibet's feudal society was forcibly pressured to assimilate to Communist Chinese society, often through severe repression of the Tibetan people. The traditional domain of Tibet was broken up as the Tibetan Autonomous Region (TAR) was established in 1965 and adjoining Tibetan-inhabited areas were incorporated in the neighboring provinces of Gansu, Qinghai, Sichuan, and Yunnan.

The United Nations again attempted to restrain China's repressive policies by passing a resolution in December 1965 calling for the protection of human rights in Tibet. The Indian delegate at the UN even accused the PRC of trying to "obliterate the Tibetan people" (International Alert 1990, 8).

Central government policies were especially severe during the Cultural Revolution of 1966–1976, when nearly all Buddhist monasteries and religious symbols were destroyed and all manifestations of Tibetan culture outlawed. The Tibetan government-in-exile estimates that more than 300,000 Tibetans were killed by Chinese forces and twice as many died due to famine and imprisonment. In 1976 the Chinese government acknowledged that mistakes had been made in Tibet, attributing them to the Gang of Four and the Cultural Revolution.

Conflict Management Efforts

In 1979, Deng Xiaoping embarked on a campaign of economic and social liberalization that paved the way for limited contacts and negotiations with Tibetan representatives. (See table 9.11: Management Initiative I, August 1979–April 1982, for details.) Although the Dalai Lama refused an offer to visit Tibet, he was allowed to dispatch a fact-finding mission to the region in August. The mission was reportedly greeted by proindependence demonstrations and calls for the return of the Dalai Lama.

In response to the negative report issued by the fact-finding mission, Party Secretary Hu Yaobang visited Tibet in May 1980. Shocked by his findings, Hu announced far-reaching reforms such as the promotion of Tibetan culture, economic

Table 9.11: Management Initiative Tibetans I, August 1979–April 1982

Conflict Phase at Onset of Initiative: Phase I. Conventional Mobilization

Motives

Chinese Government
- Desire for international support for its economic liberalization program, which could be furthered by reducing world censure regarding its policies in Tibet.
- The offer of talks along with economic development proposals for the region aim to allay Tibetan resentment against Chinese rule.
- The regime is also likely testing the degree of popular support for the Dalai Lama.

Tibetans
- They are hopeful that a new era of liberalization will lead to a comprehensive dialogue on Tibet's status. This is the first offer by either side to hold talks.
- There is broad concern among Tibetans in exile due to reports of widespread repression and the destruction of Tibetan cultural symbols during the Cultural Revolution.

Interacting Motives
- Both parties are hopeful that this new era will lead to better relations.

Management Techniques

Principals:
- Chinese government: Norm-based appeals; concessions; incentives; communications
- Tibetans: Norm-based appeals; observation

Short-Term Consequences:
- The strong support received by the Dharamsala fact-finding missions likely raises Chinese fears of a potential escalation of the conflict.
- It becomes clear that the Dalai Lama retains widespread adherence within Tibet.

Long-Term Consequences:
- Although no progress occurs in talks between the two sides, this first step paves the way for future negotiations.

---

reforms that included an end to collectivization and tax holidays, and the reduction of Han cadres in Tibet (Bray 1990, 222–223). His announcement was followed by the visit of the second Dharamsala fact-finding mission. Since these representatives were also greeted by proindependence supporters, their visit was cut short and another mission scheduled for the following year was canceled. Exploratory talks were still held between Tibetan representatives and Beijing in April 1982. No progress was reported and no further talks were held until 1984.

In an effort to placate Tibetan aspirations, China launched a major economic development program and relaxed some religious laws in the Himalayan region. Tibetans were allowed to openly display pictures of the Dalai Lama for the first time since the Cultural Revolution and the rebuilding of temples was authorized. However, the economic policies also led to mass immigrations of Han Chinese into Tibet, some voluntary and others through government-sponsored programs. This raised fears among Tibetans that they would become a minority in their homeland. The benefits of development programs were also reported to disproportionately accrue to the Han, while Tibetans remained the poorest group in the region. Further, Tibetans and other minorities were supposed to be exempt from China's birth control policies, but reports documented continual practices of forced abortions and sterilizations.

The second effort to reach a settlement on the Tibet question occurred in September 1984 when a Dharamsala delegation visited Beijing. (See table 9.12: Management Initiative II, November 1984–September 1985, for details.) Talks between the two sides continued until December. A Tibetan proposal calling for the acceptance of Tibet's historical status, its right to self-determination, the right to reunify the traditional area of Tibet, and its creation as a zone of peace was rejected by Chinese authorities. While no further negotiations were held, a Dharamsala delegation visited Tibetan areas in Gansu and Qinghai provinces (Wangyal 1994, 200–201).

The decline of communism in Eastern Europe coupled with increasing international censure of the Chinese regime likely influenced the Dalai Lama to put forth a five-point peace proposal in September 1987. (See table 9.13: Management Initiative III, September 1987, for details.) The proposal called for Tibet to be transformed into a zone of peace; the abandonment of China's population transfer policy; respect for the Tibetans' fundamental human rights and democratic freedoms; protection of the environment and an end to nuclear testing in Tibet; and the opening of negotiations on the future status of Tibet. The Chinese government angrily rejected the proposal and castigated the United States for allowing its presentation in Washington. China asserted that it essentially sought the creation of an independent state.

Within Tibet, the proposal sparked widespread demonstrations in support of independence and the Dalai Lama. More than twenty people were reported killed during an October 1 demonstration. Chinese attempts to repress the protestors resulted in hundreds of arrests, the closure of temples, and a ban on foreigners entering Tibet.

These efforts to quell Tibetan dissent drew the condemnation of the international community. The European Union expressed its support for the five–point proposal while the U.S. Congress passed a nonbinding resolution that accused the PRC of human rights violations in Tibet. Various NGOs such as Amnesty International, Human Rights Watch, and the International Campaign for Tibet also attempted to highlight the military actions of the Chinese regime.

The next year, the Dalai Lama put forth another peace proposal during a visit to the European, in Strasbourg. (See table 9.14: Management Initiative IV, June 1988–November 1988, for details.) Referring to it as the final compromise the plan provided for Chinese control over foreign and defense policy in return for complete internal autonomy. Independence for the Tibetans was formally excluded as the Dalai Lama's primary concern was now the cultural survival of the Tibetans. Some reports indicated that by now the Tibetans were a minority in the region due to massive migrations of Han Chinese.

Table 9.12: Management Initiative Tibetans II, November 1984–September 1985

Conflict Phase at Onset of Initiative: Phase I. Conventional Mobilization

Motives

Chinese Government
- The regime likely believes that it can obtain concessions as it expects economic growth to have subdued resistance within Tibet.
- Attempt to improve its international image due to the high degree of world attention Tibet garners.

Tibetans
- They are hopeful that as China opens up to the world, it will be more likely to loosen its control over Tibet. It has been more than twenty-five years since the Dalai Lama fled the region.

Management Techniques

Principals:
- Chinese government: Concessions
- Tibetans: Proposals; observation

Short-Term Consequences:
- China continues its relaxation of economic and religious restrictions in Tibet.
- The Panchem Lama, Tibet's second holiest leader, urges the Dalai Lama to return home while also asserting that talks can only continue if he renounces independence.

Long-Term Consequences:
- The failure to make any progress leads the Dalai Lama to seek greater international support for and involvement in the Tibetan issue. Relations between the two principals worsen as China rejects these efforts.
- Chinese rule over Tibet likely gains some legitimacy as West German Chancellor Kohl visits the area in 1987. He is first Western leader to do so since the 1950 invasion.

While stating that the "One Country, Two Systems" formula adopted in Hong Kong and Macau and offered to Taiwan was not possible for Tibet, Beijing agreed to open talks with the Dalai Lama. China rejected the Strasbourg proposal as the framework for negotiations, asserting that it did not relinquish the concept of independence. Talks were set for January 1989 in Geneva.

In the meantime, divisions within the Tibetan movement in exile erupted. Referring to the Strasbourg proposal as a sellout, the Tibetan Youth Congress advocated an armed struggle. The Dalai Lama contended that any agreement would be subject to the ratification of all Tibetans. Within Tibet, the inability of security forces to halt repeated demonstrations resulted in the dismissal of the region's Communist Party leader. Hundreds were injured and up to twenty died during demonstrations in Lhasa in December and an unprecedented march was held by Tibetan students in Tianamen Square.

Table 9.13: Management Initiative Tibetans III, September 1987

Conflict Phase at Onset of Initiative: Phase I. Conventional Mobilization

Motives

Tibetans
- The Dalai Lama hopes to revive talks with China as no negotiations have been held during the past three years.
- The Dalai Lama also hopes that talks will help to avoid a splintering of the Tibetan movement since a growing minority favors the use of violent tactics.

Management Techniques

Principals:
- Chinese government
- Tibetans: Proposals; concessions

Third Parties:
- United States: Norm-based appeals, resolutions
- European Union: Norm-based resolutions
- International nongovernmental human rights organizations: Norm-based appeals, condemnations

Short-Term Consequences:
- Shift to Phase IIIa. Low-Level Hostilities.
- China expands its international campaign to limit the mobilization efforts of the Tibetans. It is particularly successful with regard to India, as the timing coincides with regional attempts to promote a rapproachment between the two neighbors.

Long-Term Consequences:
- Active resistance to Chinese rule in Tibet expands to include segments of society that have not been politically active since the 1950s. The Panchem Lama, for instance, who previously provided some support for the regime, publicly criticizes Chinese rule of the region.
- Emergence of the sporadic use of violent strategies by a minority within Tibet.
- Divisions within the Tibetan community intensify between those who support the Dalai Lama's nonviolent approach and others who favor the use of violent methods.
- Beijing retrenches on its easing of economic and religious restrictions while reactivating its use of repression.

Reported Chinese objections to the inclusion of officials of the Tibetan government-in-exile and a foreign legal adviser led Beijing to cancel the scheduled Geneva talks (Wangyal 1994, 202). As of mid-2000, this was the last time that the two sides were close to reaching the negotiating table.

Since the early 1990s, there has been an escalation in both the campaign for Tibetan autonomy and/or independence, and the Chinese government's efforts to suppress its supporters. A year of martial law was lifted in early 1990, after what was described as the most serious challenge to Chinese rule since the 1959 uprising. However, from 1994 onward, China successively increased its political and military control of the Himalayan region. Special army units are in place in Tibet in addition to regular Chinese

Table 9.14: Management Initiative Tibetans IV, June 1988–November 1988

Conflict Phase at Onset of Initiative: Phase IIIa. Low-Level Hostilities

Motives

Chinese Government
- The regime hopes that offering to hold talks will help reduce unrest within Tibet and stop it from spreading to Tibetan areas in nearby provinces.
- Beijing is seeking to improve its international image, which has suffered due to its military crackdown in Tibet.
- Talks with the Tibetans are expected to help deflect domestic attention from the country's economic difficulties and its emerging prodemocracy movement

Tibetans
- The Dalai Lama hopes the concessions in his new proposal will help to reduce growing violence/repression within Tibet. He is now concerned about the survival of Tibetan people and their culture.
- The Tibetans are likely hoping that growing international condemnation of Chinese suppression will pressure the government to return to the negotiating table.

Interacting Motives
- Both parties are concerned about escalating violence in Tibet and are seeking to defuse the situation.

Management Techniques

Principals:
- Chinese Government
- Tibetans: Norm-based appeals; proposals; concessions

Third Parties:
- Nongovernmental human rights organizations: Norm-based appeals, condemnations

Short-Term Consequences:
- Shift to Phase IIIb. High-Level Hostilities. This coincides with growing Chinese concern over the expansion of the prodemocracy movement, largely led by students in major urban centers, and the collapse of communism in the USSR and Eastern Europe that has led to the emergence of an active separatist campaign among the country's Muslim Uighur population.
- Divisions among Tibetans become more prominent as a new generation favors the use of violence to obtain independence.
- The Dalai Lama is awarded the Nobel Peace Prize.
- India and China take the first formal step to normalizing relations when Indian Prime Minister Rajiv Gandhi visits Beijing in December 1988.

Long-Term Consequences:
- Shift to Phase II. Militant Mobilization.
- Beijing expands its campaign of political, and religious restrictions, while continuing economic development policies to counter aspirations for autonomy/secession within Tibet.
- Tensions between the Dalai Lama and China deepen, especially over his restoration of relations with Taiwan and the appointment of a successor for the Panchem Lama. It appears that Beijing is now waiting for the Dalai Lama's death in order to choose his successor and thereby gain influence over the Tibetans. China expands its regional ties with Nepal and India; both countries have large numbers of Tibetan residents.
- While the Tibetan issue continues to garner international attention, as of mid-2000 no active efforts have been undertaken to help resolve the dispute.

forces, and work teams are stationed in key monasteries. The number of political prisoners has at least doubled since the mid-1990s; more than 1,200 Tibetans, mostly monks and nuns, were reported to be in custody in 1998. Official reports note periodic confiscations of weapons and explosives.

Beijing's retrenchment on policies enacted during the early 1980s liberalization phase especially targeted any manifestations of Tibetan culture—religion and education being at the forefront. In 1995 the disputed succession of the Panchem Lama, the second holiest religious leader in Tibet, directly pitted the government's authority against that of the Dalai Lama. The tenth Panchem Lama died in January 1989. Beijing's rejection of the Dalai Lama's chosen successor and the subsequent government appointment of a new Panchem Lama engendered widespread discontent that resulted in numerous demonstrations and riots in Tibet and neighboring India. In mid-1999, in what appeared to be another challenge to the Dalai Lama's religious authority, the government-appointed Panchem Lama took up residence in Lhasa. He was reported to be urging Tibetans to obey President Zemin and to embrace the Communist Party. No information has been available about the whereabouts of the Dalai Lama's chosen successor since the young boy was detained in 1995.

Restrictions on religious practices include a ban on the public and private display of pictures of the Dalai Lama, limitations on the number of monks and nuns in monasteries, and direct oversight of religious sites to promote patriotic education. The patriotic education campaign, which began in 1996, requires monks and nuns to denounce the Dalai Lama and sign a pledge of allegiance to China. It was expanded to include ordinary citizens in 1998. Tibetan language schools have also been closed and the use of the Tibetan language in postsecondary institutions eliminated.

In the economic arena, China continues its development efforts and is actively promoting foreign investment and tourism in order to appease Tibetans. More than $1.5 billion would reportedly be spent by 2000 to help raise the living standards of Tibetans. In 1995, China publicly acknowledged that minorities in the country did not even have the basic necessities and it vowed that all minorities would be provided with adequate food and clothing by 2000.

As of mid-2000, China still refuses to hold direct talks with the Dalai Lama, while simultaneously asserting that it is more than willing to do so if the spiritual leader renounces his support for Tibetan independence. Meanwhile, the Dalai Lama repeatedly contends that he is only seeking autonomy and the preservation of the Tibetan culture and religion. The most recent effort to bring the two sides to the negotiating table ended in November 1998 after some eighteen months of informal contacts.

In comparison to many ethnopolitical groups, the Tibetans continue to attract the attention of Western governments and various NGOs. The European Union, for instance, regularly passes resolutions condemning China's human rights practices in Tibet. However, no country to date has challenged Beijing's claim that Tibet is a part of China. The unique role of the Dalai Lama, who won the Nobel Peace Prize in 1989, is perhaps the major reason for Tibet's international exposure. His spiritual, nonviolent approach and frequent travels around the world not only generate much interest in

Tibetan Buddhism but also serve to maintain attention to the status of the Tibetans and Chinese practices in the region.

From the early 1960s until 1996, only sporadic violent attacks have occurred in the context of the Tibetan campaign. But a growing minority of Tibetans, especially members of the Tibetan Youth Congress, are now questioning what the Dalai Lama's nonviolent strategy has achieved over the past forty years. The self-immolation of a Tibetan activist in New Delhi in April 1998 has been referred to as a turning point in the nonviolent struggle. This was the first such death in more than four decades and it led the Tibetan Youth Congress, which has about 10,000 members in India, to assert that further violence will occur. Reports from the UN, NGOs, and Tibetans suggest that repression within Tibet is hardening and that there have been at least seven bomb blasts in the past three years along with violent resistance by monks and Tibetan political prisoners. The fragmentation of the Tibetan movement remains a distinct possibility.

The future status of the institution of the Dalai Lama is also in doubt. Were the current Dalai Lama to die in the near future, it is not clear how his successor will be chosen. Tibetan practice mandates that the Panchem Lama determines the next incarnation. The current Panchem Lama was chosen by Beijing while the Dalai Lama's choice remains in custody.

A major security crackdown, deepening restrictions on religious and educational practices, continued migrations of Han Chinese into Tibet, and limited economic benefits for most Tibetans make it very likely that the Tibetan campaign will escalate to a higher level in comparison to recent decades. Along with the Taiwanese, the Tibetans and the Muslim Uighurs are perceived by the Chinese leadership as the primary threats to the country's territorial integrity. Any potential Chinese accommodation in Tibet is likely to be influenced by the regime's effort to avoid a precedent that could be seized upon by Taiwan, and secondarily, the Uighurs. The Muslim independence campaign turned increasingly violent in 1996; the potential for a similar development in Tibet should not be discounted.

Conclusions:
Lessons for Managing Separatist Conflicts

Repeated efforts were made to contain, manage, and transform each of the four conflicts examined in this chapter. Of the fourteen major initiatives we analyzed only two were "successful" in the sense that they led to a substantial and sustained reduction of armed hostilities based on accommodation of the interests of the contending parties. Mizo III in 1984–1986 resulted in a shift from low-level hostilities (Phase IIIa) to settlement (Phase VI). Moros III in 1993–1996 contributed to a shift from high-level hostilities to acceptance (by most principals) and implementation of a regional autonomy plan (Phase V). But this 14:2 tabulation is misleading. The successful negotiations in Mizoram and Moro Mindanao in both instances built on previous initiatives. The Mizo I negotiations of 1975–1978 set the framework for the Mizo II initiative in 1980–1982, which resulted in agreements on many of the issues in dispute and set the stage for negotiations in 1984 that culminated in the 1986 accord in which Mizoram gained full statehood in the Indian Union. Similarly in the Moro case, the autonomy agreement being implemented in Moro Mindinao in 1996–2000 derived from the Tripoli Agreement negotiated between the Marcos regime and the Moro National Liberation Front in 1976, with the mediation of the Organization of the Islamic Conference (OIC). The intervening years of fighting, and the initiatives of 1986–1987 (Moros II) and 1993–1996 (Moros III), were part of a deadly strategic game about how to interpret and implement the terms of the Tripoli Agreement.

It is not unduly optimistic to expect that if and when enduring settlements are reached in Tibet and Kashmir, they will build on previous initiatives. But on what elements of those initiatives? Tibetan demands, as formulated by the Dalai Lama, have shifted away from independence and toward protection of Tibetan culture and religion. The government in Beijing, which was receptive to Tibetan cultural concerns in the early 1980s, has racheted up repression in response to militant mobilization within Tibet that the exile organization seemingly cannot control. The parameters of successful accommodation are likely to be these: on the part of Beijing, acceptance of Tibetan cultural and religious autonomy, a gradual stand-down of military and security forces, and more even-handed development policies; and on the part of Tibetans, a cessation of militant action within Tibet and the end of organized exile opposition, signaled by the return of the Dalai Lama—or, more likely, his eventual successor—to Tibet. In Kashmir, political moderates represented by the National Conference have controlled the state government since the 1996 elections. But there is little short-term prospect that Muslim militants can be drawn into conventional politics because the Indian government has refused to enter into talks with them, except for a brief period in 1994–1996, and their Pakistani sponsors have little interest in accommodation. As in the past, political developments in Kashmir are hostage to the bitter rivalry, now a nuclear one, between India and Pakistan.

Unilateral efforts by governments to end separatist conflicts are not as likely to be effective as the negotiated settlements characterized above. Such efforts failed in the early stages of both the Mizo and Moro conflicts. In 1972 Indira Gandhi's government made Mizoram a union territory (and created three other new states in the northeast) in an attempt to defuse autonomy movements in the region. The Mizoram territory was established without negotiating a settlement with the Mizo National Front; warfare continued. In 1979 the Marcos government implemented its version of the autonomy plan outlined in the Tripoli Agreement of 1976 on terms that were rejected by the MNLF, who also continued to fight. A parallel can be drawn with Chinese reforms in Tibet in the mid-1980s. Beijing launched a major economic development program and lifted some religious restrictions on Tibetan Buddhism. The policies were based on Beijing's perceptions of what was needed in Tibet rather than negotiations with Tibetans. Later talks failed to address the exiled leadership's concerns for Tibetan autonomy and militant mobilization soon began within Tibet.

It is useful to take a closer look at the conflict management techniques employed by principals and by third parties. The purpose is not to ascertain "what works" in the

Table 9.15:
Techniques Used in Fourteen Asian Initiatives to Manage Separatist Conflicts

Type of Technique	Used by Principals	Used by Third Parties
Symbolic Techniques		
Appeals	24	16
Resolutions	0	2
Condemnations	7	7
Communications	1	5
Subtotals	32	30
Accommodative Techniques		
Proposals	9	3
Concessions	21	1
Incentives	8	1
Subtotals	38	5
Interventionist Techniques		
Observation	2	6
Mediation	0	2
Coercive diplomacy	0	1
Peacekeeping	0	0
Military intervention	3	5
Subtotals	5	14

larger sense, but what is attempted and by whom. When specific techniques are cataloged, as they are in table 9.15, it is evident that some are used with greater relative frequency by third parties, others by principals. We can distinguish between symbolic, accommodative, and interventionist techniques. Third-party actions are mainly symbolic in character, including appeals, resolutions, condemnations, and communications. These make up about 60 percent of all third-party initiatives. Principals also issue many appeals, but what they do most distinctively is issue proposals and offer concessions and incentives to their challengers. As suggested above, the domestic management of these conflicts follows principally from the substance of concessions and incentives, and from the gradual—or sometimes abrupt—movement of one or both principals toward accommodation. The interventionist techniques include observation missions, mediation, coercive diplomacy, and military intervention. These are mainly the tools of third parties. The three instances of military intervention that are attributed to "principals" refer to actions in Kashmir by Pakistan, which we categorize as a principal. The two observation

Table 9.16:
Types of Techniques Used to Manage Four Separatist Conflicts, by Country

Conflict and Type of Technique	Used by Principals	Used by Third Parties
Mizos in India, Three Initiatives		
Symbolic techniques	6	0
Accommodative techniques	8	0
Interventionist techniques	0	2
Moros in Philippines, Three Initiatives		
Symbolic techniques	6	8
Accommodative techniques	8	3
Interventionist techniques	0	5
Tibetans in China, Four Initiatives		
Symbolic techniques	4	7
Accommodative techniques	8	0
Interventionist techniques	2	0
Kashmiris in India, Four Initiatives		
Symbolic techniques	16	15
Accommodative techniques	14	2
Interventionist techniques	3	7

missions attributed to principals were visits by exiled representatives of the Dalai Lama to Tibet that were authorized by the Beijing government.

The two settled separatist conflicts differ markedly in the patterns of techniques employed, as shown in table 9.16. In the Mizo case the only third-party engagement was military support in the form of base areas for Mizo rebels in Bangladesh and Burma. Appeals for accommodation or settlement came only from the principals. And concessions and incentives by principals were instrumental in conflict settlement, as the case study account makes clear. The Moro conflict was much more internationalized, with third parties playing an active role throughout. Libya and Malaysia provided military support for the Moros in the early stages of the conflict. The critical factors that led to and sustained negotiations were the communications, proposals, and mediation of the OIC, and the willingness of the principals to make concessions and offer incentives in response to prompting by third parties.

Kashmir is the most internationalized of all the conflicts, as is evident from the high level of third-party engagement using all types of techniques. The UN has been engaged since 1948 and, along with the European Union, the United States, and the

OIC has been the source of appeals to end the conflict. Condemnations have been issued mainly from international NGOs concerned with human rights violations. Four principals have a stake in this conflict: India, Pakistan, Kashmiri militants, and the National Conference. Pakistan is the principal source of condemnations and military intervention, India the source of most concessions and incentives, including those which led to the 1996 elections and the victory of the National Conference.

The contrasts provided by the four cases suggest that the engagement of external third parties is neither necessary nor sufficient for successful management and transformation of separatist conflicts. The Mizoram conflict was settled without any positive international engagement, whereas the OIC was instrumental in brokering a settlement of the Moro conflict. The Tibetan conflict has prompted episodic symbolic responses by the United States, the European Union, and human rights NGOs with no discernible effect. The Kashmir dispute has had more substantial and intense third-party engagement than any of the other conflicts, but the level of armed hostilities has remained essentially unchanged since 1989.

A related observation is that the major regional powers—China and India—seem impervious to international efforts to promote or broker agreements to separatist conflicts by comparison with the Philippines, a lesser power that is more susceptible to international influence. An alternative interpretation is that the superpowers and the UN have chosen not to embark on a full-scale diplomatic and political campaign to persuade China or India to deal more constructively with Tibet and Kashmir. Regional organizations have not done so either: ASEAN as a matter of principle avoids engagement in internal conflicts of member states, and the South Asian Association for Regional Cooperation (SAARC) is also inactive. The European Union has taken positions on both Tibet and Kashmir, and sent an observer mission to the latter, but seems to have no influence on Chinese and Indian policy. Only the Organization of the Islamic Conference (OIC) can claim a successful mediating role.

These broad comparisons need a more nuanced interpretation. First, the instrumental role of the OIC at several stages in the Moro conflict was due to the vulnerabilities of the principals. Our analysis of the Moro initiatives makes clear that Misuari, the leader of the Moro National Liberation Front, and the successive governments of Marcos, Aquino, and Ramos all had incentives for reducing hostilities. To use William Zartman's term (1989), the conflict was at several points "ripe for resolution," or at least ripe for constructive engagement by a third party. In Kashmir there was also an opening from late 1993 to mid-1997 between Pakistan and India, because both countries had prime ministers willing to engage in constructive dialogue. The OIC supported the process symbolically, but the electoral victory of Hindu nationalists (the BJP) in 1998 halted the dialogue, not least because the BJP's platform called for taking back Pakistani-controlled Azad Kashmir. The subsequent rounds of nuclear and ballistic missile tests by both countries, and Pakistan's aborted incursion across the LOC in mid-1999, have ended for the indefinite future any prospects for third-party initiatives. The protracted rivalry between India and Pakistan has trumped third-party initiatives at conflict management in Kashmir.

The second nuance has to do with the impact of communal electoral politics on the management of separatist conflict. Some Mizo leaders had participated in electoral politics in the union territory since the early 1970s. In 1984 the Mizo leaders of the local Congress Party pushed hard for the resumption of talks between the New Delhi government and the rebels; their participation seems to have been critical for the successful outcome of negotiations. It is possible that the elected Muslim government of Kashmir, the National Conference, might play a similar "domestic third-party" role if and when a new opportunity arises for conflict management. Elected communal parties have two analytically distinct roles in the process of conflict management and transformation. First, electoral politics provides an alternative mode of participation for people who might otherwise support militants; in the settlement phase they may give former militant leaders access to power, as happened in Mizoram. Second, communal parties in office usually have a vested interest in ending armed conflict and potentially can bring credible pressure to bear on other principals to engage in dialogue and negotiations.

Autonomy negotiations and agreements do not necessarily deal with all the issues that prompted open conflict. Three of the four Asian separatist movements analyzed here have been motivated in large part by resistance to large-scale immigration that threatens the local culture and alienates traditional lands. The immigrant groups are Bengalis in Mizoram, Christians in historically Muslim Mindinao, and Han Chinese in Tibet. Only the Mizoram agreement restricts continued immigration. Dominant groups in the Philippines and China support continued immigration and the likely marginalization of the local population. The same three regions are also among the poorest in their respective countries. The Mizo and Moro agreements call for more investment and development funds but implementation is uncertain. Only the political demands for autonomy and participation have been met, in substantial part, by the two agreements.

To summarize, these are our principal conclusions about the management of armed conflicts where challenging groups seek autonomy or independence. Though based only on four Asian cases, it is plausible to think that they are relevant elsewhere.

- Successful settlements of protracted separatist conflicts usually are reached following a series of negotiations punctuated by periods of warfare. Failed negotiations often lay the groundwork for future negotiations.

- Unilateral reforms by governments aimed at ending separatist conflicts are unlikely to succeed. Successful settlements are more likely to emerge from negotiations that engage all principals and involve mutual accommodations.

- Third-party conflict management initiatives are most likely to be effective when the principals have their own reasons for seeking a settlement. In most separatist conflicts the issues and personalities of domestic politics trump third-party initiatives.

- Participation of communal parties in electoral politics and regional administration contribute to the mitigation and transformation of separatist conflicts. The opening of conventional political opportunities for moderates tends to marginalize fighting groups. For most separatists expedient participation in autonomy arrangements trumps militancy.

Notes

We would like to thank Ishtiaq Ahmed and Robert Tomes for their valuable comments on an earlier version.

1. The settlements are more accurately characterized as relatively successful. Some Moro factions continue to fight in hopes of gaining additional concessions. There is no armed conflict in Mizoram but, as in Moro Mindinao, significant underlying social and economic issues (documented in the case studies) remain unresolved. For purposes of case selection for this chapter a settlement is characterized as "successful" if it is based on negotiated accommodations of group interests and leads to a substantial and sustained phase shift away from armed conflict (see text below).

2. In addition to the references noted in the text, all the case studies rely on detailed chronologies compiled from Nexis Library Reports and other information resources of the Minorities at Risk project. For more details on the Minorities at Risk information resources see the project's Web site at www.bsos.umd.edu/cidcm/mar.

3. The imposition of economic sanctions and international condemnations following the 1998 Indian and Pakistani nuclear tests are not included in the Kashmiris IV Conflict Management Initiative as they do not specifically address the Kashmir dispute.

Part III
A Prototype Information System for Early Warning Networks

10
A Comparative Look at Early Warning Indicators: PIOOM, the State Failures Project, and CEWS Cases

Alex P. Schmid

In this chapter, the countries analyzed in case studies in this volume will be looked at through a different lens. They will be treated as potential or actual cases of "state failure," and two sets of quantitative early warning indicators for state failure will be tested for their forecasting power with the benefit of hindsight.

Conflict prevention requires both timely information and political will and strength to act upon it. Very often it is assumed that the main problem is not one of forecasting outbreaks of violent conflict but the generation of "political will" to intervene. Emphasis is therefore often put on removing obstacles in the way of creating such political will, while early warning—or, more precisely, early detection based on reliable indicators—is often taken for granted, and considered as being a mere technical data collection problem. What is often forgotten is that a reliable early warning system can actually help to generate political will (Gurr and Harff 1996, 80). Many people are not even aware how many ongoing conflicts there are, living with the happy assumption that

Table 10.1: Number of Armed Conflicts between 1993 and 1999 (PIOOM)

	1993	mid-1995	end 1996	end 1997	mid-1998	end 1999
HICs	22	22	19	17	16	26
LICs		39	42	70	70	80
VPCs	84[a]	40	74	74	114	178
Total	106	101	135	161	200	284

[a] LICs and VPCs were not separated in 1993.

there has been a decline of large scale wars. This decline was, until mid-1998, real, as far as full-scale, high-intensity conflicts (HICS—with more than 1,000 deaths per twelve months), is concerned, but is mistaken with regard to low-intensity conflicts (LICs—with between 100 and 1,000 deaths per year), and violent political conflicts (VPCs—with fewer than 100 deaths per year), as shown in table 10.1. Forecasting remains a difficult (some would say impossible) task and there are, in the field of early warning, still too few systematic attempts to test the predictive power of individual indicators or group of indicators empirically. Such testing can be done in two ways:

1. Prospective: Establish which past forecasts turned out to be correct, copy the methodology, and reapply it to present cases for which one requires forecasts.

2. Retrospective: Engage in postdiction, i.e., "forecast" with indicators and models created after the phenomenon to be forecasted has already occurred. Apply these indicators to past situations where the outcome is known, using data antedating those outcomes.

Each method has its problems. A major disadvantage of the first method is that many of the correct forecasts might have turned out right for the wrong reasons, i.e., the forecaster just happened to be right not due to the quality of his methodology but due to sheer luck. Another problem is that one is usually not given access into the "kitchen" of successful forecasters since they tend to keep their methodology secret for national security or commercial reasons.

The second method has the advantage of a more experimental design, where various variables and their predictive strength in a model can be individually assessed, applying them to a variety of cases—the outcome of which is already known. Such tests can be reproduced again and again as the methodology is open to scrutiny. Both methods suffer from the problem that the flow of events is not linear, that there may be new intervening factors that did not exist in the past, affecting the expected outcome.

It is the second method that will be applied in this chapter. At the time of writing (summer 1998), one of the two sets of indicators tested here—the CIA-financed State Failure project commissioned by the office of U.S. Vice President Al Gore—was still shrouded in some secrecy and neither the data nor the details of the methodology utilized were fully in the public domain.[1]

Definition and Focus of Early Warning

What is early warning? It involves "a process of communicating judgments about threats early enough for decision makers to take action to deter whatever outcome is threatened; or failing that, to manage events in such a way that the worst consequences are mitigated" (McCarthy 1997, 15). The definition of early warning used by the London-based NGO Forum on Early Warning and Early Response (FEWER) closely parallels the above from the U.S. intelligence community in that it defines early warning as "the systematic collection and analysis of information coming from areas of crises for the purposes of:

1) anticipating the escalation of violent conflict,

2) development of strategic responses to these crises, and

3) the presentation of options to critical actors for the purposes of decision-making" (cited in Schmeidl and Adelman, 1997)

Early warning signals have been sought for a variety of conflict situations (see table 10.2). In this chapter an attempt will be made to compare two sets of early warning indicators in terms of their predictive power in the field of "state failure." One set of indicators to be retested is derived from the U.S. government-financed State Failure project (see Esty et al. 1998, 1999). The other set of indicators is based on an alternative

Table 10.2: Focus of Various Early Warning Efforts (Dependent Variables)

Conflict Escalation (PIOOM; see Jongman and Schmid 1994)
Genocide/Politicide/Democide (Harff 1996; Rummel 1995, 1997)
Refugee Flows (Schmeidl and Jenkins 1998)
Humanitarian Crises (HEWS; see Ahmed and Kassinis 1998)
Internal Displacement (GEWS)
State Failure (CIA; see Esty et al. 1999)
Ethnopolitical Rebellion (Gurr and Marshall 2000)
Famine (FAO; see Rashid 1998)
Gross Human Rights Violations (Hamm 1998)

operationalization of "state failure" proposed by PIOOM (Schmid 2000). The U.S. State Failure project is one of the mega-projects in the field of social sciences, wherein social scientists not confined by financial restraints sought to collect more than 2 million pieces of data, covering 166 countries for a period of forty years. A replication of this entire project with alternative indicators is far beyond the means of this chapter. Our goal is much more modest: take the leading half dozen indicators from the State Failure (SF) project and see how well these forecast in comparison with an alternative set of indicators based on the work of Pierson (1996, 8) as operationalized by PIOOM (referred to below as the PP project). The utility of such a comparison was pointed out fifteen years ago by Gurr and Lichbach (1986, 4): "Comparison of the forecasts indicates the degree of accuracy with which empirical theory can predict aspects of conflict. Comparison among forecasts make it possible to say which model provides the most accurate forecasts, and of what conflict properties; and which countries' conflict is most readily explained."

Simple as such a postdictive exercise may seem, there are considerable theoretical, conceptual, methodological, and data problems involved even in such a modest exercise as envisaged here. The countries selected for this comparison are listed in table 10.3, which also indicates the Repression levels, on a 1–5 Political Terror Scale (PTS) developed by Stohl et al. (see Appendix for details), and provides conflict and repression data for two small control groups, one of developing countries not experiencing state failure and an analogous group of developed countries.

The U.S. Government's State Failure Study

There are several definitions of what constitutes "State Failure" or "State Collapse." Helman and Ratner, for instance, characterized a failed state as one "utterly incapable of sustaining itself as a member of the international community" (1992–1993, 5). States that come to mind as typical cases of "state failure" in recent years are Somalia, Liberia, Sierra Leone, Afghanistan, and, more recently, Congo (Zaire). If a broader definition is taken, other countries such as Albania and Colombia might also fall under this concept. Some formerly split states have been reunited, e.g., the two Yemens and the two Germanies, whereby one of them is an obvious example of "state failure." The greatest recent failure is the collapse of Soviet Union, which split into fifteen successor states, some of them, including perhaps even Russia itself, tottering on the brink of collapse. What is a "collapsed state"? Zartman offers this description:

> Collapse means that the basic functions of the state are no longer performed, as analyzed in various theories of state. As the decision-making center of government, the state is paralyzed and inoperative: laws are not made, order is not preserved, and societal cohesion is not enhanced (Vadie & Birnbaum . . .). As a symbol of identity, it has lost its power of conferring a name on its people and a meaning to their social action (Dyson . . .; Migdal . . .). As a territory, it is no longer assured security and provisionment by a central

Table 10.3: Level of Conflict (VPC, LIC, or HIC) in 1998 for Countries in the Sample and Level of Political Repression (PTS, 1 = low, 5 = high)

Country	VPC	LIC	HIC	PTS
Countries with State Failures				
Mozambique		x		3
Sierra Leone			x	5
Sudan	4x	2x	x	5
Algeria		x	x	5
Nigeria	5x	4x		4
Angola		2x		4
South Africa		2x		3
China/Tibet	2x	x		4
India/Kashmir	14x	5x	3x	4
Bangladesh	2x	x		4
Philippines	x	x		3
Burundi			x	5
Rwanda			x	5
Zaire/Congo		4x		5
El Salvador	x			3
Guatemala		x		3
Macedonia	x			2
Moldova				2
Russia/Chechnya	2x	x		3
(Mexico/Chiapas)	4x	x		3
Control Group I: Developing Countries				
Thailand		x		3
Tunisia		x		2
Tanzania				3
Kazakhstan				2
Costa Rica				1
Control Group II: Developed Countries				
Spain	x			1
Germany				1
Australia				1
United States	x			1
Belgium	x			1
Italy				1
France	x			1

Note: See text for definitions of categories. The numbers preceding the x's indicate the number of ongoing conflicts in a country of each type. Conflict data are from the PIOOM databank. Since the Chiapas conflict in Mexico was not in the original SF dataset, Mexico is not used for the comparisons that follow.

sovereign organization (Poggi . . .). As the authoritative political institution, it has lost its legitimacy, which is therefore up for grabs, and so has lost its right to command and conduct public affairs (Weber . . .; Ferrero . . .). As a system of socioeconomic organization, its functional balance of inputs and outputs is destroyed; it no longer receives support from nor exercises control over its people, and it no longer is even the target of demands, because its people know that it is incapable of providing supplies. No longer functioning, with neither traditional nor charismatic nor institutional sources of legitimacy, it has lost the right to rule. . . . State collapse . . . is the breakdown of good governance, law, and order. (Zartman, 1995a:5–6)

Total state collapse has occurred in only eighteen cases between 1955 and 1996, according to the researchers of the updated Phase II State Failure report (Esty et al. 1999, 68). However, short of complete collapse there are many weak states that manifest instability, lawlessness, conflict, and violence. It is on such manifestations of state failure that the team of researchers of the State Failure project concentrated. The SF project team used a rather broad and indirect definition of "state failure," namely the presence and magnitude of four categories of events:

- *Revolutionary wars*, defined as sustained military conflicts between insurgents and central governments, aimed at displacing the regime. The forty-one cases of the original data set included:

- Large scale and intense guerrilla and civil wars with more than 250,000 deaths, for example, mujahidin warfare against the Khalq regime in Afghanistan, 1978–1992.

- Large scale and intense guerrilla and civil wars with between 10,000 and 250,000 deaths, for example, the Sandinista guerrilla war against the Somoza regime in Nicaragua, 1978–1979.

- Small scale guerrilla wars and rebellions that result in 1,000 to 10,000 deaths, for example, left-wing guerrilla warfare against the Colombian government, since 1984 (currently escalating).

- *Ethnic wars*, defined as secessionists civil wars, rebellions, protracted communal warfare, and sustained episodes of mass protest by politically organized communal groups. The sixty cases of the original data set included:

- Large scale and intense ethnic wars with more than 250,000 deaths; for example, the rebellion by southern Sudanese, 1983 to the present.

- Large scale and intense wars with between 100,000 and 250,000 deaths; for example, the Kurdish rebellion against the Khomeini regime in Iran, 1979–1984.

- Small scale communal wars and rebellions with 1,000 to 10,000 deaths, for example, the Intifada campaign in the Israeli-occupied territories, 1988–1994.

- Protracted episodes of violent communal rioting, clashes, and terrorism; for example, violent protest by Azerbaijanis against Soviet policies, 1987–1991.

- *Genocides and politicides*, defined as sustained policies by states or their agents, and, in civil wars, by contending authorities, that result in the deaths of a substantial portion of members of communal or political groups. In genocides the victimized groups are targeted primarily because of their communal (ethnic, religious) characteristics. In politicides, by contrast, victims are targeted mainly because of their political opposition to the state or dominant group. The forty-six cases of the original data set included:

- Episodes involving more than 250,000 deaths, for example, the Khmer Rouge killings and starvation deaths in Cambodia, 1975–1979.

- Events involving between 100,000 and 250,000 deaths, for example, the civilian death toll from massacres and starvation during the Renamo's rebellion against the government of Mozambique, 1976–1992.

- Events involving between 10,000 and 100,000 deaths; for example, Tutsi army massacres of Hutus in Burundi, 1993.

- Events involving fewer than 10,000 deaths; for example, the victims of the military's "dirty war" against left-wing movements in Argentina, 1976–1980.

- *Adverse or disruptive regime transitions*, defined as major, abrupt shifts in patterns of governance, including state collapse, periods of severe regime instability, and shifts toward authoritarian rule. The cases (n = 80) include:

- Collapse of central state authority for two or more years; for example, the collapse of central government in Somalia, 1989 to the present.

- Transition toward autocratic rule by revolution or coup, for example, the military coup against the Allende regime in Chile, 1973.

- Abrupt transitions toward autocratic rule by nonviolent means; for example, the replacement of democratic institutions by one-party rule in Sierra Leone in 1978.

- Violent regime instability accompanied by revolution or coup, with no increase in autocracy, for example, north-south rivalry and civil war after the attempted merger of North and South Yemen in 1990.

Such an encompassing definition results in a large number of "state failures"—no fewer than 243 individual episodes were identified for the period 1955–1994. A number of them showed more than one of the four characteristics described above—hence the 243 episodes of "state failure" were consolidated into 113 cases (Esty et al. 1999, 31–32).

Table 10.4: Phenomena covered by the Task Force's State Failure Definition

1) Regime crises	24.5%
2) War and regime crisis and genocides/politicides	19.8%
3) Ethnic war	18.9%
4) War and regime crisis	14.2%
5) Revolutionary war	10.4%
6) War and genocide/politicide	5.7%
7) Regime crisis and genocide/politicide	2.8%
8) Ethnic and revolutionary war	1.9%
9) Genocide/politicide	1.9%

This empirical definition was apparently chosen for its operational advantages but it is not without problems. One of them is the heterogeneity of the phenomenon under investigation.[2] The 113 consolidated cases of state failure consisted of the single cases and combinations of cases summarized in table 10.4.

In order to establish the forecasting power of indicators in such cases of "state failure," the SF Task Force members took a control group of countries not experiencing state failure. For each year in which a consolidated case began, three cases were selected (at random) from countries in which no problem-set events of any type or magnitude were under way. Yet the control set also included countries that had at one period or another experienced state failure (as defined by the authors of the project) themselves, though, not within plus or minus three years of the time they were taken as control cases. This creates, in our view, the problem of a polluted control group. It might have been wiser to compare the state failure countries only with countries with an unblemished record. Since data were collected for no less than 166 countries, that should not have been a problem.[3]

Indicators Used in the State Failure Project

While the dependent variable was state failure (identified as any or a combination of revolutionary war, ethnic wars, violent or abrupt regime transitions, or genocides and politicides), the task force looked for explanatory independent variables in three different fields:

1) political and leadership variables

2) demographic and societal variables

3) economic and environmental variables

Indicators were selected from an extensive list of potential causal variables, based on existing theories as well as mere hunches what factors might have an impact on state failure. In addition to supposedly causal variables linking independent to dependent factors, the project also collected data on general dimensions such as size of total population and total area of the country. More than 2 million pieces of data were collected for 166 countries in the problem or in the control group for the period 1955–1995, utilizing in each case for the values of the indicators data reflecting the situation two years prior to the manifestation of state failure. If, for instance, a state failure crisis broke out in 1965, then the task was to obtain data for 1963 for both the state failure and the control cases.

The data were, where possible, selected from existing open sources like the World Bank, the United Nations, etc. Other data that were deemed necessary, e.g., on "ethnic discrimination" and on the "ethnic identity of ruling elites" had never been assembled before on a universal scale and were hand-coded specifically for this project. Where data for the selected year were not available, the most recent value prior to that year was incorporated into the data set.

While data on no less than 617 explanatory (independent) variables were originally sought, problems of data quality and completeness reduced the set of data ultimately utilized. In the end the test run was done with twenty-four political variables; twenty-one demographic/social variables; and thirty environmental/economic variables. Each of these seventy-five variables was statistically tested individually by the statisticians and mathematicians in the project in order to examine their capacity to differentiate between the states that suffered some kind of state failure and the states that during the relevant period did not suffer a crisis or failure. The variables listed in table 10.5 were identified, after a series of stepwise regressions, for their superior ability to discriminate between likely state failures and countries not experiencing such crises.

For the first two indicators the theoretical link to state failure is not directly obvious. With regard to infant mortality (number of children that die in the first year of their lives per 1,000 live-born children) the analysts of the task force sought to explain the predictive power of their best-scoring variable in these terms:

> Infant mortality is a marker that represents a basket of independent conditions. . . . Infant mortality [the ratio of reported deaths of infants under one year old per thousand live births] is indicative of the quality of life in society. . . . Its importance as an indicator of stability is likely due to its inverse association with popular discontent. Regimes that are unwilling or unable to raise the quality of life to international standards are at risk of popularly based challenges. The relationship is likely to be more pronounced in democratic countries where discontented publics have greater opportunities to organize opposition. (Esty et al. 1995, 35–36)

While there is some plausibility to this explanation, infant mortality remains a problematic indicator for at least one group of countries, namely those where large numbers of babies

Table 10.5: Leading State Failure Indicators (from Esty et al., 1995)

1) Infant mortality (reported deaths to infants under one year old per thousand live births)
2) Trade openness (ratio that measures the value of imports plus exports divided by gross domestic product)
3) Democracy, measured dichotomously as more or less democratic
4) Youth bulge (ratio of the 15–29-year age group to 30–54-year group)
5) Regime durability (number of years since last major, abrupt change in regime)
6) Ethnicity of Ruling Elite (whether the elite demographically represents a minority or majority group or the population as a whole)

are not immediately registered and entered in government statistics. In such countries infant mortality rates might, for early warning purposes, not be such a reliable datum. Even in developed states statistics on infant mortality need not be accurate. Take the former East German state, which failed in 1990. In East Germany officially only 9.2 out of 1,000 live born babies were dying in 1988—a rate almost as good as West Germany (8.6) and better than the United Kingdom (9.5) or the United States (10.0).[4] One reason why East Germany apparently had a very low infant mortality rate was because midwives were instructed to drown children who had visible deficiencies rather than try to save them and exposing them to the risk of dying in the first year of their life—in which case they would have entered the infant mortality statistics.

The second most powerful predictor found by the task force behind the SF project was involvement in international trade, as measured by trade openness. It was associated with smaller risk of state failure in both developed and less developed countries and in all contexts. In line with this, a reduction of trade barriers would be likely to improve national stability, other things being equal. In the words of the SF researchers:

> This finding suggests that policies or measures—including internal factors such as dependable enforcement of contracts, modest or low corruption, and improved infrastructure, as well as bilateral and multilateral efforts to eliminate trade barriers—that help to foster higher levels of international trade could help prevent political crises. Interestingly, it appears that it is the involvement in international trade itself, and not the eventual prosperity that such trade provides, that is the key to this effect. The work of Etel Solingen has shown that free trade, if sustained, helps bring together coalitions of elite actors that support the rule of law and stable property relationships, as a condition for building wealth (Esty et al. 1999, 67, citing Solingen 1998).

Trade openness was operationalized as the sum of exports and imports as a ratio of the gross domestic product. However, as an indicator it is problematic in one sense, since

Table 10.6: International Trade in Goods and Services as Percentage of GDP, Selected Countries and Road Density, late 1980s.

	High Risk of Failure Countries		"Healthy" Countries	
	Trade Openness		Trade Openness	
Yugoslavia	16.5 [5.02]	India	15.8 [2.21]
Somalia	17.8 [2.75]	Japan	17.7 [9.23]
Liberia	40.1 [2.79]	Austria	44.2 [14.19]
Afghanistan	35.0 [1.33]	Sweden	35.9 [15.59]
Rwanda	14.7 [1.77]	United States	11.7 [25.68]

Note: Road density, shown in brackets, is expressed in terms of thousands of kilometers of paved road per million inhabitants. The data are from *The Economist* (1990, 154–155) and Kurian (1991, 190–192).

it does not take into account the size of a country's domestic market in comparison to its foreign market. This can lead to distortions. As table 10.6 makes clear, some countries with a large internal market like the United States score not very differently than a country like Rwanda. table 10.6 lists some failed states and some strong states for the late 1980s and indicates that, at least in these cases, the indicator does not seem to be able to select high-risk of state failure countries from countries not likely to experience such a crisis.

Trade openness is taken to express a country's integration into the world market. According to the SF project authors, trade openness correlates strongly with road density. We therefore used this indicator as a possible substitute indicator where the size of the internal market might distort the value of the trade openness indicator. This substitution, however, does not solve all problems, as the close score of India to Liberia reveals. The correlation between trade openness and road density also is less obvious in the small sample in table 10.6 than found in the SF project.

Democracy was analyzed in Phase I of the SF project as a dichotomous variable, and is so treated in the analysis that follows. One of the most important modifications of Phase II was a further differentiation of the political system variable, distinguishing between "full democracies," "partial democracies," and "autocracies." Using such a trichotomized measure of democracy, the SF researchers discovered that "partial democracies" were far more vulnerable to state failure-type crises than are either full democracies or autocracies. Other things being equal, "partial democracies" were on the average three times more likely to experience state failure. Furthermore, it was found on the basis of an updated problem set, revised data, and new control cases, "that states with above-average trade openness, other things being equal, have one-half the failure risk of countries with below-average trade openness. In addition, countries with above-world median levels of infant mortality have, other things being equal, three times the risk of state failure as compared with countries with below-median levels of infant mortality" (Esty et al. 1999, 53).

The remaining leading "state failure" indicators from the Phase I study—youth bulge, regime duration, and ethnicity of the ruling elite—raise fewer question marks and will not be discussed here.

Forecasting with the State Failure Model

How successful were the original forecasts made by the State Failure Task Force? The four type of events identified as manifestations of state failure were forecasted, with data two years prior to the occurrence of the event, with an accuracy of between 66 and 70 percent, depending on the method chosen (neural net analysis or regression analysis) and depending on the subtype of state failure selected (apparently ethnic war could be forecasted with 78 percent accuracy while abrupt regime changes were forecast in 69 percent of all cases) (Esty et al. 1995, viii–ix; Esty et al. 1998, 37).

The model could have been used to forecast state failures in 1996 (based on 1994 data). However, no such forecasts have been published by the authors of the SF project. Presumably it would have been politically too sensitive to make public government-financed assessments about how well or how badly some "friendly" states (such as Brazil or Saudi Arabia) might do in such a test. A high-level State Department official reportedly discouraged the publication of any results of the SF Phase I study on grounds that it could complicate the conduct of U.S. foreign policy.[5] Publication of forecasts might also have contributed to a self-fulfilling prophecy.

Some sound scientific reasons why the SF task force did not make or release forecasts were offered by the authors of the task force reports, who identified several problems associated with the use of past indicators for future forecasts:

1) The international environment of the past might have changed with the end of the Cold War and what was a good predictor then might no longer be a good predictor.

2) The forecasts are based on a rather broad definition of "state failure" and might not apply to other manifestations of state failure (e.g., in Albania where the "pyramid schemes" led to the temporary collapse of the state).

3) Since the accuracy of the forecasts was about 70 percent, it means that the model can be wrong in more than 58 states out of the 192 existing states. Such a high rate of "false alarms" would not be increasing confidence in an early warning model based on these indicators alone.

A 70 percent success rate in forecasting looks, at first sight, impressive—but it is not. For public early warning purposes one has to find indicators that perform better than those utilized by the SF project. One strategy to increase the number of accurate forecasts is to add a different type of variables than those utilized by the task force. The most notable absence in SF set of indicators was the lack of predictors related to external (rather than domestic) variables. International political and economic factors can impact very strongly on domestic affairs and contribute to state failure. By introducing some foreign affairs-related indicators it should be possible to increase the percentage of accurate forecasts. And if one combines such a statistical model-based with Delphi-type expert assessments, the accuracy of forecasts can probably be brought beyond the 80 percent threshold, which would be "good enough" for some types of forecasts.[6] That this is not unrealistic has been demonstrated later in a subsequent phase of the SF project in which 80 percent of past genocide/politicide cases could be successfully classified (Harff, Surko, and Unger, forthcoming). Any early warning system that aspires to credibility should be able to minimize the number of "false positives"—warnings that were misplaced—and, most important, to minimize "false negatives"—crises not anticipated.

Forecasting State Failure with Alternative Indicators

What follows is an alternative analysis of the risks of state failure, based on the work of Pierson in *The Modern State* (1996). Pierson does not deal explicitly with state failure. However, he offers a list of nine characteristics of the modern state based on the question, "What should a [well-functioning] state be and what should it do?" This he contrast with the question, "What are states actually like?" (1996, 6).The difference between the actual condition of a state and the ideal-type state can be measured. The closer an existing state is to the ideal-type the more strength it has. On the other hand, the further away a state is from the ideal-type, the closer it would be to "state failure." Pierson (1996, 8) offers this list of nine of the most important features of the modern state:

1) (monopoly) control of the means of violence

2) territoriality

3) sovereignty

4) constitutionality

5) impersonal power

6) the public bureaucracy

7) authority/legitimacy

8) citizenship, and

9) taxation

For our operationalization of state strength/state failure we use this list. Our alternative working definition of state failure is as follows: A "failing state" is one that scores low on several of these nine dimensions. While continued state failure will ultimately lead to state collapse, the process is reversible since state failure is a gradual process (except in the case of foreign invasion and occupation). As a likely consequence of waning state strength, those holding state power are tempted to take recourse to human rights violations in their attempts to quell protest and rebellion.

This working definition differs substantially from the one proposed by the SF project, which, as mentioned above, defined state failure in terms of the occurrence of revolutionary and ethnic wars, violent or abrupt regime transitions, or genocides and politicides. However, the outcome might in fact not be too different since we assume that, if several or all of these nine variables show low values, at least one of the four phenomena listed in the SF definition is indeed likely to occur. We also assume that state failure as defined on the basis of the Pierson list is likely to result in higher levels of human rights violations in an affected country. The outcome then, should show a great deal of overlap.

While the SF project uses two indicators (infant mortality and trade openness) where the theoretical link between causal variable and the outcome of state failure is not self-evident (there is no direct causal link between high infant mortality rates and state failure), the Pierson variables are more directly linked to the outcome (e.g., if a state does not manage to extract any taxes it is very likely to fail).

Testing

The following comparison of the two sets of indicators does not replicate the original SF project in all details, partly because some of them were not in the public domain when the variables were tested. While in the original SF project the measurement of the indicators was taken two years before the outbreak of a state failure, this replication uses a lead period of only one year. Since most indicators are structural they do not change much from one normal year to the next. In addition, the analysts from the SF project could not always find data two years before the "event" and had to take the closest available data prior to state failure, from one to three years or more. In order to make the data comparable, we have ranked all fifteen indicators (the six from the SF project and the nine PP variables) on a 1-5 scale, whereby 1 is indicative for a very satisfactory condition (e.g., infant mortality is very low) and 5 stands for a very ominous or bad condition. The scaling is done in such a way that the world median score falls under 3, the half-way position between very bad and very good. Since the world median is not always the same in the period under consideration (more than thirty years), we have to assess it for each of the case years. The maximum score a country can get for the SF indicators is 30 (six indicators x 1 to 5 values), the minimum score is 6 (six x 1 to 5 values). For the Pierson indicators the maximum is 45 (9 x 5) and the minimum is 9 (9 x 1). In order to make the two final scores comparable, they are both expressed as percentages (maximal scores of 30 and 45 respectively equal a 100 percent risk of state failure while 6 and 9 equal a zero percent risk). Once the total scores are calculated, the countries will be categorized under one of the following risk levels:

1) High risk of state failure	(81–100%)
2) High to moderate risk of state failure	(61–80%)
3) Moderate risk of state failure	(41–60%)
4) Moderate to low risk of state failure	(21–40%)
5) Low risk of state failure	(20% or less)

The test cases selected for comparative testing here are listed in table 10.7. They are chosen from the larger sample of 113 countries and episodes used in the SF project.

Results

The details of the operationalization (including tables 10.16 through 10.20) are omitted here but can be downloaded from the CEWS Web site: www.usc.edu/dept/LAS/ir/cis/cews. What follows here is a brief discussion of some of the results contained in tables 10.8 to 10.10. How do the two sets of indicators compare? If the definition of state failure of the SF project is taken, the forecasts based on the sum of the six indicators are as a whole superior, as shown in the comparison in table 10.11. The PP indicators did not do so well, despite their intuitive plausibility. The State Failure indicators placed three upcoming state failures correctly in the high risk category and an additional ten in the high moderate risk category, while the Pierson/PIOOM indicators managed to place only one in the top category and only half in the second category.

With regard to the nonfailing developing countries, the differences between the two sets of indicators are less marked. When it comes to the second control group of developed nonfailing countries, the PP indicators place one country (Italy) in a slightly higher category but the differences are relatively small, though bigger than for the first control group of developing countries. The overall average forecasting power of the six SF indicators is about 63 percent, while the respective value for the PP indicators for the twenty test countries is about 58 percent, 5 percentage points lower than the SF indicators.

Since we do not know how close these ten control group countries actually came one year after the measurement to a higher risk of state failure, we cannot establish how well the two sets of indicators do in this regard. Categorywise the two sets do not diverge greatly. Percentagewise the SF indicators score slightly higher for the developing countries control set while the PP indicators score higher for the developed countries in terms of clearly assigning nonfailing countries to the lowest risk category.

Table 10.7: Countries with State Failure, According to the State Failure Project

	Pre-crisis test year	(SF minus 1 year)
Mozambique	1978	SF, 1979–92
Philippines	1968	SF: 1969–92
Sierra Leone	1977	SF: 1967–71;1978
Sudan	1982	SF: 1955–1972;1983–
Algeria	1961	SF: 1962–63
Nigeria	1979	SF: 1964–70;1980–84
Angola	1974	SF: 1975–95
South Africa	1989	SF: 1990–93
China/Tibet	1979	SF: 1950–75;1980–
India/Kashmir	1989	SF: 1952–
Bangladesh/ Chittagong Hills	1973	SF: 74–75
Burundi	1961	SF: 1962–
Rwanda	1993	SF: 1959–
Zaire	1991	SF: 1959-65;1977–85;1992–
El Salvador	1976	SF: 1977–92
Guatemala	1965	SF: 1966–
Mexico/Chiapas	1992	SF: No (only later added)
Serbia/Macedonia	1989	SF: 1981–83;1990–93
Czechoslovakia	1967	SF: 1968
USSR/Moldova (Russia)	1989	SF: 1986–91(USSR);1991–
USSR/Chechnya (Russia)	1990	SF: 1986–91(USSR);1991–

The expectation that the PP indicators would do better because they included two foreign-directed indicators (sovereignty and territoriality) was not supported, at least not in the case of the 1968 Warsaw Pact invasion of Czechoslovakia. Here the SF indicators scored significantly higher than the PP indicators: 54.2 percent versus 39.3 percent.

The conclusion is unmistakable: the six SF indicators are, as a set, superior to the set of nine PP indicators when it comes to identifying the risks of state failure as defined by the SF project. Does that mean that the Pierson/PIOOM indicators should be thrown into the experimental dustbin? Not yet. Several things ought to be considered before such a drastic decision is taken. First, individual indicators (rather than sets of indicators) ought to be looked at. It might be that some of these score quite high but their forecasting power is, as it were, undone by the "bad company" of less useful indicators they are in. The second point concerns the definition of state failure. The PP indicators might be not so bad after all in forecasting other types of state failure than those four contained in the State Failure Task Force working definition. Let us first look at some individual indicators.

Comparing the Top Six Indicators of the SF and PP Sets

In the original SF project seventy-five indicators were tested. From these the six top scorers retested here emerged. The best indicator turned out to be infant mortality, followed by trade openness, and, in descending order, the remaining four. If our operationalization in the retest has been carried out correctly, the same order of forecasting power should emerge for indicators assessing the twenty countries (excluding Mexico) in the main sample as in the original SF project. This is indeed the case, as shown in table 10.13.

Only two PP indicators manage to rise above the average of the SF indicators. These are "taxation" and "monopoly of violence." Therefore it should be useful to include these two in future tests. On the other hand, two Pierson indicators score very badly. These are "territoriality" and "impersonal power." If we reduce our set of indicators also to half a dozen, leaving out the two lowest scoring ones and the hard to measure "quality of bureaucracy" score, the picture brightens considerably. The average score then rises from 58 percent to 64.9 percent, which is less than 2 percentage points worse than the combined six SF leading indicators as determined by sophisticated statistical methods.

If we would throw out "sovereignty" as the lowest scoring of the top six PP indicators and replace it with "corruption"—an indicator we dropped for lack of sufficient (historical) data, but one which measured almost as high as "taxation," 80 percent as opposed to 83.9 percent—the six most powerful PP indicators could have scored even higher—69.1 percent—as opposed to 66.4 percent for the leading six SF indicators. Given the fact that the Pierson indicators were not pretested, the top six of them do rather well.

Redefining "State Failure"

The above data are all geared to the SF project's definition of "state failure," a definition that is problematic in many ways. A look at the list of supposedly failed states contained in the SF project data set (Phase I) indicates the there might be problems in utilizing such a broad definition encompassing so many forms of violence and conflict. The list of cases of state failure includes countries like Great Britain (due to Northern Ireland) but excludes Spain (with a comparable Basque problem). Hungary and Czechoslovakia are listed for 1956 and 1968 respectively due to the Soviet invasions. Other cases where a sitting regime was overthrown by a superpower, as with the U.S. intervention in Grenada and Panama in the 1980s, are, however, not included (Panama features as state failure only in 1968; the exclusion of Grenada can be explained by the 500,000 inhabitants threshold used in the SF project). On the basis of only partial access to the

Table 10.8: Country Scores for the Six Leading State Failure Indicators

	IM	RD	D	YB	Re	E	total	%
Countries with State Failures								
Algeria 1961	5	2	4	4	5	3	23	70.8
Angola 1974	5	4	5	4	5	3	26	83.3
Bangladesh 1973	5	5	3	4	5	2	24	75.0
Burundi 1961	5	4	5	4	5	5	28	91.7
El Salvador 1976	3	4	3	5	4	1	20	58.3
Guatemala 1965	3	4	2	4	4	4	21	62.5
Mozambique 1978	4	4	5	4	5	4	26	83.3
Nigeria 1979	5	4	3	4	4	4	24	75.0
Philippines 1968	4	4	4	5	3	2	22	66.7
USSR/Chechnya 1990	1	4	3	1	1	4	14	33.3
USSR/Moldova 1989	2	1	4	1	1	4	13	29.2
Rwanda 1993	5	4	4	5	3	3	24	75.0
Sierra Leone 1977	5	4	3	3	4	2	21	62.5
South Africa 1989	3	1	4	2	1	5	16	41.7
Sudan 1982	5	5	3	4	4	3	24	75.0
Zaire 1991	5	5	4	4	3	2	23	70.8
Control Group I: Developing Countries								
China/Tibet 1979	3	5	4	4	3	2	21	62.5
Czechoslovakia 1967	2	3	2	2	3	4	16	41.7
India 1989	4	2	3	4	1	2	16	41.7
Macedonia 1989	2	2	3	2	1	3	13	29.2
Mexico 1992	2	1	3	5	1	2	14	33.3
Control Group II: Developed Countries								
Costa Rica 1987	1	1	1	4	1	2	10	16.7
Kazakhstan 1994	2	1	2	2	5	2	14	33.3
Tanzania 1992	5	4	2	5	3	2	21	62.5
Thailand 1985	2	3	3	4	5	1	18	50.0
Tunisia 1995	2	1	3	3	2	1	12	25.0

Note: IM = infant mortality, RD = road density, D = Democracy, YB = youth bulge, Re = regime durability, E = ethnicity of ruling elite

Table 10.9: Scores and Percentages for the PIOOM/Pierson Indicators

	Mo	Te	ES	Co	IP	Cr	Au	Ci	Ta	To	%
Algeria 1961	5	3	4	4	2	nd	5	3	nd	26	67.8
Angola 1974	5	3	4	4	3	nd	5	5	nd	29	78.6
Bangladesh 1973	4	2	3	3	2	5	1	5	5	30	58.3
Burundi 1961	3	3	4	4	3	nd	2	5	5	29	65.6
El Salvador 1976	5	2	3	3	2	nd	4	2	5	26	55.2
Guatemala 1965	5	2	2	3	3	nd	4	3	5	27	59.4
Mozambique 1978	5	1	5	4	2	nd	3	5	nd	25	64.3
Nigeria 1979	2	2	2	3	3	5	3	4	2	26	47.2
Philippines 1968	4	2	2	2	3	4	3	1	5	26	47.2
USSR/Chechnya 1990	1	3	2	2	2	4	3	1	5	23	38.9
USSR/Moldova 1989	1	3	2	2	2	nd	3	1	nd	14	25
Rwanda 1993	5	1	4	4	2	nd	5	4	5	30	68.7
Sierra Leone 1977	4	1	3	4	3	nd	5	5	4	29	65.6
South Africa 1989	4	4	2	4	4	3	4	2	1	28	52.8
Sudan 1982	4	2	3	4	4	nd	4	5	5	31	71.9
Zaire 1991	5	2	5	5	5	nd	4	3	4	33	78.1
	Mo	Te	ES	Co	IP	Cr	Au	Ci	Ta	To	%
China 1979	2	2	1	4	2	3	1	3	5	23	38.9
Czechoslovakia 1967	1	2	3	4	2	nd	3	1	nd	16	34.6
India 1989	5	2	3	3	3	4	3	5	5	33	66.6
Macedonia 1989	4	5	2	3	2	nd	3	2	5	26	58.1
Mexico 1992	2	1	3	2	1	4	2	2	5	22	36.1
	Mo	Te	ES	Co	IP	Cr	Au	Ci	Ta	To	%
Costa Rica 1987	2	1	5	1	1	2	1	1	5	19	27.7
Kazakhstan 1994	1	1	1	2	2	4	1	1	nd	13	16.1
Tanzania 1992	1	2	5	2	4	nd	5	4	4	27	61.3
Thailand 1985	2	2	3	3	3	4	2	1	4	24	41.7
Tunisia 1995	2	1	4	2	4	3	4	3	5	28	52.8

Notes: To transform the absolute scores into percentages, a coefficient was created (9 x 5 = 45), from which 9 was subtracted (lowest possible score). The difference between highest score (45) and lowest (9) is 36. Dividing 100 by 36, one obtains the coefficient 2.777. This coefficient is then multiplied with the total score to obtain a percentage value. In cases of missing data different coefficients are used (3.126 if one piece of data is missing; 3.571 in case two pieces are missing; and 4.1666 in case of three missing values).

Mo = monopoly of violence; Te = territoriality; ES = external sovereignty; Co = constitutionality; IP = impersonal power; Cr = corruption in the public bureaucracy; Au = authority/legitimacy of government as expressed in election outcomes; Ci = citizenship; Ta = taxation; To = total.

Table 10.10: Final Scores

Test Countries	SF Score	Risk Level	PP Score	Risk Level
Algeria 1961	70.8%	(IV)	67.8%	(IV)
Angola 1974	83.3%	(V)	78.6%	(IV)
Bangladesh 1973	75.0%	(IV)	58.3%	(III)
Burundi 1961	91.7%	(V)	65.6%	(IV)
El Salvador 1976	58.3%	(III)	56.2%	(III)
Guatemala 1965	62.5%	(IV)	59.4%	(III)
Mozambique 1978	83.3%	(V)	64.3%	(IV)
Nigeria 1979	75.0%	(IV)	47.2%	(III)
Philippines 1968	66.7%	(IV)	47.2%	(III)
USSR/Chechnya 1990	33.3%	(II)	38.9%	(II)
USSR/Moldova 1989	29.2%	(II)	25.0%	(II)
Rwanda 1993	75.0%	(IV)	68.7%	(IV)
Sierra Leone 1977	62.5%	(IV)	65.6%	(IV)
South Africa 1989	41.7%	(III)	52.8%	(III)
Sudan 1982	75.0%	(IV)	71.9%	(IV)
Zaire 1991	70.8%	(IV)	78.1%	(IV)
China 1979	62.5%	(IV)	44.4%	(III)
Czechoslovakia 1967	54.2%	(III)	39.3%	(II)
India 1989	41.7%	(III)	66.6%	(IV)
Macedonia 1989	29.2%	(II)	62.5%	(IV)
Mexico 1992	33.3%	(II)	36.1%	(II)
Control Group I: Developing States				
Costa Rica 1987	16.7%	(I)	22.2%	(II)
Kazakhstan 1994	33.3%	(II)	17.8%	(I)
Tanzania 1992	62.5%	(IV)	53.1%	(III)
Thailand 1985	50.0%	(III)	41.7%	(III)
Tunisia 1995	29.2%	(II)	50.0%	(III)
Control Group II: Developed States				
Spain 1990	16.6%	(I)	20.0%	(I)
Germany 1990	8.3%	(I)	0.0%	(I)
Australia 1992	4.2%	(I)	2.8%	(I)
United States 1990	4.2%	(I)	5.5%	(I)
Belgium 1995	4.2%	(I)	2.8%	(I)
Italy 1997	0.0%	(I)	25.0%	(II)
France 1974	8.3%	(I)	13.9%	(I)

Note: The percentage range is divided into five segments, representing the five levels of risks of state failure, with high percentage scores signaling high risk and low percentage scores standing for lower risk levels.

Table 10.11: Comparison of Forecasts of State Failure for Twenty Countries Using SF and PP Indicators

	SF	PP
1) High risk of state failure (81–100%)	3	0
2) High moderate risk of state failure (61–80%)	10	10
3) Moderate risk of state failure (41–60%)	4	7
4) Moderate low risk of state failure (21–40%)	3	3
5) Low risk of state failure (20% or less)	0	0

Table 10.12: Forecasting Power of the Two Sets of Indicators

	SF	PP
A. Twenty Test Countries	66.085%	57.92%
B. Control Group I Scores	100 - 41.66% = 58.34%	100 - 37.06% = 62.94%
C. Control Group II Scores	100 - 6.54% = 93.46%	100 - 10% = 90%

Table 10.13: Forecasting Power of Individual Indicators in the SF Project on a 1–5 Scale

1) Infant mortality:	79.7%
2) Road density:	67.2%
3) Democracy:	67.2%
4) Youth bulge:	65.6%
5) Regime durability:	64.1%
6) Ethnicity of ruling elite:	54.7%
SF Average for the 20 test cases:	66.4%

reports of the State Failure research team, it was often hard to follow the logic of the compilers of the list. Why are some countries considered state failures for all the years and others only for certain years? The list of 113 cases appears to be heterogeneous, incomplete, and, to some extent, arbitrary.

In addition, the four types of events that are said to constitute state failure are themselves quite diverse for a single concept like state failure. They range from

Table 10.14: Forecasting Power of PP Indicators on the 1-5 scale

1) Taxation	83.9%
2) Monopoly of Violence	68.7%
3) Authority/Legitimacy	65.6%
3) Constitutionality	60.1%
5) Citizenship	59.4%
6) Sovereignty	51.6%
7) Impersonal Power	43.7%
8) Territoriality	31.2%
PP Average for the 20 test cases	58.0%

Note: For Quality of Bureaucracy, operationalized as corruption-proneness, not enough data were available to determine a representative score; the provisional score is 80%.

nonviolent transitions to autocratic rule to genocides involving more than 250,000 deaths. They range from protracted episodes of rioting, violent clashes, and terrorism to large scale and intense guerrilla warfare and civil wars. The differences among the categories are large. The differences within categories are also big, encompassing events involving fewer than 10,000 deaths to more than 250,000 deaths, and events ranging from "transitions towards autocratic rule" by revolution, coup, or other nonviolent means to "the collapse of central state authority for two or more years."

The establishment of autocratic rule, which can serve to save a state from failure, is placed in the same category as a collapse of central state authority. A state like Israel, which, by most accounts, is a "success," is placed under state failure while a failure like East Germany is only mentioned in the control set for 1955, 1972, and 1980. The sample of 113 consolidated cases contains a rather mixed bag of small public order events, and larger internal troubles, both violent and nonviolent, whereby a change of government toward a weak democracy by nonviolent means is not counted as state failure while a change from a weak government by nonviolent means toward perhaps state-saving autocratic rule is included in the sample.

Another definition of state failure might yield better results for the PP indicators and worse ones for the SF indicators. A retest of both sets of indicators with an alternative working definition of state failure should be done as a next step. The definition of "failure" would involve the establishment of a threshold among the 1–5 score values of the nine PP indicators and perhaps also a weighing among them.

While the retesting of the two sets of indicators with a different definition of state failure is beyond the scope of this chapter, in conclusion we also suggest adding to the nine Pierson-derived indicators, above, a consequentialist outcome of state failure, namely the likelihood of gross human rights violations as an instrument used by those holding state power to compensate for the loss of legitimacy due to their failure to run the state well. Unfortunately, this part of an alternative definition of state failure can not be tested with the limited sample of countries we have utilized here. However, Clair Apodaca has recently done a similar test with a larger sample, examining the link between human rights abuses and refugee flows, utilizing the same political terror scale (PTS) we used in table 10.3 and the Appendix below (Apodaca 1998; see also Gibney, Apodaca, and McCann 1996).

In particular, Apodaca looked at the human rights record in three consecutive years prior to a refugee flow, the year of the flow itself, and two subsequent years for twenty developing countries that experienced refugee migration from 1984 to 1994 (excluding the breakup of the Soviet Union as a case). She also used a control group of fifty-five developing countries not experiencing refugee outflows. She found that countries with good human rights records rarely produce refugees, while countries experiencing levels of repression in the 3.5–4.5 range of the political terror scale accounted for 70 percent of the refugee flows. Apodaca found a general pattern in the form of an increase in human rights violations from an average score of 2 three years prior to flight, to just over 3.5 when refugees flee. She also found that nonrefugee-producing countries do not exhibit the general staircase pattern of increasing human rights abuse levels of refugee-producing countries. Nonrefugee-producing countries generally had a stable human rights rating hovering around 2.5 from 1985 through 1994 on the 1–5 scale (see operationalization details on the CEWS Web site). However, fourteen out of the fifty-five countries (25 percent) in the control group also suffered a step progression of human rights violations without subsequent refugee flows, indicating that the increase of such violations is an important but not a sufficient indicator for impending refugee flight. Nevertheless, she was confident enough to conclude on the basis of her data that, "The monitoring of human rights is an appropriate method of forecasting probable refugee crises."[7]

Unfortunately, there are too few cases with PTS-data available in our sample to retest her findings. The PTS longitudinal data series in our possession start only in 1980. They exclude the developed countries for which scores were only introduced later by Jongman (Jongman and Schmid 1999). Looking at three specific cases from our sample of twenty countries there is no clear indications that the trend she observed in a larger sample exists.

Conclusion

The competitive test between the two sets of indicators has been won by the set of indicators from the State Failure project. Yet the definition of "state failure" in that project remains problematical due to its broad character. A different definition of state failure might to some extent turn the tables, allowing the PP indicators to do better. Two, probably three, of the PP indicators—taxation, monopoly of violence, and corruption—do well and should be included in further tests of the results, past and future, of the SF project. If only the six top indicators from Pierson are used and run against the top SF Task Force indicators, they appear to do quite well. Clearly, further testing with larger samples is required.

Yet one should not only look at state failure. While it is clearly useful to look at state strength/failure when assessing the risks a country runs, risk assessments would be much improved if researchers also could measure and assess the effects of "society cohesion/society fragmentation." Once this has been done, one should then look at the relationship between state and society. Internal conflict risks are highest if the state is at odds with society or segments thereof. The quality of that relationship might, in the end, offer the best indicators for forecasting a country's future.[8] At the same time, one should never loose sight of the importance of the geopolitical context in which a country is forced to operate.

It also should be kept in mind that macrostructural quantitative indicators alone will be able to assess only the (in-)capacities of states and societies. States' intentions and determination are a matter of political culture and elite decisionmaking and can be accessed only by other than quantitative methods. Quantitative indicators are unable to gauge the state of mind of the political decision makers. For assessing motivations, the judgment of political analysts remains crucial.

However, a combination of various forecasting techniques might substantially increase the number of accurate forecasts. Three approaches should be used simultaneously:

1) field-based monitoring by local observers

2) expert assessments by regional specialists

3) monitoring structural quantitative background variables

Taken together, the combination of all three kinds of early warning instruments is likely to yield substantively enhanced forecasts that might be "good enough" for creating political will to avoid disaster.[9] However, the importance of the creation of solid time-series and cross-country data for longitudinal and comparative analysis cannot be overemphasized. This requires continuous work. There are no short-cuts to accurate early detection and early warning.

Notes

I would like to thank the students of my 1998 course, "What Makes and Breaks States and Societies," at Erasmus University, Rotterdam, for their help in data collection on their countries of origin. At Leiden University I would like to thank Loek Becker Hoff for his help in hand coding and collecting data and providing some of the tables. This chapter was written before the author joined the United Nations and all views or opinions expressed here are his sole responsibility.

1. When this chapter was drafted the State Failure project reports had not been made publically available, though enough information from them was circulated in the early warning research community to understand most of its logic, methodology, and data bases (see Esty et al. 1998). In the meantime there has been considerable disclosure, especially on the task force's work in its

second phase (see Esty et al. 1999). Most of the task force's database will be made available to the research community in late 2000.

2. State Failure researchers have acknowledged that the original operationalization was too heterogenous for some theoretical and analytical purposes and, in forthcoming reports on the project's third phase, they report the results of analyses of specific types of "failures" (for example, Harff, Surko, and Unger, forthcoming). A related problem was that successive episodes of events fall under the definition within one country in the period under consideration. In Iraq, for example, four successive Kurdish rebellions were identified between 1961 and 1992 (1961–1970, 1973–1975, 1981–1988, 1991–present). Similarly, different kinds of state failures often cooccur, for example, an ethnic war and regime collapse followed by a politicide. Instances where rebellions or crises overlapped or came in quick succession (less than five years elapsing between the beginning and end of successive events) were termed consolidated cases. Of the 113 cases analyzed in Phase I, sixty-two were single events and fifty-one were complex cases involving multiple and/or successive events. In the most recent "problem set," each case is scored on a set of annual magnitude measures. The case descriptions and magnitude codes can be accessed by researchers who want to reanalyze the data at www.bsos.umd.edu/cidcm/stfail.

3. "During troubled periods they suffered state failure and were included in the problem set; during noncrisis periods, they were randomly selected as control set cases" (Esty et al. 1995, 2). In subsequent phases of the SF project new sets of control cases were obtained, as before, by randomly selecting to match every country-year that preceded a state failure by two years, three countries that had experienced no crises for the preceding five years. Changing the control sets did not, according to the researchers, make a difference in any of the global model results (personal communication).

4. Kurian (1991, 232) notes that "Infant mortality rates are sensitive to even very small improvements in national health care, and medical experts are adamant that delivering routine health care and social services to pregnant women could significantly reduce them. Infant mortality has been declining in all parts of the world, although noticeably slower in Africa. Fifteen of the top twenty nations in infant deaths are African.... Worldwide, the differences in infant mortality rates for developed and developing countries are quite marked. Thirty-six times as many infants die at birth in Afghanistan as in Japan." Kurian also suggests a related reason why infant mortality might not be such a robust indicator for "state failure," noting that "The definition of an infant varies. Some countries require breathing to establish a live birth, while others recognize any signs of life" (231).

5. Personal communication from T. R. Gurr, a task force member.

6. Gurr and Harff, both members of the task force, write that "Initial results of the State Failure project . . . suggest that early warning research using macro-indicators can correctly classify at best 75 percent of state failures vs. nonstate failures" (Gurr and Harff 1996, 86). This is in line with the conclusion of Hamm (Mercator University, Duisburg) that "structural data are of only limited use for early warning. Rather a combination of quantitative and qualitative analysis seems more appropriate" (Hamm 1998, 2).

7. The countries studied were Togo, Kuwait, Bhutan, Mali, Mauritania, Senegal, Liberia, Sierra Leone, Kenya, Zimbabwe, Niger, Suriname, Chile, South Yemen, Somalia, Djibouti, Mozambique, Bangladesh, Burma, and Sri Lanka. Of the twenty cases one involved a country with a score of 2 or below, there were four cases with a score of 3, fourteen with scores of 3.5 to 4.5, and two cases with a score of 5 (Apodaca 1998, 85).

8. PIOOM has developed two different monitoring instruments: a State Strength/State Failure meter and a Society Cohesion/Society Fragmentation meter (see Schmid 2000).

9. The parallel use of several methodologies of forecasting is also emphasized in the Phase II report of the State Failure project: "In order to bridge the gap between the two-thirds accuracy of our statistical model, and the better than 90 percent accuracy required for effective policy responses, the skills of individual country analysts and policy makers in assessing rapidly changing local conditions remain absolutely crucial" (Esty et al. 1999, 66).

Appendix: Stages in Conflict and Repression

Five Stages of Political Terror Scale

With number of cases at each stage in 1996, from Gibney, Apodaca, and McCann (1996).

Level 1: 56 Countries

Countries... under a secure rule of law, people are not imprisoned for their views, and torture is rare or exceptional.... Political murders are extraordinarily rare.

Level 2: 55 Countries

There is a limited amount of imprisonment for nonviolent political activity. However, few are affected, torture and beatings are exceptional.... Political murder is rare.

Level 3: 49 Countries

There is extensive political imprisonment, or a recent history of such imprisonment. Execution or other political murders and brutality may be common. Unlimited detention, with or without trial, for political views is accepted.

Level 4: 18 Countries with almost 3 Billion People

The practices of Level 3 are expanded to larger numbers. Murders, disappearances, and torture are a common part of life.... In spite of its generality, on this level violence affects primarily those who interest themselves in politics or ideas.

Level 5: 12 Countries with about 250 million People

The violence of Level 4 has been extended to the whole population.... The leaders of these societies place no limits on the means or thoroughness with which they pursue personal or ideological goals.

Table 10.15: Five Stages of Conflict and Two Crises Thresholds

Stage I: Peaceful Stable Situation
High Degree of Social Stability & Regime Legitimacy

Stage II: Dispute & Tension Situation
Growing Levels of Systemic Strain and Increasing Social and Political Cleavages, Often Along Factional Lines

Political Crisis

Stage III: Violent Political Conflict
Erosion of Political Legitimacy of the National Government and/or Rising Acceptance of Factional Politics

Stage IV: Low-Intensity Conflict
Open Hostility and Armed Conflict among Factional Groups; Regime Repression and Insurgency

Humanitarian Crisis

Stage V: High-Intensity Conflict
Open Warfare among Rival Groups and/or Mass Destruction and Displacement of Sectors of the Civilian Population

Source: Pioom, Leiden University

11
A Synthetic Framework for Extensible Conflict Early Warning Information Systems

Thomas Schmalberger and Hayward R. Alker

Over the past years, considerable effort has been invested to develop early warning systems that take account of the changing nature of intergroup (including but not limited to interstate) conflicts. As suggested in the preface and chapter 1, recently there have been more internal than international conflicts, making more relevant to violent conflict prevention the role of regional organizations such as the OAU, OAS or OSCE, as well as NGOs specializing in related challenges.

This increased complexity has required not only the rethinking of jurisdictional issues, but the development of different, often more decentralized and network-oriented, methods to collect and analyze data for the monitoring and interpretation of conflict situations by the increasing variety of agencies directly concerned with such conflicts.[1] It also has required the development of different concepts of the internationally relevant dimensions of such conflicts, and new policy instruments to prevent, abate, or diffuse them. Acknowledging the challenge that the changing nature of such conflicts presents for the international community, early in the post–Cold War era, UN Secretary General

Boutros Boutros-Ghali called upon the academic community to "improve information available ... for purposes of preventive diplomacy" (Boutros-Ghali 1992).

As amply evidenced by earlier chapters in this volume, the challenge of corroborating and synthesizing what is known about conflict early warning in a way that allows both for continued scholarly investigations and improved practical applications is a difficult task. Differing conceptual frameworks often get in the way of such synthetic efforts, and the lessons of particular case studies or comparisons do not obviously apply to new cases similar in some respects, but different in others. Such efforts are the principal purpose of Part III; in chapter 2, this cluster of tasks was referred to as Stage 2 of the CEWS Research Project.

There are both qualitative and quantitative dimensions to such an exercise, several of which we shall focus on in this chapter, while others will be addressed later. Perhaps the most obvious problem is the qualitative one, i.e., the increasingly heterogenous character of "intergroup conflicts" or "contemporary conflicts" that fall within the post–Cold War focus of the CEWS project. Without a unifying way of recognizing conflict commonalities and differences, comparisons and preventively oriented, context-sensitive learning would not be possible. Using a Simmelian concept of social conflict, we shall try to synthesize the different conceptions of conflict found in the peace research, political science and international studies literatures, and in the other chapters of this volume. Recognizing that conflicts may also be psychological phenomena, and that they may often be represented in terms of oppositional concepts that are not particularly focused on intergroup social relations, for our purposes we shall henceforth use "conflicts" to mean "social conflicts." The approach developed here and in the next chapter offers a graphical way that both peacemakers and scholars may find helpful for thinking more clearly about context-sensitive conflict interventions and alternative conflict trajectories.

Quantitatively oriented early warning indicator approaches, such as those at the focus of Alex Schmid's comparisons in chapter 10, raise a related issue: how to conform these approaches to the more qualitative insights of conflict life-cycle approaches? Although the PIOOM project does have a qualitatively sophisticated conception of the states of conflict, including "political" and "humanitarian" crisis thresholds, the State Failures project does not appear to be so focused, making "life-cycle" comparisons difficult.[2] Even the ambitious, initial proposal of chapter 1 sidestepped the possible uses of news-based event data for early warning indicator construction purposes. However, Vorkunova and Harff in Part II, many of the approaches that Davis and Gurr review (1998), and the proponents of FEWER practice (reviewed in chapter 13) find these quantitative approaches to have value.

Even when we recall that each chapter of Part II was written within the spirit of the CEWS guidelines presented in chapter 2—calling for preventively focused, life-cycle structured, trajectory comparisons—our task here is not an easy one. For example, event data researchers tend to build up their quantifiable codings from preliminary chronologies, while narratively oriented "life cycle" theorists link these concepts to the qualitatively meaningful structure (or "plot") of their conflict narratives. Can the different representations be shown to correspond?

Finally, for us there is the problem of extensibility. As argued in chapter 2, any moderately large effort to develop a conflict early warning information system can offer at best only a useful prototype. The approach should allow both scholars, policy-oriented observers, parties to conflicts, and peacemakers to add in their own perspectives, as well as new cases, or subsequent episodes of the cases already coded, without too much difficulty. When the authors, their source materials, and the underlying rationales of earlier or later studies are not copresent with those of a prototypical study, as well as the views of those they are studying, this integration can be a very difficult one.

We will begin the development of an integrative framework by building up and incorporating some of the conceptual ideas proposed by, and/or entailed in, this volume's previous contributions. This discussion will reveal gaps between the concerns of scholarly forecasters and practical interveners, between scholarly categories and participant perspectives, and among paradigmatic epistemologies; it should demonstrate the extent to which the proposed framework is capable of bridging them. To test the validity of this framework we will then illustrate how it is capable of integrating the narratives and/or chronologies of the various contributions.[3] Notice though that this framework has a different objective than any of the other contributions, and uses them only to test its applicability. The diversity of these contributions in terms of methods, data, and geographical and analytical focus was intended not only to illustrate how differently conflict early warning research can be conducted, but also to describe the challenge that an integrative framework faces.

Let it be clear. Each of these contributions stands on its own, has its own merits, develops its own insights into international conflict, and derives its own lessons. To integrate these contributions into a common framework neither negates nor diminishes the value of any of them. On the contrary, if an integrative framework is unable to adequately incorporate any of the given contributions, the applicability of the framework, and not the value of the contribution, is compromised. It would be another project, of far larger dimensions, to engage CEWS authors in a reanalysis of their uses of their own primary materials. Our approach here attempts to allow and facilitate the addition and discussion of new perspectives, but not to prejudge the outcomes of such contributions.

Toward an Integrative Framework for Conflict Early Warning Systems

The most important conceptual problem blocking the contemporary integration of different conflict early warning systems is to develop a concept of conflict that is broad enough to incorporate both paradigmatic or epistemological differences as well as the rich variety of intergroup conflicts falling under some degree of international concern. This means recognizing the different explicit and implicit definitions and notions of conflict that are being used in the literature without eliminating the more detailed distinctions they entail.

A solution to this problem cannot be found in identifying a lowest common denominator. In some cases, there is not any such common element. For instance, in his seminal work, Schelling (1970, 5) wrote that "to study the strategy of conflict is to take the view that most conflict situations are essentially bargaining situations." Conflicts are therefore a subset of bargaining situations, which themselves usually mix elements of conflict and cooperation. So describing bargaining as an essential and distinguishing feature of conflicts will not work logically.

And there is a disciplinary problem here too: bargaining is the subject matter par excellence of modern economics and its derivative paradigms. Whereas in some religious or ethnic identity conflicts studied by sociologists, recognition is a prerequisite to bargaining, many bargaining situations would not be seen at all as instances of identity conflicts. Bargaining theorists would say that recognition could be bargained over. Both might be right in some fashion, but different disciplines often try to rest their theories on different foundational concepts, or "unmoved movers," and the matter is hard to resolve.

An earlier synthesizer, the American peace researcher and international lawyer Quincy Wright was more interested in ontological questions, taking what we would now call an experientially grounded, sociological approach to the phenomenology of conflict. He wrote that "conflict may designate a duel, a household brawl, a strife between political factions, a fight between street urchins, a suppression of a rebellion, or a war between nations. . . . Each of these forms of conflict has, of course, its peculiarities, but the sociologist, by comparison and analysis, distinguishes the universal from the particular aspect of each conflict" (Wright 1983, 238). Thus, in Wright's (and our own) view, the study of conflict needs to concern itself with identifying what the constitutive elements are that distinguish conflict situations from other situations that are not conflicts. Although this view does by no means exclude that bargaining can occur in conflict situations, bargaining cannot be used as a defining feature uniquely or modally/statistically to identify conflicts.

Since we are interested in developing a concept of conflict that can help us to better describe and forecast alternative possible trajectories of particular intergroup conflicts, we must identify not only the constitutive variables of conflict as a generic, atemporal form of social interaction, but also the different forms of conflict that are created when the constitutive variables are given particular values. Each distinctive form of conflict shares the constitutive variables of a generic notion of conflict, but distinguishes itself from other forms of conflict by the values that are attributed to these variables.

We will develop our conceptual framework of conflict in two steps. First, we will introduce three variables that constitute conflict in its generic form, and can help us to identify and distinguish different forms of conflict. This step includes a discussion of how the different notions of conflict used in the contributions to this project can be accommodated in this framework. Second, bringing time into the analysis, we explore the consequences of the fact that conflict forms are constituted in time. We shall be able to describe how different forms of a conflict come into and go out of existence at different times, allowing their description as conflict phases. This should facilitate our goal of developing the "practical grammars of action (and habit) making [peacemaking successes and failures] possible" (Alker 1988, lesson 8; see also chapter 2).

Composing Forms of Conflict

War, violent conflict, ethnic conflict, and genocide are some of the concepts that are often used to describe either the same or different intergroup situations in which many people lose their lives due to an organized use of force. Similarly, these notions are often contrasted with domestic or international crisis situations in which no or only a few lives are lost. Although each author usually defines these concepts so as to avoid contradictions, the individual definitions often make it difficult to cumulate and synthesize related findings. We need additionally to ask: what are the defining characteristics of a conflict regardless of whether or not human life is lost? Before we can begin to make distinctions between particular forms of conflict, we must determine what exactly it is that makes them intergroup conflicts in the first place.

Recall from chapter 2 the notion of a conflict that is conceived of as a living social organism with a life history. In analytically unpacking this notion, we are helped by the social theorist Simmel, who argued that conflict is a form of sociation. Sociation "synthesizes all human interests, contents, and processes into concrete units. . . . [It] continuously emerges and ceases and emerges again. Even where its external flux and pulsation are not sufficiently strong to form organizations proper, they link individuals together" (Simmel 1950, 5, 10). Sociation is therefore understood as the general process by which individuals and groups interact with each other. Depending on how they interact with each other different social forms are created that distinguish one kind of interaction from another; that is, the form of an interaction is abstracted from its pragmatic context even though the interaction itself can only be understood to be what it is in its pragmatic context. Simmel identified several social forms such as exchange, domination, and conflict.[4]

Adopting this notion of social forms, conflict becomes a living form, a social organism that comes into being, can be transformed, and dies. That is, a conflict has an organic life cycle. For Simmel as well as Galtung and Rupesinghe in their nonWestern mode (see chapter 2), the driving force behind this life cycle are those oppositions created in interactions that permit a relationship between individuals or groups to continue, and thus to produce and maintain the form that is characteristic of a particular conflict. This characteristic is to "resolve divergent dualisms; it is a way of achieving some kind of unity" (Simmel, 1955, 13). This unity can involve the opposing group in which case the underlying dualism is resolved, and the form of sociation is transformed into one that is not a conflict. In this case a conflict can be said to have been settled. This notion is thus compatible with the one developed in the literature on conflict transformation, understood as "a flexible, yet comprehensive process, by which ultimately a culture of negotiation and accommodation displaces a culture of violence and provides ordinary people with the means to prevent any return to barbarity" (Rupesinghe 1995, viii).

But the creation of unity can also involve the adoption of different ways of expressing the underlying opposition. In this case, a conflict continues but takes on a different form. For instance, the opposition underlying a crisis can be expressed in the mutual exchange of threats while the same opposition in a war can be expressed in the conquest or destruction of the other. Consequently, the generic form of conflict takes on more concrete forms that are distinguished from each other by the way in which the underlying opposition is expressed. This notion is compatible with much of the literature on international crisis where an underlying opposition is dealt with differently in a crisis than in a war.[5] However, this notion goes beyond this literature in that it allows to distinguish different forms of conflict irrespective of the actors or issues involved, and thus allows us to address domestic, interethnic, transnational, as well as interstate conflicts.

To distinguish qualitatively different forms of conflict, what are the variables that we need to look for? The first variable flows directly from our conception of conflict and describes an oppositional relation between groups. This variable can be found in virtually all treatises on human conflict, although it is conceptualized differently. Following Lund's classification of analytical frameworks in chapter 6, three conceptualizations of a conflictual opposition can be distinguished. In structural theories, an opposition emerges from a society's history, economy, and social structure that positions different groups against each other. Consequently, the opposition underlying a conflict results from the conditions that endow groups with different characteristics, or, in other words, the difference between groups puts them into a conflictual position with respect to each other. An instance of such a conception is Schmid's, in chapter 10, in which he identifies indicators that point at situational characteristics that are likely to pit groups against each other so as to result in state failure. In action theories, an opposition emerges from "the behavior of major political leaders and their governments . . . in response to evolving events," he writes. An opposition is created by the way in which groups interact with each other, and not by the difference of the groups per se. In fact, groups are formed and distinguish themselves in their actions toward each other. For instance, Vorkunova describes in chapter 5 the actions and responses that created the oppositions underlying the conflicts in Chechnya and Moldova. Finally, approaches that focus on political institutions and processes are concerned with how a conflictual opposition can be avoided or mitigated by the existence or creation of institutions and processes that help to accommodate diverging claims and interests. An opposition is thus the result of the absence or inefficiency of mechanisms that prevent a divergence of beliefs to turn into a conflictual opposition. The contributions by Gounden–Solomon and Anderlini–Garcia–Rupesinghe elaborate on how this process can be reversed, and Lund explores cases in which the existence of adequate mechanisms has prevented a conflictual opposition to develop.

In order to integrate these different conceptions our first variable can be operationalized by identifying minimally the parties to a conflict. This allows us to distinguish conflicts that involve different parties. For instance, Vorkunova shows in her analysis of the war in Chechnya that the conflict was transformed when the Russian support for counterrevolutionary forces was revealed, that is, Russia became a party to the conflict while it had been considered a mediator before. However, we prefer to also identify the issue(s) that define what the conflict is about. Although the parties to a conflict can remain the same, the issues that separate them can change, and thus redefine a conflict. For instance, in Padilla's account of the civil war in Guatemala, the parties remained the same while their differences changed from promoting and resisting the establishment of a socialist regime to the promotion and repression of democratic reforms. Similarly, the same parties can be engaged in several conflicts that are about different issues, and yet are together embedded in a larger conflict. For example, Gurr and Khosla describe the conflict between India and Pakistan over Kashmir as consisting of several other conflicts involving the same parties but different issues.

An opposition is not sufficient to uniquely identify different forms of conflict, however. For instance, a crisis can be characterized by the same opposition as a civil war. As a second variable we therefore choose the use of violence. The use of violence is the single most common variable used in the literature to distinguish types of conflicts, and therefore promises not only a great integrative potential, but also points at one of the key defining characteristics of some forms of conflict. Violence is often operationalized in terms of the number of casualties, and is subsequently classified into different types according to the parties or issues involved so that ethnic conflict, interstate war, or revolutionary wars are distinguished. However, the quantification of violence is easily misleading because it does not link conflictual behavior to the casualties it produces. It is the conflictual behavior that we need to capture, however, because it expresses the opposition underlying the conflict and thus distinguishes violence from other forms of conflict. For instance, a sporadic or incidental use of violence can produce more casualties than the regular and systematic use of violence. Yet, it is precisely the regular and systematic use of violence that indicates that violence is considered a permissible and justifiable way of dealing with each other. If violence occurs in other forms of conflict, such as a crisis, it is usually considered to be an aberration or a provocation, but not a justifiable means for engaging with another conflict party.

On the other hand, the special concern of authors like Fein and Lund (as reviewed in chapter 1), Gurr, Harff, and Schmid with politically motivated mass killings (politicide) and genocide surely needs our attention. Thus while not measuring the use of violence quantitatively in terms of the number of casualties, we recognize a certain ordinality of violence associated with its regular and systematic occurrence, perhaps further increased by doing away with meaningful restraints on its exercise.

Although the use of violence allows the analyst to distinguish violent forms of conflict from others, it does not allow us to identify and distinguish among those forms of conflict that do not involve systematic violence, nor to illuminate the early warner's preoccupation with violent situations that could get much worse.[6] For instance, a crisis is preceded by a dispute, and a limited war can become a total one. Each can be considered as different forms of conflict because their underlying oppositions are expressed differently. As a third variable we therefore introduce opposition-relevant sequential expectations. Notice how this variable interactively combines with notions of oppositional parties, issues, and claims in the composition/construction of a fuller definition of the intergroup conflict. Composing music or thoughts is more than merely additively or multiplicatively sequencing notes or words.

Opposition-relevant sequential expectations—"expectations" for short—are usually not used as indicators in the existing literature, although they are often used implicitly. We find expectations a most useful variable because it not only allows one to distinguish violent and nonviolent forms of conflict, it connects them. For instance, a dispute is characterized by the expectation of a possible, subseqent crisis. If a crisis does occur, it continues the underlying opposition of the dispute, and in fact is premissed on its nonresolution, so that a different mode of behavior is justified. Similarly, a dispute might be resolved precisely because a crisis is expected as a real successive possibility.

Notice that oftentimes more than one form of conflict can be expected, without the necessity or ability being assumed that we can meaningfully assign probabilities or "odds" to such possibilities. For instance, in a crisis situation a settlement as well as an outbreak of violence can be expected, but the empirical basis for odds calculation, a large set of comparable cases, may not exist.The defining quality of opposition-relevant sequential expectations is not only which form of conflict can, but also which ones cannot be, expected. Consequently, a dispute is characterized as much by the expectation of a crisis as by the nonexpectation of an outbreak of violence.

Recognizing opposition-relevant sequential expectations as a constitutive variable of social conflicts is a necessary early step toward operationalizing significant historicities in the lives of a people, in discovering conflict life cycles and grammar-like possibilities for conflict transformation within historically focused social expectations (Alker 1988; Schmalberger 1998; see chapter 2). Importantly, the phenomena of a group's, people's, or society's history become empirically researchable.

Narratives have been distinguished from chronologies of events on the basis of the narrative structures meaningfully connecting and unifying the events in time and space. (Alker 1996a; chapters 4, 6, 8, 10, and 11). Opposition-relevant sequential expectations can be operationalized best from narrative accounts that map out the various possibilities perceived to exist in participants' and/or observers' minds at important junctures of a conflict, or describe the reasoning that lead the conflicting parties to their actions. Only for sequential representations in which the context of a conflict is not conveyed, expectations cannot be so operationalized. These analyses can only be partly integrated into our framework.

In the language of conventional formal logic, we argue that the three variables opposition (conceived of in terms of parties and issues), the more or less regularized use of violence, and sequential expectations are necessary and sufficient to distinguish forms of intergroup conflict that are the focus of the present research project. In this sense, with a heightened awareness of the historical complexities of the possibly contested social predications involved, we consider them to be constitutive variables of intergroup conflict. This implies that together they define a situation as being a conflict; depending on their contingent properties, that is, the values they are given, they define different forms of conflict.

Based on our preventively focused concern with alternative conflict trajectories and these three variables—opposition, use of violence, and sequential expectations—we nonexhaustively choose to distinguish four forms of conflict particularly useful for present purposes. Just as one example, note that many issues of Lund's "normal" diplomacy (figure 1.3) or of typical legislative politics do not belong in the universe of table 11.1 at all: they do not have associated with them the realistic possibility of the use of violence. The nonexhaustive character of these highlighting distinctions should be evident from the fact that the top three of the conflict forms in table 11.1 are defined in terms of the existence of an expectation that a subsequent, more violent form of conflict is a real possibility. Of course diminutions in violence are also often possible, but for our purposes, we define these three forms in an escalatory fashion. The closeness of fit of these distinctions to those independently evolved by Gurr and Khosla in chapter 9 is particularly encouraging.

For future reference, let us spell out these definitions of our four highlighted forms of conflict:

- *Dispute.* A conflict begins with a dispute that is characterized by opposing claims that are expressed in ways that use existing institutional processes. This alone does not distinguish a dispute from other disagreements and define any political process. The distinguishing characteristic is rather the expectation of a crisis as a real possibility, that is, the existing institutions for accommodating divergent claims and interests are threatened or expected to be disabled or sidestepped. No violence connected to the dispute occurs.

- *Crisis.* The opposition underlying a crisis is expressed in ways that use the existing institutional processes but their substitution with violence is openly threatened or expected. Contrary to a dispute in which not the use but the threat of using violence is expected, a crisis is characterized by the expectation of a regular and systematic use of violence. In fact, incidental and sporadic violence can already occur and give further reason to believe that the way in which the underlying opposition is expressed might soon involve the regular and systematic use of violence.

- *Limited violence.* The regular and systematic use of violence implies that the underlying opposition is no longer expressed within the existing institutional processes to peacefully accommodate diverging claims. In fact, the legitimacy or usefulness of these processes is called into question, and the systematic and regular use of force is considered justified and permissible. However, even if the regular and systematic use of force is justified, not all uses of force are equally justified. For instance, a government might engage in selective military actions against a group of rebels without unduly implicating the civilian population in that region, or unduly interfering with the everyday activities of the rest of the population. We can therefore distinguish a form of conflict that is characterized by a restrained use of force from another form of conflict that is characterized by the unrestrained use of force. We call the former a form of limited violence and the latter a form of massive violence. They usually, but not necessarily, coincide with lower and higher numbers of casualties.[7] The defining characteristic of a form of limited violence is that an unrestrained use of force, and thus a form of massive violence, can be expected.

- *Massive violence.* Massive violence is characterized by the regular, systematic, and unrestrained use of force. Institutional processes for peacefully accommodating diverging claims are disabled or avoided, and the opposition underlying the conflict is expressed in using the full range of violent means available. For instance, a government might feel compelled, and could thus justify, that its military actions do not discriminate between the group of rebels against which the actions are directed from the civilian population among which the rebels operate. Notice that our definition of an underlying opposition is sufficiently broad to not only include conflictual behavior that involves the mutual use of violence but also the exclusive use of violence by one group against another. If such violence is used in an unrestrained manner not only war but also genocide and politicide can be characterized in this manner. The unrestrained use of force gives rise to the expectation of destruction or elimination of a party.

The four forms of conflict and their respective values for the three constitutive variables of conflict are represented in table 11.1.

The variables determining the distinctions among forms of conflict in table 11.1 also determine how these forms can be assembled into a sequence so as to represent a particular conflict narrative or data story. More specifically, the specific version of "opposition-related sequential expectations" included in the table mutually defines one form in terms of another form of conflict. The focus on escalation in the first three rows of the table fulfills our desire to develop preventively focused coding practices aimed at generating early warnings about violent conflict, even if it allows only escalatory expectations, thus truncating typical ideas of conflict life cycles.[8] Only the destructive de-escalation of eliminative "conflict resolution," e.g., genocidal "final solutions," is highlighted.

Table 11.1 also demonstrates the compositional approach of our framework. We can build forms of conflict by combining the three constitutive variables of the generic notion of conflict. Forms of conflict are by no means the only relevant phenomena we can address, however. Other phenomena that are pertinent to a suggestive and empirically measurable conceptualization of intergroup conflict can be developed using the same approach. This can be demonstrated with a phenomenon that one recurrently observes

Table 11.1: Forms of Conflict

Form of conflict	Variable		
	Opposition underlying conflict	Use of violence	Sequential expectation
Dispute	divergent claims are accommodated within existing institutional processes	none	possible threats of using violence
Crisis	divergent claims are accommodated within existing institutional processes	incidental and sporadic	possible use of limited or massive violence
Limited violence	divergent claims are expressed by the use of violence	regular, systematic, and restrained	possible use of massive violence
Massive violence	divergent claims are expressed by the use of violence	regular, systematic, and unrestrained	destruction, elimination, unconditional surrender

in conflictual situations, namely divergent perspectives. Many practitioners have pointed out that a recurrent obstacle to conflict mediation is the divergence of perspectives among the participants in a conflict. In the scholarly literature this divergence has often been subsumed under the opposition underlying a conflict when in fact the definition of such an opposition is contingent on particular perspectives. This implies that the constitutive variables of a particular intergroup conflict are not contested but rather that the parties to a conflict attribute different values to them and therefore produce different conflict descriptions.

The conceptualization of divergent perspectives allows us, in turn, to address a feature of conflict that is mostly identified by traditional historians, lawyers, and practitioners, and to a lesser extent by contemporary social scientists, namely claims for recognition and legitimacy. Claims for recognition and legitimacy express and characterize the relationship between divergent perspectives. Hence, each perspective is grounded in the three constitutive variables to which different values are attributed, and issues of legitimacy and recognition are expressed in those differences. For instance, a government that does not recognize the conflicting party interprets the underlying opposition differently than that party. Often it can be observed that whereas the acquisition of arms by a rebel group is understood by them as a means to defend themselves against government repression, the government interprets this action as a terrorist attempt to undermine the political and social order. This divergence of perspectives affects also the use of violence, for a rebel group might resort to the regular and systematic use of violence that is interpreted by the government as sporadic and incidental occurrences of violence. This might be due to the limited resources available to the rebels but it also might be due to the government's refusal to admit its inability to preserve the existing order.

The divergence of perspectives also affects the sequential expectations of the conflicting parties. Precisely because the conflicting parties can find themselves engaged in different forms of conflict, their opposition-relevant sequential expectations differ. For instance, a rebel group that is already engaged in an all-out war against the government can expect this war only to be stopped or resolved, while the government employs only parts of its police and military forces to fight terrorists, and can still further unleash its use of force. The operationalization of claims to recognition and legitimacy is difficult because many analyses aim at producing a convergent rather than a divergent picture of a conflict. However, a divergence of perspectives can be inferred from a convergent account if it reports from one of the participants' point of view. This usually casts the opponent in particular terms spelling out one perspective, and at the same time, providing hints about the other perspective.[9]

At this point a cautionary note about the limited aspirations of the CEWS project is warranted. Although we claim that the three variables are constitutive of intergroup conflicts, that dispute, crisis, limited, and massive violence can be identified and distinguished by them, and that the subsidiary concept of legitimacy and recognition adds identity-relevant descriptive richness to our conceptualization, in this study we do not directly validate these claims empirically. The methodology we are developing is primarily aimed at integrating different conflict early warning frameworks and historical or empirical accounts or data sets that are premised on different grounds. In our efforts, we are treating these accounts and interpretations as given, as if they were primary sources. This practice is justified because we do not here aim to make substantive claims about any of the cases included beyond those warranted by the experts in our research project. However, just as this methodology can extensibly be applied to new cases and revised analyses of older cases, it could be applied to primary sources of specific cases, and it could be applied to the empirical testing of our hypothesis that the three variables—opposition, use of violence, and expectations—are indeed constitutive of conflict.[10] Surely such additional efforts are worthwhile for scholars to undertake, and representable and arguable in the heuristically suggestive, practically oriented, extensible information system we seek to construct.

Phase Structures for Data Stories about Conflict Life Cycles

Although the variable of sequential expectations of the nearly atemporal definitions of forms of conflict in table 1.1 hint at trajectory possibilities, we want to embed these forms in historical time by further redefining forms of conflict as conflict phases. This will allow corresponding definitions of two useful new phase types—conflict abatement and conflict settlement—and more adequately descriptive data stories built up from observations and correspondingly enriched conflict life-cycle notions. Of several plausible ways to do this, we shall here proceed by thinking of each value of our constitutive variables as possibly changing in time, and enriching our conception of sequential expectations to include both previous phase contexts, the suspension of increasingly violent expectations, and the possibility of new conflict episodes. Once we have done this, we shall be in a position to grammatically describe and explain how conflict phases can be combined into a variety of possible phase sequences.

As reviewed in chapters 1 and 2, the notion of conflict phases is widely used to separate out an historical period or moment when key variables are relatively unchanged. Because the four forms of conflict defined above—dispute, crisis, limited, and massive violence—are more concrete manifestations of our generic notion of conflict, all we have to do to turn these forms of conflict into conflict phases is to specify corresponding phases as periods when the respective values of our constitutive variables do not change, short of one modification: the expectation of further escalation is temporarily suspended.

Most of the chapters in Part II explore how de-escalation can be brought about at earlier stages and in less destructive ways. When exclusive, such an emphasis tends to not incorporate a prognostic component for detecting when a renewed escalation can erupt. For our attempt to integrate information relevant to movement in both directions, we need to specify not only how forms of conflict are created but also how they are abated or dissolved. For this purpose we introduce the notion of "abatement."

Abatement Phase

A situation that is characterized by the suspension of escalatory expectations can result from a multitude of developments, such as a truce agreement or the defeat of one of the conflicting parties. These situations do not represent a wholly new form of conflict, such as a dispute or a crisis, or the resolutional end of a conflict. Rather they describe a transitional phase of the existing form of conflict. We shall call such phases "abatements" and attempt to characterize them in ways consistent with the distinctions among forms of conflict given above.

An abatement phase marks the end of an escalatory trajectory and represents a potential turning-point in a conflict. It demarcates the end of a particular conflict episode that is started every time a new escalatory trajectory begins. From such a transitional phase, a conflict episode slowly dissipates its venom without being formally resolved, and it moves toward the resolutional completion of its life cycle, or toward a new escalatory episode.

Because the fuller characterization of such phases depends on the prior conflict phase that is being abated, we say that this kind of description is context sensitive. Not surprisingly four such variants need to be defined—abatement phases corresponding to dispute, crisis, limited violence, and massive violence phases—all of which presume that the conflict defining opposition persists. In terms of our three constitutive variables, an abatement phase corresponding to a dispute phase would be one where opposition persists, no violence occurs and expectations of a subsequent crisis are suspended. Similarly, in an abatement phase corresponding to a crisis phase, violence does not occur, and the expectation of subsequent systematic violence is suspended. An abatement following a limited violence phase is one in which both systematic violence and the expectation of massive subsequent violence are suspended, although sporadic violence can still occur. Finally, an abatement phase corresponding to a massive violence phase has the same violence pattern as one following a limited violence phase, combined with the suspension of expectations that the destruction or elimination of opposed parties is to occur.

An abatement phase is the transitional stage from where a conflict can move toward its resolution or a renewed escalation. However, conflict re-escalation doesn't mean that the clock has been turned back, because grammatically structured histories are much more than linear sequences of events. Thus a truce agreement that has been broken indicates a new episode has begun in a protracted, i.e., multiepisodic conflict. Its renewed escalatory path makes possible new kinds of events, such as acts of revenge linked to remembered earlier violations of trust, and the hardening of parties' attitudes toward each other. In such a situation a mediation effort was not only unsuccessful but may also have been counterproductive.[11] If the potential created in the temporary de-escalation is realized, on the other hand, the opposition underlying the various forms of conflict is resolved and the entire conflict is settled. In such a situation, as we see in the Southern African case studies of chapters 7 and 8, a mediation was able to transform a conflict, involving a rewriting of shared accounts of one or several groups' pasts.

Settlement Phase

In terms of a conflict's three constitutive variables, a settlement phase may be said to be characterized by the dissolution of its foundational opposition, the absence of the use of violence, and no expectation of violence or the threat of violence in subsequent periods. Unlikely in practice, a completely efficient eliminative genocide or total war victory that eliminates all potential rulers legitimated by an earlier order, might be said to fit this definition. Were one to include specific recognition relationships in the definition of a settlement phase, one could define a settlement phase as entered into when and if the conflicting parties resolve the opposition underlying the conflict in a noneliminative fashion, establish or reconstitute mutually recognized actors and/or institutional processes in which opposing claims are accommodated, and end intergroup violence and the expectation that other such episodes of the same conflict might begin again.

Abatements happen more often than eliminative or genuine conflict settlements. For instance, Gurr and Khosla report that the Tripoli Agreement reached in 1976 accommodated the Moros' claim for autonomy for which they had fought for more than fifteen years. However, during this time the ethnic composition of the population had changed and made autonomy based on referendums unlikely. A new escalation began when the Moros called the Tripoli Agreement into question and pressed for independence. Although the opposition underlying the conflict between the Moros and the Philippine government remained essentially the same, it was articulated differently within its identity-related dimension. That is, the escalatory trajectory leading up to the Tripoli Agreement was characterized by claims for autonomy whereas the escalatory trajectory following the agreement was characterized by claims for independence.

A Grammar of Multi-Episode Phase Sequences

Conflicts can get more complicated, because historical movements do not always move linearly through the stages in an ideal typical conflict life cycle. Reescalations happen. Building on our newly crafted notions of abatement and settlement phases, a more adequate account of the sequential composition of conflict phases into one or more conflict episodes is graphically represented in figure 11.1. Like a formal grammar, the figure specifies the legitimate successor states for each possible phase of a particular episode. As suggested above abatements end an episode, and may lead to a new episode beginning in any of the four conflict phases, while a settlement phase terminates a conflict.

The distinction among conflict episodes is a useful way to represent some of the larger themes of a conflict's history, and to connect them to the more detailed aspects of a conflict trajectory. In other words, a more context-sensitive representation of conflict is produced if the history of a conflict is structured in terms of thematically coherent conflict episodes that are not simply recorded as a timeless sequence of previous conflict phases, but whose reinterpretations can be traced and their effects on the further unfolding of a conflict trajectory can be explained.

Why a particular possible phase sequence occurs is not explained by a grammar of conflict phases, or the typical narrative written within its constraints. But when escalatory and de-escalatory phase sequences are recognized, we have a minimal data story, episode, or narrative definable within the guiding ideal type of a conflict life cycle and a grammar of its possible variations. The need for further explanations is partly fulfilled and partly focused and stimulated by such coherence generating accounts, depending on the motivational-situational richness of its details. Whenever we have sufficient contextual information we can identify the common and evolving themes that connect phase sequences and form distinct conflict episodes. In the absence of such

Figure 11.1. A Grammar of Possible Conflict Phase Sequences

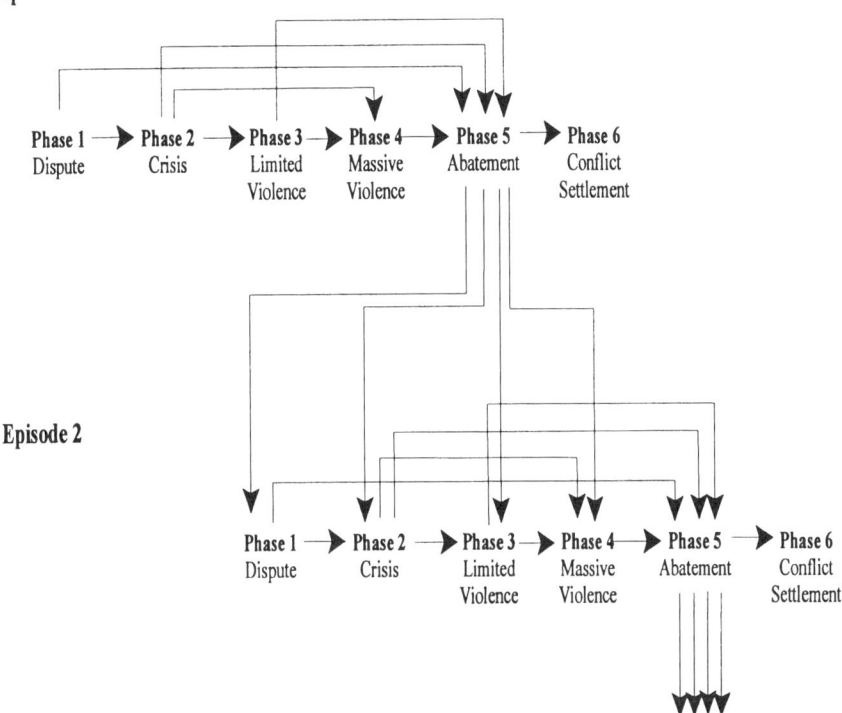

information we can still separate conflict episodes from each other by dint of the nominal definition of an abatement phase, but we cannot describe what these episodes were about and how they differed from each other.

Adding Multiple Perspectives and Historical Transformations

With some reality constraints, our approach allows for different conflict parties or observers to have different accounts of the same historical sequences, including disagreements about what phase a conflict is in, when and why it changes to a new phase. Rebels being repressed in Guatemala or Sierra Leone, for example, will be much more willing to see systematic limited or unrestrained governmental violence directed against them and the people they are supposedly fighting for than governments committed to (and *perhaps* believing that) a noncrisis or nonwarring characterization of their country's state of affairs.

Although, in principle, disagreement can also exist about abatement phases, we have only observed two instances in which this is the case. In Sierra Leone the rebels released hostages as an act of conciliation but it was not recognized as such by the government. Similarly, in Kashmir the rebels implemented a unilateral cease-fire that was not recognized by the Indian government. The few disagreements about abatement phases make for fairly convergent separations of conflicts into conflict episodes. However, the themes characterizing them differ according to the perspectives of the participants who describe them as sequences consisting of different conflict phases. A settlement phase, on the other hand, requires that the perspectives of the conflicting parties are convergent, and consequently, that they recognize each other. It is particularly interesting to observe how an agreement over a dominant interpretation of the conflict history represents an important aspect of the activities during a settlement phase.

A slip of the fingers—substituting "conflict focused sequential expectations" for "opposition focused sequential expectations"—shows the recursive, compositional way historical memories work, sometimes differently for different continuing parties, societies, or communities, sometimes convergently. Initial oppositions of parties and issues, combined with the use of violence and sequential expectations, constitutively define an intergroup conflict. In subsequent conflict phases, such conflict eggs become conflict chickens pregnant in their memories, habits, and practices with more conflict eggs, some of which may eventually produce offspring able to fly.

The thematic coherence within, and the thematic connections between, conflict episodes become particularly significant if they are redefined retrospectively, involving multiple perspectives. Time ordered collective self-understandings are being constructed; such historicities help constitute and differentiate the continuing entities bearing them. For one or several such communities or parties, episodes are recognized, and multiepisodic histories constructed. In rare historical moments of interparty reconciliation, these may be transformatively reconstructed and synthesized. To the extent that we can reliably and validly catch such dynamics within the framework of our historical-compositional approach, controversies about a society's past or its future prospects—its *contested historicities*—have become comparable and further researchable. So does the more or less integrative reshaping of collective memories by truth and reconciliation commissions, as well as journalists, historians, politicians, and textbook writers. All this historical richness and compositional complexity is suggested to the preventively oriented mind by the sensitive reading of historical conflict accounts, specifically by the narratively based Guatemalan and Southern African case studies of chapters 3, 7, and 8. The adequacy of our approach will be tested below.

We have now finally arrived at the full specification of our integrative framework for graphically describing in a comparable fashion differently specified conflict accounts. This framework is built up from three constitutive variables—opposition (parties and thematically described issues), uses of violence, and sequential expectations—which allow us to distinguish and mark for further investigation six different conflict phases defined in terms of the values attributed to these variables. If the parties to the conflict do not recognize each other they attribute different values to those variables, and thus produce different interpretations of the conflict. This divergence needs to be resolved if the conflict is to be settled. The six conflict phases can be combined into a grammatically limited number of possible sequences that can be separated into conflict episodes. Each episode represents a distinct unit of the conflict's history; the embedded order of conflict episodes defines a conflict as a whole. Transformations in collective memories are also possible on some occasions, reconciliatory rewritings of history that can bring parties together in a new beginning for a society, or transformations that set parties further apart.

This framework is designed in an easily extensible fashion to integrate a great variety of empirical analyses and narratives of conflict so as to produce a common, cumulative, and comparable representation of intergroup conflicts, their transformations and their resolutions. As a tool for conflict early warning research it permits us analytically and visually to examine the actual historical structure of conflicts, to examine how this structure can be or was redefined, and to explore how it could have been changed. Hopefully, it can contribute to a better understanding of particular conflicts and their transformative possibilities by both theory-building generalists, comparative historians of conflict prevention practices, and peacemakers. As a tool for the practice of conflict early warning it represents a heuristic device for the identification and forecasting of possible conflict trajectories. However, at this point these possibilities are merely conceptual and do not adequately take account of the empirical context in which particular conflicts unfold. Applied to particular conflicts some of these possibilities may not exist or may exist only under particular circumstances. Chapter 12 will show how a more context-sensitive representation of possible conflict trajectories can be developed by systematically comparing the various conflicts that are integrated into our framework.

A First Test of the Integrative Potential of Our Framework

At the outset of this chapter we discussed the dual use of our methodology. If used for the empirical analysis of conflicts the primary sources used are reports, narratives, and other accounts of the participants involved. Alternatively, we can focus on the accounts of scholarly analysts guided by guidelines more or less like those explicated in chapter 2. Following the grammar of conflict phases for such representations in figure 11.1, we want to be able to produce what could be called empirically grounded "trajectory graphs," in which multiple episodes, multiple perspectives, phase-change possibilities, and history-rewriting transformations could be clearly and suggestively shown. The focus of the rest of this chapter will be on reliably producing such graphs from the different kinds of evidence and analysis provided by CEWS contributors.

When we try extensibly to code old or new conflict reports in terms of the three constitutive variables described in the previous section, we are concerned with the correspondence between our nominal distinctions and those of the respective analysis/ narrative/chronology. Account-specific coding procedures would then be applied to identify the three variables and to distinguish conflict phases, phase transitions, separable episodes, and their transformations. The validity of the codings can be assured or challenged through continuous comparison within and across accounts, whatever their format. Moreover, we can assure the reliability of our coding by using different individuals or teams each coding the same material, a procedure only partly followed in the development of the prototypical CEWS data set now available on the CEWS Web site.[12]

We have preceded in such a manner with all contributions to the CEWS project, succeeding to our relative satisfaction in approximately twenty out of twenty-two cases narratively or chronologically described by CEWS contributors. We will not discuss all cases but rather will illustrate with two differently formatted conflict accounts the wide applicability of our framework. The first is Harff's study of the genocide in Burundi based on event chronologies familiar to many quantitative international relations methodologists, but alien to the narratively structured understandings of many peacemakers. Harff uses chronologically ordered news accounts that are coded in terms of accelerators and de-accelerators that are subsequently quantified.

Harff's Study of Burundi

The genocide in Burundi is one of three cases that Harff uses to test her argument that "the close monitoring of prespecified events believed to be contributing factors to genocidal violence gives us a tool to predict the onset and magnitude of genocide" (Harff, chapter 4).[13] Extending other work that focuses on the identification and monitoring of factors for the timely detection of state failure, Harff develops an accelerator model to trace, and eventually predict, the path along which a conflict moves toward or away from particular kinds of state failure namely genocide and politicide. The objective of her model is to develop an early warning capability that provides reliable estimates of conflict potential; generates "warnings" months in advance of serious escalation; and enables analysts to differentiate among different types of conflict.

The first objective pays tribute to the general philosophy of conflict early warning research, namely conflicts and their escalation are not inevitable but can be prevented and mitigated. As Harff argues, massacres and genocides "are not inevitable and should not be blamed on traditional communal animosities." However, these animosities can form the background against which "the right mix of incentives and provocations" can produce violent conflict. By identifying and forecasting when such a mix is produced one cannot only warn of their occurrence but also devise actions for their prevention. Translated into the language of our integrative framework, this means that the opposition underlying a conflict is not the mere difference between groups, but the concrete manifestation of an opposition in the actions used by members of different groups. By the same token, an opposition can be resolved and a conflict can be transformed while the differences between groups may persist.

Harff's second objective, the timely warning of conflict escalation, is concerned with a forecasting capability that provides diplomats with sufficient time to take action. However, she is aware that not only the timing for mediation but also the selection of particular mediation tools is key to a successful prevention or mitigation of violent conflict. Contrary to other work that focuses only on successful mediation, Harff also incorporates how mediation efforts "at inappropriate times [can] sometimes contribute to renewed or prolonged fighting" (Harff, chapter 4). However, it might be disputed whether timely detection and warning is measured best in calendar time. Escalation unfolds within particular contexts that determine the time between a particular conflictual occurrence and the outbreak of violence. In some situations an escalation may proceed faster than in others. Escalation measured in social time would provide a more context-sensitive representation, and would in fact measure not the succession of predefined stages but rather escalatory trajectories that can consist of different stages and that can last for different periods. A modest step into this direction is our use of expectations as a constitutive variable of conflict.

Finally, Harff's third objective, the differentiation of different types of conflict, is fully compatible with our framework, and can be derived from the various possible combinations of our constitutive variables.

Similar to our generic notion of conflict Harff also builds her analysis on "the assumption that all conflicts proceed through stages of development similar to life cycles" (Harff, chapter 4). Yet, whereas we derive conflict phases from the generic notion of conflict, Harff argues that her analysis permits only the selective use of phase categories. She provides two arguments for why conflict phases are ill-suited to capture her research interest. First, she holds that original conflict phase research is premised on action-reaction processes which are atypical for pure forms of genocide. Her definition of genocide includes the "promotion, execution and/or implied consent of sustained policies by governing elites or their agents— or in case of civil war, either of the contending authorities—that result in the deaths of a substantial portion of a communal and/or politicized communal group." This widely shared definition of genocide can be fully incorporated into our conflict phase framework, however. The definition distinguishes two groups that are in a conflictual opposition to each other. Our first conceptual variable captures such an opposition, that is, we ask minimally for the identification of opposing groups and preferably also for the issues characterizing this opposition. The definition further specifies that sustained violence is used and tolerated, and results in substantial deaths. This is synonymous with our operationalization of a massive violence phase that is characterized by the systematic, regular, and unrestrained use of force. In addition, our operationalization of a massive violence phase is forward-looking rather than post-hoc, and specifies that the elimination of a group can be expected. This does not contradict the definition of genocide but rather adds a refining feature.

Harff's second argument for the limited use of conflict phases states that action-reaction processes do not fit her analytical categories of accelerators and de-accelerators. These categories are conceptualized as events that do not necessarily prompt reactions or are necessarily related to each other. However, much of the earlier conflict phase literature is also based on events, and focuses on the distinction of conflict phases for the identification of factors qua events that account for a phase shift, and thus for a movement toward or away from more violence. Harff's focus on identifying factors that move a conflict toward or away from genocide and politicide is similar. Our framework is capable of integrating conflict research that is based on events data as long as we can translate the analytical categories used into our constitutive variables. However, research that uses event data cannot be integrated to the same extent as other analyses and narratives that use more context-sensitive data. We discuss these limitations by illustrating how Harff's accelerator model can be accommodated with our use of conflict phases.

Harff uses news reports from the Reuters World Service and codes them as events. An example of coded events are the following excerpts from the chronologically order data set she provided for Burundi. They are dated January 1, 1993, and January 11, 1993, respectively:

> Rwandan rebels killed eight civilians and seriously injured five others when they shelled a government military post in the northern Ruhengeri region, state radio said on Tuesday. The radio said rebels of the Rwandan Patriotic Front (RPF) shelled an army unit late on Monday at Kidaho commune in Ruhengeri in violation of a cease-fire signed.

> Young supporters of President Juvenal Habyarimana blocked Rwanda's lifeline trade route to Tanzania on Monday to protest against what they described as his minority role in a new government. Youths belonging to the ruling National Movement for Democracy and Develoment (MNRD) went on the rampage on the main Kibungo-Rusumo road linking the tiny central African state to Tanzania, officials said. Witnesses said the youths beat up people and looted property and cars, forcing the closure of the route used for tea and coffee exports and most imports.

Both events are coded as accelerators of the class "occurrence of violent opposition by kindred groups in neighboring countries, or increase in refugee flows (displaced people)." Whereas the first event is coded as "physical injury," the latter is coded as "riots." We could apply our coding procedures to the events identified in the data set but we would then incorporate Harff's data set and not her analysis of this data set. In both cases we are confronted with the same set of problems, however. First, the list of events is ordered only by their chronological occurrence, and we are unable to determine whether and which events are related to each other. One event may be related to another event that occurs at a much earlier or later point in time. Conversely, two events that occur in a chronologically successive order may be unrelated to each other. Consequently, the historical context in which these events occurred, and which is precisely characterized by the order in which they are related to each other, is irretrievably lost. For the integration of such research into our framework this implies that we can distinguish conflict phases based on our minimum requirements but we cannot describe the thematic coherence of conflict episodes and their ordering within the wider historical context of the entire conflict.

Second, the reliance on a single news service is bound to produce a biased and impartial picture of a conflict. News services report on occurrences in foreign countries that they deem to be newsworthy. This leaves out a great deal of events and actions that are relevant for the participants in a conflict, and it is unsuited to convey the historical context in which the participants understand these events and actions. Moreover, news services often have to rely on official sources for information because other sources are suppressed or difficult to contact. The examples above illustrate this point. It must be noted, however, that Harff does provide for contending perspectives in her analysis. As one of her eight accelerator groups she provides for the aggressive posturing or actions by opposition groups. However, it also must be noticed that virtually no events have been coded as such.

In our attempt to integrate Harff's accelerator model we have used her eight groups of accelerators and translated them into indicators for conflict phases, i.e., we attributed values to our constitutive variables based upon the events and actions identified as accelerators. By replicating Harff's quantification in terms of indicators for conflict phases we tried to distinguish conflict phases. The translation of accelerators into indicators for conflict phases is excerpted in table 11.2.[14]

Notice that many indicators for conflict phases cannot be uniquely identified, that is, many accelerators are not sufficiently discriminatory to provide only one value per constitutive variable. However, in most cases a small range of values can be determined that defines a corresponding range of conflict phases. We have identified nine such ranges.

1) Any phase that describes a range of events that cannot be attributed to any specific conflict phase, or any conflictual situation for that matter[15]
2) Any but a settlement phase
3) Any but a dispute or settlement phase
4) Dispute or a crisis phase
5) Crisis phase
6) Crisis or limited violence phase
7) Limited or massive violence phase
8) Massive violence phase
9) Abatement phase

Indicators for an abatement phase cannot be derived from the three constitutive variables, for this would require that we know how the respective event is related to previous events. Our conceptualization of an abatement phase is intrinsically context-sensitive because its defining features are contingent upon those that define the conflict phase they abate. The same applies to the identification of a settlement phase that depends on the characteristics of not only the preceding conflict phase but the preceding conflict episodes. In the absence of such contextual information we simply considered all de-accelerators as indicators for an abatement phase.

Based on the translation of accelerators and de-accelerators into indicators for conflict phases we replicated their quantification, that is, we produced the same addition of events per month as Harff but in terms of indicators for conflict phases. This representation allowed us to identify conflict phases. We grouped together those events that pointed most to the threat of use or use of violence until an abatement phase was reached. We identified an abatement phase by the number of indicators for such a phase as long as it was greater than the number of indicators for other phases and no indicators were present that included the systematic use of violence. The replication of Harff's quantification in terms of conflict phases is represented in figure 11.2.

Based on the representation in figure 11.2 we can retell the development of the genocide in Burundi in terms of conflict phases. In the beginning of 1993, Burundi was

Table 11.2: Excerpt of Harff's Genocide Accelerators Translated into CEWS Phases

Accelerators for paths leading to genocide	Opposition	Use of Violence	Expectation	Indicators for conflict phases
1.1 Declaration against the government	government and opposition group abroad	?[16]	?	1.1 Any but Settlement Phase
1.2 Threats of physical action	government and opposition group abroad	no or sporadic	use of violence	1.2 Crisis Phase
1.3 Marches, demonstrations	government and opposition group abroad	no or sporadic	threats of or use of violence	1.3 Dispute or Crisis Phase
1.4 Riots	government and opposition group abroad	sporadic	use of violence	1.4 Crisis Phase
1.5 Physical destruction of property	government and opposition group abroad	sporadic or systematic	use of violence or elimination	1.5 Any but Dispute and Settlement Phase
1.6 Physical injury	government and opposition group abroad	sporadic or systematic	use of violence or elimination	1.6 Any but Dispute and Settlement Phase

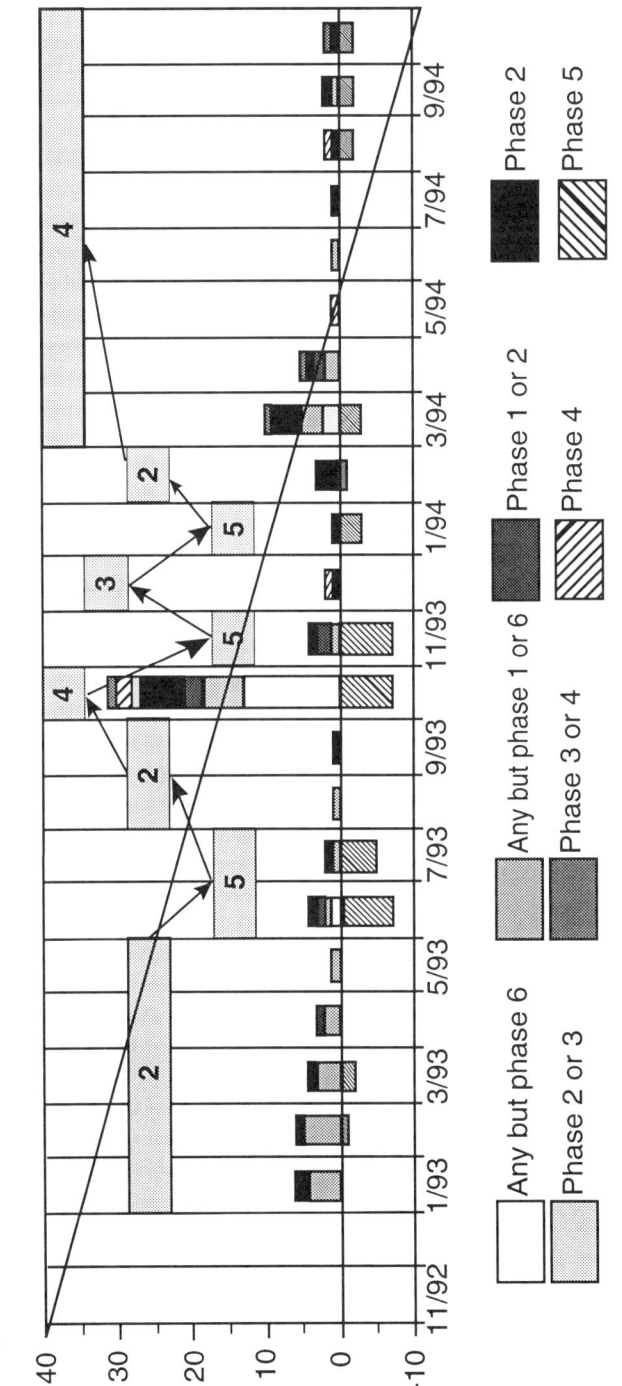

Figure 11.2: Replication of the Case of Burundi in Terms of Conflict Phases

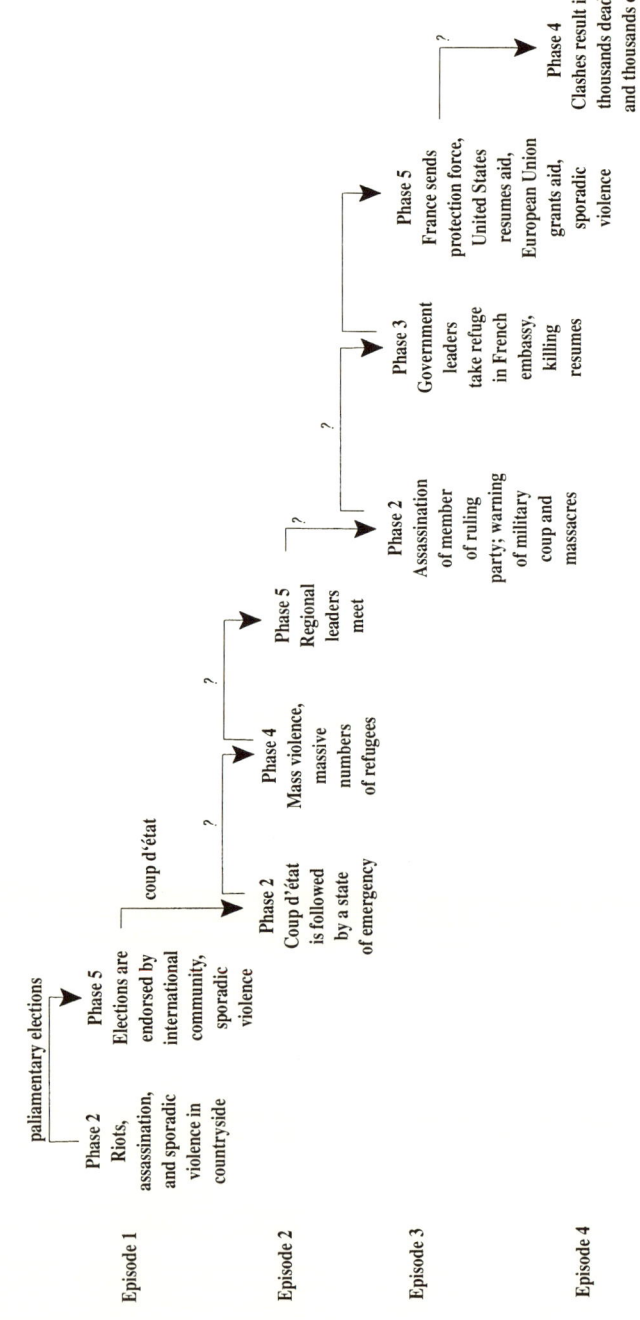

Figure 11.3: Trajectory Graph of the Case of Burundi

in a crisis phase that shifted into an abatement phase in the summer. Two months later the conflict resumed in a crisis phase that lasted for another two months and escalated to a short but massive violence phase. Another brief abatement phase ensued but the conflict resumed again in a short limited violence phase. After another abatement phase during the month of January 1994 the conflict escalated again, first into a crisis phase and later into a prolonged massive violence phase.

This description is largely consistent with Harff's account but differs in one important respect. Harff's account ends on a positive note, namely she writes that "in September Burundi selects its new president to replace the interim government—Ntibantuganya, a Hutu, is elected and a Tutsi prime minister is reappointed. In October a new power sharing agreement is reached between the political factions" (Harff, chapter 4). This assessment would suggest that the conflict entered at least an abatement if not a settlement phase. However, the occurrence of events that imply the systematic use of violence is inconsistent with our definition of an abatement phase. Two days before the power sharing agreement was reached Burundi troops are reported to have killed twenty people and set houses ablaze in response to an attack by an armed gang that had wounded eight soldiers. And twelve days after the agreement was reached at least twenty people were killed in clashes between the army and gunmen; clashes had erupted for more than a week and had made hundreds of civilians flee their homes. Consequently, in our replicated account the conflict continued in a massive violence phase.

This account is now structured in terms of conflict phases, which makes it comparable to other cases. As a first step toward a comparison we have designed a common graphic representation. The "trajectory graph" representation of the case of Burundi is presented in figure 11.3.

A Second Test of the Integrative Potential of Our Framework

After more than forty years the civil war in Guatemala was resolved in a long process that culminated in the signature of a final peace accord in September 1996. In chapter 3, Padilla examines and reviews the various steps that transformed the conflict in Guatemala with a special focus on mediating efforts that helped to bring about such a transformation. Contrary to Harff, whose focus is on the general escalatory trajectory leading to genocide, Padilla focuses on the de-escalation of a particular case of civil war. His analytically structured, richly grounded, qualitative historical narrative is based on other analyses, documents, a book, length chronology, and his personal experience.

More specifically, he examines how the civil war in Guatemala—which had claimed hundreds of thousands of lives—was not only resolved so as to put an end to violence, but was transformed so as to build a new civil society in which divergent claims and interests can be accommodated within newly established institutional processes. However, one also needs to take into account that Padilla lived through the conflict himself and undoubtedly brings some of his own observations and identifications to bear on the analysis.

Padilla's analytical framework is informed by the notion of conflict transformation, that is, the participants to the conflict "agreed not only to address the causes of conflict as an essential element of the negotiations, but they also agreed to promote both democratization and sustainable development as a fundamental means for both conflict resolution and *peace building*, using the term in the sense of Galtung 'overcoming the contradictions at the root of conflict formation'" (emphasis in the original, Padilla, chapter 3). The notion of conflict transformation is fully compatible with our framework and describes the processes that characterize the settlement phase in a conflict. However, Padilla's analysis does not make any reference to conflict phases as an analytical category. Moreover, he provides a historical analysis of the period preceding the settlement of the conflict only to the extent that it brings out the contradictions underlying the conflict that are being overcome during the settlement phase. This analysis fills only a few pages. But in those pages he paints a remarkably rich picture of the civil war in Guatemala.

Before we can apply our coding procedures to the narrative, we have to identify a chronological order of the events that are being described at different locations in the narrative. This chronological order differs from the one in Harff's analysis in that calendar time is not the ordering principle but the thematic relations between events and actions. For instance, in his introduction Padilla anticipates his conclusions by attributing the beginning of the civil war to the "violent U.S. intervention in Guatemala (1954)" (Padilla, chapter 3). However, in the description of the historical roots of the civil war he positions the U.S. intervention also in the wider historical context of Great Power interventions dating back to the nineteenth century. The theme of this wider conflict in which the U.S. intervention is but one instance can be described as a struggle for independence whereas the theme of the civil war that was triggered by the American intervention can be described as a struggle for democracy. The two themes are not contradictory but rather the one is embedded in the other. However, the theme of democracy does not figure in Padilla's account of the early years of the civil war in which he positions the Guatemalan government against communist rebels. It is only toward the end of the civil war that democracy becomes a guiding theme. This again is not a shortcoming of the author—whose analysis we here accept at face value—but rather the result of a historicized analysis of the civil war in Guatemala. The challenge for us is to adequately represent the multiple layers and reinterpretations that Padilla provides us with in terms of our integrative framework.

Padilla portrays the Guatemalan conflict from 1954 to 1996 as an episode of a long struggle for independence from the imperial reach of the United States and Great Britain.[17] This episode began with the election of a new Guatemalan government in 1951. The newly elected President Arbenz "wanted to compete with the U.S.-owned monopolies in railroads and electricity . . . [and] . . . enacted an agrarian reform that affected the interest not only of Guatemalan landowners but also of the United Fruit Company" (Padilla, chapter 3). However, the reason for why neither the U.S. administration nor the Guatemalan government saw the reforms purely in these terms, was that "the strong nationalism and ideological rhetoric of the leftist politicians, the influence of the small Guatemalan communist party within the government, and the international context of cold war and U.S.–USSR confrontation" provided the background against which the reforms were understood. We can infer two phases from this. First a dispute phase was created that pitted the U.S. administration against the newly elected Guatemalan government. Apart from the tangible U.S. interests that were likely to suffer under the new government, the government was perceived as communist "mainly because of the agrarian reform . . . but also because of its nationalist and modernization policies." No violence occurred but the expectation of a crisis existed once U.S. corporate interests were directly affected by the proposed agrarian reform. Once this reform was implemented the conflict shifted into a crisis phase in which the use of force could be anticipated.

In an interview to clarify this point, Padilla confirmed this interpretation, adding that violence was expected to come from guerrilla groups who were known to be supported by the U.S. administration. However, no systematic violence was actually used. Instead, the United States supported an "invasion of the country by a small military corps under the command of colonel Carlos Castillo Armas in June 1954 [which] was just a smoke curtain in order to prepare the conditions for the coup d'etat organized by U.S. Ambassador John D. Peurifoy" (Padilla, chapter 3). Neither the invasion nor the coup d'etat encountered any significant resistance. Hence, the conflict shifted into an abatement phase between the United States and Guatemala as well as between the new Guatemalan government and the new Guatemalan opposition. No systematic violence was used and the previous expectation of such violence was suspended. Thus, a conflict episode was concluded.

However, this episode was embedded in different historical contexts qua wider conflicts that depended on the perspective of the respective participants. From the U.S. perspective, the covert operation leading to the toppling of the Arbenz regime was a successful episode in its attempt to the stem the communist tide in the Western hemisphere. The reforms announced and implemented by the Arbenz government had not been considered legitimate because they had been understood to aim at the establishment of a communist regime. From the perspective of the new Guatemalan government, the old order that had preceded the Guatemalan revolution, and its political, economic, and social reforms, was reestablished. The reforms had not been considered legitimate because they had aimed at transforming the oligarchic structure of society. From the perspective of the previous Guatemalan government and now suppressed opposition, the U.S.-sponsored coup d'etat marked the end of the Guatemalan revolution that had begun in 1944. The old oligarchic structure had not been considered legitimate, which had been the reason for its reform.

The result of this first conflict episode was the creation of a new opposition that characterized the civil war that was to follow. After the successful coup d'etat "an authoritarian regime was established, the leftist parties were outlawed, hundreds of people went to exile and others, less fortunate, were killed or imprisoned, and, of course, the agrarian law was repealed" (Padilla, chapter 3). A new conflict episode began but was interpreted differently by the new rulers and the new opposition respectively due to their mutual refusal to recognize the other. Padilla's account allows us to reconstruct better the insurgents' perspective, for his language reveals his favored point of view.[18] The repressive actions taken by the government were regarded as a consolidation and maintenance of the political order, which is equivalent to a dispute phase. The violence employed was part of the institutional policing processes but the evasion of communist opposition groups gave rise to the expectation of sporadic violence in the form of terrorist attacks, assassination attempts, etc. Members of the communist party, on the other hand, went underground and started to "organize a resistance movement." This implies that they found themselves in a crisis phase from which they expected the systematic use of violence.

An escalatory phase shift occurred when a failed rebellion attempt by members of the army led to the collaboration with the underground leftist movement and the formation of a guerrilla organization. From the perspective of the government, the conflict shifted from a dispute to a crisis phase because sporadic attacks were launched by the rebels and a more systematic use of violence could be expected. For the rebels, on the other hand, the conflict shifted from a crisis to a limited violence phase because they were now in a position to allocate and employ considerable means of violence in a systematic fashion but could expect a more massive use of violence if the government retaliated more forcefully. Such retaliations occurred in 1967–1970 when two rebel groups, the FAR and the MR13, "were defeated by the army in a ruthless and bloody military campaign" (Padilla, chapter 3). During those three years, the rebels found themselves in a massive violence phase in which defeat or destruction could be expected. The government, on the other hand, shifted into a limited violence phase, not only because it used force systematically against armed rebels but also because it accompanied these actions with "a wave of terror against real or suspected communist leaders or leftist intellectuals and by the operation of death squads in charge of political assassinations and 'disappearances' of people."[19] However, the defeat of the rebel forces shifted the conflict into another abatement phase, that is, the military defeat did not permit the rebels to continue their use of force and the expectation of a more massive use of violence was suspended. The abatement concluded another conflict episode, which from the government's perspective had been about the maintenance of the existing political and social order but from the rebels' perspective had been about the establishment of a socialist regime.

Following their defeat, the "survivors of the military and terror campaign of the 1960s reorganized the guerrillas for a second stage of the revolutionary war in the mid–1970s as 'political and military organizations.' " They established their strongholds in regions mainly populated by indigenous people, distributed their military operations in distinct geographical areas, and in 1982 formed an alliance with the Communist Party. The alliance was called National Guatemalan Revolutionary Unity (URNG). Previously, the rebels had followed the doctrine of Che Guevara, according to which guerillas form the core of a revolution. After their defeat, the rebels adopted the doctrine of Nguyen Vo Giap, according to which a revolution must be carried by the popular masses. This doctrine proved to be more successful, for the military campaigns of the rebels found widespread public support. Thus, a new conflict episode had begun. The new guerrilla organization was able to systematically use violence on a limited scale, that is, targets were selectively chosen. However, more massive uses of violence could be expected, especially in light of previous retaliatory actions by the government. From the government's perspective, on the other hand, these attacks were considered sporadic uses of violence, but the formation of an alliance between guerrilla groups that enjoyed popular support gave rise to the expectation of more systematic violence. Such violence was initiated by the government, which launched "monstrous and ruthless military campaigns" against the civilian, mostly indigenous, population in 1981, 1982, and 1983. These campaigns shifted the conflict from a crisis to a limited violence phase for the government, and from a limited to a massive violence phase for the rebels. The result was again defeat of the rebel forces, which shifted the conflict again into a phase of abatement.[20]

While the Guatemalan government continued to deny legitimacy to the rebels's claims, the guerilla organization lobbied abroad for its cause and obtained international support from various political groups in North America and Western Europe. Padilla asserts that "it is not clear if at the time the insurgents were genuinely committed to a negotiated settlement of the armed conflict, but in any case their political discourse and actions were addressed in that direction." This confirms the interpretation that the conflict had entered a phase of abatement. This also confirms the interpretation that up to this point the rebels had not been recognized, either by the Guatemalan government or by the international community. However, what prompted a change in the eyes of the international community? Padilla emphasizes that the brunt of government attacks was borne by the indigenous population. He also points out that international support came primarily from humanitarian groups, such as Amnesty International, because of human rights violations committed by the government. This begs the question of what made the international community react in the 1980s and not earlier.

We can explain this change by the creation of a new opposition that had not existed before. As Padilla asserts, "the conflict was transformed in the middle of the 1980s from an ideological conflict to a conflict about governance and democracy." This implies that previously, the Guatemalan government launched campaigns against communist rebels whereas it was now committing massacres against innocent people in its fight against democratic reformers. Padilla writes that the attacks against the indigenous population do not render the conflict into an ethnic one, because the rebels, not the indigenous population, were the target of attacks. In an interview he explained further that the prevalent racism among the elites permitted the large number of casualties inflicted on the indigenous population to be considered as acceptable collateral damage. Yet, this view is precisely what caused international outrage and de-legitimized the actions of the Guatemalan government. Conversely, the changing objective of the rebels from establishing a socialist regime to establishing a democratic regime that coincided with their widespread popular support, especially among the indigenous population, endowed the rebels with legitimacy and rendered them into democratic reformers. Padilla asserts that "the support and solidarity from democratic countries of North America and Europe . . . were decisive in the change of mentality and attitude of the guerilla commanders, who changed their Marxist-Leninist ideology for a democratic and pragmatic approach."

As the rebels' interpretation became more dominant among the Guatemalan society at large as well as among the international community, the history of the conflict began to be re-interpreted. The conflict episode that had started with the institution of a new government in 1954 was no longer regarded as a fight between a government and communist rebels but between an authoritarian regime and democratic reformers. The reinterpretation of the conflict episodes describing the civil war also affected the interpretation of the preceding episode, because it was "unchained by the U.S. intervention in 1954 . . . In order to contain an absolutely unreal take over of 'communism' (and of the Soviet Union) in Guatemela, Washington played the sorcerer's apprentice, liberating forces impossible to control afterwards, evil forces that sowed the seeds of discord, violence, and civil war in the country."[21] Contrary to the interpretation that had prevailed during the height of the civil war, the civil war was now regarded as "a revolutionary war between insurgents and the government aimed at displacing the authoritarian regime imposed by the U.S. intervention of 1954 through guerrilla warfare."

Although both parties were in a phase of abatement, the road to a final settlement was initially blocked by the government's resistance to recognize the rebels' claims. Padilla argues that although the Central American peace process, symbolized in the Esquipulas Accord signed in 1986, put pressure on the Guatemalan government, "the army refused arguing that the Esquipulas accord stipulated negotiations with the 'legal' opposition not with armed rebels."[22] The establishment of the National Commission on Reconciliation (CNR) headed by Catholic Bishop Quezada brought together representatives of the URNG with different sectors of Guatemalan society. While the URNG agreed to institutional reforms based upon democracy, human rights, and social welfare, and refrained from committing acts of sabotage during the presidential elections in 1990–1991, the government continued to refuse to directly talk with the rebels. Finally in April 1991 the government agreed to initiate direct talks with the rebels without conditions. Negotiations resulted in the Queretaro Agreement in July 1991 but further negotiations remained in an impasse until January 1994. During this period the United Nations served as an observer and was chosen as an alternative to the Organization of American States (OAS), which is generally considered to be the preferred instrument of U.S. foreign policy toward Latin America. A number of states formed the Group of Friendly Nations and facilitated the peace process.

A settlement phase was entered when the deadlock in negotiations was broken in January 1994. The United Nations was given the more active role as a "mediator," Bishop Quezada was called back to chair the newly established Civil Society Assembly, and the Group of Friends served as witnesses of honor. The issues that were considered to be at the heart of the conflict were: the absence of democracy and the rule of law;

Figure 11.4: Trajectory Graph of the Case of Guatemala

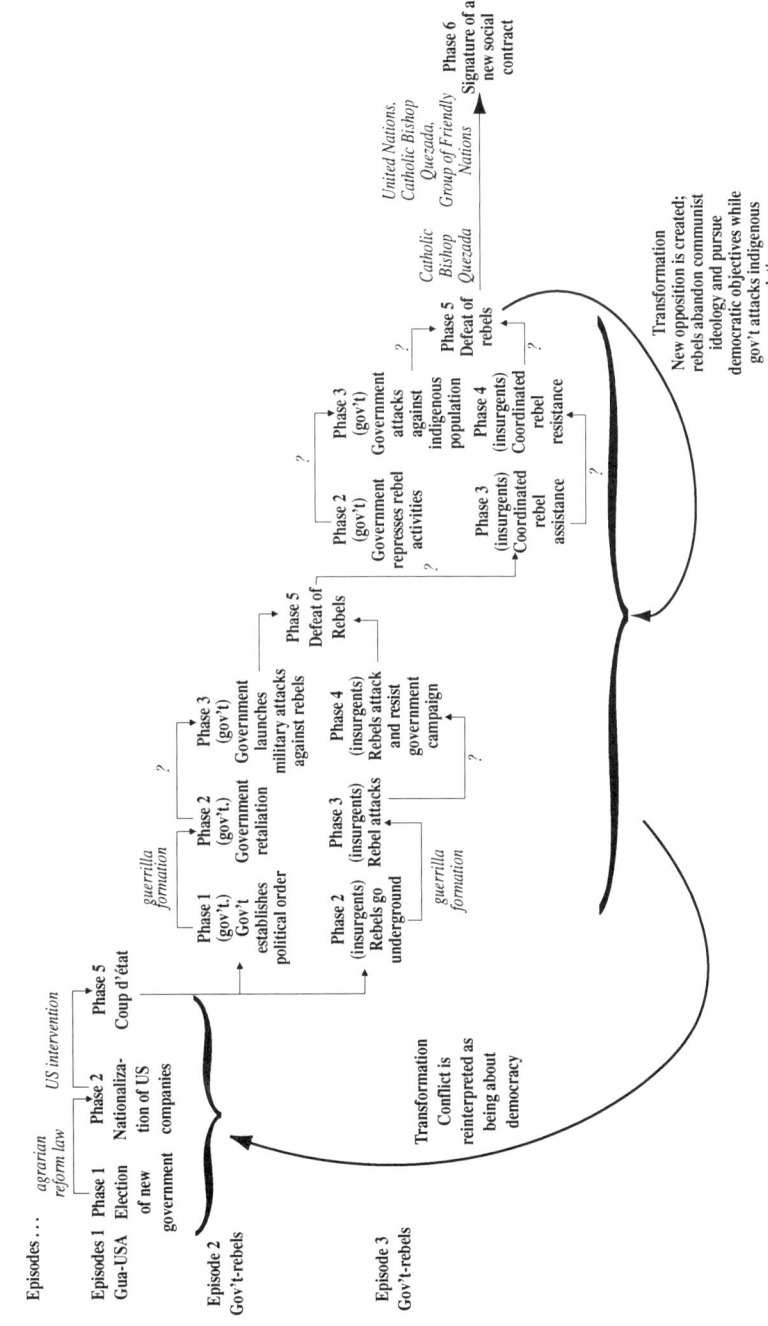

human rights violations; the role of the army in a democratic society; economic, social, and agrarian inequalities; and the recognition of indigenous people. The resolution of these issues removed any expectations about a renewed conflict. A definitive cease-fire and the disarmament of the rebel forces was signed with the final accord in 1996.

A Multiepisode, Multiparty, Trajectory Graph, with Transformations

A multiepisode, multiparty trajectory graph of the civil war in Guatemala is presented in figure 11.4. Its construction has been based on the constitutive theory of conflict phases, phase-transitions, episodes, and transformations given earlier in this chapter. Note that the history transforming rewrites by parties and peacemakers of a newly constituted Guatemalan society and polity are represented there with large braces.

Our detailed, framework, based reconstructions of Padilla's account have been buttressed by frequent citations to Padilla's text, as represented in chapter 3, and to Schmalberger's 1998 interview with him, in which he followed the validating procedure of discussing with an author his or her analytical understandings of the trajectory graph until that point where its summary of a larger chronology/narrative was accepted as adequate. Our readers should also check on these correspondences.

Because our trajectory graphing approach is extensible, their own rewrites of this history could also be overlain on this graph, added to it, or presented separately for comparative purposes. In chapter 12 we shall discuss procedures for adding historically grounded alternatives to this and similar figures.

Notes

1. Davis and Gurr (1998) give an excellent review of a variety of early warning approaches and methodologies. Written from the perspective of the Forum on Early Warning and Early Response, chapter 13 also expertly reviews recent practices in this area.

2. At the first CEWS London meeting, John Amoda defended the relevance of "state failure" conceptualizations. Indeed, his approach has a number of similarities to both of those reviewed in chapter 10, including a humanitarian intervention threshold. His narrative of the Sudan conflict is part of the CEWS data set; his own, realistic framework for analyzing this and his other cases is made available on the CEWS Web site. Although Amoda's conceptual framework influenced the development of the guidelines-inspired framework of this chapter, Alker and Schmalberger were not able to confirm his two other narratives and/or chronologies to it.

3. This chapter improves upon the earlier set of proposed constitutive categories presented in Alker, Schmalberger, Blum, Schjølset, (1999), thus providing indirect evidence for the claim in our earlier, collaborative paper that meaning-focused, or constitutive, research hypotheses are at least indirectly testable.

4. Since all social forms are forms of sociation and sociation is based on reciprocity, an opposition that prevents individuals from continuing their relationship also makes any social form impossible. "When the last trace of reciprocity in a relationship has disappeared, it no longer exists as a social fact; society in Simmel's sense, has ceased to be" (Levine 1971, xxxiv).

5. Notice that international crises are usually defined as involving, among other things, a threat to the nation's security. This characteristic cannot easily be translated to other crisis situations that do not involve states, which suggests that the definition of international crisis does not sufficiently capture the defining features of a crisis.

6. Structural approaches to conflict can only identify a conflict potential without explaining why, when, and how the difference between groups realizes this potential. Harff tries to fill this gap with her accelerator model which is to "link the background conditions to the onset or avoidance of state failure" (Harff, chapter 4).

7. The focus on conflictual behavior rather than the number of casualties is also shared by the contributors to this volume. For instance, Harff distinguishes particular types of behavior, such as mass arrests or mass executions, rather than merely counting the casualties they produce. Also, Gurr and Khosla, (chapter 9) distinguish the "limited, localized, selective use of disruptive and violent strategies" from "intense, widespread, and organized armed violence."

8. For instance, many of Harff's accelerators are various forms of threats that imply an impending, subsequently expected event. Similarly, Gurr and Khosla define one of their phases, militant mobilization, in terms of expectations.

Table 11.3: A Perspectives–Sensitive Typology of Conflicts

Form of Conflict	Relation between convergent/divergent perspectives	Type to conflict
Dispute	mutual recognition of each other's identity	international or domestic dispute
Crisis	mutual recognition of each other's identity	international or regime crisis
	a party's identity is not recognized	international or domestic terrorism
Limited Violence	mutual recognition of each other's identity	international intervention or civil war
	a warring party's identity is not recognized	guerrilla war
	a nonwarring party's identity is not recognized	persecution
Massive Violence	mutual recognition of each other's identity	international war
	a warring party's identity is not recognized	civil war
	a nonwarring party's identity is not recognized	genocide

9. One could further develop this analysis with a view to adding on to the forms of conflict distinguished in table 11.2.

10. Indirectly, we validate our hypotheses as to the necessary and contingent constitutive elements of conflict by succeeding in integrating the results of this and other projects within our proposed framework. More work on the validity of our theorizing viz-à-viz conflict participants is clearly needed.

11. Recall Harff's telling arguments about "foolish" international threats to withdraw support, and the inappropriateness of Western preferred problem-solving devices for sharply divided nonWestern countries already at war. Even the Arusha Accords of 1993 may have been counterproductive (Harff, chapter 4).

12. The CEWS Web site is located at www.usc.edu/dept/LAS/ir/cis/cews/

13. Like the other citations to chapters in this volume, we shall leave to the reader the designation of the relevant pages from which the quoted citations are taken. Since this chapter was written on the basis of earlier chapter drafts, some differences in such matchups might occur due to editing; this editing has tried not to modify statements of substantive positions.

14. The full table is accessible on the CEWS Web site at www.usc.edu/dept/LAS/ir/cis/cews/.

15. No such event has been coded, however, which is the reason for why it is left out from the replication of conflict phases in figure 11.2.

16. Variables that cannot be given any or any discriminatory values are marked. We have removed the de-accelerators from an earlier version of this table because they are there treated as corresponding to abatement conflict phases.

17. The creation of Guatemela was itself the result of the imperial practice of *divide et impera*. The Central American Federal Republic, established in 1821, dissolved into its five republics in 1838 of which Guatemala was one. In 1859, the British "forced the Guatemalan government to give up Belize . . . in order to legitimize the occupation of the Guatemalan territory known afterwards as 'British Honduras.'" The U.S. intervention in Guatemala in the 1950s is "a historical example of the 'big stick' policy that Washington applied to Central America in those years." This and the remainder of quotations from Padilla in this chapter, unless explicitly noted, are taken from a late draft text version of chapter 3.

18. For instance, Padilla describes the actions of the army as "ruthless and bloody military campaigns," a "wave of terror against real or suspected leaders or leftist intellectuals," "the operation of death squads in charge of political assassinations and 'disappearances' of people." On the other hand, he describes the rebels' activities as "military effort," or he does not mention their activities at all.

19. Notice how our framework, when augmented, permits to capture the different policies used by the Guatemalan state. Based on the combination of the four variables—opposition, violence, expectation, and recognition—we can specify that the government found itself in a guerrilla war with the rebel forces while it persecuted nonwarring portions of the population. Both types of conflict fall within the characteristics of a limited violence phase.

20. The two-part description "was not able to resist" and "military stalement" is coded as defeat. Regardless of whether the rebels were defeated or a stalement was reached, the conflict entered once again into an abatement phase.

21. Contrast Padilla's assessment of "absolutely unreal takeover of 'communism'" with his earlier assessment of "strong nationalism and ideological rhetoric of the leftist politicians, the influence of the small Guatemalan Communist Party within the government, and the international context of US–USSR confrontation" forming an explosive cocktail.

22. Padilla argues implicitly that the government was prevented from resuming violent actions against the rebels because the international community observed closely the Guatemalan situation. This suggests, however, that the government's legitimacy had been significantly curtailed, for it could no longer argue that its military operations were needed to restore the political order. Although it appears that the government lost its legitimacy when it launched massive attacks against the indigenous population, this process needs to be made explicit.

12
Exploring Alternative Conflict Trajectories with the CEWS Explorer

Thomas Schmalberger and Hayward R. Alker

The rationale of our research on potentially violent intergroup conflicts is to better understand past conflicts in order to prevent future violence and to abate or terminate current violence. The underlying assumption of these efforts is that violent situations are not the predetermined outcome of forces beyond the control of the relevant actors in those situations. It is rather the interaction between these actors that makes the escalation of conflicts possible, and consequently avoidable. Conflict early warning research is precisely concerned with identifying indicators for when a situation can possibly turn more violent, and if a conflict with the possibility of violence has already erupted, when a further escalation can possibly occur. Conflict mediation, management and resolution, on the other hand, are concerned with designing strategies to avoid those possibilities, and to seize those opportunities that can abate or resolve such a conflict. Hence, an intrinsic component of conflict research is the identification, assessment, and exploration of possibilities, and thus, counterfactual analysis.

Counterfactual analysis can be undertaken in different ways and for different purposes. Some use counterfactual analysis to probe theoretical propositions.[1] Others use it to make historical claims about the evitability or inevitability of specific events.[2] And still others use counterfactual analysis for the discovery of more general patterns.³ However, in the past counterfactual analysis has often been met with suspicion because, by its very nature, it deals with speculation. For this reason counterfactual analysis has for a long time been in disrepute among philosophers, historians, and social scientists alike.⁴ More recently, counterfactual analysis has become respectable, if not fashionable in those disciplines.⁵ Yet, with the exception of philosophy, where major advances in possible world semantics have established a firm ground for talking about possibilities, other disciplines are still struggling with the development of methodologies that make counterfactual analysis a systematic and rigorous element of their research.⁶

It must be noted though that historians and social scientists do not resort to counterfactual arguments by choice but by necessity, for, as Max Weber explained, any claim about the importance of a particular event involves counterfactual claims stating that under different conditions this event would not have occurred (Weber 1949). In fact, learning from history is premised on counterfactual reflection, for if we want to draw lessons from the past, we need to know what could have happened in order to bring about or to avoid similar occurrences in the future. However, the problem that scholars face is to assess the validity of counterfactual arguments, that is, to determine the conditions under which some claims are to be considered possible while others are not. In a recent collection of essays on counterfactual analysis in international relations, the authors have identified several criteria for judging "the legitimacy, plausibility, and insightfulness of specific counterfactuals," and thus for adjudicating what is to be considered possible.⁷ Similar criteria have been applied in a recent study on preventive diplomacy (Jentleson 2000). Yet, although these criteria are plausible for all practical purposes, they fail to address the nature of possibilities upon which their systematic exploration hinges.

In an attempt to develop a more systematic methodology for the study of counterfactuals in conflict research, we will begin with a discussion of what the study of possibilities entails. In a second step, we will apply the results of this discussion to the integrative framework developed in chapter 11. We will argue that this framework lends itself for a systematic exploration of possibilities, and we will illustrate, with the twenty cases of the CEWS project, how a set of rules can be formulated whose application produce empirically grounded counterfactual scenarios. In a third step, we will discuss, and illustrate, how these rules can be built into a computer simulation that allows one to generate scenarios of alternative pasts and futures that inform further analysis as well as policy making. In a fourth and final step, we will present the CEWS Web site as a prototypical attempt to bring the research products of the CEWS project (and others like it) to bear on the development of an information system that provides institutional assistance and expertise to peacemakers in the field.

The Study of Possibilities

The nature of possibilities has intrigued philosophers since Aristotle and his presocratic predecessors. It involves a variety of problems ranging from ontological conundrums about nonexistent possibles such as unicorns to the ontological status of possible worlds as such.[8] A tension seems to exist between the frequent reference to possibilities in our everyday description of the world and the meaning we give to those possibilities when we refer to them. Some philosophers have contended that speaking of possibilities is nothing but a rhetorical device for referring to actual events, and have declared possibilities as *entia non grata*.[9] Such a drastic conclusion is not only unsatisfactory but also unwarranted. Our evocation of possibilities is more than just a way of speaking about the actual world; it helps us to constitute it.[10] Whenever we make a decision we are confronted with several possibilities. These possibilities are relative to the actual world we are in, and from this perspective represent possible futures. By choosing one of them, we actualize it, while all other possibilities remain unactualized. From this new perspective these possibilities represent now possible pasts, and although we cannot go back and choose another one, we take them into account when we judge our decision.[11] Whenever we make judgments about why an event actually occurred or why an action was actually taken, we at least implicitly, if not explicitly, make statements about how it could or could not have occurred or could have been made differently. Yet when we speak of possibilities do we refer to them as if they existed like parallel universes, one in which we do something, one in which we do something else, and still another one in which we do not do anything at all? Or do we refer to possibilities as if they were the product of our imagination and they do not exist as such? What is the relation between possible worlds and the actual world? Can we visit a possible world to explore it, and if we cannot, how do we know what is happening in it? These are but some of the questions that philosophers have tried to answer.[12] Their discussion has resulted in a systematic approach for talking about possibilities and is now known as possible world semantics.[13]

Possible world semantics is a formal system that uses possible worlds to determine the truth value of statements, claims and inferences, and has proved to be an important, if not essential, tool for philosophical analysis[14] (Stalnaker 1984). Based on possible world semantics one can state that an individual or a phenomenon exists in different possible worlds. This individual or phenomenon consists of some essential properties by which it is characterized in all possible worlds, and of some contingent properties by which it is characterized in only some but not in other possible worlds. Hence, one can systematically engage in counterfactual analysis by first determining a set of essential properties of those individuals or phenomena that are to be examined, and then by determining a set of contingent properties with which these individuals or phenomena are altered in different worlds.[15] For instance, the essential properties of "John F. Kennedy" are those properties that made him "John F. Kennedy" as opposed to "Robert Kennedy," and contingent properties are, for instance, "Republican," "Democrat," "president," "mayor," "carpenter," etc. One can then specify possible worlds in which "John F. Kennedy" had been a "Republican" or a "mayor," but not a "woman" or "Robert Kennedy."[16] Consequently, counterfactual analysis consists of determining the possible worlds in which some but not all contingent properties hold true with respect to the world that is at the basis of the particular counterfactual.[17]

Scholars critical of this approach to counterfactual analysis usually disapprove of the essentialism it entails. As Quine has argued "essentialism is abruptly at variance with the idea, favored by Carnap, Lewis, and others, of explaining necessity by analyticity. For the appeal to analyticity can pretend to distinguish the essential and the accidental traits of an object relative to how the object is specified, not absolutely" (1961,155). However, this assessment assumes falsely that essentialism is committed to absolute essences. Although philosophers since Plato have pondered over absolute essences, essences do not necessarily have to be absolute. According to Rescher, "there are various different and *alternative* bases upon which the essential/accidental distinction can be placed, and one cannot establish any one of these as universally and uniquely *correct*, but rather can only maintain one or another of them as functionally *suitable* within the concrete setting of a particular problem-context" (1975, 22; emphasis in the original). On this reading essences are context-specific and can and do change over time. For instance, the essential properties of "ethnic conflict" involves a concept of "ethnicity" that is fairly young, that is, the essence of "ethnicity" itself consists of elements that have been assembled in this particular form only for a relatively short period of time.[18] To apply the notion of "ethnic warfare" to a historical context in which the concept of "ethnicity" was not known or was understood differently, creates an anachronism that yields little or no insight. This fallacy does not only apply to actual historical situations but also to counterfactual historical situations in which the essential properties of a phenomenon that exist in one historical context are transposed to another historical context, although the phenomenon did not actually have those properties at that time, if it existed at all. Thus, because essences are context-specific, a counterfactual analysis that makes operations on them is bound to the same context.[19]

Although many philosophers embrace possible world semantics and the essentialism it entails, they disagree over how one ought to conceive of possible worlds and how one ought to engage in their exploration. One can distinguish between those scholars who maintain that many possible worlds exist parallel to the actual world, and those who hold that possible worlds exist as stipulations. The former view is often referred to as *Realism* for its belief in the real existence of possible worlds. The latter view is usually referred to as *Actualism* for its grounding of essences in the actual world.[20] According to the most prominent Realist perspective, usually associated with the work of David Lewis, individuals exist in different possible worlds.[21] But because nothing can be in two places at once, each individual is slightly different in each possible world, different in precisely the way in which an individual did one thing as opposed to another. It follows therefore that individuals in different possible worlds can resemble each other to varying degrees but they cannot be identical (Lewis 1968, 1973). For this reason Lewis has introduced the notion of counterparts to emphasize that "they resemble you more closely than do the other things in their worlds. But they are not really you" (Lewis 1968, 115). The most practical implication of this approach is that possible worlds can be compared in terms of how close they are with respect to each other. If one were to devise a scale of relevant properties, one could measure the similarity of or the distance between various worlds.

However, this approach comes with two major disadvantages. First, it entails an extreme form of essentialism that comes awfully close to determinism. For if every slight change of what an individual could have done but did not do creates a possible world in which this individual is slightly different, then the implication is that "nothing could have been different in any way from the way it actually is" (Stalnaker 1986, 126). However, this seems to undermine the basic rationale of counterfactual analysis by which the essential properties are held constant while the contingent properties are changed in order to explore how some things could have been different from the way they actually are, but not others.

A second disadvantage is related to the first. Because every slight change in what an individual could have done creates a possible world consisting of a totality of objects, the objects in that world are similar but not identical to other objects in other worlds. Thus, a world is essential as a whole whereas none of its parts are. This makes a comparison of worlds difficult, if not impossible, because one has forfeited the very criterion by which those properties that are really relevant qua essential are distinguished from those that are merely contingent. One can therefore encounter a situation in which an individual, an object, or a phenomenon in one world shares more properties with a counterpart in another world than the one which originally gave rise to the creation of this world. For instance, the world in which "John F. Kennedy" had been a "carpenter" can entail an individual that is a "Democrat" and "won the presidential election," and would therefore share more properties with the individual in another world in which "John F. Kennedy" was a "Democrat" and "won the presidential election."

The Actualist approach to counterfactual analysis avoids these difficulties by grounding the essential properties in the actual world. Although various versions of this approach exist, they have in common that nonactual possible worlds are not concrete objects that exist in some nonactual place, but are abstract objects that actually exist but are uninstantiated (Stalnaker 1986, 121). By making the actual world the ground from which essential properties are derived implies that these essences are "not absolute (categorical) and metaphysical, but relative (hypothetical) and empirical in nature . . . if the actual world that furnishes our de facto starting point were different, we would arrive at a different view of the 'essential' properties of an individual. In this sense, our essentialism is not absolute but *empirically relativized to the descriptive constitution of the actual world."* (Rescher 1975, 34; emphasis added). The empirical foundation of essences implies both, that they are discovered in the description of the actual world and that the act of discovery is one of theorizing and abstraction. Essences are thus not concrete but abstract properties, and they are not intrinsic to the actual world but contingent upon its description. This can be applied to all phenomena be they natural or social. For instance, Watson and Crick discovered empirically and formulated theoretically the essence of DNA (deoxyribose nucleid acid). They found that DNA consists of a double-stranded molecule twisted into a helix. Each spiraling strand is connected to a complementary strand by hydrogen bonding between the paired bases adenine (A), thymine (T), cytosine (C), and guanine (G). A and G are connected by two hydrogen bonds. G and C are connected by three hydrogen bonds. Notice that the four bases alone, or any combination of them, do not form DNA. It is rather the particular configuration discovered by Watson and Crick that forms the essence of DNA regardless of whether it is found in different individuals, species, or organisms. What distinguishes different individuals, species, and organisms are their contingent properties such as the order of paired bases.[22] Notice though, that what enabled Watson and Crick to discover this essence was the particular description of genetic information in terms of modern biochemistry.

The essences of social phenomena can be discovered in a similar combination of empirical research and theorizing. For instance, Polanyi discovered how the so-called hundred-year peace preceding the First World War was built upon a particular configuration of four essential political economic institutions—the market economy, the gold standard, the liberal state, and the balance of power. Although each European power had set up, participated in, and was constrained by these institutions differently, reflecting the contingent properties of this political economic system, they nonetheless shared its essential properties. Moreover, Polanyi described how these essential properties developed and disintegrated historically, thus forcefully demonstrating the historical contingency of social essences (Polanyi 1975).[23]

Our interest in counterfactual analysis is a similar one. We are concerned with developing a systematic methodology that enables us to identify and explore past and future conflict trajectories. This requires us to first identify the social essences of conflict. This step resembles the specification of ceteris paribus conditions. However, these conditions are not assumed for all practical or theoretical purposes but they rather represent the empirically discovered and theoretically formulated conditions under which particular conflicts are constituted in their respective historical context. The second step explores how such conflicts can have different properties in other worlds. For this purpose we must determine a set of contingent properties based on which we can determine whether or not they hold true in some but not in other possible worlds. Without anticipating the details of how we operationalize these steps, a few remarks are needed to specify what they do and do not entail.

First, by speaking of the actual world we do not refer to the totality of all objects that currently exist but only of those that are relevant for our analysis. If one speaks of the actual world of genetic information, the only objects that are relevant are those related to the chemical compounds and processes forming DNA irrespective of the multitude of things happening in other domains at the same time. Similarly, when we speak of the actual unfolding of a particular conflict we are concerned only with those occurrences that directly pertain to the conflict in question, regardless of the many other events that unfold concurrently. For this reason it is appropriate to conceive of the actual world not as a universe but as a state of affairs, and more specifically, as a particular description of a state of affairs.[24] This implies, second, that the actual world is not "out there" to be grasped, but rather is constituted in the description one gives of it. And since a conflict, or any other phenomenon for that matter, can be described differently, we may well have to deal with different conflicts, although these descriptions appear to refer to the same event.

The same points apply to possible worlds. Thus, third, a possible world is a description of a state of affairs and entails only those phenomena that are currently under examination. Hence, the set of contingent properties that is used to determine the range of possible worlds contains only those elements that are related to the essence of the phenomenon under investigation. In Kripke's words *"a possible world is given by the descriptive conditions we associate with it"* (1980, 44; emphasis in the original). This implies also that different descriptions of a conflict yield different possible worlds in which different contingent properties hold true. This means, fourth, that possible worlds are not discovered as if they were parallel universes in the way that Realists conceive of them. Rather, possible worlds are stipulated for the purpose of exploring the possibilities by which a particular phenomenon can be modified or transformed.[25] In other words, in our explorations of how a particular conflict could or could not have developed differently we do not discover a novel form of conflict but rather test the conditions under which known forms of conflict develop.

It follows, fifth, that the range of possible worlds is limited to those worlds in which particular sets of contingent properties hold true under the conditions provided by the essential properties of the respective phenomenon so that no additional criterion of plausibility is required for determining what is possible and what is not. Hence, the common practice of defining ad-hoc plausibility criteria for determining a range of possibilities can be substituted with a systematic qua logical derivation of possibilities from the constitutive elements of the phenomenon under investigation.[26] And finally, the exploration of possible modifications or transformations of a particular phenomenon is not concerned with the causal relations but with the descriptive, and thus, constitutive relations that are expressed by these possibilities. Hence, one of the most serious weaknesses of many approaches to counterfactual analysis in the social sciences can be avoided because as Sylvan and Majeski explain, "the problem, as almost every scholar is aware, is that simple causal relations among political phenomena are scarce; but to bring in all the relevant causal relations implies the specification of a large and complex system, which probabilistically, is characteristic only of the actual world and not of any possible worlds. Strictly speaking, if one really believes that political science research revolves only around the exploration of highly complex causal systems, then one cannot advocate the undertaking of even limited counterfactual analysis" (Sylvan and Majeski 1998, 89).[27]

With these general remarks in mind we can now begin to think about how the theoretical framework developed in the previous chapter can be used for the systematic exploration of past and future conflict trajectories.

Developing the Basis for Exploring Counterfactual Conflict Trajectories

Our goal in chapter 11 was to develop a framework that is able to integrate a great variety of conflict studies. We showed how fairly diverse approaches to different conflicts can be accommodated in this framework so as to provide a common basis for knowledge cumulation and case comparisons. More pragmatically speaking, the integrative framework can be used to establish a database that can be continuously extended and updated regardless of the theoretical approach, method, or narrative style in which a conflict case was originally developed. The main purpose of the database is to collect analyses of conflict in a standardized format that enables and facilitates the quick retrieval and comparison of conflicts and their respective historical structure. However, the practical and theoretical value of this database can be further enhanced if it also permits a user to undertake systematic counterfactual analyses. As we noted earlier, counterfactual analysis is an integral part of conflict research. But it is also a critical element in the assessment and development of strategies to prevent, mediate, or resolve particular conflicts. Consequently, any conflict database gains tremendously in value if it is able to not only store information in a standardized manner, but also has a built-in potential for counterfactual analysis that can be applied for both, the exploration of alternative conflict histories and the forecasting of future conflict trajectories.[28]

The integrative framework developed in the previous chapter lends itself naturally for the kind of counterfactual analysis proposed by scholars working within the Actualist approach. The natural affinity between the two derives from the importance attributed to the narrative constitution of conflictual events, which enables us to identify the essential and contingent properties of the respective conflict. We consider it to be a particular achievement that our framework is capable to partly recover narrative descriptions from quantitative studies, which by their very nature are not conducive to a systematic exploration of counterfactual scenarios.[29] This might seem counterintuitive, for many prognostic tools from weather to stock market forecasts rely on quantified data. However, they are concerned with probabilities and not with possibilities. Those two concepts are often conflated although they are quite different. Probabilities describe the correlation between occurrences and not the constitutive relations that make an occurrence this as opposed to another phenomenon. Consequently, they can inform us about the distribution of actually observed occurrences but can tell us little about those occurrences that are not observed, but are nonetheless possible. This implies, first, that many previously unobserved occurrences cannot be forecast but can only be considered post hoc, and second that the distribution of probabilities is characteristic only of the actual world whereas no compelling reason exists to believe that it is also characteristic of any other possible world. Our concern, on the other hand, is to identify the trajectories a conflict can possibly take irrespective of whether or how often such a trajectory has been previously observed. It is precisely the determination of possible past and future trajectories that enables scholars and practitioners to better assess the opportunities for preventing, abating, or resolving a conflict.[30] And since scholars and practitioners learn about, discuss, report, and decide on conflicts in linguistic form, it is therefore critical to obtain data in the form of narrative descriptions from which the essential and contingent properties can be elicited that are at the basis of systematically exploring possible conflict trajectories.[31] This is exactly what our theoretical framework is designed to accomplish.

We started the development of our theoretical framework with a generic definition of conflict whereby conflict is understood to be a social form. The concept of a social form entails a notion of essences, for it distinguishes those features that characterize a particular social form across different contexts (i.e., its essential properties) from those features that characterize the specific content of a social form in its respective context (i.e., its contingent properties). Moreover, a social form is not to be understood like a lifeless physical structure but rather like a living organism that can grow, decay, or transform into something else. In Simmel's terms, a conflict is a social form that "resolves divergent dualisms; it is a way of achieving some kind of unity" (1955, 13). We identified five ways in which such a unity can be achieved; one resolves the conflict in the sense that it is being transformed into another social form that is not conflictual; the others produce the more concrete forms of conflict, which we called dispute, crisis, limited violence, and massive violence. We described these forms of conflict in terms of constitutive, and thus, essential properties. They are the opposition underlying the conflict, the use of violence, and the expectation of another form of conflict. Whereas opposition and violence refer to the actual state of affairs, sequential expectations refer to those events that describe possible states of affairs. It is immaterial how likely or plausible such expectations are, for what matters to us is that the participants (or, the observer who reports on the participants' perspective) consider a certain course of events to be possible, for only those events that participants consider to be possible can be actively pursued or prevented by them.

The mere distinction between forms of conflict does not allow us to describe the historical development of a conflict, however. Yet, we are particularly interested in describing how one form of conflict can possibly transform into another form of conflict or into an altogether different social form. We have therefore introduced the notion of a phase so that each form of conflict consists of its respective phase and a corresponding abatement phase. For instance, a dispute is a form of conflict that is distinguished into a dispute phase and an abatement phase. One of the defining features of a dispute phase is that a crisis can be expected. If this expectation materializes the conflict shifts into a crisis phase, whereas if this expectation is temporarily suspended the conflict shifts into an abatement phase. Consequently, the participants' expectations of how their conflict can possibly escalate or de-escalate provides us with the logical possibilities of conflict trajectories.

Although the development of our theoretical framework may appear to be metatheoretical it takes into account existing theories that have been empirically tested, a synthesis of the existing literature on conflict, and an integration of the various contributions to the CEWS project. It is for this reason that we can confidently assert—although strictly speaking not empirically validate—that the three variables—opposition, use of violence, and sequential expectations—are indeed constitutive of conflict. Notice, though, that we do not claim that these essential properties of conflict are essential in an absolute sense. Following the Actualist approach, we contend that the properties we consider to be essential of conflict derive from the particular theoretical perspective we apply to describe the lifecycle of conflicts. From a different theoretical perspective other essential properties may be discovered. However, the theoretical perspective applied to studying conflicts is not to be confused with the divergence of perspectives that participants of a conflict may have. Our theoretical framework is capable of integrating divergent participants' perspectives into the same representational structure. This presupposes that all participants conceive of conflict in the same way although they may attribute different values to the essential properties, and thus disagree over the particular form of conflict they consider themselves to be engaged in. Consequently, the logical possibilities deriving from our theoretical framework apply equally to different participants' perspectives.

It must be emphasized, though, that these logical possibilities are de-contextualized and must necessarily be so because they are derived from the essential properties of conflict that describe conflicts across different contexts. Based on these logical possibilities no interesting counterfactual conflict trajectories can be explored, for they merely reproduce our theoretical framework. In order to develop nontrivial counterfactual scenarios we need to define a set of contingent conflict properties that specify the context in which some conflict trajectories are possible while others are not. To determine these contingent properties we need to systematically compare all available conflict cases, which requires that these cases can be compared. Our theoretical framework was designed for precisely this end; it provides coding procedures that can be applied to a great variety of conflict studies and result in a common, and thus, comparable representation of conflict that can be collected in a database.

The database that grew out of the CEWS project is a prototype and illustrates with the twenty cases which were part of the CEWS project that a great variety of conflict studies can be accommodated in a common representational structure. This structure consists of distinct conflict phases that are grouped in conflict episodes and describe the histories of a conflict from the participants' perspective.[32] Although we have identified such a structure for each conflict we do not yet know how this structure developed in any other than a purely chronological order. A chronology can inform us only that certain conflict phases were possible before or after another conflict phase by dint of their mere actual occurrence. However, a chronological order cannot inform us about why these possibilities existed. Our objective must therefore be to express the chronological order as a sequential order, which implies that we need to be able to formulate rules characterizing the conditions under which one conflict phase can follow another one. We can start to abduce rules by systematically comparing identical phase triples across all available coded conflict narratives.[33] The reason for why we have to compare three instead of two contingent phases is that our theoretical framework determines which conflict phase can or cannot follow another conflict phase. Hence, comparing pairs of conflict phases would merely reproduce our coding procedures. On the other hand, comparing sequences composed of more than three conflict phases would jump a few steps ahead, because before we can explain how a sequence of four or more phases creates the conditions for a particular conflict phase to follow, we need to explain how each of these phases became possible in the first place.[34]

The question becomes then which three consecutive conflict phases to choose. In principle, any combination of three consecutive conflict phases could be selected. However, this would disregard the episodic nature of conflicts as well as our claim that conflicts unfold in cycles. Similar to a conflict in general, a conflict episode is characterized by a life cycle, that is, an episode is distinct from other episodes and entails escalation (or at least a potential for escalation) and de-escalation. Although a new episode can include other actors or issues—and can thus be distinguished in those terms—it also is different if actors and issues remain unchanged. The mere fact that a new conflict episode grows out of a previous de-escalation, which had at least temporarily abated the conflict, implies that a renewed escalation is not a mere continuation of a previous one, but a new one for which the abatement has made a historical difference. Our focus on consecutive conflict phases should therefore be on escalation and de-escalation.

The abductive process of comparing consecutive conflict phases consists of three steps:

1. Associating empirically observed phase triples with the logical phase triples provided by our theoretical framework. This allows us to exclude those logical possibilities that do not occur empirically, and to focus on those that do.

2. Classifying identical conflict phases into phase types. This provides us with a description of the conditions under which particular conflict phases can follow others.

3. Formulating rules that characterize the conditions under which some but not other conflict phases can be combined.

Step 1: Associating Empirically Observed Phase Triples with Logical Phase Triples

In the first step, all empirical escalation and de-escalation sequences are identified and compared across all coded narratives in the CEWS database. The aim of this procedure is to associate empirical instances with their logical corrolary in order to exclude those logical possibilities for which no corresponding empirical context can be found. An escalation sequence consists of a phase triple, whereby the second phase is an escalation with respect to the first phase. A de-escalation sequence, on the other hand, consists of a phase triple whereby the second phase is a de-escalation with respect to the first phase. The principle of this procedure is to compare empirical phase pairs A-B and to determine which of the logical possibilities—C, D, E—follow this combination.[35] Logically possible escalation sequences are:

$$
\begin{array}{lll}
1\text{-}2 \Rightarrow 3 & 2\text{-}3 \Rightarrow 4 & 3\text{-}4 \Rightarrow 5 \\
1\text{-}2 \Rightarrow 4 & 2\text{-}3 \Rightarrow 5 & \\
1\text{-}2 \Rightarrow 5 & &
\end{array}
$$

5-1 => 2	5-2 => 3	5-3 => 4	5-4 => 5
	5-2 => 4	5-3 => 5	
	5-2 => 5		

Logically possible de-escalation sequences are:

1-5 => 1	2-5 => 1	3-5 => 1	4-5 => 1
1-5 => 2	2-5 => 2	3-5 => 2	4-5 => 2
1-5 => 3	2-5 => 3	3-5 => 3	4-5 => 3
1-5 => 4	2-5 => 4	3-5 => 4	4-5 => 4
1-5 => 6	2-5 => 6	3-5 => 6	4-5 => 6

Step 2: Classifying Identical Conflict Phases into Phase Types

After having collected those phase triples that are empirically observed, we compare them for similar contexts. The aim of this procedure is to classify the second phase in the phase triple in order to account for the subsequent third phase. Following an established tradition in linguistics we proceed in such a way that "where two elements occur in environments which are almost but not quite identical, we may be able to collect them into one distributional class by setting up a chain of equivalences connecting the two almost identical environments" (Harris 1952, 319). Hence, by comparing sequences of the form A-B => C and contrasting them against sequences of the form A-B => D and A-B => E we can classify phase B into the phase types $B_{1,2,...n}$.[36] A phase type expresses the specific characteristics that set it apart from other type s of the same phase and might explain why a sequence A-B_1 can be followed by phases C and D but not by a phase E. The determination of these combinatorial possibilities is the objective of the remaining third step. For this step, however, it is important to notice that a phase type is maintained only if all instances fit the descriptive conditions of the respective type. As long as an instance can fit into more than one phase type or does not fit into any of the phase types, the classification needs to be adjusted. Although the requirement of a unique fit may appear to be overly restrictive, it is necessary because the membership of a particular instance to a particular class can be established only if the conditions for membership assign unambiguously and completely each instance to one and only one class.[37] Our comparison of all coded conflict narratives in the CEWS database resulted in the phase types described in table 12.1. Notice though that these phase types are preliminary and might be refined as more cases are included in the database.

Before we proceed to the third and last step of our analysis, let us put the identification of phase types into the larger scheme of our theoretical framework. The distinction of phase types parallels our earlier distinction of the generic social form of conflict into more concrete forms of conflict, namely dispute, crisis, limited violence, and massive violence. From the perspective of the generic form of conflict the more concrete forms of conflict result from applying different values (contingent properties) to

Table 12.1: Conflict Phase Types

Conflict Phase	Conflict Phase Type	Description
Phase 1: Dispute Phase	1a: Separation from opponent	The expectation of a crisis arisis from discussions/claims for autonomy or independence. This differs from 2c in that the discussions or claims are made with a view to resolving disagreements within the existing political system.
	1b: Reform	The expectation of a crisis arises from discussions, claims, and efforts to reform the existing political, social, or economic system.
	1c: Disagreement	The expectation of a crisis arises from a disagreement over the interpretation of a previously concluded agreement.
Phase 2: Crisis Phase	2a: Formation or support of armed groups	The expectation of systematic violence arises from the formation of armed groups or the receipt of economic, military, or political assistance by existing armed groups.
	2b: Suppression of opponent	The expectation of systematic violence arises from the suppression, confinement, or elimination of members of the other party.
	2c: Separation from opponent	The expectation of systematic violence arises from the declaration that one party separates itself unilaterally from a common social or political order. This includes declarations of autonomy or independence.
Phase 3: Limited Violence Phase	3a: Overt repression	A conflict party employs open but limited force against a group without encountering any noticable violent response.
	3b: Overt attacks	A conflict party engages in the systematic use of force against an armed opponent.
Phase 4: Massive Violence Phase	4a: Massacres	A conflict party employs massive force against a group without encountering any noticable violent response.
	4b: War	A conflict party engages in the massive use of force against another warring party.
Phase 5: Abatement Phase	5a: Defeat of a party	A violent conflict is temporarily abated by the military defeat of an opponent.
	5b: Regime change	A conflict is temporarily abated by the installation of a new government.
	5c: Negotiation	A conflict is temporarily abated when the protagonists engage in attempts to stop further violence or to resolve the conflict.
	5d: Concession	A conflict is temporarily abated when one of the protagonists changes his policy toward the other and can be understood as making a concession.
	5e: Change in legitimacy	A conflict is temporarily abated when one of the protagonists acquires or looses the legitimacy that had justified his previous actions.

the constitutive variables (essential properties) of conflict. For instance, systematic but restrained use of violence is a contingent property of conflict, that is, regardless of whether or not the use of violence is systematic and unrestrained in a particular situation, this situation still characterizes a conflict, only in a different form such as a dispute or a crisis. However, in order to distinguish a dispute or a crisis from limited violence we have to change our focus. We now take for granted the essential properties of conflict as a social form and concentrate on identifying the essential properties of each form of conflict. From this perspective, the use of systematic but restrained violence is essential for distinguishing limited violence from other forms of conflict. Once we add a temporal dimension to the purely nominal distinction of forms of conflict, and therefore speak of conflict phases, we can begin to explore phase transitions, and thus, conflict trajectories and histories. But to account for phase transitions, not in the sense of factors that cause or bring about a particular transition, but rather in the sense of particular aspects of a phase that make a transition to another phase possible or impossible, we need to focus on conflict phases and distinguish them into types. Thus, we take for granted the essential properties of each conflict phase and focus now on how even more fine-grained distinctions can be made.

This highlights three important points about our analysis. First, the essential/contingent distinction is dependent on what we choose to make relevant for our analysis. Essential and contingent properties do not exist in the abstract but only with reference to a particular phenomenon. Second, the embedded nature of our essential/contingent distinction reflects our constructivist qua compositional approach. This embedded nature is clarified in table 12.2.

Third, our concern with preventively oriented representations of conflict is reflected in the distinction of phase types. We do not focus on particular instruments or management techniques but on the kinds of situations that make certain phase transitions possible. We therefore do not make any statements about whether a proposal, a condemnation, or an appeal should be made in order to bring about a certain situation, because it is not the use of these instruments as such but rather their content and the manner in which they are made that produces certain results. But to account for how certain instruments are understood and reacted to in their respective context exceeds the capacity of even the largest research enterprises. An experienced conflict mediator who is familiar with a particular conflict situation brings more tacit knowledge to this situation than can ever be made fully explicit and, thus, be examined systematically. However, what we are able to do is to specify the situations that do or do not make particular phase transitions possible. Experienced conflict mediators can then apply their knowledge and expertise to devise and employ instruments that aim at bringing about such situations. Hence, our analysis does not aim at substituting expert knowledge but rather at providing experts with a tool that will help them better employ their expertise.

Table 12.2: Composition of Conceptual and Empirical Categories

Concept	Empirical Category					
Social Form	Conflict					
Form of Conflict	Dispute	Crisis	Limited Violence	Massive Violence		
Conflict Episode	(Not specified)[38]					
Conflict Phase	Dispute Phase	Crisis Phase	Limited Violence Phase	Massive Violence Phase	Abatement Phase	Settlement Phase
Phase Type	a) Separation from opponent b) Reform c) Disagreement	a) Formation of armed groups b) Suppression of opponent c) Separation from opponent	a) Repression of opponent b) Overt attacks	a) Massacres b) War	a) Defeat of a party b) Regime change c) Negotiations d) Concessions e) Change in legitimacy	(Not specified)[39]

Step 3: Formulating Rules

In the third and final step of our analysis we compare all phase triples that result from the previous two steps with a view to abstracting general rules about the conditions that characterize particular phase transitions. More concretely, we collect all empirical phase triples that correspond to their logical corollary (step 1) and distinguish them by dint of their respective phase types (step 2) in order to abstract rules from them. An excerpt of the result of steps 1 and 2 is represented in tables 12.3 and 12.4.[40] The complete tables can be viewed on the CEWS Web site.[41]

The complete tables of escalation and de-escalation sequences show that only those logical possibilities have no empirical corollary that relate to a dispute phase that is abated. More specifically, the only existing 1-5 => z triple is one in which x stands for a settlement phase and, thus, for the resolution of the conflict. Based on the limited number of cases we cannot make any strong claims about the absence of the other 1-5 => z triples. However, we can put forward two hypotheses that may explain these absences. First, the focus of conflict studies is mostly on cases that reach a stage from which violence could at least have been expected, if not observed. Consequently, the selection of cases is often biased in favor of those that are known to have been violent, whereas those that never reached a potentially violent stage are neglected. This includes

Table 12.3: Excerpt of Escalation Sequences

Phase Triple x-y = > z	Conflict Episode	Types of Conflict Phases x xt-y yt = > z	Conditions for Phase Transition x xt-y yt = > z
1-2 = > 3	Chiapas-1	1b-2a = > 3	1b-2a = > 3
	El Salvador-1	1b-2a = > 3	
	Guatemala-2	1b-2a = > 3	
	Moros-1	1b-2a = > 3	
	Kosovo-1	1a-2b = > 3	1ac-2b = > 3
	Kosovo-4	1c-2b = > 3	
	Tibet-1	1c-2b = > 3	

Table 12.4: Excerpt of De-Escalation Sequences

Phase Triple x-y = > z	Conflict Episodes	Types of Conflict Phases x xt-y yt = > z	Conditions for Phase Transition x xt-y yt = > z
2-5 = > 2	Guatemala-12	2a-5b = >2	2a-5b = > 2
	Kosovo-12	2b-5c = >2	2ab-5c = >2
	Mozambique-12	2a-5c = >2	
	Rwanda-12	2b-5c = >2	
	Sierra Leone-12	2b-5c = >2	
	South Africa-12	2a-5c = >2	
	Tibet-23	2b-5c = >2	
	Burundi-12	2b-5e = >2	
	Chechnya-23	2b-5e = >2	
	Molodova-12	2c-5e = >2	2bc-5e = >2

also those cases that have been successfully resolved before they reached a violent stage, which reiterates the concern about the often neglected and less visible successes of conflict prevention expressed in chapter 2. The reason why we have an instance of 1-5 => 6 is that Michael Lund followed an important specification of the CEWS guidelines and specifically selected cases that were abated before violence could erupt, or in his words, cases in that the "dog didn't bark." As long as more of these cases are not being studied it remains difficult to draw lessons about how conflicts can be abated or settled in their early stages. Second, the phase triples 1-5 => 3 and 1-5 => 4 appear to defy proportionality. It is hard to imagine that the failed abatement of a dispute can immediately lead to the use of systematic violence. However, a greater number of cases is needed to test this hypothesis.[42]

Based on the classification of phase transitions in terms of phase types we can now begin to classify the conditions for these transitions, or in other words, "after discovering which sequences occur in equivalent environments, we can group them together into one equivalent class" (Harris 1952, 320). The aim of this procedure is to develop more abstract rules that can generate all observed phase transitions as well as all other phase transitions that have not been observed but are possible on the basis of empirically established logical equivalences. Two modes of abstraction are being used. One mode abstracts on preceding phases. For instance, the phase sequences 3a-5a=>1 and 4a-5a => 1 can be aggregated to (3 4) a-5a => 1, which expresses a rule according to which an abatement brought about by the defeat of one of the conflicting parties and which was preceded by either overt repression or massacres can lead to a renewed dispute.[43] In conjunction with other abstracted rules that use the phase pairs (3 4) a-5a the range of possible phase transitions can be determined. The other mode abstracts on phase types. For instance, the phase sequences 1a-2a => 3 and 1a-2c => 3 can be aggregated to 1a-2 (a c) => 3. In this case the conditions for a particular phase transition are not uniquely discriminated by phase types. Only further research can determine whether the respective phase types can be refined to account for differences or whether the exisiting phase types accurately classify the same phase transition. Table 12.5 illustrates an excerpt of the general rules for phase transitions based on abstractions made on the results entailed in the complete version of tables 12.3 and 12.4. The complete table of rules for phase transitions can again be viewed on the CEWS Web site.

Table 12.5: Excerpt of Rules for Phase Transitions

Rule Number	Phase Transition	Rule	Description
R1	if 2a then 1	- 5b	A new dispute phase is entered after a regime change did not resolve previous differences that lead to the formation or support of armed groups. The only alternative is =>2.
	=> 1		
R2	if (3 4) b then 1	- 5c	A new dispute phase is entered after the negotiations are being disputed that abated limited or massive violence. Alternatives are => 2, => 3, => 6 for 3b and => 2 and => 6 for 4b.

Based upon thirty rules, all 153 actually observed phase transitions can be reproduced, and therefore the phase trajectories of all twenty cases can be reconstructed. Moreover, the same rules that generate the actual cases can now be used to generate an even greater number of counterfactual cases. However, the actual or counterfactual phase trajectories that are generated by these rules merely line up phases that are possible with respect to the preceding phase pair. Although this allows us to generate conflict episodes we cannot determine the conditions under which particular conflict episodes affect possible phase sequences in later conflict episodes. This limitation is not the result of our approach but rather of the limited number of cases we have included in our analysis. If we added more cases we could apply similar procedures to conflict episodes, that is, similar to the classification of phase types we could classify types of conflict episodes and abstract rules about how particular types of conflict episodes affect the possibilities for past and future phase sequences. We would then be able to develop a more complete set of rules that would enable us to better address the historical dimension of conflict trajectories. More specifically, a systematic comparison of conflict episodes would enable us to:

- Explain and reproduce how a particular combination of phases produces a historical reinterpretation, and how this reinterpretation affects the production of future phase sequences and the possibilities for settling a conflict. We discussed in the previous chapter how in the case of Guatemala such an historical reinterpretation affected the further course of a conflict trajectory and eventually contributed to the settlement of the conflict. However, we were only able to observe that it had occurred. By including more cases in which historical reinterpretations are observed would allow us to not only explain why in the case of Guatemala a reinterpretation occurred at this point in the conflict but also at which other points it could have occurred in this or in other cases.

- Explain and reproduce how several conflicts are embedded into larger conflicts and how the unfolding and settlement of a conflict is dependent on the larger conflict into which it is embedded. Several of the conflicts we examined were set against a particular historical context, such as colonial struggles or the Cold War. By including more cases we would be able to determine not only how a conflict can be embedded into one of them but also how a past or ongoing conflict can be invoked to set the background for the creation and unfolding of a new conflict.

Although the limitations imposed by the small set of cases restrict our ability to address more fully the historical dimension of conflicts as seen from the parties' perspectives, we are nonetheless able to address to a certain degree the relationship between those perspectives. Parties can interpret their situation differently and have different expectations about how this situation can evolve. However, these differences must unfold within certain

Table 12.6: Excerpt of Divergent Phase Sequences

Phase Sequence	Conflict Episode
2a > 2a-**5c**-3a-**5c**-2a-2a-**5c** < 3b (Mexican government)	Chiapas-123
2a > 3b-**5c**-3a-**5c**-2a-3b-**5c** < 3b (Zapatistas)	

constraints if the parties are not to be disconnected from each other's reality. We can identify some of these constraints by comparing all divergent phase sequences. Table 12.6 presents an excerpt of all instances of divergent phase sequences found in the twenty cases that we examined.[44] A complete table can again be viewed on the CEWS Web site.

Three regularities can be observed in the complete version of table 12.6. First, in all instances, divergent perspectives are characterized by one party that consistently considers itself to be in a lower phase than the other. We can therefore speak of a dominant party that tends to have a less serious interpretation of the conflict than the one that is dominated. In future analyses we may want to examine in greater detail whether and how it is possible to change this relation. From our current analysis we can merely suggest that a change in legitimacy (Phase 5e) may produce not only a redefinition of which party dominates a conflict, but also may instantiate a reinterpretation of the conflict's history. The case of Guatemala supports this hypothesis. Second, in all instances in which a party is defeated, divergent perspectives converge. It appears odd, however, that in the cases of Guatemala, Kashmir, and the Mizos a defeat is followed by a settlement of the conflict.[45] What seems to be going on is that the defeat of one of the parties is followed by a change in legitimacy (Phase 5e), and it is this change, and not the defeat, that sets the stage for a settlement. However, more detailed examination is required to test this hypothesis. Third, in all instances in which parties enter into negotiations divergent perspectives converge. In all other instances, divergent perspectives are possible within the confines of the rules established above. These three regularities can again be expressed as rules and complete our analysis of phase trajectories. In the next section we will discuss how these rules can be translated into a computer simulation that permits the exploration of counterfactual scenarios.

Designing a Computer Simulation for the Exploration of Conflict Trajectories

In the beginning of this chapter we argued that learning from history requires counterfactual reflection. The purpose of our counterfactual explorations is to learn about the successes and failures of preventing, mitigating, and resolving violent conflicts. We are specifically interested in identifying how past conflicts could have developed differently, for if we can make statements about the trajectories a conflict can possibly take, we can also describe the kinds of situations that lead to more or less violence, and consequently, we can warn of impending humanitarian disasters and inform about opportunities for mitigating or resolving violent conflicts. At the basis of such a counterfactual exploration is the derivation of rules that reproduce the unfolding of actual conflict trajectories and establish the logical equivalences for systematically producing counterfactual trajectories. We discussed in the previous section how such rules can be derived from a systematic analysis of empirical cases. However, applying these rules for generating actual or counterfactual scenarios quickly becomes a complex enterprise. It is therefore most useful to translate these rules into computational procedures so that the generation of conflict trajectories can be computed by a program, and the user has merely to decide which of the available alternatives to select. We have developed such a program and called it the CEWS Explorer. How we designed the program requires some explanation.

Notice that by applying our coding procedures to conflict narratives or chronologies we in fact interpreted the interpretation of our contributors. More specifically, we categorized interpretations into conflict phases and their respective types. We labeled conflict phases in terms of numbers and conflict phase types in terms of letters, and expressed the relationship between them as sequences of the form x xt-y yt => z; x designates the first phase, xt the type of the first phase, y the phase following the first phase, and yt its correponding phase type. Z is then the phase that can possibly follow the phase pair x xt-y yt. We called sequences of this form rules because they express empirically validated relations between categories, that is, we have established that in all cases in which a particular x xt-y yt is observed a particular z can possibly follow. To label conflict phases and their respective types in terms of numbers and letters is a first step toward formalizing the relations between categories. Notice, however, that these labels stand for situation descriptions and therefore need to be read/interpreted as such. For instance, a rule of the form 1a-2a => 3 is to be read as:

A situation in which

1a: the expectation of a crisis arises from discussions, claims, and efforts to reform the existing political, social, or economic system, and develops into a situation in which

2a: the expectation of systematic violence arises from the formation of armed groups or the receipt of economic, military, or political assistance by existing armed groups can possibly develop into a situation in which

3: violence is used in a systematic but restrained manner.

Recall from the previous section that our categorization of phase types required the unambiguous and complete assignment of each observed instance to one and only one phase type.[46] This requirement meets the definition of a function in logic so that each of the rules we have abstracted can be expressed as a compound of functions. However, to translate these rules into computational procedures does not only imply the translation of phase transitions into a computer language but also the specification of when and how particular rules for phase transitions are to be applied. We therefore speak of a function when we describe what a set of rules does, and we speak of a procedure when we describe the process by which these rules are executed[47] (Harvey and Wright 1994, 43–44). More specifically, we speak of an effective procedure as "a set of rules which tells us, from moment to moment, precisely how to behave" (Minsky 1967, 106). What makes a procedure effective is that, when executed, a precisely specified set of rules (compound function) consitutes a particular object, namely a phase that can possibly follow a particular phase pair, or a phase type that can possibly be associated with a phase.

A rule, as the one used above, can therefore be represented in a particular programming language as the following effective procedure.[48]

```
(define (R1 x xt y yt)
  (if (and
    (equal? x 1)
    (equal? xt 'a)
    (equal? y 2)
    (equal? yt 'a))
    '(3)
    '()))
```

The procedure R1 executes, first, the function *(equal? x 1)* and returns either the value true or false depending on whether the argument of x is the number 1. It then executes the next function *(equal? xt 'a)* and again returns either the value true or false depending on whether the argument of xt is the letter a. When all functions of the form *(equal? . . .)* have returned a value, function *(and . . .)* is executed. Depending on whether all incorporated functions have returned the value true, the value true or false is returned. Finally, the function *(if . . .)* is executed and depending on whether the function *(and . . .)* returned the value *true* either the value 3 or *false* is returned. Hence, the procedure R1 returns a value that designates the next possible phase 3 only if the arguments (the input) are identical to the sequence 1b-2a. Consequently, a procedure that takes the arguments of a phase pair and executes all procedures developed from the thirty rules identified above, returns values that represent the range of possible next phases of this particular phase pair.[49]

However, we are not interested only in computing the range of next phases of only one phase pair. We are rather interested in generating entire scenarios in which one phase from the range of next possible phases (output) becomes the second phase (input) for the generation of yet another range of possible next phases, and so on. However, selecting a phase from the range of next possible phases is not a matter of computation but rather of analytical interest. Therefore, the user must decide which of the possible next phases will be actualized, be it for reproducing an actual case, exploring particularly violent trajectories, particularly successful abatements or settlements, specific alternatives of particular cases, or any other analytical focus one may have. However, the selection of a next possible phase does not automatically determine which phase type is associated with it. Neither are all phase types of a particular phase applicable in particular contexts. Therefore a range of possible phase types must be determined. This can be achieved by using a procedure that takes all phase types of a particular phase as arguments (e.g., a, b, c for Phase 1), and executes the same thirty procedures that are being used for the computation of possible next phases. Those phase types with which next possible phases can be associated are the ones that are applicable in this particular context. The user can then choose the phase type from the available range of possible phase types. Hence, a user can continuously generate conflict trajectories until the conflict is settled, no possible next phases or phase types are being returned, or she decides to stop.

However, this does not yet permit a user to explore conflict trajectories that involve divergent perspectives. To explore the possibilities and constraints of divergent perspectives, a set of meta-rules must be incorporated that affect the computation of possible next phases and phase types. In the previous section we have formulated three such rules. The first determines the relationship between divergent perspectives in terms of dominance, that is, the range of possible next phases for the dominant perspective cannot include any phases on a higher escalatory stage than the ones of the dominated perspective. The second determines that the defeat of one of the parties (5a) leads to a necessary convergence of perspectives, i.e., once one party enters a 5a the other must also enter a 5a, regardless of what other phases and phase types the thirty procedures may return. Finally, the third meta-rule determines another neccessary convergence of perspectives, namely one that is brought about when one party enters into negotiations (5c) with the other.

Together these procedures allow a user to generate actual or counterfactual conflict trajectories. However, we are interested not only in the generation of conflict trajectories but also in their comparison with relevant other actual or counterfactual conflict trajectories. It is precisely by identifying relevant historical precedents or similarities that more general lessons can be drawn. For this reason we made a database an integral part of the CEWS Explorer. We have included all cases of the CEWS project in this database so that we can continue any one of them at any point in its actual phase sequence in order to explore the possible future trajectories it can take or the past trajectories it could have taken. Any newly generated conflict trajectory can then be added to the database for further explorations or comparisons. To enable comparisons a case list needs to be defined. The definition of a case list consists of two independent selections: a selection of the cases against which a particular conflict trajectory is to be compared, and a mode of comparison that determines which aspects of a conflict trajectory is to be compared. Four modes of comparison exist. The coarsest mode compares phase triples irrespective of the phase types that are associated with it. This implies that all cases included in the case list are being compared with respect to the phase triple generated in the simulation. A more fine grained mode compares identical phase triples including their respective phase types. This implies that comparisons are made on a more specific set of similarities or contexts. A third mode compares phase sequences irrespective of the phase types associated with conflict phases but in terms of conflict episodes. This implies that only those cases will be returned that have the exact sequence of phases as the one that is generated by the simulation. Finally, the most context-sensitive mode makes comparisons to only those cases that have identical phase sequences in terms of conflict episodes including their associated phase types.

The integration of the database into the simulation provides a user with a powerful tool to systematically engage in counterfactual analysis. However, we have stated earlier that our analysis of the twenty cases of the CEWS project was merely illustrative, and by no means final. We therefore did not want to design a computer program that requires substantial knowledge of programming to make changes to the rules we have identified in our illustrative analysis. In addition, we may, for experimental reasons, want to change the set of rules, or develop more specialized sets of rules for particular historical periods. Consequently, we designed the CEWS Explorer so that it is extensible to the greatest extent possible. This implies that the definitions of phase types can be changed. How such a change will affect the set of rules and meta-rules cannot be determined computationally, for it is a matter of empirical research and validation. For instance, the addition of another phase type may leave the exisiting rules unaffected and merely require the formulation of additional rules. The modification or deletion of a phase type, on the other hand, may affect many existing rules because all empirically observed phase transitions need to be compared again, and new rules need to be abstracted from the result of this comparison. However, the possibility for these kinds of changes needs to be, and is being, provided by the CEWS Explorer. Once new rules have been formulated, they can be easily incorporated into the program, that is, the user enters the values of phases and phase types, and the program adds them in their appropriate form as computational procedures to the simulation. Moreover, the program makes sure that all procedures are abstracted to the greatest extent possible, that is, all procedures that can be merged without altering what they are doing will be combined into one procedure.[50] The same mechanism is applied to meta-rules that constrain the possibilities of divergent perspectives to unfold.

Figure 12.1 represents a functional flow chart of the CEWS Explorer emphasizing the integration of its three modules; the simulation, the database, and the program that allows a user to make changes to the CEWS Explorer.

With the aid of the CEWS Explorer we can now illustrate how one can systematically engage in counterfactual explorations. For this purpose let us discuss again the case of Guatemala.

Exploring Alternative Trajectories of the Conflict in Guatemala

Recall that in the previous chapter we illustrated how we had coded Padilla's narrative in order to arrive at a graphic representation of the Guatemalan civil war. Now that we have built on this analysis we can reproduce the Guatemalan civil war computationally,

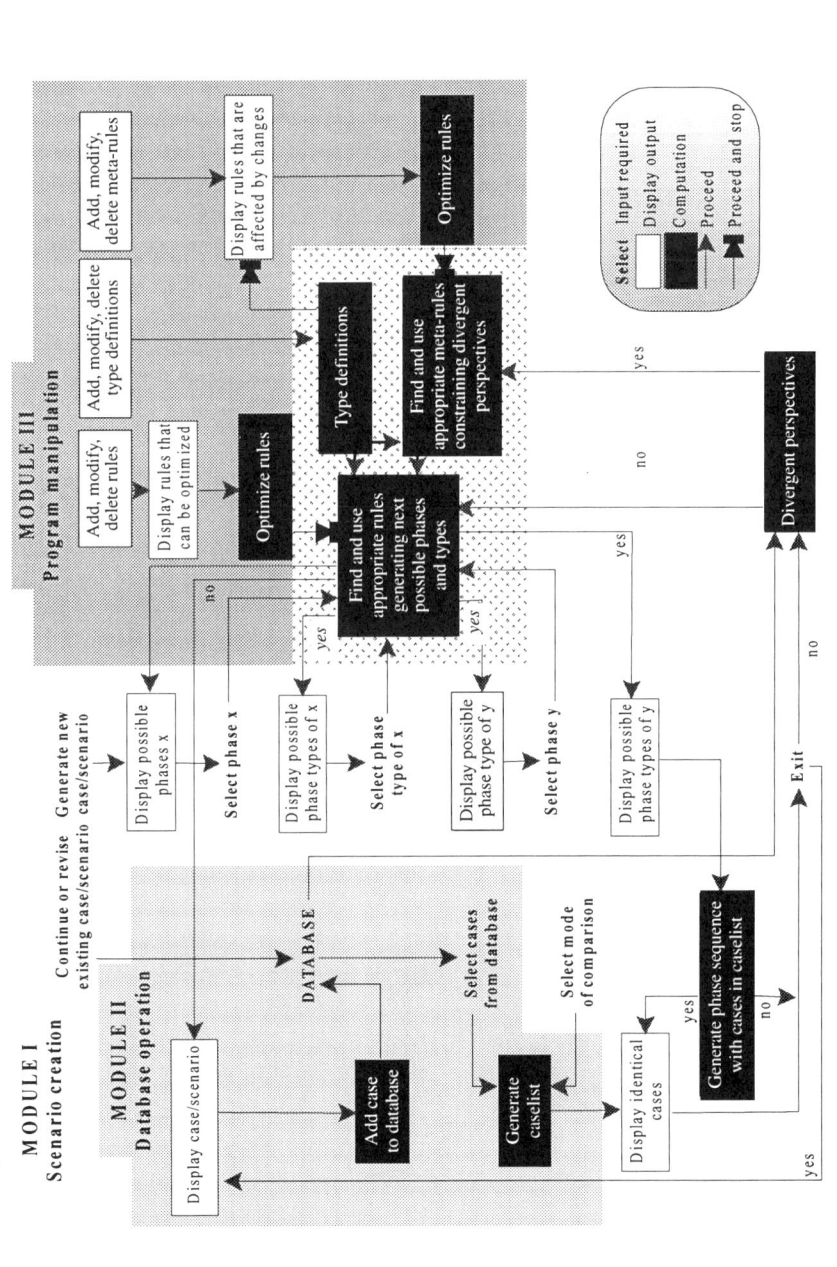

Figure 12.1: Functional Flow Chart of the CEWS Explorer

Figure 12.2: Actual First Episode of the Conflict in Guatemala, Plus Explorer Alternatives

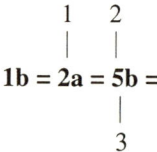

and represent it again graphically. However, now we are in a position to display not only the actual phase sequence that characterized the conflict, but also the alternatives that existed at each node in the sequence. Contrasting the actual with the range of possible alternative phases allows us to better assess the limitations and opportunities to prevent a more violent conflict or to move the conflict on to a less violent trajectory. Hence, whenever a new case is added to the database of the CEWS Explorer, it represents one of the many possible phase trajectories that can be generated with the rules described above. In addition, each case includes the range of possible alternatives that existed at each node.[51] Figure 12.2 introduces the graphic representation of computationally generated phase sequences by using the first episode of the conflict in Guatemala. (For phase type definitions, refer to table 12.1.)

The phase sequence in the middle row, i.e., 1b-2a-5b, represents the actual phase sequence. The phases branching off the actual phases represent the alternatives that the empirically based grammar in the CEWS Explorer suggest to have been possible. For example, instead of moving into an abatement phase (5b) the conflict could have stayed in a crisis phase (2) or moved into a limited violence phase (3). Remember though that we can provide a much more detailed account of a conflict's trajectory than just in terms of phase descriptions. As noted above, the combination of numbers and letters is merely a formal shorthand for situation descriptons. Consequently, the first episode of the Guatemalan conflict is properly described as follows:

A situation somewhat more expansively graphed in figure 11.4 in which

> 1b   the expectation of a crisis arises from discussions, claims, and efforts to reform the existing political, social, or economic system,

> is followed by a situation in which

> 2a   the expectation of systematic violence arises from the formation of armed groups or the receipt of economic, military, or political assistance by existing armed groups,

> which in turn is followed by a situation in which

> 5b   a conflict is temporarily abated by the installation of a new government.

This description in terms of situational characteristics can now be matched to the specific description in Padilla's account.

1b The newly elected President Arbenz "wanted to compete with the U.S. owned monopolies in railroads and electricity . . . [and] . . . enacted an agrarian reform that affected the interest not only of Guatemalan landowners but also of the United Fruit Company" (Padilla, chapter 3).

2a The United States supported an "invasion of the country by a small military corps under the command of colonel Carlos Castillo Armas in June 1954 [which] was just a smoke screen in order to prepare the conditions for the coup d'etat organized by the U.S. Ambassador John D. Peurifoy."

5b "Afterward an authoritarian regime was established."

This contrast validates the match between the specific description of the beginning of the Guatemalan civil war and the sequence of typical situation descriptions. It also emphasizes an important point about the use of the CEWS Explorer: the CEWS Explorer combines typical situation descriptions into typical conflict trajectories or stories. If a user wants to generate conflict trajectories that are to represent specific situations, she must use her own expertise and imagination to relate the specific content of her narrative to the general narrative form provided by the program. This is precisely why the CEWS Explorer is especially useful for supporting practitioners in their attempt to identify, assess, and design instruments to move a conflict into a different direction. To illustrate how the CEWS Explorer can be used toward this end, we will now explore episode by episode the limitations and opportunities for a less violent conflict in Guatemala.

According to Padilla's account, the first episode of the conflict is particularly important because the civil war had its "roots in the violent U.S. intervention in Guatemala (1954) aimed to overthrow the democratic and legally elected government of President Jacobo Arbenz Guzmán." We can thus assert that if the conflict between the governments of Guatemala and the United States had been resolved differently, the ensuing civil war could have been avoided. Yet, how could this have been achieved?

A look at alternative vertical paths generated for the first episode in figure 12.2 shows that once the agrarian reform law had been passed the two countries found themselves in a dispute situation that could have either continued (1) or escalated into a crisis situation (2). However, this conclusion must be taken with a grain of salt, because the reason why we do not have the possibility of an abatement after a dispute phase, i.e., a 1b-5 sequence, is that we have not observed an empirical instance of this sequence. As we noted above, this does not seem to reflect a particular aspect of conflict, but rather a negligence on the part of researchers to study cases in which conflict resolution has been successful in very early stages of a conflict. We therefore caution against concluding that an early resolution of the dispute between Guatemala and the United States was impossible.

Even if we did argue that no possibility for an early resolution existed, we would still not argue that the U.S. covert operation, which brought about a regime change, was therefore necessary. In fact, we can ask what other possibilities existed to follow the U.S. military support of Guatemalan reactionary forces? Figure 12.2 indicates three possibilities, namely the imposition of an authoritarian regime (5b), which is the possibility that was realized, the continuation of military support (2), and an escalation in the form of an overt intervention (3). However, these are not the only possibilities, for each phase can be further distinguished into phase types. Thus, when we enter an abatement phase (5), after the U.S. military support raises the specter of an outbreak of violence (2a), it can take three forms: a regime change (5a), negotiations (5c), and a change in legitimacy (5e). The regime change was actualized and set the stage for a prolonged civil war. How could the other two possibilities have affected the conflict? A negotiation could have been brought about by a UN intervention. Padilla mentions this option when he writes that "President Arbenz tried to obtain the intervention of the United Nations in 1954 in order to find a solution for the interstate conflict with the United States." This would have prevented an armed overthrow of the government and left the Arbenz regime in power. However, would this abatement have been temporary, or could it have resulted in an early settlement? A continuation of this scenario reveals that the abatement would have been temporary, and that the only ensuing possibilities would have been a prolongation of negotiations (5c), a renewed crisis in which the use of systematic violence was again expected (2), or an armed intervention (3). We can thus conclude that a UN intervention in 1954 would have, for some time, prevented the use of violence and the overthrow of the Arbenz regime. But it would not have been able to resolve the conflict or prevent the civil war.

Would the only remaining possibility, namely a change in legitimacy, have made a difference? Padilla describes how we can imagine such a change in legitimacy to have taken place. He explains that "if both the Guatemalan ruling economic class and the Eisenhower administration could have waited for the elections programmed for the year 1956, they could have had a democratic solution with the election of a more 'conservative' Guatemalan administration, as it was the case in the Nicaraguan elections of 1990, when Daniel Ortega was defeated by Violeta Chamorro." Translated into our conceptual language, the Arbenz regime would have lost not only its power but also its legitimacy, for the ideas that it stood for would have been discredited. Such a situation could have lead to a settlement of the conflict, either immediately following the elections or after negotiations. Consequently, a civil war could have been prevented if the elections of 1956 had brought about a change in government. Figure 12.3 displays this alternative phase sequence, with actual phase types in boldface.

Figure 12.3: Avoiding the Civil War through a Change in Legitimacy

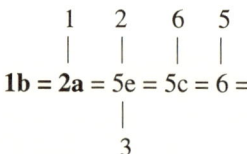

Figure 12.4: Actual Second Episode of the Conflict in Guatemala

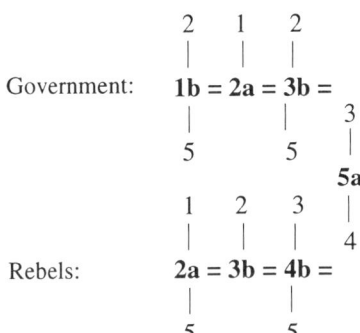

Let us continue our counterfactual explorations with the second episode of the conflict in Guatemala. This episode begins after the Arbenz regime had been overthrown, and an authoritarian government had taken its place. The actual phase sequence of the second episode is represented in figure 12.4.

Figure 12.4 shows divergent perspectives where, by convention, the dominant party's perspective is represented on top, and the dominated party's perspective on the bottom. When the two perspectives converge they are represented together in one row. So let us assess what was to become the Guatemalan civil war, and whether and how it could have been abated earlier. The actual phase sequences indicate that the government considered itself in a dispute (1b) whereas the rebels deemed their situation to be one of a crisis (2a). The possibility of an abatement (5) at this point is merely a prolongation of the previous regime change (5b), and does not offer any other forms of abatement. Both parties could have started on a lower conflict level, but they would have escalated sooner or later. It is both interesting and terrifying to notice that a possibility for preventing violence does not occur before one of the parties reaches a stage where violence is already being used systematically. In the actual scenario, this opportunity arose when the rebels suffered from limited violence (3b) inflicted by government troops. Instead of escalating further, into a limited violence phase (3) in the case of the government, and into a massive violence phase (4) in the case of the rebels, they could have also entered an abatement phase (5). This abatement could again have taken various forms, namely a renewed regime change (5b), negotiations (5c), or a change in legitimacy (5e). Let us discuss each of these possible changes in these contested historicities in turn.

Another regime change (5b) would have come about if the rebels had been successful in their attempt to restore the previous government and its reforms. This would have meant a defeat of the ruling elites including their U.S. supporters (5a). This, in turn, would have delegitimized the elites and legitimized the former rebels and current

Figure 12.5: Settling the Civil War through a Regime Change

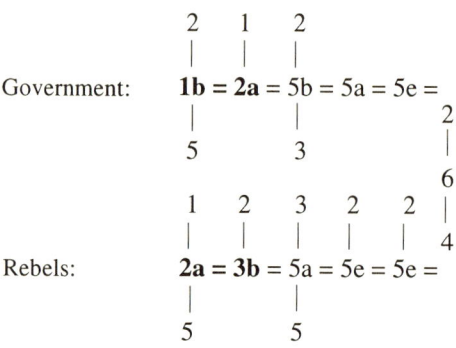

leaders (5e). A settlement would have been possible. However, a renewed escalation would have been possible also, either in the form of a crisis (2) or a full-fledged counterattack by the ruling elites (4). This scenario is represented in figure 12.5.

Negotiations would have been another alternative to the further escalation in the actual scenario. Padilla provides no indication how such negotiations could have been brought about. In such a situation it is particularly useful to select a mode of comparison that tells the CEWS Explorer which aspects of a phase sequence are to be matched between the simulated case and the cases stored in the database. One of the five cases in which a match can be found is the one of Chiapas.[52] A closer look at this case reveals that an important factor in bringing about negotiations was the temporary recognition of the rebels, primarily because of the considerable pressure that the international community brought to bear on the Mexican government. We can use this analogy to our counterfactual scenario about the conflict in Guatemala. This would have meant that the rebel's concerns would have been considered legitimate, and that for this reason the government would have agreed to enter into negotiations. However, negotiations would not have immediately led to a resolution of the conflict. Instead a new episode would have been started in which the government would have temporarily experienced an escalation, either because the rebels would not have suspended their military preparations (2a), or because the government would have employed limited violence (3). Only if the government had stayed in a crisis phase (2a) while the rebels would have indicated a further interest in negotiations (5c), would the possibility for a settlement (6) have arisen. However, at each node of this counterfactual phase sequence the possibility of a renewed escalation would have existed. figure 12.6 shows the graphic representation of this counterfactual scenario.

Figure 12.6: Settling the Civil War through Negotiations

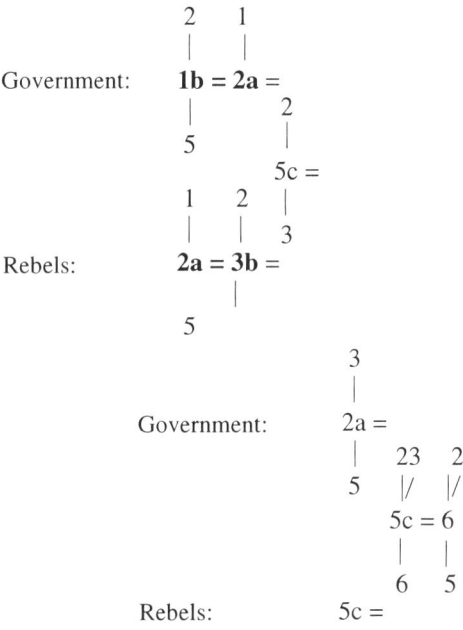

Finally, the actions by the authoritarian Guatemalan regime could have produced a change in legitimacy. Again, Padilla does not provide any clues about how this could have been brought about. Comparisons to other cases reveal that Moldova and South Africa contain partly matching phase sequences. However, they are not close matches because Moldova contains a convergent 3b-5e perspective and South Africa a convergent 2a-5e perspective. In no other case do we have a divergent perspective consisting of a 3b-5e and a 2a-5e sequence. Without any empirical analogy we can imagine, however, that the authoritarian regime would have been delegitimized by its actions, perhaps less so internationally than domestically. This change in the domestic climate would have paved the way for negotiations and an eventual settlement of the conflict.[53] It is especially noteworthy that after a change in legitimacy only possibilities for other forms of abatement or a settlement exist. This can be misleading because next to negotiations (5c) the possibility of a regime change (5b) exists. If this latter option were to be realized the authoritarian regime would have regained power and the rebels would have pursued an escalatory path. Figure 12.7 shows the phase sequence in which a change in legitimacy resulted in successfully concluded negotiations.

Another aspect of the second episode in the Guatemalan civil war is worth elaborating on. Notice that once the parties had used considerable violence against each

Figure 12.7: Settling the Conflict through a Change in Legitimacy

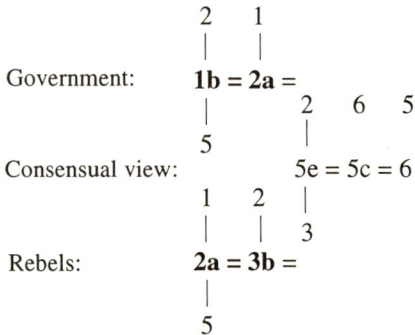

other, i.e., the government considered itself to be in a limited violence phase (3b) while the rebels considered themselves in a massive violence phase (4b), the only possibility for an abatement was the defeat of one of the parties (5a). As we have seen in the previous three scenarios, possibilities for an abatement would have existed only one phase earlier. This suggests that an abatement, let alone a settlement, is the more difficult to produce the more the parties are invested in the systematic use of violence. This is further underscored by the beginning of the next episode, which is characterized by a renewed escalation on a higher level.

Let us therefore explore the third and final episode of the actual conflict in Guatemala. Figure 12.8 displays this episode graphically.

Figure 12.8: Actual Third Episode in the Conflict of Guatemala, and Alternatives

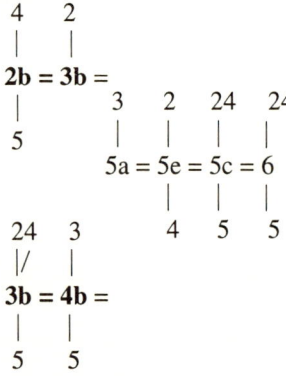

The beginning of this episode appears to replicate the previous one. However, there are several significant differences. First, the rebels could have started in a crisis phase (2), which would have enabled a replication of their previous escalatory trajectory. Instead they continued their armed struggle (3b), which eliminated any possibility to abate the conflict at this point, short of prolonging the defeat that the government had inflicted on them (5a). Second, the government did not operate with respect to the mobilization of rebels (2a) as it had previously, but with respect to their suppression (2b). This difference affected the possibilities for a subsequent abatement. Whereas in the previous episode an abatement was possible in three forms (as alternatives to the systematic use of violence) only two forms of abatement would have been possible at this point, namely negotiations (5c) and a change in legitimacy (5e). A regime change (5b) would no longer have been possible. Most importantly, neither negotiations nor a change in legitimacy would be able to produce a path leading to a settlement. This finding is confirmed by Padilla, who argued in a personal communication that a settlement would not have been possible at this stage.

Once the conflict escalated, another defeat of the rebels was inevitable. As noted above, the use of systematic violence makes it extremely difficult to produce possibilities for an abatement, let alone a settlement. The fact that the Guatemalan conflict was actually settled gains even more significance if one considers the numerous possibilities that existed to start new violent episodes. Instead of producing a change in legitimacy (5e), the conflict could have continued with another crisis (2) or even massive violence (4). These possibilities were not realized because of the international pressure that was exerted on the Guatemelan regime, on the one hand, and the ideological switch of the rebels, on the other. This combination created the environment in which the Central American peace process could influence the further development of the conflict in Guatemala, which culminated in the Esquipulas Accord. According to Padilla, "without the Esquipulas agreement of 1987 there could not have been a peace process in Guatemala." More specifically, the Esquipulas agreement put the conflict onto a path towards a settlement which included not only the resolution of the causes of the conflict but also the promotion of democratization and sustainable development. This path proceeded first through a stage of negotiations before it finally reached a stage in which the conflict was settled. However, possibilities existed at both stages, which could have terminated the peace process and prolonged the civil war. In view of these alternatives it is all the more remarkable how the perseverant and creative efforts of mediators built a foundation on which the Guatemalan people can live together peacefully after more then forty years of violence.

Our illustration of how the CEWS Explorer can be used to simulate alternative conflict trajectories has helped us to better assess the limitations and opportunities of resolving the Guatemalan civil war. However, we do not want to create the impression that our counterfactual explorations claim to be irrefutable. On the contrary, our claims are contestable, which is not only an intrinsic feature of any counterfactual, and thus, speculative analysis, but is also a practice that we expressly encourage. A major advantage of the CEWS Explorer is that it generates counterfactual conflict trajectories in a transparent and reproducible manner. Any of the counterfactual scenarios can be contested on its own grounds, if evidence can be found that contradicts any of the categories or rules. Objections of this sort can be used to improve the CEWS Explorer as well as to exchange experiences and knowledge about conflict trajectories in particular or related cases.

Hence, the CEWS Explorer not only represents a technical tool for generating conflict scenarios but also provides a common structure to talk about actual and counterfactual conflict trajectories for better assessing instruments and requirements for the prevention, abatement, and resolution of violent conflicts. To exploit this potential to the fullest extent, the CEWS Explorer is intended to be integrated into a Web site where it serves as a globally accessible information system for the collection, analysis, and exchange of conflict data.

The CEWS Web Site:
A Prototype of an Electronic Information System

The CEWS Web site was developed concurrently to the present volume to, at least, partly pursue the objectives set out in the original Proposal 2, namely to develop an inexpensive, replicable, extensible preventive information storing and handling system[54] (see chapter 1). Initially, the CEWS Web site was mainly designed to introduce the CEWS project to a wide audience, to present our analytical framework, and to demonstrate its applicability and usefulness by featuring the trajectory graphs of all coded CEWS cases. A particular concern was to provide a great deal of transparency so that each trajectory graph is complemented with the original narrative or chronology that served as raw data, and our notes on how we coded this data to arrive at a reconstruction of the narrative/ chronology in terms of graphically represented conflict phases. Transparency is needed to invite interested scholars and practitioners to engage with our analysis, and to confirm, add to, or contest our interpretations. We illustrated how such an exchange can be envisaged as an integral component of the Web site, namely in the form of annotations that can be added to any object in the trajectory graph. At this stage we had thus addressed some of our main concerns. Our Web site enabled us to store preventive information in an inexpensive, replicable and extensible manner.

However, we had not yet developed the analytical structure necessary to build a full-fledged database with the capability to make specific searches and comparisons. The development of the CEWS Explorer has made this possible. With the help of the CEWS Explorer one can compare various aspects of phase sequences as they unfold, that is, a phase sequence is not only matched to other phase sequences, but it is matched to them within its particular context of possible phase trajectories. In addition, a list of relevant cases can be defined for specific purposes to further specify the context (e.g., geographical area, type of conflict) in which comparisons are to be made. Due to administrative and technical obstacles the CEWS Explorer is currently only available as a separate application that can be downloaded for free from the CEWS Web site. Ideally the CEWS Explorer would be accessible on-line. However, we added the rules underlying the CEWS Explorer to the CEWS Web site and linked them to their corresponding trajectory graphs. Users can now make comparisons within and across cases in terms of identical phase sequences, but they cannot explore counterfactual phase sequences. Hence, we have reached our objective of developing an information handling system only to a limited extent.

Taking the CEWS Web site to the next level, where it would become a fully operational information system, requires, first, the complete integration of the CEWS Explorer in the Web site, and, second, complete interactivity of all other components. Only then would it be able to serve as facilitator for and node in a network of scholars and practitioners. This information system would not aim at substituting existing information systems including other databases and modes of analysis. On the contrary, it would aim at integrating them so that the knowledge entailed in diverse but incompatible and incomplete information systems be cumulated and made accessible to a wide audience. The guiding principle of such an information system would be that it be continuously updated, modified, and used by a network of scholars, practitioners, and their institutions.

We have tried to lay the groundwork for such an information system when, with help from Jafer Adibi and Leila Kaqhazian, we designed the CEWS Web site with three strategies in mind. They can be read as a road map to an operational information system.

The strategy of integration aims at developing an analytical method that is used to make a diverse set of conflict data—ranging from systematically collected and quantified event data to individual reports of participants—comparable. Once this data can be compared, it can be analyzed, lessons can be learned, and the otherwise incompatible or lost knowledge can be cumulated. We developed and tested such a method in chapter 11.

For the development of an information system, which is both a network in the technical and in the social sense, it is important that this analytical method be applied by members of the community in order to expand and modify the database. After all, the purpose of such an analytical method is not to compete with other methods but rather to provide a common language with which a diverse range of people can share and converse with each other about a diverse set of conflict-related information. For this reason we designed our analytical method in such a way that no extensive theoretical or methodological skills are needed to apply it. The basic rules for coding a case are explained on the Web site and can be studied in greater detail in this volume. This is crucial to assure that a wide variety of people can easily and quickly participate in the integration, and thus, cumulation effort.

If more fully developed, each participant can code cases, draw on-line trajectory graphs, and submit the corresponding raw data and his/her coding notes to a volunteer editor who makes them available on the Web site. In this way no central institution is required to develop and maintain the information system.

The strategy of simulation aims at providing practitioners and scholars with an analytical tool that helps them to make prognoses about possible future trajectories of a conflict and to learn from past actual and counterfactual conflict trajectories. Some of their principal activities to explore what is and is not possible in a particular situation and to assess whether a particular situation can be brought about or avoided. A simulation is therefore a valuable tool to learn from past conflicts, to assess future trajectories of current conflicts, and to stimulate creative decision making to prevent, abate, or resolve violent conflicts.

The advantage of a network-based information system is that actual and counterfactual conflict trajectories can be examined and assessed individually as well as collectively. Each node in a phase sequence as well as the phase sequence itself are potentially contestable, and an exchange of information, lessons learned, and experiences gained may help to arrive at timelier and more effective decisions. Especially institutions with little experience in matters of conflict mediation may benefit from the experience and knowledge of others and their assessment of past and future conflict trajectories. Local prevention and mediation efforts can thus be supported globally.

The simulation was developed in such a way that it can be easily modified to correspond to new empirical findings or to meet particular analytical needs. The basic procedures for empirical rule development are explained on the Web site and in greater detail in this volume. Again they are simple and do not require extensive background knowledge or training.

If more fully developed, the simulation is accessible on-line and can be used, expanded, and modified either individually within a personal profile or collectively via a volunteer editor. Chat rooms or news groups can be created for the general exchange of information, or more specifically tailored toward particular cases, episodes, phase sequences, or other relevant subjects.

The strategy of communication aims at building an institutional and an informational network. The more institutions participate in the development and application of the information system, the more they will form a community that can coordinate additional activities through the same or other channels, which will help to prevent, abate or resolve violent conflicts more effectively or more quickly. To form an institutional network that spans the entire globe a technology must be used that is widely available, affordable, and provides instant connectivity. Such a technology exists in the form of the Internet.

The Internet is an ideal technology to create and maintain networks, not only in the technical sense by which people are enabled to communicate with each other, but also in the social sense by which people who communicate with each other form communities. If such a network is not centrally organized, either technically or administratively, it entirely rests on the members of this community to develop and maintain their network themselves in a decentralized manner. Several of such communities exist, including those in the area of conflict prevention and resolution who communicate with each other via chat rooms, news groups, list servers, or e-mail.

However, these communication channels are mostly disconnected from institutional memories to which all participants can relate and build upon. An information system that uses all three strategies—integration, simulation and communication—in a complementary manner will maximize the value and scope of existing institutional memories, and support situation assessments and decision making within a global network of individuals and institutions who operate at the locations where conflicts are to be prevented, mitigated, or resolved.

The contributions in this volume in conjunction with the CEWS Web site have created a promising platform from which scholars, practitioners, and their institutions can start to develop a fully operational information system that is capable of effectively supporting conflict mediation efforts in the post–Cold War era.

Notes

1. For a discussion and references to the recent relevant American literature in international relations see Fearon (1991) and Tetlock and Belkin (1996). Influenced by Simon and Rescher (1966) and Harold Guetzkow's Simulated International Processes Project, Alker's own work on counterfactual simulations commenced with Alker and Christensen (1972).

2. See e.g., Geiss (1967) on why the World War I was inevitable and Ferguson (1999) on why Great Britain could have refrained from entering World War II.

3. See Cederman (1996) and Schmalberger (1998).

4. According to Rescher, philosophers "from Hume to the logical positivists of the 1930s and their later congeners, such as W. V. O. Quine and Nelson Goodman" have found metapysical speculation distasteful (Rescher 1975, 1) Similary, historians have found counterfactual analysis ill-devised for historical analysis. A. J. P. Taylor wrote that "a historian should never deal in speculations about what did not happen" Taylor (1954). See also Fischer (1970) and McClelland (1975).

5. Some of the most influential philosophical works on counterfactuals are collected in Linsky (1971), Loux (1979), and Tooley (1999). An example of an historian's foray into counterfactual analysis is Ferguson (1999).

6. In philosophy a major change of attitude about counterfactuals occurred when Saul Kripke introduced a technique that allows one to make claims about the necessity, contingency, and possibility of inferences by quantifying the number of entities in terms of "some" or "all." See Kripke (1980) for a fairly nontechnical discussion. Based on Kripke's work, Sylvan and Majeski have developed an innovative, nonprobabilistic methodology for the study of historical counterfactuals, and Schmalberger has developed a related methodology for the study of counterfactual state interactions. See Sylvan and Majeski (1998) and Schmalberger (1998).

7. The criteria are: 1) clarity, i.e., defining dependent and independent variables; 2) logical consistency, i.e., the connecting principle that links the antecedent with the consequent is logically consistent; 3) historical consistency, i.e., historical facts are altered only minimally; 4) theoretical consistency, i.e., the connecting principle is consistent with well-established theoretical generalizations; 5) statistical consistency, i.e., the connecting principle is consistent with well-established statistical generalizations; 6) projectability, i.e., the implication of a counterfactual argument can be observed in the actual world (Tetlock & Belkin 1996, 18).

8. For a discussion of the philophical treatment of possibilites throughout history see Rescher (1969, 1973).

9. See especially Quine (1948, 1960).

10. For a detailed explanation of this argument see Husserl (1970a, 1970b, 1973b, 1977), Schutz (1967), and Schutz and Luckmann (1973).

11. See especially Husserl (1973a) and the distinction between "in order to" motives and "because of" motives in Schutz (1967) and Schutz and Luckmann (1973).

12. For a critical discussion of these questions see Goodman (1978, 1983).

13. In the 1960s Saul Kripke developed a model structure for semantic modal logic that has made possible world semantics an integral part of various strands of logic. See Kripke (1980). Possible world semantics is truth-conditional and set-theoretic, that is, the conditions under which a sentence is true and the meaning of a sentence is identified with a set of possible worlds. For instance, the sentence "Tom eats" consists of a subject and a verb category. If "Tom eats" is true all other elements of the set that satisfy the conditions for being the subject category are also true. Consequently, "Bob eats," "John eats," and "Sue eats" are all possible combinations, if the conditions for the subject category are names. See Cresswell (1988).

14. The truth value of a claim is understood in Tarski's terms as a formally correct and materially adequate "sentential function which contains no free variables," i.e., "a sentence is true if it is satisfied by all objects, and false otherwise" (Tarski 1944).

15. The literature on possible world semantics is vast. For a fairly nontechnical presentation of some of the most important arguments, including a comprehensive list of references and an application to international relations, see Sylvan and Majeski (1996).

16. According to Kripke, the essential properties of individuals are contained in their genetic code, which makes each one of them unique. (Kripke 1980). Consequently, "John F. Kennedy" cannot be a "woman" or "Robert Kennedy" because this would alter the essential properties, as opposed to the contingent properties of "John F. Kennedy's" genetic make-up. If one wants to explore possible worlds in which "John F. Kennedy" is a "woman," one must determine the essential properties of "John F. Kennedy" in another way than by his genetic code so that gender can be a contingent as opposed to an essential property. Without anticipating too much from our later discussion on essential properties it should be mentioned here that essential properties are not to be understood as universally but as contextually essential.

17. Notice that the world that is at the basis for counterfactual analysis need not be the actual world. Because we need to know the essential properties of the phenomenon we want to examine counterfactually, we also need to know how these properties are assembled—actually as well as counterfactually. However, a possible world is always related to the world from which it was evoked rendering counterfactual claims world-specific. See e.g., Kripke (1980), Lewis (1968).

18. For a study of the concept of ethnicity and its relation to ethnic conflict, see Eller (1999).

19. By context we refer to the relations between meaning concepts that can be understood and used by members of a particular social group at a particular moment in time.

20. For a discussion of these two perspectives see Chihara (1998).

21. It may seem esoteric to believe in the existence of parallel worlds, but the basis from which Realists derive this belief is that mathematical objects such as numbers or sets exist. Following a line of reasoning that was developed by Russell and Whitehead, Realists argue that the existence of possible worlds should be accepted because they permit the deduction of mathematical statements which we believe to be true—statements that could not be proved without the existence of possible worlds. See Chihara (1998, 84).

22. Notice that the essential properties of DNA can be further broken down into the essential properties of the DNA of mammals or human DNA, depending on which phenomenon is to be described. This implies that no absolute basis exists on which essences are grounded but rather that essences establish the ground that is relevant for a particular phenomenon, that is, they constitute the phenomenon in question.

23. See also Schmalberger (1998) on the constitutive relations of threats in international politics.

24. This implies that the actual world can be described differently, thus depicting different states of affairs from which different essences can be derived that give rise to different counterfactuals.

25. This also implies that, contrary to the Realist conception of possible worlds, nothing new can be discovered in a possible world in the sense that no new phemonenon can be discovered. But this does not imply that nothing new can be learned. By exploring possible worlds more can be learned about the contingent properties of the phenomenon under investgation, and thus more can be learned about the phenomenon as such. See Rescher (1973, 1975).

26. In the absence of a systematic methodology to determine the validity of counterfactual claims, an arbitrary collection of plausibility criteria is often used to separate those claims that are to be considered really possible, in the sense of plausible, from those that are to be considered not really possible, in the sense of implausible. See e.g., Tetlock and Belkin (1996). However, the plausibility of a claim is unrelated to its possibility. Many claims that appear to be plausible are impossible and many claims that are implausible are possible. The virtue of possible world semantics, on the other hand, is that the attribution of truth values to counterfactual claims determines unequivocally and systematically the set of possible alternatives.

27. A formal attempt to engage in counterfactual analysis based on causal relations can be found in Simon and Rescher (1966). It demonstrates, however, that a complete structure of causal relations is required in order to deductively arrive at a specification of possibilities. For most social phenomena such a complete structure of causal relations is too complex to be exhaustively defined.

28. Bloomfield's CASCON and Sherman's SHERFACS are examples of alternative information systems that permit simulations of conflict trajectories.

29. Notice that the recovery of narrative descriptions from quantified data requires access to at least the coding procedures, and preferably also to the raw data that underlie the quantitative analysis.

30. This is not to say that scholars and practitioners are not also interested in the weighing of those potentials. But, before a possibility can be given a weight with respect to others, the range of possibilities must be determined. In this project we are not concerned with scaling possibilities, and leave this task for future research.

31. Notice that the phenomenon of conflict can be constituted in linguistic and nonlinguistic manners, depending on the activities through which actors constitute it. Hence, the process of constituting a conflict differs between those actors who are engaged in the actual fighting on the front line and those actors who receive reports about the fighting and decide on military or political strategies. Whereas the former are engaged in activities that employ a variety of sign systems of which language is but one, the latter employ primarily language.

32. In cases in which we have only one perspective on a conflict we can speak only of a history of the respective conflict, whereas in all other cases in which we have at least two perspectives we can speak of different histories of a conflict.

33. The concept of abduction was developed by Peirce. He distinguished three modes of inference: deduction, induction, and abduction. Deduction arrives at a necessary conclusion by drawing on an assumed rule and a case. From the assumed rule "all humans are mortal"

and the case "Socrates is a human" the conclusion follows that "Socrates is mortal." The deductive mode proves that the result is a particular instance of a case. Induction derives a rule from an observation and a case. Thus, from the observation "Socrates is mortal" and the case "Socrates is a human" the rule "all humans are mortal," is included. The inductive mode allows one to infer the existence of similar instances that are not observed. Finally abduction derives a case from an observation and a hypothetical rule. From the observation "Socrates is mortal" and the hypothetical rule "all humans are mortal" the case can be derived that "Socrates is a human." Hence, abduction is the only mode of inference that generates a set of which the observation is an element. Peirce argued that in perception only abductive inferences are used while scientific research employs all three modes of inference. See Peirce (1932, 5:181, 6:452–485). Abductive inferences are central to many theoretical concerns in the social sciences. For instance, ethnomethodology examines how subjects make abductive inferences in particular settings to theorize about the methods that are being used to identify and produce these settings (Garfinkel 1967). Abductive inferences also underlie the examination of practical reasoning in the way that it has been espoused by philosophers from Aristotle to Wittgenstein. For a discussion about the relevance of practical reasoning for the study of international relations, see Alker (1996a).

34. In this project we did not attempt to go beyond a simple descriptive grammar. If one wanted to develop a more sophisticated generative grammar that can deal with historical rewritings, one requires a fairly large universe of cases. For an example, see Schmalberger (1998).

35. The logical possibilities enumerated below are equivalent to their graphical representation in the previous chapter.

36. As a notational convention => is to be read as "can possibly be followed by," and not as "must necessarily be followed by."

37. If elements of a set are unambiguously and completely assigned to a set, their assignment can be expressed as functions. Constitutive relations must by definition fulfill the criteria of functions, and they therefore lend themselves naturally for computational explorations. We will see in the next section how this can be achieved. For an accessible introduction on this subject, see McCawley (1981).

38. Due to the small number of conflict episodes in our database, and the lack of sufficiently detailed information on the historical as opposed to the chronological evolution of our cases, we were not able to define conflict episodes in any other than a purely nominalistic manner. With more cases that represent more of the historical evolution of particular conflicts, conflict episodes can be distinguished in the same manner as forms of conflicts, conflict phases, and phase types. A comparison of different types of conflict episodes might then account for the resumption and resolution of conflicts as well as for the different ways in which conflicts can be embedded in others.

39. Due to the small number of cases in our study we have not been able to further distinguish settlement phases.

40. Following our previous notational convention according to which => stands for "can possibly be followed by" a condition of the form "if 1-2a then 5" is to be read as "if phase 2a follows phase 1, then 5 can possibly be followed by Phase 5." Notice that 2a stands for a particular type of crisis and is not to be understood as an aggregate of indicators or factors.

41. The CEWS Web site is: www.usc.edu/dept/LAS/ir/cis/cews.

42. This would imply that the essential properties of forms of conflict would have to be redefined, which would, of course, affect the rest of our analysis. We want to emphasize once again,

however, that the purpose of our current endeavors is to develop a prototype that can demonstrate the feasibility and usefulness of our approach, and does not constitute a fully developed system.

43. Notice that the phase type designated with "a" refers to different situations depending on whether it is associated with Phase 3 or Phase 4. In the former case it designates "overt repression" whereas in the latter case it designates "massacres."

44. Divergent phase sequences are demarcated by <. . .>, that is before and after these markers the perspectives on the respective phases converge. ?? indicates that we have no information about this conflict phase because our data does not include the beginning of a conflict or ends before a conflict is settled.

45. In the cases of Guatemala and the Mizos the entire conflict is settled, whereas in the case of Kashmir only an embedded conflict, namely the independence of Bangladesh, is settled, whereas the larger conflict continues.

46. We applied the same logic to the coding of conflict phases. Although different parties can have different interpretations of the conflict phase they consider themselves to be in, they nontheless consider themselves to be in only one conflict phase at a time.

47. To exemplify the distinction betwen functions and procedures with a simpler example consider the following functions: The function $f(x) = 3x + 12$ and $g(x) = 3 (x + 4)$ are identical in the sense that they bring into correpondence the same starting value (e.g., 3) with the same resulting value (e.g., 21). However, the procedure $f(x) = 3x + 12$ and $g(x) = 3 (x + 4)$ are different because in $f(x)$ the function $(3x)$ is calculated first, and its value (e.g., 9) is then added with 4 whereas in $g(x)$ the function $(x + 4)$ is calculated first, and its value (e.g., 7) is then multiplied by 3.

48. We used Scheme as programming language for developing our computer simulation. Scheme is one of several dialects of Lisp and distinguishes itself from others by its simplicity. Several introductions to Scheme exist. Eisenberg and Abelson (1990), Harvey and Wright (1994) Springer and Friedman (1989) are among the best text authors. The most comprehensive is Abelson and Sussman with Sussman (1985). A number of freeware Scheme implementations can be obtained at swissnet.ai.mit/scheme-home.html or cs.indiana.edu/scheme-repository/home.html. We used MIT Scheme.

49. In addition to the twenty-nine rules identified in the complete table 5 we have included a rule 3(ab), 4b-5e => 6. We discussed this rule above as one that is hypothetical at this stage.

50. The two modes of abstraction presented in the previous section are used as templates for merging procedures, that is, the phase transitions 1a-2a => 3 and 1b-2a => 3 will be merged to 1(ab)-2a => 3 and the phase transitions 1a-2a => 3 and 1a-2b => 3 will be merged to 1a-(2ab) => 3.

51. If a case cannot be reproduced with the existing rules an anomaly exists requiring that the set of rules be redefined. The CEWS Explorer provides this capability. The user must only add a new or modify an existing rule, and the program performs the necessary abstractions and changes on the rest of the rules. It must be emphasized though that changes to the rules presuppose an empirical validation in exactly the way described in the previous and this chapter. This requirement obviously does not apply if rules are changed for analytical purposes so that scenarios can be explored whose premise is not only what would have happened if this as opposed to that phase had followed, but rather what would have happened if particular phase sequences had been possible for which no empirically based corollary has been found.

52. The other cases are Moldova, Moros, Sierra Leone, and South Africa. Moldova and South Africa are not close matches to Guatemala because the sequence 2a-5c is shared by both parties of the conflict. In Guatemala only the government considers itself in a 2a-5c sequence

whereas the rebels consider themselves in a 3b-5c sequence. Similarly, in the case of the Moros, only the government finds itself in a 3b-5c sequence whereas the rebels are in a 4b-5c sequence. Still another variation can be found in the case of Sierra Leone, where the government is in a 2a-5c sequence and the rebels in a 4b-5c sequence. Only Chiapas is a close match because it shares identically structured divergent perspectives.

53. This situation differs from the one at the end of the third and final episode of the Guatemalan civil war in that a change in legitimacy is not the result of a defeat of one the parties. We will return to this situation later.

54. The CEWS Web site is at www.usc.edu/dept/LAS/ir/cis/cews/index.html.

Part IV
Sharing Informational Resources within Global CEW Networks

13
A Review of Research and Practice in Early Warning and Early Response: Lessons Learned and Policy Issues

Kumar Rupesinghe and David Nyheim
with Maha Khan

This chapter[1] charters the complex waters of early warning research and practice. It seeks to draw out an understanding of future directions and key policy issues in early warning by reviewing and assessing the work of key experts in the field. The chapter looks at definitions of early warning, provides a rough overview of the historical milestones in the early warning literature, situates early warning in relation to different kinds of responses to conflict, and reviews lessons learned in early warning methodology and practice. It concludes with a review of policy implications and future directions for the field.

Definitions of Early Warning

Early warning is a broad concept. Nowhere is this better illustrated than in the definitions that are propounded in early warning literature. Not surprisingly, definitions differ according to the orientation of the author: the identity of their audience; their focus for early warning; whether they concentrate on policy or on research; and their perspective, whether it is embedded at the international or at the grassroots level.

Assumptions and Objectives

Typically, many definitions of early warning assume a conflict continuum and that there is a steady escalation of a crisis. Like forecasting the progress of an illness, early warning in this respect is prognostic and supposes that there is a certain pattern of events where frequently conflicts lead to violence. In a number of definitions, early warning is not just a process of information gathering but is also intrinsically linked to response. Information derived through early warning processes informs and advises actors who are in the best position to proactively affect a situation.

Jongman and Schmid's definition is very much in this vein and refers to early warning as "prognosis (forecasting) or projection on the basis of collected and processed information. More clearly than monitoring, it is designed to have an alerting function, identifying critical situations with a high escalation potential so that timely action can be taken to reverse the trend or, at least, to soften its impact through contingency planning" (Jongman and Schmid 1994). Lund's definition, however, moves away from the prognostic view that a certain pattern of events will occur unhindered if there is not intervention of some sort. Instead he prefers to define early warning as an exercise in risk assessment that involves "judging the probability that certain events lead to violence or other crises. This requires reliable information on a range of possible common events—border crises, disintegrating regimes, civil wars, genocide, human rights abuses, refugee flows—and estimating where these are most likely to emerge" (Lund 1997).

In addition to differences in assumptions, definitions of early warning will differ on the point of what one warns about, or why. These differences are illustrated in the following definitions. Dorn defines early warning as: "The act of alerting a recognized authority (e.g., UN Security Council) to the threat of a new (or renewed) armed conflict at a sufficiently early stage for that authority to attempt to take preventive action" (Dorn 1997). Rusu describes it as "the ability to predict the possible movement or displacement of people as a result of nature, conflict or coercion" (Rusu 1997). The fact that this definition encompasses a different phenomenon (which may or may not involve violence) implies also the need to look at other nonviolence related factors. Acharya and Dewitt say that early warning "[i]nvolves monitoring of developments in political, military, ecological, and other areas (such as natural disasters, refugee flows, threats of famine, and the spread of disease) that may, unless mitigated, lead to outbreak of violence or major humanitarian disasters" (Acharya and Dewitt 1997).

Methods

For the most part, the definitions surveyed see early warning methodology as basic intelligence gathering with the monitoring of event indicators in a systematic way.

Another critical element of early warning methodology is the need for analysis in order to formulate a truly informed response action. Diller's definition, for example, describes the process of early warning as a multifaceted mechanism "of monitoring, recording, analysing, and transmitting information about escalating conflict to enable responses to avert or mitigate destructive consequences" (Diller 1997). Some definitions, such as Lund's or Acharya and Dewitt's above, elaborate to give a list of some of the crisis indicators although it can be argued whether there is the space in any definition for a typology, broad and succinct enough to encompass all the indicators. Tishkov and Ustinova stress the analytical sources and areas subject to analysis: "By early warning we mean based on in-depth local/comparative analysis the ability to assess sociocultural and political situation in a multiethnic milieu for the purpose to diagnose existing potential threats for social actors and system and to deliver a proper message for timely response" (Tishkov 1997).

Warning-Response

While many of the definitions focus on early warning as an information gathering function, others prefer to emphasize the response aspect and the interface between ascertaining a threat and prompting a response. For example McCarthy is very clear about how important this link actually is and defines early warning as: "A process of communicating judgments [emphasis added] about threats early enough for decision makers to take action to deter whatever outcome is threatened; or failing that, to manage events in such a way that the worst consequences are mitigated" (McCarthy 1997). Making sure a warning is communicated successfully to relevant actors is not de facto and many of the definitions recognize that those who would respond must hear the forecasters. Rusu's definition describes early warning as a "coherent international mechanism for information collection, verification, and exchange in the interests of early warning . . . a decentralized system that could be viewed as authoritative" (Rusu 1997) [emphasis added]. Going back to Jongman and Schmid's definition they too remarked: "The warning should be issued by a source that has authority with target groups, otherwise it might be ignored or the wrong sort of action might be taken" (Jongman and Schmid 1994).

If there is any "product" as far as an early warning is system is concerned then it is clearly the information that is passed on to policy actors. Not too many of the definitions allude to the nature of the information product; whether it is merely a report or analysis of a particular situation, or whether this information is supplemented by a range of policy options. FEWER's definition stresses the role of early warning in the development of options for response: "The systematic collection and analysis of information coming from areas of crises for the purpose of: (a) anticipating the escalation of violent conflict; (b) development of strategic responses to these crises; and (c) the presentation of options to critical actors for the purposes of decisionmaking" (FEWER 1997). In many of the definitions the link with specific conflict prevention policies is stated. Stoel defines early warning as: "Information about escalatory developments . . . far enough in advance in order for them [OSCE bodies, AS] to react timely and effectively, if possible leaving them time to employ preventive diplomacy and other noncoercive and nonmilitary preventive measures" (NIIR 1996).

Preliminary Conclusions

From this overview it is clear that early warning is a multidimensional concept. The definitions surveyed raise important divergences and challenges in thinking. Six of these are listed below.

- A number of definitions assume a linear pattern of conflict. Others stress its fluidity and dynamic nature.
- Most definitions emphasize prediction prior to the start of a crisis, rather than the escalation or de-escalation during the conflict continuum.
- The great variety of objectives for early warning is a reflection of the many different directions in the field.
- Methodologically, there is little agreement on what indicators to use, information sources, and analytical approaches.
- How to communicate early warning (beyond having it issued from an authoritative source) remains a challenge.
- The overall paradigm that is reflected in many definitions is one of intervention, particularly from the north in the south. Information is extracted, responses defined, and interventions follow.

Milestones in the Early Warning Literature

Prior to the end of the Cold War, there was very little literature dealing specifically with early warning. While many writers such as Lewis Richardson, Pitrim Sorokin, Quincy Wright, Lincoln Bloomfield, Johan Galtung, Tedd Gurr, Ernst Haas, Nazli Choucri, and Robert North, plus the researchers at SIPRI, had prepared a lot of the ground work for future research on early warning by examining the causes of violence and mapping paths of conflict and conflict management, it is J. David Singer and Michael D. Wallace who stand out as early pioneers of research on early warning. In their 1979 edited volume *To Augur Well: Early Warning Indicators in World Politics,* they introduced the application of social science research, and specifically correlation models, to develop early warning indicators for forecasting conflicts (Adelman and Suhrke 1996). In the intervening period up until the beginning of the 1990s, the actual practice of early warning, other than for military purposes, was almost totally restricted to the aims of preventing humanitarian disaster. Organizations, such as the UN's Ad Hoc Working Group on Early Warning Regarding New Flows of Refugees and Displaced Persons (established in 1991) were set up but nothing concrete or systematic emerged.

As reviewed in chapter 1, the major catalyst for the proliferation of early warning literature in recent years has been the end of the Cold War. The transformation of the international system that occurred following the shift from East-West bipolarity to the "New World Order" prompted new concerns as attention turned away from ideology and focused on the viability of the existing nation state system. Symptomatic of this change was the reemergence of issues, among national and international actors, of identity, ethnicity, religion, language, ecology, and nationalism. For the international community, traditional efforts designed to prevent interstate conflicts were replaced by fresh threats to international stability posed by communal conflicts, ethnic strife, genocide, politicide, democide, refugee flows, and humanitarian disaster.

As recalled in the Preface to this volume, at the beginning of the 1990s the United Nations began to realize that its role, firmly embedded in the traditional concept of collective security, needed to be reevaluated. Conflict and upheaval were more commonly becoming intrastate phenomena and the United Nation's existing mandate was not flexible enough to take into account these alterations in the patterns of conflict. In 1991, the Security Council called on UN Secretary General Boutros Boutros-Ghali to formulate a new vision for the UN. In 1992, the Commission on Internal Conflicts and Their Resolution (ICON), formed under the auspices of the International Peace Research Association (IPRA), produced a report on "Early Warning and Conflict Resolution" that was to become the locus of UN-related interest in these topics. That same year Boutros-Ghali produced *An Agenda for Peace* (1992), which mapped out the proposed activities of the United Nations in the New World Order. In this document he alluded to the threat posed to the cohesion of states and proposed a series of recommendations for the UN that included peacekeeping, preventative diplomacy peacemaking (including enforcement actions), and recognized the importance of pre- and postconflict, development-linked peacebuilding (Rupesinghe 1995). At the heart of the new agenda was the realisation that the new emerging types of conflict required early warning capabilities to enhance the effectiveness of preventive diplomacy.

In *An Agenda for Peace*, Boutros-Ghali called on NGOs and academics to address the changing mix of conflicts in the world. Whether in response to this call or not, between 1992 and 1994 a range of governments, academics, IGOs, and NGOs took up the cause of early warning and developed new concepts and models.

Going beyond the literature review of chapter 1, in their excellent recent review, Davies and Gurr (1998) provide an overview of the types of early warning research. table 13.1 summarizes their findings.

Model-based researchers, such as Ted Gurr, have focused on minorities and communal violence and have developed correlation models. Barbara Harff's work on genocide and politicide used a sequential model, which took into account context and defined so-called accelerators in conflict situations. This type of research, which was essentially based on a retrospective analysis of conflict, was also adopted by Albert Jongman and Alex Schmid of PIOOM (Interdisciplinary Program of Research on Root Causes of Human Rights Violations) in the Netherlands. However, their focus was on

Table 13.1 Overview of Davies and Gurr Findings (1998)

Types of early warning research include those looking at:
1. arms flows (e.g., Hilterman*)
2. ethnopolitical conflict (e.g., Gurr*)
3. environmental conflict (e.g., Baechler*)
4. intrastate conflict (e.g., Schmid*);
5. genocide, gross human rights violations (e.g., Harff*)
6. state failure (e.g., Esty*)
7. food crises (e.g., Rashid*)
8. refugee flows (e.g., Schmeidl and Jenkins*)
9. political instability (e.g. Schrodt and Gerner*)

Research is also being conducted on early warning according to the *different stages* of conflict. This research focuses on:
1. background conditions ("structural tensions")
2. crisis escalation ("dynamic factors or accelerators")
3. trigger incidents leading to full blown crisis

Six kinds of information sources are used for early warning:
1. in country situation studies (e.g., Human Rights Watch)
2. screening of public news sources
3. field reports from NGOs, IGOs
4. coded assessments by country experts
5. databases of structural indicators
6. episodic databases on past crises

Refers to chapter in Davies and Gurr (1998).

codifying human rights violations. Helen Fein of the Institute for the Study of Genocide in Massachusetts developed a different model based on response. Her model tried to identify strategic moments in crisis situations for the purpose of averting genocide and politicide.

John Davies's (University of Maryland) and Phil Schrodt's (University of Kansas) work on event data characterized another trend developing in early warning research. It represented a coming of age of research into conflict within the context of the information revolution. Davies's Global Events Data System (GEDS) and the system set up at the University of Kansas (KEDS) (see Schrodt and Gerner 1997) monitored and coded information derived from global media sources thus converting the information collated into rough trends analyses. What was different about these models, as opposed to previous ones (such as Gurr's and Harff's), was the tracking of conflicts quantitatively in near real-time, rather than retrospectively.

Away from model-based research of the conventional sort, a number of authors preferred to analyze and observe conflict using a narrative or qualitative approach.

Howard Adelman, Sharon Rusu, Hayward Alker, Michael Lund, and Kumar Rupesinghe emerged as leading lights in this respect though they all had different focuses to their work. While Adelman and Rusu concentrated on early warning in relation to refugees and humanitarian emergencies, Alker, Rupesinghe, and Lund focused more on conflict resolution and prevention. The research and literature produced by this group began to yield a picture of how conflicts evolved, the changing nature of conflict, and how early warning systems needed to develop, and introduced the idea of linking particular responses to different points during the conflict continuum (see Rupesinghe and Kuroda 1992).

As this research evolved, events elsewhere in the world marked another watershed in the history of early warning. The failure of the international community to both foresee and react to the events that developed in Rwanda illustrated more sharply than ever the need for effective early warning systems. While a number of researchers attempted to derive lessons from the Rwandan experience, others took on the task of addressing the practicalities of creating effective early warning systems. The emerging theme seemed to be the need to link warning with response. Schmeidl (1997), for example, described the need to develop realistic strategic options to avert humanitarian disasters. Others stress that early warning per se needed to be firmly response oriented, and looked for institutionalized approaches of action following warning. A notable feature of the post-Rwanda literature was also the focus, in the context of early warning, on peacebuilding and longer-term structural responses rather than shorter-term conflict prevention measures. MacFarlane (1998) and others stressed the importance of addressing the "deeper" causes of conflict, tackling issues such as the need to strengthen civil society, and address constitutional issues, inequality, and democratization. See chapters 11 and 12 for an important, new, synthetic conceptual-operational approach to early warning.

The latter period of the 1990s has been characterized by a process of raising early warning and the policy agendas of governments and multilateral agencies, as well as establishing operational conflict early warning systems. Thinkers such as Martin Ennals, Rudolfo Stavenhagen, Asbjørn Eide, and Kumar Rupesinghe set the stage for nongovernmental early warning efforts. In 1992, International Alert (founded by Ennals) spearheaded a major advocacy campaign for early warning and response in different parts of the world. This campaign focused on: (a) fostering policy changes among Western governments; (b) encouraging the formation of networks and institutions, particularly in conflict affected regions; and (c) designing early intervention models that required closer cooperation with local actors.

The establishment of operational early warning networks such as the Forum on Early Warning and Early Response (FEWER), systematic information collection, and dissemination systems such as the Integrated Regional Information Network (IRIN) and ReliefWeb, and processes such as the UN Framework Team for Early Warning, resulted from a greater understanding of the role of early warning for effective preventive action (Rupesinghe, 1998). Once the ongoing successes and failures of such projects become apparent (see the penultimate section below for preliminary lessons learned) a further proliferation of early warning literature in a more practical vein can be expected.

Preliminary Conclusions

With changes and events in the post–Cold War era, research into early warning has moved to become increasingly operational. A number of trends and challenges can be identified:

- Thinking in the field has advanced significantly in the last ten years with a solid body of research now in place on early warning concepts, models, and processes.
- Quantitative models and systems for early warning are increasingly enabling the policy-making community to track and process large quantities of relevant information.
- Qualitative research is stressing the need for early warning to identify opportunities for response at all stages of a conflict continuum.
- Early warning analysis is increasingly accepted in different policy communities as a corner-stone for the development of effective responses to conflict.
- Quantitative and qualitative research continue on parallel paths with limited cross-fertilisation. Part III of this volume is dedicated to the needed, more effectively linking of these styles of research.
- Nongovernmental and intergovernmental systems are becoming more operational. It is critical to now learn how to do real time and policy relevant early warning.

Linking Early Warning to Preventive Action

The need to link warning to response emerges clearly from the above discussion. However, the role that early warning plays in relation to different types of preventive action remains to be more clearly delineated. Below is an overview of early warning in relation to conflict prevention, preventive diplomacy, genocide prevention, and the prevention of complex humanitarian emergencies.

Conflict Prevention

Conflict prevention has been defined as "actions, policies, procedures or institutions undertaken in particularly vulnerable places and times in order to avoid the threat or use of armed force and related forms of coercion by states or groups as the way to settle the political disputes that can arise from the destabilising effects of economic, social, political and international change" (Schmid 1998a).

Conflict prevention can also include action taken after the eruption of violent conflict to avoid its recurrence. "Conflict prevention can occur at two points in a typical conflict's life history: 1) when there has not been a violent conflict in recent years, and before significant violence signals possible escalation, conflict prevention aims to keep a conflict from escalation; and 2) when there has been a recent violent conflict but peace is being restored, conflict prevention aims to avoid a relapse or re-igniting of violence" (Lund 1997).

We are looking, therefore, at a broad set of structural or dynamic measures that can be applied prior, during, or in the aftermath of conflict. Early warning can be viewed as a resource for conflict prevention in a number of ways:

- systematic monitoring/analysis of a volatile situations sheds important light on conflict dynamics that may assist in identifying appropriate preventive activities
- systematic monitoring/analysis of actual conflict situations will help identify windows of opportunity for peacemaking
- systematic monitoring/analysis of postconflict situations will enable an understanding of critical issues (poverty, arms availability, etc.) that need to be addressed for peacebuilding and consolidation.

In view of the above, two important challenges for early warners can be identified. First, early warning aimed toward identifying the outbreak of violence and assist in crisis management needs to be effective enough to automatically trigger a political reaction from the appropriate actors when a certain threshold in the conflict continuum is reached. And second, the relative strengths of different types of organizations involved in early warning need to be better understood. The ability of intergovernmental organisations (IGOs) such as the United Nations to effectively warn or respond to crises is often inhibited by the notion of state sovereignty, the high levels of consensus required between member states for action and effort to move a cumbersome bureaucratic machinery into gear. NGOs, both local and international, are not bound by state sovereignty, and can respond faster to potential or actual conflict situations. However, access to state actors may be limited, as are resources available for large scale action.

Preventive Diplomacy

As explained in Alex Schmid's *Thesaurus* (Schmid 1998a) the term preventive diplomacy refers to a variety of bilateral and multilateral nonmilitary official and unofficial efforts, which are preferably taken at the early stages of conflict by third parties (states, international organisations, NGOs, and others) to mobilize forces of moderation against a deteriorating security situation in a target country. Preventive diplomacy in contrast with "traditional diplomacy," involves unilateral and multilateral efforts "to pressure, cajole, arbitrate, mediate, or lend 'good offices' to encourage dialogue and facilitate a nonviolent resolution of the crisis" (Carnegie Commission 1997, xx–ii). For International Alert, preventive diplomacy represents measures that are taken to prevent the breakdown of peaceful conditions. It aims to prevent existing tensions from escalating into violence and to contain the spread of conflict when it occurs" (International Alert et al. 1993).

Preventive diplomacy is very much an integral part of conflict prevention that can be applied at the early stages of a crisis, or for the resolution of a conflict. Early warning is a resource for preventive diplomacy in a number of ways:

- the predictive aspect of early warning and identification of crises, may give more time to preventive diplomacy efforts
- the sustained monitoring/analysis of a crisis or conflict will help identify and understand grievances and stakes for different conflicting parties
- response-oriented early warning, as carried out by FEWER members, involves also the identification of key conflict protagonists, as well as mapping out which organizations/institutions have the capability to affect the situation. Both of these elements are critical for facilitating preventive efforts

It is vitally important, therefore, that forecasters have a credible and respected voice with policy makers.

Genocide Prevention

A genocide is "any of the following acts committed with the intent to destroy, in whole or in part, a national, ethnic, racial or religious group, such as: a) killing members of the group; b) causing serious bodily or mental harm to members of the group; c) deliberately inflicting on the group conditions of life calculated to bring about its physical destruction in whole or in part; d) imposing measures intended to prevent births within the group; and e) forcibly transferring children of the group to another group" (UN 1948 Convention on Genocide). The term "politicide" refers to lethal mass violence against unarmed people for political reasons. Other terms coined have been "democide" and "ethnocide."

There is a dual purpose for early warnings with regard to preventing genocide:

1. It is critical to build up public awareness of the impending disaster.
2. Sustained monitoring/analysis can assist in developing and planning specific preventive responses.

A number of problems are associated with genocide prevention. As Harff explains, "Typically, we know that there is a genocide in the making just prior to escalation. Governments, faced with an imminent crisis of massive proportion, may opt out totally rather than commit massive resources to stop ongoing slaughters. Policy makers are more likely to do something at earlier stages of a conflict, at a time when preventive or early conflict resolution type measures may prove adequate to halt escalation. Once involved, however, governments are less likely to abandon conciliatory or punitive measures" (Harff 1996). Furthermore, the involvement of early warning in cases of genocide is problematic. Early warning, in some cases, can publicize and hence encourage genocide rather than prevent it. Early warning in this case must be timely and targeted to policy makers before it becomes too difficult for them to react. Early warning must also be clothed in languages that are understandable to everyone involved in the conflict, if it is to be effective in spreading awareness among key actors.

Prevention of Complex Humanitarian Emergencies

A complex humanitarian emergency (CHE) is a natural or manmade disaster with economic, social, and political dimensions, "a profound social crisis in which a large number of people die and suffer from war, disease, hunger, and displacement owing to man-made and natural disasters, while some others may benefit from it" (Väyrynen 1991). CHEs, therefore, are interrelated with violent conflict though not exclusively associated with it.

Early warning is emerging as an increasingly used and useful tool in dealing with humanitarian emergencies: early warning may help identify potential "hot spots" for potential humanitarian crises, and the analysis of causes and possible consequences of a conflict related humanitarian disaster will assist in planning appropriate contingency measures.

There are several methodological issues related to early warning for CHEs. As already suggested, the problem with trying to conceptualise early warning and CHEs is the fact that they occur for the most part as a result of numerous phenomena (Schmeidl and Jenkins 1998). Model development will require the accumulation of comparative data on patterns and relative importance of accelerators in crisis and control situations (Harff and Gurr, 1998).

The methodological problems associated with straight forecasting of CHEs have prompted numerous authors to suggest a movement away from the focus on straight forecasting, to research on prevention, conflict management, contingency, and the analysis and development of effective strategic options for response.

Preliminary Conclusions

It is clear that early warning can and does play a critical part in conflict prevention, preventive diplomacy, genocide prevention, and the prevention/mitigation of complex humanitarian emergencies. The value added of early warning in relation to these is in broad terms:

- The identification of potential crises gives time for planning and implementing responses.
- Public early warning, and response oriented early warning, may assist in generating political will for action.
- Systematic monitoring/analysis of a volatile or actual conflict situation sheds important light on conflict dynamics, grievances/stakes that need to be addressed, and possible windows of opportunity for peacemaking.

Among the critical issues identified in this section is the need for forecasters to: a) have good access to decisionmakers; b) understand who can do what in a given situation; c) ascertain the impact of an early warning on conflict dynamics; and d) work on developing effective strategies for response.

Early Warning Methodology and Practice

The previous discussion has sought to provide a rough sketch of early warning at the conceptual and theoretical level, as well as a sense of the role of warning in relation to different types of preventive action. An overview of applied early warning methods, and practice-based lessons learned from FEWER is provided below.

Overview of Applied Early Warning Initiatives

More than twenty NGO/academic and IGO early warning initiatives existed in 1998. These have been surveyed on different occasions by FEWER as well as by the University of Maryland (Davies and Gurr 1998). The unpublished FEWER overview, summarized below, provides a sense of the diversity of initiatives in the field. The categories used to group the different initiatives are: (a) research and model-based initiatives; (b) action-oriented networks; (c) initiatives based in conflict regions; (d) international nongovernmental systems; and (e) intergovernmental initiatives. For each of the categories, key activities are summarized, and sources as well as target audiences identified.

Research and Model-based Initiatives

Examples of these include the Accelerators Project, Minorities at Risk Project, CEWS, GEDS, KEDS, and PANDA. Emphasis is placed on developing models of conflict and identifying key indicators. The CEWS project in particular takes a broader view that also includes assessing response strategies. Information sources used are primarily from the news/media sector and/or expert assessments, and the target audience is academic and governmental in North America and Europe.

Action-oriented Networks

These include the European Commission's Conflict Prevention Network (CPN), as well as the International Rescue Committee. Expert analyses are used to assess situations of concern. The primary target audience is intrainstitutional and the humanitarian aid community.

Initiatives Based in Conflict Regions

These include EAWARN (Russian Academy of Sciences), Africa Peace Forum (APFO), and ACCNET (ACCORD in South Africa). Emphasis is placed on documenting and reporting on conflict situations. All these initiatives take a networking approach, linking a range of analysts and organizations. Sources used are usually local and some international media/news sources. The audience is local actors in conflict areas and international groups.

International Nongovernmental and Think Tank Systems

These include the International Crisis Group, PIOOM Foundation, Forced Migration Project, and Uppsala Conflict Data Project. Emphasis is placed on providing analyses of or information on various conflict situations. International and local experts are used, and a variety of information sources. The target audience is primarily international.

Intergovernmental Initiatives

These include the above mentioned CPN, as well as Organization for Security and Cooperation in Europe/High Commissioner for National Minorities, UN framework team on early warning, UN High Commissioner for Refugees/Center for Documentation and Research, and the Organization of African Unity. Experts are frequently used for the production of specific analyses on countries of concern. A networking principle is taken linking/pooling different sources of information. The primary audience is intrainstitutional or the humanitarian community.

Preliminary Conclusions

Some basic observations may be drawn from this overview:

- There is a great diversity of objectives, approaches, methods, and sources among early warning initiatives.
- The academic and field links are weak. Rarely are model or research initiatives applied to actual or potential conflict situations.
- The implicit direction of information flows appears as relatively extractive, from areas of conflict to external actors and audiences.
- Only a limited amount of initiatives are locally based and managed by organizations in conflict areas, and focus on dissemination information to grassroots audiences.

Case-Study: Lessons from Applied Early Warnings by FEWER Members

As a response to the Rwandan genocide of 1994 a core group of the foremost researchers, practitioners, and policy-making institutions involved in the field of early warning and conflict prevention joined to form the Forum on Early Warning and Early Response (FEWER). As of mid-2000, FEWER is a global multisectoral and multidisciplinary network of more than twenty-five organizations with a stated goal of providing early warning and informing peacemaking and peacebuilding efforts. Members of the FEWER network operate early warning networks in the Caucasus,[2] Great Lakes,[3] West Africa,[4] Central Asia,[5] and Southeast Asia.[6] In 1998 and 1999, FEWER members predicted the outbreak of violence in the Democratic Republic of the Congo and Daghestan-Chechnya (UNDP 2000). Lessons learned from this work are outlined in relation to early warning systems and approaches to early response.

Early Warning

The networks for early warning have adopted three principles:

1. An emphasis on ensuring that local perspectives on the causes and dynamics of violent conflict, as well as what should be done to promote peace, are heard in different policy-making communities. Early warning efforts are led and implemented by networks of local organizations in conflict prone/affected regions.
2. The need to build upon existing early warning initiatives, and to create synergy among these. Operational cooperation between local early warning networks, and initiatives such as the Global Events Data System (University of Maryland) and the Country Indicators for Foreign Policy (Norman Paterson) are critical preconditions for rigorous early warning analysis.
3. A focus on ensuring that warning is linked to appropriate responses—and a peace that is owned by multiple stakeholders (local, regional and international). Network members work to convene actors who can respond in different conflict situations, map out their capacities, and assist them in planning integrated strategies for peacemaking and peacebuilding.

The main lessons learned from this work are summarized below in terms of what emerges as good practice for: a) early warning methods; b) information/data sources; and c) analytical processes.

a) Prediction and trends definition in early warning requires an understanding of three elements: i) conflict generating factors (dynamic and structural/local and international); (ii) stakeholder agendas and grievances; and (iii) peace generating factors (structural and dynamic peace developments, effectiveness of peacemaking/building activities, etc.). A simplified equation is therefore: (i) + (ii) − (iii) = trends.

b) Effective early warning requires the use of a range of data sources and analytical methods. Three categories of information sources can be listed: (i) local (e.g., events and perceptions not covered by the media); (ii) dynamic newswire reports (e.g., Reuters, ITAR-TASS, BBC); and (iii) structural data (e.g., World Bank, UNDP data, etc.). Relevant data from these sources needs to be identified and analyzed using both qualitative and quantitative methods.

c) The best analysis emerges from a dynamic process among local, regional, and international analysts. Given the complexity and specificity of violent conflicts, it is critical that the main source for the analysis is local.

In view of the above, FEWER's "good practice" system is schematically presented below, using the Caucasus as an example. Key organizations involved include the Russian

Figure 13.1: Early Warning Systems in Practice

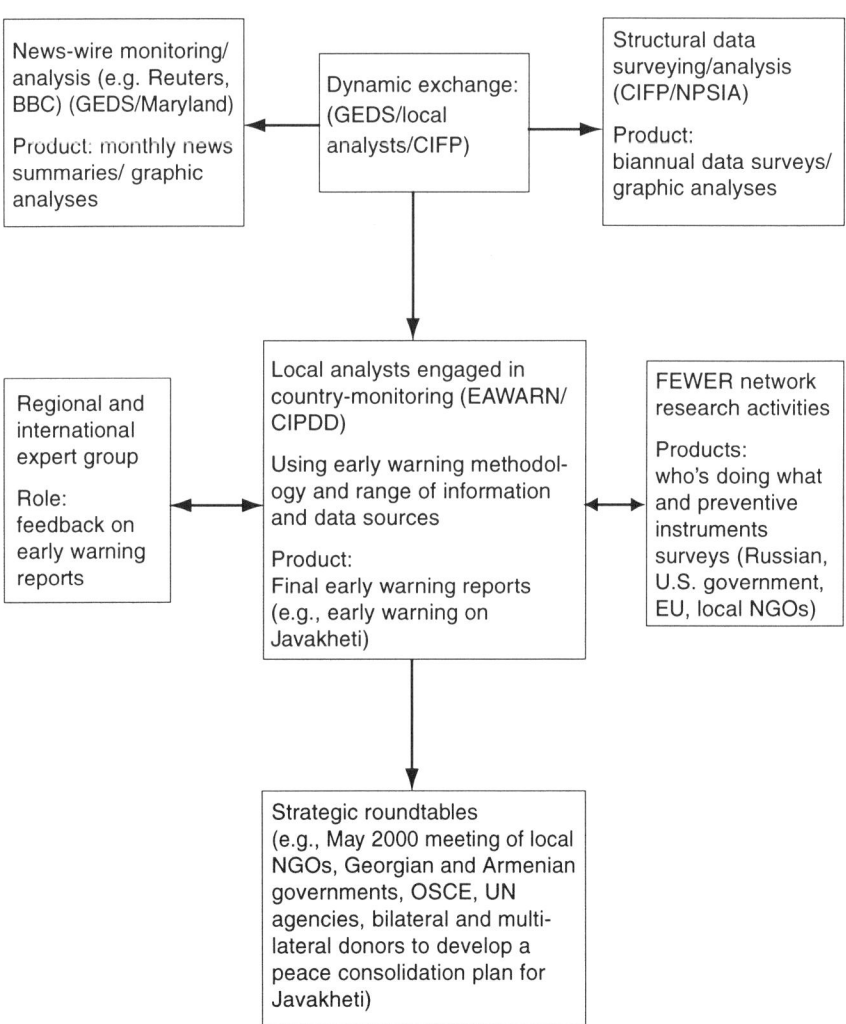

Academy of Sciences/EAWARN (EAWARN, Russia), Caucasian Institute for Peace, Democracy and Development (CIPPD, Georgia), and the Global Events Data System project (University of Maryland). An interface with the Country Indicators for Foreign Policy project (Norman Paterson School, Canada) is being established and is included for purposes of illustration. See www.fewer.org/caucasus/index.htm for access to reports.

The operational relevance of the system described above can be further illustrated with a brief (and simplified) summary of early warning issues in Javakheti—and who would (and does) provide relevant information and analysis.

The schematic presentation of a "good practice" early warning system, and the simplified analysis of the situation in Javakheti, underscores the value added and role played by the different organizations involved: a) the CIFP project can play an important role in providing structural data on statehood (civil liberties and political rights), minorities, and economic trends; b) GEDS data and analysis sets the stage for real time perspectives ethnic tensions, presence of Russian bases, and Armenian-Georgian cooperation; and c) the CIPDD, through its local network, is able to assess the importance of different indicators and understand the agendas and grievances of key stakeholders.

A number of challenges and advantages are linked to such a system. These are summarized below in relation to: a) the use of local analysts; b) newswire sources; and c) information sharing and the use of expert feedback. In relation to the use of local analysts, their expertise and analytical capacities may in some cases need to be strengthened and bias needs to be managed carefully. A dynamic and interactive process for the production of reports is necessary. However, the use of local analysts enables a solid understanding of conflict generating factors, and culturally specific issues (e.g., how a situation is perceived) that are not picked up by external experts. Critically, local experts are able to define what are sustainable peace objectives that response efforts should aim for.

The challenge with newswire monitoring is that coverage is infrequent. Areas that are not in the media spotlight receive scant attention until a conflict breaks. Real time monitoring is problematic, as "reliable" trends become visible only on a monthly basis. Nonetheless, the use of newswire monitoring (e.g., of Reuters, ITAR-TASS, BBC, etc.) offers important additional information sources for the local analysts. This enables the analyst to inquire of a broader regional perspective. Also, the reports produced locally have greater credibility among decisionmakers, as they are also based on the monitoring of hundreds of articles and reports.

Information sharing and expert feedback also suffer from problems of bias. Bias is present both locally and internationally. The management of a system of information sharing and expert feedback is highly resource intensive and time-consuming. However, the key advantages of information sharing and expert feedback lie in opening additional sources for local analysts and adding to the rigour and credibility of the work done.

Generic challenges to the system are threefold. First, rigorous early warning is time-consuming. By the time a report has gone through the system, its value may have decreased in terms of timeliness. Second, local analysts are constantly exposed to security risks due to their reporting activities. Although sources used are purely open ones,

Table 13.2 Case Study Example: Javakheti

Conflict generating factors		Stakeholder agendas/grievances			Peace-generating generating factors	
Indicator	Source	Issue		Source	Indicator	Source
Weak Georgian statehood	CIPDD and CIFP[1]	Armenians and Russians: ambivalent to Georgian citizenship		CIPDD	Evolving Georgian statehood	CIPDD and CIFP[2]
Socioeconomic isolation	CIPDD	Armenians: isolation reflects governmental discrimination		CIPDD		
Ethnic tensions	GEDS,[3] CIFP,[4] CIPDD	Resource scarcity creates Armenian, Russian, and Georgian tensions		CIPDD	Strong Armenian-Georgian relations	GEDS[5]
Presence of Russian bases	CIPDD and GEDS[6]	Mixed perception: bases provide jobs, but should go		CIPDD		
Repatriation of Meskhetian Turks	CIPDD	General perception: return will increase hardship		CIPDD		
Economic underdevelopment	CIPDD and CIFP[7]	Armenians: poverty reflects governmental discrimination		CIPDD	Seasonal migration of labor to Russia	CIPDD

Trends
Trends drawn out from assessing the balance between: (i) conflict generating factors; (ii) stakeholder agendas and grievances; and (iii) peace generating factors

1. Data on political rights and civil liberties.
2. Data on political rights and civil liberties.
3. Media reports on ethnic violence incidents in Armenia, Russia, and Georgia involving different groups.
4. Data on minorities and minorities at risk.
5. Media reports on Georgian and Armenian cooperation.
6. Media reports on negotiations regarding the withdrawal of Russian bases in the Caucasus, and Russian troops fighting in Chechnya.
7. Data on economic growth and government expenditure.

certain governments and groups may see this work as subversive. And third, it is critical that the use of local and dynamic data is complemented by structural data on economic and other indicators in the regions covered.

Early Response

As outlined above, preemptive and concerted responses to early warning of violent conflicts is one of the most important challenges facing policy makers today.[14] In a forthcoming introduction to a FEWER-EastWest Institute (EWI) publication on linking warning to response in the Caucasus, Glenys Kinnock, European Parliament member and chair of FEWER, Marton Krasznai of the OSCE Conflict Prevention Center, and John Mroz of EWI identify critical obstacles for effective and responses to potential conflicts. Political will, they argue, is hampered by the lack of:

- appropriate planning and implementation frameworks to bring together the range of actors, and methodology needed to plan for integrated action
- knowledge about what one can do, what others are doing, or instruments that can be used to promote peace
- knowledge about what peace-building approaches work, even if there is an understanding about what can be done
- accountability among policy makers as early warning information, and responses to this information are normally confidential, or outside of the public domain

The need to address the obstacles of political will and the complexity of peace-building work (see table 13.3) has informed the two principles that underpin the response activities of FEWER members. First, responses to conflict need to be concerted and integrated. NGOs, governments, and intergovernmental organizations have to work together, at different levels (local, regional, and international), and in different sectors (such as diplomacy, development, trade, and security) to comprehensively address the causes and dynamics of conflict. Second, responses to conflict should link short-term peacemaking with longer-term peace-building efforts, and ensure that peace processes and the definition of peace objectives are inclusive and owned by conflict-affected or conflict-prone communities.

In 1999 and 2000, together with the East-West Institute, the FEWER network moved to address the "who can do what" question in the Caucasus by surveying the regional conflict prevention instruments of the U.S. and Russian governments, European Union institutions, and Caucasian NGOs. A methodology was developed (see table 13.3) for planning and implementing integrated responses to potential and actual conflicts, thus helping to link warning with response. The methodology itself was used in Javakheti (an "early warning" situation) and yielded the plan described in table 13.4. The surveys, methodology, and work on the selected case

Table 13.3: Methodology for Developing and Implementing Integrated Peace-Building Plans

(i) Survey existing conflict/peace-related activities and actors in a given region.

(ii) Convene a group of peace-building actors (local, regional and international) for a strategic roundtable. This "coalition of the willing" is asked to:

    a) discuss conflict factors, their interconnectedness and relative importance

    b) define and agree on longer-term peace objectives for the region

    c) identify key potential spoilers

    d) identify key preventive instruments (developmental, diplomatic, security, economic, etc.) that can address (a), (b), and (c)

    e) divide up roles and responsibilities among key actors (local, regional, and international) who can play a role in building peace

    f) decide on the time-frame for activities and identify possible donors

From this roundtable a macrolevel plan is formulated which indicates the broad areas for action and key actors who need to be involved.

(iii) Carry out a needs assessment and feasibility study in the conflict prone/affected region to validate and elaborate on the plan (identification of microprojects). This study also involves extensive consultation with local stakeholders, in addition to those who took part in the roundtable.

(iv) Develop project proposals for microlevel activities and compile these into an appeal. Organize a donor meeting.

(v) Establish a steering group and subgroups on different issue areas of implementers and donors to oversee the implementation process. Identify an agency that will put in place a communication strategy for ensuring information flows implementing organizations.

(Javakheti, Georgia) are accessible on the FEWER Web site at: www.fewer.org/caucasus/index.htm.

The methodology is based on convening a broad "coalition of the willing" to work through a prepared analysis of a potential conflict situation. Rather than offering options for response in the analytical report, convened participants develop their own plans and divide roles and responsibilities among themselves. The identification of appropriate instruments for response is based on surveys of the regional conflict prevention activities of key actors.

The plan of action is subsequently validated through further consultations, situation analyses, and roundtables.

The implementation process involves establishing a steering group that oversees activities, setting up a restricted Web site where progress is posted along with other useful activities, and identifying an NGO that "chases up" information on progress.

Key challenges for the development and implementation of the peace-building plans include:

Table 13.4: Summary of the Javakheti Integrated Peace-Consolidation Plan

Agencies involved in the process include the Armenian, Georgian, Russian, U.S., British, and German governments, OSCE (headquarters and local missions), UN (UNOMIG, UNHCR, UN volunteers), European Union (TACIS, council and commission), Council of Europe, NATO, local and international think tanks.

The conflict-generating factors identified are:
1) regional instability
2) social-political isolation
3) economic underdevelopment (poor infrastructure
4) potential ethnic tensions
5) patrimonial social structures

Long-term objectives for the region include:
1) establishment of a prosperous economic zone
2) integration (political/social) and multiculturalism
3) good governance (civil society development)
4) improved regional relations (Turkish-Armenian-Georgian-Russian relations)

It was noted that the repatriation of the Meskhetian population should figure among the objectives, but that it is clearly not a priority area, given its larger national and international character. First, research must be conducted regarding the actual number of people who are willing to go back based upon individually informed decisions, not upon dissatisfaction with harassment policies or denial of residence permits (propiska).

Envisaged responses encompass:
1) strengthen local self-governance
2) conduct regional projects and cross-border cooperation
3) guarantee multilingual education and broadcasting
4) organize professional (re)training
5) develop SMEs
6) engage in NGO capacity building
7) raise awareness and promote information exchange (Georgia<->Dzhavakheti);
8) stimulate interconfessional and interethnic dialogue
9) build basic infrastructure
10) conduct research into and establish a management plan for the repatriation of the Meskhetian population

- the methodology is most suitable in preconflict situations, rather than actual high-intensity conflict situations
- the planning of responses to subnational potential conflicts needs to address also other conflict generating issues at a national level

- a low-profile approach is required for the roundtables themselves, and midlevel policy makers should attend in order to avoid rapid politicisation of the work

Preliminary Conclusions

A number of challenges for operational early warning and responses activities have been identified above.

- The range of objectives, methods, and approaches in the field needs to be addressed in order to come closer to an understanding of what constitutes "good practice" in early warning. This will mean creating more effective synergy between qualitative and quantitative approaches, and the research-practice communities.
- Although there is an emerging trend to draw on the value of local analytical capacities, and move away from a more extractive and interventionist paradigm, current efforts are far too limited. Stronger links between local and international early warning capabilities still need to be forged.
- Current "good practice" efforts need further streamlining and resources in order to make them fully effective and enhance the timeliness of analyses produced.
- Approaches to tackle bias, as it emerges from local, newswire, and international expert sources, remain to be fully developed.
- Generating responses to early warning remains a difficulty for warners. Inclusive methods and processes to link warning with response in a variety of different conflict contexts, need to be strengthened.

Policy Analysis and Future Directions

The broadness of the above discussion reflects the wealth of the research and applied practice that has gone into the early warning field over the last two decades. This book, and its contributors provide a range of perspectives on the way forward. Below, therefore, we will only highlight some key issues that we consider of particular importance.

Early Warning

Four key principles and directions emerge from the literature and practice surveyed in this chapter. First, warners need to provide early warning and directions for response at all stages of the conflict continuum. The value of warning is reduced if its focus is solely on predicting the outbreak of violence. Second, the development of cost-effective and streamlined early warning systems requires the marrying of multiple approaches, local and international research, research and practice, and quantitative and qualitative methods. Third, emphasis needs to be placed on strengthening local early warning capacities in regions of conflict. The voices from conflict prone and affected communities should be made more audible by supporting local groups and enhancing their credibility. Fourth, making early warning available to the general public will help generate more political will for appropriate response and reduce the accountability deficit of responders.

Early Response

Three principles and directions can be outlined. First, it is clear that early warning analyses need to serve as the basis for response. A common understanding of conflict dynamics among a coalition of responders is a precondition of effective preventive action. Second, warning should inform both short-term peacemaking and long-term peace-building efforts, and the use of a range of preventive instruments. Integrated action is critical for the achievement of sustainable peace. Third, the definition of responses needs to be based on inclusive processes involving a range of local, regional, and international actors. Top-down or select interventionist approaches do not work.

In addition to the principles outlined above, some final conclusions can be drawn on future directions for the early warning field. These are described below in relation to (a) the interventionist paradigm; (b) developments in the information and communication technology field; and (c) the management of source and analytical bias.

Interventionist Paradigm

It is clear that an interventionist approach to preventive action is flawed. As emerges from Leonardt and Nyheim's (1999) metaphor, effective responses to conflict require integrated action, and action that is owned by communities in conflict prone/affected areas. This points to the need to ensure that local perspectives are fully available to responders through early warning analyses, and that the response definition process is both inclusive and comprehensive. The approach of FEWER members to linking warning and response is one promising alternative to the interventionist paradigm.

Information and Communication Technology (ICT)

Information is often abundant in conflict situations. Policy makers frequently complain about information overload and the poor timeliness of early warning analyses. Initiatives such as the GEDS and KEDS projects are promising developments that enhance our ability to process quickly large amounts of information. The current revolution in the ICT field makes it possible to electronically access digital information and knowledge by virtually anyone, anytime, and anywhere. A key challenge for warners will be to capitalize on these developments.

Bias

Bias in early warning is to be found both in the information sources used, as well as emerging analyses. It is important to move away from the standard concern of local sources being biased. Early warning is also an act of writing history. It is safe to estimate that more than 90 percent of U.S. history, for example, has been written by Americans. Bias is a local, as well as an international phenomenon. It will be found in external "expert" analyses of a situation, multilateral fact-finding mission reports, as well as in local situation reports. Different sources of information used for early warning will be biased. Newswire coverage of situations will be profoundly skewed as governments and other powers "spin" policy and the coverage of their actions (Iraq, Kosovo, etc.) in the media. Part of the future challenge for warners will be to access the broadest range of sources, and find mechanisms for the effective management of bias.

Notes

1. This chapter draws on the wealth of experience and expertise in the early warning field. It is largely a summary and analysis of research by CEWS academics and FEWER members and staff. Specific thanks go to Sally Chin, Rohini Deshmukh, Kristina Mitchell, and Ross Ashworth, previously at the FEWER Secretariat. Also, to our CEWS colleagues whose groundbreaking research will take the field forward in years to come.

2. Led by the Russian Academy of Sciences/EAWARN (Russia), with Caucasian Institute for Peace, Democracy and Development (Georgia), and the GEDS group of the University of Maryland.

3. Led by the Africa Peace Forum (Kenya), and supported by the GEDS group of the University of Maryland.

4. Led by the West Africa Network for Peacebuilding (Ghana).

5. Led by the Russian Academy of Sciences/EAWARN (Russia), with the FAST group of the Swiss Peace Foundation (Switzerland).

6. Led by the Gaston Z. Ortiga Peace Institute (Philippines).

7. Data on political rights and civil liberties.

8. Data on political rights and civil liberties.

9. Media reports on ethnic violence incidents in Armenia, Russia and Georgia involving different groups.

10. Data on minorities and minorities at risk.

11. Media reports on Georgian and Armenian cooperation.

12. Media reports on negotiations regarding the withdrawal of Russian bases in the Caucasus, and Russian troops fighting in Chechnya.

13. Data on economic growth and government expenditure.

14. Leonhardt and Nyheim (1999) draw a useful metaphor in their comparison of peacebuilding with house construction.

> Bricks and material are peace-building activities, processes and principles.
> The builders are the communities, NGOs, governments and IGOs who

implement projects. The environment of the house is the context of conflict and peace. The architecture is the vision and objective we define for peacebuilding. And the inhabitants of the house are those communities who have to live with the "peace" that is built.

The metaphor helps us understand the different elements required for responding to warning, namely what activities are required, who does what, who works with whom, what are the objectives, and who owns them. It places emphasis on the need to ensure that proper situation analyses inform responses to conflict and that processes are in place for integrated planning and implementation of activities that are owned by local communities, and thus become more sustainable.

References

Abelson, H., and G. J. Sussman with J. Sussman. (1995). *Structure and Interpretation of Computer Programs.* Cambridge, MA: MIT Press.
Acharya, A., and D. Dewitt. (1997). "Fiscal Burden Sharing." In *Reconceiving International Refugee Law,* edited by J. C. Hathaway. The Hague: Martinus Nijhoff.
Ackermann, A. (1996). "The Former Yugoslav Republic of Macedonia: A Relatively Successful Case of Conflict Prevention in Europe." *Security Dialogue* 27 (4): 409–424.
Ackermann, A., and A. Pala. (1996). "From Peacekeeping to Preventive Deployment: A Study of the United Nations in the Former Yugoslav Republic of Macedonia." *European Security* 5 (1): 83–97.
Adelman, H., and A. Suhrke. (1996). "Early Warning and Response: Why the International Community Failed to Prevent the Genocide." *Disasters* 20 (4): 295–304.
Adelman, H., and A. Suhrke. (1999). *The Path of a Genocide: The Rwanda Crisis from Uganda to Zaire.* New Brunswick, NJ: Transaction Publishers.
Adelman, H. (1993). "Towards an Early Warning System." In *Report from the Phase 3, May 27–28, 1993 Workshop.* York, Ontario: Center for Refugee Studies.
Adibi, J., H. R. Alker, M. Malita, and L. T. Vest Jr. (1998). "PARIS: A Prototype Action Recommender's Information Support System for Conflict Prevention." *Romanian Journal of International Affairs* 4 (1): 75–108.
Agropromyshlenij kompleks of the Soviet Union. (1990). Moscow.
Ahmed, A., and E. V. Kassinis. (1998). "The Humanitarian Early Warning System (HEWS): From Concept to Practice" In Davies and Gurr eds. (1988).
Ahmed, I. (1996). *State, Nation and Ethnicity in Contemporary South Asia.* London and New York: Pinter.
Ali, S. M. (1993). *The Fearful State: Power, People and Internal War in South Asia.* London: Zed Books.
Alker, H. R. (1974). "Are There Structural Models of Voluntaristic Social Action?" *Quality and Quantity* 8: 199–246.

Alker, H. R. (1988). "Emancipatory Empiricism: Towards the Renewal of Empirical Peace Research." In *Peace Research: Achievements and Challenges,* edited by P. Wallenstein, Boulder, CO: Westview.

Alker, H. R., Jr. (1993). "Making Peaceful Sense of the News: Institutionalizing International Conflict-Management Event Reporting Using Frame-Based Interpretive Routines." In *International Event-Data Developments: DDIR Phase II,* edited by R. L. Merritt, R. G. Muncaster, and D. A. Zinnes. Ann Arbor: University of Michigan Press.

Alker, H. R. (1994a). "Early Warning Models and/or Preventive Information Systems?" In Gurr and Harff, eds. (1994).

Alker, H. R. (1994b). "Globalizing the Conflict Prevention Knowledge Base: A Proposal of the Conflict Early Warning Systems (CEWS) Research Program of the International Social Science Council." From the Center for International Studies, School of International Relations, University of Southern California to the Carnegie Corporation of New York, covering the period January 1, 1995, until May 1, 1997. Photocopy.

Alker, H. R. (1996a). *Rediscoveries and Reformulations: Humanistic Methodologies for International Studies.* Cambridge: Cambridge University Press.

Alker, H. R. (1996b). "Draft Guidelines for Contributors to the CEWS Comparative Study of Conflict Prevention Successes and Failures." Photocopied memo of six pages in length, July 29, 1996.

Alker, H. R., Jr., and C. Christensen. (1972). "From Causal Modeling to Artificial Intelligence: The Evolution of a UN Peacemaking Simulation." In LaPonce and Smoker, eds., *Eperimentation and Simulation in Political Science.* Toronto: University of Toronto Press.

Alker, H. R., and K. Mushakoji. (2000). "Three Times for Tomorrow." In *Time in the Making and Possible Futures,* edited by E. R. Larreta, coordinated by C. Mendes. Rio de Janeiro: UNESCO/ISSC/EDUCAM.

Alker, H. R., Jr., and W. J. Greenberg. (1971). "The UN Charter: Alternative Pasts and Futures." In *The United Nations: Problems and Prospects,* edited by E. H. Fedder. St. Louis: University of Missouri Press.

Alker, H. R., Jr., and W. J. Greenberg. (1977). "On Simulating Collective Security Regime Alternatives." In *Thought and Action in Foreign Policy,* edited by G. M. Bonham and M. J. Shapiro. Basel: Birkhauser Verlag.

Alker, H. R., and F. L. Sherman. (1995). "Historical Possibilities for Collective Security-Seeking Practices." In *Las Naciones Unidas a los Cincuenta Anos,* edited by M. S. Vazquez. Mexico, D.F.: Fondo de Cultura Economica.

Alker, H. R., Jr., and F. L. Sherman. (1982). "Collective Security-Seeking Practices since 1945." In *Managing International Crises,* edited by D. Frei. Beverly Hills, CA: Sage.

Alker, H. R., T. R. Gurr, and K. Rupesinghe. (1995). "Conflict Early Warning Systems: An Initial Research Program." Presented at the Annual Meeting of the International Studies Association, Chicago, February 21–24.

Alker, H. R., T. Schmalberger, A. Blum, and A. Schjølset. (1999). "Testable Understandings of Structured Histories: With Examples from a Comparative Study of Conflict Prevention Successes and Failures." Paper presented at the Annual Meeting of the International Studies Association, Washington, DC. Available at www.usc.edu/dept/LAS/ir/cis/cews.html.

Amnesty International. (1990). *The Philippines: A Summary of AI's Concerns.* London: AIP.

Amnesty International. (1991). *Report on the Philippines.* London: AIP.

Amnesty International. (1992). *People's Republic of China—Repression in Tibet 1987– 1992.* New York: Amnesty International.

Amnesty International. (1995). *Sierra Leone: Human Rights Abuses in a War Against Civilians.* London: AIP.

Andersen, W. K. (1990). "Multiethnic Conflict and Peacemaking: The Case of Assam." In Montville.

Angola Update. (1994). 3 (9, 10, 12).

Angola Update. (1997). 6 (2).

ANGOP, various numbers between no. 90 (February 10, 1988) and no. 166 (August 20, 1991). UK: Agencia Angola Press.

Annan, K. (1999). "Keynote Address to the Conference on Preventing Deadly Conflict Among Nations in the Twenty-First Century." University of California at Los Angeles, April, 22, UN Press Release SG/SM/6534.

Annan, K. (1999). "The Causes of Conflict and the Promotion of Durable Peace and Sustainable Development in Africa." New York: United Nations.

Annan, K. (1999). "Facing the Humanitarian Challenge: Towards a Culture of Prevention."

Apodaca, C. (1998). "Human Rights Abuses: Precursor to Refugee Flight?" *Journal of Refugee Studies* 11 (1): 80–93.

Appel, H., and J. Gould. (2000). "Identity Politics and Economic Reform: Examining Industry-State Relations in the Czech and Slovak Republics." *Europe-Asia Studies* 52 (1): 111–131.

Appleby, J. et al. (1996). *Knowledge and Postmodernism in Historical Perspective.* New York: Routledge.

Arbatov, Aleksei, Abram Chayes, Antonia Handler Chayes, and Lara Olson, eds. (1997). *Managing Conflict in the Former Soviet Union. Russian and American Perspectives.* Cambridge, MA: MIT Press.

Ashworth, G. (1977). "Muslims in the Philippines." In *World Minorities, Vol. 1*, edited by G. Ashworth (pp. 125–130). London: Quartermaine House Ltd. for Minority Rights Group.

Ataman, Yuri. (1999). "Moldova." In *International Mediation—Case Studies and General Conclusions*, ed. Lars Truedson. Report from a seminar coorganized by the Olof Palme International Center and the Stockholm International Peace Research Institute, SIPRI. Stockholm: The Olof Palme International Center.

Ayres, R. W. (1998). "Strategies and Outcome in Post–Soviet Nationalist Secession." *International Politics* 35: 135–163.

Azar, E. E. (1980). "The Conflict and Peace Data Bank (COPDAB) Project." *Journal of Conflict Resolution* 24 (1): 143–152.

Banks, A. S., et al., eds. (various years). *Political Handbook of the World.* New York: McGraw-Hill.

Barnett, R. ed. (1994). *Resistance and Reform in Tibet.* Bloomington: Indiana University Press.

Baxter, C., Y. K. Malik, C. H. Kennedy, and R. C. Oberst. (1987). *Government and Politics in South Asia.* Boulder, CO: Westview Press.

Behera, N. C., P. M. Evans, and G. Rizvi. (1997). *Beyond Boundaries: A Report on the State of Non-Official Dialogues on Peace, Security, & Cooperation in South Asia.* Toronto, Ontario: University of Toronto-York University.

Bercovitch, J., ed. (1996). *Resolving International Conflicts: The Theory and Practice of Mediation.* Boulder, CO: Lynne Rienner.

Bercovitch, J., T. Agnoson, and D. Willie. (1991). "Some Conceptual Issues and Empirical Trends in the Study of Successful Mediation in International Relations." *Journal of Peace Research*, 28 (1): 7–17.

Beska, V. P. (1995). "Non-Governmental Organizations, Early Warning, and Preventive Diplomacy: The Case of Macedonia." Unpublished manuscript, Faculty of Philosophy, University St. Cyril and Methodius, Skopje.

Bhaumik, S. (1996). *Insurgent Crossfire: Northeast India.* New Delhi and London: Lancer Publishers.

Biberaj, E. (1993). *Kosova: The Balkan Powder Keg.* London: Research Institute for the Study of Conflict and Terrorism.

Blank, S., and T. Young. (1992). *Challenges to Eastern European Security in the Nineties.* Carlisle, PA: Strategic Studies Institute, U.S. Army War College.

Blazyca, G. (1998). "The Politics of Economic Transformation." In *Developments in Central and East European Politics,* edited by S. White, J. Bhatt, and P. G. Lewis. Durham, NC: Duke University Press.

Bloomfield, L. P. (1988). "Computerizing Conflicts." *Foreign Service Journal,* June 1988: 46–49.

Bloomfield, L P., and A. Leiss. (1969). *Controlling Small Wars: A Strategy for the 1970s.* New York: Knopf.

Bloomfield, L. P., and A. Moulton. (1997). *Managing International Conflict: From Theory to Policy, a Teaching Tool Using CASCON.* New York: St. Martin's Press.

Bookman, M. Z. (1994). "War and Peace: The Divergent Breakups of Yugoslavia and Czechoslovakia." *Journal of Peace Research* 31 (2): 175–187.

Bordas, S., et al. (1995). *Counter-Proof: The Examination of the Slovak-Hungarian Relationship with Sociologic and Ethnopsychological Methods in Slovakia.* Nap Publishers.

Boutros-Ghali, B. (1992). *An Agenda for Peace: Preventive Diplomacy, Peacemaking and Peacekeeping.* New York: United Nations.

Bowers, S. (1994). "Tibet Since Mao Zedong." *Journal of Social, Political & Economic Studies* 19 (4) (Winter): 409–432.

Bray, J. (1990). "China and Tibet—An End to Empire." *World Today* (December): 221– 224.

Brecher, M., and J. Wilkenfeld. (1989). *Crisis, Conflict, and Instability.* Oxford: Pergamon Press.

Brecher, M., J. Wilkenfeld, and S. Moser. (1988). *Crises in the Twentieth Century,* Vol. I. Oxford: Pergamon Press.

Brecke, P. (1998). "Finding Harbingers of Violent Conflict: Using Pattern Recognition to Anticipate Conflicts." *Conflict Management and Peace Science* 16 (1): 31–56.

"Bringing in Buthelezi. How the IFP was drawn into the election." (1994). *Track Two* 3 (2/3).

Brown, M. E., and S. Ganguly, eds. (1997). *Government Policies and Ethnic Relations in Asia and the Pacific.* Cambridge, MA: MIT Press.

Burgerman, S. D. (1995). "The United Nations Secretary General as Third Party to the Salvadoran Peace Process." *Estudios Internacionales.* No. 12.

Camplisson, Joe, and Michael Hall. (1996). *Hidden Frontiers. Addressing Deep-Rooted Violent Conflict in Northern Ireland and the Republic of Moldova.* Newtownabbey: Island Publications.

Carnegie Commission on Preventing Deadly Conflict. (1997). *Preventing Deadly Conflict, Final Report.* Washington, DC: Carnegie Commission on Preventing Deadly Conflict.

Carment, D., and P. James, eds. (1998). *Peace in the Midst of Wars: Preventing and Managing International Ethnic Conflicts.* Columbia University of South Carolina Press.

Casino, E. S. (1987). "Interethnic Conflict in the Philippine Archipelago." In *Ethnic Conflict: International Perspectives,* edited by J. Boucher, D. Landis, and K. A. Clark. London: Sage Publications.

Cassidy, M. (1995). *A Witness for Ever: The Dawning of Democracy in South Africa. Stories Behind the Story.* United Kingdom: Hodder & Stoughton Ltd.

Cederman, L-E. (1996). "Rerunning History: Counterfactual Simulation in World Politics." In Tetlock and Belkin.

Central Intelligence Agency. (various years). *The World Factbook.* Washington, DC: Brasseys. See also on-line: www.odci.gov/cia/publications/factbook/country-frame.html.

Chadda, M. (1997). *Ethnicity, Security, and Separatism in India.* New York: Columbia University Press.

Chayes, A., and A. H. Chayes. (1996). *Preventing Conflict in the Post–Communist World.* Washington, DC: Brookings Institution.

Chihara, C. S. (1998). *The Worlds of Possibility: Modal Realism and the Sematics of Modal Logic.* Oxford: Clarendon Press.

Choedon, Y. (1990). "Ethnic, Social, and Religious Conflict—Rights of Minorities." In *Ethnic, Social and Religious Conflict—The Rights of Minorities*, occasional paper from presentations of the Working Group on Minorities, World Congress on Human Rights, New Delhi, India, December. London: Minority Rights Group.

Clapham, C. (1998). "Rwanda: The Perils of Peacemaking." *Journal of Peace Research* 35 (2): 193–210.

Clark, I. (1997). *Globalization and Fragmention: International Relations in the Twentieth Century.* Oxford: Oxford University Press.

Coalition for Peace. (1993). "Basic Peace: Peace Agenda of Four Sectors." Quezon City: Coalition for Peace.

Comprehensive Agreement on Human Rights and Humanitarian Law. (1998). Government of the Republic of the Philippines and the National Democratic Front, March 16.

Conference on Security and Cooperation in Europe, Mission to Moldova. (1993). *Report* No. 13, November 16.

Cranna, M. (1994). "The Kashmir Conflict." In *The True Cost of Conflict: Seven Recent Wars and Their Effect on Society*, edited by Michael Cranna. New York: The New Press.

Cresswell, M. J. (1988). *Semantical Essays.* Boston: Kluwer.

Daily News (1994). Articles focused on the IFP's involvement in the 1994 elections, January–mid-April.

David, S. R. (1997). "Internal War: Causes and Cures." *World Politics* 49 (4) (July): 552–576.

Davies, J., and T. R. Gurr, eds. (1998). *Preventive Measures: Building Risk Assessment and Crisis Early Warning Systems.* Lanham, MD: Rowman & Littlefield.

Day, A. J., ed. (1987). *Border and Territorial Disputes.* Harlow, England: Longman.

Day, A. J., and H. W. Degenhardt, eds. (1980). *Political Parties of the World.* Harlow, England: Longman.

Dedring, J. (1992). "Socio-political Indicators for Early Warning Purposes." In Rupesinghe and Kuroda, ed.

DeNevers, R. (1999). "Slovakia." In *The Cost of Conflict*, edited by M. Brown and R. Rosecrance. Lanham, MD: Rowman & Littlefield.

Der Derian, J., and M. Shapiro, eds. (1989). *International/Intertextual Relations: Postmodern Rereadings of World Politics.* Lexington, MA: Lexington Books.

Deutsch, K. W., B. Fritsch, H. Jaguaribe, and A. Markovits. (1997). *Problems of World Modeling: Political and Social Implications.* Cambridge, MA: Ballinger Publishing Company.

Diller, J. M. (1997). *Handbook on Human Rights in Situations of Conflict.* Minneapolis: Minnesota Advocates for Human Rights.

Diplomaticheskij vestnik. (1994). No. 21–22: 47–51.

Dixon, W. J. (1996). "Third-Party Techniques for Preventing Conflict Escalation and Promoting Peaceful Settlement." *International Organization* 50 (4) (Autumn): 653–681.

Dorn, A W. (1997). "Early (and Late) Warning by the UN Secretary-General: Article 99 Revisited." In Schmeidl and Adelman, eds.

Drew, E. (1994). *On the Edge: The Clinton Presidency.* New York: Simon and Schuster.

Dueck, J., and a HURIDOCS Task Force. (1993). "HURIDOCS Standard Formats: A Tool for Documenting Human Rights Violations." Oslo: HURIDOCS. Current versions should be available from the HURIDOCS Secretariat, 2 rue Jean-Jacquet, CH1201 Geneva, Switzerland.

Duffy, G. (1994). "Events and Versions: Reconstructing Event Data Analysis." In Duffy ed. (1994).

Duffy, G., ed. (1994). *New Directions in Events Data Analysis.* Special issue, *International Interactions.* 20 (1–2): 1–167.

Duleba, A. (1997). "Democratic Consolidation and the Conflict over Slovakian International Alignment." In *Slovakia: Problems of Democratic Consolidation and the Struggle for the Rules of the Game,* edited by S. Szomolnyi and J. Gould. New York: Columbia International Affairs Online.

Economist, The (1990). *Book of Vital World Statistics.* London: Hutchinson.

Eisenberg, M., and Abelson, H. (1990). *Programming in Scheme.* Cambridge, MA: The MIT Press.

Eller, J. D. (1999). *From Culture to Ethnicity to Conflict: An Anthropological Perspective on International Ethnic Conflict.* Ann Arbor: University of Michigan Press.

Emizet, K. N. F. (1997). *Zaire after Mobutu: A Case of a Humanitarian Emergency.* Helsinki: UNU World Institute for Development Economics Research, Research for Action 32.

Esty, D. C., et al. (1995). *Working Papers State Failure Task Force Report.* McLean, VA: Science Applications International Corporation.

Esty, D. C., J. A. Goldstone, T. R. Gurr, B. Harff, P. T. Surko, A. N. Unger, and R. Chen. (1998). "The State Failure Project: Early Warning Research for U.S. Foreign Policy Planning." In Davies and Gurr.

Esty, D. C., J. A. Goldstone, B. Harff, M. Levy, G. D. Dabelko, P. T. Surko, and A. N. Unger (1999). "State Failure Task Force Report: Phase II Findings." The Woodrow Wilson Center, *Environmental Change & Security Project Report,* 5 (Summer): 49–72.

European Centre for Conflict Prevention in cooperation with IFOR and the Coexistence Initiative of State of the World Forum. (1999). *People Building Peace: 35 Inspiring Stories from Around the World.* Utrecht: European Center for Conflict Prevention.

European Platform for Conflict Prevention and Transformation in cooperation with PIOOM and the Berghof Research Institute for Constructive Conflict Management, eds. (1998). *Prevention and Management of Violent Conflicts.* Utrecht: European Center for Conflict Prevention.

European Platform for Conflict Prevention and Transformation, in cooperation with the African Center for the Constructive Resolution of Disputes. (1999). *Searching for Peace in Africa: An Overview of Conflict Prevention and Management Activities,* edited by M. Mekenkamp, P. van Tongeren, and H. van de Veen. Utrecht: European Platform for Conflict Prevention and Transformation.

Evans, G., and S. Whitefield. (1998). "The Structuring of Political Cleavages in Post–Communist Societies: The Case of the Czech Republic and Slovakia." *Political Studies* 46 (1): 115–139.

Falla, R. (1992). *Massacres de la Selva. Ixcán, Guatemala (1975–1982)* Guatemala: Editorial Universitaria.

Falla R. (1995). *Las Masacres en Rabinal: Estudio Histórico Antropológico de las Masacres de Plan de Sánchez, Chichupac y Rio Negro.* Guatemala: Equipo de Antropología Forense de Guatemala.

Fearon, J. D. (1991). "Counterfactuals and Hypothesis Testing in Political Science." *World Politics* 43 (2): 169–195.

Fein, H. (1993a). "Accounting for Genocide After 1945: Theories and Some Findings." *International Journal of Group Rights* 1: 79–106.

Fein, H. (1993b). *Genocide: A Sociological Perspective.* London: Sage Publications for the International Sociological Association.

Fein, H. (1994). "Tools and Alarms: Uses of Models for Explanation and Anticipation." In Gurr and Harff, eds.

Ferguson, N., ed. (1998). *Virtual History: Alternatives and Counterfactuals.* London: Papermac.

Ferguson, N. (1999). *The Pity of War: Explaining World War I.* New York: Basic Books.

Ferrer, M. C., and A. Raquiza, eds. (1993). *Motions for Peace: A Summary of Events Related to Negotiating the Communist Insurgency in the Philippines 1986–92.* Quezon City, Philippines: Coalition for Peace.

FEWER. (1997). *Mission Statement.* Forum on Early Warning and Early Response. York, England: FEWER, February 19.

FEWER and the EastWest Institute (forthcoming). *Linking Warning to Response in the Caucasus.* London: FEWER.

Fischer, D. H. (1970). *Historians' Fallacies.* New York: Harper Colophon Books.

Fisher, R. J., and L. Keashly. (1991). "The Potential Complementarity of Mediation and Consultation within a Contingency Model of Third Party Intervention." *Journal of Peace Research* 28 (1): 29–42.

Freedom House Survey Team. (various years). "Freedom in the World." *The Annual Survey of Political Rights and Civil Liberties.* New York: Freedom House.

Gagnon, V. P. (1994–1995). "Ethnic Nationalism and International Conflict: The Case of Serbia." *International Security* 19 (3): 130–166.

Gallagher, T. (1998). "The Balkans: Bulgaria, Romania, Albania, and the Former Yugoslavia." In *Developments in Central and East European Politics,* edited by S. White, J. Bhatt, and P. G. Lewis. Durham, NC: Duke University Press.

Galtung, J. (1995). *Choose Peace: A Dialogue Between Johan Galtung and Daisaky Ikeda.* Trans. and edited by R. L. Gage. Boulder, CO: Pluto Press.

Galtung, J. (1996). *Peace by Peaceful Means: Peace and Conflict, Development and Civilization.* Oslo: International Peace Research Institute.

Ganguly, S. (1996a). "Conflict and Crisis in South and Southwest Asia." In *The International Dimensions of Internal Conflict,* edited by M. E. Brown. Cambridge, MA: MIT Press.

Ganguly, S. (1996b). "Explaining the Kashmir Insurgency: Political Mobilization and Institutional Decay." *International Security* 21 (2) (Fall): 76–107.

Ganguly, S. (1997a). *The Crisis in Kashmir: Portents of War, Hopes of Peace.* New York: Woodrow Wilson Center.

Ganguly, R. (1997b). "The Move Towards Disintegration: Explaining Ethnosecessionist Mobilization in South Asia." *Nationalism and Ethnic Politics* 3 (2) (Summer): 101–130.

Garcia, E., (1993). *Participative Approaches to Peacemaking in the Philippines*. Tokyo: United Nations University.

Garcia E., ed. (1993). *Participation in Governance: The People's Rights*. Quezon City, Philippines: Ateneo de Manila University Press.

Garfinkel, H. (1967). *Studies in Ethnomethodology*. Englewood Cliffs, NJ: Prentice Hall.

Gastil, R. D. (1986). *Freedom in the World: Political Rights and Civil Liberties, 1985– 1986*. New York: Freedom House.

Geiss, I. (1967). *July 1919, the Outbreak of the First World War: Selected Documents*. New York: Scribner's.

George, A. L. (1979). "Case Studies and Theory Development: The Method of Structured, Focused Comparison." In *Diplomatic History: New Approaches in History, Theory and Policy*, edited by P. G. Lauren. New York: Free Press.

George, A. L., and J. E. Holl. (1996). *The Warning-Response Problem and Missed Opportunities in Preventive Diplomacy*. New York: Carnegie Commission on Deadly Conflict.

George, A. L., and T. J. McKeown. (1985). "Case Studies and Theories of Organizational Decision Making." In *Advances in Information Processing in Organizations*, vol. 2. Greenwich, CT: JAI Press.

George, T. J. S. (1980). *Revolt in Mindanao: The Rise of Islam in Philippine Politics*. Kuala Lumpur, Malaysia: Oxford University Press.

Gibney, M., C. Apodaca, and J. McCann. (1996). "Refugee Flows, the Internally Displaced and Political Violence (1980–1993): An Exploratory Analysis." In *Whither Refugee? The Refugee Crisis: Problems and Solutions*, edited by A. P. Schmid. Leiden, the Netherlands: PIOOM.

Gleijeses, Piero (1991). *Shattered Hope. The Guatemalan Revolution and the United States, 1944–1954*. Princeton, NJ: Princeton University Press.

Goodman, N. (1978). *Ways of Worldmaking*. Cambridge: Hackett.

Goodman, N. (1983). *Fact, Fiction, and Forecast*, 4th ed. Cambridge, MA: Harvard University Press.

Gopinath, A. (1991). "International Aspects of the Thai Muslim and Philippine Muslim Issues: A Comparative Study." In *Internationalization of Ethnic Conflict*, edited by K. M. de Silva and R. J. May. London: International Center for Ethnic Studies.

Gordenker, L. (1992). "Early Warning: Conceptual and Practical Issues." In Rupesinghe and Kuroda eds. (1992).

Graeger, Nina. (1995). "Moldova and Transdniestr." In *Conflicts in the OSCE Area*. Oslo: International Peace Research Institute.

Gurr, T. R. (1992). "Designing Early-Warning Systems for Conflict-Prevention and Humanitarian Assistance: A Proposal for Coordinated Social Science Planning and Research." Draft 3.1, typescript. College Park. University of Maryland.

Gurr, T. R. (1993a). *Minorities at Risk: A Global View of Ethnopolitical Conflict*. Washington, DC: U.S. Institute of Peace Press. See also the *Minorities at Risk Dataset* on-line at: www.bsos.umd.edu/cidcm/mar.

Gurr, T. R. (1993b). "Why Minorities Rebel: A Global Analysis of Communal Mobilization and Conflict since 1945." *International Political Science Review* 14: 161– 201.

Gurr, T. R. (1994a). "Testing and Using a Model of Communal Conflict for Early Warning." In Gurr and Harff, eds.

Gurr, T. R. (1994b). "Peoples Against States: Ethnopolitical Conflict and the Changing World System." *International Studies Quarterly* 38 (3) (September): 347–377.

Gurr, T. R. (1998). "A Risk Assessment Model of Ethnopolitical Rebellion." In Davies and Gurr, eds.

Gurr, T. R. (2000). *Peoples Versus States: Minorities at Risk in the New Century*. Washington, DC: US Institute of Peace Press.

Gurr, T. R., and B. Harff, eds. (1994). *Early Warning of Communal Conflicts and Humanitarian Crises*. A Special Issue of *The Journal of Ethno-Development* 4 (1).

Gurr, T. R., and B. Harff. (1994a). "Conceptual, Research, and Policy Issues in Early Warning Research: An Overview." In Gurr and Harff, eds.

Gurr, T. R., and B. Harff. (1994b). *Ethnic Conflict in World Politics*. Boulder, CO: Westview Press.

Gurr, T. R., and B. Harff. (1996). *Early Warning of Communal Conflicts and Genocide: Linking Empirical Research to International Responses.* Monograph Series on Governance and Conflict Resolution. Tokyo: United Nations University.

Gurr, T. R., and M. I. Lichbach. (1986). "Forecasting Internal Conflict: A Competitive Evaluation of Empirical Theories." *Comparative Political Studies* 19 (1) (April): 3– 38.

Haas, E. B. (1968). *Collective Security and the Future International System*. Denver: Graduate School of International Affairs Studies Monograph Series.

Haas, E. B. (1993). "Collective Conflict Management: Evidence for a New World Order?" In *Collective Security in a Changing World,* edited by T. G. Weiss. Boulder, CO: Lynne Rienner.

Haass, R. N. (1990). *Conflicts Unending: The United States and Regional Disputes*. New Haven, CT: Yale University Press.

Haass, R. N. (1998). *Intervention: The Use of American Military Force in the Post–Cold War World,* revised edition. A Carnegie Endowment Book. Washington, DC: Brookings Institution Press.

Hagerty, D. T. (1995–1996). "Nuclear Deterrence in South Asia: The 1990 Indo-Pakistani Crisis." *International Security* 20 (3) (Winter): 79–114.

Hamm, B. (1998). "The Usefulness of Structural Data for Early Warning Models." Pan-European International Relations and International Studies Association, Vienna, September.

Hannum, H. (1990). *Autonomy, Sovereignty, and Self-Determination—The Accommodation of Conflicting Rights*. Philadelphia: University of Pennsylvania Press.

Harff, B. (1992a). "Bosnia and Somalia: Strategic, Legal, and Moral Dimensions of Humanitarian Intervention." *Report from the Institute for Philosophy and Public Policy* 12 (3/4) (Summer/Fall): 1–7.

Harff, B. (1992b). "Recognizing Genocides and Politicides." In *Genocide Watch*, edited by H. Fein. New Haven, CT: Yale University Press.

Harff, B. (1996). "Early Warning of Potential Genocide: The Cases of Rwanda, Burundi, Bosnia, and Abkhazia." In Gurr and Harff.

Harff, B. (1998). "Early Warning of Humanitarian Crises: Sequential Models and the Role of Accelerators." In Davies and Gurr (pp. 70–78).

Harff, B., and T. R. Gurr. (1988). "Toward Empirical Theory of Genocides and Politicides: Identification and Measurement of cases since 1945." *International Studies Quarterly* 32 (3): 359–371.

Harff, B., and T. R. Gurr. (1992). "Victims of the State: Genocides Politicides and Group Repression since 1945." *Estudios Internacionales* no. 6 (July–December): 96–119.

Harff, B., and T. R. Gurr. (1998). "Systematic Early Warning of Humanitarian Emergencies." *Journal of Peace Research* 35 (5): 551–579.

Harff, B., P. T. Surko, and A. N. Unger. (forthcoming). "Risk Assessment and Early Warning of Genocides and Political Mass Murder: Two Empirical Studies." *Journal of Conflict Resolution.*

Harris, Z. S. (1952). *Structureal Linguistics.* Chicago: University of Chicago Press.

Hart, K., et al., eds. (1995). *Why Angola Matters.* Cambridge: African Studies Centre, University of Cambridge.

Harvey, B., and M. Wright. (1994). *Simply Scheme.* Cambridge, MA: MIT Press.

Hayner, P. B. (1994). "Fifteen Truth Commissions—1974 to 1994: A Comparative Study." *Human Rights Quarterly* 16(4): 591–665.

Hedges, C. (1999). "Kosovo's Next Masters?" *Foreign Affairs* 78 (3) (May/June): 24–42.

Helman, G.B., and S. R. Ratner. (1992–1993). "Saving Failing States." *Foreign Policy* 89 (Winter): 3–20.

Helsinki Committee for Human Rights in Serbia (1995). *Hate Speech as Freedom of Speech.* Belgrade.

Heraclides, A. (1991). *The Self-Determination of Minorities in International Politics.* London: Frank Cass.

Hudson, V., ed. (1990). *Artificial Intelligence and International Politics.* Boulder, CO: Westview.

Hume, C. (1994). *Ending Mozambique's War, The Role of Mediation and Good Offices.* Washington DC: U.S. Institute for Peace Press.

Husserl, E. (1970a). *The Crisis of European Sciences and Transcendental Phenomenology: An Introduction to Phenomenological Philosophy,* trans. with an introduction by D. Carr. Evanston, IL: Northwestern University Press.

Husserl, E. (1970b). *Logical Investigations,* trans. J. N. Findlay. New York: Humanities Press.

Husserl, E. (1973a). *Experience and Judgment: Investigations in a Genealogy of Logic,* revised and edited by L. Landgrebe, trans. J. S. Churchill, and K. Ameriks. Evanston, IL: Northwestern University Press.

Husserl, E. (1973b). *The Idea of Phenomenology,* trans. by W. P. Alston and G. Nakhnikian, introduction by G. Nakhnikian. The Hague: Nijhoff.

Husserl, E. (1977). *Cartesian Meditations: An Introduction to Phenomenology,* 6th ed., trans. D. Cairns. The Hague: Nijhoff.

Independent Electoral Commission. (1994). *Report of the Independent Electoral Commission, The South African Elections of April 1994.* South Africa: IEC.

International Alert. (1990). *Tibet—An International Consultation.* London: International Alert, July 6–8.

International Alert. (1997). *A Time of Hope and Transformation: Sierra Leone Peace Process, Reports and Reflections.* London: International Alert.

International Alert, United Nations University, National Institute for Research Advancement. (1993). *Preventive Diplomacy: A UN/NGO Partnership in the 1990s.* Report of a roundtable on preventive diplomacy and the United Nation's agenda for peace. London: International Alert, January 28–30.

International Peace Research Institute. (1996). Report of the workshop on "An Agenda for Preventive Diplomacy: Theory and Practice," October 16–19, Skopje: International Peace Research Institute.

IRIPAZ. (1992). *Cronologias de los Procesos de Paz: Guatemala y El Salvador*, vols. I and II. Guatemala: IRIPAZ.
Isakovic, Z. (1999). "Diplomacy and the Conflict in Kosovo—Notes on Threats and Fears." Center for Peace and Conflict Research, Institute of Internatoinal Politics and Economics, Belgrade, Yugoslavia. Paper prepared for presentation at the ISA Annual Convention, February 16–20, Washington, DC.
Izvestiya (1992). October 15.
Jenkins, J. C., and D. Bond. (1998). "Conflict Carrying Capacity, Political Meltdowns and Reconstruction: A Framework for the Early Warning of Political System Vulnerability." Minneapolis: International Studies Association.
Jentleson, B. W., ed. (2000). *Opportunities Missed, Opportunities Seized: Preventive Diplomacy in the Post–Cold War World*. Lanham, MD: Rowman and Littlefield.
Jentleson, B. W., and M. S. Lund. (unpublished). "Preventive Diplomacy: An Idea in Search of a Strategy." Prepared for the first session of "Preventive Diplomacy in the Post–Cold War Period: Challenge and Opportunities for the United States" a study group sponsored by the U.S. Institute of Peace in collaboration with the Policy Planning Staff, U.S. Department of State.
Jonas, S. (1991). *The Battle for Guatemala: Rebels, Death Squads and US Power*. Boulder, CO: Westview Press.
Jongman, A. J. (1984, 1988). "World Directory of Terrorist Organizations and Other Groups, Movements and Parties Involved in Political Violence As Initiators or Targets of Armed Violence." In *Political Terrorism*, edited by A. P. Schmid. Amsterdam: North-Holland Publications.
Jongman, A.J., and A. P. Schmid. (1994). *Monitoring Human Rights. Manual for Assessing Country Performance*. Leiden: PIOOM.
Kadian, R. (1993). *The Kashmir Triangle: Issues and Options*. Boulder, CO: Westview Press.
Kalven, J. (1977). "The Kashmiri." In *World Minorities*, vol.1, edited by G. Ashworth. Middlesex, England: Quartermaine House for Minority Rights Group.
Kant, I. (1784, reprint 1963). "Idea for a Universal History from a Cosmopolitan Point of View," trans. and reprinted in *Kant on History,* edited by L. W. Beck. New York: Macmillan/Library of Liberal Arts.
Kaplan, R. D. (1994). *Balkan Ghosts: A Journey Through History.* New York: Vintage Books.
Kaufman, C. (1996). "Possible and Impossible Solutions to Ethnic Civil Wars," *International Security* 20 (4):136–175.
Keesing's Record of World Events. (1989–1996). Vols. 35–42. United Kingdom: Longman Group Ltd.
Kelley, J. (2000). "The Role of European Institutions' Use of Norms & Membership Incentives on Ethnic Politics." Paper for Annual Meeting of the American Political Science Association.
Kolstoe, P., A. Edemsky, and N. Kalashnikova. (1993). "The Dniester Conflict: Between Irredentism and Separatism." *Europe-Asia Studies* 45 (6): 973–1000.
Kriesberg, L. (1998). *Constructive Conflicts: From Escalation to Resolution.* Lanham, MD: Rowman & Littlefield.
Kripke, S. (1980). *Naming and Necessity.* Cambridge, MA: Harvard University Press.
Kurian, G. T. (1991). *The New Book of World Rankings,* 3rd ed. New York: Facts on File.
Kurian, G. T. (1998). *Fitzroy Dearborn Book of World Rankings.* Chicago: Fitzroy Dearborn Publications.
Kuroda, M. (1993). "Selected Early Warning Systems, Methods and Mechanisms." An unpublished working paper.

Kusy, M. (1997). "The State of Human and Minority Rights in Slovakia." In *Slovakia: Problems of Democratic Consolidation and the Struggle for the Rules of the Game,* edited by S. Szomolnyi and J. Gould. New York: Columbia International Affairs Online.

Le Bot, Y. (1992). *La Guerre en Terre Maya. Communauté, Violence et Modernité au Guatemala.* Paris: Editions Khartala.

Leatherman, J., P. D. DeMars, Gaffney, P. and R. Väyrynen. (1999). *Breaking Cycles of Violence: Conflict Prevention in Intrastate Crises.* West Harford, CT: Kumarian Press.

Lebed, Alexander. (1997). *My Life and My Country.* Chicago: Regnery.

Lent, T. (1996). "The Search for Peace and Justice in Guatemala: NGOs, Early Warning, and Preventive Diplomacy." In *Vigilance and Vengeance: NGOs Preventing Ethnic Conflict in Divided Societies,* edited by R. I. Rotberg (pp. 73–92). Washington, DC: Brookings Institution Press.

Leonardt, M., and D. Nyheim. (1999). "Promoting Development in Areas of Actual or Potential Violent Conflict: Approaches in Conflict Impact Assessment and Early Warning." Presented at the Global Development Network conference in Bonn. Washington, DC.: World Bank.

Levine, D. N., ed. (1971). *Georg Simmel: On Individuality and Social Forms. Selected Writings.* Chicago: The University of Chicago Press.

Levy, J. (1996). "Contending Theories of International Conflict: a Level of Analysis Approach." In *Managing Chaos: Sources of and Responses to International Conflict,* edited by C. Crocker and I. Hampson with P. Aall. Washington, DC: U.S. Institute of Peace.

Lewis, D. (1968). "Counterpart Theory and Quantified Modal Logic." *The Journal of Philosophy* 65: 113–126.

Lewis, D. (1973). *Counterfactuals.* Oxford: Basil Blackwell.

Licklider, R. (1993). *Stopping the Killing: How Civil Wars End.* New York: New York University Press.

Lindgren, G., K. A. Nordquist, and P. Wallensteen, eds. (1991). *Peace Processes in the Third World.* Uppsala, Sweden: Department of Peace and Conflict Research.

Linsky, L., ed. (1971). *Reference and Modality.* London: Oxford University Press.

Linter, B. (1994). *Burma in Revolt: Opium and Insurgency Since 1948.* Boulder, CO: Westview Press.

Literaturnaya Rossia. (1992). No. 31.

Little, D., and S. W. Hibbard. (1994). *Sino-Tibetan Coexistence—Creating Space for Tibetan Self-Direction.* Washington, DC: U.S. Institute of Peace.

Loux, M. J., ed. (1979). *The Possible and the Actual: Readings in the Metaphysics of Modality.* Ithaca, NY: Cornell University Press.

Lund, M. S. (1993). "Europe's Tool Box for Conflict Prevention." Chapter 10 in *Post–Cold War European Security and Conflict Management: The Roles of Multilateral Organizations.* Draft manuscript. Washington, DC: U.S. Institute of Peace.

Lund, M. S. (1996). *Preventive Diplomacy and American Foreign Policy: A Guide to the Post–Cold War Era.* Washington, DC: U.S. Institute of Peace.

Lund, M. S. (1996). *Preventing Violent Conflicts: A Strategy for Preventive Diplomacy.* Washington, DC: U.S. Institute of Peace Press.

Lund, M. S. (1997). *Preventing and Mitigating Violent Conflicts: A Revised Guide for Practitioners.* Washington, DC: Creative Associates International.

Lund, M. S. (1999). "'Preventive Diplomacy' for Macedonia, 1992–1998: From Containment to Nation-Building." In *Opportunities Seized, Opportunities Missed: Success and Failures in Post–Cold War Preventive Diplomacy,* edited by B. Jentleson (pp. 173–210). Lanham, MD: Rowman & Littlefield.

Lusaka Protocol. (1995). Free Angola Information Service Inc.
MacFarlane S. N. (1998). *Peace Support Operations and Humanitarian Action: A Conference Report.* Halifax, Nova Scotia: Centre for Foreign Policy Studies, Dalhousie University.
Madale, N. T. (1984). "The Future of the Moro National Liberation Front (MNLF) As a Separatist Movement in Southern Philippines." In *Armed Separatism in Southeast Asia*, edited by L. Joo-Jock and S. Vani. Singapore: Institute of Southeast Asian Studies.
Majul, C. A. (1985). *The Contemporary Muslim Movement in the Philippines.* Berkeley, CA: Mizan Press.
Maki, J. (1994). "Away from Confrontation." War Report (October/November): 18–19.
Malcolm, N. (1998). *Kosovo: A Short History.* New York: New York University Press.
Mallery, J. C. (1994). "Beyond Correlation: Bringing Artificial Intelligence to Events Data." In Duffy, ed.
March, A., and R. Sil. (1999). *The "Republic of Kosova" (1989–1998) and the Resolution of Ethno-Separatist Conflict: Rethinking "Sovereignty" in the Post–Cold War Era.* Philadelphia: Browne Center for International Politics, University of Pennsylvania.
Maxwell, N. (1980). *India, The Nagas and the North-East.* London: Minority Rights Group.
May, R. J. (1988). "The Moro Movement in Southern Philippines." *Ethnic Studies Report* 6 (2) (July): 52–84.
May, R. J. (1992). "The Religious Factor in Three Minority Movements: The Moro of the Philippines, the Malays of Thailand, and Indonesia's West Papuans." *Contemporary Southeast Asia* 13 (4) (March): 396–414.
Maynes, C. W. (1993). "Containing Ethnic Conflict." *Foreign Policy* 90 (Spring): 3–21.
McCarthy, M. O. (1997). "Potential Humanitarian Crises: The Warning Process and Roles for Intelligence." In Schmeidl and Adelman, ed.
McCawley, J. D. (1981). *Everything That Linguists Have Always Wanted to Know About Logic: But Were Ashamed to Ask.* Chicago: Chicago University Press.
McClelland, P. (1975). *Causal Explanation and Model-Building in History, Economics, and the New Economic History.* Ithaca, NY: Cornell University Press.
McColm, R. B. (1993). *Freedom in the World, 1992–1993: The Annual Survey of Political Rights and Civil Liberties 1992–1993.* New York: Freedom House.
Mercado, E. R. (1984). "Culture, Economics and Revolt in Mindanao: The Origins of the MNLF and the Politics of Moro Separatism." In *Armed Separatism in Southeast Asia*, edited by L. Joo-Jock and S. Vani. Singapore: Institute of Southeast Asian Studies (pp. 151–175).
Merritt, R. L., R. G. Muncaster, and D. A. Zinnes, eds. (1993) *International Event-Data Developments: DDIR Phase II.* Ann Arbor: University of Michigan Press.
Miall, H. (1992). *The Peacemakers: Peaceful Settlement of Disputes since 1945.* New York: St. Martin's Press.
Minority Rights Group International. (1997). *World Directory of Minorities.* London: Minority Rights Group.
Minsky, M. L. (1967). *Computation.* Englewood Cliffs, NJ: Prentice Hall.
Montville, J. V. (1990). *Conflict and Peacemaking in Multiethnic Societies.* Lexington, MA: Lexington Books.
Moreno, P. R. (1998). "Condiciones de Posibilidad para la Solucion Negociada de un Conflicto Armado." Presented at the Encuentro Sobre Conflictos y Experiencias de Intermediacion en America Latina, Universidad Autonoma de Barcelona, Barcelona, May 27.

Moynihan, D. P. (1993). *Pandemonium: Ethnicity in International Politics.* Oxford: Oxford University Press.

Munuera, G. (1994). *Preventing Armed Conflict in Europe: Lessons from Recent Experience.* Chaillot Paper 15/16. Paris: Institute for Security Studies, Western European Union.

Nahaylo, B. (1992). "Moldovan Conflict Creates New Dilemmas for Ukraine." *RFE/RL Research Report* 1 (20).

National Institute for Policy Studies. (1992). *Back to the Barracks, The Military in Democratic Transition.* Quezon City, Philippines: National Institute for Policy Studies.

National Peace Conference [The Philippines]. (1993) "Basic Peace: Peace Agenda of Four Sectors." National Peace Conference, 1993.

National Peace Conference[The Philippines]. (1998). "Social Reform Should Form the Core of Governance: The Basic Sectors' Agenda for the Post-Ramos Administration." National Peace Conference, February 1998.

Netherlands Institute of International Relations (NIIR). (1996). *Conflict Prevention and Early Warning in the Political Practice of International Organisations.* The Hague: Clingendael.

Nezavisimaya gazeta.(1992). April 1.

Nezavisimaya gazeta. (1994). March 2.

Nezavisimaya gazeta. (1998). February 10.

Nezavisimaya gazeta. (1999). February 26.

Novoe vremya. (1993). No. 29.

Organization for Security and Cooperation in Europe, Mission to Moldova. (1996). *Spot Report* 22, August 12.

Organization for Security and Cooperation in Europe, Mission to Moldova (1996). "Memorandum on the Fundamentals of Normalizing the Relations between the Republic of Moldova and Trans-Dniestria." Annex to *Spot Report 16*, June 20.

Organization for Security and Cooperation in Europe, Mission to Moldova (1996). "Memorandum on the Fundamentals of Normalizing the Relations between the Republic of Moldova and Trans-Dniestria." Annex to *Spot Report 18*, July 11.

Organization for Security and Cooperation in Europe, Mission to Moldova. (1997). *Monthly Report 7*, April 22.

Organization for Security and Cooperation in Europe Mission in Skopje (1995–1996). *OSCE Skopje Reports.* August 1995 to October 1996, Nos. 73–90.

Owen, D. (1995). *Balkan Odyssey.* New York: Harcourt and Brace.

Padilla, L. A. (1994). "The Peace Process in Central America: A Comparative Analysis of Mediation in El Salvador and Guatemala." In *War and Peace: Essays of Conflict and Change*, edited by E. Garcia. Quezon City, Philippines: Claretian Publications.

Padilla, L. A. (1995). "The United Nations and Conflict Resolution in Central America: Peace Making and Peace Building in Internal Armed Conflict." *Estudios Internacionales* 12: 92–104.

Papp, D. S. (1993). "The Angolan Civil War and Namibia. The Role of External Intervention." In *Making War and Making Peace. Foreign Investment in Africa*, edited by D. Mock. Washington, DC: U.S. Institute of Peace Press.

Peirce, C. S. (1932). *Collected Papers*, vol. 1–8, edited by C. Harthorne, P. Weiss, and A. Burks. Cambridge, MA: Harvard University Press.

Petocz, K. (1994). "A Minority Under Pressure." *War Report* (October/November): 35–36.

Pierson, C. (1996). *The Modern State.* London: Routledge.

Polanyi, K. (1975). *The Great Transformation.* New York: Octagon Books.

Prunier, G. (1995). *The Rwanda Crisis, 1959–1994: History of a Genocide.* London: Christopher Hurst.
Quine, W. V. O. (1948). "On What There Is." *Review of Metaphysics* 2.
Quine, W. V. O. (1960). *Word and Object.* Cambridge, MA: MIT Press.
Quine, W. V. O. (1961). *From a Logical Point of View.* Cambridge, MA: Harvard University Press.
Regan, P. M. (1996). "Conditions of Successful Third-Party Intervention in Intrastate Conflicts." *Journal of Conflict Resolution* 40 (2): 336–359.
Rescher, N. (1969). "The Concept of Nonexistent Possibles." In *Essays in Philosophical Analysis,* edited by N. Rescher. Pittsburgh: Pittsburgh University Press.
Rescher, N. (1973). "The Ontology of the Possible." In *Logic and Ontology,* edited by M. Munitz. New York: New York University Press.
Rescher, N. (1975). *A Theory of Possibility: A Constructivistic and Conceptualistic Account of Possible Individuals and Possible Worlds.* Pittsburgh: University of Pittsburgh Press.
Richards, P. (1997). "Fighting for the Rain Forest: War, Youth and Resources in Sierra Leone" (unpublished manuscript).
Rodil, B. R. (1993). *The Lumad and Moro of Mindanao.* London: Minority Rights Group International Report, no. 2.
Rosenau, J. (1990*). Turbulence in World Politics. A Theory of Change and Continuity.* Princeton, NJ: Princeton University Press.
Rothchild, D. (1997). *Managing Ethnic Conflict in Africa.* Washington, DC: Brookings Institution Press.
Rothchild, D., et al. (1990). "The Road to Gbadolite: Great Powers and African Mediators in Angola." Presented at the African Studies Association, Baltimore, November.
Rummel, R. J. (1995). "Democracy, Power, Genocide and Mass Murder." *Journal of Conflict Resolution* 39 (1) (March): 3–26.
Rummel, R. J. (1997). *Statistics of Democide, Genocide and Mass Murder since 1900.* Charlottesville, VA: Center for National Security Law, School of Law.
Rupesinghe, K. (1988). "Ethnic Violence, Human Rights and Early Warning." In *UNESCO Yearbook for Peace and Conflict Studies.* Westport, CT: Greenwood Press.
Rupesinghe, K. (1992). "The Disappearing Boundaries between Internal and External Conflicts." In *Internal Conflict and Governance.* New York: St. Martin's Press.
Rupesinghe, K., ed. (1992). *Internal Conflict and Governance.* New York: St. Martin's Press.
Rupesinghe, K. (1994). "Conflict Transformation in Multiethnic Societies." In *War and Peacemaking,* edited by E. Garcia, Quezon City, Philippines: Claretian Publications.
Rupesinghe, K. (1995). "Conflict Transformation." In Rupesinghe, ed.
Rupesinghe, K., ed. (1995). *Conflict Transformation.* Basingstoke, UK: Macmillan Press.
Rupesinghe, K. (1998). "The Northern Ireland Peace Agreement: Lessons to be Learned." London: International Alert.
Rupesinghe, K., and M. Kuroda, eds. (1992). *Early Warning and Conflict Resolution.* London: Macmillan Press.
Rupesinghe, K., and M. Rubio C., eds. (1994). *The Culture of Violence.* Tokyo: The UN University Press.
Rupesinghe, K., with S. N. Anderlini. (1998).*Civil Wars, Civil Peace, Introduction to Conflict Resolution.* London: Pluto Press.
Rupesinghe, K., and V. Tiskhov, eds. (1994). *Ethnicity and Power in the Contemporary World.* Tokyo: The UN University Press.

Rupesinghe, K., P. King, and O. Vorkunova, eds. (1992). *Ethnicity and Conflict in a Post-Communist World*. London: Macmillan Press.

Rusu, S. (1997). "Early Warning and Information: The Role of ReliefWeb." In Schmeidle and Adelman.

Salim, A. S. (1997). "Address by the Secretary-General of the OAU at the Second Meeting of the Chiefs of Defense Staff of Member States of the OAU Central Organ." Harare, October 25.

Schelling, T. C. (1970). *The Strategy of Conflict*. Reprint, New York: Oxford University Press.

Schlesinger, S. (1978). "How Dulles Worked the Coup d'Etat." *The Nation*, October.

Schlesinger, S., and S. Kinzer. (1983). *Bitter Fruit: The Untold Story of the American Coup in Guatemala*. Garden City, NY: Doubleday.

Schmalberger, T. (1998). "Dangerous Liaisons: As Theory of Threat Relationships in International Politics." Ph.D. dissertation, Geneva. The dissertation and a later version of the related simulation are available at www-rcf.usc.edu/~thomass/index.html.

Proceedings. Center for International and Security Studies, York University, Toronto.

Schmeidl, S. (1995). "From Root Cause Assessment to Preventive Diplomacy: Possibilities and Limitations of the Early Warning of Forced Migration." Ph.D. dissertation, Department of Sociology, Ohio State University, Columbus.

Schmeidl, S. (1997). "Exploring the Causes of Forced Migration: A Pooled Time-Series Analysis, 1971–1990." *Social Science Quarterly* 778 (2): 284–308.

Schmeidl, S., and H. Adelman, eds. (1997). *Synergy in Early Warning: Conference Proceedings*. Toronto, Canada, March 15–18.

Schmeidl, S., and J. C. Jenkins (1998). "The Early Warning of Humanitarian Disasters. Problems in building an early warning system." *International Migration Review* 32 (2): 471–486.

Schmid, A. P., ed. (1997). *Violent Crime and Conflicts*. Milan, Italy: ISPAC.

Schmid, A. P. (1998a). "Indicator Development: Conceptual, Methodological and Data Issues Involved in Forecasting Conflict Escalation." In Davies and Gurr.

Schmid, A. P., ed. (1998). *Violent Crime and Conflict*. Milan, Italy: ISPAC.

Schmid, A. P. (2000). *Thesaurus and Glossary of Early Warning and Conflict Prevention Terms*. London: FEWER.

Schmid, A. P., and A. J. Jongman. (1988). *Political Terrorism. A New Guide to Actors, Authors, Concepts, Data Bases, Theories, and Literature*. Cambridge, MA: Center for International Affairs, Harvard University, North-Holland Publications.

Schmid, A. P., and A. J. Jongman, eds. (1992). *Monitoring Human Rights Violations*. Leiden, The Netherlands: COMT.

Schmidt, F. (1996). "Teaching the Wrong Lesson in Kosovo." *Transition* (12 July): 37–39.

Schopflin, G. (1994). "The Hungarian Exception? The Quiet National Question." *War Report* (October/November): 15–17.

Schrodt, P. A., and D. J. Gerner. (1997). "Empirical indicators of Crisis Phase in the Middle East, 1979–1995." *Journal of Conflict Resolution* 41 (4): 329–352.

Schutz, A. (1967). *The Phenomenology of the Social World*, trans. by G. Walsh and F. Lehnert, with an introduction by G. Walsh. Evanston, IL: Northwestern University Press.

Schutz, A. and T. Luckmann. (1973). *The Structures of the Life-World*, translated by R. M. Zaner and H. T. Engelhardt, Jr. Evanston, IL: Northwestern University Press.

Sengulane, D., and J. P. Goncalves. (1998). "A Calling for Peace: Christian Leaders and the Quest fo Reconciliation in Mozambique." In *ACCORD*, Issue 3, edited by J. Armon, D. Hendrickson and A. Vines, Conciliation Resources.

Sherman, F. L. (1994). "SHERFACS: A Cross-Paradigm, Hierarchical and Contextually Sensitive Conflict Management Data Set." *International Interactions* 20 (1–2) (August): 79–100.

Simmel, G. (1950). *The Sociology of Georg Simmel,* trans., edited and with an introduction by K. H. Wolff. New York: The Free Press.

Simmel, G. (1955). *Conflict. The Web of Group-Affiliations* trans. by K. H. Woolf and R. Bendix, with a foreword by E. C. Hughes. New York: The Free Press.

Simon, H. A., and N. Rescher. (1966). "Cause and Counterfactual." *Philosophy of Science* 33 (40): 323–340.

Singer, J. D., and M. D. Wallace, eds. (1979). *To Augur Well: Early Warning Indicators in World Politics.* Beverly Hills, CA: Sage.

Singer, M. R. (1990). "Prospects for Conflict Management in the Sri Lankan Ethnic Crisis." In Montville.

Spencer, W. (1994). "Implications for Policy Use: Policy Uses of Early Warning Models and Data for Monitoring and Responding to Humanitarian Crises." In Gurr and Harff, eds., (pp. 111–116).

Springer, G., and D. P. Friedman. (1989). *Scheme and the Art of Programming.* Cambridge, MA: The MIT Press.

Stalnaker, R. (1984). *Inquiry.* Cambridge, MA: MIT Press.

Stalnaker, R. (1986). "Counterparts and Identity." In *Studies in Essentialism,* edited by P. A. French et al., Midwest Studies in Philosophy, vol. II. Minneapolis: University of Minnesota Press.

Stavenhagen, R. (1990). *The Ethnic Question: Conflicts, Development, and Human Rights.* Tokyo: United Nations University Press.

Steinberg, J. B. (1993). "International Involvement in the Yugoslavia Conflict." In *Enforcing Restraint: Collective Intervention in Internal Conflicts,* edited by L. F. Damrosch. New York: Council on Foreign Relations.

Stockholm International Peace Research Institute. (various years). *World Armaments and Disarmaments Yearbook.* London: Taylor and Francis.

Stroschein, S. (1996). *The Components of Existence: Hungarian Minorities and Interethnic Relations in Romania, Slovakia and Ukraine.* New York: Institute on East Central Europe, Columbia University.

Suhrke, A., and L. G. Noble. (1977). "Muslims in the Philippines and Thailand." In *Ethnic Conflict in International Relations,* edited by A. Suhrke and L. G. Noble (178–212). New York: Praeger Publishers.

Sunday Tribune. (1994). January–mid-April.

Surroi, V. (1996). "The Albanian National Question: The Post Dayton Payoff." *War Report* (May) The Institute for War and Peace Reporting.

Sylvan, D., and S. Majeski. (1998). "A Methodology for the Study of Historical Counterfactuals." *International Studies Quarterly* 42 (1): 79–108.

Szayna, T. S. (1994) *Ethnic Conflict in Central Europe and the Balkans: A Framework and U.S. Policy Options.* Santa Monica, CA: Arroyo Center, Rand.

Tan, S. K. (1987). "Moro Secessionism in the Philippines." *Ethnic Studies Report* 5 (2) (July): 1–8.

Tarski, A. (1944). "The Semantic Concept of Truth." In *Philosophy and Phenomenological Research* 4 (3): 341–376.

Taylor, A. J. P. (1954). *The Struggle for Mastery in Europe, 1848–1918.* London: Oxford University Press.

Teleki, I. (1998). "Loss and Lack of Recognition: Identifying Fears in the Slovak-Hungarian Relationship." *Slovo* 10 (1/2):199–218.

Tetlock, P. E., and A. Belkin, eds. (1996). *Counterfactual Thought Experiments in World Politics: Logical, Methodological, and Psychological Perspectives.* Princeton, NJ: Princeton University Press.

Tishkov, V. (1997). "EARWARN: An Overview." Moscow: Russian Academy of Sciences, Institute of Ethnology.

Tishkov, V. (1999). "Ethnic Conflicts in the Former U.S.S.R: The Use and Misuse of Typologies and Data." *Journal of Peace Research* 36 (5): 571–591.

Tooley, M., ed. (1999). *Necessity and Possibility: The Metaphysics of Modality.* New York: Garland.

Touval, S. (1992). "Gaining Entry to Mediation in Communal Strife." In *The Internationalization of Communal Strife,* edited by M. I. Midlarsky. London and New York: Routledge.

Troebst, S. (1994). "Macedonia: Powder Keg Defused?" *RFE/RL Research Report* 3 (4): 33–41.

Troebst, S. (1998). *Conflict in Kosovo: Failure of Prevention? An Analytical Documentation, 1992–98.* ECMI Working Paper #1, May.

Turner, B., ed. (1998). *The Statesman's Yearbook 1988–89.* London: Macmillan.

United Nations (1948). *Convention on Genocide.* New York: United Nations.

United Nations (1997). *The Sex and Age Distribution of the World Population: The 1996 Revision.* New York: United Nations.

United Nations Department of International Economic and Social Affairs. (various years). *Demographic Yearbook.* New York: United Nations.

United Nations Development Program. (1995). *Report on Sierra Leone.* New York: United Nations.

United Nations Development Program. (2000). *Human Development Report 2000.* New York: Oxford University Press.

United Nations Educational, Scientific and Cultural Organization. (1997). *Statistical Yearbook 1997.* Lanham, MD: UNESCO Publications.

United States Department of State. (various years). *Country Reports on Human Rights Practices.* Washington, DC: U.S. Government Printing Office.

Unknown. "Moldova: fused." *Eastern Europe Newsletter* 6 (6).

Update on Angola. (1995). *The African Communist* Third Quarter.

Vankovska-Cvetkovska, B. (1999). "Between Preventive Diplomacy and Conflict Resolution: The Macedonian Perspective of the Kosovo Crisis." Paper presented at the 40th Annual Convention of the International Studies Association, February.

Varshney, A. (1991). "India, Pakistan, and Kashmir: Antinomies of Nationalism." *Asian Survey* 31 (11) (November): 997–1019.

Väyrynen, R. (1991). "To Settle or to Transform? Perspectives on the Resolution of National and International Conflicts." In *New Directions in Conflict Theory, Conflict Resolution, and Conflict Transformation.* London: SAGE Publications.

Väyrynen, R. (1995). "Structure, Culture, and Territory: Three Sets of Early Warning Indicators." Paper prepared for the Theme Panel: Early Warning and Conflict Prevention in Intrastate Conflicts. The 36th Annual Convention of the International Studies Association, Chicago, February 21–25.

Vines, A. (1991). *Renamo Terrorism in Mozambique.* Monograph published by the Centre for Southern African Studies, University of York in association with J. Currey. Bloomington: Indiana University Press.

Vines, A. (1995). "Angola and Mozambique: The Aftermath of Conflict." *Conflict Studies*, 280 (May/June).
Vines, A. (1998). "Sant' Egidio and the Mozambican Peace Process." In *ACCORD*, Issue 3, edited by J. Armon, D. Hendrickson and A. Vines, Conciliation Resources.
Vines, A. (no date). "No Democracy without Money, the Road to Peace in Mozambique," CIIR briefing paper.
Walker, J. (1993). "International Mediation of Ethnic Conflicts." *Survival* 35 (1) (Spring): 102–117.
Wallensteen, P., ed. (1995). "The 1995 Executive Seminar on Third Parties and New Challenges to Conflict Resolution." Uppsala, Sweden: Department of Peace and Conflict Research, Uppsala University.
Wallensteen, P., ed. (1998). *Preventing Violent Conflicts: Past Record and Future Challenges*. Uppsala, Sweden: Department of Peace and Conflict Research, Report No. 48.
Wallensteen, P.. and K. Axell. (1994). "Conflict Resolution and the End of the Cold War, 1989–1993." *Journal of Peace Research* 31 (3): 333–349.
Wallensteen, P., and M. Sollenberg. (1998). "Armed Conflict and Regional Conflict Complexes, 1989–1997." *Journal of Peace Research* 35 (5): 621–634.
Walter, B. F. (1997). "The Critical Barrier to Civil War Settlement." *International Organization* 51 (3) (Summer): 335–364.
Wangyal, T. (1994). "Sino-Tibetan Negotiations Since 1959." In *Resistance and Reform in Tibet*, edited by Robert Barnett. Bloomington: Indiana University Press.
Weber, M. (1949). "Objective Possibility and Adequate Causation in Historical Explanation." In *The Methodology of the Social Sciences*. New York: The Free Press.
Wehr, P., and J. P. Lederach. (1992). "Mediating Conflict in Central America." *Journal of Peace Research* 28 (1): 85–98.
Weithmann, M. (1993). "Macedonia—Land Between Four Fires." *Aussenpolitik* (3): 261–270.
Wendt, A. (1999). *Social Theory of International Politics*. New York: Cambridge University Press.
Wirsing, R. G. (1994). *India, Pakistan, and The Kashmir Dispute: On Regional Conflict and Its Resolution*. New York: St. Martin's Press.
Woodward, S. L. (1994). *Balkan Tragedy: Chaos and Dissolution After the Cold War*. Washington, DC: Brookings Institution.
World Bank. (1995). "World Debt Tables 1994–1995: External Finance for Developing Countries." Washington, DC: World Bank.
World Bank. (various years). *World Development Report*. Washington, DC: Oxford University Press.
Wright, Q. (1983). *A Study of War*. Abridged by L. L. Wright. Chicago: The University of Chicago Press.
Zalaquett, J. (1993). "Report of the Chilean National Commission on Truth and Reconciliation," vol. 1. Notre Dame, IN: University of Notre Dame Press.
Zartman, I. W. (1989) *Ripe For Resolution*. New York: Oxford University Press.
Zartman, I. W., ed. (1994). *Reconstructing the State in Africa*. Boulder, CO: Lynne Rienner.
Zartman, I. W., ed. (1995a). *Elusive Peace: Negotiating an End to Civil Wars 1995–1996*. Washington, DC: Brookings Institution Press.
Zartman, I. W., ed. (1995b). *Collapsed States: The Disintegration and Restoration of Legitimate Authority*. Boulder, CO: Lynne Rienner.
Zartman, I. W., and C. Knudsen. (2000). "Peace Agreements: The Case of Angola." *Case Study Series* No. 1. Durban, South Africa: ACCORD.

Zefova, A. (1992). "The Integration of the Hungarian Minority in Slovakia—the Language Problem." In *Minorities in Politics: Cultural and Language Rights,* edited by J. Plichtova. Bratislava. Committee of the European Cultural Foundation.

Zielonka, J. (1992). *Security in Central Europe.* Adelphi Paper No. 272, London: The International Institute for Strategic Studies.

Index

AAAS. *See* American Association for the Advancement of Science
Abdullah, Farooq, 269
Abelson, Robert, 48
Abidjan Accord (1997), 216
Abir, Jafer, 387
Abkhazia, 118
ACCNET-ACCORD Electronic Network, 408
Accord of Identity and Rights of the Indigenous Peoples, 74
Acharya, A., 398–99
actualism, 357, 361
Adams, Richard, 72
Adelman, Howard, xvi, 8, 19, 403
Adibi, J, H., 48
Afgan war, 122
Afghanistan, 294
Africa: disputes in, 21, *22, 101, 102;* genocide in, 83; internal conflicts, 6, 240; North, 246; and refugees, 179; and Soviet Union, 34; and Third World, 44; West, 21, *22,* 213, 410
African National Congress (ANC), 180, 182, 185–86, 190, 205, 207
African Peace Forum (APFO), 408
"African Renaissance," 195

Agenda for Peace, An (Boutrous-Ghali), xiv–xv, 103, 401
"Agenda for Preventive Diplomacy: Theory and Practice, An," 103–04
Agrarian-Democratic Party, 114, 117
Agreement for a Firm and Lasting Peace in Guatemala (1996), 58
Agreement of Identity and Rights of the Indigenous People, 58
Agreement of Nonaggression and Good Neighborliness, South Africa, 207
Ahmed, I., 242
Alatas, Ali, 255
Albania, Albanians, 131–33, 138–45, 150–56, 160–65, 170–71, 294, 302
Albright, Madeline, 167
Algabid, Hamid, 255
Ali Bhutto, Zulfikar, 263
Ali Jinnah, Mohammed, 263
Alker, Hayward R., xv–xvi, xviiin13, 87, 403
All Party Hurriyat Conference (APHC), 269, 271
All People's Party, 213
Allende, Salvador, 297
American Assiciation for the Advancement of Science (AAAS), 30n14

441

Amnesty International, 16, 24, 62, 75n7, 97, 220–21, 227, 276
Amoda, John, 350n2
AMRSP. *See* Association of Major Religious Superiors in the Philippines
ANC. *See* African National Congress
Anderlini, Sanam Naraghi, 44
Angola, 179–95, 204
Annan, Kofi, 29n8, 179
Annenberg Center for Communications at the University of Southern California, 47
Antall, Josef, 153, 159–60, 175
apartheid, 181, 192, 205, 208
APFO. *See* African Peace Forum
APHC. *See* All Party Hurriyat Conference
Apodaca, Clair, 312
Aquino, Benigno, 218
Aquino, Croazon, 218, 227, 251
Arabs, 98
Arbenz, Jacobo, 56, 60, 71–72, 75n5, 345, 379–81
Arellano, Rossely, 77n16
Arévalo, Joan José, 60
Argentina, 297
Aristotle, 49, 355
Armas, Carlos Castillo, 60–61, 345, 379
Armas, Castillo, 60–61, 77n16
Armenian-Georgian cooperation, 412
ARMM. *See* Autonomous Region of Muslim Mindanao
Arnault, Jean, 66
Aronson, Bernard, 77n21
Arusha Accords (1993), 91, 93–95, 99
ASEAN. *See* Association of Southeast Asian Nations
Asia, 6, 245, *283–84,* 286–87, 342, 410
assimilation, 139
Association for Progressive Computing, 35
Association of Major Religious Superiors in the Philippines (AMRSP), 220
Association of Southeast Asian Nations (ASEAN), 248, 285
Association of Workers of Slovakia (ZRS), 158
ASSR. *See* Supreme Soviet of Chechen-Inguish

Austria, 149
Austro-Hungarian Empire, 105, 136–37, 147
autocratic rule, 312
Autonomous Region of Muslim Mindanao (ARMM), 251, 255
autonomy, 13, 114, 147, 155–58, 162, 247 282, 286–87
Avturkhanov, Umar, 121
Azar, Ed, xviii, 87
Azerbaijan, 106

Badinter Commission, 169
Baker, James, 187
Balkan Ghosts (Kaplan), 137
Balkan Wars of 1912, 138
Balkans, 105, 117, 131, 177n1
Bangladesh, 17, 255–57, 260–65, 269, 284
Banyarwandans, 95
Basic Accord for the Search of Peace by Political Means, 63
Battle of the Polje Fields (1389), 151
Beijing, 275, 280–81, 284
Belarus, 113, 167
Belgium, 90, 93–95, 97–98
Belgrade, 141, 155, 160–61
Belize, 60
Bercovitch, Jacob, 24
Berisha, Saul, 162
Berlin Wall, 66, 208
Bessarabia, 104–05
Betts, Wendy, 177
Bharatiya Janata Party (BJP), 269, 271–72
Bhutto, Benazir, 265–66
Bicesse Accords, 181, 184–89, 191–93
Bio, Julius Maada, 215
birthrate, 142, 145, 151
BJP. *See* Bharatiya Janata Party
Black Sea, 123
Bloomfield, Lincoln, xvi, 8, 16, 20–27, 36, 42, 47–48, 87, 243, 400
Bohemia, 140, 143–44, 147
Borneo, 247
Bosnia, 17, 128, 132, 160–61, 168
Bosnia-Herczegivina, 169
Boutrous-Ghali, Boutrous, xiv–xv, xviin8, 19, 43, 66, 74n1, 103, 318–19, 401

Braudel, F., 44
Brazil, 302
Brecher, Michael, 10, 23, 36
Brecke, Peter, xvi
Brussels, 95
Budapest, 159
Buddhism, 37, 273–74, 282
Buddhist Lamas, 273–74
Bukovina Popular Assembly, 105
Bulgaria, 113, 132, 138, 141, 149, 161, 169
Bulgarians, 105
Burbulis, Gennady, 119
Burma, 241, 255–57, 260, 284
Burundi: accelerators of conflict, *89,* 340–41; colonialism in, 82, 88; conflict in, 81, 88, 95, 99–100, *341*–42, 343; coup in, 88, 90–91, 93–94, 99; democracy in, 91; economics in, 91; elections in, 88, 90; French protection forces in, 90; genocide in, 83; Harff on, 336–343; Hutus in, 81, 294; massacres in, 88, 90–91, 93; and Organization of African Unity, 17, 90; refugees from, 90
Bush, Pres. George, 77n21, 169, 171
Buthelezi, Gatsha, 182
Buthelezi, Mangosuthu, 180, 190, 193
Butterworth, Robert L., 48

Cabot, John Moors, 60, 72, 76n12
CACIF. *See* Committee of Commercial, Agricultural, Industrial, and Financial Organizations, Guatemala
Cambodia, 297
Camplisson, Joe, 109, 116
Canada, 6–7, 19, 24, 62–63, 98, 170
Carnap, Rudolph, 357
Carnegie Commission, 33–34, 37, 40–41, 45, 53n16
Carnegie Commission on Preventing Deadly Conflicts, 203
Carnegie Corporation, xviin2, 4, 29n2, 32–33, 49–50, 51n2, 55n24
Carnogursky, Jan, 158
Carrington, Lord Peter, 187
CASCON. *See* Computer-Aided System for the Analysis of Conflicts

Caspian oil, 123
Castro, Fidel, 76n13
Catholic Bishops' Conference of the Philippines (CBCP), 220
Catholic Church, 56, 62–65, 77n16, 98, 140–41, 198, 208–09
Catholic Relief Service, 171
Caucasian Institute for Peace, Democracy, and Development (CIPPD), 412
Caucasian wars, 118
Caucasus, 118, 123, 410–11, 414
CBCP. *See* Catholic Bishops' Conference of the Philippines
Center for International Development, University of Maryland, 87
Center for International Studies at University of Southern California, xviin2
Center for Refugee Studies, 25
Center for Refugee Studies at York University, xvi
CENTO. *See* Central Treaty Organization
Central America, 58–59, 72–73, 233, 235, 348, 352n17
Central American Federal Republic, 59
Central European Cooperation Committee, 166
Central Intelligence Agency (CIA), 53n21, 72, 76n13, 78n25, 293
Central Treaty Organization (CENTO), 262
Cerezo, Vinicio, 58
CEWS. *See* Conflict Early Warning Systems
Chamorro, Violeta, 76n12, 380
Charlemange, 148
CHE. *See* Complex Humanitarian Emergencies
Chechen-Ingush Republic, 118–19
Chechen-Ingush Supreme Soviet, 119–20
Chechen National Congress (CNC), 118–19
Chechen war, 123
Chechnya, 118–23, 132, 323–24
Chiapas, 382, 393–94n52
Chikane, Rev. Frank, 187
Chile, 297
China, 241–42, 256–57, 265, 274–81, 285
Chisinau, 105, 110, 112–114, 117
Chissano, Joaquim, 207, 211

Choueri, Nazli, 400
Christian Democratic Movement (KDH), 158
Christian-Democratic Popular Front, 114
Christianity, 148, 246–48, 254
CIA. *See* Central Intelligence Agency
CIDCM. *See* Center for International Development, University of Maryland
CIPPD. *See* Caucasian Institute for Peace, Democracy, and Development, 412
CIS. *See* Confederation of Independent States
Civic Democratic Party, 143
Civil Society Assembly, Guatemala (ASC), 66
Clinton, Hillary, 167
Clinton, Pres. William, 171, 273
CNC. *See* Chechen National Congress
CNR. *See* National Commission on Reconciliation, Guatemala
COCTA. *See* Committee on Conceptual and Terminology Analysis
Coexistence Initiative of the State of the World Forum, 52n11
Cohen, Herman J., 187
Cold War: and Europe, 6, 136, 151; history of, 5, 139, 182, 400; implications of, 7, 44, 84, 318, 370; shift in, 241–42; and Soviet Union, 143–44; and third world, 182; world after, 3, 5–8, 66, 141, 145–49, 174, 240, 302, 404, xii–xiii
colonialism, 82, 88, 193–94, 217, 370
Columbia, 58
Commission on International Conflicts and Their Resolution (ICON), xiii, 401
Committee for the Consolidation of Peace, 212
Committee of Commercial, Agricultural, Industrial, and Financial Organizations, Guatemala (CACIF), 63
Committee on Conceptual and Terminology Analysis (COCTA), 25
communism, 65, 71, 137–40, 143, 152, 208, 219, 276
Communist Party, 61, 115–17, 130–32, 147–48, 159, 222
Communist Party, Philippines (PKP), 218
"Comparative Study of Conflict Prevention Success and Failures, A," 40

Complex Humanitarian Emergencies (CHE), 407
Comprehensive Agreement of Human Rights and Humanitarian Law, 222
Computer-Aided System for the Analysis of Conflicts (CASCON), xviiin13, 23, 26, 30n17, 36, 47–48, 391n28
computer simulation of conflict trajectories, 372–76
Confederation of Independent States (CIS), 111–13
Conference on Conflict and Cooperation in Europe (CSCE), 110, 115, 159, 168–69
Conference on Security and Cooperation in Europe (CSCE), 166, 169, 171
conflict: accelerators of, 86–87, 99, 408; alarms and responses, *40;* analysis of, 18, 135, 358–61, 387; aspects of, 38, 385; case studies of, 33, 373, *413;* causes of, 142, 186–87, 231–32; civil, 152; definition of, 43, 391n31; development, 83, 87–88; dominant parties in, 372; early warning systems for, xviin8 10, 18, 27, 82–83, 291–317; and economics, xiv,139, 255; escalation of, 10, 83, 86–88, 364, *369;* forms of, 322–23, 326–28, *328,* 362; groups in, *173;* in Guatemala, 4, 56–78; handling practices, 19; histories of, 10, 42, 333–34, 359; humanitarian, xiv; intensity of, *292,* 292–93, *295;* international, xii, 7, 13, 73–74, 165; and International Alert, 5; intervention in, 35–36, 42, 87–88; levels of, *295, 317;* life cycles of, *9,* 10, 32, 37–39, 42–45, 50, 330–31, 362, 364; management, xiii, 17, 36, 44, 45, 243–44, *252–54,* 257, *258–59,* 260, *261,* 400; management failure, 243; mediation, 23–24, 36, 328; military, xiv; and national interest, 7; phases of, 21, 42, 50, 86–88, 95, 124, 243–44, *249–50, 252, 261,* 330–33, *340–41,* 362–67, *366, 370,* 373–74; and politics, xv, 134, *384;* prevention, xv, 4, 10, 16–20, 33–38, 42–45, 56, 103, 128, 134, 403–07; reconstruction, 183; research on, xv, 4,

18, 355, 370, 408–09; resolution, 10, 36, 59, 65, 73, 77n18, 184–93, 354–55, 403; root causes of, 129–30, 139, 186–87; Rupesinghe's definition of, 56; sequence, 205–07; and third-party intervention, 66–67; trajectories of, 360–64, 372–76; transformation, 37–38, 67, 182–83, 196, 229–33 368; triggers, 86–87; types of, 18, 33, 83, 84–85, *351, 368;* and violence, 213

Conflict Early Warning Systems (CEWS): case studies from, 16–17, 37, 39, 41–46, 369, 386; codebooks and coding, 24, 48, 373; and conflict prevention, 20; coordinators for, 18; databases, 21, 23–24, 35–36, 305, 363–64, 375–76, 392n38; design of, 44–46, 319–20, 329; Explorer, 354–94; framework of, 46, 55n29, 329, 364–65; funding for, xvi–xvii, xviin2, 3–4, 19, 39–40, 50, 54n26; goals of, 3–4, 21, 34, 37, 56, 87; guidelines for, 40–41, 44–46; and International Alert, 34; intervention tools, 28; knowledge base of, 25–26; methodology of, 45, 329, 372–75, 387; models of, 4, 388; networks, 28; origins of, xii–xvii; participation in, 45; phases of, 21, 23, 42, 46–47, 339, *340,* 364–65, *366,* 373–74; process of, 35; project meetings of, 32; research program of, 5–8, 20–21, 27–28; Schmalberger on, 4; steering committee of, 18–19, 30n15, 32–39, 50n1, 54n27; strategies of, 386–87; trajectory studies, 385–86; transformation, 36, 77n18; Web site for, 4, 48–50, 305, 313, 350n2 372, 386–89

Congo, 81, 128, 179, 210, 294, 410. *See also* Zaire

Contadora Group, 66, 78n22

Costa Rica, 59, 63

Côte D'Ivoire. *See* Ivory Coast

Council of Europe, 166, 167

Country Indicators for Foreign Policy project, 410, 412

CPN. *See* European Commission, Conflict Prevention Network of

Creanga, Gen. Pavel, 113

Crimea, 131–32

Crimean War, 104

crisis, 326, 339

Croatia, 17, 131–32, 136–38, 159–60, 169

CSCE. *See* Conference on Security and Cooperation in Europe.

CSEMADOK (Democratic Association of Hungarians in Slovak), *153*

CSFR. *See* Czech and Slovak Federation

Cuba, 61, 72, 76n13, 181, 186

Cuban Missile Crisis, 49

Czech and Slovak Federation (CSFR), 143, 147

Czech Republic, 140, 143–44, 147–49, 157, 166

Czechoslovakia, 131, 137, 140–43, 153–54, 159, 165–66, 306–07

Dalai Lama, 274–77, 280–82

Daoism, 37

Data Development in International Relations (DDIR), xviiin12

Davies, John L., xvi, 87, 402

Dayton Accords, 163–64, 171

DDIR. *See* Data Development in International Relations

de Klerk, Frederik W., 185, 191

Debray, Regis, 61

Decade of Peace", 220

Declaration of Transdniestria State (1998), 116

demagoguery, 156

democracy: and ethnic mobilization, 156; and governance, 57, 152–53; and human rights, 56; and peace, 59, 67; as political solution to conflict, 63, 74, 301; in Zaire, 95, 97–99

Democratic Association of Hungarians in Slovak (CSEMADOK), 153

Democratic League of Kosova (LDK), 145, 151, 155, 162, 164, 170–71

Deng Xiaoping, 274

Desai, Moraji, 257

determinism, 358

Deutsch, Karl, 7, 16

Dewitt, D, 398–99

Dhlakhama, Afonso, 205, 208, 238n7
Dienstbier, Jiri, 166
Diller, J. M., 399
Diokno, Jose W., 219
diplomacy: international, 172, 355; Lund on, 10, 103; nonconventional, 196–241; preventative, xiii, 36, 39, 43, 103, 123, 128, 401, 405–06; Rupseinghe on, 192; and Russia, 117; United Nations role in, xiii–xiv
disarmament, 233–34
dispute, 326
Dixon, W. J., 242–44
Dniester: armed forces of, 111; autonomy for, 114; region of, 104, 111, 118; republic of, 110–11
Dniester River, 104–05
Dniestrian Republic Guard, 109–10
Dominican Republic, 72
Dorn, A. W., 398
Dubosari region, 117
Dudaev, Djohar, 119–22
Duffy, Gavan, xvi, xviiin15, 8, 23, 25–26, 47
Dulles, Allen, 60, 72, 76n12
Dulles, John Foster, 60, 72, 76n12

Early Warning and Conflict Resolution (Kuroda, Rupesinghe), xiii–xiv, 16,
early warning systems: bias of, 419; challenges to, 412–13; and conflict phases, 86, 407; definitions of, 293–94, 397–98, 400, 404, 410; forecasts for, 302–03, 314; four principles of, 417–18; framework of, 320–21; indicators for, 291–93, 302–03, *308–11;* initiatives, 354, 408; methods of, 292–93, 316n9, 398–99, 404, 408–10; models for, xviin8, 10, 18, 27, 82–83, *293, 402, 404, 411;* networks, 410; objectives of, 398–99; and responses, 399, 418
Eastern Europe, 104–05, 130–31, 144, 166, 276. *See also* Europe
EAWARN. *See* Network on Ethnological Monitoring and Early Warning of Conflict
EC. *See* European Community

ecology. *see* environment
ECOMOG-ECOWAS Cease-fire Monitoring Group, 212, 217
economics: and Balkan states, 174; in Burundi, 91; and competition, 142–43, 146, 178n5; and conflict, xiv, 139, 175, 202, 242, 255, 308; decline in, 142–43, 173–75; growth in, 142–43; and international policy, 303; and labor, 142; of Macedonia, xiv, 144–45; of Moldova, 105–06, 108, 114, 116–17; and peace, 234–35; reforms in, xii, 63–64, 135, 143, 146; of Slovakia, 144; in Third World nations, 130; in Yugoslavia, 144, 163, 174
Ecuador, 63
EGP. *See* Guerrilla Army of the Poor, Guatemala
Egypt, 98
Eide, Asbjørn, 403
Eisenhower, Dwight, 380
El Escorial, 66
El Salvador, 38, 58, 62, 72–73
Elías, Jorge Serrano, 64
Emizet, Kisangani, 95
England. *See* United Kingdom
Enlightenment, 6, 29n3
Ennals, Martin, 403
environment, xiv, 23, 44, 401
Eritrea, 179
Esquipulas Peace Accord, 58, 62. 72, 75n8
Esquipulas II Peace Accord, 59, 73
essentialism, 358
Essy, Amara, 214
Estonia, 131
Ethiopia, 179
ethnic, ethnicity: affinities, 131–32; balance, 132; beliefs, 86, 157–58; conflict, 83, 132–33, 155, 173–76, 177n2, 298; and democratic influence, 156; discrimination in Slovakia, 155; groups, 58, 83, 131, 142; homogeneity, 149; identity, 136, 170; nationalism, 146; relationship patterns, 136–39; studies, 25; wars, 82–83, 85, 294, 304, 315n2, 357
Eurasia, 132

Europe: and Albania, 145; and Cold War, 6, 136, 151; and human rights, 65; and Kosovo, 171; social thought of, 6; and Stability Pact, 168; Western, 19, 29n3, 62
European Center for Conflict Prevention, 52n11
European Commission, Conflict Prevention Network of (CPN), 408–09
European Community: and African refugees, 90, 94; Association Agreements, 165; boundaries of, 7; and Eastern Europe, 169; and Kashmir, 284; and Kosovo, 171; and North Atlantic Treaty Organization, 166–69; trade in, 166; on Zairean massacre, 97–98
European Community Association Agreement, 167
European Free Trade Area (EFTA), 166
European Parliament, 414
European Union (EU). *See* European Community
EWI (East West Institute), 414

FAO. *See* Food and Agriculture Organization
FAR. *See* Rebel Armed Forces, Guatemala
Farabundo Marti National Liberation Front, El Salvador (FMLN), 58, 62
Fascism, 138
Fein, Helen, 8, 10, 13, 20, 23–26, 42, 47, 84, 324, 402
FEWER. *See* Forum for Early Warning and Early Response
Finland, 170
Finno-Ugric. *See* Hungary, Hungarians
Fisher, Ronald, 56, 76n14, 77n20
FLEC. *See* Front of the Liberation of the Cabinda Enclave, Angola
FMLN. *See* Farabundo Marti National Liberation Front, El Salvador
Food and Agriculture Organization (FAO), 20
Forced Migration Project, 409
Forum for Early Warning and Early Response (FEWER), xiii–xv, 5, 46, 50, 55n29, 293, 319, 399, 403, 408–18

Framework Agreement of January 1994 (Guatemala), 55
France, 90, 93, 97–98, 100, 172, 210
Frelimo, 204–05
Front of the Liberation of the Cabinda Enclave, Angola (FLEC), 182–83, 188
FRY, Federal Republic of Yugoslavia. *See* Yugoslavia
Fuerzas Armadas Rebeldes (FAR), 61

Gagauz, 108–09
Galtung, Johan, 29n7, 34, 37, 46, 56, 59, 124, 322, 344, 400
Gandhi, Indira, 256–57, 260, 263, 282
Gandhi, Mahatma, 162
Gandhi, Rajiv, 260
Ganguly, S., 242
Garcia, Ed, 34, 44
Gates, Robert, 266
Gbadolite Peace Accords, 192
GDP. *See* gross domestic product
GEDS. *See* Global Events Data Systems Maryland
General Peace Agreement, Mozambique (GPA), 234
genocide: accelerators of, *340;* in Africa, 83; definition of, 74–75n4, 83–87, 297; Gurr on, 23; and human rights violations, 13, 398; prevention of, 406–07; processes leading to, *14;* in Rwanda, 82, 90–91, 93–94, 99, 409; and State Failure Project, 298–304; structural preconditions of, *14, 85*
Genscher, Hans Dietrich, 169
George, Alexander, 37, 39, 53n16
Georgia, Republic of, 106
Germany, 90, 118, 137–38, 147–49, 157, 172, 204, 300, 312
Gersony, Robert, 207
Gersony Report, 207, 211
Ghana, 215
Gleijeses, Piero, 72
Gligorov, Kiro, 160–62, 169, 175
Global Events Data Systems, Maryland (GEDS), 23, 87, 402, 408, 410, 412

globalization, 5, 20, 130
Gopinath, A., 242
Gorbachev, Mikhail, 115, 130
Gore, Al, 293
Gouden, Vasu, 179–95
governments: coalition, 13
Gowda, H. D. Deve, 269
GPA. *See* General Peace Agreement, Mozambique
Grachev, Gen. Pavel, 113
Graeger, Nina, 105, 109
Great Britain. *See* United Kingdom
Greece, 132, 144, 161, 169
Green Net, 35
Grenada, 307
gross domestic product (GDP), 142–44, *301*
Grotius Society, 7
Grozny, 120–23
GRP, Republic of the Philippines. *See* Philippines
Grupo de Contadora, 58
Guatemala: communism in, 61, 71; conflict in, 4, 56–78, 333, 348, *349,* 353n22, 371–72, 376, 378–84, 393–94n52; creation of, 352n17; Cubans in, 61; democracy restored in, 60; and Esquipulas Peace Accord, 60, 72; governance of, 57, 385; guerrilla warfare in, 57–58, 343–45; indigenous peoples of, 57–58; liberation army in, 60–61; Mayans in, 58; peace process in, 56–78; Solidarity Committees in, 62; Spanish invasion of, 58; and United Fruit Company, 60; United Nations mission in, 66; U.S. corporations in, 60; U.S. intervention in, 56–57, 60, 71, 348, 379–80
Guatemalan National Revolutionary Unity (URNG), 57, 63, 66, 348
Guatemalan Peace Accords, *67–71*
Guerrilla Army of the Poor, Guatemala (EGP), 61
guerrilla warfare, 57–57, 122, 163–64, 224–26, 296, 312, 347
Guevara, Ernesto "Ché", 61, 346
Gujral, I. K., 271

Gurr, Ted Robert, xvi, xviiin11, 3–31, 34–35, 40–44, 56, 87, 294, 324–26, 401, and Minorities at Risk survey, 83
Guzmán, Jacobo. *See* Arbenz, Jacobo

Haas, Ernst, xvi, 10, 20, 28, 47–48, 400
Habayarimana, Juvenal, 90, 100
Habermas, Jürgen, 6, 46
Habsburgs, 136, 147–48
Hague Declaration of 1992, 222
Hall, Michael, 109, 116
Harff, Barbara, xvi, 8, 13, 17–23, 42–43, 245, 324, 336–43, 406
Havana, 59
Havel, Vaclav, 159
HCNM. *See* High Commissioner of National Minorities
Helsinki agreements, 112
Helsinki foreign ministers' conference, 110
heterogeneity, 82, 86, 139, 298
HIC. *See* high-intensity conflict
High Commissioner of National Minorities (MCNM), 168, 170
high-intensity conflict (HIC), 292
Hindus, 271, 273
history, 10, 328, 333–34, 355, 359, 371
Hoff, Loek Becker, 314
Holl, Jane, 33, 53n16
Holocaust, 87
Holy Roman Empire, 148
Honduras, 58, 59, 60
Hong Kong, 277
Horn, Gyula, 153
Hudson, M., 26
human rights: and democracy, 56; and Europe, 65; institutional changes of, 63; and rule of law, 65, 67, 77n19; violations, 13, 26, 163, 202, 232, 312–13, 398
Human Rights Information and Documentation System (HURIDOCS), 24, 30n14, 30n15, 52n9
Human Rights Watch, 16, 276
humanitarian crises forecast models, *12,* 13
Hungarian revolution, 147
Hungarian Socialist Party Alliance of Free Democrats, 153

Hungary, Hungarians, 132–37, 140–44, 146–49, 151–55, 159–60, 164–68, 175, 307
Huntington, Samuel, 177n1, 178n7
Hurd, Douglas, 187
HURIDOCS. *See* Human Rights Information and Documentation System
Husserl, Edmund, 49
Hutus: in Burundi, 81; militias, 91; refugees, 94; and Tutsi, 17, 81–82, 88, 90, 99–100, 297
HZDS. *See* Movement for a Democratic Slovakia

ICON. *See* Commission on Internal Conflicts and Their Resolution
ICRC. *See* International Committee of the Red Cross
ICT. *See* Information and Communication Technology
ideology, 86, 104, 146
IERRIS. *See* International Emergency Reduction, Readiness and Response Information System
IFP. *See* Inkatha Freedom Party
IGO. *See* International Governmental Organization
IMF. *See* International Monetary Fund
IMPD. *See* Institute for Muliparty Democracy
India, 241, 243, 245, 256–57, 263–65, 272–73, 282, 285, 301, 324
Indian Union, 260
indigenous peoples, 13, 38, 57–58, 74, 77n16, 256
Indonesia, 222, 241–42, 255
infant mortality, 142, 299–300, 302, 304, 307, 315n3
Information and Communication Technology (ICT), 418
Inkatha Freedom Party (IFP), 180–81, 185, 187–88, 190, 192
Institute for Multiparty Democracy (IMPD), 192
Institute for the Study of Genocide, 402
Inter-University Consortium, 23
Interdisciplinary Research Program on Root Causes of Human Rights Violations

(PIOOM), 4, 23, 39, 46, 291–92, *292*, 294–306, *309, 310*, 319
Internal Macedonian Revolutionary Organization Democratic Party for Macedonian National Unity (VMRO-DPMNU), 150, 154
International Alert (London), 4–5, 18–20, 27–28, 32–35, 199, 212–16, 224–31, 405–06
International Committee of the Red Cross (ICRC), 214–15, 225, 227
international crisis, 351n5
International Crisis Group, 409
International Emergency Reduction, Readiness and Response Information System (IERRIS), 28
International Governmental Organization (IGO): archives of, 36; and conflict studies, 45; and mediation, 38, xiii; role of, 401, 404–05
International Monetary Fund (IMF), 144, 169, 171
International Peace Research Association (IPRA), xiii, xv, 29n7, 34, 401
international policy, 135
International Rescue Committee, 408
International Social Science Council (ISSC), xii, xv–xvi, 27–28, 32, 34, 54n24, 54n27, 55n16
International Studies Association (ISA), 7
Internet, 3, 25, 28, 388–89
Intifada, 296
IPRA. *See* International Peace Research Association, xiii, xv
Iran, 72, 248, 294
Iraq, 190, 419
ISA. *See* International Studies Association
Islam, 141, 246
Islamabad, 271–72
Islamic Conference (eighth), 249, 266
Israel, 38, 192, 294, 312
ISSC. *See* International Social Science Council
Italy, 138, 149, 171–72, 198, 209, 221, 305
Ivory Coast, 199, 212–16, 225, 228
Izvestiya, 113

Jabidah Massacre, 247
Jammu and Kashmir Liberation Front (JKLF), 265–66
Janta Dal party, 257, 272
Japan, 19, 98, 217–18, 247
Javakheti, Georgia, 412, *413*, 414–16
Javakheti Integrated Peace Consolidation Plan, *416*
Jeddah Accord, 251
Jentleson, Bruce, 33
Jericho Operation, 256
Jews, 105–06
JKLF. *See* Jammu and Kashmir Liberation Front
JMPC. *See* Joint Politico-Military Commission, Angola
Joint Politico-Military Commission, Angola (JMPC), 189
Joint Verification Committee, Mozambique (JVC), 233; Mission, 210
Jonas, Susan, 72, 76n11
Jongman, A. J., 8, 313, 398–99
Journal of Ethno-Development on Early Warning of Communal Conflicts and Humanitarian Crises, xvi, 7, 20, 24
JVC. *See* Joint Verification Committee, Mozambique

Kansas Event-Data Systems (KEDS), 23, 402, 408
Kant, Immanuel, 5–7
Kaplan, Robert, 137, 177n1
Kaqhazian, Leila, 387
Kargil incursion, 273
Karl-I-Bond, 97–98
Kashmir, 241, 245–46, 262–66, *264, 267–68, 270,* 282–85, 324, 372
Kazakhstan, 106, 118
KDH. *See* Christian Democratic Movement
Keashly, Loraleigh, 76n14, 77n20
KEDS. *See* Kansas Event-Data Systems
Kennan, George, 73
Kennedy, John F., 356, 358
Kennedy, Robert F., 356
Kenya, 187, 208, 210, 228
Khasavurt Agreements, 122

Khasbulatov, Ruslan, 119
Khmer Rouge, 297
Kilgali, 93–94
Kinnock, Glenys, 414
Kinshasa University, 98
Kinzer, Stephen, 72
Kissinger, Henry, 187
KLA. *See* Kosovo Liberation Army
Klaus, Vaclav, 143, 157
Kodry, 106
Kohl, Helmut, 167
Kosovo: Albanians in, 133, 138–41, 155; antagonism, 17; autonomy for, 155; civil war in, 133; economy in, 151; ethnic cleansing of, 172, 175; and Europe, 171; and European Community, 171; and international community, 135, 164; Serbs in, 132–33, 150–51, 172; unemployment in, 145; U.S. sanctions on, 145; United States presence in, 171–72; violence in, 136; and Yugoslavia, 145, 155, 170–73, 176
Kosovo Liberation Army (KLA), 163, 176
Kosovo Verification Mission, 172
Kovacs, Michael, 158–59
Kozyrev, Andrei, 112
Krasznai, Marton, 414
Kravchuk, Leonid, 110, 112
Kremlin, 122–23
Kripke, Saul, 49, 360, 389n6, 390n13, 390n16
Kurdish rebellion, 296, 315n2
Kuroda, Michiko, xiii, xv, 24

Lalthanhawla, Chief Minister, 260
Lancaster House Agreement, 205
Latin America, 44, 232, 348
Lawson, Brian, 34
LDK. *See* Democratic League of Kosova
League of Nations, 5, 36, 52n12
League of Prizren, 151
Ledbed, Gen. Alexander, 113, 122–23
Lederach, John Paul, 34, 56
Lee, Shin-wa, 23
Leiss, Amelia, 21, 36, 87, 243
Leonhardt, Manuela, 419–20n14
Lewis, David, 357

Liberia, 213–14, 294, 301
Libya, 248–49, 284
LIC. *See* low-intensity conflicts
Line of Control (LOC), 265, 273, 285
Linter, B., 242
LISP. *See* List processing computer programming language
List processing computer programming language (LISP), 47, 55n31
Literaturnaya Rossiya, 113
Lithuania, 106
LOC. *See* Line of Control
Lodge, Henry Cabot, 60, 72, 76n12
London, 4–5, 18
low-intensity conflicts (LIC), 292
Lucunschi, Petru, 115
Lund, Michael: and Alker, xviiin13; on Bloomfield, 36; on diplomacy, 10, 103; and early warning methodology, 323, 369, 398, 403; and Institute of Peace, 10, 42, 54n27, 103
Lushai Hills, 255–56

Macau, 277
Macedonia: Albanians in, 131, 150–51, 154; antagonism in, 17; economy of, 144–45; ethnic conflicts in, 155, 160, 170, 175; independence for, 133, 150; industry in, 149; nationalism in, 150–51; parliament, 161; religion in, 141; Serbs in, 132–33, 137–41, 149–50, 154–55, 160–64; and Slovakia, 135, 172, 174–76; and World War I, 137; and Yugoslavia, 145, 154, 161, 168–69, 174
MacFarlane, S. N., 403
Machel, Graca, 207–08
Madrid, 66
Magyars, 136, 148–49, 159
Malaysia, 247–48, 263, 284
Mallery, John, 25–26
Managing Small Wars (Bloomfield, Leiss), 36
Mandela, Nelson, 97, 182, 185–86, 190, 193
Marcos, Ferdinand, 218
Marcos, Fidel, 248, 251
Marinalá, Jurún, 60
Marxism, 6, 65, 186, 205, 348

Maskhadov, Aslan, 122
Massachusetts Institute of Technology, 25
Matsangaissa, Andre, 205
Mayans, 58
Mbeki, Thabo, 190, 195
MCC. *See* Mozambican Christian Council
McCarthy, M. O., 399
McCarthyism, 57
Mdlalose, Frank, 188
Meciar, Vladimir, 143, 148, 153, 157–59, 164, 167–68, 174–75
mediation: conflict, 23–24, 36; definition of, 64, 76–77n14, 77n20; international, 56; and International Governmental Organization, xiii
Mefford, Dwain, 17, 48
Mefford, T., 26
Menchú, Rigoberta, 62
Mercy Corps International, 171
Merritt, Richard, xvi, xviiin12
Mexico, 58, 63–64, 66, 307
Meyer, Roelf, 188
Middle East, 30–31n17, 190, 251
MILF. *See* Moro Islamic Liberation Front
Milosevic, Slobodan, 139, 150–51, 155, 161–64, 171–74, 176
MIM. *See* Muslim Independence Movement
Mindanao, 251, 254
Minorities at Risk (Gurr), 23
Minorities at Risk Project, 408
MINUGUA. *See* United Nations Mission in Guatemala
missionaries, 81, 255
Misuari, Nur, 248, 250, 254–55
Mizo National Front (MNF), 256–57, 260
Mizos, 241, 243, 246, 255–57, 260, 281–86, 372
MNF. *See* Mizo National Front
MNLF. *See* Moro National Liberation Front
mobilization for protest, *11*
Mobutu Sese Seko, 81–82, 95, 98–100
Modern State, The (Pierson), 303
modern state indicators, 303–04
Moldova: and Chisinau delegation, 114; conflict tracking in, 323, 383; constitution of, 115; economics of, 105–06, 108,

114, 116–17; ethnicity of, 106, 108–09; independence of, 108; nationalism, 108–09, 117; Parliament of, 110, 112, 115–17; Republic of, 115–16, 132, 393n52; and Romania, 106, 109; Russian army in, 111–13, 116; society in, 132; socioeconomic development of, 106; and Soviet Union, 105–06; and Transdniestria, 116; and Turkey, 104
Moldova-Dniester Conflict, 104–09, 111, 117, 123–24, *125*
Moldovan Popular Front, 106
Mongol invasion of 1241, 148
Monsanto, Pablo, 76n13
Montenegro, 163
Moore, G. E., 49
Moravchik, Josef, 158
Moravia, 147
Morgenthau, Hans, 73
Moro Islamic Liberation Front (MILF), 250–51, 254–55
Moro National Liberation Front (MNLF), 217, 222, 247–48, 250–51, 254, 285
Moros, 241, 246–48, *249–50,* 251, 282–85, 286n1, 332
Moscow, 59, 116–121
Moulton, Allen, 47–48
Movement for a Democratic Slovakia (HZDS), 147–48, 157–58
Movement for the Popular Liberation of Angola (MPLA), 194
Mozambican Christian Council (MCC), 208
Mozambique, 196–205, 207–12, 223–25, 228–36, 297
MPLA. *See* Movement for the Popular Liberation of Angola
MSPA. *See* Multi-Sectoral Peace Advocates
Mugabe, Robert, 205
Multi-Sectoral Peace Advocates (MSPA), 221
Museveni, Yoweri Kaguta, 91, 93–94
Mushakoji, Kinhide, 39, 46–47
Muslim Independence Movement (MIM), 247–48
Muslim United Front, 265
Muslims, 138, 141, 150, 242, 246–48, 254, 262–65, 272–73, 281, 286

Nairobi Peace Initiative, 214
Namibia, 184, 190
National Cease-fire Committee (NCC), 219
National Commission on Reconciliation, Guatemala (CNR), 65–66, 77n21, 348
National Conference on Democratic Reform, 98
National Democratic Front, Philippines (NDF), 218, 221–22
National Guatemalan Revolutionary Unity (URNG), 58, 61–65, 67, 346
National Peace Accord (NPA), 180, 221
National Peace Conference (NPC), 199, 221–222, 235
National Provisional Ruling Council, Sierra Leone (NPCR), 199, 213, 215, 225
National Unification Committee, 251
National United Committee of Trade Unions (CNUS), 62
nationalism: in Albania, 151–52, 160; and discrimination, 108; and ethnicity, 146, 158; and independence, 106, 401; in Macedonia, 151; in Moldova, 106, 108–09, 117; in Serbia, 151–52, 160; in Slovakia, 147–49, 153, 159; in Yugoslavia, 150–51
NATO. *See* North Atlantic Treaty Organization
Nazis, 118, 137–38, 157
NCC. *See* National Cease-fire Committee
Ndadaye, Melchoir, 90, 93
NDF. *See* National Democratic Front, Philippines
negotiations, 180, 197, 200, 209–10, 382, *383*
Nehru, Jawaharak, 262
Nepal, 269
Netherlands, 221–22
Network on Ethnological Monitoring and Early Warning of Conflict (EAWARN), 412
New Delhi, 257, 272
New Directions in Events Data Analysis (Duffy), 47
New People's Army (NPA), 218, 251
New World Order, 401
New York Accords, 192
NGO. *See* nongovernmental organization

Nicaragua, 58–62, 72, 296, 380
Nigeria, 98, 212–13, 215
Nobel Peace Prize, 62, 280
nongovernmental organization (NGO): in Africa, 94, 100; case studies of, 198–99, 227–28, 232; in Central America, 36–38, 41, 45, 62, 223; definition of, xiii, xv, 13; and early warning systems, 293; in Eastern Europe, 152, 168, 171–72; in peace process, 201, 236–37, 280–81, 318; in Philippines, 222, 230; role of, 196, 199, 223–25, 245, 401, 404–05, 415; and Tibet, 280
Nordstrom, Carolyn, 34
North, Robert, 400
North Atlantic Cooperation Council (NACC), 167
North Atlantic Treaty Organization (NATO): alliances of, 84; and European Community, 16, 167–69; expansion of, 116; Partnership for Peace, 165; and Serbia, 172; and Yugoslavia, 133
North Caucasian republics, 118–19, 122–23
North-Eastern Areas Reorganization Act, 256
Norway, 63, 66, 170, 192
NPA. *See* National Peace Accord
NPA. *See* New People's Army
NPC. *See* National Peace Conference
NPRC. *See* National Provisional Ruling Council, Sierra Leone
Nyheim, David, 5, 419–20n14

OAS. *See* Organization of American States
OAU. *See* Organization for African Unity
Office for Research and Coordination of Information (ORCI), xv–xvi, xviiin13, 28
OIC. *See* Organization of the Islamic Conference
Okumu, Washington, 187, 193
Ollman, Bertell, 49
Operation Merdeka, 247
Operation Turquoise, 94
Opportunities Missed, Opportunities Seized: Preventive Diplomacy in the Post-Cold War Era (Jentleson, ed), 177

ORCI. *See* Office for Research and Coordination of Information
Organization for African Unity (OAU): and Burundi, 90; and conflict prevention, 20, 318, 409; mediations by, 17; and Mobutu, 98; and Rwanda, 17; Salim on, 195; and Sierra Leone, 199; summit conference, 94; and United Nations, 94, 100, 214
Organization for Security and Cooperation in Europe (OSCE), 115, 118, 170–72, 414
Organization of American States (OAS), 59, 318
Organization of the Islamic Conference (OIC), 222, 248, 250–51, 254, 282, 285
Ortega, Daniel, 76n12, 380
OSCE. *See* Organization for Security and Cooperation in Europe.
Oslo Agreement, 64–65
Oslo Peace Accords, 192
Ottoman Empire, 118, 137–38, 148, 149
Oxfam, 171

Padilla, Luis Alberto, 4, 44, 56–78, 327, 343–47, 353n22, 376–80, 383–85
Pakistan, 241, 256–57, 262–63, 272–73, 282–83, 285, 324
Palestine, 38, 192
Panama, 58, 307
Panchem Lama, 280
PANDA. *See* Protocol for the Assessment of Nonviolent Direct Action
PARIS-in-LA Project, 47–48
Paris Peace Treaty, 160
Partido Guatemalteco del Trabajo (PGT), 61
Party for Democratic Prosperity (PDP), 154
Peace: consolidation plan for, *416;* culture of, 235–36; and democracy, 59; and economics, 234–35; and Guatemala, 56–78; integrated plan for, *415;* international research on, xiii–xiv; life cycle of process, 200; negotiation for, 200–205; phases of process, 200–05, *201;* process of, 183, 200–205, 230–31; researchers, 34, 36, 39, 46, 73, 176–77, 179–80, 200; studies of, 242–43; and Third Party intervention, 62–67

peacekeeping:case studies, 245–46; elements of, 74n1, 197, 234–38; and peace initiatives, 72, xii–xiii; role of, 34, 192–93, United Nations role in, xiv–xv, 5, 72, 91, 93
PeaceNet, 28
Peasant United Committee, Guatemala (CUC), 62
People on Arms Organization, Guatemala (ORPA), 61
"Peoples against States: Ethnopolitical Conflict and Changing World Systems" (Gurr), 7, 13
Perez de Cuellar, Javier, 38
Persia, 118
Peurifoy, John D., 60, 345, 379
PGT. *See Partido Guatemalteco del Trabajo*
Philippines, 196, 199, 217–27, 230, 235, 241–42, 246–50, 254, 285, 332
philosophy, 49, 355–57
Pierson, C., 294, 303–05, 307, 312–14, 391–92n33
PIOOM. *See* Interdisciplinary Research Program on Root Causes of Human Rights Violations
PKP. *See* Communist Party, Philippines
Plato, 357
pluralism, 19
Poland, 149, 165–66
Polanhy, K., 359
political terror scale (PTS), 294, 312–13, 316
politicide: definition of, 74–75n4, 83–86, 297; Gurr on, 23; and human rights violations, 13; processes leading to, *14;* and rivalries, 82; and State Failure Projects, 298–304; structural preconditions of, *85;* and types of, 87
politics, 130, 197, 287, 291, 359
polity leaders, *156*
Polje Field, 138
Poltoranin, Milhail, 119
Portugal, 184, 193, 204, 209–10
Prague, 147, 158–59
"Presumption of Anarchy in World Politics, The," (Wendt), 29n5
Prishtina, 151, 171

Prishtina University, 151
Protestantism, 136, 141, 208
Protocol for the Assessment of Nonviolent Direct Action (PANDA), 408
Prut River, 104–05
PTS. *See* political terror scale
Public against Violence (VPN), 148, 157–59
Pulikovskih, Gen. Constantin, 122

Quadripartite Commission, 249
Queretaro Agreement, 65, 348
Quezada, Bishop. *See* Toruño, Rodolfo Quezada
Quinlan, J. R., 26, 48

Ramaphosa, Cyril, 188
Ramos, Fidel, 251, 254
Rao, Narasimha, 266
Reagan, Ronald, 77n21, 78n26, 238n5
realism, 357, 360
realist, 7, 390n21, 391n24
Rebel Armed Forces, Guatemala (FAR), 61, 76n13
Red Crescent, 20
Red Cross, 20, 199, 214, 221, 225
Reformation, 136
refugees: and Africa, 179; aid to, 94; and Albania, 163; case law for, 25; flow of, 26–27, 171, 313, 398; Hutu, 94: in Rwanda, 90, 93–94; and Ukraine, 110; and United Nations, xv; in Zaire, 94
Regan, P. M., 242
regimes, 86, 244–45, 297–98, 302, 304, 312
RELATUS Computational System, 25
Relief Net, 28
Renamo (Resistencia Nacional Mocambicana), 198, 205–07, 210–12, 225–26, 229–33, 238n7, 297
Reschner, N., 357
Reuters World Service, 87, 412
Revolution in the Revolution (Debray), 61
Revolutionary United Front of Sierra Leone (RUF/SL), 199, 212–16, 225, 227, 229, 239n20
Rhodesia, 204–05
Ribbentrop-Molotov Pact (1940), 105
Richardson, Lewis, 400

Rights Watch, 24
Risk Assessment, 82–83, 304–05, 313–14
Romania, 104–09, 113, 116, 137, 149, 159–60
Rome General Peace Accord, 211
Rowland, Tiny, 203, 208–09, 211–12, 238n3
RPF. *See* Rwanda Patriotic Front
RUF/SL. *See* Revolutionary United Front of Sierra Leone
Rugova, Ibrahim, 151, 162–65
Rupesinghe, Kumar: on conflict definition, 51n6, 56, 322; on conflict prevention, 8, 25, 56; on conflict transition, 42, 44, 182–83; on cultures of tolerance, 43; on diplomacy, 190, 192; on early warning models, 403; and International Alert, 5, 18–19, 32–34; and International Peace Research Association, xiii, xv–xvi, 29n7
Russia: in Caucasus, 118; and Chechnya stalemate, 120–23; diplomacy of, 117; ethnicity of, 131; independence of, 108, 294; people of, 105. *See also* Soviet Union (USSR)
Russian: Civil War, 105; constitution, 121; Empire, 118; Federation, 115–20, 122–23; Foreign Ministry, 111–12; National Army, 112, 122; Parliament, 110; Revolution, 104
Russian State Bank, 110
Russian 14th Army, 111–13, 116, 118
Russo-Turkish war, 104
Rusu, Sharon, 398–99, 403
Rwanda: accelerators of conflict, *92;* conflict in, 81, 88, 99–100, 301, 403; genocide in, 82–83, 90–91, 93–94, 99, 409; and Organization for African Unity, 17; protests in, 90; refugees in, 90, 93
Rwanda Patriotic Front (RPF), 91, 93, 100
Ryan, Eric, 34

SAARC. *See* South Asian Association for Regional Cooperation
SADF. *See* South African Defense Force
Salim, Ahmed Salim, 195
Sandinistas, 58–59, 62
Sandino, Augusti Cescar, 60
Sankoh, Foday, 213

Sant Egidio, 198, 209–11, 224–26, 231–32, 238n7
Saudi Arabia, 248, 302
Savimbi, Jonas, 180–81, 187, 190
Sayyaf, Abu, 254–55
Schank, Roger, 48
Schlesinger, Stephen, 72
Schmalberger, Thomas, 4, 32–55, 389n6
Schmeidl, S., 403
Schmid, Alex, 4, 30n15, 39, 46, 51n4, 324, 398–99, 405
Schneidl, Susan, 23
School of International Relations at the University of Southern California, 39
Scrodt, Phil, 402
SDUM. *See* Social Democratic Union of Macedonia
SEATO. *See* South-East Asian Treaty Organization
security systems, *8*
Semenov, Vladimir, 111
Senegal, 214
Serb Radical Party, 150
Serb Renewal Party, 155
Serbia, Serbs: and Albanians, 138–39, 145, 155–56, 162–65, 170–71; and bombing, 172; and Croatia, 131; and Kosovo, 132, 133, 150–51, 172; and Macedonia, 132–33, 137–41, 149–50, 154–55, 160–64; and nationalism, 151–52, 160; and United Nations sanctions, 161
Sese Seko, Mobutu, 192
Seselj, Vojislav, 150
Sharif, Nawaz, 269, 271, 273
SHERFACS. *See* Sherman, Frank, management data set of (SHERFACS)
Sherman, Frank, xvi, 7, 17, 23, 42, 47–48, 87, 243
Sherman Frank, management data set of (SHERFACS) *6, 21, 22, 23, 28, 42, 47,* 391n28
Sierra de las Minas, 61
Sierra Leone, 34, 196–200, 212–19, 223–36, 287, 294, 333, 393n52
Sierra Leone People's Party, 213
Silesia, 147

Simla Agreement, 265
Singapore, 263
Singer, J. David, xvi, 47, 400
Slavic, 140
Slovak National Council, 153
Slovak National Party (SNS), 147, 158
Slovak Socialist Republic. *See* Slovakia
Slovakia: agriculture in, 140; autonomy of, 147; and Czechoslovakia, 140; democratization, 140, 148; economic changes in, 144, 174; and ethnicity, 137, 155, 175; and Hungary, 133, 136–37, 146–48, 152–53, 159–60, 164–68; independence for, 147; industry in, 140; language of, 140; and Macedonia, 135, 172, 174–76; nationalism, 147–49, 153, 159; official language of, 148; parliament of, 148, 167; political status, 143–44; workers of, 158; and Yugoslavia, 174–75
Smirnov, Igor, 110–11
Snegur, Mircea, 108, 110–12, 114, 116
SNS. *See* Slovak National Party
Social Democratic Union of Macedonia (SDUM), 154
social structure, 134–35, 139, 175, 314, 329, 350n4, 362
Socialist Party, 114
sociology, 10, 34, 36–37, 134, 176, 177n2, 328, 359
Sokalski, Henryk, 170
Solidarity Committees, 62
Solingen, Etel, 300
Solomon, Hussein, 179–95
Somalia, 128, 186, 294, 297
Sorokin, Pitrim, 400
South Africa: and African National Congress, 205; Agreement of Nonaggression and Good Neighborliness, South Africa, 207; and Angola, 179–95; and conflict resolution, 184–93; conflicts in, 38, 235, 383, 393n52, Parliament of, 189; and Zaire, 97
South African Defense Force (SADF), 184
South Asian Association for Regional Cooperation (SAARC), 271, 285

South-East Asian Treaty Organization (SEATO), 262
Southern Philippine Council for Peace and Development (SPCPD), 254
Soviet bloc system, 132
Soviet Union (USSR): and Africa, 13; army of, 147; and Cold War, 143–44; and Eastern Europe, 104–05; end of, 13, 65, 108, 132, 294; and India, 265; and Moldova, 105–06; states of, 131. *See also* Russia
Spain, 58–59, 63, 66, 77n21, 217, 246, 307
Spanish Embassy in Guatemala City, 66
SPCPD. *See* Southern Philippine Council for Peace and Development
Spencer, Metta, 13, *15,* 42
Sri Lanka, 17, 241–42
State Failure Project, 82–84, 291–94, 296–303, *306,* 306–07, *308, 309, 310,* 311
State Failure Project Reports, indicators, 296–97, *298, 300,* 302–04, *306,* 307, *308–12,* 313–14, 314–15n1
State Failure Task Force, 46–47, 53n21 84, 86, 298, 300–301, 306–07
Stavenhagen, Rudolfo, 403
Stevens, Siaka, 213
Strasser, Valentine, 213
Sulu Archipelago, 246
Supreme Soviet. *See* Soviet Union (USSR)
Supreme Soviet of Chechen-Inguish (ASSR), 118–19
Sweden, 170
Swiss National Science Foundation, 49
Sylvan, David, 49, 360
Syracuse University, xvi
Szuros, Matyas, 159

Taiwan, 277
Tanzania, 88, 93–94
TAR. *See* Tibetan Autonomous Region
Tatarstan, 132
Tetovo University, 170
Thailand, 242
think tank systems, 409
third-party intervention, 66–67, 74, 76n14, 77n2, 242, 244, 283, 286

Tianamen Square, 277
Tibet, 241, 245–46, 274–80, *275, 277–79,* 282
Tibetan Autonomous Region (TAR), 274
Tibetan Youth Congress, 277, 281
Tibetans, 273–78, 280–87
Tikhomirov, Gen. Vyachelslav, 122
Tiraspol. *See* Chisinau
Tito, 138, 144, 162
To Augur Well: Early Indicators in World Politics, 400
Togethernet, 28
tolerance, 43
Toruño, Rodolfo Quezada, 63–66, 348
trade, 165, 300–302, *301,* 304, 307
trajectories of conflict, 358–86
Transdniester Moldavoam Soviet Socialist Republic, 109
Transdniestria, 104–05, 108–09, 111–14, 116–17
Transylvania, 136
Treaty of Paris, 217
Treaty of Trianon (1920), 137, 140, 160
Tripoli Agreement, 248, 250, 254, 282, 332
trust, 223–24
Tsaran, Anatol, 114
Tshisekedi, Etienne, 95, 97–98
Tuminez, Astrid, 45
Turkey, 104, 148, 154
Turks, 138, 151
Tutsi: and Hutus, 17, 81–82, 88, 99–100, 297; political leaders of, 90
Tutu, Desmond, 187–88, 193
Tydings-McDuffe Act, 217–18

UFCO. *See* United Fruit Company
Uganda, 88, 90, 93–94, 97–100
Ukraine, 104–13, 116–17, 132, 166
Ukrainians, 105
UN. *See* United Nations (UN)
UNAVEM II. *See* United Nations Angola Verification Mission II
UNDP. *See* United Nations Development Program
UNESCO. *See* United Nations Educational, Social and Cultural Organization

UNHCR. *See* United Nations High Commission for Refugees
UNICEF. *See* United Nations Children's Fund
Union for Total Independence of Angola (UNITA), 180–81, 184, 189–90, 194
UNIPOM. *See* United Nations India-Pakistan Observation Mission
UNITA. *See* Union for Total Independence of Angola
United Fruit Company (UFCO), 60, 72, 344, 379
United Kingdom, 172, 208, 210, 300, 307
United Liberation Movement for Democracy, 213
United Nations Ad Hoc Working Group on Early Warning Regarding New Flow of Refugees and Displaced Persons, 400
United Nations Angola Verification Mission II (UNAVEM II), 189
United Nations Children's Fund (UNICEF), 220
United Nations Development Program (UNDP), 26, 213
United Nations Educational, Social and Cultural Organization (UNESCO), xviin1
United Nations High Commission for Refugees (UNHCR), 19–20, 23, 28, 52n9, 53–54n22, 93, 409
United Nations Human Rights Commission, 75n7
United Nations India-Pakistan Observation Mission (UNIPOM), 263
United Nations Mission in Guatemala (MINUGUA), 66
United Nations Operations in Mozambique (UNOMOZ), 234
United Nations Preventative Deployment Force (UNPREDEP), 170–71
United Nations Protection Force (UNPROFOR), 171
United Nations Secretary General, xiv,103, 170
United Nations Security Council, xiv, 90, 93–94, 99, 111–12, 172, 262, 398, 401
United Nations (UN): charter of, 5, 59, 73; and crisis management, 36; and diplomacy, xiii–xiv; *Human Development Report,*

26; and International Governmental Organization, xiii, 13, 405; intervention practices of, 48, 65–66, 229, 233; and Kashmir, 284–85; as mediators, 58–59, 66, 71, 199; and nongovernmental organization, xiii, xv, 234; and Organization of African Unity, 94, 100; peacekeeping tasks of, xiv–xv, 5, 72–73, 91, 93, 99, 169–70; and refugees, xv; research programs of, 25; role of, 7, 13, 21, 28, 73; statistical world reports by, xvi, 299;

United Nations University (UNU), 28

United States, 5–6; and African conflicts, 90, 98; and China, 265; and early conflict warning, 18–19; foreign policy of, 59, 72, 300, 302; and Guatemala, 56–57, 66, 71, 348, 379–80; and international trade, 301; and Kashmir, 284–85; and Kosovo, 171–72, nongovernmental organizations in, 62; and United Nations, 5–6; yearbooks of, 21

United States Congress, 217

United States Constitution, 72

United States Department of Defense's Advanced Research Projects Agency, 25

United States Human Rights Documentation and Information Network, 24

United States Institute of Peace, xvi, xviiin13, 10

United States Secretary of State, 60, 72

United States State Department, 207

University of Kansas, 402

University of Maryland, xvi, 87, 402, 408, 412

University of San Carlos, 62

University of Southern California, 39–40, 47, 54n23

UNOMOZ. *See* United Nations Operations in Mozambique

UNPREDEP. *See* United Nations Preventative Deployment Force

UNPROFOR. *See* United Nations Protection Force

Unseld, Sigrid, 26

UNSG. *See* United Nations Secretary General

UNU. *See* United Nations University

Uppsala Conflict Data Project, 409

URGN. *See* National Guatemalan Revolutionary Unity

URNG. *See* Guatemalan National Revolutionary Unity

USSR. *See* Soviet Union

Vajpayee, Atal Bihari, 272
van der Stoel, Max, 168, 170
Váryen, Raimo, 77n18, 104
Vatican, 198, 203, 209, 212, 224
Velvet Revolution, 147, 152
Vendrell, Francesc, 65
Venezuela, 58, 66
Vest, Thomas, Jr., 33
Vietnam, 72, 262
violence: and conflict, 213; cycles of, 82; escalation of, 172–74, 176; factors of, 106, 129–30, 143, 152, 202, 331; intervention in, 134; levels of, 326–27, 331, 373, 381; patterns of, 398; prevention of, xii–xiii, 16, 44, 46, 134, 354; quantification of, 324; reduction of, 39; symptoms of, 124, *125, 126–27;* types of, 124, 378; violent political conflicts (VPC), 292, *295*

Visegrad Four, 166–67
Visegrad Triangle, 166
VMRO-DPMNU. *See* Internal Macedonian Revolutionary Organization Democratic Party for Macedonian National Unity
Vo Giap, Nguyen, 61, 346
Vojvodina, 136, 159–60, 169
Vorkunova. Olga A., 44
VPC *(*violent political conflicts), 292, *295*
VPN. *See* Public against Violence

Walachia, 104
Walker, William, 60
Wallace, Michael D., 400
Walter, J., 242–43
Warsaw Pact, 147, 306
Weber, Max, 355
Wendt, Alexander, 29n5
West Africa. *See* Africa
Western Europe. *See* Europe

Wilkenfeld, Johnathan, 10, 23, 36
Women's Union for Support of Transdniestria, 112
World Bank, 94, 145, 166, 169, 171, 255, 299
World War I, 5, 137–38, 149, 359
World War II, 5, 138, 159, 194, 247, 263
World Wide Web, 35. *See also* Internet
Wright, Quiney, 321, 400

Ydígoras Fuentes, Miguel, 61, 76n13
Yeltsin, Boris, 111–13, 120–22
Yemen, 294, 297
York conference, 8, 26
York Report, 23
youth bulge, 142, 302
YPA. *See* Yugoslav People's Army
Yugoslav People's Army (YPA), 161
Yugoslavia: Albanians in, 155–56, 164; economic changes in, 144, 163, 174; ethnic communities in, 130–31; and Kosovo, 145, 155, 170–73; and Macedonia, 145, 154, 161, 168–69, 174; martial law in, 155–56; nationalism, 150–51; neutrality in, 164; and North Atlantic Treaty Organization, 133; people's army, 161; regional interventions in, 13, 137; and Slovakia, 174–76; and United Nations sanctions, 144; war in, 132–33, 164–65, 186

Zaire: accelerators of conflict, *96;* democratic conference in, 97; democratization in, 95, 97–100; elections in, 97; and European Community, 97–98; fighting in, 93, 294; genocide in, 83, 99; massacres in, 82; news agency of, 95; protests in, 90; refugees in, 94; risk factors in, 86; and South Africa, 97. *See also* Congo
Zambia, 210
ZANU. *See* Zimbabwean African National Union
Zartman, I. W., 294, 296
Zimbabwean African National Union (ZANU), 205
Zinnes, Dina, xvi
ZRS. *See* Association of Workers of Slovakia
Zulu, 180, 186–87, 189, 191
Zuma, Jacob, 188

About the Contributors

Hayward R. Alker is John A. McCone Professor in the School of International Relations at the University of Southern California. He is a former president of the International Studies Association and served as coordinator of the CEWS project.

Sanam Naraghi Anderlini is currently the senior policy adviser on the global campaign entitled, "Women Building Peace: From the Village Council to the Negotiating Table." She is also the managing editor of the Forum on Early Warning and Early Response and has written on the role of women in preventing violent conflict.

Ed Garcia serves as senior policy advisor for International Alert, a nongovernmental organization working for the peaceful resolution and transformation of violent conflict.

Vasu Gounden is the founder and executive director of ACCORD, a continent-wide conflict management organization based in Durban, South Africa. He is a mediator, trainer, and researcher in the field of conflict management.

Ted Robert Gurr is Distinguished University Professor at the University of Maryland, College Park, and directs the Minorities at Risk project there. He is also a former president of the International Studies Association.

Barbara Harff is professor of political science at the U.S. Naval Academy and has written extensively on cases, causes, and consequences of genocide and political mass murder.

Maha Khan is a journalist with *Risk Magazine* and a freelance writer on conflict in international relations. She is currently compiling research for a book on U.S. nuclear bases in Britain during the Cold War.

Deepa Khosla is a doctoral candidate in the Department of Government and Politics, University of Maryland, and a senior research assistant with the Minorities at Risk project.

Michael S. Lund is senior associate at Management Systems International and professorial lecturer at the School of Advanced International Studies, Johns Hopkins University, both in Washington, D.C. He has researched and written extensively on recent conflict prevention cases and instruments, and was formerly associated with the U.S. Institute of Peace.

David Nyheim is director of the FEWER Secretariat. He has held a number of policy and research/teaching positions in the European Commission, University of Louvain and University of London.

Luis Alberto Padilla is the founder and president of the International Relations and Peace Reseach Institute in Guatemala (IRIPAZ). He has also held positions as Secretary General of the Latin American Council for Peace Research, Guatemalan Vice Minister for Foreign Affairs, ambassador and permanent Guatemalan representative at the UN European office in Geneva, Switzerland, and professor of international relations at San Carlos University, Guatemala.

Kumar Rupesinghe is currently the chair of Quality Management Systems, International. From 1992–1998 he was Secretary General of International Alert and Chair of FEWER. Previously he was deputy director of the International Peace Research Institute and Chair of HURIDOCS.

Thomas Schmalberger is a consultant with Deloitte Consulting in Zurich. Previously, he was a researcher at the United Nations and has taught at the Graduate Institute of International Studies in Geneva.

Alex P. Schmid holds the Synthesis Chair on Conflict Resolution at the Erasmus University in Rotterdam, and is officer-in-charge of the Terrorism Prevention Branch of the United Nations in Vienna. He was, until recently, coordinator of the Interdisciplinary Research Programme on Causes of Human Rights Violations (PIOOM) and was one of the founding members of FEWER. He has also served on the executive board of the International Scientific and Professional Advisory Council of the UN Crime Prevention and Criminal Justice Programme.

Hussein Solomon lectures in the Department of Political Science, University of Pretoria (South Africa) and is a senior associate of ACCORD.

Olga A. Vorkunova is affiliated with the Centre for Development and Peace Studies FORUM Institute of World Economy and International Relations and the Russian Academy of Sciences.